Turn the page...

for tools to use in the classroom the workplace to improve your w. and communication skills, with...

The Student Toolbox CD-ROM

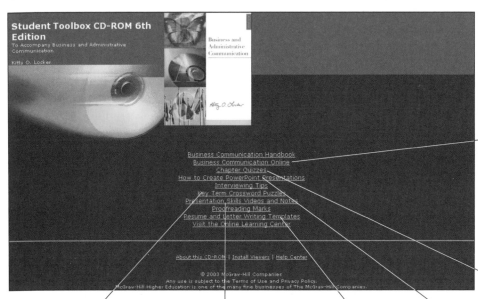

With each new copy of the text, you will receive (for free!) this new CD. Use it to:

Access Business Communication Online– a resource full of activities and assessments to help you evaluate and improve your communication skills.

Prepare for exams by taking the chapter quizzes.

Try your hand at crossword puzzles for each chapter – a fun way to review the key terms in the book.

View video clips and accompanying notes on nonverbal messages, presentation skills, and interview techniques.

Practice writing letters and creating résumés with the Word templates based on documents in the text.

Create a PowerPoint presentation. This Word document leads you through the basic steps.

Use this CD as your "toolbox" to help you achieve success in your course and as a resource in your future career.

SIXTH EDITION

Business and Administrative Communication

KITTY O. LOCKER
The Ohio State University

McGraw-Hill
Irwin

Boston   Burr Ridge, IL   Dubuque, IA   Madison, WI   New York   San Francisco   St. Louis
Bangkok   Bogotá   Caracas   Kuala Lumpur   Lisbon   London   Madrid   Mexico City
Milan   Montreal   New Delhi   Santiago   Seoul   Singapore   Sydney   Taipei   Toronto

McGraw-Hill Higher Education

A Division of The **McGraw-Hill** *Companies*

BUSINESS AND ADMINISTRATIVE COMMUNICATION

Published by McGraw-Hill/Irwin, a business unit of The McGraw-Hill Companies, Inc., 1221 Avenue of the Americas, New York, NY, 10020. Copyright © 2003, 2000, 1998, 1995, 1992, 1989 by The McGraw-Hill Companies, Inc. All rights reserved. No part of this publication may be reproduced or distributed in any form or by any means, or stored in a database or retrieval system, without the prior written consent of The McGraw-Hill Companies, Inc., including, but not limited to, in any network or other electronic storage or transmission, or broadcast for distance learning.

Some ancillaries, including electronic and print components, may not be available to customers outside the United States.

This book is printed on acid-free paper.

domestic   2 3 4 5 6 7 8 9 0 WCK/WCK 0 9 8 7 6 5 4 3 2
international 1 2 3 4 5 6 7 8 9 0 WCK/WCK 0 9 8 7 6 5 4 3 2

ISBN 0-07-246958-7

Publisher: *John E. Biernat*
Senior sponsoring editor: *Andy Winston*
Developmental editor: *Sarah Reed*
Senior marketing manager: *Ellen Cleary*
Lead project manager: *Mary Conzachi*
Manager, new book production: *Melonie Salvati*
Director of design BR: *Keith J. McPherson*
Producer, Media technology: *Jennifer Becka*
Supplement producer: *Betty Hadala*
Photo research coordinator: *David A. Tietz*
Photo researcher: *Inge King*
Cover and interior design: *Michael Warrell*
Typeface: *10.5/12 Palatino*
Compositor: *Carlisle Communications, Ltd.*
Printer: *Quebecor World Versailles Inc. (WCK)*

Library of Congress Control Number: 2002103614

INTERNATIONAL EDITION ISBN 0-07-115111-7

Copyright © 2003. Exclusive rights by The McGraw-Hill Companies, Inc. for manufacture and export. This book cannot be re-exported from the country to which it is sold by McGraw-Hill. The International Edition is not available in North America.

www.mhhe.com

To my husband, Bob Mills, with love

Kitty O. Locker is an Associate Professor of English at The Ohio State University in Columbus, Ohio, where she coordinates the Writing Center and teaches courses in business and technical discourse and in research methods. She has taught as Assistant Professor at Texas A&M University and the University of Illinois.

She has also written *The Irwin Business Communication Handbook: Writing and Speaking in Business Classes* (1993), coauthored *Business Writing Cases and Problems* (1980, 1984, 1987), and co-edited *Conducting Research in Business Communication* (1988). She has twice received the Alpha Kappa Psi award for Distinguished Publication in Business Communication for her article " 'Sir, This Will Never Do': Model Dunning Letters 1592–1873" and for her article " 'As Per Your Request': A History of Business Jargon." In 1992 she received the Association for Business Communication's Outstanding Researcher Award.

Her research in progress includes work on collaborative writing in the classroom and the workplace, and the emergence of bureaucratic writing in the correspondence of the British East India Company from 1600 to 1800.

Her consulting work includes conducting tutorials and short courses in business, technical, and administrative writing for employees of URS Greiner, Ross Products Division of Abbott Laboratories, Franklin County, the Ohio Civil Service Employees Association, AT&T, the American Medical Association, Western Electric, the Illinois Department of Central Management Services, the Illinois Department of Transportation, the A. E. Staley Company, Flo-Con, the Police Executive Leadership College, and the Firemen's Institute. She developed a complete writing improvement program for Joseph T. Ryerson, the nation's largest steel materials service center.

She has served as the Interim Editor of *The Bulletin of the Association for Business Communication* and, in 1994–95, as President of the Association for Business Communication (ABC). She edited ABC's *Journal of Business Communication* from 1998 to 2000.

In 1998, she received ABC's Meada Gibbs Outstanding Teacher Award.

 Sixth Edition

August 1, 2002

Dear Student:

Business and Administrative Communication (BAC) takes the mystery out of writing and speaking effectively.

As you read,

- Use the Chapter Outline to preview what you'll learn. Check your understanding with the Summary of Key Points at the end of the chapter.

- Note the terms in boldface type and their definitions. In later chapters, the fast-forward and rewind arrows identify the page where the term is first defined.

- Use items in the lists when you prepare your assignments or review for tests.

- Use the examples, especially the paired examples of effective and ineffective communication, as models to help you draft and revise. Comments in red ink signal problems in an example; comments in blue ink note things done well.

The side columns offer anecdotes and examples that show the principles in the text at work in a variety of business and administrative situations. Some readers like to read all the sidebars first, then come back to read the chapter. Other readers prefer to take a break from the page to read the sidebar. The logos identify the kind of example:

International examples show how to apply or modify the principles when you communicate with international audiences.

Ethical and Legal examples alert you to ethical decisions and legal implications of business and administrative communication.

Technology examples show how technology can help create better messages and how technological changes affect the way people produce, transmit, and interpret business messages.

On-the-Job examples show the principles in the text at work.

Just-for-Fun anecdotes show the lighter side of business communication. Skip them if you're in a hurry, or read them just for enjoyment.

 McGraw-Hill Irwin

In addition, gold ribbons identify sidebar classics. These oldies but goodies are still relevant to today's business world.

When you prepare an assignment,

- Review the analysis questions in Chapter 1. Some assignments have "Hints" to help probe the problem. Some of the longer assignments have preliminary assignments analyzing the audience or developing reader benefits or subject lines. Use these to practice portions of longer documents.

- If you're writing a letter or memo, read the sample problems in Chapters 7, 8, and 9 with a detailed analysis, strong and weak solutions, and a discussion of the solutions to see how to apply the principles in this book to your own writing.

- See the Toolbox CD-Rom for practice exercises, more sample solutions with evaluations, and templates for letters, memos, and résumés.

- Remember that most problems are open-ended, requiring original, critical thinking. Many of the problems are deliberately written in negative, ineffective language. You'll need to reword sentences, reorganize information, and think through the situation to produce the best possible solution to the business problem.

- Learn as much as you can about what's happening in business. The knowledge will not only help you develop reader benefits and provide examples but also make you an even more impressive candidate in job interviews.

Business and Administrative Communication can help you develop the communication skills required for success in the 21st century. Have a good term—and a good career!

Cordially,

Kitty O. Locker
locker.1@osu.edu

BAC Sixth Edition

August 1, 2002

Dear Professor:

Business and Administrative Communication (BAC) can make your job teaching business communication just a little bit easier.

You'll find that this edition of BAC is as flexible, specific, interesting, comprehensive, and up-to-date as its predecessors. The features teachers and students find so useful have been retained: the anecdotes and examples, the easy-to-follow lists, the integrated coverage of ethics and international business communication, the analyses of sample problems, problems, the wealth of in-class exercises and out-of-class assignments. But a good thing has become even better. This edition of BAC is the most effective teaching tool yet.

Major Changes in the Sixth Edition

Six major changes make the text even more useful:

- Chapters 9 and 10 have been combined into a single chapter, "Persuasive Messages." The persuasion coverage from the previous Chapter 10 now appears in Appendix D, "Crafting Logical Arguments," where it accompanies the Toulmin logic coverage.

- Chapter 10, "Sales, Fund-Raising, and Promotional Messages," includes new coverage of brochure copy, valuable in the case of businesses that rely on product managers rather than outside agencies to write advertising copy.

- Each chapter now features one or two InSite examples (screen captures) that illustrate the role of the World Wide Web in business communication.

- Coverage of job search and résumé material has been expanded to include keywords and summary of qualifications in résumés, behavioral interviews, sending a résumé by e-mail, and online job boards.

- The new Manager's Hot Seat video lessons accompanying the text show unscripted managers responding to unpredictable situations to promote class discussion.

- New and revised chapter opening statements by business professionals and marginal sidebars keep the text up-to-date.

Features Retained

BAC retains the features that have made it the number one book in business communication:

- **BAC is flexible.** Choose the chapters that best fit your course and your students. Choose from in-class exercises, messages to revise, problems with hints, and cases presented as they'd arise in the workplace. Many problems offer several options: small group discussions, individual writing, group writing, or oral presentations.

- **BAC is specific.** BAC provides specific strategies, specific guidelines, and specific examples. BAC takes the mystery out of creating effective messages.

- **BAC is interesting.** Anecdotes from a variety of fields show business communication at work. The lively side columns from *The Wall Street Journal* and a host of other sources keep students turning pages and provide insights into the workplace that business students demand.

- **BAC is comprehensive.** BAC includes international communication, communicating across cultures in this country, ethics, collaborative writing, organizational cultures, graphs, and technology as well as traditional concerns such as style and organization. Assignments allow students to deal with international audiences or to cope with ethical dilemmas.

- **BAC is up-to-date.** The sixth edition of BAC incorporates the latest research and practice so that you and your students stay on the cutting edge.

Supplements

The stimulating, user-friendly supplement package has been one of the major reasons that BAC is so popular.

1. The **Instructor's Resource Manual** contains

    - **Answers to all exercises,** an overview and difficulty rating for each problem, and, for several of the problems in the book, a detailed analysis, discussion and quiz questions, and a good solution.

    - **Additional transparency masters** with ready-to-duplicate examples and lecture points.

    - **Additional exercises and cases for** diagnostic and readiness tests, grammar and style, and for letters, memos, and reports.

    - **Lesson plans and class activities for each chapter.** You'll find discussion guides for transparencies, activities to reinforce chapter materials and prepare students for assignments, and handouts for group work, peer editing, and other activities.

    - **Sample syllabi** for courses with different emphases and approaches.

2. The **Test Bank** contains approximately 1,200 test items with answers and a difficulty rating for each.

3. **PowerPoint** presentation CD-Rom is available to enliven your classes.

    - Approximately 100 **color acetates** are included that represent figures in the text and expand on concepts in the chapters.

4. The **Instructor's CD-Rom** collects many features of the Instructor's Resource Manual, videos, PowerPoint slides, and lecture material in an electronic format.

5. The **Student Toolbox CD-Rom** provides an added study tool for your students in the classroom and in the workplace to help improve their overall writing and communication skills.

6. A **Computerized Test Bank** is available to qualified adopters in both Macintosh and Windows formats, and allows professors to generate and edit their own test questions.

7. All new **Manager's Hot Seat** skills videos are now included. These videos provide a wonderful jump-start to classroom discussion, as they portray real managers—unscripted—reacting to actors in the video. These videos illustrate topics and skills such as negotiation amid cultural differences, active listening, communication in the virtual workplace, and teamwork.

8. Access to the **BComm Skill Booster** is provided with each new copy of the book. The Skill Booster is an Internet-based learning reinforcement system that delivers fun, interactive lessons to help your students retain and practice what they've learned in your Business Communication course. Each lesson includes three action steps that will help them "boost" their retention of one core skill—reinforced through quizzes, exercises, tips, and Web links. Each lesson takes 10 to 15 minutes. You can choose which lessons they receive, or default to all 40.

9. The **Business Communication PowerWeb** site is an online resource that provides high-quality, peer-reviewed business communication content and Web links, as well as assessment, interactive exercises, and study tips. Access to PowerWeb is available through the accompanying text Web site.

Continuing the Conversation

You can get more information about teaching business communication from the meetings and publications of The Association for Business Communication (ABC). Contact

Professor Robert J. Myers, Executive Director
Association for Business Communication
Baruch College—CUNY
Department of Communication Studies (8-240)
One Bernard Baruch Way
New York, NY 10010
Voice: 212-312-3723; Fax: 212-312-3721; E-mail: abcrjm@cs.com

This edition incorporates the feedback I've received from instructors who used earlier editions. Tell me about your own success stories teaching *Business and Administrative Communication*. I look forward to hearing from you!

Cordially,

Kitty O. Locker

Kitty O. Locker
locker. 1@osu. edu

THANKS

All writing is in some sense collaborative. This book in particular builds upon the ideas and advice of teachers, students, and researchers. The people who share their ideas in conferences and publications enrich not only this book but also business communication as a field.

Many people reviewed the fifth edition, suggesting what to change and what to keep. Additional reviewers commented on drafts of the sixth edition or completed in-depth surveys, helping me further improve the book. I thank all of these reviewers for their attention to detail and their promptness!

Kathy Lewis-Adler, *University of North Alabama*

John Boehm, *Iowa State University*

Maureen S. Bogdanowicz, *Kapi`olani Community College*

Kendra S. Boggess, *Concord College*

Christy Ann Borack, *California State University, Fullerton; Orange Coast College, Costa Mesa*

Charles P. Bretan, *Northwood University*

Phyllis Bunn, *Delta State University*

Nancie McCoy-Burns, *University of Idaho*

Robert Callahan, *The University of Texas, San Antonio*

Danny Cantrell, *West Virginia State College*

Jay Christiansen, *California State University, Northridge*

Lynda Clark, *Maple Woods Community College**

Carla Dando, *Idaho State University**

Anna Easton, *Indiana University*

Louisa Fordyce, *Westmoreland County Community College*

Daryl Grider, *West Virginia State College*

Ed Hagar, *Belhaven College*

David Hawes, *Owens Community College*

Robert Hill, *University of LaVerne*

Kenneth Hoffman, *Emporia State University*

Carole A. Holden, *County College of Morris*

Robert W. Key, *University of Phoenix*

Donna Kienzler, *Iowa State University*

Sarah McClure Kolk, *Hope College*

Dana Loewy, *California State University, Fullerton*

Elizabeth Macdonald, *Thunderbird Graduate School of International Management*

Pamela L. Martin, *The Ohio State University*

Julia R. Meyers, *North Carolina State University*

Paul Miller, *Davidson College*

Josef Moorehead, *California State University, Sacramento*

Nancy Nygaard, *University of Wisconsin, Milwaukee*

Linda N. Peters, *University of West Florida*

Evelyn M. Pierce, *Carnegie Mellon University*

Cathy Pleska, *West Virginia State College*

Susan Plutsky, *California State University, Northridge*

Janet Kay Porter, *Leeward Community College*

Susan Prenzlow, *Minnesota State University, Mankato*

Brenner Pugh, *Virginia Commonwealth University*

Janetta Ritter, *Garland County Community College*

Mary Jane Ryals, *Florida State University*

Betty Schroeder, *Northern Illinois University*

Nancy Schullery, *Western Michigan University*

Janet Starnes, *University of Texas, Austin*

Christine Tachick, *University of Wisconsin, Milwaukee*

Bette Tetreault, *Dalhousie University*

Barbara Z. Thaden, *St. Augustine's College*

Lisa Tyler, *Sinclair Community College*

Linda Weavil, *Elon College*

Gail S. Widner, *University of South Carolina*

Jan Barton-Zimerman, *University of Nebraska, Kearney*

*A special thanks go to Carla Dando and Lynda Clark for reviewing the fifth edition supplements and providing suggestions for change in the sixth edition IM and TB.

In addition, the book continues to benefit from people who advised me on earlier editions:

Bill Allen, *University of LaVerne*

Vanessa Arnold, *University of Mississippi*

Lynn Ashford, *Alabama State University*

Dennis Barbour, *Purdue University–Calumet*

Jaye Bausser, *Indiana University–Purdue University at Fort Wayne*

Carole Bhakar, *The University of Manitoba*

Sallye Benoit, *Nicholls State University*

Raymond W. Beswick, *formerly of Synerude, Ltd.*

Randi Meryl Blank, *Indiana University*

Vincent Brown, *Battelle Memorial Institute*

John Bryan, *University of Cincinnati*

Janice Burke, *South Suburban College of Cook County*

Andrew Cantrell, *University of Illinois*

John Carr, *The Ohio State University*

Brendan G. Coleman, *Mankato State University*

John Cooper, *University of Kentucky*

Tena Crews, *State University of West Georgia*

Susan H. Delagrange, *The Ohio State University*

Mark DelMaramo, *Thiel College*

Moira E. W. Dempsy, *Oregon State University*

Gladys DeVane, *Indiana University*

Jose A. Duran, *Riverside Community College*

Dorothy J. Dykman, *Point Loma Nazarene College*

Mary Ann Firmin, *Oregon State University*

W. Clark Ford, *Middle Tennessee State University*

Paula J. Foster, *Foster Communication*
Silvia Fuduric, *Wayne State University*
Robert D. Gieselman, *University of Illinois*
Cheryl Glenn, *Pennsylvania State University*
Peter Hadorn, *Virginia Commonwealth University*
Elaine Hage, *Forsythe Technical Community College*
Barbara Hagler, *Southern Illinois University*
Robert Haight, *Kalamazoo Valley Community College*
Les Hanson, *Red River Community College, Canada*
Kathy Harris, *Northwestern State University*
Mark Harstein, *University of Illinois*
Maxine Hart, *Baylor University*
Vincent Hartigan, *New Mexico State University*
Charles Hebert, *The University of South Carolina*
Paulette Henry, *Howard University*
Elizabeth Hoger, *Western Michigan University*
Carlton Holte, *California State University, Sacramento*
Glenda Hudson, *California State University, Bakersfield*
Elizabeth Huettman, *Cornell University*
Melissa Ianetta, *University of Southern Indiana*
Susan Isaacs, *Community College of Philadelphia*
Daphne A. Jameson, *Cornell University*
Elizabeth Jenkins, *Pennsylvania State University*
Lee Jones, *Shorter College*
Paula R. Kaiser, *University of North Carolina at Greensboro*
Joy Kidwell, *Oregon State University*
Susan E. Kiner, *Cornell University*
Lisa Klein, *The Ohio State University*
Gary Kohut, *University of North Carolina, Charlotte*
Keith Kroll, *Kalamazoo Valley Community College*
Milton Kukon, *Southern Vermont College*
Linda M. LaDuc, *University of Massachusetts, Amherst*
Suzanne Lambert, *Broward Community College*
Barry Lawler, *Oregon State University*
Gordon Lee, *University of Tennessee*
Luchen Li, *Iowa State University*
Andrea A. Lunsford, *Stanford University*
John T. Maguire, *University of Illinois*
Michael D. Mahler, *Montana State University*
Iris Washburn Mauney, *High Point College*
Patricia McClure, *West Virginia State College*
Brian R. McGee, *Texas Tech University*
Yvonne Merrill, *University of Arizona*
Jayne Moneysmith, *Kent State University–Stark*

Evelyn Morris, *Mesa Community College*

Frederick K. Moss, *University of Wisconsin–Waukesha*

Frank P. Nemecek, Jr., *Wayne State University*

Cheryl Noll, *Eastern Illinois University*

Jean E. Perry, *University of Southern California*

Florence M. Petrofes, *University of Texas at El Paso*

Virginia Polanski, *Stonehill College*

Kathryn C. Rentz, *University of Cincinnati*

Naomi Ritter, *Indiana University*

Jeanette Ritzenthaler, *New Hampshire College*

Ralph Roberts, *University of West Florida*

Carol Roever, *Missouri Western State College*

Mary Saga, *University of Alaska-Fairbanks*

Kelly Searsmith, *University of Illinois*

Sherry Sherrill, *Forsythe Technical Community College*

Frank Smith, *Harper College*

Pamela Smith, *Florida Atlantic University*

Ron Stone, *DeVry University*

Judith A. Swartley, *Lehigh University*

Mel Tarnowski, *Macomb Community College*

Linda Travis, *Ferris State University*

Lisa Tyler, *Sinclair Community College*

Donna Vasa, *University of Nebraska–Lincoln*

David A. Victor, *Eastern Michigan University*

Catherine Waitinas, *University of Illinois, Champaign-Urbana*

Vicky Waldroupe, *Tusculum College*

Randall Waller, *Baylor University*

George Walters, *Emporia State University*

Judy West, *University of Tennessee–Chattanooga*

Rosemary Wilson, *Washtenaw Community College*

Janet Winter, *Central Missouri State University*

Bonnie Thames Yarbrough, *University of North Carolina at Greensboro*

Sherilyn K. Zeigler, *Hawaii Pacific University*

I'm pleased to know that the book has worked so well for so many people and appreciative of suggestions for ways to make it even more useful in this edition. I especially want to thank the students who have allowed me to use their letters and memos, whether or not they allowed me to use their real names in the text.

I am grateful to all the business people who were willing to interrupt busy schedules to write the chapter-opening statements for this book. The companies where I have done research and consulting work have given me insights into the problems and procedures of business and administrative communication. Special acknowledgment is due Joseph T. Ryerson & Son, Inc., which hired me to create the Writing Skills Program that ultimately became the first draft of this book. And I thank the organizations that permitted me to reproduce their documents in this book and in the transparency masters.

Alisha Rohde did library and Web research. Sarah Reed and Lori Bailey helped me line up the business people whose profiles open each chapter. The book continues to incorporate the contributions of Bennis Blue, Susan Carlson, Kathy Casto, Jane Greer, Ruth Ann Hendrickson, Gianna Marsella, Scott Miller, Carole Clark Papper, Paula Weston, and Andrea Williams to earlier editions.

I would also like to thank Jayne Moneysmith for authoring the Instructor's Resource Manual and Test Bank, Nina McGuffin for revising the PowerPoint presentation, and Christine Tachik for creating the transparency acetates that accompany the book.

My publisher, McGraw-Hill/Irwin, continues to provide strong editorial and staff support. I am particularly grateful to Andy Winston for his creative problem solving, patience, and encouragement, to Sarah Reed for taking care of necessary details, and to Michael Warrell and Mary Conzachi for the appearance of the book.

And, finally, I thank my husband, Robert S. Mills, who continues to provide a sounding board for ideas, encouragement, and, when deadlines are tight (as they continue to be, even on this sixth edition), weekly or nightly rides to FedEx.

A Guided Tour

The 6th Edition of Business and Administrative Communication was developed to teach you how to communicate effectively and improve your written and oral business communication skills. This knowledge will help you in your courses and, more importantly, in your future career.

Throughout this text, several pedagogical elements appear to teach readers about all the aspects of business communication. These examples in their many formats are found in every chapter and provide excellent real-world examples to underscore key concepts throughout the text.

Please take a moment to learn about this new edition and its features by paging through this visual guide outlining the text's new features.

NEW

"InSite" Boxes show the WWW at work in business communication. Corporate, small business, nonprofit, and government Web sites illustrate the resources available on the Web and show how innovative organizations use the Web to compete successfully.

It's easy to feel defensive when someone criticizes your work. If the feedback stings, put it aside until you can read it without feeling defensive. Even if you think that the reader hasn't understood what you were trying to say, the fact that the reader complained usually means the section could be improved. If the reader says "This isn't true" and you know the statement is true, several kinds of revision might make the truth clear to the reader: rephrasing the statement, giving more information or examples, or documenting the source.

Reading feedback carefully is a good way to understand the culture of your organization. Are you told to give more details or to shorten messages? Does your boss add headings and bullet points? Look for patterns in the comments, and apply what you learn in your next document.

Using Boilerplate

Boilerplate is language—sentences, paragraphs, even pages—from a previous document that a writer includes in a new document. In academic papers, material written by others must be quoted and documented. However, because businesses own the documents their employees write, old text may be included without attribution.

In some cases, boilerplate may have been written years ago. For example, many legal documents, including apartment leases and sales contracts, are almost completely boilerplated. In other cases, writers may use boilerplate they wrote for earlier documents. For example, a section from a proposal describing the background of the problem could also be used in the final report after the proposed work was completed. A section from a progress report describing what the writer had done could be used with only a few changes in the methods section of the final report.

InSite

www.wisc.edu/writing/Handbook/Proofreading.html

The University of Wisconsin Writing Center offers tips on proofreading. For more proofreading links, visit the BAC Web site.

Review and Revision*

In my most recent experience, 2½ years in a Sales and Marketing Division of a major international corporation, . . . all important writing that is generated by the corporation is reviewed at three or more levels. That means that if a middle manager sends a letter to all or some dealers, the letter will be reviewed by his or her boss (usually a vice president) and a senior vice president. If the contents are sensitive, possibly vulnerable to unfavorable media review, the letter may be reviewed by all senior vice presidents, the legal [staff], and the president/CEO.

If a senior vice president writes a letter, any letter [going] outside the company, it is reviewed by the president and by the management level just below him.

All letters going outside the company and written at or below the middle management level are heavily reviewed, sometimes harshly reviewed.

*Quoted from Carol Elizabeth King, Rensselaer Polytechnic Institute, Troy, NY, "Re: Reviews?" posting to bizcom@ebbs.english.vt.edu, January 27, 1998.

FIGURE 5.6

✓ CHECKLIST   Questions to Ask Readers

Outline or planning draft
- ☐ Does the plan seem on the right track?
- ☐ What topics should be added? Should any be cut?
- ☐ Do you have any other general suggestions?

Revising draft
- ☐ Does the message satisfy all its purposes?
- ☐ Is the message adapted to the audience(s)?
- ☐ Is the organization effective?
- ☐ What parts aren't clear?
- ☐ What ideas need further development?
- ☐ Do you have any other suggestions?

Polishing draft
- ☐ Are there any problems with word choice or sentence structure?
- ☐ Did you find any inconsistencies?
- ☐ Did you find any typos?
- ☐ Is the document's design effective?

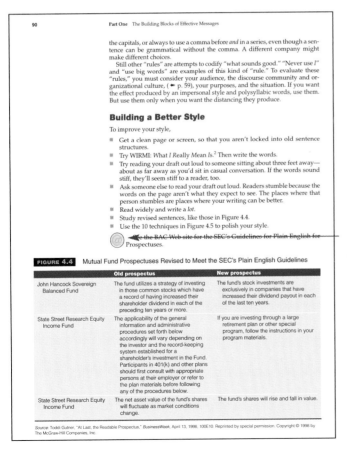

Sidebars offer fun and innovative examples of the text principles at work. They appear in the margins of every chapter of the text and cover a variety of topics: International, Legal/Ethical, Just for Fun, On the Job, and Technology. "Classic" sidebars are highlighted with a gold ribbon as well.

"@ links" in the text let you know that the textbook Web site has links to more information about the topic. On the Web, the links are organized by chapter. Click on them, and you'll find additional Web sites, information, and content to enrich the chapter discussions.

Business Communication, Management, and Success

Dave Seifert
Strategic Communication Manager, Hallmark Cards

Hallmark Cards is the world's leading personal expression company and is virtually synonymous with consumers' preferred brand of greeting cards. Dave communicates strategies and solutions for Hallmark's international division and provides counsel to senior managers.

www.hallmark.com

"In today's highly competitive marketplace, good communication matters more than ever."

In today's highly competitive marketplace, good communication matters more than ever. Employees want to know where the organization is headed and how they can help. Customers want to know how your product provides value for them that can't be found elsewhere. Other stakeholders want to know how your organization affects them. You can only meet those needs if you communicate effectively.

Organizational communication used to mean delivering information to selected audiences. Today, it means strategically addressing opportunities and needs so that your organization can achieve its goals. That means shaping messages and delivery mechanisms to connect with each audience in ways that are timely, relevant and credible.

A few years ago, Hallmark Cards closed a manufacturing facility in a town in Kansas because the company had excess capacity at other facilities. Communicating that change involved:

- Explaining the decision and, more importantly, the rationale to employees, and meeting with them individually to explain how it would affect them.

- Announcing the decision to local news media, where this would be perceived as bad news unless correctly understood.

- Talking to local political leaders to make sure they understood why this would occur and what steps Hallmark would take to help them find another user for the facility.

The project involved not only internal and external communicators from Hallmark but also key staff from operations, human resources and public affairs. It took planning and thinking—always the biggest parts of writing and editing.

Good communication isn't easy, but it's som[...] cation is about what the receivers will to hear[...]

It's about connecting your organization's [...] sense, whether you're involved or not.

And it's about telling the truth, with contex[...]

Most importantly, good communication is a[...] gic" means—getting out ahead of events by co[...] goals and progress.

Kevin Thomson, chairman of the Marketing [...] that "winning the hearts and minds" of empl[...] day. It might be said that's also true of all stake[...]

And what better way to win hearts and min[...]

"Inside Perspectives" open each chapter. Real business people explain how they use the chapter concepts in their work.

Checklists for the most important messages appear throughout the book. Use them to plan your message and to check your draft.

FIGURE 9.12   A Good Solution to the Sample Problem

Jennifer M. Kirkland   2   October 10, 2003

According to the accounting department, Nakamura makes a net profit of $10 on every TV set we sell. And, as you know, with the boom in TV sales, we sell every set we make. Those 18,600 units we don't produce are costing us $186,000 a year.

Shows where numbers in paragraph 1 come from

Bringing down the temperature to 78° (the minimum allowed under federal guidelines) from the present summer average of 112° will require an investment of $500,000 to insulate and air-condition the tube room. Extra energy costs for the air-conditioning will run about $30,000 a year. We'll get our investment back in less than three years. Once the investment is recouped, we'll be making an additional $150,000 a year—all without buying additional equipment or hiring additional workers.

Additional benefit

By installing the insulation and air-conditioning this fall, we can take advantage of lower off-season rates. Please authorize the Purchasing Department to request bids for the system. Then, next summer, our productivity can be at an all-time high.

Tells reader what to do

Reason to act promptly

Ends on positive note of problem solved, reader enjoying benefit

---

✓ CHECKLIST   Checklist for Problem-Solving Persuasive Messages

☐ If the message is a memo, does the subject line indicate the writer's purpose or offer a reader benefit? Does the subject line avoid making the request?
☐ Does the first sentence interest the reader?
☐ Is the problem presented as a joint problem both writer and reader have an interest in solving, rather than as something the reader is being asked to do for the writer?
☐ Does the message give all of the relevant information? Is there enough detail?
☐ Does the message overcome objections that readers may have?
☐ Does the message avoid phrases that sound dictatorial, condescending, or arrogant?
☐ Does the last paragraph tell the reader exactly what to do? Does it give a deadline if one exists and a reason for acting promptly?

And, for all messages, not just persuasive ones,
☐ Does the message use you-attitude and positive emphasis?
☐ Is the style easy to read and friendly?
☐ Is the visual design of the message inviting?
☐ Is the format correct?
☐ Does the message use standard grammar? Is it free from typos?

Originality in a problem-solving persuasive message may come from
☐ A good subject line and common ground.
☐ A clear and convincing description of the problem.
☐ Thinking about readers and giving details that answer their questions, overcome objections, and make it easier for them to do as you ask.
☐ Adding details that show you're thinking about a specific organization and the specific people in that organization.

FIGURE 7.2 A Positive Letter *(continued)*

Professor Adrienne Prinz
March 7, 2003
Page 2

IFI offices are equipped with Pentium computers with Access, WordPerfect, and Excel. Is there any software that we should buy for cataloguing or research? Are there any office supplies that we need to have on hand June 2 so that you can work efficiently?

In the meantime,

1. Please send your written acceptance right away.

2. Let me know if you need any software or supplies.

3. Send me the name, address, and Social Security number of your research assistant by May 1 so that I can process his or her employment papers.

4. If you'd like help finding a house or apartment in Atlanta, let me know. I can give you the name of a real estate agent.

Goodwill ending

On June 2, you'll spend the morning in Personnel. Stop by my office at noon. We'll go out for lunch and then I'll take you to the office you'll have while you're at IFI.

Welcome to IFI!

Cordially,

Cynthia Yen

Cynthia Yen
Director of Education and Training

to persuade. The opportunity for the professor to study records that aren't available to the public is an implicit reader benefit; the concern for the reader's needs builds goodwill.

The memo in Figure 7.3 announces a new employee benefit. The first paragraph summarizes the policy. Paragraphs 2–5 give details. Negative elements are in paragraphs 3–5, stated as positively as possible. The last section of the memo gives reader benefits and a goodwill ending.

Subject Lines for Informative and Positive Messages

A **subject line** is the title of a document. It aids in filing and retrieving the document, tells readers why they need to read the document, and provides a framework in which to set what you're about to say.

Subject lines are standard in memos. Letters are not required to have subject lines (see Appendix A, Formats for Letters, Memos, and E-mail Messages). However, a survey of business people in the southwest United States found that 68% of them considered a subject line in a letter to be important, very

---

You-Attitude with International Audiences

When you communicate with international audiences, look at the world from their point of view.

The United States is in the middle of most of the maps sold in the United States. It isn't in the middle of maps sold elsewhere in the world.

The United States clings to a measurement system that has been abandoned by most of the world. When you write for international audiences, use the metric system.

Even pronouns and direction words need attention. *We* may not feel inclusive to readers with different assumptions and backgrounds. *Here* won't mean the same thing to a reader in Bonn as it does to one in Boulder.

Maybe the reader expects that anything you sell would meet government regulations (OSHA—the Occupational Safety and Health Administration—is a federal agency). The reader may even be disappointed if he or she expected higher standards. Simply explain the situation or describe a product's features; don't predict the reader's response.

When you have good news for the reader, simply give the good news.

Lacks you-attitude: You'll be happy to hear that your scholarship has been renewed.

You-attitude: Congratulations! Your scholarship has been renewed.

4. In positive situations, use you more often than I. Use we when it includes the reader.

Whenever possible, focus on the reader, not on you or your company.

Lacks you-attitude: We provide health insurance to all employees.

You-attitude: You receive health insurance as a full-time Procter & Gamble employee.

Most readers are tolerant of the word *I* in e-mail messages, which seem like conversation. Edit paper documents to use *I* rarely if at all. *I* suggests that you're concerned about personal issues, not about the organization's problems, needs, and opportunities. *We* works well when it includes the reader. Avoid *we* if it excludes the reader (as it would in a letter to a customer or supplier or as it might in a memo about *we* in management want *you* to do).

5. In negative situations, avoid the word you. Protect the reader's ego. Use passive verbs and impersonal expressions to avoid assigning blame.

When you report bad news or limitations, use a noun for a group of which the reader is a part instead of *you* so readers don't feel that they're singled out for bad news.

Lacks you-attitude: You must get approval from the director before you publish any articles or memoirs based on your work in the agency

You-attitude: Agency personnel must get approval from the director to publish any articles or memoirs based on their work at the agency.

Use passive verbs and impersonal expressions to avoid blaming the reader. **Passive verbs** describe the action performed on something, without necessarily saying who did it. (See Chapter 4 for a full discussion of passive verbs.) **Impersonal expressions** omit people and talk only about things.

In most cases, active verbs are better. But when your reader is at fault, passive verbs may be useful to avoid assigning blame.

Normally, writing is most lively when it's about people—and most interesting to readers when it's about them. When you have to report a mistake or bad news, however, you can protect the reader's ego by using an impersonal expression, one in which things, not people, do the acting.

Lacks you-attitude: You made no allowance for inflation in your estimate.

You-attitude (passive):   No allowance for inflation has been made in this estimate.

You-attitude (impersonal):   This estimate makes no allowance for inflation.

A purist might say that impersonal expressions are illogical: an estimate, for example, is inanimate and can't "make" anything. In the pragmatic world of business writing, however, impersonal expressions often help you convey criticism tactfully.

CONTENTS

PART TWO   Letters, Memos, and E-mail Messages   145

PART THREE Interpersonal Communication 289

PART FOUR   Reports   345

PART FIVE   Job Hunting   483

The Building Blocks of Effective Messages

Business Communication, Management, and Success

Business Communication, Management, and Success

Dave Seifert
Strategic Communication Manager, Hallmark Cards

Hallmark Cards is the world's leading personal expression company and is virtually synonymous with consumers' preferred brand of greeting cards. Dave communicates strategies and solutions for Hallmark's international division and provides counsel to senior managers.

www.hallmark.com

In today's highly competitive marketplace, good communication matters more than ever. Employees want to know where the organization is headed and how they can help. Customers want to know how your product provides value for them that can't be found elsewhere. Other stakeholders want to know how your organization affects them. You can only meet those needs if you communicate effectively.

Organizational communication used to mean delivering information to selected audiences. Today, it means strategically addressing opportunities and needs so that your organization can achieve its goals. That means shaping messages and delivery mechanisms to connect with each audience in ways that are timely, relevant and credible.

A few years ago, Hallmark Cards closed a manufacturing facility in a town in Kansas because the company had excess capacity at other facilities. Communicating that change involved:

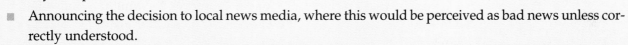

"In today's highly competitive marketplace, good communication matters more than ever."

- Explaining the decision and, more importantly, the rationale to employees, and meeting with them individually to explain how it would affect them.

- Announcing the decision to local news media, where this would be perceived as bad news unless correctly understood.

- Talking to local political leaders to make sure they understood why this would occur and what steps Hallmark would take to help them find another user for the facility.

The project involved not only internal and external communicators from Hallmark but also key staff from operations, human resources and public affairs. It took planning and thinking—always the biggest parts of writing and editing.

Good communication isn't easy, but it's something that anyone can do well. To start, good communication is about what the receivers will to hear/read, not what the deliverer wants them to hear/read.

It's about connecting your organization's desired outcomes to current activities in ways that make sense, whether you're involved or not.

And it's about telling the truth, with context that enhances understanding.

Most importantly, good communication is all about being intentional. That's really what being "strategic" means—getting out ahead of events by communicating on a regular basis about your organization's goals and progress.

Kevin Thomson, chairman of the Marketing & Communications Agency Ltd. in Marlow, England, says that "winning the hearts and minds" of employees is the most important factor in business success today. It might be said that's also true of all stakeholders.

And what better way to win hearts and minds than through effective communication?

Lessons from the Best*

The best manufacturing plants in the United States "focus on people, communicate, and have common goals."

"Communication—both formal and informal—is the key to ingraining your company philosophy and goals into each and every employee," points out Darryl Miller, Plant Manager, Aeroquip Corporation, New Haven, IN (air-conditioning components).

"Open . . . lines of communication develop trust, encourage new ideas, eliminate intimidation and skepticism, and aid in building a brighter future for employees and the company," says Steve McGowen, Plant Manager, Halliburton Energy Services, Carrollton, TX (equipment for the oil and gas industries).

"We use group meetings, required readings, a shift newsletter, a monthly newspaper, daily electronic and hard-copy news sheets, all-hands meetings, team meetings, and even public-address announcements to keep people informed. Communication is like dairy farming—you milk the cows but they never stay milked. It has to be a process the organization uses constantly," notes John R. Dew, Manager of Mission Success, Lockhead Martin Utility Services, Paducah, KY (enriched uranium).

*Quotations from Michael A. Verespie, "Lessons from the Best," *Industry Week*, February 2, 1998; INDUSTRYWEEK.COM/Current Articles/asp/articles/ asp?ArticleD=262, visited site December 15, 1998.

Business depends on communication. People must communicate to plan products; hire, train, and motivate workers; coordinate manufacturing and delivery; persuade customers to buy; and bill them for the sale. Indeed, for many businesses and nonprofit and government organizations, the "product" is information or services rather than something tangible. Information and services are created and delivered by communication. In every organization, communication is the way people get their points across and get work done.

Communication takes many forms: face-to-face or phone conversations, informal meetings, e-mail messages, letters, memos, and reports. All of these methods are forms of **verbal communication,** or communication that uses words. **Nonverbal communication** does not use words. Pictures, computer graphics, and company logos are nonverbal. Interpersonal nonverbal signals include smiles, who sits where at a meeting, the size of an office, and how long someone keeps a visitor waiting.

Communication Ability = Promotability

Even in your first job, you'll communicate. You'll read information; you'll listen to instructions; you'll ask questions; you may solve problems with other workers in teams. In a manufacturing company, hourly workers travel to a potential customer to make oral sales presentations. In an insurance company, clerks answer customers' letters. Even "entry-level" jobs require high-level skills in reasoning, mathematics, and communicating. As a result, communication ability ranked first among the qualities that employers look for in college graduates.[1]

Richard Todd at the Federal Reserve Bank of Minneapolis tries to find people who can write and read critically:

> Good writing is one of two key abilities I focus on when hiring; the other is the ability to read critically. I can train people to do almost anything else, but I don't have time to teach this.[2]

Communication becomes even more important as you advance. Annette Gregorich, Vice President of Human Resources for Multiple Zones International, says,

> I've actually seen people lose promotions because they couldn't write a proposal or stand in front of the management team and make a presentation.[3]

Good communication skills are crucial if you want (or need) to change jobs. According to career counselor Andrew Posner,

> Transferable skills—[the ability to] analyze, write, persuade, and manage—are what will facilitate a career change.[4]

As a result, good writers earn more. Linguist Stephen Reder has found that among people with two- or four-year degrees, workers in the top 20% of writing ability earn, on average, more than three times as much as workers whose writing falls into the worst 20%.[5]

"I'll Never Have to Write Because . . ."

Some students think that a secretary will do their writing, that they can use form letters if they do have to write, that only technical skills matter, or that they'll call rather than write. Each of these claims is fundamentally flawed.

Claim 1:   Secretaries will do all my writing.
Reality: Downsizing and voice mail have cut support staffs nationwide. Of the secretaries who remain, 71% are administrative assistants whose duties are managerial, not clerical.[6]

Claim 2:   I'll use form letters or templates when I need to write.
Reality: A **form letter** is a prewritten, fill-in-the-blank letter designed to fit standard situations. Using a form letter is OK if it's a good letter. But form letters cover only routine situations. The higher you rise, the more frequently you'll face situations that aren't routine, that demand creative solutions.

Claim 3:   I'm being hired as an accountant, not a writer.
Reality: Almost every entry-level professional or managerial job requires you to write e-mail messages, speak to small groups, and write e-mail and paper documents. People who do these things well are more likely to be promoted beyond the entry level.

Claim 4:   I'll just pick up the phone.
Reality: Important phone calls require follow-up letters, memos, or e-mail messages. People in organizations put things in writing to make themselves visible, create a record, to convey complex data, to make things convenient for the reader, to save money, and to convey their own messages more effectively. "If it isn't in writing," says a manager at one company, "it didn't happen." Writing is an essential way to make yourself visible, to let your accomplishments be known.

The Managerial Functions of Communication

According to Henry Mintzberg, managers have three basic jobs: to collect and convey information, to make decisions, and to promote interpersonal unity.[7] Every one of those jobs is carried out through communication. Managers collect relevant information from conversations, the grapevine, phone calls, memos, reports, databases, and the Internet. They convey information and decisions to other people inside or outside the organization through meetings, speeches, press releases, videos, memos, letters, e-mail messages, and reports. Managers motivate organizational members in speeches, memos, conversations at lunch and over coffee, bulletin boards, and through "management by walking around."

Effective managers are able to use a wide variety of media and strategies to communicate. They know how to interpret comments from informal channels such as the company grapevine; they can speak effectively in small groups and in formal presentations; they write well.

Communication—oral, nonverbal, and written—goes to both internal and external audiences. **Internal audiences** (Figure 1.1) are other people in the same organization: subordinates, superiors, peers. **External audiences** (Figure 1.2) are people outside the organization: customers, suppliers, unions, stockholders, potential employees, government agencies, the press, and the general public.

The Importance of Listening, Speaking, and Interpersonal Communication

Informal listening, speaking, and working in groups are just as important as writing formal documents and giving formal oral presentations. As a newcomer in an organization, you'll need to listen to others both to find out what you're supposed to do and to learn about the organization's values and culture. Informal chitchat, both about yesterday's game and about what's happening at work, connects you to the **grapevine,** an informal source of company information. You may be asked to speak to small groups, either inside or outside your organization.[8] Networking with others in your office and in town and working with others in workgroups will be crucial to your success.

Legal Implications of Business Writing*

Letters and memos create legal obligations for organizations.

When a lawsuit is filed against an organization, the lawyers for the plaintiffs have the right to subpoena documents written by employees of the organization. These documents may then be used as evidence that an employer fired an employee without adequate notice or that a company knew about a safety defect but did nothing to correct it.

Organizations whose actions are irresponsible or negligent deserve to be condemned by their own words. But a careless writer can create obligations that the writer does not intend and that the organization does not mean to assume.

Careful writers and speakers think about the larger social context in which their words may be read. What might those words mean to other people in your field? What might they mean to a judge and jury?

*Based on Elizabeth A. McCord, "The Business Writer, the Law, and Routine Business Communication: A Legal and Rhetorical Analysis," *Journal of Business and Technical Communication* 5.2 (April 1991): 173–99.

Listening at Pillsbury*

Top managers in some companies are isolated. Pillsbury managers avoid that problem by encouraging anonymous phone calls.

Pillsbury employees can sound off to a recording machine. Another company provides verbatim anonymous transcripts. Pillsbury's CEO gets them all.

Some comments report problems: delayed pension benefits or expense reimbursements.

Many comments suggest ideas or provide genuinely useful knowledge. One caller suggests a new topping for Pillsbury's frozen pizza. Another notes that the time clock in Eden Prairie, Minnesota, was five minutes fast. Still another notes that a certain retail product isn't on the local grocery store shelf.

Some comments support managers' decisions. Dozens of employees phoned in to applaud the action of one manager in shutting down a plant during a snowstorm.

Pillsbury's managers listen. And as a result, in small, important ways, the company is changing the way it does business.

*Based on Thomas Petzinger, Jr., "Two Executives Cook Up Way to Make Pillsbury Listen," *The Wall Street Journal,* September 27, 1996, B1.

FIGURE 1.1   The Internal Audiences of the Sales Manager—West

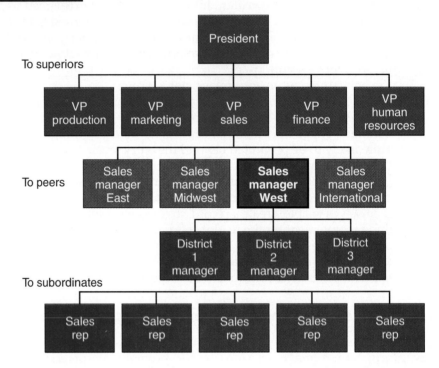

FIGURE 1.2   The Corporation's External Audiences

Source: Daphne A. Jameson

These skills remain important as you climb the corporate ladder. In fact, a study of 15 executives judged good performers by their companies showed that these executives spent most of their time in informal contact with other people. They asked questions; they joked; they schmoozed; they nudged people toward the direction they wanted them to go. These informal discussions and meetings took 76% of these executives' work time. The resulting interactions with thousands of employees and outsiders enabled them to promote their agendas.[9]

The Documents That Writers in Organizations Write

People in organizations produce a large variety of documents. Figures 1.3 and 1.4 list a few of the specific documents produced at Joseph T. Ryerson & Son. Ryerson, a subsidiary of a Fortune 500 company, has 25 plants across the United States; it fabricates and sells steel, aluminum, and plastics to a wide variety of industrial clients.

All of the documents in Figures 1.3 and 1.4 have one or more of the **three basic purposes of organizational writing:** to inform, to request or persuade, and to build goodwill. When you **inform,** you explain something or tell readers something. When you **request or persuade,** you want the reader to act. The word *request* suggests that the action will be easy or routine; *persuade* suggests that you will have to motivate and convince the reader to act. When you **build goodwill,** you create a good image of yourself and of your organization—the kind of image that makes people want to do business with you.

Most messages have multiple purposes. When you answer a question, you're informing, but you also want to build goodwill by suggesting that you're competent and perceptive and that your answer is correct and complete. In a claims adjustment, whether your answer is *yes* or *no,* you want to suggest that the

FIGURE 1.3   Internal Documents Produced in One Organization

Document	Description of document	Purpose(s) of document
Transmittal	Memo accompanying document, telling why it's being forwarded to the receiver	Inform; persuade reader to read document; build image and goodwill
Monthly or quarterly report	Report summarizing profitability, productivity, and problems during period. Used to plan activity for next month or quarter	Inform; build image and goodwill (report is accurate, complete; writer understands company)
Policy and procedure bulletin	Statement of company policies and instructions (e.g., how to enter orders, how to run fire drills)	Inform; build image and goodwill (procedures are reasonable)
Request to deviate from policy and procedure bulletin	Persuasive memo arguing that another approach is better for a specific situation than the standard approach	Persuade; build image and goodwill (request is reasonable; writer seeks good of company)
Performance appraisal	Evaluation of an employee's performance, with recommended areas for improvement or recommendation for promotion	Inform; persuade employee to improve
Memo of congratulations	Congratulations to employees who have won awards, been promoted, or earned community recognition	Build goodwill

| FIGURE 1.4 | External Documents Produced in One Organization |

Document	Description of document	Purpose(s) of document
Quotation	Letter giving price for a specific product, fabrication, or service	Inform; build goodwill (price is reasonable)
Claims adjustment	Letter granting or denying customer request to be given credit for defective goods	Inform; build goodwill
Job description	Description of qualifications and duties of each job. Used for performance appraisals, setting salaries, and for hiring	Inform; persuade good candidates to apply; build goodwill (job duties match level, pay)
10-K report	Report filed with the Securities and Exchange Commission detailing financial information	Inform
Annual report	Report to stockholders summarizing financial information for year	Inform; persuade stockholders to retain stock and others to buy; build goodwill (company is a good corporate citizen)
Thank-you letter	Letter to suppliers, customers, or other people who have helped individuals or the company	Build goodwill

reader's claim has been given careful consideration and that the decision is fair, businesslike, and justified.

Two of the documents listed in Figure 1.4 package the same information in different ways for different audiences. The 10-K report filed with the Securities and Exchange Commission (SEC) and the annual report distributed to stockholders contain essentially the same information, but differing purposes and differing audiences create two distinct documents. The 10-K report is informative, designed merely to show that the company is complying with SEC regulations. The annual report, in contrast, has multiple purposes and audiences. Its primary purpose is to convince stockholders that the company is a good investment and a good corporate citizen. Annual reports will also be read by employees, stockbrokers, potential stockholders, and job applicants, so the firm creates a report that is persuasive and builds goodwill as well as presenting information.

The Cost of Correspondence

Writing costs money. In 1996, according to the Dartnell Institute, a short one-page business letter cost between $13.60 and $20.52, depending on how it was produced.[10] Dartnell's estimates assume that an executive dictates a letter in 10 minutes. But a consultant who surveyed employees in seven industries found that most of them spent 54 minutes planning, composing, and revising a one-page letter.[11] Her respondents, then, each spent over $84 at 1996 prices to create a one-page letter. Dartnell no longer calculates the cost of a business letter, but it seems likely that costs have not fallen. One company in Minneapolis writes 3,000 original letters a day. If each of those letters is written in slightly less than an hour, it spends at least $252,000 a day just on outgoing correspondence.

In many organizations, all external documents must be approved before they go out. A document may **cycle** from writer to superior to writer to another superior to writer again 3 or 4 or even 11 times before it is finally approved. The cycling process increases the cost of correspondence.

Longer documents can involve large teams of people and take months to write. An engineering firm that relies on military contracts for its business calculates that it spends $500,000 to put together an average proposal and $1 million to write a large proposal.[12]

Good communication is worth every minute it takes and every penny it costs. In fact, in a survey conducted by the International Association of Business Communicators, CEOs said that communication yielded a 235% return on investment.[13]

The Costs of Poor Correspondence

When writing isn't as good as it could be, you and your organization pay a price in wasted time, wasted efforts, and lost goodwill.

Wasted Time

Bad writing takes longer to read. Studies show that up to 97% of our reading time is taken not in moving our eyes across the page but in trying to understand what we're reading. How quickly we can do this is determined by the difficulty of the subject matter and by the document's organization and writing style.

Second, bad writing may need to be rewritten. Many managers find that a disproportionate amount of their time is taken trying to explain to subordinates how to revise a document.

Third, ineffective writing may obscure ideas so that discussions and decisions are needlessly drawn out. People inside an organization may disagree on the best course, and the various publics with which organizations communicate may have different interests and values. But if a proposal is clear, at least everyone will be talking about the same proposed changes, so that differences can be recognized and resolved more quickly.

Fourth, unclear or incomplete messages may require the reader to ask for more information. A reader who has to supplement the memo with questions interrupts the writer. If the writer is out of the office when the reader stops by or calls, even more time is wasted, for the reader can't act until the answer arrives.

Wasted Efforts

Ineffective messages don't get results. A reader who has to guess what the writer means may guess wrong. A reader who finds a letter or memo unconvincing or insulting simply won't do what the message asks.

One company sent out past-due bills with the following language:

> Per our conversation, enclosed are two copies of the above-mentioned invoice. Please review and advise. Sincerely, . . .

The company wanted money, not advice, but it didn't say so. The company had to write third and fourth reminders. It waited for its money, lost interest on it— and kept writing letters.

Lost Goodwill

Whatever the literal content of the words, every letter, memo, or report serves either to build or to undermine the image the reader has of the writer.

Part of building a good image is taking the time to write correctly. Even organizations that have adopted casual dress still expect writing to appear professional and to be free from typos and grammatical errors.

The Cost Was Classified*

Fuzzy building instructions have added hundreds of thousands of dollars to building costs. And a single hyphen omitted by a supervisor at a government-run nuclear installation may hold the cost record for punctuation goofs. He ordered rods of radioactive material cut into "10 foot long lengths"; he got 10 pieces, each a foot long, instead of the 10-foot lengths required. The loss was so great it was classified [as secret by the federal government].

*Quoted from William E. Blundell, "Confused, Overstuffed Corporate Writing Often Costs Firms Much Time—and Money," *The Wall Street Journal*, August 21, 1980, 21.

FIGURE 1.5   A Form Letter That Annoyed Customers

Nelson Manufacturing

600 N. Main Street   317-281-3000
Indianapolis, IN   46204   fax 317-281-3001

Where are date,
Inside address?
No excuse for not adding these!

Sexist!
Gentlemen:
Stuffy   *emphasizes the*
writer, not the reader

Please be advised that upon reviewing your credit file with us, we find the information
herein outdated. In an effort to expedite the handling of your future orders with us, and to
wrong allow us to open an appropriate line of credit for your company, we ask that you send an
word updated list of vendor references. Any other additional financial information that you can
(also supply would be to both of our benefits.
stuffy)   *Prove it!*   *What*
                                                                            information?

main
point
is
buried

May we hear from you soon?

Sincerely,

Messages can also create a poor image because of poor audience analysis
and inappropriate style. The form letter printed in Figure 1.5 failed because it
was stuffy and selfish. Four different customers called to complain about it.
When you think how often you are annoyed by something—a TV commercial,
a rude clerk—but how rarely you call or write the company to complain, you
can imagine the ill will this letter generated.

As the comments in red show, several things are wrong with the letter in Figure 1.5.

1. **The language is stiff and legalistic.** Note the obsolete (and sexist) "Gentlemen:" "Please be advised," "herein," and "expedite."
2. **The tone is selfish.** The letter is written from the writer's point of view;
   there are no benefits for the reader. (The writer says there are, but, without
   a shred of evidence, the claim isn't convincing.)
3. **The main point is buried** in the middle of the long first paragraph. The
   middle is the least emphatic part of a paragraph.
4. **The request is vague.** How many references does the supplier want? Are
   only vendor references OK, or would other credit references, like banks,
   work too? Is the name of the reference enough, or is it necessary also to
   specify the line of credit, the average balance, the current balance, the years
   credit has been established, or other information? What "additional financial information" does the supplier want? Annual reports? Bank balance?
   Tax returns? The request sounds like an invasion of privacy, not a reasonable business practice.
5. **Words are misused** (*herein* for *therein*), suggesting either an ignorant writer
   or one who doesn't care enough about the subject and the reader to use the
   right word.

Benefits of Improving Correspondence

Better writing helps you to

- **Save time.** Reduce reading time, since comprehension is easier. Eliminate the time now taken to rewrite badly written materials. Reduce the time taken asking writers "What did you mean?"

- **Make your efforts more effective.** Increase the number of requests that are answered positively and promptly—on the first request. Present your points—to other people in your organization; to clients, customers, and suppliers; to government agencies; to the public—more forcefully.

- **Communicate your points more clearly.** Reduce the misunderstandings that occur when the reader has to supply missing or unclear information. Make the issues clear, so that disagreements can surface and be resolved more quickly.

- **Build goodwill.** Build a positive image of your organization. Build an image of yourself as a knowledgeable, intelligent, capable person.

Criteria for Effective Messages

Good business and administrative writing meets five basic criteria: it's clear, complete, and correct; it saves the reader's time; and it builds goodwill.

1. **It's clear.** The meaning the reader gets is the meaning the writer intended. The reader doesn't have to guess.

2. **It's complete.** All of the reader's questions are answered. The reader has enough information to evaluate the message and act on it.

3. **It's correct.** All of the information in the message is accurate. The message is free from errors in punctuation, spelling, grammar, word order, and sentence structure.

4. **It saves the reader's time.** The style, organization, and visual impact of the message help the reader to read, understand, and act on the information as quickly as possible.

5. **It builds goodwill.** The message presents a positive image of the writer and his or her organization. It treats the reader as a person, not a number. It cements a good relationship between the writer and the reader.

Whether a message meets these five criteria depends on **the interactions among the writer, the audience, the purposes of the message, and the situation.** No single set of words will work in all possible situations.

Trends in Business and Administrative Communication

Both business and business communication are changing. Ten trends in business, government, and nonprofit organizations affect business and administrative communication: a focus on quality and customers' needs, entrepreneurship and outsourcing, teams, diversity, globalization, legal and ethical concerns, balancing work and family, the end of the job, the rapid rate of change, and technology.

Focus on Quality and Customers' Needs

In general, satisfaction with quality and customer service is falling.[14] That's a problem for companies, notes direct marketing expert James Rosenfield:

> Unhappy customers in industrialized countries historically tell 15 people about their experiences. [On the Internet] with one keystroke, you can now tell 150 or 1,500 or 15,000![15]

Bumping the Lamp*

"Bumping the lamp" is part of Disney's corporate culture. The phrase refers to a scene in *Roger Rabbit* in which a character bumps into a lamp and makes it shake. The lamp's shadow shakes, too—a touch of excellence that only a few moviegoers will notice. "Bumping the lamp" means achieving a level of excellence—whether or not it's noticed.

The emphasis on customer service continues even when families leave a Disney theme park. Every year, 20,000 guests lock their keys in their cars. Cast members (as employees are called) roam the parking lots to help families get into their cars—no phone call to a locksmith, no waiting, no fee.

*Based on Robert Hiebeler, Thomas B. Kelly, and Charles Ketterman, *Best Practices: Building Your Business with Customer-Focused Solutions* (New York: Simon & Schuster, 1998), 197.

Superior customer service pays. Bank customers who described themselves as most satisfied were much more profitable for the company than were customers who were merely "satisfied." Espresso Connection, an 11-store chain of drive-through coffee bars based in Everett, Washington, increased per-store profits by 50% by beefing up training to include *how* to provide good service: "Never close the window on a customer after a purchase even it's raining." "On sunny days, don't hide behind sunglasses." In Concord, Massachusetts, Debra Stark has built a $2.5 million gourmet health food store by "slather[ing] attention" on customers. She even employs a registered nurse to ensure that the herbal remedies customers buy won't interfere with other medicines they may be taking.[16]

Offering superior customer service doesn't always mean spending extra money. Southwest Airlines customer service agent Sharron Mangone convinced an entire gate area to join in a "biggest hole in the sock" contest while they waited for their plane. The Peninsula Beverly Hills hotel offers 24-hour-a-day check-in, a benefit for all guests but particularly those who arrive after all-night international flights. The major expense: replacing noisy vacuum cleaners with quiet handheld ones so that some maids can start (and leave) work earlier. Online florist Proflowers.com's CEO Bill Strauss realized that customers most often called to ask "Have the flowers been delivered?" So he sends confirmation e-mails to customers when flowers are ordered, shipped, and signed for—and saves money in the process.[17]

Communication is at the center of the focus on quality and customers' needs. Brainstorming and group problem solving are essential to develop more efficient ways to do things. Then the good ideas have to be communicated throughout the company. Innovators need to be recognized. And only by listening to what customers say—and listening to the silences that may accompany their actions—can an organization know what its customers really want.

"We want to give employees and customers the best experience they've ever had," says John Yokoyama, owner of the Pike Place Fish Market in Seattle. Tossing fish through the air is just one sign of a creative environment that fosters customer satisfaction and intense employee loyalty. January is normally a slow month for fish sales. Employees came up with the idea of phoning everyone who had mail-ordered fish from Pike Place the year before. As a result, Pike Place's sales hit a record high.

Entrepreneurship and Outsourcing

Since 1980, the number of businesses in the United States has risen faster than the civilian labor force. Estimates of the number of entrepreneurs vary widely. *Free Agent Nation* author Daniel H. Pink claims the number of "free agents" who work only for themselves rose from 25 million in 1998 to 33 million in 2000. The US Small Business Administration, in contrast, claims that self-employment declined during the 1990s and that fewer than 10 million people were self-employed in 2000.[18] Whatever the number, entrepreneurship is so popular that many business schools now offer courses, internships, or whole programs in starting and running a business.

For links to Web sites providing information about starting your own company, see the BAC Web site.

Some established companies are trying to match the success and growth rate of start-ups by nurturing an entrepreneurial spirit within their organizations. Innovators who work within organizations are sometimes called **intrapreneurs.** Researchers at 3M can spend 15% of their time working on ideas that don't need management approval; Post-it Notes and the Scotch-Brite Never Rust wool soap pad are two products that came out of 3M's "skunk works." Thermo Electron lets managers "spin out" promising new businesses. Xerox employees write business proposals competing for corporate funds to develop new technologies.[19]

Dan Lauer left a 10-year career in banking to make toys. His Waterbabies became the second-biggest-selling baby doll ever—and made him a millionaire. He's now invented Sea Pets, a line of realistic bathtub toys. The whale sings two real whale songs and spouts water from its blowhole. The shark's jaws open and close on its tuna prey, which in turn "bleeds" a red, nonstaining tub tint.

Should Companies Care?*

Some businesses have been forced to become entrepreneurial because of outsourcing. **Outsourcing** means going outside the company for products and services that once were made by the company's employees. Companies can outsource manufacturing (Flextronics designs and builds the routers Cisco sells), customer service (ScriptSave answers questions about prescription drug benefits for members of health insurance companies), and accounting (Virtual Growth provides accounting services for companies with 12–15 employees). Outsourcing is often a win–win solution: the company saves money, and the outsourcer makes a profit. Started in 1995, Virtual Growth grossed $12 billion in 1999.[20]

Entrepreneurs have to handle all the communication in the organization: hiring, training, motivating, and evaluating employees; responding to customer complaints; drafting surveys; writing business plans; and making presentations to venture capitalists.

Outsourcing makes communication more difficult—and more important—than it was when jobs were done in-house. It's harder to ask questions, since people are no longer down the hall. And it's easier for problems to turn into major ones. Some companies now are creating a "Chief Resource Officer" to monitor contracts with vendors so that lines of communication will be clear.

Teams

To produce quality products while cutting costs and prices, more and more companies are relying on cross-functional teams. A team of 10 middle managers from various departments at the North Island Naval Depot improved the process of manufacturing replacement parts for fighter planes. They cut the time needed to manufacture and deliver a part by 42% and saved the Navy—and thus taxpayers—$1.7 million in a year and a half.[21] Teams at Dettmers Industries in Stuart, Florida, make a product in 80 hours—down from 140 hours three years before. Though employees earn more—sometimes much more—than workers in comparable local industries, the company's labor costs have remained steady, while sales are up 50% and profit margins are twice the industry standard.[22]

The prevalence of teams puts a premium on learning to identify and solve problems, to share leadership, to work *with* other people rather than merely delegating work *to* other people, to resolve conflicts constructively, and to motivate everyone to do his or her best job. To learn more about working in teams, see Chapter 12 ➡.

Diversity

Teams put a premium on being able to work with other people—even if they come from different backgrounds.

Women, people of color, and immigrants have always been part of the US workforce. But for most of our country's history, they were relegated to clerical, domestic, or menial jobs. Even when men from working-class families began to get college degrees in large numbers after World War II, and large numbers of women and minorities entered the professions in the 1960s and 1970s, only a few made it into management. Now, US businesses realize that barriers to promotion hurt the bottom line as well as individuals. Success depends on using the brains and commitment as well as the hands and muscles of every worker.

In the last decade, we have also become aware of other sources of diversity beyond those of gender and race: age, religion, class, regional differences, sexual orientation, physical disabilities. Helping each worker reach his or her po-

Diversity allows businesses to draw ideas from many traditions. At Xerox, co-workers "pass the rock" in a Native American talking circle. Only the person holding the stone can speak, forcing everyone to learn to listen.

tential requires more flexibility from managers as well as more knowledge about intercultural communication. And it's crucial to help workers from different backgrounds understand each other—especially when continuing layoffs make many workers fear that increased opportunities for someone else will come only at a cost to themselves.

Treating readers with respect has always been a principle of good business and administrative communication. The emphasis on diversity simply makes it an economic mandate as well. To learn more about diversity and the workforce, read Chapter 11, and see the BAC Web site.

Globalization

In the global economy, importing and exporting are just the start. More and more companies have offices and factories around the world. To sell $200 million worth of appliances in India, Whirlpool adapts appliances to local markets and uses local contractors who speak India's 18 languages to deliver appliances by truck, bicycle, and even oxcart. Citibank is also active in India, financing 10,000 truckers, most with fewer than 30 trucks. Diebold owns and manages automated teller machines (ATMs) in China, France, and Brazil. In Latin America, consumers use banks to pay everything from utility bills to taxes, and Diebold's ATMs handle these services. Sometimes global products can even open up new opportunities at home. Diebold supplied the electronic voting machines for Brazil's 2000 presidential election and now—in the wake of the controversial US 2000 elections—expects US demand to surge.[23]

For Web sites on doing international business, see the BAC Web site.

All the challenges of communicating in one culture and country increase exponentially when people communicate across cultures and countries. Succeeding in a global market requires **intercultural competence,** the ability to communicate sensitively with people from other cultures and countries, based on an understanding of cultural differences. To learn more about international communication, see Chapter 11.

Legal and Ethical Concerns

Legal fees cost US businesses hundreds of thousands of dollars. The price of many simple items, such as ladders, is inflated greatly by the built-in reserve to protect the manufacturer against lawsuits. Companies are finding that clear, open communication can reduce lawsuits by giving all the parties a chance to shape policies and by clarifying exactly what is and isn't being proposed.

For more information about legal issues and links to pages discussing the value of clear legal writing, see the BAC Web site.

Ethical concerns don't carry the same clear dollar cost as legal fees. But over the last 25 years, Clinton's impeachment, Ivan Boesky's insider trading, Beechnut's allowing fake apple juice to be sold in its baby food, Watergate, the savings and loan debacle, and experiments suggesting that many business people and business students were willing to commit fraud[24] have left many consumers with a deep distrust of both business and government. To regain public trust and to avoid further regulation, business and government must both act ethically and convince the public that they are doing so.

To help clients encourage good people to do the right thing, KPMG Peat Marwick, a Big Five accounting firm, offers an "ethics audit" to increase discussion of ethical issues in the workplace and identify places where an organization's system may break down.[25]

For links to Web sites showing how some companies work to maintain high ethical standards, see the BAC Web site.

As Figure 1.6 suggests, language, graphics, and document design—basic parts of any business document—can be ethical or manipulative. Persuasion and gaining compliance—activities at the heart of business and orga-

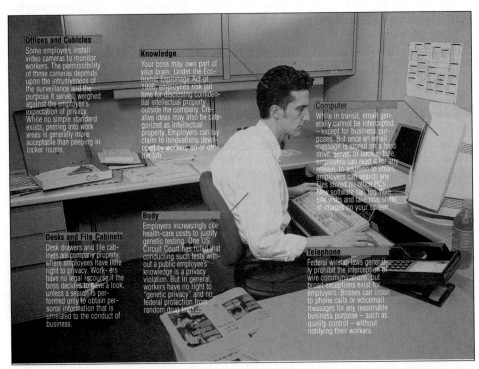

In 2001, 78% of medium-to-large US companies monitored their employees electronically. Of the companies surveyed, 31% reported firing someone for misusing the telephone, e-mail, or the Web.

nizational life—can be done with respect or contempt for customers, co-workers, and subordinates.

Ethical concerns start with telling the truth and offering good value for money. Organizations must be concerned about broader ethical issues as well: being good environmental citizens, offering a good workplace for their employees, contributing to the needs of the communities in which they operate.

Balancing Work and Family

The Wall Street Journal now runs a regular column on Work and Family. The Montgomery Work/Life Alliance reports that 78% of workers cited balancing work/life issues as their first priority. Companies are trying to respond. More than 60% of Fortune 500 companies offer flextime, telecommuting, or some other kind of flexible option. To make itself more family-friendly, Ernst & Young tells people not to check their e-mail on weekends or vacations, limits consultants' travel, and tries to redesign work loads so people won't burn out.[26] Xerox and First Tennessee National Corp. are among companies that have found that taking workers' family needs into consideration produces clear gains in productivity and customer service.[27]

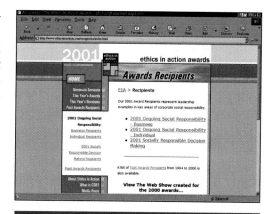

InSite

www.ethicsinaction.com/recipients/index.html

The Ethics in Action Awards recognize businesses and individuals in British Columbia and Ontario who are "doing the right thing."

FIGURE 1.6	Ethical Issues in Business Communication

How the message is conveyed	What the message is	The larger organizational context of the message
Language, Graphics, and Document Design • Is the message audience-friendly? Does it respect the audience? • Do the words balance the organization's right to present its best case with its responsibility to present its message honestly? • Do graphics help the audience understand? Or are graphics used to distract or confuse? • Does the design of the document make reading easy? Does document design attempt to make readers skip key points? **The Tactics Used to Shape Response** • Are the arguments logical? • Are the emotional appeals used fairly? Do they supplement logic rather than substituting for it? • Does the organizational pattern lead the audience without undue manipulation? • Are the tactics honest? That is, do they avoid deceiving the audience?	• Is the message that is communicated an ethical one that treats all parties fairly and is sensitive to all stakeholders? • Have interested parties been able to have input into the decision or message? • Does the audience get all the information it needs to make a good decision? • Is information communicated in a timely way, or is information withheld to reduce the audience's power? • Is information communicated in a schema the audience can grasp, or are data "dumped" without any context?	• How does the organization treat its employees? How do employees treat each other? • How sensitive is the organization to stakeholders such as the people who live near its factories, stores, or offices and to the general public? • Does the organization support employees' efforts to be honest, fair, and ethical? • Do the organization's actions in making products, buying supplies, and marketing goods and services stand up to ethical scrutiny? • Is the organization a good corporate citizen, helpful rather than harmful to the community in which it exists? • Are the organization's products or services a good use of scarce resources?

Succeeding in the 21st Century*

Alesandro Lanto, senior consultant for Personnel Decisions International [suggests five ways to succeed in the 21st century:]

- **Be willing to go the extra mile.** Find ways to stay motivated and show that you're doing more than the bare minimum.

- **Be flexible and demonstrate a continuous desire to learn.** Don't moan and complain when new ways of working are implemented. Instead, aquaint yourself with them, and use them to continue getting results.

- **Recognize that globalization will change the rules.** Don't take those changes personally. Getting over assumptions about the way things "should" be done will be critical to success on the job.

- **When in doubt, pick up the phone.** Don't rely on e-mail for all your communication. Remember that technology is a means to an end: customer satisfaction. It's not an end in itself.

- **Demonstrate "strategic orientation."** Make it a point to stay informed—in your company and your industry. Broaden your competencies by perfecting your analytical proficiency, strategic and tactical reasoning and cross-functional thinking skills.

*Quoted from Robyn D. Clarke, "Workforce 2000," *Black Enterprise*, February 2000, 102. © 2000 Black Enterprise Magazine, New York, NY. Reprinted with permission.

Balancing work and family requires using ways other than physical presence to demonstrate one's commitment to and enthusiasm for organizational goals. It may require negotiating conflicts with other workers who have different family situations or who raised children years ago when fewer companies were family-friendly. The downside of this trend is that sometimes work and family life are not so much balanced as blurred. Many employees study training videos and CDs, write e-mail, and participate in conference calls on what used to be "personal time." Lori D. Lewis, Hewlett-Packard's Worldwide Reseller Channel Manager for Disk Drives, reports that she has approved prices on a cellular phone on the ski slopes.[28] This flexibility is necessary in an age of downsizing and doing business in many time zones, but it means that she, like many managers, is essentially on call all the time.

For links to Web sites on balancing work and family life, see the BAC Web site.

The End of the Job

In traditional jobs, people did what they were told to do. Now, they do whatever needs to be done. As one man explains,

> [At the old company,] my work could be represented by a small circle labeled "Me" inside of a much larger one labeled "Not Me." At Corsair, a third circle, nearly as large as the first, is inserted between the other two, and it is labeled, "Maybe Me."[29]

Indeed, research suggests that the most effective workers don't see work as assigned tasks. Instead, they define their own goals based on the needs of customers and clients.[30]

With flatter organizations, workers are doing a much wider variety of tasks. Teams of hourly workers at Weyerhaeuser visit customers in the United States and in Japan to see the demands that high-speed printing makes on their newsprint. When they come back from a trip, they make presentations for two or three weeks to co-workers at the plant.[31]

Your parents may have worked for the same company all their lives. You may do that, too, but you have to be prepared to job-hunt—not only when you finish your degree but also throughout your career. That means continuing to learn—keeping up with new technologies, new economic and political realities, new ways of interacting with people.

Rapid Rate of Change

Jack Welch, CEO of General Electric, is widely acknowledged as the leading master of corporate change in our time. He says,

> You've got to be on the cutting edge of change. You can't simply maintain the status quo, because somebody's always coming from another country with another product, or consumer tastes change, or the cost structure does, or there's a technology breakthrough. If you're not fast and adaptable, you're vulnerable. This is true for every segment of every business in every country in the world.[32]

But change is stressful. Many people, especially those who have felt battered by changes in the workplace, fear that more change will further erode their positions. Even when change promises improvements, people have to work to learn new skills, new habits, and new attitudes. To reduce the stress of change, scholars suggest reducing the number of major, radical changes and relying more on frequent, small, incremental changes.[33]

Rapid change means that no college course or executive MBA program can teach you everything you need to know for the rest of your working life. You'll need to remain open to new ideas. And you'll need to view situations and options critically, so that you can evaluate new conditions to see whether they demand a new response. But the skills you learn can stand you in good stead for the rest of your life: critical thinking, computer savvy, problem solving, and the ability to write, to speak, and to work well with other people.

Technology

Technology is so pervasive that almost all office employees need to be able to navigate the Web and to use word processing, e-mail, spreadsheet, database, and presentation software. Most colleges have short courses to help students master the fine points of these programs; take these courses or play around with the software to become proficient.

Technology provides new opportunities and saves companies money. On-line ticket sales have brought in new patrons and record receipts for the New York City Ballet and the San Francisco Opera. Air-conditioner manufacturer Carrier gets most of its customer service calls when it's hot outside. By opening up its service contract to online bidding, Carrier found a call center that also had a seasonal business—but was busy in cold weather. Carrier also uses the Web to confirm international sales, cutting confirmation time from six days to six minutes.[34]

Intranets—Web pages just for employees—give everyone in an organization access to information. Ace Hardware started its message board to cut the cost of mailing out weekly newsletters to franchise owners and answering their phone questions. But an added benefit is that dealers share ideas with each other. Tom Green, an Ace dealer in Pittsburg, California, wrote up his success in giving away a few cans of paint to attract corporate customers. Other dealers copied his idea, with equal success. A dealer in Fitchburg, Massachusetts, won new business from a major hotel and convention center, while a dealer in Bulkhead, Arizona, won a multimillion-dollar supply contract. Energy giant Royal Dutch/Shell Group saved $200 million in 2000 alone from the

Someone's Monitoring Your E-Mail*

E-monitors scan for keywords and note when something questionable is sent or viewed. Says Rob Spence of Ireland's Baltimore Technologies, "If I want to screen every outgoing e-mail that has the word 'résumé,' . . . I can do that."

Your home computer may not be private, either. In 2000, a federal judged ruled that a company had the right to copy the entire hard drive of the home computer of an employee suspected of organizing a sick-out.

*Paragraph 1 quoted from Ann Therese Palmer, "Workers, Surf at Your Own Risk," *BusinessWeek*, 2001, 14. Paragraph 2 based on Dana Hawkins, "Data on Home Computers Not Necessarily Your Own," *U.S. News & World Report*, February 28, 2000, 85.

Energy traders use the Net to add or draw power from a grid when demand or prices change.

E-Mail Acronyms

The following abbreviations often show up in e-mail messages:

BTW   By the way
FAQ   Frequently asked
        questions
IMHO   In my humble opinion
OTOH   On the other hand
TTYL   Talk to you later

ideas exchanged on its message boards. And it earned $5 million in new revenue when an engineering team in Africa was able to get the solution to a problem from teams in Europe and Asia that had already faced similar situations.[35]

Extranets—Web pages for customers or suppliers—save time and money and improve quality. Two hours after dropping off a load of cranberries, growers can log on to Ocean Spray's extranet to find out how much they earned and how their berries compare to those of other growers. The information helps growers make decisions about harvesting the rest of the crop. Growers benefit by earning more money; Ocean Spray gets higher quality and cuts waste by 25%.[36]

Modems, faxes, and videophones allow employees to work at home rather than commute to a central office. Fax, e-mail, pagers, and text typewriter (TTY) telephones enable deaf and other hearing-impaired employees to fill a variety of jobs. Fax and e-mail make it easy to communicate across oceans and time zones. Teleconferencing makes it possible for people on different continents to have a meeting—complete with visual aids—without leaving their hometowns.

Technological change carries costs. Technology makes it easier for companies to monitor employees—even when they're out of the office. While technology creates new jobs, it eliminates old ones, requiring employees to retrain. Acquiring technology and helping workers master it requires an enormous capital investment. Learning to use new-generation software and improved hardware takes time and may be especially frustrating for people who were perfectly happy with the old software. And the very ease of storing information and sending messages means that managers have more information and more messages to process. **Information overload** occurs when messages arrive faster than the human receiver can handle them. In the information age, time management depends in part on being able to identify which messages are important so that one isn't buried in trivia.

The technology of office communication also affects the way people interpret messages. Readers expect all documents to be well designed and error free—even though not everyone has access to a laser printer or even to a computer. E-mail and faxes lead people to expect instant responses, even though thinking and writing still take time.

Writing E-Mail Messages

When you start a new job, you may have a short grace period before you have to write paper documents. But most employers will expect you to "hit the ground running" with e-mail. It's likely that you'll respond to—and perhaps initiate—e-mail messages during your very first week at work.

E-mail communities develop their own norms. If possible, lurk a few days—read the messages without writing anything yourself—before you enter the conversation.

Follow these guidelines to be a good "netizen":

- Never send angry messages by e-mail. If you have a conflict with someone, work it out face-to-face, not electronically.

- Use full caps to emphasize only a single word or two. Putting the whole message in caps is considered as rude as shouting.

- Send people only messages they need. Send copies to your boss or CEO only if he or she has asked you to.

- When you respond to a message, include only the essential part of the original message so that the reader understands your posting. Delete the rest. If the quoted material is long, put your response first, then the original material.

As you write e-mail messages, keep these guidelines in mind:

- Although e-mail feels informal, it is not private, as a conversation might be. Your employer may legally check your messages. And a message sent to one person can be printed out or forwarded to others without your knowledge or consent. Don't be indiscreet on e-mail.

- All the principles of good business writing still apply. Use you-attitude and positive emphasis (➡ Chapter 2). Use reader benefits (➡ Chapter 3) when they're appropriate. Use the pattern of organization that fits the purpose of the message (➡ see Chapters 7, 8, and 9).

- Because e-mail feels like talking, some writers give less attention to spelling, grammar, and proofreading. Many e-mail programs have spell checkers; use them. Check your message for grammatical correctness and to be sure that you've included all the necessary information.

- Reread and proofread your message before sending it out.

- E-mail messages have to interest the reader in the subject line and first paragraph. If the message is longer than one screen, the first screen must interest the reader enough to make him or her continue. E-mail messages to people who report directly to you are easy, because people will read anything from their supervisors. But writing to people who are not in a direct reporting relationship or to people outside your unit or organization takes more care.

Understanding and Analyzing Business Communication Situations

The best communicators are conscious of the context in which they communicate; they're aware of options.

Ask yourself the following questions:

- **What's at stake—to whom?** Think not only about your own needs but also about the concerns your boss and your readers will have. Your message will be most effective if you think of the entire organizational context—and the larger context of shareholders, customers, and regulators. When the stakes are high, you'll need to take into account people's emotional feelings as well as objective facts.

- **Should you send a message?** Sometimes, especially when you're new on the job, silence is the most tactful response. But be alert for opportunities to learn, to influence, to make your case. You can use communication to build your career.

- **What channel should you use?** Paper documents and presentations are formal and give you considerable control over the message. E-mail, phone calls, and stopping by someone's office are less formal. Oral channels are better for group decision making, allow misunderstandings to be cleared up more quickly, and seem more personal. Sometimes you may need more than one message, in more than one channel.

- **What should you say?** Content for a message may not be obvious. How detailed should you be? Should you repeat information that the audience already knows? The answers will depend on the kind of document, your purposes, audiences, and the corporate culture. And you'll have to figure these things out for yourself, without detailed instructions.

- **How should you say it?** How you arrange your ideas—what comes first, second, and last—and the words you use shape the audience's response to what you say.

How to Solve Business Communication Problems

When you're faced with a business communication problem, you need to develop a solution that will both **solve the organizational problem and meet the psychological needs of the people involved.** The strategies in this section will help you solve the problems in this book. Almost all of these strategies can also be applied to problems you encounter on the job.

- **Understand the situation.** What are the facts? What can you infer from the information you're given? What additional information might be helpful? Where could you get it?

- **Use the six questions for analysis in Figure 1.7 to analyze your audience, your purposes, and the situation.** Try to imagine yourself in the situation, just as you might use the script of a play to imagine what kind of people the characters are. The fuller an image you can create, the better.

- **Brainstorm solutions.** In all but the very simplest problems, there are *several* possible solutions. The first one you think of may not be best. Consciously develop several solutions. Then measure them against your audience and purposes: Which solution is likely to work best?

- **If you want to add or change information, get permission first.** You can add facts or information to the problems in this book only if the information (1) is realistic, (2) is consistent with the way real organizations work, and (3) does not change the point of the problem. If you have any questions about ideas you want to use, *ask your instructor.* He or she can tell you *before* you write the message.

  Sometimes you may want to use a condition that is neither specified in the problem nor true in the real world. For example, you may want to assume you're sending a letter in April even though you're really writing it in October. Change facts *only with your instructor's approval.*

  When you use this book to create messages on the job, you can't change facts. That is, if it's October, you can't pretend that it's April just because it may be easier to think of reader benefits for that time of year. But it may be possible to change habits that your company has fallen into, especially if they no longer serve a purpose. Check with your supervisor to make sure that your departure from company practice is acceptable.

Use this process to create good messages:[37]

Answer the six questions for analysis in Figure 1.7.

Organize your information to fit your audiences, your purposes, and the situation.

Make your document visually inviting.

FIGURE 1.7   Questions for Analysis

1. Who is (are) your audience(s)? What characteristics are relevant to this particular message? If you are writing or speaking to more than one person, how do the people in your audience differ?

2. What are your purposes in writing?

3. What information must your message include?

4. How can you build support for your position? What reasons or reader benefits will your reader find convincing?

5. What objection(s) can you expect your reader(s) to have? What negative elements of your message must you de-emphasize or overcome?

6. What aspects of the total situation may affect reader response? The economy? The time of year? Morale in the organization? The relationship between the reader and writer? Any special circumstances?

Revise your draft to create a friendly, businesslike, positive style.

Edit your draft for standard English; double-check names and numbers.

Use the response you get to plan future messages.

Answer the Six Questions for Analysis.

The six questions in Figure 1.7 help you analyze your audience(s), purpose(s), and the organizational context.

1. **Who is (are) your audience(s)? What characteristics are relevant to this particular message? If you are writing or speaking to more than one person, how do the people in your audience differ?**

   How much does your audience know about your topic? How will they respond to your message? Some characteristics of your readers will be irrelevant; focus on ones that matter *for this message*. Whenever you write to several people or to a group (like a memo to all employees), try to identify the economic, cultural, or situational differences that may affect how various subgroups may respond to what you have to say.

2. **What are your purposes in writing?**

   What must this message do to solve the organizational problem? What must it do to meet your own needs? What do you want your readers to do? To think or feel? List all your purposes, major and minor. Specify *exactly* what you want your reader to know or think or do. Specify *exactly* what kind of image of yourself and of your organization you want to project.

   Even in a simple message, you may have several related purposes: to announce a new policy, to make readers aware of the policy's provisions and requirements, and to have them feel that the policy is a good one, that the organization cares about its employees, and that you are a competent writer and manager.

3. **What information must your message include?**

   Make a list of the points that must be included; check your draft to make sure you include them all. If you're not sure whether a particular fact must be included, ask your instructor or your boss.

   To include information without emphasizing it, put it in the middle of a paragraph or document and present it as briefly as possible.

4. **How can you build support for your position? What reasons or reader benefits will your reader find convincing?**

   Brainstorm to develop reasons for your decision, the logic behind your argument, and possible benefits to readers if they do as you ask. Reasons and reader benefits do not have to be monetary. Making the reader's job easier or more pleasant is a good reader benefit. In an informative or persuasive message, identify at least five reader benefits. In your message, use those that you can develop most easily and most effectively.

   Be sure the benefits are adapted to your reader. Many people do not identify closely with their companies; the fact that the company benefits from a policy will help the reader only if the saving or profit is passed directly on to the employees. Instead, savings and profits are often eaten up by returns to stockholders, bonuses to executives, and investments in plants and equipment or in research and development.

5. **What objection(s) can you expect your reader(s) to have? What negative elements of your message must you de-emphasize or overcome?**

   Some negative elements can only be de-emphasized. Others can be overcome. Be creative: Is there any advantage associated with (even though not caused by) the negative? Can you rephrase or redefine the negative to make the reader see it differently?

Just a Deadline, No Directions*

School assignments are spelled out, sometimes even in writing. In the workplace, workers are less likely to get details about what a document should include. The transition can be disorienting. One intern reported, "I was less prepared than I thought. . . . I was so used to professors basically telling you what they want from you that I expected to be, if not taught, then told, what exactly it was that they wanted these brochures to accomplish. . . . They have not taken the time to discuss it—they just put things on my desk with only a short note telling me when they needed it done. No directions or comments were included."

*Intern's quotation from Chris M. Anson and L. Lee Forsberg, "Moving Beyond the Academic Community," *Written Communication* 7, no. 3 (April 1990): 211.

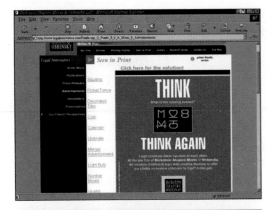

6. **What aspects of the total situation may affect reader response? The economy? The time of year? Morale in the organization? The relationship between the reader and writer? Any special circumstances?**

    Readers may like you or resent you. You may be younger or older than the people you're writing to. The organization may be prosperous or going through hard times; it may have just been reorganized or may be stable. All these different situations will affect what you say and how you say it.

    Think about the news, the economy, the weather. Think about the general business and regulatory climate, especially as it affects the organization specified in the problem. Use the real world as much as possible. Think about interest rates, business conditions, and the economy. Is the industry in which the problem is set doing well? Is the government agency in which the problem is set enjoying general support? Think about the time of year. If it's fall when you write, is your business in a seasonal slowdown after a busy summer? Gearing up for the Christmas shopping rush? Or going along at a steady pace unaffected by seasons?

    To answer these questions, draw on your experience, your courses, and your common sense. Read *The Wall Street Journal* or look at a company's Web site. Sometimes you may even want to phone a local business person to get information. For instance, if you needed more information to think of reader benefits for a problem set in a bank, you could call a local banker to find out what services it offers customers and what its rates are for loans.

Organize Your Information to Fit Your Audiences, Your Purposes, and the Situation.

You'll learn several different psychological patterns of organization later in this book. For now, remember these three basic principles:

1. Put good news first.
2. In general, put the main point or question first. In the subject line or first paragraph, make it clear that you're writing about something that is important to the reader.
3. Disregard point 2 and approach the subject indirectly when you must persuade a reluctant reader.

Make Your Document Visually Inviting.

A well-designed document is easier to read and builds goodwill. To make a document visually attractive

- Use subject lines to orient the reader quickly.
- Use headings to group related ideas.
- Use lists and indented sections to emphasize subpoints and examples.
- Number points that must be followed in sequence.
- Use short paragraphs—usually six typed lines or fewer.

If you plan these design elements before you begin composing, you'll save time and the final document will probably be better.

The best physical form for a document depends on how it will be used. For example, a document that will be updated frequently needs to be in a loose-leaf binder so the reader can easily throw away old pages and insert new ones.

Revise Your Draft to Create a Friendly, Businesslike, Positive Style.

In addition to being an organizational member or a consumer, your reader has feelings just as you do. Writing that keeps the reader in mind uses **you-attitude.** Read your message over as if you were in your reader's shoes. How would you feel if *you* received it?

Good business and administrative writing is both friendly and businesslike. If you're too stiff, you put extra distance between your reader and yourself. If you try to be too chummy, you'll sound unprofessional. When you write to strangers, use simple, everyday words and make your message as personal and friendly as possible. When you write to friends, remember that your message will be filed and read by people you've never even heard of: avoid slang, clichés, and "in" jokes.

Sometimes you must mention limitations, drawbacks, or other negative elements, but don't dwell on them. People will respond better to you and your organization if you seem confident. Expect success, not failure. If you don't believe that what you're writing about is a good idea, why should they?

You emphasize the positive when you

- Put positive information first, give it more space, or set it off visually in an indented list.
- Eliminate negative words whenever possible.
- Focus on what is possible, not what is impossible.

Edit Your Draft for Standard English; Double-Check Names and Numbers.

Business people care about correctness in spelling, grammar, and punctuation. If your grasp of mechanics is fuzzy, if standard English is not your native dialect, or if English is not your native language, you'll need to memorize rules and perhaps find a good book or a tutor to help you. Even software spelling and grammar checkers require the writer to make decisions. If you know how to write correctly but rarely take the time to do so, now is the time to begin to edit and proofread to eliminate careless errors. Correctness in usage, punctuation, and grammar is covered in Appendix B ➡.

Always proofread your document before you send it out. Double-check the reader's name, any numbers, and the first and last paragraphs.

Use the Response You Get to Plan Future Messages.

Evaluate the **feedback,** or response, you get. The real test of any message is "Did you get what you wanted, when you wanted it?" If the answer is *no,* then the message has failed—even if the grammar is perfect, the words elegant, the approach creative, the document stunningly attractive. If the message fails, you need to find out why.

Analyze your successes, too. You know you've succeeded when you get the results you want, both in terms of objective, concrete actions and in terms of image and goodwill. You want to know *why* your message worked. Often, you'll find that the principles in this book explain the results you get. If your results are different, why? There has to be a reason, and if you can find what it is, you'll be more successful more often.

Can Business Change the World?*

Joseph White, Dean of the University of Michigan Business School, says:

"The most moving experience that I've had in recent years was a meeting with Desmond Tutu in Cape Town. I asked him, 'What are your greatest concerns about the future of South Africa?' He said, 'We have 30 million people living on hope. If the economy and society don't deliver measurable improvements over the next five years, I don't know what's going to happen here.' Now, if you're a 25-year-old student and you're looking for a challenge, then look no further: Archbishop Tutu just delivered it to you.

"That opportunity reflects a fundamental difference between the current generation of business people and the previous generation. . . . If the dream 25 years ago was to join a big company and to pursue a career involving steady advancement, the dream now is to cultivate an economic entity that creates tremendous value, that provides opportunity for others, and that may even change the world."

*Quotation from Polly Labarre, ed., "Unit of One," *Fast Company,* January 1999, 74.

**They Needed
to Proofread**

- One woman mailed out a cover letter for a $750,000 contract asking the reader "to take a moment not to read and sign this contract."

- One man mailed a letter to a male friend with the salutation, "Dear Ms. Weeks."

- In 1990, just hours before the graduation ceremony, the head of the U.S. Naval Academy discovered that the 1,600 diplomas conferred degrees from the "U.S. Navel Academy."

Summary of Key Points

- Communication helps organizations and the people in them achieve their goals. The ability to write and speak well becomes increasingly important as you rise in an organization.

- People put things in writing to create a record, to convey complex data, to make things convenient for the reader, to save money, and to convey their own messages more effectively.

- **Internal documents** go to people inside the organization. **External documents** go to audiences outside: clients, customers, suppliers, stockholders, the government, the media, and the general public.

- The three basic purposes of business and administrative communication are **to inform, to request or persuade, and to build goodwill.** Most messages have more than one purpose.

- A one-page business letter that took 10 minutes to dictate cost between $13.60 and $20.52 in 1996. Poor writing costs even more since it wastes time, wastes effort, and jeopardizes goodwill.

- Good business and administrative writing meets five basic criteria: it's **clear, complete,** and **correct;** it **saves the reader's time;** and it **builds goodwill.**

- To evaluate a specific document, we must know the interactions among the writer, the reader(s), the purposes of the message, and the situation. No single set of words will work for all readers in all situations.

- Ten trends affecting business and administrative communication are a focus on quality and customers' needs, entrepreneurship and outsourcing, teams, diversity, international competition and opportunities, legal and ethical concerns, balancing work and family, the end of the job, the rapid rate of change, and technology.

- To understand business communication situations, ask the following questions:
    - What's at stake—to whom?
    - Should you send a message?
    - What channel should you use?
    - What should you say?
    - How should you say it?

- The following process helps create effective messages:
    - Answer the six numbered questions for analysis below.
    - Organize your information to fit your audiences, your purposes, and the situation.
    - Make your document visually inviting.
    - Revise your draft to create a friendly, businesslike, positive style.
    - Edit your draft for standard English; double-check names and numbers.
    - Use the response you get to plan future messages.

- Use these six questions to analyze business communication problems:
    1. Who is (are) your audience(s)? What characteristics are relevant to this particular message? If you are writing or speaking to more than one person, how do the people in your audience differ?
    2. What are your purposes in writing?
    3. What information must your message include?
    4. How can you build support for your position? What reasons or reader benefits will your reader find convincing?

5. What objection(s) can you expect your reader(s) to have? What negative elements of your message must you de-emphasize or overcome?

6. What aspects of the total situation may affect reader response? The economy? The time of year? Morale in the organization? The relationship between the reader and writer? Any special circumstances?

■ A solution to a business communication problem must both solve the organizational problem and meet the needs of the writer or speaker, the organization, and the audience.

CHAPTER 1   Exercises and Problems

Getting Started

1.1   Letters for Discussion—Landscape Plants

Your nursery sells plants not only in your store but also by mail order. Today you've received a letter from Pat Sykes, complaining that the plants (in a $572 order) did not arrive in a satisfactory condition. "All of them were dry and wilted. One came out by the roots when I took it out of the box. Please send me a replacement shipment immediately."

The following letters are possible approaches to answering this complaint. How well does each message meet the needs of the reader, the writer, and the organization? Is the message clear, complete, and correct? Does it save the reader's time? Does it build goodwill?

1.

Dear Sir:

I checked to see what could have caused the defective shipment you received. After ruling out problems in transit, I discovered that your order was packed by a new worker who didn't understand the need to water plants thoroughly before they are shipped. We have fired the worker, so you can be assured that this will not happen again.

Although it will cost our company several hundred dollars, we will send you a replacement shipment.

Let me know if the new shipment arrives safely. We trust that you will not complain again.

2.

Dear Pat:

Sorry we screwed up that order. Sending plants across country is a risky business. Some of them just can't take the strain. (Some days I can't take the strain myself!) We'll send you some more plants sometime next week and we'll credit your account for $372.

3.

Dear Mr. Smith:

I'm sorry you aren't happy with your plants, but it isn't our fault. The box clearly says, "Open and water immediately." If you had done that, the plants would have been fine. And anybody who is going to buy plants should know that a little care is needed. If you pull by the leaves, you will pull the roots out. Since you don't know how to handle plants, I'm sending you a copy of our brochure, "How to Care for Your Plants." Please read it carefully so that you will know how to avoid disappointment in the future.

We look forward to your future orders.

4.

Dear Ms. Sykes:

Your letter of the 5th has come to the attention of the undersigned.

According to your letter, your invoice #47420 arrived in an unsatisfactory condition. Please be advised that it is our policy to make adjustments as per the Terms and Conditions listed on the reverse side of our Acknowledgment of Order. If you will read that document, you will find the following:

"... if you intend to assert any claim against us on this account, you shall make an exception on your receipt to the carrier and shall, within 30 days after the receipt of any such goods, furnish us detailed written information as to any damage."

Your letter of the 5th does not describe the alleged damage in sufficient detail. Furthermore, the delivery receipt contains no indication of any exception. If you expect to receive an adjustment, you must comply with our terms and see that the necessary documents reach the undersigned by the close of the business day on the 20th of the month.

5.

Dear Pat Sykes:

You'll get a replacement shipment of the perennials you ordered next week.

Your plants are watered carefully before shipment and packed in specially designed cardboard containers. But if the weather is unusually warm, or if the truck is delayed, small root balls may dry out. Perhaps this happened with your plants. Plants with small root balls are easier to transplant, so they do better in your yard.

The violas, digitalis, aquilegias, and hostas you ordered are long-blooming perennials that will get even prettier each year. Enjoy your garden!

1.2   E-Mail Messages for Discussion—Announcing a Web Page

The Acme Corporation has just posted its first Web page. Ed Zeplin in Management Information Systems (MIS), who has created the page, wants employees to know about it.

The following e-mail messages are possible approaches. How well does each message meet the needs of the reader, the writer, and the organization? Is the message clear, complete, and correct? Does it save the reader's time? Does it build goodwill?

1.

Subject: It's Ready!

I am happy to tell you that my work is done. Two months ago the CEO finally agreed to fund a Web page for Acme, and now the work of designing and coding is done.

I wanted all of you to know about Acme's page. (Actually it's over 100 pages.) Now maybe the computerphobes out there will realize that you really do need to learn how to use this stuff. Sign up for the next training session! The job you save may be my own.

If you have questions, please do not hesitate to contact me.

L. Ed Zeplin, MIS

2.

Subject: Web Page

Check out the company Web page at www.server.acme.com/homepage.html

3.

Subject: Visit Our Web Page

Our Web pages are finally operational. The 100 pages were created using DreamWeaver, a program designed to support HTML creation. Though the graphics are sizable and complex, interlacing and code specifying the pixel size serve to minimize download time. Standard HTML coding is enhanced with forms, Java animation, automatic counters, and tracking packages to ascertain who visits our site.

The site content was determined by conducting a survey of other corporate Web sites to become cognizant of the pages made available by our competitors and other companies. The address of our Web page is www.server/acme/com/homepage.html. It is believed that this site will support and enhance our marketing and advertising efforts, improving our outreach to desirable demographic and psychographic marketing groups.

L. Ed Zeplin, MIS

Voice: 713-555-2879 Fax: 713-555-2880 e-mail: zeplin.1@acme.com

"Only the wired life is worth living."—Anonymous

4.

Subject: Web Page Shows Acme Products to the World, Offers Tips to Consumers, and Tells Prospective Employees about Job Possibilities

Since last Friday, Acme's been on the World Wide Web. If you have a computer with Internet access, check out the page at www.server.acme.com/homepage.html. You can't view the page if you don't have a computer or if you're still using a Mac SE or a 286.

I have included pages on our products, tips for consumers, and job openings at Acme in the hope of making our page useful and interesting. Content is the number one thing that brings people back, but I've included some snazzy graphics, too.

When I asked people for ideas for the company pages, almost nobody responded. But if seeing the page inspires you, let me know what else you'd like. I'll try to fit it into my busy schedule.

So check it out. But don't spend too much time on the Web: you need to get your work done, too!

L. Ed Zeplin, MIS
zeplin.1.caacme.com
Today's Joke
Fun Links

5.

Subject: How to Access Acme's Web Page

Tell your customers that Acme is now on the Web:
www.server.acme.com/homepage.html

Web pages offer another way for us to bring our story to the public. Other companies have found that Web pages increase sales, often reaching customers far from normal sales and distribution channels. Our advertisements and packaging will feature our Web address. And people who check out our Web page can learn even more about our commitment to quality, protecting the environment, and meeting customer needs.

If you'd like to learn more about how to use the Web or how to create Web pages for your unit, sign up for one of our workshops. For details and online registration, see www.server.acme.com/training.

If you have comments on Acme's Web pages or suggestions for making them even better, just let me know.

L. Ed Zeplin
zeplin.1@acme.com

1.3   Discussing Strengths

Introduce yourself to a small group of other students. Identify three of your strengths that might interest an employer. These can be experience, knowledge, or personality traits (like enthusiasm).

Communicating at Work

1.4   Understanding the Role of Communication in Your Organization

Interview your supervisor to learn about the kinds and purposes of communication in your organization. Your questions could include the following:

- What channels of communication (e.g., memos, e-mail, presentations) are most important in this organization?
- What documents or presentations do you create? Are they designed to inform, to persuade, to build goodwill—or to do all three?
- What documents or presentations do you receive? Are they designed to inform, to persuade, to build goodwill—or to do all three?
- Who are your most important audiences within the organization?

- Who are our most important external audiences?
- What are the challenges of communicating in this organization?
- What kinds of documents and presentations does the organization prefer?

As Your Instructor Directs,

a.   Share your results with a small group of students.
b.   Present your results in a memo to your instructor.
c.   Join with a group of students to make a group presentation to the class.
d.   Post your results online to the class.

Memo Assignments

1.5   Introducing Yourself to Your Instructor

Write a memo (at least 1½ pages long) introducing yourself to your instructor. Include the following topics:

Background: Where did you grow up? What have you done in terms of school, extracurricular activities, jobs, and family life?

Interests: What are you interested in? What do you like to do? What do you like to think about and talk about?

Achievements: What achievements have given you the greatest personal satisfaction? List at least five. Include things that gave *you* a real sense of accomplishment and pride, whether or not they're the sort of thing you'd list on a résumé.

Goals: What do you hope to accomplish this term? Where would you like to be professionally and personally five years from now?

Use complete memo format with appropriate headings. (See Appendix A ➡ for examples of memo format.) Use a conversational writing style; check your draft to polish the style and edit for mechanical and grammatical correctness. A good memo will enable your instructor to see you as an individual. Use specific details to make your memo vivid and interesting. Remember that one of your purposes is to interest your reader!

1.6   Introducing Yourself to Your Collaborative Writing Group

Write a memo (at least 1½ pages long) introducing yourself to the other students in your collaborative writing group. Include the following topics:

Background: What is your major? What special areas of knowledge do you have? What have you done in terms of school, extracurricular activities, jobs, and family life?

Previous experience in groups: What groups have you worked in before? Are you usually a leader, a follower, or a bit of both? Are you interested in a quality product? In maintaining harmony in the group? In working efficiently? What do you like most about working in groups? What do you like least?

Work and composing style: Do you like to talk out ideas while they're in a rough stage or work them out on paper before you discuss them? Would you rather have a complete outline before you start writing or just a general idea? Do you want to have a detailed schedule of everything that has to be done and who will do it, or would you rather "go with the flow"? Do you work best under pressure, or do you want to have assignments ready well before the due date?

Areas of expertise: What can you contribute to the group in terms of knowledge and skills? Are you good at brainstorming ideas? Researching? Designing charts? Writing? Editing? Word processing? Managing the flow of work? Maintaining group cohesion?

Goals for collaborative assignments: What do you hope to accomplish this term? Where does this course fit into your priorities?

Use complete memo format with appropriate headings. (See Appendix A ➡ for examples of memo format.) Use a conversational writing style; edit your final draft for mechanical and grammatical correctness. A good memo will enable others in your group to see you as an individual. Use details to make your memo vivid and interesting. Remember that one of your purposes is to make your readers look forward to working with you!

1.7   Describing Your Experiences in and Goals for Writing

Write a memo (at least 1½ pages long) to your instructor describing the experiences you've had writing and what you'd like to learn about writing during this course.

Answer several of the following questions:

- What memories do you have of writing? What made writing fun or frightening in the past?

- What have you been taught about writing? List the topics, rules, and advice you remember.

- What kinds of writing have you done in school? How long have the papers been?

- How has your school writing been evaluated? Did the instructor mark or comment on mechanics and grammar? Style? Organization? Logic? Content? Audience analysis and adaptation? Have you gotten extended comments on your papers? Have instructors in different classes had the same standards, or have you changed aspects of your writing for different classes?

- What voluntary writing have you done—journals, poems, stories, essays? Has this writing been just for you, or has some of it been shared or published?

- Have you ever written on a job or in a student or volunteer organization? Have you ever typed other people's writing? What have these experiences led you to think about real-world writing?

- What do you see as your current strengths and weaknesses in writing skills? What skills do you think you'll need in the future? What kinds of writing do you expect to do after you graduate?

Use complete memo format with appropriate headings. (See Appendix A ➡ for examples of memo format.) Use a conversational writing style; edit your final draft for mechanical and grammatical correctness.

2

Building Goodwill

Building Goodwill

Stephen Hlibok
Vice President, Merrill Lynch & Co.

Stephen Hlibok is a Certified Financial Manager who helps serve more than 4,500 deaf and hard-of-hearing clients. Merrill Lynch, the largest financial service firm in the United States, also provides special services for blind and visually impaired people and for families of children with disabilities.

www.ml.com
www.fc.ml.com/Stephen_Hlibok

Revising for you-attitude makes the message more persuasive and builds goodwill. When I helped write a 51-page document proposing that Merrill Lynch create a division to serve investors who were deaf and hard of hearing, we used language and arguments that focused on the company. When I write a letter to an individual investor, you-attitude is one way I present information from the reader's point of view. You-attitude also means respecting the reader. Many potential clients really don't understand finances, so I often need to explain the basics. You-attitude helps me do that in a way that isn't condescending.

As a stockbroker and financial planner, there are times when I can't use positive emphasis. I have to make sure that clients understand the risk of a specific investment. And when news is bad, I give solid facts. If the stock market is down 17%, it would be unprofessional to say, "Your portfolio retains 83% of its value."

Building goodwill also means speaking the client's language. I started my position three months before October 19, 1987—Black Monday—the day the Dow Jones Industrial Average plunged 508 points. On that day, stockbrokers were flooded by calls from worried clients. Due to time constraints, deaf people found face-to-face appointments hard to come by, and brokers did not have the necessary telecommunications equipment to communicate with people who used American Sign Language.

With determination and guts, I helped build a bridge between Wall Street and the deaf community. Merrill Lynch recognized the potential untapped community and became the first Wall Street brokerage firm to establish the Deaf and Hard of Hearing Investors' Services Division. The division reflects the company's involvement in a diverse, cross-cultural workforce.

Merrill Lynch's own slogan is "You should know no boundaries." Growing up in a deaf household, I never thought or believed I couldn't do anything I wanted to because of my deafness. I want to instill the same attitude among other deaf and disabled people.

The Internet is a revolution for the deaf community because it helps to solve our communication needs and reduce obstacles. Within five years, videoconferencing should be standard, and there'll be plenty of flying hands!

"Revising for you-attitude makes the message more persuasive and builds goodwill."

All Work Is Social*

Establishing good working relationships can help us secure the cooperation of the people we need to accomplish our tasks. If we delay building good relationships until we really need them, it will be too late.

*Quoted from "Be a Social Worker," *Fast Company*, May 1999, 228.

Goodwill smooths the challenges of business and administration. Companies have long been aware that treating customers well pays off in more sales and higher profits. Government organizations now realize that they need citizen support—goodwill—to receive funding. Goodwill is important in internal as well as external documents. More and more organizations are realizing that treating employees well is financially wise as well as ethically sound. Sears Roebuck found that improvements in employee attitudes produced predictable improvements in revenue. Northern Telecom of Toronto, MCI Communications, and Electronic Data Systems have also found that internal goodwill has a measurable effect on the bottom line.[1] Researcher Jim Collins found that the most financially successful companies put "people first, strategy second." Another study found that companies that "manage people right" outperformed other companies by 30% to 40%.[2]

You-attitude, positive emphasis, and bias-free language are three ways to help build goodwill. Writing that shows you-attitude speaks from the reader's point of view, not selfishly from the writer's. Positive emphasis means focusing on the positive rather than the negative aspects of a situation. Bias-free language is language that does not discriminate against people on the basis of sex, physical condition, race, age, or any other category. All three help you achieve your purposes and make your messages friendlier, more persuasive, more professional, and more humane. They suggest that you care not just about money but also about your readers and their needs and interests.

You-Attitude

Putting what you want to say in you-attitude is a crucial step both in thinking about the reader's needs and in communicating your concern to the reader.

How to Create You-Attitude

You-attitude is a style of writing that looks at things from the reader's point of view, emphasizing what the reader wants to know, respecting the reader's intelligence, and protecting the reader's ego.

To apply you-attitude, use the following five techniques:

1. **Talk about the reader, not about yourself.**
2. **Refer to the reader's request or order specifically.**
3. **Don't talk about feelings, except to congratulate or offer sympathy.**
4. **In positive situations, use *you* more often than *I*. Use *we* when it includes the reader.**
5. **In negative situations, avoid the word *you*. Protect the reader's ego. Use passive verbs and impersonal expressions to avoid assigning blame.**

As we look at examples of these techniques, note that many of the you-attitude revisions are *longer* than the sentences lacking you-attitude. You-attitude sentences have *more* information, so they are often longer. They are not wordy, however. **Wordiness** means having more words than the meaning requires. We can add information and still keep the writing tight.

1. Talk about the reader, not about yourself.

Readers want to know how they benefit or are affected. When you provide this information, you make your message more complete and more interesting.

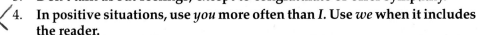

Lacks you-attitude: I have negotiated an agreement with Apex Rent-a-Car that gives you a discount on rental cars.

You-attitude:	As a Sunstrand employee, you can now get a 20% discount when you rent a car from Apex.

The first sentence focuses on what the writer does, not on what the reader receives. Any sentence that focuses on the writer's work or generosity lacks you-attitude, even if the sentence contains the word *you*. Instead of focusing on what we are giving the reader, focus on what the reader can now do.

Lacks you-attitude:	We are shipping your order of September 21 this afternoon.
You-attitude:	The two dozen Corning Ware starter sets you ordered will be shipped this afternoon and should reach you by September 28.

The reader is less interested in when we shipped the order than in when it will arrive. Note that the phrase "should reach you by" leaves room for variations in delivery schedules. If you can't be exact, give your reader the information you do have: "A UPS shipment from California to Texas normally takes three days." If you have absolutely no idea, give the reader the name of the carrier, so the reader knows whom to contact if the order doesn't arrive promptly.

2. Refer to the reader's request or order specifically.

When you write about the reader's request, order, or policy, refer to it specifically, not as a generic *your order* or *your policy*. If your reader is an individual or a small business, it's friendly to specify the content of the order; if you're writing to a company with which you do a great deal of business, give the invoice or purchase order number.

Lacks you-attitude:	Your order . . .
You-attitude (to individual):	The desk chair you ordered . . .
You-attitude (to a large store):	Your invoice #783329 . . .

3. Don't talk about feelings except to congratulate or offer sympathy.

In most business situations, your feelings are irrelevant and should be omitted.

Lacks you-attitude:	We are happy to extend you a credit line of $5,000.
You-attitude:	You can now charge up to $5,000 on your American Express card.

The reader doesn't care whether you're happy, bored stiff at granting a routine application, or worried about granting so much to someone who barely qualifies. All the reader cares about is the situation from his or her point of view.

It *is* appropriate to talk about your own emotions in a message of congratulations or condolence.

You-attitude:	Congratulations on your promotion to district manager! I was really pleased to read about it.

In internal memos, it may be appropriate to comment that a project has been gratifying or frustrating. In the letter of transmittal that accompanies a report, it is permissible to talk about your feelings about doing the work. But even other readers in your own organization are primarily interested in their own concerns, not in your feelings.

Don't talk about the reader's feelings, either. It's distancing to have someone else tell us how we feel—especially if the writer is wrong.

Lacks you-attitude:	You'll be happy to hear that Open Grip Walkway Channels meet OSHA requirements.
You-attitude:	Open Grip Walkway Channels meet OSHA requirements.

The Enlightened Manager*

Building goodwill comes from attitudes, not just from words. Enlightened managers assume that workers

- Want to do a good job.
- Can improve.
- Want to be needed, respected, and appreciated.
- Prefer meaningful work.
- Are whole people, with lives outside work.
- Will make good decisions when they have good information.

*Based on "Do You Have What It Takes to Be an Enlightened Manager?" *Inc.*, October 1998, 47–51.

Maybe the reader expects that anything you sell would meet government regulations (OSHA—the Occupational Safety and Health Administration—is a federal agency). The reader may even be disappointed if he or she expected higher standards. Simply explain the situation or describe a product's features; don't predict the reader's response.

When you have good news for the reader, simply give the good news.

Lacks you-attitude:	You'll be happy to hear that your scholarship has been renewed.
You-attitude:	Congratulations! Your scholarship has been renewed.

4. In positive situations, use you more often than I. Use we when it includes the reader.

Whenever possible, focus on the reader, not on you or your company.

Lacks you-attitude:	We provide health insurance to all employees.
You-attitude:	You receive health insurance as a full-time Procter & Gamble employee.

Most readers are tolerant of the word *I* in e-mail messages, which seem like conversation. Edit paper documents to use *I* rarely if at all. *I* suggests that you're concerned about personal issues, not about the organization's problems, needs, and opportunities. *We* works well when it includes the reader. Avoid *we* if it excludes the reader (as it would in a letter to a customer or supplier or as it might in a memo about what *we* in management want *you* to do).

5. In negative situations, avoid the word you. Protect the reader's ego. Use passive verbs and impersonal expressions to avoid assigning blame.

When you report bad news or limitations, use a noun for a group of which the reader is a part instead of *you* so readers don't feel that they're singled out for bad news.

Lacks you-attitude:	You must get approval from the director before you publish any articles or memoirs based on your work in the agency.
You-attitude:	Agency personnel must get approval from the director to publish any articles or memoirs based on their work at the agency.

Use passive verbs and impersonal expressions to avoid blaming the reader. **Passive verbs** describe the action performed on something, without necessarily saying who did it. (See Chapter 4 ➡ for a full discussion of passive verbs.) **Impersonal expressions** omit people and talk only about things.

In most cases, active verbs are better. But when your reader is at fault, passive verbs may be useful to avoid assigning blame.

Normally, writing is most lively when it's about people—and most interesting to readers when it's about them. When you have to report a mistake or bad news, however, you can protect the reader's ego by using an impersonal expression, one in which things, not people, do the acting.

Lacks you-attitude:	You made no allowance for inflation in your estimate.
You-attitude (passive):	No allowance for inflation has been made in this estimate.
You-attitude (impersonal):	This estimate makes no allowance for inflation.

A purist might say that impersonal expressions are illogical: an estimate, for example, is inanimate and can't "make" anything. In the pragmatic world of business writing, however, impersonal expressions often help you convey criticism tactfully.

You-Attitude beyond the Sentence Level

Good messages apply you-attitude beyond the sentence level by using content and organization as well as style to build goodwill.

To create goodwill with content,

- Be complete. When you have lots of information to give, consider putting some details in an appendix, which may be read later.
- Anticipate and answer questions the reader is likely to have.
- When you include information the reader didn't ask for, show why it is important.
- Show readers how the subject of your message affects them.

To organize information to build goodwill,

- Put information readers are most interested in first.
- Arrange information to meet your reader's needs, not yours.
- Use headings and lists so that the reader can find key points quickly.

Consider the letter in Figure 2.1. As the red marginal notes indicate, many individual sentences in this letter lack you-attitude. Fixing individual sentences could improve the letter. However, it really needs to be totally rewritten.

Figure 2.2 shows a possible revision of this letter. The revision is clearer, easier to read, and friendlier. Check the BAC Web site for another example of a letter revised to improve you-attitude.

Positive Emphasis

Some negatives are necessary. As Stephen Hlibok points out, when you have bad news to give the reader—announcements of layoffs, product defects and recalls, price increases—straightforward negatives build credibility. (See Chapter 8 ➡ on how to present bad news.) Sometimes negatives are needed to make people take a problem seriously. Wall Data improved the reliability of its computer programs when it eliminated the term *bugs* and used instead the term *failures.* In some messages, such as disciplinary notices and negative performance appraisals, your purpose is to deliver a rebuke with no alternative. Even here, avoid insults or global attacks on the reader's integrity or sanity. Being honest about the drawbacks of a job reduces turnover. And sometimes negatives create a "reverse psychology" that makes people look favorably at your product. Rent-a-Wreck is thriving. (The cars really don't look so bad.)[3]

But in most situations, it's better to be positive. Annette N. Shelby and N. Lamar Reinsch, Jr., found that business people responded more positively to positive than to negative language and were more likely to say they would act on a positively worded request.[4] Martin Seligman's research for Met Life found that optimistic salespeople sold 37% more insurance than pessimistic colleagues. As a result, Met Life began hiring optimists even when they failed to meet the company's other criteria. These "unqualified" optimists outsold pessimists 21% in their first year and 57% in the next.[5]

Positive emphasis is a way of looking at things. Is the bottle half empty or half full? You can create positive emphasis with the words, information, organization, and layout you choose.

Create positive emphasis by using the following five techniques:

1. Avoid negative words and words with negative connotations.
2. State information positively. Focus on what the reader can do rather than on what you won't or can't let the reader do.
3. Justify negative information by giving a reason or linking it to a reader benefit.

You-Attitude on the Web*

You-attitude means seeing things from the audience's point of view. GE Polymerland, which sells plastic pellets that become CD cases, car bumpers, and bedpans, has created a profitable Web site by making life easier for its customers.

On the Web, customers can search for plastics by name, number, or characteristics and download the certification sheets that specify the characteristics of each plastic. Downloading a new certification sheet let one client complete an overnight job when he couldn't find his original copy of the information.

Letting customers find fast, accurate information is good for the company, too. Online orders cut the company's costs 3 to 4%. Online sales were expected to bring in more than $1.5 billion in 2001. But, as Peter Foss, President of GE Polymerland, says, "We didn't do all of this because it was the next big thing. We did it because it seemed like a great way to serve our customers."

*Based on Cheryl Dahle, "Adventures in Polymerland," *Fast Company,* May 2000, 353–61.

FIGURE 2.1   A Letter Lacking You-Attitude

SIMMONS STRUCTURAL STEEL

450 INDUSTRIAL PARK
CLEVELAND, OH 44120
(216) 555-4670
FAX: (216) 555-4672

December 11, 2003

Ms. Carol McFarland
Rollins Equipment Corporation
18438 East Night Hawk Way
Phoenix, AZ 85043-7800

Dear Ms. McFarland:

Legalistic

Not you-attitude

We are now ready to issue a check to Rollins Equipment in the amount of $14,207.02. To receive said check, you will deliver to me a release of the mechanic's liens in the amount of $14,207.02.   *Sounds dictatorial*

Lacks you-attitude

Focuses on negative

Before we can release the check, we must be satisfied that the release is in the proper form. We must insist that we be provided with a stamped original of the lien indicating the document number in the appropriate district court where it is filed. Also, either the release must be executed by an officer of Rollins Equipment, or we must be provided with a letter from an officer of Rollins Equipment authorizing another individual to execute the release.

Hard to read, remember

Please contact the undersigned so that an appointment can be scheduled for this transaction.   *Jargon*

Sincerely,

Kelly J. Pickett

Kelly J. Pickett

4.   If the negative is truly unimportant, omit it.

5.   Put the negative information in the middle and present it compactly.

Now, let's see how to apply each of these techniques.

1. Avoid negative words and words with negative connotations.

Figure 2.3 lists some common negative words. If you find one of these words in a draft, try to substitute a more positive word. When you must use a negative, use the *least negative* term that will convey your meaning.

FIGURE 2.2   A Letter Revised to Improve You-Attitude

450 INDUSTRIAL PARK
CLEVELAND, OH 44120
(216) 555-4670
FAX: (216) 555-4672

December 11, 2003

Ms. Carol McFarland
Rollins Equipment Corporation
18438 East Night Hawk Way
Phoenix, AZ 85043-7800

Dear Ms. McFarland:

Starts with main point from the reader's point of view

Let's clear up the lien in the Allen contract.

Focuses on what reader gets

Rollins will receive a check for $14,207.02 when you give us a release for the mechanic's lien of $14,207.02. To assure us that the release is in the proper form,

1. Give us a stamped original of the lien indicating the document's district court number, and

2. Either
   a. Have an officer of Rollins Equipment sign the release
      or
   b. Give us a letter from a Rollins officer authorizing someone else to sign the release.

List makes it easy to see that reader needs to do two things—and that the second can be done in two ways.

Call me to tell me which way is best for you.   *Emphasizes reader's choice*

Sincerely,

Kelly J. Pickett

Kelly J. Pickett
Extension 5318   *Extension number makes it easy for reader to phone.*

The following examples show how to replace negative words with positive words.

Negative: We have failed to finish taking inventory.

Better: We haven't finished taking inventory.

Still better: We will be finished taking inventory Friday.

Negative: If you can't understand this explanation, feel free to call me.

Better: If you have further questions, just call me.

Still better: Omit the sentence.

The Wait from This Point*

Waiting is a negative word and a negative experience. Disney World's FASTPASS system reduces the experience. But when waiting is necessary, Disney World uses the negative word to create reverse psychology that results in a positive feeling. Helpful signs tell you how long the wait will be from various points in line. If you're not ready to wait that long, you leave.

If you do stay in line, you'll be pleasantly surprised: the line will move faster than advertised.

The signs deliberately overstate the wait. Recently, the sign at the Indiana Jones Adventure ride advised a wait of 25 minutes. It actually took less than 20.

"It's part of the psychology," says Tony Baxter, Vice President of Conceptual Development at Disney's imagineering unit.

*Based on Jeff Rowe, "Waiting in Line Is All Part of the Amusement at Theme Parks," *The Columbus Dispatch*, June 14, 1996, 1C; and Walt Disney World, "Parks & More: Disney's FASTPASS," disneyworld.disney.go.com/waltdisneyworld/parksandmore/fastpass; visited site August 29, 2001.

FIGURE 2.3   Negative Words to Avoid

afraid	error	lacking	trivial
anxious	except	loss	trouble
avoid	fail		wait
bad	fault	**Some mis- words:**	weakness
careless	fear	misfortune	worry
damage	hesitate	mistake	wrong
delay	ignorant	missing	
delinquent	ignore	neglect	**Many un- words:**
deny	impossible	never	unclear
difficulty		no	unfair
	Many in- words:	not	unfortunate
Some dis- words:	inadequate	objection	unfortunately
	incomplete	problem	unpleasant
disapprove	inconvenient	reject	unreasonable
dishonest	insincere	sorry	unreliable
dissatisfied	injury	terrible	unsure
eliminate			

If a sentence has two negatives, substitute one positive term.

Negative: Never fail to back up your disks.

Better: Always back up your disks.

When you must use a negative term, use the least negative word that is accurate.

Negative: Your balance of $835 is delinquent.

Better: Your balance of $835 is past due.

Getting rid of negatives has the added benefit of making what you write easier to understand. Sentences with three or more negatives are very hard to understand.[6]

Beware of **hidden negatives:** words that are not negative in themselves but become negative in context. *But* and *however* indicate a shift, so, after a positive statement, they are negative. *I hope* and *I trust that* suggest that you aren't sure. *Patience* may sound like a virtue, but it is a necessary virtue only when things are slow. Even positives about a service or product may backfire if they suggest that in the past the service or product was bad.

Negative: I hope this is the information you wanted.
[Implication: I'm not sure.]

Better: Enclosed is a brochure about road repairs scheduled for 2004–06.

Still better: The brochure contains a list of all roads and bridges scheduled for repair during 2004–06. Call Gwen Wong at 555-3245 for specific dates when work will start and stop and for alternate routes.

Negative: Please be patient as we switch to the automated system.
[Implication: You can expect problems.]

Better: If you have questions during our transition to the automated system, call Melissa Morgan.

Still better: You'll be able to get information instantly about any house on the market when the automated system is in place. If you have questions during the transition, call Melissa Morgan.

Negative: Now Crispy Crunch tastes better.
                      [Implication: it used to taste terrible.]

Better: Now Crispy Crunch tastes even better.

Removing negatives does not mean being arrogant or pushy.

Negative: I hope that you are satisfied enough to place future orders.

Arrogant: I look forward to receiving all of your future business.

Better: Call Mercury whenever you need computer chips.

When you eliminate negative words, be sure to maintain accuracy. Words that are exact opposites will usually not be accurate. Instead, use specifics to be both positive and accurate.

Negative: The exercycle is not guaranteed for life.

Not true: The exercycle is guaranteed for life.

True: The exercycle is guaranteed for 10 years.

Negative: Customers under 60 are not eligible for the Prime Time discount.

Not true: You must be over 60 to be eligible for the Prime Time discount.

True: If you're 60 or older, you can save 10% on all your purchases with RightWay's Prime Time discount.

Legal phrases also have negative connotations for most readers and should be avoided whenever possible. The idea will sound more positive if you use normal English.

Negative: If your account is still delinquent, a second, legal notice will be sent to you informing you that cancellation of your policy will occur 30 days after the date of the legal notice if we do not receive your check.

Books I'll buy another day...

Some stores might say, "Put books you don't want here." But Bookseller Joseph Best in Lexington, KY, uses positive emphasis.

**Side Effects?
What Side
Effects?***

The US Food and Drug
Administration (FDA) requires
full-length ads recommending
specific drugs for specific
medical conditions to list major
side effects. Some products
attempt to get around the rule
by preparing two short ads.

A Xenical TV ad discusses
obesity, morphing a chubby
baby into a heavyset woman. It
doesn't name the drug. The
second ad uses the same
images and music and names
the drug, but says nothing
about losing weight. The ads
total 45 seconds, as long as
some "full-length" TV ads, but
never mention the side effects.

Claritin used the same
technique in magazine ads
picturing celebrity Joan
Lunden. A first small ad says in
large type, "Joan Clears the Air
About Seasonal Allergies." No
product is mentioned. The
second small ad reads, "Joan
Lunden Asks: Curious about
Claritin?" Neither ad mentions
side effects.

The FDA declared the Claritin
ads "misleading" and forced
the company to stop using
them. The FDA is exploring the
issues in TV ads and may end
up rewriting its rules.

But whether the rules change
or not, it isn't ethical to omit
negatives if customers need
the information to make
decisions.

*Based on Chris Adams, "Xenical
Ads Avoid Listing Unpleasant Side
Effects," *The Wall Street Journal*,
April 3, 2001, B1, B6.

Better:	Even if your check is lost in the mail and never reaches us, you still have a 30-day grace period. If you do get a second notice, you will know that your payment hasn't reached us. To keep your account in good standing, stop payment on the first check and send a second one.

2. Focus on what the reader can do rather than on limitations.

Eliminate double negatives. When there are limits, or some options are closed, focus on the alternatives that remain.

Negative:	We will not allow you to charge more than $1,500 on your VISA account.
Better:	You can charge $1,500 on your new VISA card.
or:	Your new VISA card gives you $1,500 in credit that you can use at thousands of stores nationwide.

As you focus on what will happen, **check for you-attitude.** In the last example, "We will allow you to charge $1,500" would be positive, but it lacks you-attitude.

When you have a benefit and a requirement the reader must meet to get the benefit, the sentence is usually more positive if you put the benefit first.

Negative:	You will not qualify for the student membership rate of $25 a year unless you are a full-time student.
Better:	You get all the benefits of membership for only $25 a year if you're a full-time student.

3. Justify negative information by giving a reason or linking it to a reader benefit.

A reason can help your reader see that the information is necessary; a benefit can suggest that the negative aspect is outweighed by positive factors. Be careful, however, to make the logic behind your reason clear and to leave no loopholes.

Negative:	We cannot sell computer disks in lots of less than 10.
Loophole:	To keep down packaging costs and to help you save on shipping and handling costs, we sell computer disks in lots of 10 or more.

Suppose the customer says, "I'll pay the extra shipping and handling. Send me seven." If you can't or won't sell in lots of less than 10, you need to write:

Better:	To keep down packaging costs and to help customers save on shipping and handling costs, we sell computer disks only in lots of 10 or more.

If you link the negative element to a benefit, be sure it is a benefit the reader will acknowledge. Avoid telling people that you're doing things "for their own good." They may have a different notion of what their own good is. You may think you're doing customers a favor by limiting their credit so they don't get in over their heads and go bankrupt. They may think they'd be better off with more credit so they could expand in hopes of making more sales and more profits.

4. If the negative is truly unimportant, omit it.

Omit negatives only when

- The reader does not need the information to make a decision.
- You have already given the reader the information and he or she has access to the previous communication.
- The information is trivial.

The following examples suggest the kind of negatives you can omit:

Negative: A one-year subscription to *PC Magazine* is $49.97. That rate is not as low as the rates charged for some magazines.

Better: A one-year subscription to *PC Magazine* is $49.97.

Still better: A one-year subscription to *PC Magazine* is $49.97. You save 43% off the newsstand price of $87.78.

Negative: If you are not satisfied with Interstate Fidelity Insurance, you do not have to renew your policy.

Better: Omit the sentence.

5. Put the negative information in the middle and present it compactly.

The beginning and end are always positions of emphasis. Use these positions for ideas you want to emphasize. Put negatives in the middle of a paragraph rather than in the first or last sentence and in the middle of the message rather than in the first or last paragraphs.

When a letter or memo runs several pages, remember that the bottom of the first page is also a position of emphasis, even if it is in the middle of a paragraph, because of the extra white space of the bottom margin. (The first page gets more attention because it is on top and the reader's eye may catch lines of the message even when he or she isn't consciously reading it; the tops and bottoms of subsequent pages don't get this extra attention.) If possible, avoid placing negative information at the bottom of the first page.

Giving a topic lots of space emphasizes it. Therefore, you can de-emphasize negative information by giving it as little space as possible. Give negative information only once in your message. Don't list negatives vertically on the page since lists take space and emphasize material.

Tone, Power, and Politeness

Tone is the implied attitude of the writer toward the reader. If the words of a document seem condescending or rude, tone is a problem. Tone is tricky because it interacts with power: the words that might seem friendly from a superior to a subordinate may seem uppity if used by the subordinate to the superior. Norms for politeness are cultural and generational. Language that is acceptable within one group may be unacceptable if used by someone outside the group.

The desirable tone for business writing is businesslike but not stiff, friendly but not phony, confident but not arrogant, polite but not groveling. The following guidelines will help you achieve the tone you want.

■ **Use courtesy titles for people outside your organization whom you don't know well.** Most US organizations use first names for everyone, whatever their age or rank. But many people don't like being called by their first names by people they don't know or by someone much younger. When you talk or write to people outside your organization, use first names only if you've established a personal relationship. If you don't know someone well, use a courtesy title:

Dear Mr. Reynolds:
Dear Ms. Lee:

■ **Be aware of the power implications of the words you use.** "Thank you for your cooperation" is generous coming from a superior to a subordinate; it's not appropriate in a message to your superior.

Different ways of asking for action carry different levels of politeness.[7]

A Soft Answer Turneth Away Lawsuits*

Lawyers usually tell individuals and companies not to admit liability, lest the admission become evidence in a lawsuit for damages. Maybe that's good advice in major crises where the CEO has a responsibility to stockholders to reduce the company's legal liability.

But one soft drink company found that sincere apologies satisfied people, so they didn't sue.

The company had a spate of complaints about exploding bottles. But instead of giving people a form to fill out and saying, "Contact our risk department," service representatives were told to empathize and apologize.

The company's liability expenses went down $2 million in a year.

*Based on Cynthia Crossen, "The Simple Apology after Poor Service Is in Very Sorry State," *The Wall Street Journal*, November 29, 1990, B8; and Lisa Tyler, "Liability Means Never Being Able to Say You're Sorry: Corporate Guilt, Legal Constraints, and Defensiveness in Corporate Communication," *Management Communication Quarterly* 11, no. 1 (August 1997): 51–73.

Positive Emphasis in Canada*

In the United States, ask someone "How are you?" and you'll probably get the standard response: "Fine, thank you" or even "Terrific!" In Canada, the standard response is "Not bad."

The words that create goodwill vary from culture to culture. Canadians—like people in Great Britain, New Zealand, and other Commonwealth countries—tend to understate and downplay. As a result, positive emphasis will be a bit less positive than it would be in the United States.

You-attitude takes precedence over every other principle: use the language that works for your audience.

*Based on Margot Northey, personal communication, October 28, 1993, Montreal, Canada; and Roger Graves, " 'Dear Friend'(?): Culture and Genre in American and Canadian Direct Marketing Letters," *The Journal of Business Communication* 34, no. 3 (July 1997): 235–52.

Order: (lowest politeness)	Turn in your time card by Monday.
Polite order: (midlevel politeness)	Please turn in your time card by Monday.
Indirect request: (higher politeness)	Time cards should be turned in by Monday.
Question: (highest politeness)	Would you be able to turn in your time card by Monday?

Higher levels of politeness may be unclear. In some cases, a question may seem like a request for information to which it's acceptable to answer, "No, I can't." In other cases, it will be an order, simply phrased in polite terms.

You need more politeness if you're asking for something that will inconvenience the reader and help you more than the person who does the action. Generally, you need less politeness when you're asking for something small, routine, or to the reader's benefit. Some discourse communities, however, prefer that even small requests be made politely.

| Lower politeness: | To start the scheduling process, please describe your availability for meetings during the second week of the month. |
| Higher politeness: | Could you let me know what times you'd be free for a meeting the second week of the month? |

Generally, requests sound friendliest when they use conversational language.

| Poor tone: | Return the draft with any changes by next Tuesday. |
| Better tone: | Let me know by Tuesday whether you'd like any changes in the draft. |

■ **When the stakes are low, be straightforward.** Messages that beat around the bush sound pompous and defensive.

Poor tone:	Distribution of the low-fat plain granola may be limited in your area. May we suggest that you discuss this matter with your store manager.
Better tone:	Our low-fat granola is so popular that there isn't enough to go around. We're expanding production to meet the demand. Ask your store manager to keep putting in orders, so that your grocery is on the list of stores that will get supplies when they become available.
or	Store managers decide what to stock. If your store has stopped carrying our low-fat granola, the store manager has stopped ordering it. Talk to the manager. Managers try to meet customer needs, so if you say something you're more likely to get what you want.

■ **When you must give bad news, consider hedging your statement.** John Hagge and Charles Kostelnick have shown that auditors' suggestion letters rarely say directly that firms are using unacceptable accounting practices. Instead, they use three strategies to be more diplomatic: specifying the time ("currently, the records are quite informal"), limiting statements ("it appears," "it seems"), and using impersonal statements that do not specify who caused a problem or who will perform an action.[8]

Reducing Bias in Business Communication

Everything we do in good business communication attempts to build goodwill. Bias-free language and bias-free visuals help sustain the goodwill we work so hard to create.

Bias-free language is language that does not discriminate against people on the basis of sex, physical condition, race, age, or any other category. It includes all readers, helps to sustain goodwill, is fair and friendly, and complies with the law. Bias-free language and visuals are also profitable. As Stephen Hlibok points out, Merrill Lynch tapped into a new, underserved market when it established its Deaf and Hard of Hearing Investors' Services Division.

Check to be sure that your language is nonsexist, nonracist, and nonagist. When you talk about people with disabilities or diseases, talk about the people, not the condition. When you produce newsletters or other documents with photos and illustrations, choose a sampling of the whole population, not just part of it.

Making Language Nonsexist

Nonsexist language treats both sexes neutrally. Check to be sure that your writing is free from sexism in four areas: words and phrases, job titles, courtesy titles, and pronouns.

Words and phrases

If you find any of the terms in the first column in Figure 2.4 in your writing or your company's documents, replace them with terms from the second column.

Not every word containing *man* is sexist. For example, *manager* is not sexist. The word comes from the Latin *manus* meaning *hand;* it has nothing to do with maleness.

Avoid terms that assume that everyone is married or is heterosexual.

Biased: You and your husband or wife are cordially invited to the dinner.

Better: You and your guest are cordially invited to the dinner.

Job titles

Use neutral titles which do not imply that a job is held only by men or only by women. Many job titles are already neutral: *accountant, banker, doctor, engineer, inspector, manager, nurse, pilot, secretary, technician,* to name a few. Other titles reflect gender stereotypes and need to be changed.

If you need a substitute for a traditional word, check the US Department of Labor's *Job Title Revisions to Eliminate Sex- and Age-Referent Language* from the *Dictionary of Occupational Titles,* 4th ed., 1991.

Instead of	Use
Businessman	A specific title: executive, accountant, department head, owner of a small business, men and women in business, business person
Chairman	Chair, chairperson, moderator
Foreman	Supervisor (from *Job Title Revisions*)
Salesman	Salesperson, sales representative
Waitress	Server
Woman lawyer	Lawyer
Workman	Worker, employee. Or use a specific title: crane operator, bricklayer, etc.

Courtesy titles

Memos normally use first and last names without courtesy titles. Letters, however, require courtesy titles in the salutation *unless* you're on a first-name basis with your reader. (See Appendix A ➡ for examples of memo and letter formats.)

R-E-S-P-E-C-T*

Most major airlines and hotel chains provide disability training to employees. . . . I recognize when someone has been trained—to offer me a Braille menu, use my name when addressing me, or take a moment to orient me to a new environment. What I appreciate even more, though, is . . . simple, common courtesy.

I don't care how many pages in an employee manual somewhere are devoted to . . . the dos and don'ts of interacting with someone who is deaf, blind, or mentally retarded. Among hundreds of experiences in airports and hotels, the one distinction that separates the (mostly) pleasing from the (occasionally) painful in my encounters has been the honest friendliness and respect with which I have or have not been treated.

Ask me where I'd like to sit, whether I need help getting there, and what other kinds of help I need.

Please, assume that I know more about my disability than anyone else ever could.

Respect me as you do any other customer who is paying for the same service, and have the grace to apologize if something does go wrong.

Too many companies, it seems to me, are busy shaking in their boots over the imagined high cost of accommodating people with disabilities when, in many instances, a good old-fashioned refresher course in manners would cover most bases.

*Quoted from Deborah Kendrick, "Disabled Resent Being Patronized," *Columbus Dispatch,* July 21, 1996, 3B.

FIGURE 2.4   Getting Rid of Sexist Terms and Phrases

Instead of	Use	Because
The girl at the front desk	The woman's name or job title: "Ms. Browning," "Rosa," "the receptionist"	Call female employees *women* just as you call male employees *men*. When you talk about a specific woman, use her name, just as you use a man's name to talk about a specific man.
The ladies on our staff	The women on our staff	Use parallel terms for males and females. Therefore, use *ladies* only if you refer to the males on your staff as *gentlemen*. Few businesses do, since social distinctions are rarely at issue.
Manpower Manhours Manning	Personnel Hours or worker hours Staffing	The power in business today comes from both women and men. If you have to correspond with the US Department of Labor's Division of Manpower Administration, you are stuck with the term. When you talk about other organizations, however, use nonsexist alternatives.
Managers and their wives	Managers and their guests	Managers may be female; not everyone is married.

- When you know your reader's name and gender, use courtesy titles that do not indicate marital status: *Mr.* for men and *Ms.* for women. There are, however, two exceptions:

  1. If the woman has a professional title, use that title if you would use it for a man.

     Dr. Kristen Sorenson is our new company physician.
     The Rev. Elizabeth Townsley gave the invocation.

  2. If the woman prefers to be addressed as *Mrs.* or *Miss,* use the title she prefers rather than *Ms.* (You-attitude takes precedence over nonsexist language: address the reader as she—or he—prefers to be addressed.) To find out if a woman prefers a traditional title,

     a. Check the signature block in previous correspondence. If a woman types her name as *(Miss) Elaine Anderson* or *(Mrs.) Kay Royster,* use the title she designates.

     b. Notice the title a woman uses in introducing herself on the phone. If she says, "This is Robin Stine," use *Ms.* when you write to her. If she says, "I'm Mrs. Stine," use the title she specifies.

     c. Check your company directory. In some organizations, women who prefer traditional titles can list them with their names.

     d. When you're writing job letters or crucial correspondence, call the company and ask the receptionist which title your reader prefers.

Ms. is particularly useful when you do not know what a woman's marital status is. However, even when you happen to know that a woman is married or single, **you still use *Ms.* unless you know that she prefers another title.**

In addition to using parallel courtesy titles, use parallel forms for names.

Not Parallel	Parallel
Members of the committee will be Mr. Jones, Mr. Yacone, and Lisa.	Members of the committee will be Mr. Jones, Mr. Yacone, and Ms. Melton.
	or
	Members of the committee will be Irving, Ted, and Lisa.

- When you know your reader's name but not the gender, either
  1. Call the company and ask the receptionist, or
  2. Use the reader's full name in the salutation:
     Dear Chris Crowell:
     Dear J. C. Meath:
- When you know neither the reader's name nor gender, you have three options:
  1. Use a letter format that omits the salutation. The AMS Simplified letter format (see Appendix A) includes the inside address and uses a subject line but omits the salutation and complimentary close.
     SUBJECT: RECOMMENDATION FOR BEN WANDELL
  2. Use the reader's position or job title:
     Dear Loan Officer:
     Dear Registrar:
  3. Use a general group to which your reader belongs:
     Dear Investor:
     Dear Admissions Committee:

Terms that are meant to be positive (Dear Careful Shopper: or Dear Concerned Citizen:) may backfire if readers see them as manipulative flattery.

Although many people claim to dislike Dear Friend: as a salutation in a form letter, research shows that letters using it bring in a higher response than letters with no salutation.

Pronouns

When you write about a specific person, use the appropriate gender pronouns:

In his speech, John Jones said that . . .

In her speech, Judy Jones said that . . .

When you are writing not about a specific person but about anyone who may be in a given job or position, traditional gender pronouns are sexist.

Sexist: a. Each supervisor must certify that the time sheet for his department is correct.

Sexist: b. When the nurse fills out the accident report form, she should send one copy to the Central Division Office.

There are four ways to eliminate sexist generic pronouns: use plurals, use second-person *you*, revise the sentence to omit the pronoun, or use pronoun pairs. Whenever you have a choice of two or more ways to make a phrase or sentence nonsexist, choose the alternative that is the smoothest and least conspicuous.

The following examples use these methods to revise sentences *a* and *b* above.

1. Use plural nouns and pronouns.

   Nonsexist: a. Supervisors must certify that the time sheets for their departments are correct.

Note: When you use plural nouns and pronouns, other words in the sentence may need to be made plural too. In the example above, plural supervisors have plural time sheets and departments.

Avoid mixing singular nouns and plural pronouns.

Nonsexist but lacks agreement: a. Each supervisor must certify that the time sheet for their department is correct.

Since *supervisor* is singular, it is incorrect to use the plural *their* to refer to it. The resulting lack of agreement is acceptable orally but is not yet acceptable to many readers in writing. Instead, use one of the four grammatically correct ways to make the sentence nonsexist.

Ms.* in Any Language

Other countries are also developing nonsexist courtesy titles for women.

- United States
  Miss
  Mrs.
  Ms.
- France
  Mademoiselle (Mlle.)
  Madame (Mme.)
  Mad.
- Spain
  Señorita (Srta.)
  Señora (Sra.)
  Sa.
- Denmark
  Frøken
  Fru
  Fr.
- Japan
  San
  San
  San

*Based on Mary Ritchie Key, *Male/Female Language* (Metuchen, NJ: Scarecrow Press, 1975), 50; John C. Condon and Fathi Yousef, *An Introduction to Intercultural Communication* (Indianapolis: Bobbs-Merrill, 1975), 50; and Silvia Fuduric, Letter to the Author, January 19, 1998.

Attempts To Create a Unisex Pronoun*

For 150 years, people have attempted to coin a unisex pronoun. None of the attempts has been successful.

Date	**he or *she***	**his or *her***	**him or *her***
1850	ne	nis	nim
1884	le	lis	lim
1938	se	sim	sis
1970	ve	vis	ver
1977	e	e's	em
1988	ala	alis	alum

*Based on Dennis E. Baron, "The Epicene Pronoun: The Word That Failed," *American Speech* 56 (1981): 83–97; and Ellen Graham, "Business Bulletin," *The Wall Street Journal*, December 29, 1988, A1.

2. Use *you*.

Nonsexist: a. You must certify that the time sheet for your department is correct.

Nonsexist: b. When you fill out an accident report form, send one copy to the Central Division Office.

You is particularly good for instructions and statements of the responsibilities of someone in a given position. Using *you* also may shorten sentences, since you write "Send one copy" instead of "You should send one copy." It also makes your writing more direct.

3. Substitute an article (*a, an,* or *the*) for the pronoun, or revise the sentence so that the pronoun is unnecessary.

Nonsexist: a. The supervisor must certify that the time sheet for the department is correct.

Nonsexist: b. The nurse will
   1. Fill out the accident report form.
   2. Send one copy of the form to the Central Division Office.

4. When you must focus on the action of an individual, use pronoun pairs.

Nonsexist: a. The supervisor must certify that the time sheet for his or her department is correct.

Nonsexist: b. When the nurse fills out the accident report form, he or she should send one copy to the Central Division Office.

Making Language Nonracist and Nonagist

Language is **nonracist** and **nonagist** when it treats all races and ages fairly, avoiding negative stereotypes of any group. Use these guidelines to check for bias in documents you write or edit:

- **Give someone's race or age only if it is relevant to your story.** When you do mention these characteristics, give them for everyone in your story—not just the non-Caucasian, non-young-to-middle-aged adults you mention.

- **Refer to a group by the term it prefers. As preferences change, change your usage.** Fifty years ago, *Negro* was preferred as a more dignified term than *colored* for African Americans. As times changed, *Black* and *African American* replaced it. Surveys in the mid-1990s showed that almost half of blacks aged 40 and older preferred *Black,* but those 18 to 39 preferred *African American.*[9]

   Oriental has now been replaced by *Asian.*

   The term *Latino* is the most acceptable group term to refer to Mexican Americans, Cuban Americans, Puerto Ricans, Dominicans, Brazilianos, and other people with Central and Latin American backgrounds. (*Latina* is the term for an individual woman.) Better still is to refer to the precise group. The differences among various Latino groups are at least as great as the differences among Italian Americans, Irish Americans, Armenian Americans, and others descended from various European groups.

   Eskimo is the accepted term for native people in Alaska. However, First Nation people in Canada prefer the term *Inuit,* which means *the people.*

   Older people and *mature customers* are more generally accepted terms than *Senior Citizens* or *Golden Agers.*

- **Avoid terms that suggest that competent people are unusual.** The statement "She is an intelligent black woman"

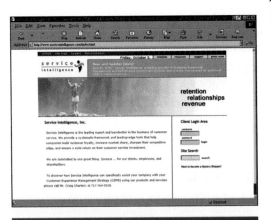

InSite

www.serviceintelligence.com/index.html

You-attitude, positive emphasis, and bias-free language build goodwill with words, just as service, quality, and reliability build goodwill with actions.

Technology helps blind people contribute fully as members of the workforce. This Braille keyboard allows a computer engineer to key in commands and data. Computer programs such as JAWS can read computer screens out loud.

suggests that the writer expects most black women to be stupid. "He is an asset to his race" suggests that excellence in the race is rare. "He is a spry 70-year-old" suggests that the writer is amazed that anyone that old can still move.

Talking about People with Disabilities and Diseases

A disability is a physical, mental, sensory, or emotional impairment that interferes with the major tasks of daily living. According to the US Census Bureau, 21% of Americans currently have a disability; the number of people with disabilities will rise as the population ages.[10]

■ *People-first language* **focuses on the person, not the condition. People-first language** names the person first, then adds the condition. Use it instead of the traditional noun phrases that imply the condition defines the person.

Instead of	Use	Because
The mentally retarded	People with mental retardation	The condition does not define the person or his or her potential.
Cancer patients	People being treated for cancer	

■ **Avoid negative terms, unless the audience prefers them.** You-attitude takes precedence over positive emphasis: use the term a group prefers. People who lost their hearing as infants, children, or young adults often prefer to be called *deaf,* or *Deaf* in recognition of Deafness as a culture. But people who lose their hearing as older adults often prefer to be called *hard of hearing,* even when their hearing loss is just as great as that of someone who identifies him- or herself as part of the Deaf culture.

Just as people in a single ethnic group may prefer different labels based on generational or cultural divides, so differences exist within the disability

Positive Emphasis Is Good for Your Health*

According to a 30-year study by the Mayo Clinic, optimists live almost 20% longer than pessimists. Optimists are better at coping with stress and have more disease-fighting T-cells.

Optimists and pessimists tell themselves different stories. Optimists feel powerful; pessimists feel doomed. When bad things happen, pessimists believe the cause is permanent. Optimists, in contrast, believe that the cause is temporary or an aberration—a disruption of normally good progress.

Experts believe we can learn to be optimistic. If you tend to be pessimistic,

- Set realistic goals so that you can succeed.
- Look for lessons. When you learn something from a bad experience, you can change the way you respond in the future.
- Look for silver linings.
- Think happy thoughts. When something minor goes wrong, focus on a good memory.
- Smile. Smiling—even when you don't initially feel happy—can improve your mood.

*Based on Donald D. Hensrud, "How to Live Longer (and Love It)," *Fortune,* April 30, 2001, 210; and Judith Newman, "Sailing Through the Blues," *Reader's Digest,* January 2001, 145–48.

community. Several disabled people explain their choices in the video clip on the BAC Web site.

Using the right term requires keeping up with changing preferences. If your target audience is smaller than the whole group, use the term preferred by that audience, even if the group as a whole prefers another term.

Some negative terms, however, are never appropriate. Negative terms such as *afflicted, suffering from,* and *struck down* also suggest an outdated view of any illness as a sign of divine punishment.

Instead of	Use	Because
Confined to a wheelchair	Uses a wheelchair	Wheelchairs enable people to escape confinement.
AIDS victim	Person with AIDS	Someone can have a disease without being victimized by it.
Abnormal	Atypical	People with disabilities are atypical but not necessarily abnormal.

Choosing Bias-Free Photos and Illustrations

When you produce a document with photographs or illustrations, check the visuals for possible bias. Do they show people of both sexes and all races? Is there a sprinkling of various kinds of people (younger and older, people using wheelchairs, etc.)? It's OK to have individual pictures that have just one sex or one race; the photos as a whole do not need to show exactly 50% men and 50% women. But the general impression should suggest that diversity is welcome and normal.

Check relationships and authority figures as well as numbers. If all the men appear in business suits and the women in maids' uniforms, the pictures are sexist even if an equal number of men and women are pictured. If the only blacks and Latinos pictured are factory workers, the photos support racism even when an equal number of people from each race are shown.

In 1997, as Marilyn Dyrud has shown, only 22% of the images of humans in clip art files were women, and most of those showed women in traditional roles. An even smaller percent pictured members of minority groups.[11] Don't use biased clip art or stock photos: create your own bias-free illustrations.

Summary of Key Points

- **You-attitude** is a style of writing that looks at things from the reader's point of view, emphasizing what the reader wants to know, respecting the reader's intelligence, and protecting the reader's ego.
  1. Talk about the reader, not about yourself.
  2. Refer to the reader's request or order specifically.
  3. Don't talk about feelings except to congratulate or offer sympathy.
  4. In positive situations, use *you* more often than *I*. Use *we* when it includes the reader.
  5. In negative situations, avoid the word *you*. Protect the reader's ego. Use passive verbs and impersonal expressions to avoid assigning blame.
- Apply you-attitude beyond the sentence level by using organization and content as well as style to build goodwill.
- **Positive emphasis** means focusing on the positive rather than the negative aspects of a situation.
  1. Avoid negative words and words with negative connotations.
  2. Focus on what the reader can do rather than on limitations.

3. Justify negative information by giving a reason or linking it to a reader benefit.

4. If the negative is truly unimportant, omit it.

5. Put the negative information in the middle and present it compactly.

■ The desirable tone for business writing is businesslike but not stiff, friendly but not phony, confident but not arrogant, polite but not groveling. The following guidelines will help you achieve the tone you want:

■ Use courtesy titles for people outside your organization whom you don't know well.

■ Be aware of the power implications of the words you use.

■ When the stakes are low, be straightforward.

■ When you must give bad news, consider hedging your statement.

■ Writing should be free from sexism in four areas: words and phrases, job titles, courtesy titles, and pronouns.

■ *Ms.* is the nonsexist courtesy title for women. Whether or not you know a woman's marital status, use *Ms. unless* the woman has a professional title or unless you know that she prefers a traditional title.

■ Traditional pronouns are sexist when they refer to a class of people, not to specific individuals. Four ways to make the sentence nonsexist are to use plurals, to use *you*, to revise the sentence to omit the pronoun, and to use pronoun pairs.

■ Bias-free language is fair and friendly; it complies with the law. It includes all readers; it helps to sustain goodwill.

■ Check to be sure that your language is nonsexist, nonracist, and nonagist. When you talk about people with disabilities or diseases, use the term they prefer. When you produce newsletters or other documents with photos and illustrations, picture a sampling of the whole population, not just part of it.

 For a self-test on the concepts in this chapter, visit the BAC Web site.

CHAPTER 2   Exercises and Problems

Getting Started

2.1   Evaluating the Ethics of Positive Emphasis

The first term in each line below is negative; the second is a positive term that is sometimes substituted for it. Which of the positive terms seem ethical? Which seem unethical? Briefly explain your choices.

junk bonds	high-yield bonds
second mortgage	home equity loan
tax	user fee
nervousness	adrenaline
problem	challenge
price increase	price change
for-profit hospital	tax-paying hospital

2.2   Eliminating Negative Words and Words with Negative Connotations

Revise each of the following sentences to replace negative words with positive ones. Be sure to keep the meaning of the original sentence.

1. You will lose customer goodwill if you are slow in handling returns and issuing refunds.

2. Do not put any paper in this box that is not recyclable.

3. When you write a report, do not make claims that you cannot support with evidence.

4. Do not fail to back up your hard disk every day.

5. I am anxious to discuss my qualifications in an interview.

2.3   Using Passives and Impersonal Expressions to Improve You-Attitude and Positive Emphasis

Revise each of these sentences to improve you-attitude and positive emphasis, first using a passive verb, then using an impersonal expression (one in which things, not people, do the action). Are both revisions equally good? Why or why not?

1. You did not supply all of the information necessary to process your claim.
2. The credit card number you supplied has expired.
3. You did not send us your check.
4. You did not include all the necessary information in your letter.
5. By failing to build a fence around your pool, you have allowed your property to violate city regulations against health hazards.

2.4   Focusing on the Positive

Revise each of the following sentences to focus on the options that remain, not those that are closed off.

1. Housing applications that arrive December 1 or later cannot be processed.
2. You cannot use flextime unless you have the consent of your supervisor.
3. As a first-year employee, you are not eligible for dental insurance.
4. I will be out of the country October 25 to November 10 and will not be able to meet with you then.
5. You will not get your first magazine for at least four weeks.

2.5   Identifying Hidden Negatives

Identify the hidden negatives in the following sentences and revise to eliminate them. In some cases, you may need to add information to revise the sentence effectively.

1. The seminar will help you become a better manager.
2. Thank you for the confidence you have shown in us by ordering one of our products. It will be shipped to you soon.
3. This publication is designed to explain how your company can start a recycling program.
4. I hope you find the information in this brochure beneficial to you and a valuable reference as you plan your move.
5. In thinking about your role in our group, I remember two occasions where you contributed something.

2.6   Improving You-Attitude and Positive Emphasis

Revise these sentences to improve you-attitude and positive emphasis. Eliminate any awkward phrasing. In some cases, you may need to add information to revise the sentence effectively.

1. We cannot provide vegetarian meals unless you let us know at least three days in advance.
2. We are pleased to provide free e-mail accounts to students.
3. You'll be happy to know that we have installed an ATM for your convenience.
4. We're swamped. We won't be able to get your order out to you until Friday morning.
5. If the above information is unclear, or if further information on this or any other topic is necessary, please do not hesitate to contact me.
6. I have been using e-mail both in my internship and in classes. I realize that almost everyone now does have experience with e-mail, but at least I won't be behind.
7. I am anxious to discuss this problem with you.
8. Medical certification can delay shutoff of electrical service for nonpayment of bills. If someone in your home needs electricity to assure health and well-being, signing up for our medical certification will delay disconnection for 30 days.
9. I had a difficult time evaluating the Web page. The sheer size of the site made it difficult to weed through. After considerable time, I decided that, although it is huge, the site is thorough and well designed.
10. We cannot process your request for a reservation because some information is missing.

2.7 Improving You-Attitude and Positive Emphasis

Revise these sentences to improve you-attitude and positive emphasis. Eliminate any awkward phrasing. In some cases, you may need to add information to revise the sentence effectively.

1. Don't drop in without an appointment. Your counselor or caseworker may be unavailable.

2. Although I was only an intern and didn't actually make presentations to major clients, I was required to prepare PowerPoint slides for the meetings and to answer some of the clients' questions.

3. At DiYanni homes we have more than 30 plans that we will personalize just for you.

4. Please notify the publisher of the magazine of your change of address as soon as possible to prevent a disruption of subscription service.

5. I'm sorry you were worried. You did not miss the deadline for signing up for a flexible medical spending account.

6. We are in the process of upgrading our Web site. Please bear with us.

7. You will be happy to hear that our cell phone plan does not charge you for incoming calls.

8. The employee discount may only be used for purchases for your own use or for gifts; you may not buy items for resale. To prevent any abuse of the discount privilege, you may be asked to justify your purchase.

9. I apologize for my delay in answering your inquiry. The problem was that I had to check with our suppliers to see whether we could provide the item in the quantity you say you want. We can.

10. If you mailed a check with your order, as you claim, we failed to receive it.

2.8 Improving You-Attitude and Positive Emphasis

Revise these sentences to improve you-attitude and positive emphasis. Eliminate any awkward phrasing. In some cases, you may need to add information to revise the sentence effectively.

1. The company cannot make its revenue goals without increasing sales in Japan.

2. We can arrange for our services to reach you within 24 hours.

3. Starting January 1, the company will create a new program that lets full-time employees volunteer one hour a week on company time.

4. I'm very sorry that you were worried. I'm happy to tell you that our special offer has not yet expired.

5. I hope this answers your question. If you still do not understand, do not fail to ask for more information.

6. Once you choose which days you want off, you can't change them after December 15 unless you have holidays remaining.

7. Next Tuesday will not be a problem. Our service crew is not overbooked and will not have trouble fitting you in.

8. I realize that Wednesday at 10 AM is not a convenient time for everyone, but I was unable to arrange a time that is good for everyone.

9. You cannot accept gifts from anyone with whom you, as an employee of the Environmental Protection Agency, deal, because some citizen might suspect that your enforcement decision had been subject to undue influence.

10. If you supplied receipts with your request for reimbursement, as you claim, they have been lost.

2.9 Eliminating Biased Language

Explain the source of bias in each of the following, and revise to remove the bias.

1. We recommend hiring Jim Ryan and Elizabeth Shuman. Both were very successful summer interns. Jim drafted the report on using rap music in ads, and Elizabeth really improved the looks of the office.

2. All sales associates and their wives are invited to the picnic.

3. Although he is blind, Mr. Morin is an excellent group leader.

4. Unlike many blacks, Yvonne has extensive experience designing Web pages.

5. Chris Renker
Pacific Perspectives
6300 West Coronado Blvd.
Los Angeles, CA
Gentlemen:

6. Enrique Torres has very good people skills for a man.

7. *Parenting 2000* shows you how to persuade your husband to do his share of child care chores.

8. Mr. Paez, Mr. O'Connor, and Tonya will represent our office at the convention.

9. Sue Corcoran celebrates her 50th birthday today. Stop by her cubicle at noon to get a piece of cake and to help us sing "The Old Grey Mare Just Ain't What She Used to Be."

10. Because older customers tend to be really picky, we will need to give a lot of details in our ads.

E-Mail Messages

2.10   Advising a Hasty Subordinate

Three days ago, one of your subordinates forwarded to everyone in the office a bit of e-mail humor he'd received from a friend. Titled "You know you're Southern when . . . ," the message poked fun at Southern speech, attitudes, and lifestyles. Today you get this message from your subordinate:

> Subject: Should I Apologize?
>
> I'm getting flamed left and right because of the Southern message. I thought it was funny, but some people just can't take a joke. So far I've tried not to respond to the flames, figuring that would just make things worse. But now I'm wondering if I should apologize. What do you think?

Answer the message.

2.11   Responding to a Complaint

You're Director of Corporate Communications; the employee newsletter is produced by your office. Today you get this e-mail message from Caroline Huber:

> Subject: Complaint about Sexist Language
>
> The article about the "Help Desk" says that Martina Luna and I "are the key customer service representatives 'manning' the desk." I don't MAN anything! I WORK.

Respond to Caroline. And send a message to your staff, reminding them to edit newsletter stories as well as external documents to replace biased language.

Communicating at Work

2.12   Evaluating You-Attitude and Positive Emphasis in Documents That Cross Your Desk

Identify three sentences from items that cross your desk that use (or should use) you-attitude and positive emphasis. If the sentences are good, write them down or attach a copy of the document(s) marking the sentence(s) in the margin. If the sentences need work, provide both the original sentence and a possible revision.

As Your Instructor Directs,
a.   Turn in the sentences and revisions.
b.   Share the sentences and revisions with the class in a brief oral presentation.
c.   Discuss the sentences and revisions with a group of students. What patterns do you see?

Letter and Memo Assignments

2.13   Evaluating Bias in Visuals

Evaluate the portrayals of people in one of the following:
■   Ads in one issue of a business magazine
■   A company's annual report
■   A company's Web page.

Do the visuals show people of both sexes and all races? Is there a sprinkling of people of various ages and physical conditions? What do the visuals suggest about who has power?

As Your Instructor Directs,

a. Share your findings orally with a small group of students.

b. Post your findings in an e-mail to the class.

c. Summarize your findings in a memo to your instructor.

d. Present your findings in an oral presentation to the class.

e. Join with a small group of students to create a written report.

2.14   Revising a Memo

Revise the following memo to improve you-attitude and positive emphasis.

> Subject: Status of Building Renovations
>
> We are happy to announce that the renovation of the lobby is not behind schedule. By Monday, October 9, we should be ready to open the west end of the lobby to limited traffic.
>
> The final phase of the renovation will be placing a new marble floor in front of the elevators. This work will not be finished until the end of the month.
>
> We will attempt to schedule most of the work during the evenings so that normal business is not disrupted.
>
> Please exercise caution when moving through the construction area. The floor will be uneven and steps will be at unusual heights. Watch your step to avoid accidental tripping or falling.

2.15   Revising a Form Letter

You've taken a part-time job at a store that sells fine jewelry. In orientation, the manager tells you that the store photographs jewelry it sells or appraises and mails the photo as a goodwill gesture after the transaction. However, when you see the form letter, you know that it doesn't build much goodwill—and you say so. The manager says, "Well, you're in college. Suppose you rewrite it."

Rewrite the letter. Use square brackets for material (like the customer's name) that would have to be inserted in the form letter to vary it for a specific customer. Add information that would help build goodwill.

> Dear Customer:
>
> We are most happy to enclose a photo of the jewelry that we recently sold you or appraised for you. We feel that this added service, which we are happy to extend to our fine customers, will be useful should you wish to insure your jewelry or need to identify it should you have the misfortune of suffering a loss.
>
> We trust you will enjoy this additional service. We thank you for the confidence you have shown by coming to our store.
>
> Sincerely,
> Your Sales Associate

3

Adapting Your Message to Your Audience

Adapting Your Message to Your Audience

Catarino Lopez

Associate Creative Director, Bromley Communications

Bromley is the second-largest Hispanic Advertising Agency in the United States. Cat Lopez has worked on a variety of blue-chip accounts including Coca-Cola, Anheuser-Busch, Polaroid, Procter & Gamble, Western Union, The American Legacy Foundation, and Burger King.

www.bromcomm.com

Whenever a new project comes up, we start by analyzing our audience. Who are we talking to? What's their nationality? Are they male or female? How old are they? What's their socio-economic status? Do they speak English or Spanish or both? How long have they been in the United States? Are they already using the product? And so forth. We then take that information and develop a target profile to help us zero in on the consumer.

Once we identify a target audience, we can then think about how we are going to reach them. A spot is no good if the intended target never sees it. Will television programming reach this audience? If not, how else can we reach them? Print, television, radio? And most importantly, what does the media budget allow?

After answering all those questions, we develop a creative brief. Determining the consumers' "hot buttons" is always a major point of discussion. Now that you know who you're talking to, how do you create a message that will appeal to them? How do you communicate the benefits of the product in a relevant manner? A single-minded approach is a good start. Figure out the one thing you want the ad to communicate and go for it. Keep it simple.

> *"Whenever a new project comes up, we start by analzying our audience."*

There have been and will continue to be many discussions on what is good creative. Good creative is not showing people what they can't see. It's showing them what they should have seen all along if they were only looking. An answer so simple that it was right in front of their face the whole time. Sounds easy. It's not.

Some of us get there with luck. A very few with pure brilliance. The rest of us get there with a lot of hard work. Trying to figure out who your audience is and then getting into their brains to develop an insight takes a lot of time and dedication. Anybody can create an ad. Very few can create an ad that works.

To create an ad that works you need information. That information needs to be communicated between people and departments. Good communication skills are essential—especially now in the electronic age when face-to-face contact diminshes by the day. All the information an agency collects will be useless if it is not communicated clearly to all those involved. Clear communication goes beyond the advertising itself. As communication professionals, everything we say, everything we write must be communicated as clearly as possible.

If you want to succeed in the ad game, polish your skills. Practice speaking in public. Write clearly worded memos, letters, and marketing plans. Place every word in the right place. Look at those who have made names for themselves in the industry. Read what they've written. Listen to them speak. While they are all different and come from a variety of backgrounds, they all have one thing in common: They're all excellent communicators.

Multiple Audiences for an Industry Report*

A consulting company was hired to write a report on how potential changes would affect manufacturing, safety, and cost of a consumer product.

The primary audience was the federal government, which would set the regulations for the product. Within this audience were economists, engineers, and policymakers.

The group of manufacturers that hired the consulting firm was both the initial audience and a gatekeeper. If it didn't like the report, it wouldn't send it on to the federal government.

Secondary audiences included the general public, other manufacturers of the product, and competitors and potential clients of the consulting company.

Industry reviewers emerged as a watchdog audience. They read drafts of the report and commented on it. Although they had no direct power over this report, their goodwill was important for the consulting company's image—and its future contracts. Their comments were the ones that authors took most seriously as they revised their drafts.

*Based on Vincent J. Brown, "Facing Multiple Audiences in Engineering and R&D Writing: The Social Context of a Technical Report," *Journal of Technical Writing and Communication* 24, no. 1 (1994): 67–75.

Knowing who you're talking to is fundamental to the success of any message. You need to identify your audiences, understand their motivations, and know how to reach them.

Identifying Your Audiences

The first step in analyzing your audience is to decide who your audience is. Organizational messages have multiple audiences:[1]

1. The **initial audience** is the first audience to get your message. Sometimes the initial audience tells you to write the message.
2. A **gatekeeper** has the power to stop your message instead of sending it on to other audiences. The gatekeeper therefore controls whether your message even gets to the primary audience. Sometimes the supervisor who assigns the message is also the gatekeeper; sometimes the gatekeeper is higher in the organization. In some cases, gatekeepers may exist outside the organization.
3. The **primary audience** will decide whether to accept your recommendations or will act on the basis of your message. You must reach the primary audience to fulfill your purposes in any message.
4. The **secondary audience** may be asked to comment on your message or to implement your ideas after they've been approved. Secondary audiences also include lawyers who may use your message—perhaps years later—as evidence of your organization's culture and practices.
5. A **watchdog audience,** though it does not have the power to stop the message and will not act directly on it, has political, social, or economic power. The watchdog pays close attention to the transaction between you and the primary audience and may base future actions on its evaluation of your message.

As the following examples show, one person can be part of two audiences. Frequently, a supervisor is both the initial audience and the gatekeeper. Sometimes the initial audience is also the primary audience who will act on the message.

Dawn is an assistant account executive in an ad agency. Her boss asks her to write a proposal for a marketing plan for a new product the agency's client is introducing. Her **primary audience** is the executive committee of the client company, who will decide whether to adopt the plan. The **secondary audience** includes the marketing staff of the client company, who will be asked for comments on the plan, as well as the artists, writers, and media buyers who will carry out details of the plan if it is adopted. Her boss, who must approve the plan before it is submitted to the client, is both the **initial audience** and the **gatekeeper.**

Joe works in the data processing unit of a bank. He must write a monthly progress report describing his work. This month, he has worked on implementing a centralized system for handling customers' checks. His boss is **both a primary and an initial audience.** His boss will write a performance appraisal evaluating his work, so Joe wants to present his own efforts positively. The boss may also include paragraphs from Joe's progress report in a memo to the president of the bank, who wants to know when the bugs in the system will be worked out. The president is thus also a **primary audience.** The **secondary audience** includes the bank's customer service representatives, who must answer customer questions and deal with complaints about the new system, and sales representatives from the computer company that sold the hardware to the bank, who want to be sure that bank personnel are able to use the equipment effectively.

Ways to Analyze Your Audience

The most important tools in audience analysis are common sense and empathy. **Empathy** is the ability to put yourself in someone else's shoes, to feel with that person. Empathy requires that one not be self-centered. In all probability, the audience is *not* just like you. Use what you know about people and about organizations to predict likely responses.

Analyzing Individuals

When you write or speak to people in your own organization and in other organizations you work closely with, you may be able to analyze your audience as individuals. You may already know your audience. It will usually be easy to get additional information by talking to members of your audience, talking to people who know your audience, and observing your audience.

The **Myers-Briggs Type Indicator** uses four dimensions to identify ways that people differ.[2] One of these is well known: introvert-extravert. Introverts get their energy from within; extraverts are energized by interacting with other people. The other three dimensions in the Myers-Briggs scale are sensing-intuitive, thinking-feeling, and perceiving-judging. Sensing-intuitive measures the way someone gets information. Sensing types gather information through their senses. Intuitive types see relationships. Thinking-feeling measures the way someone makes decisions. Thinking types use objective logic to reach decisions. Feeling types make decisions that feel "right," without necessarily being able to define the path they took to make the decision. Judging-perception measures the degree of certainty someone needs. Judging types like closure. Perceptive types like possibilities.

The poles on each of these scales represent a preference, just as we have a preference for using either our right or our left hand to write. If necessary, we can use the opposite style, but we have less practice in it and use it less easily.

You can find out your own personality type by taking the Myers-Briggs Type Indicator at your college's counseling center or student services office. Some businesses administer the Myers-Briggs Type Indicator to all employees. Even when you don't have official results, you can often make accurate guesses about someone's type by close observation.

As Figure 3.1 suggests, you'll be most persuasive if you play to your audience's strengths. Indeed, many of the general principles of business communication reflect the types most common among managers. Putting the main point up front satisfies the needs of judging types, and some 75% of US managers are judging. Giving logical reasons satisfies the needs of the nearly 80% of US managers who are thinking types.[3]

Analyzing the Organizational Culture and the Discourse Community

Be sensitive to the culture in which your audiences work and the discourse community of which they are a part. **Organizational culture** is a set of values, attitudes, and philosophies. An organization's culture is revealed verbally in the organization's myths, stories, and heroes and nonverbally in the allocation of space, money, and power. A **discourse community** is a group of people who share assumptions about what channels, formats, and styles to use for communication, what topics to discuss and how to discuss them, and what constitutes evidence.

See the BAC Web site for sample analyses of specific companies.

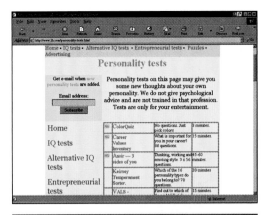

InSite

www.2h.com/personality-tests.html

Before you analyze your audience, analyze yourself—so that you can see what you and your audience share and how you differ.

My Boss Was an Introvert

I'm sure my former department chair was an introvert. How could I tell? The main clue was that he wrote out the introductory remarks he made at faculty meetings. Clearly, this man didn't like speaking spontaneously; even in this low-stress situation, he wanted to prepare his words.

The clincher was the way he responded to requests. I quickly learned that I should put even simple requests in writing—I was more likely to get what I wanted. If I asked for something orally, he had to say something immediately—and the easiest thing to say was *no*.

FIGURE 3.1   Using Myers-Briggs Types in Persuasive Messages

If your audience is	Use this strategy	Because
An introvert	Write a memo and let the reader think about your proposal before responding.	Introverts prefer to think before they speak. Written documents give them the time they need to think through a proposal carefully.
An extravert	Try out your idea orally, in an informal setting.	Extroverts like to think on their feet. They are energized by people; they'd rather talk than write.
A sensing type	Present your reasoning step-by-step. Get all your facts exactly right.	Sensing types usually reach conclusions step-by-step. They want to know why something is important, but they trust their own experience more than someone else's say-so. They're good at facts and expect others to be, too.
An intuitive type	Present the big picture first. Stress the innovative, creative aspects of your proposal.	Intuitive types like solving problems and being creative. They can be impatient with details.
A thinking type	Use logic, not emotion, to persuade. Show that your proposal is fair, even if some people may be hurt by it.	Thinking types make decisions based on logic and abstract principles. They are often uncomfortable with emotion.
A feeling type	Show that your proposal meets the emotional needs of people as well as the dollars-and-cents needs of the organization.	Feeling types are very aware of other people and their feelings. They are sympathetic and like harmony.
A perceiving type	Show that you've considered all the alternatives. Ask for a decision by a specific date.	Perceiving types want to be sure they've considered all the options. They may postpone coming to closure.
A judging type	Present your request quickly.	Judging types are comfortable making quick decisions. They like to come to closure so they can move on to something else.

Source: Modified and reproduced by special permission of the publisher, Consulting Psychologist Press, Inc., Palo Alto, CA, from *Introduction to Type®* 6th Ed. By Isabel Briggs Myers. Copyright 1998 by Consulting Psychologist Press, Inc. All rights reserved. Further reproduction is prohibited without the publisher's written consent.

In an organization that values equality and individualism, you can write directly to the CEO and address him or her as a colleague. In other companies, you'd be expected to follow a chain of command. Even if you know the name of the real decision maker, you'd be expected to send your message through your boss—and to be deferential to your superiors. Some organizations prize short messages; some expect long, thorough documents. Some cultures expect people to float trial balloons; others prefer that people work out all the details before they propose a change. Messages that are consistent with the organization's culture have a greater chance of succeeding.

Every organization—businesses, government agencies, nonprofit organizations, even colleges—has a culture. An organization's culture is constructed by the people who found the organization and change it.

You can begin to analyze an organization's culture by asking the following questions:

- Is the organization tall or flat? Are there lots of levels between the CEO and the lowest worker, or only a few?
- How do people get ahead? Are the organization's rewards based on seniority, education, being well-liked, making technical discoveries, or serv-

Ben & Jerry's corporate culture fosters informality and spontaneity. Work is interrupted with announcements that the Ben & Jerry's hot air balloon is about to take off from the parking lot, or that "SCOOP U," the in-house scoop shop, is open. The culture at software company Siebel Systems is professional and competitive. Employees can't eat at their desks. Men wear suits; women wear pantsuits or skirted suits with pantyhose. Employees are rated, and every year the lowest 5% are fired.

Culture Clash*

Kathy Wheeler learned [about corporate culture] the hard way . . . when she left Hewlett-Packard for Apple Computer. . . . Wheeler had felt comfortable with . . . HP culture: collaboration, consensus seeking, rock-solid engineering ability. Those were the qualities HP prized, and Wheeler had them big. At Apple, she says, everything was different. Suddenly she encountered a culture that exalted heroes and admired slick user interfaces. Those who got ahead were not for the most part the most skilled engineers but rather the "evangelists"—brash marketers of Apple products to the outside world. Before long, Wheeler says, she was deeply unhappy. "When you're used to being valued for one set of accomplishments," she says, "and what's actually being valued are accomplishments you either don't feel comfortable with or just aren't able to deliver on, the discomfort is pretty profound." Fourteen months after arriving at Apple, Wheeler returned to HP, notwithstanding Apple's efforts to keep her. "I admire Apple to a large extent," she says. "But I wouldn't work there again because of the cultural issues."

*Quoted from Matt Siegel, "The Perils of Culture Conflict," *Fortune,* November 9, 1998, 257–58.

ing customers? Are rewards available only to a few top people, or is everyone expected to succeed?

- Does the organization value diversity or homogeneity? Does it value independence and creativity or being a team player and following orders? What stories do people tell? Who are the organization's heroes and villains?
- How important are friendship and sociability? To what extent do workers agree on goals, and how intently do they pursue them?

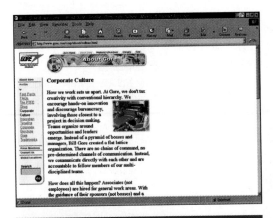

InSite

www.gore.com/corp/about/culture.html

W. L. Gore & Associates, Inc., maker of Gore-Tex, is one of many companies whose Web pages describe the corporate culture of the organization.

- How formal are behavior, language, and dress?
- What are the organization's goals? Making money? Serving customers and clients? Advancing knowledge? Contributing to the community?

Two companies in the same field may have very different cultures. In the mid-1980s, researcher Jennifer Chatman found that employees of Touche Ross (now Deloitte & Touche) rated informality as the firm's number one value. At Arthur Andersen, informality was the last of 54 values. More recently, Chatman found that new hires who "fit" the company's culture were more likely to stay with the job, more productive, and more satisfied than those who did not fit the culture.[4]

Organizations, like nations, can have subcultures. For example, manufacturing and marketing may represent different subcultures in the same organization: they may dress differently and have different values.

To analyze an organization's discourse community, ask the following questions:

- What channels, formats, and styles are preferred for communication?
- What do people talk about? What topics are not discussed?
- What kind of and how much evidence is needed to be convincing?

A discourse community may be limited to a few people in an organization. However, some discourse communities span an entire organization or even everyone in the same field in the nation or the world. You will be a member of several overlapping discourse communities. Succeeding in a job—whether it's flipping burgers or balancing books, managing a Fortune 500 company or running a hospital—requires becoming part of a discourse community. In your college courses, you learn what questions to ask about accounting systems or marketing plans; you learn what kinds of evidence you should use to prove that a landscape plan should include perennials or that a company should sell its products in Europe.

Different organizations may represent different cultures and different discourse communities, even when they hire people from the same disciplines. Lawyers in one state agency may see the documents they write as dry, factual, and unimportant, with the real emphasis on oral arguments in negotiations or trials. Lawyers at another agency may see themselves writing multipurposed, compelling documents designed not only to carry the weight of litigation but also to enhance the organization's image in the eyes of its various publics.[5] FedEx sales representatives court large customers with frequent phone calls; UPS workers send a bid and let that speak for itself—an approach consistent with UPS's culture of humility and modesty.[6]

Analyzing Members of Groups

In many organizational situations, you'll analyze your audience not as individuals but as members of a group: "taxpayers who must be notified that they owe more income tax," "customers living in the northeast side of the city," or "employees with small children." Focus on what group members have in common. Although generalizations won't be true for all members of the group, generalization is necessary when you must appeal to a large group of people with one message. In some cases, no research is necessary: it's easy to guess the attitudes of people who must be told they owe more taxes. In other cases, databases may yield useful information. In still other cases, you may want to do original research.

If you know where your audience lives, databases enable you to map demographic and psychographic profiles of customers or employees. **Demographic characteristics** are measurable features that can be counted objectively: age, sex, race, religion, education level, income, and so on.

The BAC Web site has links that profile the demographics in your zip code. Sometimes demographic information is irrelevant; sometimes it's important. Does education matter? Well, the fact that the reader has a degree from Eastern State rather than from Harvard probably doesn't matter, but how much the reader knows about accounting may. Does age matter? Sometimes. "Generational marketing" is helping manufacturers design and market products. Ford divides consumers into six generations. Then it develops vehicles to meet the profile of each group.[7] But other marketers are finding that considering age alone is inadequate to sell to the "mature market."[8]

Psychographic characteristics are qualitative rather than quantitative: values, beliefs, goals, and lifestyles. Many marketers use the Values and Life Styles (VALS) profiles developed by the SRI research firm in California. VALS profiles divide US buyers into nine categories, including Believers, the conservative middle class who "have benefited by the rules of the game"; Strivers, conspicuous consumers who don't have lots of money but who want to be in style; Fulfilleds, ambitious, hardworking, comfort-loving people who "control nearly 50% of the buying power" in the United States; and Actualizers, highly educated people who are interested in conservation, the environment, and inner growth.[9]

To see where you fit, follow the VALS link from the BAC Web site. Knowing what your audience finds important allows you to organize information in a way that seems natural to your audience and to choose appeals that the audience will find persuasive. For example, Cindy Casselman knew that Xerox had spent an enormous amount of money on infrastructure. So she pointed out that an intranet would use that infrastructure. She also knew that presenting the intranet as a way to build a community would appeal to the then-CIO, who was interested in benefits that went beyond dollars and cents.

Often it's useful for a company to identify customer segments. Taco Bell identified two groups of high-potential customers: *penny pinchers,* who visit Taco Bell frequently but don't spend much on a visit, and *speed freaks,* who are more interested in convenience than price. To attract these consumers, Taco Bell lowered prices on its core menu items and reengineered its production, cutting wait time by 71%. These changes tripled sales and—even with lower prices—raised profits $20 million.[10]

Choosing Channels to Reach Your Audience

Communication channels vary in speed, accuracy of transmission, cost, number of messages carried, number of people reached, efficiency, and ability to promote goodwill. Depending on the audience, your purposes, and the situation, one channel may be better than another.

A written message makes it easier to

- Present extensive or complex financial data.
- Present many specific details of a law, policy, or procedure.
- Minimize undesirable emotions.

Messages on paper are more formal than e-mail messages. E-mail messages are appropriate for routine interchanges with people you already know. Paper is better for someone to whom you're writing for the first time.

Oral messages make it easier to

- Use emotion to help persuade the audience.
- Focus the audience's attention on specific points.

A Young Manager Adapts to Older Audiences*

When James Ferguson became a manager at the age of 21, he realized he would trigger "conflict right, left and center" if he came on as a young hotshot. . . .

[H]e was . . . supervising a staff of 12, all of them older. He drew on tactics he had learned as head of his college newspaper, where he had to enlist and motivate a staff of volunteers. . . . [I]nstead of trying to assert control, he talked with each of [his subordinates], asking "what are the good and bad things about your job, and what do you want to change[?]" . . .

He incorporated their suggestions into his own plan, which he then sold to upper management. "But my staff owned the plan; they'd been part of the decision-making process," he says. With all employees, but particularly with older ones who are more apt to challenge a younger boss's judgment, "you've got to be a good listener and enroll their thoughts. They're not going to like everything you decide, but at least they'll know you listened."

*Quoted from Carol Hymowitz, "Young Managers Learn How to Bridge the Gap with Older Employees," *The Wall Street Journal,* July 21, 1998, B1.

Kids and Cul-de-sacs

Norma Rae-Ville

Latino America

Military Quarters

Mid-City Mix

American Dream

Young Influentials

Gray Power

Shotguns and Pickups

Market research firm Claritas, Inc., combines demographic and psychographic data to identify the zip codes that are most likely to have one of 62 lifestyle clusters, including "Kids and Cul-de-sacs" (upscale suburban families), "Mid-City Mix" (African American singles and families), and "Shotguns and Pickups" (rural blue-collar workers and families). Both the catchy names and the drawings are copyrighted by Claritas, Inc., 2001.

- Answer questions, resolve conflicts, and build consensus.
- Modify a proposal that may not be acceptable in its original form.
- Get immediate action or response.

Scheduled meetings and oral presentations are more formal than phone calls or stopping someone in the hall.

Important messages should use more formal channels, whether they're oral or written. Oral and written messages have many similarities. In both, you should

- Adapt the message to the specific audience.
- Show the audience how they would benefit from the idea, policy, service, or product.
- Overcome any objections the audience may have (➡ Chapter 9).

Choose the channel that best gets your message to the audience you want to reach. In the late 1990s, Cisco Systems added up to 1,200 new employees each quarter. How did it find them? One method was to seat Cisco employees in the end zones at the Stanford-Berkeley football game. Whenever a team scored, employees held up placards. Hits on Cisco's Web site rose 10% in the days after the game.

- Use you-attitude and positive emphasis (◀▥ Chapter 2).
- Use visuals to clarify or emphasize material.
- Specify exactly what the audience should do.

Sometimes your channel choice is determined by the audience. Some organizations still post announcements and job openings on bulletin boards because the mail staff, cleaning people, and some clerical workers don't have computers and so can't check e-mail. Even people who have access to the same channels may prefer different ones. When a university updated its employee benefits manual, the computer scientists and librarians wanted the information online. Faculty wanted to be able to read the information on paper. Maintenance workers and carpenters wanted to get answers on voice mail.[11]

The bigger your audience, the more complicated channel choice becomes, since few channels reach everyone in your target audience. When possible, use multiple channels. For example, print ads and customer service materials should contain not only 800 numbers but also street or e-mail addresses so that people who don't like to make phone calls or who have hearing impairments can contact the company.

Using Audience Analysis to Adapt Your Message

If you know your audience well and if you use words well, much of your audience analysis and adaptation will be unconscious. If you don't know your audience or if the message is very important, take the time to analyze your audience formally and to revise your draft with your analysis in mind.

As you answer these questions for a specific audience, think about the organizational culture in which the person works. At every point, your reader's reaction is affected not only by his or her personal feelings and preferences but also by the political environment of the organization, the economy, and current events.

How to Find Rich People*

1. What Will the Audience's Initial Reaction Be to the Message?

a. Will the audience see this message as highly important?

Audiences will read and act on messages they see as important to their own careers; they may ignore messages that seem unimportant to them.

When the audience may see your message as unimportant, you need to

- In a subject line or first paragraph, show your reader that this message is important and relevant.
- Make the action as easy as possible.
- Suggest a realistic deadline for action.
- Keep the message as short as possible.

b. How will the fact that the message is from you affect the audience's reaction to the words you use?

The audience's experience with you, your organization, and the subject you're writing about shapes the way he or she responds to this new message. Someone who thinks well of you and your organization will be prepared to receive your message favorably; someone who thinks poorly of you and the organization will be quick to find fault with what you say and the way you say it.

When you must write to someone who has negative feelings about your organization, your position, or you personally, you need to

- Make a special effort to avoid phrases that could seem condescending, arrogant, rude, hostile, or uncaring.
- Use positive emphasis (← p. 37) to counteract the natural tendency to sound defensive.
- Develop logic and reader benefits fully.

2. How Much Information Does the Audience Need?

a. How much does the audience already know about this subject?

It's easy to overestimate the knowledge an audience has. People outside your own immediate unit may not really know what it is you do. Even people who once worked in your unit may have forgotten specific details now that their daily work is in management. People outside your organization won't know how *your* organization does things.

When some of your information is new to the audience, you need to

- Make a special effort to be clear. Define terms, explain concepts, use examples.
- Link new information to old information that the reader already knows.
- Use paragraphs and headings to break up new information into related chunks so that the information is easier to digest.
- Test a draft of your document with your reader or a subset of your intended audience to see whether the audience can understand and use what you've written.

b. Is the audience's knowledge based on reading? Personal experience?

Things we have learned directly, through personal observation and experience, always seem more real and more true than things we've learned indirectly or from books. Other people may see our experience as an exception, an aberration, or a fluke; we see it as the best guide of what to expect in the future.

If you're trying to change someone's understanding of a policy or organization, you need to

- Acknowledge the audience's initial understanding early in the message.
- Use examples as well as theory or statistics to show the difference between short-term and long-term effects, or to show that the audience's experience is not universal.
- Allow the audience to save face by suggesting that changed circumstances call for new attitudes or action.

c. What aspects of the subject does the audience need to be aware of to appreciate your points?

When the audience must think of background or old information to appreciate your points, you can

- Preface information with "As you know" or "As you may remember" to avoid suggesting that you think the reader does not know what you're saying.
- Put old or obvious information in a subordinate clause.
- Put lengthy background or reminder information in a separate section with an appropriate heading or in an attachment to your letter or memo.

3. What Obstacles Must You Overcome?

a. Is your audience opposed to what you have to say?

People who have already made up their minds are highly resistant to change. When the audience will oppose what you have to say, you need to

- Start your message with any areas of agreement or common ground that you share with your reader.
- Make a special effort to be clear and unambiguous. Points that might be clear to a neutral reader can be misread by someone with a chip on his or her shoulder.
- Make a special effort to avoid statements that will anger the audience.
- Limit your statement or request to the smallest possible area. If parts of your message could be delivered later, postpone them.
- Show that your solution is the best solution currently available, even though it isn't perfect.

b. Will it be easy for the audience to do as you ask?

Everyone has a set of ideas and habits and a mental self-image. If we're asked to do something that violates any of those, we first have to be persuaded to change our attitudes or habits or self-image—a change we're reluctant to make.

When your request is time-consuming, complicated, or physically or psychologically difficult, you need to

- Make the action as easy as possible. Provide a form that can be filled out quickly; provide a stamped, self-addressed envelope if you are writing to someone in another organization.
- Break down actions into a list, so the audience can check off each step as it is completed.

The Audiences for a CPA Audit Report*

An audit report may be used by at least five different audiences:

The client, who may resent any report that isn't fully favorable.

Bankers, investors, and creditors, who make decisions based on audit reports and who may hold the CPA financially responsible for the report with a "third-party" lawsuit.

Colleagues, who use the reports, but who may have different ethical or theoretical positions.

Attorneys, who will use the reports as evidence for or against the CPA if a suit is filed.

The AICPA (American Institute of Certified Public Accountants), which sets the standards for accounting reports.

Good audit reports meet the needs and overcome the possible objections of all of these audiences.

*Based on Aletha S. Hendrickson, "How to Appear Reliable without Being Liable: C.P.A. Writing in Its Rhetorical Context," *Worlds of Writing: Teaching and Learning in Different Discourse Communities,* ed. Carolyn Matalene (New York: Random House, 1989), 323.

- Show that what you ask is consistent with some aspect of what the audience believes.
- Show how the audience (not just you or your organization) will benefit when the action is completed.

4. What Positive Aspects Can You Emphasize?

a. From the audience's point of view, what are the benefits of what you have to say?

Benefits help persuade the audience that your ideas are good ones. Make the most of the good points inherent in the message you want to convey.

- Put good news in the first paragraph.
- Use reader benefits that go beyond the basic good news of the first paragraph.

b. What experiences, interests, goals, and values do you share with the audience?

A sense of solidarity with someone can be an even more powerful reason to agree than the content of the message itself. Always use all the ethical strategies that are available to win support for your ideas.

When everyone in your audience shares the same experiences, interests, goals, and values, you can

- Consider using a vivid anecdote to remind the audience of what you share. The details of the anecdote should be interesting or new; otherwise, you may seem to be lecturing the audience.
- Make a special effort to make your writing style friendly and informal.
- Use a salutation and close that remind the audience of their membership in this formal or informal group.

5. What Expectations Does the Audience Have about the Appropriate Language, Structure, and Form for Messages?

a. What style of writing does the audience prefer?

Good writers adapt their style to suit the reader's preferences. A reader who sees contractions as too informal needs a different style from one who sees traditional business writing as too stuffy. As you write,

- Use what you know about your reader to choose a more or less distant, more or less friendly style.
- Use the reader's first name in the salutation only if you use that name when you talk to him or her in person or on the phone.

b. Are there hot buttons or "red flag" words that may create an immediate negative response?

You don't have time to convince the audience that a term is broader or more neutral than his or her understanding. When you need agreement or approval, you should

- Avoid terms that carry emotional charges for many readers: for example, *criminal, un-American, feminist, fundamentalist, liberal.*
- Use your previous experience with an individual reader or listener to replace any terms that have particular meanings for him or her.

c. How much detail does the audience want?

A message that does not give the audience the amount of or kind of detail he or she wants may fail. When you know the members of your audience, ask them how much detail they want. When you write to people you do not know well, you can

▪ Provide all the detail they need to understand and act on your message.

▪ Group chunks of information under headings so that readers can go directly to the parts of the message they find most interesting and relevant.

▪ Imitate the level of detail in similar documents to the same audience. If those documents have succeeded, you're probably safe in using the same level of detail that they do.

d. Does the audience prefer a direct or indirect structure?

Individual personality or cultural background may lead someone to prefer a particular kind of structure. You'll be more effective if you use the structure and organization your audience prefers.

e. Does the audience have expectations about formal elements such as length, visuals, or footnotes?

A document that meets the reader's expectations about length, number of visuals, and footnote format is more likely to succeed. If you can't meet those expectations, you need to

▪ Revise your document carefully. Be sure that a shorter-than-usual document covers the essential points; be sure that a longer-than-usual document is free from wordiness and repetition.

▪ Check with the audience to see whether the standards are flexible.

▪ Pretest the message on a subset of your audience to see if the format enhances or interferes with comprehension and action.

6. How Will the Audience Use the Document?

a. Under what physical conditions will the audience use the document?

Reading a document in a quiet office calls for no special care. But suppose the reader will be reading your message on the train commuting home, or on a ladder as he or she attempts to follow instructions. Then the physical preparation of the document can make it easier or harder to use.

When the reader will use your document outside an office,

▪ Use lots of white space.

▪ Make the document small enough to hold in one hand.

▪ Number items so the reader can find his or her place after an interruption.

▪ Consider using plastic to protect the document.

b. Will the audience use the document as a general reference? As a specific guide? As the basis for a lawsuit?

Understanding how your audience will use the document will enable you to choose the best pattern of organization and the best level of detail. A great deal of detail is needed in an Environmental Protection Agency inspection report that will be used to determine whether to bring suit against a company for violating

Rx for Profits*

Mr. Ost owns three of the smallest drugstores you ever saw, all located in the most bombed-out and burned-out section of [Philadelphia]. But he is doing $5 million of business a year, more than twice the average drugstore rate. . . .

[H]e noticed an assistant labeling a prescription by typewriter instead of by computer. She was translating it, she explained, because to many Spanish-speaking customers, English labels were gibberish. Afraid of confusing dosage, some wouldn't take their medicine.

With a few lines of programming code, Mr. Ost expanded a simple commitment to service into a powerful marketing weapon. He loaded some 1,000 common regimens in Spanish, any of which could be printed instead of the English equivalent with a single keystroke. Business took off. . . .

When an Asian influx hit, he leaped forward again, labeling in Vietnamese. Soon he was writing 400 prescriptions a day at his second location—half in English, 30% in Spanish and 20% in Vietnamese.

*Quoted from Thomas Petzinger, Jr., "Druggist's Simple Rx: Speak the Language of Your Customers," *The Wall Street Journal*, June 16, 1995, B1.

Different Benefits for Different Audiences*

Fluoride toothpaste sells for its decay prevention benefits in Germany, Holland, and Denmark with the basic US marketing and advertising strategy; but in England, France, and Italy, the cosmetic claims for toothpaste are more important, and the US strategy does not work.

Volvo . . . has emphasized economy, durability, and safety in America; status and leisure in France; performance in Germany; and safety in Switzerland. Price is considered to be a critical variable to Mexican consumers, but quality is of more importance to Venezuelans.

Closing [a $100,000 life insurance sale to a Chinese-American, the sales rep] stressed that Met Life was a venerable 119 years old—a standard pitch to Chinese-Americans. . . . It probably worked better than Snoopy, the "Peanuts" character used in the insurer's mainstream ads. Says Ruben Lopez, Met Life's marketing director for special projects, "The Chinese aren't going to buy life insurance from a dog."

*Quoted from Robert F. Roth, *International Marketing Communications* (Chicago: Crain, 1982), 296–97; David A. Ricks, *Big Business Blunders* (Homewood, IL: Dow Jones–Irwin, 1983), 60; and "Tapping into a Blossoming Asian Market," *Newsweek*, September 7, 1987, 47.

pollution control regulations. A memo within a company urging the adoption of pollution control equipment would need less information. Different information would be needed for instructions by the manufacturer of the equipment explaining how to install and maintain it.

If the document will serve as a general reference,

- Use a subject line to aid in filing and retrieval. If the document is online, consider using several keywords to make it easy to find the document in a database search program.
- Use headings within the document so that readers can skim it.
- Give the office as well as the person to contact so that the reader can get in touch with the appropriate person some time from now.
- Spell out details that may be obvious now but might be forgotten in six months or a year.

If the document will be a detailed guide or contain instructions,

- Check to be sure that all the steps are in chronological order.
- Number steps or provide check-off boxes so that readers can easily see which steps they've completed.
- Group steps into five to seven subprocesses if there are many individual steps.
- Put any warnings at the beginning of the document; then repeat them just before the specific step to which they apply.

If the document will be used as the basis for a lawsuit,

- Give specific observations with dates and exact measurements as well as any inferences you've drawn from those observations.
- Give a full report with all the information you have. The lawyer can then decide which parts of the information to use in preparing the case.

c. Will the document be filed?

In contemporary organizations, everything of importance will be filed. When you know that your message will be filed,

- Use a specific subject line.
- Specify details that may be forgotten six months or a year from now.
- Check both the draft and the final typed copy for accuracy, completeness, and friendliness.

Reader Benefits

Use your analysis of your audience to create effective reader benefits. **Reader benefits** are benefits or advantages that the reader gets by using your services, buying your products, following your policies, or adopting your ideas. In informative messages, reader benefits give reasons to comply with the policies you announce and suggest that the policies are good ones. In persuasive messages, reader benefits give reasons to act and help overcome reader resistance. Negative messages do not use reader benefits.

Characteristics of Good Reader Benefits

Good reader benefits meet four criteria. Each of these criteria suggests a technique for writing good reader benefits.

1. Adapt reader benefits to the audience.

When you write to different audiences, you may need to stress different reader benefits. Suppose that you manufacture a product and want to persuade dealers to carry it. The features you may cite in ads directed toward customers—stylish colors, sleek lines, convenience, durability, good price—won't convince dealers. Shelf space is at a premium, and no dealer carries all the models of all the brands available for any given product. Why should the dealer stock your product? To be persuasive, talk about the features that are benefits from the dealer's point of view: turnover, profit margin, the national advertising campaign that will build customer awareness and interest, the special store displays you offer that will draw attention to the product.

The Wall Street Journal wanted subscribers to renew their subscriptions for two more years rather than just for one. The cost of the second year was 66% of the cost of the first year. The mailing admitted that renewing for two years would tie up the money but presented the cost of the second year as "a 34% tax-free return on your money." The benefit was highly appropriate for an audience concerned about returns on investments and aware of the risk that normally accompanies high returns. *Garbage* magazine urged subscribers to respond to the first renewal notice to save the paper that an additional mailing would take. This logic was appropriate for an audience concerned about the disposal of solid waste.

2. Stress intrinsic as well as extrinsic motivators.

Intrinsic motivators come automatically from using a product or doing something. **Extrinsic motivators** are "added on." Someone in power decides to give them; they do not necessarily come from using the product or doing the action. Figure 3.2 gives examples of extrinsic and intrinsic motivators for three activities.

Intrinsic motivators or benefits are better than extrinsic motivators for two reasons:

1. There just aren't enough extrinsic motivators for everything you want people to do. You can't give a prize to every customer every time he or she places an order or to every subordinate who does what he or she is supposed to do.
2. Research shows that extrinsic motivators may actually make people *less* satisfied with the products they buy or the procedures they follow.

In a groundbreaking study of professional employees, Frederick Herzberg found that the things people said they liked about their jobs were all intrinsic

FIGURE 3.2 Extrinsic and Intrinsic Motivators

Activity	Extrinsic motivator	Intrinsic motivator
Making a sale	Getting a commission	Pleasure in convincing someone; pride in using your talents to think of a strategy and execute it
Turning in a suggestion to a company suggestion system	Getting a monetary reward when the suggestion is implemented	Solving a problem at work; making the work environment a little more pleasant
Writing a report that solves an organizational problem	Getting praise, a good performance appraisal, and maybe a raise	Pleasure in having an effect on an organization; pride in using your skills to solve problems; solving the problem itself

motivators—pride in achievement, an enjoyment of the work itself, responsibility. Extrinsic motivators—pay, company policy—were sometimes mentioned as things people disliked, but they were never cited as things that motivated or satisfied them. People who made a lot of money still did not mention salary as a good point about the job or the organization.[12] In 1996, 46% of people surveyed in a Harris poll said "success" meant family and/or children, not money.[13] A 1999 survey found that having responsibility and autonomy, the respect and recognition of superiors, and the opportunity to have ideas adopted all were more important than salary and bonuses. Many family-friendly companies have discovered that a culture of care keeps turnover low. The higher salary that a competitor might pay just doesn't overcome the advantage of working at a supportive, flexible company that values its employees.[14]

Since money is not the only motivator, choose reader benefits that identify intrinsic as well as extrinsic motivators for following policies and adopting ideas.

3. Prove reader benefits with clear logic and explain them in adequate detail.

A reader benefit is a claim or assertion that the reader will benefit if he or she does something. Convincing the reader, therefore, involves two steps: making sure that the benefit really will occur, and explaining it to the reader.

If the logic behind a claimed reader benefit is faulty or inaccurate, there's no way to make that particular reader benefit convincing. Revise the benefit to make it logical.

To learn about selling, Real Whirled participants spend two months cooking, washing, and cleaning. Their experience helps them use specific reader benefits to explain how the products solve real-world problems. Because he's used the new Whirlpool washing machine, Dan Fitzgerald is confident saying how quiet it is. He can also tell a story about how a Whirlpool microwave cooked his blueberry crisp to perfection.

Faulty logic:	Using a computer will enable you to write letters, memos, and reports much more quickly.
Analysis:	If you've never used a computer, in the short run it will take you *longer* to create a document using a computer than it would to type it. Even after you know how to use a computer and its software, the real time savings comes when a document incorporates parts of previous documents or goes through several revisions. Creating a first draft from scratch will still take planning and careful composing; the time savings may or may not be significant.
Revised reader benefit:	Using a computer allows you to revise and edit a document more easily. It eliminates retyping as a separate step and reduces the time needed to proofread revisions. It allows you to move the text around on the page to create the best layout.

If the logic is sound, making that logic evident to the reader is a matter of providing enough evidence and showing how the evidence proves the claim that there will be a benefit. Always provide enough detail to be vivid and concrete. You'll need more detail in the following situations:

a.   The reader may not have thought of the benefit before.

b.   The benefit depends on the difference between the long run and the short run.

c.   The reader will be hard to persuade, and you need detail to make the benefit vivid and emotionally convincing.

Does the following statement have enough detail?

You'll save money by using our shop-at-home service.

Readers always believe their own experiences. Readers who have never used a shop-at-home service may think, "If somebody else does my shopping for me, I'll have to pay that person. I'll save money by doing it myself." They aren't likely to think of savings from not having to pay for gas and parking, from having less car wear and tear, and from not losing the time it would take to travel to several different stores to get the selection you offer. Readers who already use shop-at-home services may believe you if they compare your items and services with another company's to see that your cost is lower. Even then, you could make saving money seem more forceful and more vivid by telling readers how much they could save and mentioning some of the ways they could use your service.

4. Phrase reader benefits in you-attitude.

If reader benefits aren't in you-attitude (◀ p. 00), they'll sound selfish and won't be as effective as they could be. A Xerox sales letter with strong you-attitude as well as reader benefits got a far bigger response than did an alternate version with reader benefits but no you-attitude.[15] It doesn't matter how you phrase reader benefits while you're brainstorming and developing them, but in your final draft, check to be sure that you've used you-attitude.

Lacks you-attitude:	We have the lowest prices in town.
You-attitude:	At Havlichek Cars, you get the best deal in town.

Psychological description (➡ Chapter 9) can help you make reader benefits vivid.

How to Identify and Develop Reader Benefits

Brainstorm lots of reader benefits—perhaps twice as many as you'll need for the final letter or memo. Then you can choose the ones that are most effective for your audience, or that you can develop most easily. The first benefit you think of may not be the best.

Reader Benefits for the Tone-Deaf*

The warranty cards returned by new owners of Steinway pianos revealed startling information: 40% of the owners couldn't play the piano. Why, then, had they bought the world's best piano rather than a less expensive one? Probably for the prestige and investment value.

So the company created a direct mail campaign that positioned Steinway as "the sound investment." Copy compared the Steinway not to other pianos but to fine wine, gold, and a Mercedes-Benz. The mailing was "extremely successful."

*Based on Alan Rosenspan, "Which Direct Mail Piece Pulled Best?" *Direct Marketing*, May 1997, 35.

Sometimes reader benefits will be easy to think of and to explain. When they are harder to identify or to develop, use the following steps to identify and then develop good reader benefits:

1. Identify the feelings, fears, and needs that may motivate your reader.
2. Identify the objective features of your product or policy that could meet the needs you've identified.
3. Show how the reader can meet his or her needs with the features of the policy or product.

1. Identify the feelings, fears, and needs that may motivate your reader.

One of the best-known analyses of needs is Abraham H. Maslow's hierarchy of needs.[16] Physiological needs are the most basic, followed by needs for safety and security, for love and a sense of belonging, for esteem and recognition, and finally for self-actualization or self-fulfillment. All of us go back and forth between higher- and lower-level needs. Whenever lower-level needs make themselves felt, they usually take priority.

Maslow's model is a good starting place to identify the feelings, fears, and needs that may motivate your audience. Figure 3.3 shows organizational motivations for each of the levels in Maslow's hierarchy. Often a product or idea can meet needs on several levels. Focus on the ones that audience analysis suggests are most relevant for your audience, but remember that even the best analysis may not reveal all of a reader's needs. For example, a well-paid manager may be worried about security needs if her spouse has lost his job or if the couple is supporting kids in college or an elderly parent.

2. Identify the features of your product or policy that could meet the needs you've identified.

Sometimes just listing the reader's needs makes it obvious which feature meets a given need. Sometimes several features together meet the need. Try to think of all of them.

Suppose that you want to persuade people to come to the restaurant you manage. It's true that everybody needs to eat, but telling people they can satisfy their hunger needs won't persuade them to come to your restaurant rather than going somewhere else or eating at home. Depending on what features your restaurant offered, you could appeal to one or more of the following subgroups:

Subgroup	Features to meet the subgroup's needs
People who work outside the home	A quick lunch; a relaxing place to take clients or colleagues
Parents with small children	High chairs, child-size portions, and things to keep the kids entertained while they wait for their order
People who eat out a lot	Variety both in food and in decor
People on tight budgets	Economical food; a place where they don't need to tip (cafeteria or fast food)
People on special diets	Low-sodium and low-calorie dishes; vegetarian food; kosher food
People to whom eating out is part of an evening's entertainment	Music or a floor show; elegant surroundings; reservations so they can get to a show or event after dinner; late hours so they can come to dinner after a show or game

FIGURE 3.3 Organizational Motivations for Maslow's Hierarchy of Needs

Self-actualization
- Using your talents and abilities.
- Finding solutions to problems.
- Serving humanity.
- Self-respect and pride.
- Being the best you can be.

Esteem, recognition
- Being publicly recognized for achievements.
- Being promoted or gaining authority.
- Having status symbols.
- Having a good personal reputation.
- Having a good corporate reputation.

Love, belonging
- Having friends, working with people you like.
- Cooperating with other people on a project.
- Conforming to a group's norms.
- Feeling needed.
- Being loyal or patriotic.
- Promoting the welfare of a group you identify with or care about.

Safety, security
- Earning enough to afford a comfortable standard of living.
- Having pleasant working conditions.
- Having good health insurance and pension plan.
- Understanding the reasons for actions by supervisors.
- Being treated fairly.
- Saving time and money.
- Conserving human and environmental resources.

Physical
- Earning enough to pay for basic food, clothing, shelter, and medical care.
- Having safe working conditions.

What Motivates Me*

"What motivates me is attaining a level of professionalism and a belief in my product and my product's ability to help my clients," says Bill Berenz, account executive at the *Milwaukee Journal Sentinel.* "I get pumped up by helping my clients be successful." . . .

"When I started out, money was important, but once I hit my financial goals, I was motivated more by learning as much as I could about the newspaper, marketing and advertising businesses so I could advance my career. . . . When the money starts coming in, motivating factors change." . . .

"You may have people who have been with a company for 25 years and have more vacation time than they know what to do with. Then you have someone like me, who has only two weeks vacation. Winning a trip with additional days off is a key motivating factor for me."

*Quoted from "What Gets You Going?" *Selling Power*, March 2001, 46.

To develop your benefits, think about the details of each one. If your selling point is your relaxing atmosphere, think about the specific details that make the restaurant relaxing. If your strong point is elegant dining, think about all the details that contribute to that elegance. Sometimes you may think of features that do not meet any particular need but are still good benefits. In a sales letter for a restaurant, you might also want to mention the nonsmoking section, your free coatroom, the fact that you are close to a freeway or offer free parking or a drive-up window, and how fast your service is.

Whenever you're writing to customers or clients about features that are not unique to your organization, it's wise to present both benefits of the features themselves and benefits of dealing with your company. If you talk about the benefits of dining in a relaxed atmosphere but don't mention your own restaurant, people may go somewhere else!

3. Show how the reader can meet his or her needs with the features of the policy or product.

Features alone rarely motivate readers. Instead, link the feature to the readers' needs—and provide details to make the benefit vivid.

Play to the Primary Audience*

When an architect gave the Worthington City Council its first official look recently at plans for developing 45 acres at the site of the United Methodist Children's Home on High Street, council president, John Coleman, didn't mince words on which audience the architect should be playing to.

As Rick Morse juggled the plans on an easel, Coleman suggested he move to the other side, because he was blocking the council's view.

"If I stand on the other side, the audience can't see," Morse said.

"They're not going to vote," Coleman said. "You can set your own priorities."

*Quoted from Carol Ann Lease, "Behind the Screens," *The Columbus Dispatch*, July 29, 1987, E1.

Weak: We have placemats with riddles.

Better: Answering all the riddles on Monical's special placemats will keep the kids happy till your pizza comes. If they don't have time to finish (and they may not, since your pizza will be ready so quickly), just take the riddles home—or answer them on your next visit.

Make your reader benefits specific.

Weak: You get quick service.

Better: If you only have an hour for lunch, try our Business Buffet. Within minutes, you can choose from a variety of main dishes, vegetables, and a make-your-own-sandwich-and-salad bar. You'll have a lunch that's as light or filling as you want, with time to enjoy it—and still be back to the office on time.

Why Reader Benefits Work

Reader benefits improve both the attitudes and the behavior of the people you work with and write to. They make people view you more positively; they make it easier for you to accomplish your goals.

Expectancy theory says most people try to do their best only when they believe they can succeed and when they want the rewards that success brings. Reader benefits tell or remind readers that they can do the job and that success will be rewarded.[17] Thus they help overcome two problems that reduce motivation: people may not think of all the possible benefits, and they may not understand the relationships among efforts, performance, and rewards.[18]

Writing or Speaking to Multiple Audiences with Different Needs

Many business and administrative messages go not to a single person but to a larger audience. When the members of your audience share the same interests and the same level of knowledge, you can use the principles outlined above for individual readers or for members of homogeneous groups. But often different members of the audience have different needs.

Rachel Spilka has shown that talking to readers both inside and outside the organization helped corporate engineers adapt their documents successfully. Talking to readers and reviewers helped writers involve readers in the planning process, understand the social and political relationships among readers, and negotiate conflicts orally rather than depending solely on the document. These writers were then able to think about content as well as about organization and style, appeal to common grounds (such as reducing waste or increasing productivity) that several readers shared, and reduce the number of revisions needed before documents were approved.[19]

When it is not possible to meet everyone's needs, meet the needs of gatekeepers and decision makers first.

Content and choice of details

■ Provide an overview or executive summary for readers who want just the main points.

■ In the body of the document, provide enough detail for decision makers and for anyone else who could veto your proposal.

■ If the decision makers don't need details that other audiences will want, provide those details in appendixes—statistical tabulations, earlier reports, and so forth.

Organizing the document

- Use headings and a table of contents so readers can turn to the portions that interest them.
- Organize your message based on the decision makers' attitudes toward it.

Level of formality

- Avoid personal pronouns. *You* ceases to have a specific meaning when several different audiences use a document.
- If both internal and external audiences will use a document, use a slightly more formal style than you would in an internal document.
- Use a more formal style when you write to international audiences.

Use of technical terms and theory

- In the body of the document, assume the degree of knowledge that decision makers will have.
- Put background information and theory under separate headings. Then readers can use the headings and the table of contents to read or skip these sections, as their knowledge dictates.
- If decision makers will have more knowledge than other audiences, provide a glossary of terms. Early in the document, let readers know that the glossary exists.

Summary of Key Points

- The **primary audience** will make a decision or act on the basis of your message. The **secondary audience** may be asked by the primary audience to comment on your message or to implement your ideas after they've been approved. The **initial audience** routes the message to other audiences and may assign the message. A **gatekeeper** controls whether the message gets to the primary audience. A **watchdog audience** has political, social, or economic power and may base future actions on its evaluation of your message.
- Common sense and empathy are crucial to good audience analysis.
- The following questions provide a framework for audience analysis:
  1. What will the audience's initial reaction be to the message?
  2. How much information does the audience need?
  3. What obstacles must you overcome?
  4. What positive aspects can you emphasize?
  5. What expectations does the audience have about the appropriate language, structure, and format for messages?
  6. How will the audience use the document?
- **Reader benefits** are benefits or advantages that the reader gets by using the writer's services, buying the writer's products, following the writer's policies, or adopting the writer's ideas. Reader benefits can exist for policies and ideas as well as for goods and services. Reader benefits tell readers that they can do the job and that success will be rewarded.
- Good reader benefits are adapted to the audience, based on **intrinsic** rather than **extrinsic motivators,** supported by clear logic and explained in adequate detail, and phrased in you-attitude. Extrinsic benefits simply aren't available to reward every desired behavior; further, they reduce the satisfaction in doing something for its own sake.

They Looked at the Audience and Saw Themselves*

Before a bank took a survey of its customers, employees were asked to describe the bank's typical customer.

The CEO answered: "About 60, upper-income, community leader." The middle managers said: "About 40, with grown children. On the way up; good, solid citizen." The tellers said: "Twenties or thirties, newly married, just starting out. Lots of energy and drive."

According to the survey, the typical customer was in the mid-30s, had been married a few years, earned $20,000 a year, had 1½ cars and 2 children.

People looked at customers but saw only themselves.

*Based on Ray Considine and Murray Raphel, *The Great Brain Robbery* (Pasadena, CA: The Great Brain Robbery, 1981), 68–69.

■ To create reader benefits,
  1. Identify the feelings, fears, and needs that may motivate your reader.
  2. Identify the features of your product or policy that could meet the needs you've identified.
  3. Show how the reader can meet his or her needs with the features of the policy or product.

■ When you write to multiple audiences, use the primary audience to determine level of detail, organization, level of formality, and use of technical terms and theory.

CHAPTER 3   Exercises and Problems

Getting Started

3.1   Identifying Audiences

In each of the following situations, label the audiences as initial, gatekeeper, primary, secondary, or watchdog:

1. Russell is seeking venture capital so that he can expand his business of offering soccer camps to youngsters. He's met an investment banker whose clients regularly hear presentations from business people seeking capital. The investment banker decides who will get a slot on the program, based on a comprehensive audit of each company's records and business plan.

2. Maria has created a Web page for her travel agency. She hopes to sell tickets for both leisure and business travel.

3. Paul works for the mayor's office in a big city. As part of a citywide cost-cutting measure, a blue-ribbon panel has recommended requiring employees who work more than 40 hours in a week to take compensatory time off rather than being paid overtime. The only exceptions will be the police and fire departments. The mayor asks Paul to prepare a proposal for the city council, which will vote on whether to implement the change. Before they vote, council members will hear from (1) citizens, who will have an opportunity to read the proposal and communicate their opinions to the city council; (2) mayors' offices in other cities, who may be asked about their experiences; (3) union representatives, who may be concerned about the reduction in income that will occur if the proposal is implemented; (4) department heads, whose ability to schedule work might be limited if the proposal passes; and (5) the blue-ribbon panel and good-government lobbying groups. Council members come up for reelection in six months.

3.2   Choosing a Channel to Reach a Specific Audience

Suppose that your business, government agency, or non-profit group had a product, service, or program targeted for each of the following audiences. What would be the best channel(s) to reach people in that group in your city? Would that channel reach all group members?

a. Renters.
b. African American owners of small businesses.
c. People who use wheelchairs.
d. Teenagers who work part-time while attending school.
e. Competitive athletes.
f. Parents whose children play soccer.
g. Hispanics.
h. People willing to work part-time.
i. Financial planners.
j. Hunters.

3.3   Identifying and Developing Reader Benefits

Listed here are several things an organization might like its employees to do:

1. Use less paper.
2. Attend a brown-bag lunch to discuss ways to improve products or services.
3. Become more physically fit.
4. Volunteer for community organizations.
5. Ease a new hire's transition into the unit.

As Your Instructor Directs,

a. Identify the motives or needs that might be met by each of the activities.
b. Take each need or motive and develop it as a reader benefit in a full paragraph. Use additional paragraphs for the other needs met by the activity. Remember to use you-attitude!

3.4   Identifying Objections and Reader Benefits

Think of an organization you know something about, and answer the following questions for it:

1. Your organization is thinking of creating a training video. What objections might people have? What benefits could videos offer your organization? Who would be easiest to convince?
2. The advisory council of State College recommends that business faculty members have three-month internships with local organizations to learn material. What objections might people in your organization have to bringing in faculty interns? What benefits might your organization receive? Who would be easiest to convince?

3. Your organization is thinking of expanding or creating a Web site. What fears or objections might people have? What benefits might your organization receive? Who would be easiest to convince?

As Your Instructor Directs,

a. Share your answers orally with a small group of students.
b. Present your answers in an oral presentation to the class.
c. Write a paragraph developing the best reader benefit you identified. Remember to use you-attitude.

3.5   Identifying and Developing Reader Benefits for Different Audiences

Assume that you want to encourage people to do one of the activities listed below:

1. Becoming more physically fit.
   Audiences: College students on the job market.
   Workers whose jobs require heavy lifting.
   Sedentary workers.
   People diagnosed as having high blood pressure.
   Managers who travel frequently on business.
   Older workers.
2. Getting advice about interior decorating.
   Audiences: Young people with little money to spend.
   Parents with small children.
   People upgrading or adding to their furnishings.

   Older people moving from single-family homes into smaller apartments or condominiums.
   Builders furnishing model homes.
3. Getting advice on investment strategies.
   Audiences: New college graduates.
   People earning more than $100,000 annually.
   People responsible for investing funds for a church or synagogue.
   Parents with small children.
   People within 10 years of retirement.
4. Gardening.
   Audiences: People with small children.
   People in apartments.
   People concerned about reducing pesticides.
   People on tight budgets.
   Retirees.
   Teenagers.

5. Buying a laptop computer.
    Audiences: College students.
    Financial planners who visit clients at home.
    Sales representatives who travel constantly.
    People who make PowerPoint presentations.

6. Teaching adults to read.
    Audiences: Retired workers.
    Business people.
    Students who want to become teachers.
    High school and college students.
    People concerned about poverty.

7. Vacationing at a luxury hotel.
    Audiences: Stressed-out people who want to relax.
    Tourists who like to sightsee and absorb the local culture.

Business people who want to stay in touch with the office even on vacation.
Parents with small children.
Weekend athletes who want to have fun.

As Your Instructor Directs,

a. Identify needs that you could meet for the audiences listed here. In addition to needs that several audiences share, identify at least one need that would be particularly important to each group.

b. Identify a product or service that could meet each need.

c. Write a paragraph or two of reader benefits for each product or service. Remember to use you-attitude.

3.6   Announcing Holiday Diversity

To better respect the religious and ethnic diversity of your employees, your organization will now allow employees to take any 10 days off during the year. (See Problem 7.4.) Any religious, ethnic, or cultural holiday is acceptable. (Someone who wants to take off Cinco de Mayo or Bastille Day can do so.) As Vice President for Human Resources, you need to announce the policy.

Pick a specific organization you know something about and answer the following questions about it:

1. What religious and ethnic groups do the employees come from?

2. How much do various groups know about each others' holidays?

3. What is the general climate for religious and ethnic tolerance? Should the message have a secondary purpose of educating people about less-common holidays?

4. Is the organization open every day of the year, or will it be closed on some holidays (e.g., Christmas, New Year's Day). If an employee chooses to work on a day when offices or factories are closed, what should he or she do? Work at home? Get a key? (How? From whom?) What kinds of tasks could a person working alone most profitably do?

3.7   Announcing a New Employee Benefit

Your company has decided to pay employees for doing charity work. Employees can spend 1 hour working with a charitable or nonprofit group for every 40 hours they work (or 1 hour a week for people who are on salary rather than paid by the hour; see Problem 7.15). As Vice President of Human Resources, you need to announce this new program.

Pick a specific organization you know something about and answer the following questions about it:

1. What proportion of the employees are already involved in volunteer work?

2. Is community service or "giving back" consistent with the organization's corporate mission?

3. Some employees won't be able or won't want to participate. What is the benefit for them in working for a company that has such a program?

4. Will promoting community participation help the organization attract and retain workers?

3.8   Announcing a Tuition Reimbursement Program

Assume that the organization has decided to reimburse workers for tuition and fees for job-related courses (see problem 7.16). As Director of Education and Training, you want to write a memo about the program which will answer employees' questions and build support for the program. Pick a specific organization that you know something about and answer the following questions about it.

1. What do people do on the job? What courses or degrees could help them do their current jobs even better?

2. How much education do people already have? How do they feel about formal schooling?

3. How busy are employees? Will most have time to take classes and study in addition to working 40 hours a week (or more)?

4. Is it realistic to think that people who get more education would get higher salaries? Or is money for increases limited? Is it reasonable to think that most people could be promoted? Or does the organization have many more low-level than high-level jobs?

5. What hassles do people encounter in their daily work? What could be done to alleviate one or more of those hassles? If things were better, how would their work lives be easier or more pleasant?

6. How much loyalty do employees have to this particular organization? Is it "just a job," or do they care about the welfare of the organization?

7. How competitive is the job market? How easy is it for the organization to find and retain qualified employees?

8. Is knowledge needed to do the job changing, or is knowledge learned five or ten years ago still up-to-date?

9. How competitive is the economic market? Is this company doing well financially? Can its customers or clients easily go somewhere else? Is it a government agency dependent on tax dollars for funding? What about the current situation makes this an especially good time to hone the skills of the employees you have?

3.9   Sending a Question to a Web Site

Send a question or other message that calls for a response to a Web site. (See Problem 9.10.) You could

- Ask a question about a product.
- Apply for an internship or a job (assuming you'd really like to work there).
- Ask for information about an internship or a job.
- Ask a question about an organization or a candidate before you donate money or volunteer.
- Offer to volunteer for an organization or a candidate. You can offer to do something small and one-time (e.g., spend an afternoon stuffing envelopes, put up a yard sign), or you can, if you want to, offer to do something more time-consuming or even ongoing.

Pick a specific organization you might use and answer the following questions about it:

1. Does the organization ask for questions or offers? Or will yours come out of the blue?

2. How difficult will it be for the organization to supply the information you're asking for or to do what you're asking it to do? If you're applying for an internship or offering to volunteer, what skills can you offer? How much competition do you have?

3. What can you do to build your own credibility so that the organization takes your question or request seriously?

3.10   Persuading Students to Use Credit Cards Responsibly

Many college students carry high balances on credit cards, in addition to student and car loans. You want to remind students on your campus to use credit cards responsibly. (See Problem 9.27.)

Answer the following questions about students on your campus:

1. What socioeconomic groups do students on your campus come from?

2. Do students on your campus frequently receive credit card solicitations in the mail? Do groups set up tables or booths inviting students to apply for credit cards?

3. What resources exist on campus or in town for people who need emergency funds? For people who are overextended financially?

4. What channel will best reach students on your campus?

5. What tone will work best to reach the students who are overextended and really need to read the document?

Communicating at Work

3.11   Analyzing Your Boss

What goals matter most to your boss? What pressures is he or she under? Does your boss want details or just the big picture? What are his or her pet peeves? Is punctuality more important than creativity and thoroughness, or vice versa? If you have a question, would your boss rather answer in person, by e-mail, or in a memo? Is he or she more approachable in the morning or the afternoon?

As Your Instructor Directs,

a. Share your answers orally with a small group of students.

b. Present your answers in an oral presentation to the class.

c. Present your answers in a memo to your instructor.

d. Share your answers with a small group of students and write a joint memo reporting the similarities and differences you found.

3.12   Analyzing Your Co-Workers

What do your co-workers do? What hassles and challenges do they face? To what extent do their lives outside work affect their responses to work situations? What do your co-workers value? What are their pet peeves? How committed are they to organizational goals? How satisfying do they find their jobs? Are the people you work with quite similar to each other, or do they differ from each other? How?

As Your Instructor Directs,

a. Share your answers orally with a small group of students.

b. Present your answers in an oral presentation to the class.

c. Present your answers in a memo to your instructor.

d. Share your answers with a small group of students and write a joint memo reporting the similarities and differences you found.

Memo Assignments

3.13   Analyzing the Audiences of Non-Commercial Web Pages

Analyze the implied audiences of two Web pages of two non-commercial organizations with the same purpose (combating hunger, improving health, influencing the political process, etc.). You could pick pages of the national organization and a local affiliate, or pages of two separate organizations working toward the same general goal.

Answer the following questions:

■ Do the pages work equally well for surfers and for people who have reached the page deliberately?

■ Possible audiences include current and potential volunteers, donors, clients, and employees. Do the pages provide material for each audience? Is the material useful? Complete? Up-to-date? Does new material encourage people to return?

■ What assumptions about audiences do content and visuals suggest?

■ Can you think of ways that the pages could better serve their audiences?

As Your Instructor Directs,

a. Share your results orally with a small group of students.

b. Present your results in an oral presentation to the class.

c. Present your results in a memo to your instructor. Attach copies of the Web pages.

d. Share your results with a small group of students and write a joint memo reporting the similarities and differences you found.

e. Post your results in an e-mail message to the class. Provide links to the two Web pages.

3.14   Analyzing an Organization's Culture

Interview several people about the culture of their organization. Possible organizations include

■ Businesses, government agencies, and nonprofit organizations.

■ Sports teams.

■ Sororities, fraternities, and other social groups.

■ Churches, synagogues, and temples.

■ Departments in a community college, college, or university.

To learn about the corporate culture, use your own experiences, interviews with employees, published sources, or the Web. Interview questions include the following:

■ Tell me about someone in this organization you admire. Why is he or she successful?

■ Tell me about someone who failed in this organization. What did he or she do wrong?

■ What ceremonies and rituals does this organization have? Why are they important?

■ Why would someone join this group rather than a competitor?

To research corporate culture on the Web, check

■ The company's site (usually under "about XYZ" or "working at XYZ"). In addition to explicit descriptions of corporate culture, check the mission and values statements and pages about employee benefits and regulations.

■ Independent sites, especially job sites. Some job sites give information about corporate cultures. Some post company recruiting videos. (What kind of employees does the company seem to be looking for?)

■ Opposition sites put up by unhappy employees and customers. To find these in a search engine, type in the company name and "opinion."

■ Articles published about the company on www.inc.com, www.fastcompany.com, www.businessweek.com, www.wsj.com, or other business Web sites.

As Your Instructor Directs,

a. Share your results orally with a small group of students.

b. Present your results orally to the class.

c. Present your results in a memo to your instructor.

d. Share your results with a small group of students and write a joint memo reporting the similarities and differences you found.

3.15   Analyzing a Discourse Community

Analyze the way a group you are part of uses language. Possible groups include

- Work teams.
- Sports teams.
- Sororities, fraternities, and other social groups.
- Churches, synagogues, and temples.
- Geographic or ethnic groups.
- Groups of friends.

Questions to ask include the following:

- What specialized terms might not be known to outsiders?
- What topics do members talk or write about? What topics are considered unimportant or improper?
- What channels do members use to convey messages?
- What forms of language do members use to build goodwill? to demonstrate competence or superiority?
- What strategies or kinds of proof are convincing to members?
- What formats, conventions, or rules do members expect messages to follow?

As Your Instructor Directs,

a. Share your results orally with a small group of students.

b. Present your results in an oral presentation to the class.

c. Present your results in a memo to your instructor.

d. Share your results with a small group of students and write a joint memo reporting the similarities and differences you found.

4

Making Your Writing Easy to Read

Making Your Writing Easy to Read

Wei Shen
Audit Manager for General Electric's Corporate Audit Staff, General Electric

General Electric (GE) is a global company with 12 individual businesses, ranging from Aircraft Engines and Medical Systems to Capital Services and NBC. The Corporate Audit Staff verifies the integrity of GE's financial statements, helps drive corporate initiatives such as Six Sigma, and provides training and development for future GE business leaders.

www.ge.com

S trong business writing skills become especially important to succeed in corporate auditing. My clients are high-level company executives. During an audit, we send frequent progress updates to keep the clients informed of our findings and needs. Clarity is essential in conveying our team's work and recommendations. Since our audits often cover very sensitive areas, and people's jobs sometimes depend on our assessment, the wording of the report must be 100% precise. Inaccurate wording could cause misunderstandings, take away all the credibility my team has worked hard to obtain, and damage our client relationship.

Some good tips I keep in mind in my writing and recommend to others include:

- Business writing should be formal but not "stuffy."
- The grammar, spelling, and punctuation have to be absolutely correct. Otherwise, you lose credibility.
- Make your writing clear, concise, and easy to read.
- Avoid complicated and obscure vocabulary and business jargon. If technical terms are essential, define them for readers who may not understand them.
- Make your writing easy to understand; don't write riddles.
- Start with your recommendation or conclusion, then follow with supporting facts and details. Readers need to know in the first sentence or two why they're reading the memo. Before you draft, first answer the question, "What do I want you to know?"

"Any memo or e-mail you write represents who you are to the reader."

Any memo or e-mail you write represents who you are to the reader. In a world connected by instant messaging, an e-mail you write could be sent to an entire organization in a matter of seconds. Your readers have tremendous influence over your career movement in the company. Therefore, you want everything you write to create a positive impression!

Good business and administrative writing should sound like a person talking to another person. Unfortunately, much of the writing produced in organizations today seems to have been written by faceless bureaucrats rather than by real people.

Using an easy-to-read style makes the reader respond more positively to your ideas. You can make your writing easier to read in two ways. First, you can make individual sentences and paragraphs easy to read, so that skimming the first paragraph or reading the whole document takes as little work as possible. Second, you can make the document look visually inviting and structure it with signposts to guide readers through it. This chapter focuses on ways to make words, sentences, and paragraphs easier to read. Chapter 6 will discuss ways to make the document as a whole easier to read.

Good Style in Business and Administrative Writing

Good business and administrative writing is closer to conversation and less formal than the style of writing that has traditionally earned high marks in college essays and term papers. (See Figure 4.1.) However, many business professors also like term papers that are easy to read and use good visual impact.

Most people have several styles of talking, which they vary instinctively depending on the audience. Good writers have several styles, too. An e-mail to your boss complaining about the delays from a supplier will be informal, perhaps even chatty; a letter to the supplier demanding better service will be more formal.

Reports tend to be more formal than letters and memos, since they may be read many years in the future by audiences the writer can barely imagine. In reports, avoid contractions, spell out acronyms and abbreviations the first time you use them, and avoid personal pronouns. Since so many people read reports, *you* doesn't have much meaning. See Chapter 14 for more about report style.

| FIGURE 4.1 | Different Levels of Style |

Feature	Conversational style	Good business style	Traditional term paper style
Formality	Highly informal	Conversational; sounds like a real person talking	More formal than conversation would be, but retains a human voice
Use of contractions	Many contractions	OK to use occasional contractions	Few contractions, if any
Pronouns	Uses *I*, first- and second-person pronouns	Uses *I*, first- and second-person pronouns	First- and second-person pronouns kept to a minimum
Level of friendliness	Friendly	Friendly	No effort to make style friendly
How personal	Personal; refers to specific circumstances of conversation	Personal; may refer to reader by name; refers to specific circumstances of readers	Impersonal; may generally refer to *readers* but does not name them or refer to their circumstances
Word choice	Short, simple words; slang	Short, simple words but avoids slang	Many abstract words; scholarly, technical terms
Sentence and paragraph length	Incomplete sentences; no paragraphs	Short sentences and paragraphs	Sentences and paragraphs usually long
Grammar	Can be ungrammatical	Uses standard edited English	Uses standard edited English
Visual impact	Not applicable	Attention to visual impact of document	No particular attention to visual impact

Keep the following points in mind as you choose a level of formality for a specific document:

- Use a friendly, informal style to someone you've talked with.
- Avoid contractions, slang, and even minor grammatical lapses in paper documents to people you don't know. Abbreviations are OK in e-mail messages if they're part of the group's culture.
- Pay particular attention to your style when you write to people you fear or when you must give bad news. Reliance on nouns rather than on verbs and a general deadening of style increase when people are under stress or feel insecure.[1] Confident people are more direct. Edit your writing so that you sound confident, whether you feel that way or not.

Good business style allows for individual variation. Figures 4.2 and 4.3 show the opening paragraphs from the CEO letters in two different annual reports. Jack Welch's hard-hitting style in Figure 4.2 conveys an image of energy and drive. Warren Buffett's wry, self-deprecating style in Figure 4.3 suggests intelligence and total integrity.

Half-Truths about Style

Many generalizations about style are half-truths and must be applied selectively, if at all.

Half-Truth 1: "Write as You Talk."

To test your style, read what you've written out loud to someone sitting about three feet away. If a passage sounds stiff and overly formal when you read it out loud, revise it; almost certainly it will sound stiff and perhaps even rude to the reader. If you wouldn't say it, don't write it.

Simple Words Save Money and Build Goodwill*

Writing consultant Rosemary Camilleri has a client that administers health care benefits for thousands of companies nationwide. A standard letter sent by the company explained to patients that part of their claim was "noncertified." People didn't understand, so they phoned or wrote to ask what the letter meant. The company had to employ nearly 50 nurses to answer the questions.

Camilleri helped employees rewrite the form letter.

The manager stopped her in the hall one day to tell her that they now have 25% fewer phone calls to field. People now understand the letter and feel they are being treated fairly.

*Based on Rosemary Camilleri, "Re: Adding Value," posting to APCC-L@listserv.acns.nwu.edu, December 3, 1997.

FIGURE 4.2 Jack Welch's Letter Uses the Standard Business Style

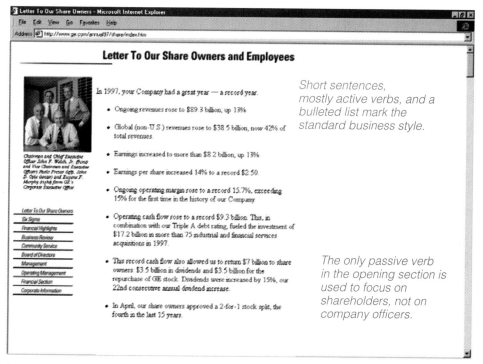

Source: [GE] Letter to Our Share Owners and Employees [1997] http://www.ge.com/annual97/share/index.htm. Reprinted with permission.

FIGURE 4.3   Warren Buffett's Letter Uses a More Individual Style

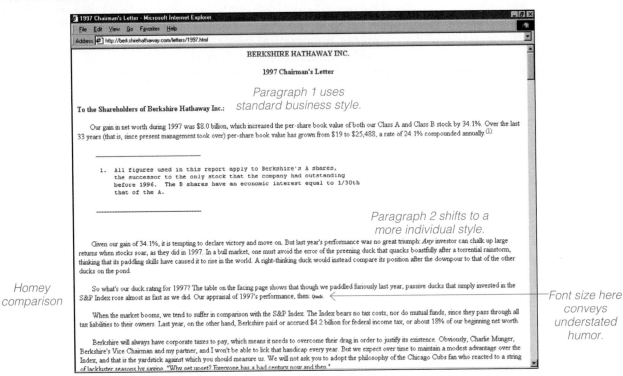

Source: Berkshire Hathaway Inc. 1997 Chairman's Letter. http://berkshirehathaway.com/letters/1997.html.

However, unless our speech is exceptionally fluent, "writing as we talk" can create awkward, repetitive, and badly organized prose. It's OK to write as you talk to produce your first draft, but edit to create a good written style.

Half-Truth 2: "Never Use *I*."

Using *I* too often can make your writing sound self-centered; using it unnecessarily will make your ideas seem tentative. However, when you write about things you've done or said or seen, using *I* is both appropriate and smoother than resorting to awkward passives or phrases like *this writer.*

Half-Truth 3: "Never Begin a Sentence with *And* or *But*."

Beginning a sentence with *and* or *also* makes the idea that follows seem like an afterthought. That's OK when you want the effect of spontaneous speech in a written document, as you may in a sales letter. If you want to sound as though you have thought about what you are saying, put the *also* in the middle of the sentence or use another transition: *moreover, furthermore.*

But tells the reader that you are shifting gears and that the point which follows not only contrasts with but also is more important than the preceding ideas. Presenting such verbal signposts to your reader is important. Beginning a sentence with *but* is fine if doing so makes your paragraph read smoothly.

Half-Truth 4: "Never End a Sentence with a Preposition."

Prepositions are those useful little words that indicate relationships: *with, in, under, at.* The prohibition against ending sentences with them is probably

Words with the right connotations sell products. In focus groups, Iomega learned that computer users either hated or were bored by the idea of data storage. But they liked the idea of getting easier access to their "stuff." So Iomega created an ad campaign for the Zip drive using the friendly, colloquial word.

based on two facts: (1) The end of a sentence (like the beginning) is a position of emphasis. A preposition may not be worth emphasizing. (2) When the reader sees a preposition, he or she expects something to follow it. At the end of a sentence, nothing does.

In job application letters, reports, and important presentations, avoid ending sentences with prepositions. Most messages are less formal; it's OK to end an occasional sentence with a preposition. Analyze your audience and the situation, and use the language that you think will get the best results.

Half-Truth 5: "Big Words Impress People."

Learning an academic discipline requires that you master its vocabulary. After you get out of school, however, no one will ask you to write just to prove that you understand something. Instead, you'll be asked to write or speak to people who need the information you have. Sometimes you may want the sense of formality or technical expertise that big words create. But much of the time, big words just distance you from your audience and increase the risk of miscommunication. When people misuse big words, they look foolish. If you're going to use big words, make sure you use them correctly.

Evaluating "Rules" about Writing

Some "rules" are grammatical conventions. For example, standard edited English requires that each sentence have a subject and verb, and that the subject and verb agree. Business writing normally demands standard grammar, but exceptions exist. Promotional materials such as brochures, advertisements, and sales and fund-raising letters may use sentence fragments to mimic the effect of speech.

Other "rules" may be conventions adopted by an organization so that its documents will be consistent. For example, a company might decide to capitalize job titles (e.g., *Production Manager*) even though grammar doesn't require the capitals, or always to use a comma before *and* in a series, even though a sentence can be grammatical without the comma. A different company might make different choices.

Still other "rules" are attempts to codify "what sounds good." "Never use *I*" and "use big words" are examples of this kind of "rule." To evaluate these "rules," you must consider your audience, the discourse community and organizational culture, (◀▥ p. 59), your purposes, and the situation. If you want the effect produced by an impersonal style and polysyllabic words, use them. But use them only when you want the distancing they produce.

Building a Better Style

To improve your style,

- Get a clean page or screen, so that you aren't locked into old sentence structures.
- Try WIRMI: *What I Really Mean Is.*[2] Then write the words.
- Try reading your draft out loud to someone sitting about three feet away—about as far away as you'd sit in casual conversation. If the words sound stiff, they'll seem stiff to a reader, too.
- Ask someone else to read your draft out loud. Readers stumble because the words on the page aren't what they expect to see. The places where that person stumbles are places where your writing can be better.
- Read widely and write a *lot.*
- Study revised sentences, like those in Figure 4.4.
- Use the 10 techniques in Figure 4.5 to polish your style.

 See the BAC Web site for the SEC's Guidelines for Plain English for Prospectuses.

FIGURE 4.4   Mutual Fund Prospectuses Revised to Meet the SEC's Plain English Guidelines

	Old prospectus	New prospectus
John Hancock Sovereign Balanced Fund	The fund utilizes a strategy of investing in those common stocks which have a record of having increased their shareholder dividend in each of the preceding ten years or more.	The fund's stock investments are exclusively in companies that have increased their dividend payout in each of the last ten years.
State Street Research Equity Income Fund	The applicability of the general information and administrative procedures set forth below accordingly will vary depending on the investor and the record-keeping system established for a shareholder's investment in the Fund. Participants in 401(k) and other plans should first consult with appropriate persons at their employer or refer to the plan materials before following any of the procedures below.	If you are investing through a large retirement plan or other special program, follow the instructions in your program materials.
State Street Research Equity Income Fund	The net asset value of the fund's shares will fluctuate as market conditions change.	The fund's shares will rise and fall in value.

Source: Toddi Gutner, "At Last, the Readable Prospectus," *BusinessWeek,* April 13, 1998, 100E10. Reprinted by special permission. Copyright © 1998 by The McGraw-Hill Companies, Inc.

FIGURE 4.5   Ten Ways to Make Your Writing Easier to Read

As you choose words,

1. Use words that are accurate, appropriate, and familiar.
2. Use technical jargon only when it is essential and known to the reader. Eliminate business jargon.

As you write and revise sentences,

3. Use active verbs most of the time.
4. Use verbs—not nouns—to carry the weight of your sentence.
5. Tighten your writing.
6. Vary sentence length and sentence structure.
7. Use parallel structure. Use the same grammatical form for ideas that have the same logical function.
8. Put your readers in your sentences.

As you write and revise paragraphs,

9. Begin most paragraphs with topic sentences so that readers know what to expect in the paragraph.
10. Use transitions to link ideas.

How Big is _Huge_?*

When two people use the same word to mean different things, bypassing occurs.

A potential client told Lois Geller that he wanted a "huge" advertising campaign for his company. She spent three weeks preparing a proposal for a $500,000 ad campaign. The client was horrified. It turned out that his budget for the whole previous year had been $10,000. To the client, a $5,000 campaign would have been "huge."

*Based on Alan Horowitz, "Can You Hear What I Hear?" _Selling Power_, July/August 2001, 70.

Ten Ways to Make Your Writing Easier to Read

Direct, simple writing is easier to read. James Suchan and Robert Colucci tested two versions of a memo report. The "high-impact" version had the "bottom line" (the purpose of the report) in the first paragraph, simple sentences in normal word order, active verbs, concrete language, short paragraphs, headings and lists, and first- and second-person pronouns. The high-impact version took 22% less time to read. Readers said they understood the report better, and tests showed that they really did understand it better.[3] Another study showed that high-impact instructions were more likely to be followed.[4] We'll talk about layout, headings, and lists in Chapter 6.

As You Choose Words

The best word depends on context: the situation, your purposes, your audience, the words you have already used.

1. Use words that are accurate, appropriate, and familiar.

Accurate words mean what you want to say. Appropriate words convey the attitudes you want and fit well with the other words in your document. Familiar words are easy to read and understand.

Some meanings have already evolved before we join the conversation. We may learn the meaning of words, of actions, or of office layouts by being alert and observant. We learn some meanings by formal and informal study: the importance of "generally accepted accounting principles," the best strategies for increasing the size of donations in a fund-raising letter, or what the trash can on a computer screen symbolizes. Some meanings are negotiated as we interact one-on-one with another person, attempting to communicate. Some words persist, even though the reality behind them has changed. In 9 of the 10 largest US cities, so-called "minorities" are already in the majority.[5] Some people are substituting the term _traditionally underrepresented groups_ for _minorities,_ but the old term is likely to remain in use for some time.

What's in a Name? (1)*

Effective brand names depend on both denotation and connotation.

At Sun Microsystems, Kim Polese called a brainstorming meeting to find a cooler name for Oak software, a product she believed would "wake up the Web." Oak became Java, now the standard for multimedia and animation on Web pages.

*Based on Bradley Johnson, "Java: Kim Polese," *Advertising Age*, June 24, 1996, s20.

What's in a Name? (2)*

Choosing product names is even more complicated when translation is involved.

When Coca-Cola was introduced in China in the 1920s, a group of Chinese characters were chosen that sounded like the English name. Unfortunately, those characters meant "bite the wax tadpole." Today, the characters used on Coke bottles in China denote "happiness in the mouth."

*Based on David A. Ricks, *Blunders in International Business* (Cambridge, MA: Blackwell, 1993), 34–36.

Some meanings are voted on. Take, for example, the term *minority-owned business.* For years, the National Minority Supplier Development Council (NMSDC) defined the term as a business in which at least 51% of the owners were members of racial or ethnic minorities. But that made it hard for businesses to attract major capital or to go public, since doing so would give more ownership to European American investors. In 2000, the NMSDC redefined *minority-owned business* as any business with minority management and at least 30% minority ownership.[6]

Accurate denotations.   To be accurate, a word's denotation must match the meaning the writer wishes to convey. **Denotation** is a word's literal or dictionary meaning. Most common words in English have more than one denotation. The word *pound,* for example, means, or denotes, a unit of weight, a place where stray animals are kept, a unit of money in the British system, and the verb *to hit.* Coca-Cola spends an estimated $20 million a year to protect its brand names so that *Coke* will denote only that brand and not just any cola drink.

When two people use the same word to mean, or denote, different things, **bypassing** occurs. For example, negotiators for Amoco and for the Environmental Protection Agency (EPA) used *risk* differently. At Amoco, *risk* was an economic term dealing with efficiency; for the EPA, the term "was a four-letter word that meant political peril or health risk."[7] Progress was possible only when they agreed on a meaning.

Problems also arise when writers misuse words.

The western part of Ohio was transferred from Chicago to Cleveland.[8]

(Ohio did not move. Instead, a company moved responsibility for sales in western Ohio.)

Three major associations of property-liability companies are poised to strike out in opposite directions.[9]

(Three different directions can't be opposite each other.)

Earn a free lunch.[10]

(A lunch one earns isn't free.)

Accurate denotations can make it easier to solve problems. In one production line with a high failure rate, the largest category of defects was *missed operations.* At first, the supervisor wondered if the people on the line were lazy or irresponsible. But some checking showed that several different problems were labeled *missed operations:* parts installed backward, parts that had missing screws or fasteners, parts whose wires weren't connected. Each of these problems had a different solution. Using accurate words redefined the problem and enabled the production line both to improve quality and to cut repair costs.[11]

Appropriate connotations.   Words are appropriate when their **connotations,** that is, their emotional associations or colorings, convey the attitude you want. A great many words carry connotations of approval or disapproval, disgust or delight. Words in the first column below suggest approval; words in the second column suggest criticism.

Positive word	Negative word
assume	guess
curious	nosy
cautious	fearful
firm	obstinate
flexible	wishy-washy

A supervisor can "tell the truth" about a subordinate's performance and yet write either a positive or a negative performance appraisal, based on the connotations of the words in the appraisal. Consider an employee who pays close attention to details. A positive appraisal might read, "Terry is a meticulous team member who takes care of details that others sometimes ignore." But the same behavior might be described negatively: "Terry is hung up on trivial details."

Advertisers carefully choose words with positive connotations. Expensive cars are never *used*; instead, they're *pre-owned, experienced,* or even *previously adored.*[12] An executive for Rolls-Royce once said, "A Rolls never, never breaks down. Of course," he added, with a twinkle in his eye, "there have been occasions when a car has failed to proceed."[13]

Words may also connote status. Both *salesperson* and *sales representative* are nonsexist job titles. But the first sounds like a clerk in a store; the second suggests someone selling important items to corporate customers.

Connotations change over time. The word *charity* had acquired such negative connotations by the 19th century that people began to use the term *welfare* instead. Now, *welfare* has acquired negative associations. Most states have *public assistance programs* instead.

Ethical implications of word choice.   How positively can we present something and still be ethical? *Pressure-treated lumber* sounds acceptable. But naming the material injected under pressure—*arsenic-treated lumber*—may lead the customer to make a different decision. We have the right to package our ideas attractively, but we have the responsibility to give the public or our superiors all the information they need to make decisions.

Familiar words.   Use familiar words, words that are in almost everyone's vocabulary. Use the word that most exactly conveys your meaning, but whenever you can choose between two words that mean the same thing, use the shorter, more common one. Try to use specific, concrete words. They're easier to understand and remember.[14]

A series of long, learned, abstract terms makes writing less interesting, less forceful, and less memorable. When you have something simple to say, use simple words.

The following list gives a few examples of short, simple alternatives:

Formal and stuffy	Short and simple
ameliorate	improve
commence	begin
enumerate	list
finalize	finish, complete
prioritize	rank
utilize	use
viable option	choice

There are four exceptions to the general rule that "shorter is better":

1. Use a long word if it is the only word that expresses your meaning exactly.
2. Use a long word if it is more familiar than a short word. *Send out* is better than *emit* and *a word in another language for a geographic place or area* is better than *exonym* because more people know the first item in each pair.
3. Use a long word if its connotations are more appropriate. *Exfoliate* is better than *scrape off dead skin cells.*
4. Use a long word if the discourse community (p. 59) prefers it.

The Ethics of Word Choice*

People can use accurate words to lie.

As a prize for visiting a condominium resort, a woman "won" an all-terrain vehicle. She had to pay $29.95 for "handling, processing, and insurance" to get it.

Then she saw her prize: a lawn chair with four wheels that converts into a wheeled cart.

The company claims it told the truth: "It is a vehicle. It's a four-wheel cart you can take anywhere—to the beach, to the pool. It may not be motorized, but [we] didn't say it was motorized."

The company may be guilty of deceptive trade practices: the courts will have to decide that. But whether or not the practice is illegal, it isn't ethical to use words that most people will misinterpret.

*Based on Carmella M. Padilla, "It's a . . . a . . . a . . . All-Terrain Vehicle, Yeah, That's It, That's the Ticket," *The Wall Street Journal*, July 17, 1987, 17.

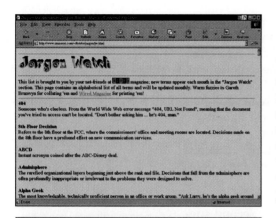

InSite

www.xmission.com/~~dtubbs/jargon/jw.html

Wired magazine lists business and computer jargon.

See the BAC Web site for links to this and other jargon dictionaries.

2. Use technical jargon sparingly; eliminate business jargon.

There are two kinds of **jargon.** The first kind of jargon is the specialized terminology of a technical field. *LIFO* and *FIFO* are technical terms in accounting; *byte* and *baud* are computer jargon; *scale-free* and *pickled and oiled* designate specific characteristics of steel. A job application letter is the one occasion when it's desirable to use technical jargon: using the technical terminology of the reader's field helps suggest that you're a peer who also is competent in that field. In other kinds of messages, use technical jargon only when the term is essential and known to the reader.

If a technical term has a "plain English" equivalent, use the simpler term:

Jargon: Foot the average monthly budget column down to Total Variable Costs, Total Management Fixed Costs, Total Sunk Costs, and Grand Total.

Better: Add the figures in the average monthly budget column for each category to determine the Total Variable Costs, the Total Management Fixed Costs, and the Total Sunk Costs. Then add the totals for each category to arrive at the Grand Total.

The revision here is longer but better because it uses simple words. The original will be meaningless to a reader who does not know what foot means.

It is especially important to replace jargon with plain English when the specialized meaning of the technical term is not in fact being used. Consider this example:

Jargon: Additional parameters for price exception reporting were established for nonstock labor buy costs.

Better: We decided to include nonstock labor buys of over $_____ in the price exception report.

The word *parameters* means factors that are held constant while other variables change. It is a term that is essential in mathematics and statistics, but it is rarely used properly in general business and administrative writing. As the revision shows, the real meaning here was simple; no technical term was needed.

The second kind of jargon is the **businessese** that some writers still use: *as per your request, enclosed please find, please do not hesitate.* None of the words in this second category of jargon are necessary. Indeed, some writers call these terms *deadwood,* since they are no longer living words. Some of these terms, however, seem to float through the air like germs. If any of the terms in the first

What's in a Name? (3)*

For Americans, "trees" are "human beings." We hug them. They are raised in nurseries. They age into "old growth." With this information, [Anthropologist Clotaire Rapaille] persuaded the Timber Association of California (timber reminded people of the logger's cry, *Timber!,* which made them think of "killing") to change its name to the California Forestry Association.

*Quoted from Jack Hitt, "Does the Smell of Coffee Brewing Remind You of Your Mother?" *The New York Times Magazine,* May 7, 2000, 73.

Prune   Dried Plum

Sales of prunes fell 14% from 1993 to 1999. To stop the slide, what had been the California Prune Board decided to change the product's name (and its own). Changing the product's name required approval from the US Food and Drug Administration, which regulates food labels. Now you don't buy prunes; you buy "dried plums."

FIGURE 4.6   Getting Rid of Business Jargon

Instead of	Use	Because
At your earliest convenience	The date you need a response	If you need it by a deadline, say so. It may never be convenient to respond.
As per your request; 65 miles per hour	As you requested; 65 miles an hour	*Per* is a Latin word for *by* or *for each.* Use *per* only when the meaning is correct; avoid mixing English and Latin.
Enclosed please find	Enclosed is; Here is	An enclosure isn't a treasure hunt. If you put something in the envelope, the reader will find it.
Forward same to this office.	Return it to this office.	Omit legal jargon.
Hereto, herewith	Omit	Omit legal jargon.
Please be advised; Please be informed	Omit—simply start your response	You don't need a preface. Go ahead and start.
Please do not hesitate	Omit	Omit negative words.
Pursuant to	According to; or omit	*Pursuant* does not mean *after.* Omit legal jargon in any case.
Said order	Your order	Omit legal jargon.
This will acknowledge receipt of your letter.	Omit—start your response	If you answer a letter, the reader knows you got it.
Trusting this is satisfactory, we remain	Omit	Eliminate *-ing* endings. When you are through, stop.

column of Figure 4.6 show up in your writing, replace them with more modern language.

As You Write and Revise Sentences

At the sentence level, you can do many things to make your writing easy to read.

3. Use active verbs most of the time.

"Who does what" sentences with active verbs make your writing more forceful.

A verb is **active** if the grammatical subject of the sentence does the action the verb describes. A verb is **passive** if the subject is acted upon. Passives are usually made up of a form of the verb *to be* plus a past participle. *Passive* has nothing to do with *past.* Passives can be past, present, or future:

were received	(in the past)
is recommended	(in the present)
will be implemented	(in the future)

To spot a passive, find the verb. If the verb describes something that the grammatical subject is doing, the verb is active. If the verb describes something that is being done to the grammatical subject, the verb is passive.

Active	**Passive**
The customer received 500 widgets.	Five hundred widgets were received by the customer.
I recommend this method.	This method is recommended by me.
The state agencies will implement the program.	The program will be implemented by the state agencies.

Writing for the Web*

People don't read on the Web; they skim. To get information to Web users,

- Start with the main point.
- Be concise. Use half as many words as you normally would.
- Use meaningful headings and subheadings (not "cute" ones).
- Highlight keywords.
- Bullet lists.
- Put only one idea in a paragraph.

*Based on Jakob Nielsen, "How Users Read on the Web," www.useit.com/alertbox/97100a/html, October 1, 1997, visited site August 7, 2001.

Verbs can be changed from active to passive by making the direct object (in the oval) the new subject (in the box). To change a passive verb to an active one, you must make the agent ("by _____" in <>) the new subject. If no agent is specified in the sentence, you must supply one to make the sentence active.

Active	**Passive**
The ⬚plant manager⬚ approved the ⬭request.⬭	The ⬚request⬚ was approved by the <plant manager.>
The ⬚committee⬚ will decide next month.	A decision will be made next month. No agent in sentence.
[You] Send the customer a ⬭letter⬭ informing her about the change.	A ⬚letter⬚ will be sent informing the customer of the change. No agent in sentence.

If the sentence does not have a direct object in its active form, no passive equivalent exists.

Active	**No passive exists**
I would like to go to the conference.	
The freight charge will be about $1,400.	
The phone rang.	

Passive verbs have at least three disadvantages:

1. If all the information in the original sentence is retained, passive verbs make the sentence longer. Passives take more time to understand.[15]
2. If the agent is omitted, it's not clear who is responsible for doing the action.
3. Using many passive verbs, especially in material that has a lot of big words, can make the writing boring and pompous.

Passive verbs are desirable in these situations:

1. Use passives to emphasize the object receiving the action, not the agent.

    Your order was shipped November 15.

    The customer's order, not the shipping clerk, is important.

2. Use passives to provide coherence within a paragraph. A sentence is easier to read if "old" information comes at the beginning of a sentence. When you have been discussing a topic, use the word again as your subject even if that requires a passive verb.

    The bank made several risky loans in the late 1990s. These loans were written off as "uncollectible" in 2001.

    Using *loans* as the subject of the second sentence provides a link between the two sentences, making the paragraph as a whole easier to read.

3. Use passives to avoid assigning blame.

    The order was damaged during shipment.

    An active verb would require the writer to specify *who* damaged the order. The passive here is more tactful.

4. Use verbs—not nouns—to carry the weight of your sentence.

Put the weight of your sentence in the verb to make your sentences more forceful and up to 25% easier to read.[16] When the verb is a form of the verb *to be*, revise the sentence to use a more forceful verb.

Weak: The financial advantage of owning this equipment instead of leasing it is 10% after taxes.

Better: Owning this equipment rather than leasing it will save us 10% after taxes.

Nouns ending in *-ment, -ion,* and *-al* often hide verbs.

~~make an adjustment~~	adjust
~~make a payment~~	pay
~~make a decision~~	decide
~~reach a conclusion~~	conclude
~~take into consideration~~	consider
~~make a referral~~	refer
~~provide assistance~~	assist

Use verbs to present the information more forcefully.

Weak: We will perform an investigation of the problem.

Better: We will investigate the problem.

Weak: Selection of a program should be based on the client's needs.

Better: Select the program that best fits the client's needs.

5. Tighten your writing.

Writing is **wordy** if the same idea can be expressed in fewer words. Unnecessary words increase typing time, bore your reader, and make your meaning more difficult to follow, since the reader must hold all the extra words in mind while trying to understand your meaning.

Good writing is tight. Tight writing may be long because it is packed with ideas. In Chapter 2, we saw that revisions to create you-attitude and positive emphasis (← pp. 34, 37, respectively) and to develop reader benefits were frequently *longer* than the originals because the revision added information not given in the original.

Sometimes you may be able to look at a draft and see immediately how to tighten it. When the solution isn't obvious, try the following strategies for tightening your writing:

a. Eliminate words that say nothing.
b. Use gerunds (the *-ing* form of verbs) and infinitives (the *to* form of verbs) to make sentences shorter and smoother.
c. Combine sentences to eliminate unnecessary words.
d. Put the meaning of your sentence into the subject and verb to cut the number of words.

You eliminate unnecessary words to save the reader's time, not simply to see how few words you can use. You aren't writing a telegram, so keep the little words that make sentences complete. (Incomplete sentences are fine in lists where all the items are incomplete.)

The following examples show how to use these methods.

a. Eliminate words that say nothing.   Cut words if the idea is already clear from other words in the sentence. Substitute single words for wordy phrases.

Wordy: Keep this information on file for future reference.

Tighter: Keep this information for reference.

or: File this information.

Wordy: Ideally, it would be best to put the billing ticket just below the CRT screen and above the keyboard.

Tighter: If possible, put the billing ticket between the CRT screen and the keyboard.

Phrases beginning with *of, which,* and *that* can often be shortened.

What I Really Mean Is . . .*

I wrote asking someone if he could "provide information for" the group he had mentioned on a Web page. He replied that he was too busy to make a submission, and added that he was in full support of the group.

I got an answer, but a useless one. I had wanted the group's address! I could have avoided confusion (and embarrassment) by simply asking, "Do you have the group's address?"

*Quoted from Margo Metegrano, Letter to the Editor, *Intercom,* May 1996, 2.

FIGURE 4.7   Words to Cut

Cut the following words	Cut redundant words	Substitute a single word for a wordy phrase	
quite	a period of three months	at the present time	now
really	during the course of the negotiations	due to the fact that	because
very	during the year of 2004	in the event that	if
	maximum possible	in the near future	soon (or give the date)
	past experience	prior to the start of	before
	plan in advance	on a regular basis	regularly
	refer back		
	the color blue		
	true facts		

Using Your Computer to Improve Style*

Laser copies look so perfect that it can be hard to edit them. But your computer can be an ally, not an enemy, as you revise and edit.

- Use the "search" or "find" command to find potential errors. One student replaces every "is" and "are" with capital letters ("IS" and "ARE") so that he can easily check his draft. Another replaces periods with several asterisks to check sentence integrity.

- Change the font or size. Putting your text in an unusual font or 24-point type can help you really see what you've said. (Just remember to change back to a standard font in a standard size before printing out the final version!)

- Ask a friend to edit, putting changes in all caps, so you can easily find them.

*Based on Todd Taylor, " 'Soft Copy' and the Illusion of Laser-Printed Text," *Technical Communication* 42, no. 1 (February 1995): 169–70.

Wordy: the question of most importance

Tighter: the most important question

Wordy: the estimate which is enclosed

Tighter: the enclosed estimate

Sentences beginning with *There are* or *It is* can often be tighter.

Wordy: There are three reasons for the success of the project.

Tighter: Three reasons explain the project's success.

Wordy: It is the case that college graduates advance more quickly in the company.

Tighter: College graduates advance more quickly in the company.

Check your draft. If you find these phrases, or any of the unnecessary words shown in Figure 4.7, eliminate them.

b. Use gerunds and infinitives to make sentences shorter and smoother.   A **gerund** is the *-ing* form of a verb; grammatically, it is a verb used as a noun. In the sentence, "Running is my favorite activity," *running* is the subject of the sentence. An **infinitive** is the form of the verb that is preceded by *to: to run* is the infinitive.

In the revision below, a gerund (*purchasing*) and an infinitive (*to transmit*) tighten the revision.

Wordy: A plant suggestion has been made where they would purchase a QWIP machine for the purpose of transmitting test reports between plants.

Tighter: The plant suggests purchasing a QWIP machine to transmit test reports between plants.

Even when gerunds and infinitives do not greatly affect length, they often make sentences smoother and more conversational.

c. Combine sentences to eliminate unnecessary words.   In addition to saving words, combining sentences focuses the reader's attention on key points, makes your writing sound more sophisticated, and sharpens the relationship between ideas, thus making your writing more coherent.

Wordy: I conducted this survey by telephone on Sunday, April 21. I questioned two groups of upperclassmen—male and female—who, according to the Student Directory, were still living in the dorms. The purpose of this survey was to find out why some upperclassmen continue to live in the dorms even though they are no longer required by the University to do so. I also wanted to find out if there were any differences between male and female upperclassmen in their reasons for choosing to remain in the dorms.

Tighter: On Sunday, April 21, I phoned upperclassmen and women living in the dorms to find out (1) why they continue to live in the dorms even though they are no longer required to do so, and (2) whether men and women had the same reasons for staying in the dorms.

d. Put the meaning of your sentence into the subject and verb to cut the number of words.   Put the core of your meaning into the subject and verb of your main clause. Think about what you *mean* and try saying the same thing in several different ways. Some alternatives will be tighter than others. Choose the tightest one.

Wordy: The reason we are recommending the computerization of this process is because it will reduce the time required to obtain data and will give us more accurate data.

Better: We are recommending the computerization of this process because it will save time and give us more accurate data.

Tight: Computerizing the process will give us more accurate data more quickly.

Wordy: The purpose of this letter is to indicate that if we are unable to mutually benefit from our seller/buyer relationship, with satisfactory material and satisfactory payment, then we have no alternative other than to sever the relationship. In other words, unless the account is handled in 45 days, we will have to change our terms to a permanent COD basis.

Better: A good buyer/seller relationship depends upon satisfactory material and satisfactory payment. You can continue to charge your purchases from us only if you clear your present balance in 45 days.

6. Vary sentence length and sentence structure.

Readable prose mixes sentence lengths and varies sentence structure. A really short sentence (under 10 words) can add punch to your prose. Really long sentences (over 30 or 40 words) are danger signs.

You can vary sentence patterns in several ways. First, you can mix simple, compound, and complex sentences. (See Appendix B ➡ for more information on sentence structure.) **Simple sentences** have one main clause:

We will open a new store this month.

Compound sentences have two main clauses joined with *and, but, or,* or another conjunction. Compound sentences work best when the ideas in the two clauses are closely related.

We have hired staff, and they will complete their training next week.

We wanted to have a local radio station broadcast from the store during its grand opening, but the DJs were already booked.

Complex sentences have one main and one subordinate clause; they are good for showing logical relationships.

When the stores open, we will have balloons and specials in every department.

Because we already have a strong customer base in the northwest, we expect the new store to be just as successful as the store in the City Center Mall.

You can also vary sentences by changing the order of elements. Normally the subject comes first.

The Value of Being Specific*

A survey of car owners revealed complaints about the fit of doors. To correct the problem, the company worked to make the doors more exactly flush with the car body. But a later survey turned up the same complaint. Confused, the company asked several owners to be part of a focus group. It turned out that the owners judged "fit of doors" by how much effort it took to close the door and by the sound the door made when it shut.

*Based on Gerald F. Smith, *Quality Problem Solving* (Milwaukee: ASQ Quality Press, 1998), 57.

The Uses of Fuzzy Language*

Specific, concrete words are usually more interesting and more forceful. But fuzzy words may be better to encourage creativity, to promote change, and to create unity.

To encourage creativity, managers should describe the goal vaguely. Santa Fe Southern Railroad wanted to create an upscale space that was flexible enough to use in many ways. Employees came up with many creative alternatives that management hadn't thought of—and that saved the company money.

Fuzzy words are also useful in promoting change. One manufacturer changed to a "cross-functional team-based system"—but let each plant decide just how to structure and implement the teams.

Metaphors and other symbols can create a sense of energy and belonging. But any metaphor is fuzzy. For example, many businesses describe workers as a "family." But many kinds of families exist, and different employees will interpret the metaphor in different ways.

*Based on Gail T. Fairhurst and Robert A. Sarr, *The Art of Framing: Managing the Language of Leadership* (San Francisco: Jossey-Bass, 1996), 36–37.

We will survey customers later in the year to see whether demand warrants a third store on campus.

To create variety, occasionally begin the sentence with some other part of the sentence.

Later in the year, we will survey customers to see whether demand warrants a third store on campus.

To see whether demand warrants a third store on campus, we will survey customers later in the year.

Use these guidelines for sentence length and structure:

- Always edit sentences for tightness. Even a 17-word sentence can be wordy.
- When your subject matter is complicated or full of numbers, make a special effort to keep sentences short.
- Use long sentences
  To show how ideas are linked to each other.
  To avoid a series of short, choppy sentences.
  To reduce repetition.
- Group the words in long and medium-length sentences into chunks that the reader can process quickly.[17]
- When you use a long sentence, keep the subject and verb close together.

Let's see how to apply the last three principles.

- **Use long sentences to show how ideas are linked to each other, to avoid a series of short, choppy sentences, and to reduce repetition.** The following sentence is hard to read not simply because it is long but because it is shapeless. Just cutting it into a series of short, choppy sentences doesn't help. The best revision uses medium-length sentences to show the relationship between ideas.

  Too long: It should also be noted in the historical patterns presented in the summary, that though there were delays in January and February which we realized were occurring, we are now back where we were about a year ago, and that we are not off line in our collect receivables as compared to last year at this time, but we do show a considerable over-budget figure because of an ultraconservative goal on the receivable investment.

  Choppy: There were delays in January and February. We knew about them at the time. We are now back where we were about a year ago. The summary shows this. Our present collect receivables are in line with last year's. However, they exceed the budget. The reason they exceed the budget is that our goal for receivable investment was very conservative.

  Better: As the summary shows, although there were delays in January and February (of which we were aware), we have now regained our position of a year ago. Our present collect receivables are in line with last year's, but they exceed the budget because our goal for receivable investment was very conservative.

- **Group the words in long and medium-length sentences into chunks.** The "better" revision above has seven chunks. In the list below, the chunks starting immediately after the numbers are main clauses. The chunks that are indented are subordinate clauses and parenthetical phrases.

  1.   As the summary shows,
  2.   although there were delays in January and February
  3.   (of which we were aware),
  4.   we have now regained our position of a year ago.
  5.   Our present collect receivables are in line with last year's,

6. but they exceed the budget
7. because our goal for receivable investment was very conservative.

The first sentence has four chunks: an introductory phrase (1), a subordinate clause (2), with a parenthetical phrase (3), followed by the main clause of the first sentence (4). The second sentence begins with a main clause (5). The sentence's second main clause (6) is introduced with *but,* showing that it will reverse the first clause. A subordinate clause explaining the reason for the reversal completes the sentence (7). At 27 and 24 words, respectively, these sentences aren't short, but they're readable because no chunk is longer than 10 words. Any sentence pattern will get boring if it is repeated sentence after sentence. Use different sentence patterns—different kinds and lengths of chunks—to keep your prose interesting.

■ **Keep the subject and verb close together.** Often you can move the subject and verb closer together if you put the modifying material in a list at the end of the sentence. For maximum readability, present the list vertically.

Hard to read: Movements resulting from termination, layoffs and leaves, recalls and reinstates, transfers in, transfers out, promotions in, promotions out, and promotions within are presently documented through the Payroll Authorization Form.

Smoother: The following movements are documented on the Payroll Authorization Form: termination, layoffs and leaves, recalls and reinstates, transfers in and out, and promotions in, out, and within.

Still better: The following movements are documented on the Payroll Authorization Form:
   ■ Termination.
   ■ Layoffs and leaves.
   ■ Recalls and reinstates.
   ■ Transfers in and out.
   ■ Promotions in, out, and within.

Sometimes you will need to change the verb and revise the word order to put the modifying material at the end of the sentence.

Hard to read: The size sequence code that is currently used for sorting the items in the NOSROP lists and the composite stock lists is not part of the online file.

Smoother: The online file does not contain the size sequence code that is currently used for sorting the items in the composite stock lists and the NOSROP lists.

7. Use parallel structure.

Parallel structure puts words, phrases, or clauses in the same grammatical and logical form. In the following faulty example, *by reviewing* is a gerund, while *note* is an imperative verb. Make the sentence parallel by using both gerunds or both imperatives.

Faulty: Errors can be checked by reviewing the daily exception report or note the number of errors you uncover when you match the lading copy with the file copy of the invoice.

Parallel: Errors can be checked by reviewing the daily exception report or by noting the number of errors you uncover when you match the lading copy with the file copy of the invoice.

Also parallel: To check errors, note
   1. The number of items on the daily exception report.
   2. The number of errors discovered when the lading copy and the file copy are matched.

When Is a Tax Cut Not a Tax Cut? When It's a Refund.*

[President George W. Bush] is smart enough to have figured one thing out: Words are weapons. . . .

The unpopular concept of school vouchers has become "opportunity scholarships." . . . Similarly, Bush has relabeled churches, which many Americans do not think should receive federal support, as "faith-based institutions." Watered-down penalties on Iraq are "smart sanctions." . . .

The upside of choosing *le mot juste* can be huge, as previous administrations have demonstrated. Reagan scored a coup when he christened the MX missile the Peacekeeper at the height of the cold war. . . . More recently, Clinton reshaped the debate over the trade with China when he ditched the elitist-sounding term "Most-Favored Nation" trade status in favor of the more egalitarian handle "Normal Trade Relations." . . .

Terminology also play[ed] a big role in [cutting] the estate tax—which is now being called the "death tax." ["Estate" is the term for the total amount of assets left by someone who dies. The term sounds like something only rich people have.] But everybody dies.

*Quoted from Richard S. Dunham, "When Is a Tax Cut Not a Tax Cut?" *BusinessWeek*, March 19, 2001, 38–39.

Writing to Be Translated*

When you know that something will be translated into another language, avoid figurative language, images, and humor. They don't translate well.

"Consider the American copywriter who prepared a campaign on snowblowers for the European market without giving a thought to translations. . . . 'Super Snow Hound' [was] the most powerful model. . . . The copywriter wrote the headline: 'Super Snow Hound Blows Up a Storm.' You can imagine the difficulty of retaining the idiom and connotations of 'blows' for snowblower and 'up a storm' for heavy duty performance in a snow storm."

*Paragraph 2 quoted from Robert F. Roth, *International Marketing Communications* (Chicago: Crain, 1982), 139.

Note that a list in parallel structure must fit grammatically into the umbrella sentence that introduces the list.

Words must also be logically parallel. In the following faulty example, *juniors, seniors,* and *athletes* are not three separate groups. The revision groups words into nonoverlapping categories.

Faulty: I interviewed juniors and seniors and athletes.

Parallel: I interviewed juniors and seniors. In each rank, I interviewed athletes and nonathletes.

Parallel structure is a powerful device for making your writing tighter, smoother, and more forceful. As Figure 4.8 shows, parallelism often enables you to tighten your writing. To make your writing as tight as possible, eliminate repetition in parallel lists; see Figure 4.9.

8. Put your readers in your sentences.

Use second-person pronouns (*you*) rather than third-person (*he, she, one*) to give your writing more impact. *You* is both singular and plural; it can refer to a single person or to every member of your organization.

Third-person: Funds in a participating employee's account at the end of each six months will automatically be used to buy more stock unless a "Notice of Election Not to Exercise Purchase Rights" form is received from the employee.

Second-person: Once you begin to participate, funds in your account at the end of each six months will automatically be used to buy more stock unless you turn in a "Notice of Election Not to Exercise Purchase Rights" form.

Be careful to use *you* only when it refers to your reader.

FIGURE 4.8   Use Parallelism to Tighten Your Writing.

Faulty

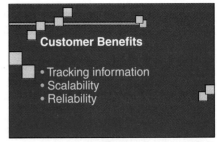

Parallel

FIGURE 4.9   Eliminate Repeated Words in Parallel Lists.

Wordy

Tight

Incorrect: My visit with the outside sales rep showed me that your schedule can change quickly.

Correct: My visit with the outside sales rep showed me that schedules can change quickly.

As You Write and Revise Paragraphs

Paragraphs are visual and logical units. Use them to chunk your sentences.

9. Begin most paragraphs with topic sentences.

A good paragraph has **unity**; that is, it discusses only one idea, or topic. The **topic sentence** states the main idea and provides a scaffold to structure your document. Your writing will be easier to read if you make the topic sentence explicit and put it at the beginning of the paragraph.[18]

Hard to read (no topic sentence):   In fiscal 2001, the company filed claims for refund of federal income taxes of $3,199,000 and interest of $969,000 paid as a result of an examination of the company's federal income tax returns by the Internal Revenue Service (IRS) for the years 1997 through 1999. It is uncertain what amount, if any, may ultimately be recovered.

Better (paragraph starts with topic sentence):   The company and the IRS disagree about whether the company is for back taxes. **In fiscal 2001, the company filed claims for a refund of federal income taxes of $3,199,000 and interest of $969,000 paid as a result of an examination of the company's federal income tax returns by the Internal Revenue Service (IRS) for the years 1997 through 1999. It is uncertain what amount, if any, may ultimately be recovered.**

A good topic sentence forecasts the structure and content of the paragraph.

Plan B also has economic advantages.

(Prepares the reader for a discussion of B's economic advantages.)

We had several personnel changes in June.

(Prepares the reader for a list of the month's terminations and hires.)

Employees have complained about one part of our new policy on parental leaves.

(Prepares the reader for a discussion of the problem.)

When the first sentence of a paragraph is not the topic sentence, readers who skim may miss the main point. Move the topic sentence to the beginning of the paragraph. If the paragraph does not have a topic sentence, you will need to write one. If you can't think of a single sentence that serves as an "umbrella" to cover every sentence, the paragraph lacks unity. To solve the problem, either split the paragraph into two or eliminate the sentence that digresses from the main point.

10. Use transitions to link ideas.

Transition words and sentences signal the connections between ideas to the reader. Transitions tell whether the next sentence continues the previous thought or starts a new idea; they can tell whether the idea that comes next is more or less important than the previous thought. Figure 4.10 lists some of the most common transition words and phrases.

Readability Formulas and Good Style

Readability formulas attempt to measure objectively how easy something is to read. However, since they don't take many factors into account, the formulas are at best a very limited guide to good style.

The Benefits of Plain English*

Allen-Bradley spent two years converting its manuals to plain English. The work is paying off in five ways. (1) Phone calls asking questions about the products have dropped from 50 a day to only 2 a month. (2) The sales force is selling more systems because people can learn about them more quickly. (3) Distributors spend less time on site teaching customers about products. (4) The clearer documents are easier to translate into Japanese, German, and French for international sales. (5) The tighter documents cost less to print, especially when translated into Arabic and German, which require 125% more space than the same content in English.

*Based on Barry Jereb, "Plain English on the Plant Floor," *Plain Language: Principles and Practice,* ed. Edwin R. Steinberg (Detroit: Wayne State University Press, 1991), 213.

FIGURE 4.10   Transition Words and Phrases

To show addition or continuation of the same idea	To introduce an example	To show that the contrast is more important than the previous idea	To show time
and	for example (e.g.)	but	after
also	for instance	however	as
first, second, third	indeed	nevertheless	before
in addition	to illustrate	on the contrary	in the future
likewise	namely	**To show cause and effect**	next
similarly	specifically	as a result	then
To introduce the last or most important item	**To contrast**	because	until
finally	in contrast	consequently	when
furthermore	on the other hand	for this reason	while
moreover	or	therefore	**To summarize or end**
			in conclusion

Computer packages that analyze style may give you a readability score. Some states' "plain English" laws require consumer contracts to meet a certain readability score. Some companies require that warranties and other consumer documents meet certain scores.

See the BAC Web site to see how to calculate the two best known readability formulas: the Gunning Fog Index and the Flesch Reading Ease Scale. As you can see when you visit the BAC Web page, readability formulas depend heavily on word length and sentence length. But as Janice C. Redish and Jack Selzer have shown,[19] using shorter words and sentences will not necessarily make a passage easy to read. Short words are not always easy to understand, especially if they have technical meanings (e.g., *waive, bear market, liquid*). Short, choppy sentences and sentence fragments are actually harder to understand than well-written medium-length sentences.

No reading formula yet devised takes into account three factors that influence how easy a text is to read: the complexity of the ideas, the organization of the ideas, and the layout and design of the document.

Instead of using readability formulas to measure style, the Document Design Center recommends that you test your draft with the people for whom it is designed. How long does it take them to find the information they need? Do they make mistakes when they try to use the document? Do they think the document is easy to use? Answers to these questions can give us much more accurate information than any readability score.

Organizational Preferences for Style

Different organizations and bosses may legitimately have different ideas about what constitutes good writing. If the style the company prefers seems reasonable, use it. If the style doesn't seem reasonable—if you work for someone who likes flowery language or wordy paragraphs, for example—you have several choices.

- Go ahead and use the techniques in this chapter. Sometimes seeing good writing changes people's minds about the style they prefer.
- Help your boss learn about writing. Show him or her this book or the research cited in the notes to demonstrate how a clear, crisp style makes documents easier to read.

■ Recognize that a style may serve other purposes than communication. An abstract, hard-to-read style may help a group forge its own identity. James Suchan and Ronald Dulek have shown that Navy officers preferred a passive, impersonal style because they saw themselves as followers. An aircraft company's engineers saw wordiness as the verbal equivalent of backup systems. A backup is redundant but essential to safety, because parts and systems do fail.[20] When big words, jargon, and wordiness are central to a group's self-image, change will be difficult, since changing style will mean changing the corporate culture.

■ Ask. Often the documents that end up in files aren't especially good; later, other workers may find these and copy them, thinking they represent a corporate standard. Bosses may in fact prefer better writing.

Building a good style takes energy and effort, but it's well worth the work. Good style can make every document more effective; good style can help make you the good writer so valuable to every organization.

Summary of Key Points

■ Good style in business and administrative writing is less formal, more friendly, and more personal than the style usually used for term papers.

■ To improve your style,
  ■ Get a clean page or screen so that you aren't locked into old sentence structures.
  ■ Try WIRMI: What *I* Really Mean Is. Then write the words.
  ■ Try reading your draft out loud to someone sitting about three feet away. If the words sound stiff, they'll seem stiff to a reader, too.
  ■ Ask someone else to read your draft out loud. Readers stumble because the words on the page aren't what they expect to see. The places where that person stumbles are places where your writing can be better.
  ■ Write a *lot.*

■ Use the following techniques to make your writing easier to read:
  As you choose words,
  1. Use words that are accurate, appropriate, and familiar. Denotation is a word's literal meaning; connotation is the emotional coloring that a word conveys.
  2. Use technical jargon only when it is essential and known to the reader. Eliminate business jargon.
  As you write and revise sentences,
  3. Use active verbs most of the time. Active verbs are better because they are shorter, clearer, and more interesting.
  4. Use verbs—not nouns—to carry the weight of your sentence.
  5. Tighten your writing. Writing is wordy if the same idea can be expressed in fewer words.
     a. Eliminate words that say nothing.
     b. Use gerunds and infinitives to make sentences shorter and smoother.
     c. Combine sentences to eliminate unnecessary words.
     d. Put the meaning of your sentence into the subject and verb to cut the number of words.
  6. Vary sentence length and sentence structure.
  7. Use parallel structure. Use the same grammatical form for ideas that have the same logical function.
  8. Put your readers in your sentences.

The Boss Won't Let Me Write That Way

When a writing consultant urged them to use *I*, the engineers in Research and Development (R&D) at one firm claimed they couldn't: "Our boss won't let us." The consultant checked with their boss, the vice president for Research and Development. He said, "I don't care what words they use. I just want to be able to understand what they write."

The vice president had a PhD and had once done experiments in R&D himself, but he'd spent several years in management. He no longer knew as many technical details as did his subordinates. Their efforts to impress him backfired: he was annoyed because he couldn't understand their reports and had to tell subordinates to rewrite them.

Moral 1: If you think your boss doesn't want you to use a word, ask. A few bosses do prize formal or flowery language. Most don't.

Moral 2: Even if your boss has the same background you do, he or she won't necessarily understand what you write. Revise your memos and reports so they're clear and easy to read.

Moral 3: What's in the file cabinet isn't necessarily a guide to good writing for your organization.

As you write and revise paragraphs,

    9. Begin most paragraphs with topic sentences so that readers know what to expect in the paragraph.

   10. Use transitions to link ideas.

■ Readability formulas are not a sufficient guide to style. They imply that all short words and all short sentences are equally easy to read; they ignore other factors that make a document easy or hard to read: the complexity of the ideas, the organization of the ideas, and the layout and design of the document.

■ Different organizations and bosses may legitimately have different ideas about what constitutes good writing.

@ See the BAC Web Site for links to pages about words and style.

CHAPTER 4   Exercises and Problems

Getting Started

4.1   Identifying Words with Multiple Denotations

a. Each of the following words has several denotations. How many can you list without going to a dictionary? How many additional meanings does a good dictionary list?

browser	log
court	table

b. List five words that have multiple denotations.

4.2   Explaining Bypassing

Show how different denotations make bypassing possible in the following examples.

a. France and Associates: Protection from Professionals

b. We were not able to account for the outstanding amount of plastic waste generated each year.

c. I scanned the résumés when I received them.

4.3   Evaluating Connotations

a. Identify the connotations of each of the following metaphors for a multicultural nation.

melting pot

mosaic

tapestry

crazy quilt

garden salad

stew

tributaries

b. Which connotations seem most positive? Why?

4.4   Evaluating the Ethical Implications of Connotations

In each of the following pairs, identify the more favorable term. Is its use justified? Why or why not?

1. wastepaper   recovered fiber
2. feedback   criticism
3. deadline   due date
4. scalper   ticket reseller
5. budget   spending plan

4.5   Correcting Errors in Denotation and Connotation

Identify and correct the errors in denotation or connotation in the following sentences:

1. In our group, we weeded out the best idea each person had thought of.
2. She is a prudent speculator.
3. The three proposals are diametrically opposed to each other.
4. While he researched companies, he was literally glued to the Web.
5. Our backpacks are hand sewn by one of roughly 16 individuals.

4.6   Using Connotations to Shape Response

Write two sentences to describe each of the following situations. In one sentence, use words with positive connotations; in the other, use negative words.

1. Chris doesn't spend time on small talk.
2. Chris often starts work on a new project without being told to do so.
3. As a supervisor, Chris gives very specific instructions to subordinates.

4.7   Choosing Levels of Formality

Identify the more formal word in each pair. Which term is better for most business documents? Why?

1. adapted to   geared to
2. befuddled   confused
3. assistant   helper
4. pilot project   testing the waters
5. cogitate   think

4.8   Eliminating Jargon and Simplifying Language

Revise these sentences to eliminate jargon and to use short, familiar words. In some sentences, you'll need to reword, reorganize, or add information to produce the best revision.

1. Computers can enumerate pages when the appropriate keystroke is implemented.
2. Any alterations must be approved during the 30-day period commencing 60 days prior to the expiration date of the agreement.
3. As per your request, the undersigned has obtained estimates of upgrading our computer system. A copy of the estimated cost is attached hereto.
4. Please be advised that this writer is in considerable need of a new computer.
5. Enclosed please find the proposed schedule for the training session. In the event that you have alterations which you would like to suggest, forward same to my office at your earliest convenience.

4.9   Changing Verbs from Passive to Active

Identify the passive verbs in the following sentences and convert them to active verbs. In some cases, you may need to add information to do so. You may use different words as long as you retain the basic meaning of the sentence. Remember that imperative verbs are active, too.

1. The business plan was written by Tyrone King.
2. The cost of delivering financial services is being slashed by computers, the Internet, and toll-free phone lines.
3. When the vacation schedule is finalized it is recommended that it be routed to all supervisors for final approval.
4. As stated in my résumé, I have designed Web pages for three student organizations.
5. Material must not be left on trucks outside the warehouse. Either the trucks must be parked inside the warehouse or the material must be unloaded at the time of receiving the truck.

4.10   Using Strong Verbs

Revise each of the following sentences to use stronger verbs:

1. The advantage of using color is that the document is more memorable.
2. Customers who make payments by credit card will receive a 1% rebate on all purchases.
3. When you make an evaluation of media buys, take into consideration the demographics of the group seeing the ad.
4. We provide assistance to clients in the process of reaching a decision about the purchase of hardware and software.
5. We maintain the belief that Web ads are a good investment.

4.11   Reducing Wordiness

1. Eliminate words that say nothing. You may use different words.
   a. There are many businesses that are active in community and service work.
   b. The purchase of a new computer will allow us to produce form letters quickly. In addition, return on investment could be calculated for proposed repairs. Another use is that the computer could check databases to make sure that claims are paid only once.
   c. Our decision to enter the South American market has precedence in the past activities of the company.
2. Use gerunds and infinitives to make these sentences shorter and smoother.
   a. The completion of the project requires the collection and analysis of additional data.
   b. The purchase of laser printers will make possible the in-house production of the newsletter.

   c. The treasurer has the authority for the investment of assets for the gain of higher returns.
3. Combine sentences to show how ideas are related and to eliminate unnecessary words.
   a. Some customers are profitable for companies. Other customers actually cost the company money.
   b. If you are unable to come to the session on HMOs, please call the human resources office. You will be able to schedule another time to ask questions you may have about the various options.
   c. Major Japanese firms often have employees who know English well. US companies negotiating with Japanese companies should bring their own interpreters.

4.12   Improving Parallel Structure

Revise each of the following sentences to create parallelism.
1. The orientation session will cover the following information:
   - Company culture will be discussed.
   - How to use the equipment.
   - You will get an overview of key customers' needs.
2. Five criteria for a good Web page are content that serves the various audiences, attention to details, and originality. It is also important to have effective organization and navigation devices. Finally, provide attention to details such as revision date and the Webmaster's address.

3. When you leave a voice-mail message,
   - Summarize your main point in a sentence or two.
   - The name and phone number should be given slowly and distinctly.
   - The speaker should give enough information so that the recipient can act on the message.
   - Tell when you'll be available to receive the recipient's return call.

4.13   Putting Readers in Your Sentences

Revise each of the following sentences to put readers in them. As you revise, use active verbs and simple words.
1. Mutual funds can be purchased from banks, brokers, financial planners, or from the fund itself.
2. Every employee will receive a copy of the new policy within 60 days after the labor agreement is signed.

3. Another aspect of the university is campus life, with an assortment of activities and student groups to participate in and lectures and sports events to attend.

4.14   Editing Sentences to Improve Style

Revise these sentences to make them smoother, less wordy, and easier to read. Eliminate jargon and repetition. Keep the information; you may reword or reorganize it. If the original is not clear, you may need to add information to write a clear revision.
1. There are many different topics that you will read about on a monthly basis once you subscribe to *Inc.*

2. With the new organic fertilizer, you'll see an increase in the quality of your tomatoes and the number grown.
3. As a manager, I am responsible for helping to promote any action or ideas that may help to improve this organization as a whole. One such idea is printing our URL on our business cards and

stationery. We could also put the URL on our invoices. I therefore recommend that when we reorder said materials, we imprint our URL on all of them so that our current and prospective customers will be able to access our Web site.

4. The county will benefit from implementing flextime.
   - Offices will stay open longer for more business.
   - Staff turnover will be lower.

- Easier business communication with states in other time zones.
- Increased employee productivity.

5. There is a seasonality factor in the workload, with the heaviest being immediately prior to quarterly due dates for estimated tax payments.

4.15   Using Topic Sentences

Make each of the following paragraphs more readable by opening each paragraph with a topic sentence. You may be able to find a topic sentence in the paragraph and move it to the beginning. In other cases, you'll need to write a new sentence.

1. At Disney World, a lunch put on an expense account is "on the mouse." McDonald's employees "have ketchup in their veins." Business slang flourishes at companies with rich corporate cultures. Memos at Procter & Gamble are called "reco's" because the model P&G memo begins with a recommendation.

2. The first item on the agenda is the hiring for the coming year. George has also asked that we review the agency goals for the next fiscal year. We should cover this early in the meeting since it may affect our hiring preferences. Finally, we need to announce the deadlines for grant proposals, decide which grants to apply for, and set up a committee to draft each proposal.

3. Separate materials that can be recycled from your regular trash. Pass along old clothing, toys, or appliances to someone else who can use them. When you purchase products, choose those with minimal packaging. If you have a yard, put your yard waste and kitchen scraps (excluding meat and fat) in a compost pile. You can reduce the amount of solid waste your household produces in four ways.

4.16   Revising Paragraphs

Revise each paragraph to make it easier to read. Change, rearrange, or delete words and sentences; add any material necessary.

a. Once a new employee is hired, each one has to be trained for a week by one of our supervisors at a cost of $1,000 each which includes the supervisor's time. This amount also includes half of the new employee's salary, since new hires produce only half the normal production per worker for the week. This summer $24,000 was spent in training 24 new employees. Absenteeism increased in the department on the hottest summer days. For every day each worker is absent we lose $200 in lost production. This past summer there was a total of 56 absentee days taken for a total loss of $11,200 in lost production. Turnover and absenteeism were the causes of an unnecessary expenditure of over $35,000 this summer.

b. One service is investments. General financial news and alerts about companies in the customer's portfolio are available. Quicken also provides assistance in finding the best mortgage rate and in providing assistance in making the decision whether to refinance a mortgage. Another service from Quicken is advice for the start and management of a small business. Banking services, such as paying bills and applying for loans, have long been available to Quicken subscribers. The taxpayer can be walked through the tax preparation process by Quicken. Someone considering retirement can use Quicken to ascertain whether the amount being set aside for this purpose is sufficient. Quicken's Web site provides seven services.

4.17   Writing Paragraphs

Write a paragraph on each of the following topics.

a. Discuss your ideal job.
b. Summarize a recent article from a business magazine or newspaper.
c. Explain how technology is affecting the field you plan to enter.
d. Explain why you have or have not decided to work while you attend college.

e. Write a profile of someone who is successful in the field you hope to enter.

As Your Instructor Directs,

a. Label topic sentences, active verbs, and parallel structure.
b. Edit a classmate's paragraphs to make the writing even tighter and smoother.

Planning, Composing, and Revising

Planning, Composing, and Revising

In preparing to write, I spend approximately one-third of my time planning. Analyzing the purpose and audience before beginning to write is one of the most important aspects of writing.

I begin by analyzing the purpose of the document—persuasive, informative, and so forth.

Secondly, I think about my audience. It's important to make sure that the audience can easily follow a document. The audience may be an individual or group of people. I write many documents that go to corporate executives, and I know that being able to write effectively is crucial in persuading them that my services will benefit their organizations.

When beginning a proposal or report, I like to start with an outline or overview. I break the document into the appropriate headings. In proposals, an overview of the document stimulates interest, persuades the audience to read the document, and prepares the reader for the detailed information inside. Starting with an outline or overview simplifies the writing process—just fill in detailed information under each of the headings you have selected.

For example, a recent client wanted to expand its current operations. I was given the task of putting together a document proposing how this expansion should happen. To begin, I identified an objective: to expand current production by adding a new building and equipment. The next step was preparing a timeline and cost estimate. Then I identified recommendations on key aspects of the project. Working out the project in my head, in notes, and in the overview saved a lot of time writing the draft.

Once the draft is complete, I go back to revise and edit—tightening up sentences, substituting words, and spell checking. Some documents need just one pass; some require multiple revisions. After revising, I spell check once again. Then I print a hard copy of the document and read it over for typos and grammatical structure. Once this is finished, I ask a colleague to review the document and make comments. If that person can easily follow the document, my audience should.

Daniel R. Zevchik

Consultant to the Pharmaceutical, Nutritional, and Food Industries; Engineering and Scientific Consulting

Daniel Zevchik composes proposals, reports, and technical documentation for a wide variety of clients. Consulting from his office in Columbus, Ohio, he provides engineering, validation, and product development services to pharmaceutical, nutritional, and food industries. His expertise helps companies overcome technical challenges with resource constraints.

drzhelp@columbus.rr.com

> *"I spend approximately one-third of my time planning."*

Skilled performances look easy and effortless. In reality, as every dancer, musician, and athlete knows, they're the products of hard work, hours of practice, attention to detail, and intense concentration. Like skilled performances in other arts, writing rests on a base of work.

The Ways Good Writers Write

No single writing process works for all writers all of the time. However, good writers and poor writers seem to use different processes.[1] Good writers are more likely to

- Realize that the first draft will not be perfect.
- Write regularly.
- Break big jobs into small chunks.
- Have clear goals focusing on purpose and audience.
- Have several different strategies to choose from.
- Use rules flexibly.
- Wait to edit until after the draft is complete.

Research shows that experts differ from novices in identifying and analyzing the initial problem more effectively, understanding the task more broadly and deeply, drawing from a wider repertoire of strategies, and seeing patterns more clearly. Experts actually composed more slowly than novices, perhaps because they rarely settled for work that was just "OK." Finally, experts were better at evaluating their own work.[2]

Thinking about the writing process and consciously adopting "expert" processes will help you become a more expert writer.

Activities in the Composing Process

Most researchers would agree that writing processes can include eight activities: planning, gathering, writing, evaluating, getting feedback, revising, editing, and proofreading. The activities do not have to come in this order. Not every writing task demands all eight.

Planning includes all the thinking you do. It includes such activities as analyzing the problem, defining your purposes, and analyzing the audience; thinking of ideas; and choosing a pattern of organization or making an outline. Planning includes not only devising strategies for the document as a whole but also generating "mini-plans" that govern sentences or paragraphs.

Gathering includes physically getting the data you need. It can mean simply getting a copy of the letter you're responding to; it can also mean conducting informal and formal research—everything from getting a computer printout or checking something on the Web to administering a questionnaire or conducting a focus group.

Writing is the act of putting words on paper or on a screen, or of dictating words to a machine or a secretary. Writing can take the form of lists, fragmentary notes, stream-of-consciousness writing, or formal drafts.

Evaluating means rereading your work and measuring it against your goals and the requirements of the situation and audience. The best evaluation results from *re-seeing* your draft as if someone else had written it. Will your audience understand it? Is it complete? Convincing? Friendly?

You can evaluate *every* activity in the process, not just your draft. Is your view of purposes adequate? Do you have enough information to write? Are your sources believable? Do your revisions go far enough?

Getting feedback means asking someone else to evaluate your work. Again, you could get feedback on every activity, not just your draft. Is your pattern of organization appropriate? Does a revision solve an earlier problem? Are there any typos in the final copy?

Revising means making changes in the draft suggested by your own evaluation or by feedback from someone else: adding, deleting, substituting, or rearranging. Revision can be changes in single words, but more often it means major additions, deletions, or substitutions as the writer measures (evaluates) the draft against purpose and audience and reshapes the document to make it more effective.

Editing means checking the draft to see that it satisfies the requirements of standard English and the principles of business writing. Here you'd correct spelling and mechanical errors and check word choice and format. Unlike revision, which can produce major changes in meaning, editing focuses on the surface of writing.

Proofreading means checking the final copy to see that it's free from typographical errors.

Note the following points about these eight activities:

- **The activities do not have to come in this order.** Some people may gather data *after* writing a draft when they see that they need more specifics to achieve their purposes.

- **You do not have to finish one activity to start another.** Some writers plan a short section and write it, plan the next short section and write it, and so on through the document. Evaluating what is already written may cause a writer to do more planning or to change the original plan.

- **Most writers do not use all eight activities for all the documents they write.** You'll use more activities when you write a certain kind of document, about a subject, or to an audience that's new to you.

Research about what writers really do has destroyed some of the stereotypes we used to have about the writing process. Consider planning. Traditional advice stressed the importance of planning and sometimes advised writers to make formal outlines for everything they wrote. But we know now that not all good documents are based on outlines.[3] George Jensen and John DiTiberio have found that extroverts do little planning and prefer to work out their ideas as they go along, while introverts prefer to work out their ideas fully before they begin writing.[4] Either method can produce good writing. A study on writer's block found that some ineffective writers spent so much time planning that they left too little time to write the assignment.[5] "Plan!" is too simplistic to be helpful. Instead, we need to talk about how much and what kind of planning for what kind of document.

Using Your Time Effectively

To get the best results from the time you have, spend only one-third of your time actually "writing." Spend at least another one-third of your time analyzing the situation and your audience, gathering information, and organizing what you have to say. Spend the final third evaluating what you've said, revising the draft(s) to meet your purposes and the needs of the audience and the organization, editing a late draft to remove any errors in grammar and mechanics, and proofreading the final typed copy.

When you first get an assignment, think about all the steps you'll need to go through so that you can plan your time for that project. Certainly two different writers might need different amounts of time to produce the same quality document. But for any one writer, different projects have different lead times, as Figure 5.1 shows.

One Writer's Process for Memos and Reports*

I was asked to prepare the business' annual marketing plan. This . . . experience . . . forced me to think about what I wanted to say, my audiences, and what they wanted and needed to know. From the beginning I recognized that I needed to explain what our industry was, how we were positioned, what our growth objectives were, and how were we going to reach them.

Writing the first draft of the plan was very daunting; I had many false starts and had to rewrite paragraphs and complete sections. Sometimes when I revisited the text, I realized that points were not clearly stated or that insight was lacking. I ended up abandoning my first plan and instead telling a story about what we had done and what we wanted to do. . . .

I begin business plans—and other documents—by outlining the key elements to include. It's useful to jot down ideas and thoughts without attempting to be grammatically correct. . . .

Once I feel basically satisfied with a draft, I go through it page by page for content, flow, and proper grammar. . . . Not surprisingly, one needs to go through more than one iteration to incorporate editorial comments, reorganize the text, and have it proofread by more than one pair of eyes!

*Quoted from Robert A. Brullo to Kitty Locker, March 22, 1999.

FIGURE 5.1 Time Lines for Various Documents
(Your actual times may vary.)

E-Mail message answering a simple question. Total time: 15 minutes

5 minutes	5 minutes	5 minutes
Read the question. Gather any information necessary for reply. Plan the message.	Draft the message.	Re-read the message. Run the message through spell check. Make small changes. Send the message.

E-Mail message answering a question that requires simple research. Total time: 2 hours

1 hour	30 minutes	30 minutes
Read the question. Think about what is needed to reply. Do research (on the Web, ask people, etc.) Analyze the information. Plan the message.	Draft the message and any attachments.	Re-read the message. Revise the message and attachments. Run the message through spell check. Send the message.

Memo explaining a new policy. Total time: 6½ hours

90 minutes	90 minutes	90 minutes	30 minutes	90 minutes
Understand the policy. Answer the questions for analysis. (◄▥ Chapter 1). Think about document design. Organize the message.	Draft.	Re-read draft. Measure draft against analysis questions and principles of business communication. Revise draft.	Ask for feedback.	Revise draft based on feedback. Run spell check. Proof by eye. Initial memo. Duplicate and distribute document.

Report recommending ways to improve customer service. Total time: 30 business days

6 days	1 day	2 days	9 days
Collect information about weaknesses in service. Plan research to gather more information. Get library sources; check the Web; plan survey or interview questions. Write proposal to do research to find solution.	Ask for feedback on proposal, research plan.	Revise proposal.	Conduct research. Analyze data. Create visuals for report. Prepare appendices.

5 days	1 day	5 days	1 day
Draft report. Evaluate draft against proposal and principles of business communication.	Ask for feedback on recommendations, report design, and visuals.	Revise report. Revise visuals. Plan oral presentation. Edit document and visuals. Run spell check. Proof by eye. Duplicate document.	Submit report. Present results orally.

Brainstorming, Planning, and Organizing Business Documents

Spend at least one-third of your time planning and organizing before you begin to write. The better your ideas are when you start, the fewer drafts you'll need to produce a good document. Start by using the analysis questions from Chapter 1 ◄ to identify purpose and audience. Use the strategies described in Chapter 3 to analyze audience (◄ p. 59) and identify reader benefits (◄ p. 70). Gather information you can use for your document.

Sometimes your content will be determined by the situation. Sometimes, even when it's up to you to think of reader benefits or topics to include in a report, you'll find it easy to think of ideas. If ideas won't come, try the following techniques:

- **Brainstorming.** Think of all the ideas you can, without judging them. Consciously try to get at least a dozen different ideas before you stop. The first idea you have may not be the best.

- **Freewriting.**[6] Make yourself write, without stopping, for 10 minutes or so, even if you must write "I will think of something soon." At the end of 10 minutes, read what you've written, identify the best point in the draft, then set it aside, and write for another 10 uninterrupted minutes. Read this draft, marking anything that's good and should be kept, and then write again for another 10 minutes. By the third session, you will probably produce several sections that are worth keeping—maybe even a complete draft that's ready to be revised.

- **Clustering.**[7] Write your topic in the middle of the page and circle it. Write down the ideas the topic suggests, circling them, too. (The circles are designed to tap into the nonlinear half of your brain.) When you've filled the page, look for patterns or repeated ideas. Use different colored pens to group related ideas. Then use these ideas to develop reader benefits in a memo, questions for a survey, or content for the body of a report. Figure 5.2 presents the clusters that one writer created about business communication in the United States and France.

- **Talk to your audiences.** As Rachel Spilka's research shows, talking to internal and external audiences helped writers involve readers in the planning process, understand the social and political relationships among readers, and negotiate conflicts orally rather than depending solely on the document. These writers were then able to think about content as well as about organization and style, appeal to common grounds (such as reducing waste or increasing productivity) that several readers shared, and reduce the number of revisions needed before documents were approved.[8]

Thinking about the content, layout, or structure of your document can also give you ideas. For long documents, write out the headings you'll use. For anything that's under five pages, less formal notes will probably work. You may want to jot down ideas to use as the basis for a draft. For an oral presentation, a meeting, or a document with lots of visuals, try creating a **storyboard,** with a rectangle representing each page or unit. Draw a box with a visual for each main point. Below the box, write a short caption or label. For an example of a storyboard, see the BAC Web site.

Letters and memos will go faster if you choose a basic organizational pattern before you start. Chapters 7, 8, and 9 give detailed patterns of organization for the most common kinds of letters and memos. You may want to customize those patterns with a planning guide[9] to help you keep the "big picture" in

Writing with Information*

Good writers write with information. Michelle Russo writes reports appraising how much a hotel is worth. Gathering information is a big part of her composing process.

She visits the site. She talks to the general manager. She gets occupancy rates, financial statements, and tax forms. She talks to the tax assessor and all the managers of competing hotels. If it's a convention hotel, she talks to the convention bureau and gets the airlines' passenger traffic counts. Gathering all this information takes about four days. When she gets back to the office, she uses databases for even more information.

*Based on Michelle S. Russo, telephone conversation with Kitty Locker, December 8, 1993.

FIGURE 5.2   Clustering Helps Generate Ideas

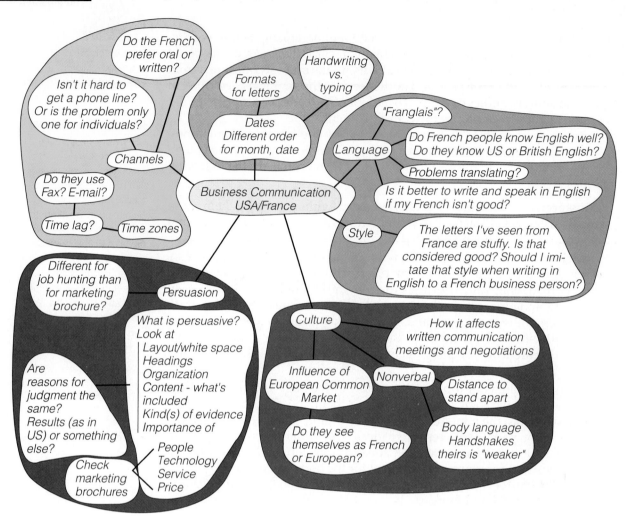

mind as you write. Figure 5.3 shows planning guides developed for specific kinds of documents.

As you plan your document, pay attention to signals from your boss and the organization's culture (◄▦ p. 59). For example, if the organization has a style manual that specifies whether *data* is singular or plural, follow its guidelines. If the organization has an ethics counselor, think about consulting him or her as you decide what to write in a situation with ethical implications. Talk to people in the organization who will be affected by what you are announcing or proposing, to better understand their concerns. In some organizations, your boss may want to see an early planning draft (see Figure 5.6 later in this chapter) to see that you're on the right track. In other organizations, you may be expected to do a great deal of revising on your own before anyone else sees the document.

Revising, Editing, and Proofreading

Good writers make their drafts better by judicious revising, editing, and proofreading. **Revising** means making changes that will better satisfy your purposes and your audience. **Editing** means making surface-level changes that

FIGURE 5.3	Customized Planning Guides for Specific Documents

Planning guide for a trip report
- The Big Picture from the Company's Point of View: We Can Go Forward on the Project.
- Criteria/Goals
- What We Did
- Why We Know Enough to Go Forward
- Next Steps

Planning guide for a proposal
- Customer's Concern #1 Our Proposal/Answer
- Customer's Concern #2 Our Proposal/Answer
- Customer's Concern #3 Our Proposal/Answer
- Customer's Concern #4 Our Proposal/Answer
- Ask for Action

Planning guide for an e-mail message
- My Purpose
- Points I Want to Make
- Document(s) to Attach
- Next Steps

Planning guide for a credit rejection
- Reason
- Refusal
- Alternative (Layaway/ Co-signer/Provide more information)
- Goodwill Ending

Source: E-mail and proposal guides based on Fred Reynolds, "What Adult Work-World Writers Have Taught Me About Adult Work-World Writing," Professional Writing in Context: Lessons from Teaching and Consulting in Worlds of Work (Hillsdale, NJ: Lawrence Erlbaum Associates, 1995), 18, 20.

make the document grammatically correct. **Proofreading** means checking to be sure the document is free from typographical errors.

What to Look for When You Revise

Every chapter in this book suggests questions you should ask as you revise. When you write to an audience you know well, you may be able to check everything at once. When you're writing to a new audience or have to solve a particularly difficult problem, plan to revise the draft at least three times. The first time, look for content and clarity. Go back to the analysis questions in Chapter 1 to make sure you've fulfilled all the necessary purposes and have reader benefits for each audience. The second time, check the organization and layout. Finally, check style and tone (← Chapter 4). Use the information in Chapter 2 to check for you-attitude, positive emphasis, and bias-free language. Use the 10 techniques in Chapter 4 to make sure sentences and paragraphs are tight, smooth, and friendly. Figure 5.4 summarizes the questions you should ask.

Often you'll get the best revision by setting aside your draft, getting a blank page or screen, and redrafting. This strategy takes advantage of the thinking you did on your first draft without locking you into the sentences in it. Use WIRMI (← p. 90) to replace awkward phrasing with what you really want to say.

As you revise, be sure to read the document through from start to finish. This is particularly important if you've composed in several sittings or if you've used text from other documents. Researchers have found that such documents tend to be well organized but don't flow well.[10] You may need to add

FIGURE 5.4

✓ CHECKLIST   Thorough Revision Checklist

Content and clarity

☐ Is your view of purposes complete? Does your document meet the needs of the organization and of the reader—and make you look good?

☐ Have you given readers all the information they need to understand and act on your message?

☐ Is all the information accurate?

☐ Is each sentence clear? Is the message free from apparently contradictory statements?

☐ Is the logic clear and convincing? Are generalizations and benefits backed up with adequate supporting detail?

Organization and layout

☐ Is the pattern of organization appropriate for your purposes, audience, and situation?

☐ Are transitions between ideas smooth? Do ideas within paragraphs flow smoothly?

☐ Does the design of the document make it easy for readers to find the information they need? Is the document visually inviting?

☐ Are the points emphasized by layout ones that deserve emphasis?

☐ Are the first and last paragraphs effective?

Style and tone

☐ Is the message easy to read?

☐ Is the message friendly and free from sexist language?

☐ Does the message build goodwill?

---

transitions, cut repetitive parts, or change words to create a uniform level of formality throughout the document.

If you're really in a time bind, do a light revision, as outlined in Figure 5.5. The quality of the final document may not be as high as with a thorough revision, but even a light revision is better than skipping revision altogether.

What to Look for When You Edit

Even good writers need to edit, since no one can pay attention to surface correctness while thinking of ideas. Editing should always *follow* revision. There's no point in taking time to fix a grammatical error in a sentence that may be cut when you clarify your meaning or tighten your style. Some writers edit more accurately when they print out a copy of a document and edit the hard copy. But beware: laser printing makes a page look good but does nothing to correct errors.

FIGURE 5.5

✓ CHECKLIST   Light Revision Checklist

☐ Are the first and last paragraphs effective?

☐ Does the design of the document make it easy for readers to find the information they need?

☐ Have you told the reader what to do?

Check to be sure that the following are accurate:

- Sentence structure.
- Subject–verb and noun–pronoun agreement.
- Punctuation.
- Word usage.
- Spelling—including spelling of names.
- Numbers.

You need to know the rules of grammar and punctuation to edit. Appendix B ➡ reviews grammar and punctuation, numbers, and words that are often confused.

See the BAC Web site for links to pages on grammar, punctuation, and editing. Most writers make a small number of errors over and over. If you know that you have trouble with dangling modifiers or subject–verb agreement, for example, specifically look for them in your draft. Also look for any errors that especially bother your boss and correct them.

How to Catch Typos

Proofread every document both with a spell checker and by eye, to catch the errors a spell checker can't find.

Proofreading is hard because writers tend to see what they know should be there rather than what really is there. Since it's always easier to proof something you haven't written, you may want to swap papers with a proofing buddy. (Be sure the person looks for typos, not content.)

To proofread,

- Read once quickly for meaning, to see that nothing has been left out.
- Read a second time, slowly. When you find an error, correct it and then *reread that line*. Readers tend to become less attentive after they find one error and may miss other errors close to the one they've spotted.
- To proofread a document you know well, read the lines backward or the pages out of order.

Always triple-check numbers, headings, the first and last paragraphs, and the reader's name.

Getting and Using Feedback

Getting feedback almost always improves a document. In many organizations, it's required. All external documents must be read and approved before they go out. The process of drafting, getting feedback, revising, and getting more feedback is called **cycling.** Dianna Booher reports that documents in her clients' firms cycled an average of 4.2 times before reaching the intended audience.[11] Susan Kleimann studied a 10-page document whose 20 drafts made a total of 31 stops on the desks of nine reviewers on four different levels.[12] Being asked to revise a document is a fact of life in businesses, government agencies, and nonprofit organizations.

You can improve the quality of the feedback you get by telling people which aspects you'd especially like comments about. For example, when you give a reader the outline or planning draft,[13] you might want to know whether the general approach is appropriate. After your second draft, you might want to know whether reader benefits are well developed. When you reach the polishing draft, you'll be ready for feedback on style and grammar. Figure 5.6 lists questions to ask.

Using Spelling and Grammar Checkers

If you use a computer to prepare your documents, use a spell checker to catch typos.

But you still need to proofread by eye.

Spell checkers work by matching words: they will signal any group of letters not listed in their dictionaries. However, they cannot tell that a word is missing or that the meaning demands *of* rather than *or, not* rather than *now,* or *manager* rather than *manger.*

Check numbers and the spelling of names. In international business communication, be sure that you have the right currency symbols: £30 million may be over twice as much as $30 million.

Writers with a good command of grammar and mechanics can do a better job than the computer grammar checkers currently available. Grammar checkers can help a writer whose command of grammar and mechanics is weak. However, since grammar checkers do not catch all errors, it's worth taking the time to master grammar and mechanics so you can edit and proofread yourself.

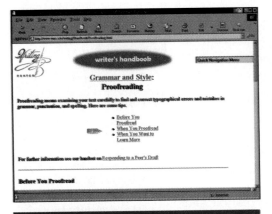

InSite

www.wisc.edu/writing/Handbook/
Proofreading.html

The University of Wisconsin Writing Center offers tips on proofreading. For more proofreading links, visit the BAC Web site.

Review and Revision*

In my most recent experience, 2½ years in a Sales and Marketing Division of a major international corporation, . . . all important writing that is generated by the corporation is reviewed at three or more levels. That means that if a middle manager sends a letter to all or some dealers, the letter will be reviewed by his or her boss (usually a vice president) and a senior vice president. If the contents are sensitive, possibly vulnerable to unfavorable media review, the letter may be reviewed by all senior vice presidents, the legal [staff], and the president/CEO.

If a senior vice president writes a letter, any letter [going] outside the company, it is reviewed by the president *and* by the management level just below him.

All letters going outside the company and written at or below the middle management level are heavily reviewed, sometimes harshly reviewed.

*Quoted from Carol Elizabeth King, Rensselaer Polytechnic Institute, Troy, NY, "Re: Reviews?" posting to bizcom@ebbs.english.vt.edu, January 27, 1998.

It's easy to feel defensive when someone criticizes your work. If the feedback stings, put it aside until you can read it without feeling defensive. Even if you think that the reader hasn't understood what you were trying to say, the fact that the reader complained usually means the section could be improved. If the reader says "This isn't true" and you know the statement is true, several kinds of revision might make the truth clear to the reader: rephrasing the statement, giving more information or examples, or documenting the source.

Reading feedback carefully is a good way to understand the culture of your organization. Are you told to give more details or to shorten messages? Does your boss add headings and bullet points? Look for patterns in the comments, and apply what you learn in your next document.

Using Boilerplate

Boilerplate is language—sentences, paragraphs, even pages—from a previous document that a writer includes in a new document. In academic papers, material written by others must be quoted and documented. However, because businesses own the documents their employees write, old text may be included without attribution.

In some cases, boilerplate may have been written years ago. For example, many legal documents, including apartment leases and sales contracts, are almost completely boilerplated. In other cases, writers may use boilerplate they wrote for earlier documents. For example, a section from a proposal describing the background of the problem could also be used in the final report after the proposed work was completed. A section from a progress report describing what the writer had done could be used with only a few changes in the methods section of the final report.

FIGURE 5.6

✓ **CHECKLIST**   Questions to Ask Readers

Outline or planning draft
☐ Does the plan seem on the right track?
☐ What topics should be added? Should any be cut?
☐ Do you have any other general suggestions?

Revising draft
☐ Does the message satisfy all its purposes?
☐ Is the message adapted to the audience(s)?
☐ Is the organization effective?
☐ What parts aren't clear?
☐ What ideas need further development?
☐ Do you have any other suggestions?

Polishing draft
☐ Are there any problems with word choice or sentence structure?
☐ Did you find any inconsistencies?
☐ Did you find any typos?
☐ Is the document's design effective?

Writers use boilerplate both to save time and energy and to use language that has already been approved by the organization's legal staff. However, as Glenn Broadhead and Richard Freed point out, using boilerplate creates two problems.[14] First, using unrevised boilerplate can create a document with incompatible styles and tones. Second, boilerplate can allow writers to ignore subtle differences in situations and audiences.

Before you incorporate old language in a new document,

- Check to see that the old section is well written.
- Consciously look for differences between the two situations, audiences, or purposes that may require different content, organization, or wording.
- Read through the whole document at a single sitting to be sure that style, tone, and level of detail are consistent in the old and new sections.

Overcoming Writer's Block

According to psychologist Robert Boice, a combination of five actions works best to overcome writer's block:[15]

1. **Participate actively in the organization and the community.** The more you talk to people, the more you interact with some of your audiences, the more you learn about the company, its culture, and its context, the easier it will be to write—and the better your writing will be.
2. **Practice writing regularly and in moderation.**
3. **Learn as many strategies as you can.** Good writers have a bag of tricks to draw on; they don't have to reinvent the wheel in each new situation. This book suggests many strategies and patterns. Try them out; memorize them; make them your own.
4. **Talk positively to yourself:** "I can do this." "If I keep working, ideas will come." "It doesn't have to be wonderful; I can always make it better later."
5. **Talk about writing to other people.** Value the feedback you get from your boss. Talk to your boss about writing. Ask him or her to share particularly good examples—from anyone in the organization. Find colleagues at your own level and talk about the writing you do. Do different bosses value different qualities? What aspects of your own boss's preferences are individual, and which are part of the discourse community of the organization? Talking to other people expands your repertoire of strategies and helps you understand the discourse community in which you write.

Technology and the Writing Process

Writers using word processing need to pay special attention to revising and proofreading their documents. Since changes are so easy to make with a word processor, some writers plan, revise, edit, and proofread less efficiently.[16] Instead of reading the whole draft through carefully, some writers skim until they reach one error. They fix it, print out the document again, but then find more errors as they read further. Even worse, because documents produced on a good printer look so neat, some writers don't revise or proofread at all. But keying in a document is no more accurate than typing on a traditional typewriter. Editing and proofreading are still necessary.

The widespread use of word processors is raising readers' expectations. Readers are more likely to ask for a revision; they care more about the physical appearance of documents. Because word processing makes it easy to correct typos, change spacing and margins, and insert graphics, readers are less tolerant of badly designed documents and of documents with obvious corrections.

Improving the Corporate Writing Process*

A fertilizer company sued several of its competitors, charging that they mislabeled their bags of composted manure. One of the defendants countersued, charging that the original company also mislabeled its bags. All the company's bags contained the same product (compost made of 7% sheep manure, 33% pig manure, and 60% cow manure), but some were called "sheep manure" while others were called "cow manure."

This inconsistency arose from a compartmentalized, linear composing process. Operations filled the bags; marketing wrote the labels. No one noticed that the labels didn't match the contents.

The case was settled out of court after much time and expense. The companies may have lost goodwill by appearing to mislead consumers. By bringing everyone together during the process of writing the labels, these companies could have saved time and money—and written better labels in the first place.

*Based on James E. Porter, "Ideology and Collaboration in the Classroom and in the Corporation," *The Bulletin of the Association for Business Communication* 53, no. 2 (1990): 21.

Reading Between the Corporate Lines*

In 2001, *The Wall Street Journal* printed excerpts from rough drafts of an Ameritrade news release. The accompanying story pointed out important changes: reducing losses for the quarter by rounding off the number and removing the hiring of a new CEO from the list of "right decisions" the company made that quarter.

How did journalists know what revisions had been made? They used "Track Changes" in Microsoft Word. (Pull down the "Tools" menu and click on "Track Changes" and then on "Highlight Changes.")

The Wall Street Journal reports that some analysts and traders routinely check electronic documents to see what changes have been made.

If you use Microsoft Word and post electronic documents but don't want to share your revising and editing with the world, you have two options. One is not to use "Track Changes" in the first place. The other option (and the one to use if your company automatically turns the feature on) is to return to the "Tools" menu and, under "Track Changes," go to "Accept or Reject Changes." Once you've accepted or rejected the changes, all of your revisions and edits are erased, and no one can find them again.

Based on Susanne Craig, "How to Read Between the Corporate Lines," *The Wall Street Journal*, May 13, 2001, C1, C16.

Summary of Key Points

- Processes that help writers write well include not expecting the first draft to be perfect, writing regularly, modifying the initial task if it's too hard or too easy, having clear goals, knowing many different strategies, using rules as guidelines rather than as absolutes, and waiting to edit until after the draft is complete.

- Writing processes can include eight activities: planning, gathering, writing, evaluating, getting feedback, revising, editing, and proofreading. **Revising** means changing the document to make it better satisfy the writer's purposes and the audience. **Editing** means making surface-level changes that make the document grammatically correct. **Proofreading** means checking to be sure the document is free from typographical errors. The activities do not have to come in any set order. It is not necessary to finish one activity to start another. Most writers use all eight activities only when they write a document whose genre, subject matter, or audience is new to them.

- To think of ideas, try **brainstorming, freewriting** (writing without stopping for 10 minutes or so), and **clustering** (brainstorming with circled words on a page).

- You can improve the quality of the feedback you get by telling people which aspects of a draft you'd like comments about. If a reader criticizes something, fix the problem. If you think the reader misunderstood you, try to figure out what caused the misunderstanding and revise the draft so that the reader can see what you meant.

- If the writing situation is new or difficult, plan to revise the draft at least three times. The first time, look for content and clarity. The second time, check the organization and layout. Finally, check style and tone.

- **Boilerplate** is language from a previous document that a writer includes in a new document. Using unrevised boilerplate can create a document with incompatible styles and tones and can encourage writers to see as identical situations and audiences that have subtle differences.

- To overcome writer's block,
  1. Participate actively in the organization and the community.
  2. Practice writing regularly and in moderation.
  3. Learn as many strategies as you can.
  4. Talk positively to yourself.
  5. Talk about writing to other people.

CHAPTER 5   Exercises and Problems

Getting Started

5.1   Interviewing Writers about Their Composing Processes

Interview someone about the composing process(es) he or she uses for on-the-job writing. Questions you could ask include the following:

- What kind of planning do you do before you write? Do you make lists? formal or informal outlines?

- When you need more information, where do you get it?
- How do you compose your drafts? Do you dictate? Draft with pen and paper? Compose on screen? How do you find uninterrupted time to compose?
- When you want advice about style, grammar, and spelling, what source(s) do you consult?
- Does your superior ever read your drafts and make suggestions?
- Do you ever work with other writers to produce a single document? Describe the process you use.
- Describe the process of creating a document where you felt the final document reflected your best work.

Describe the process of creating a document you found difficult or frustrating. What sorts of things make writing easier or harder for you?

As Your Instructor Directs,

a. Share your results orally with a small group of students.

b. Present your results in an oral presentation to the class.

c. Present your results in a memo to your instructor.

d. Share your results with a small group of students and write a joint memo reporting the similarities and differences you found.

5.2   Analyzing Your Own Writing Processes

Save your notes and drafts from several assignments so that you can answer the following questions:

- Which practices of good writers do you follow?
- Which of the eight activities discussed in Chapter 5 do you use?
- How much time do you spend on each of the eight activities?
- What kinds of revisions do you make most often?
- Do you use different processes for different documents, or do you have one process that you use most of the time?
- What parts of your process seem most successful? Are there any places in the process that could be improved? How?

- What relation do you see between the process(es) you use and the quality of the final document?

As Your Instructor Directs,

a. Discuss your process with a small group of other students.

b. Write a memo to your instructor analyzing in detail your process for composing one of the papers for this class.

c. Write a memo to your instructor analyzing your process during the term. What parts of your process(es) have stayed the same throughout the term? What parts have changed?

5.3   Checking Spelling and Grammar Checkers

Each of the following paragraphs contains errors in grammar, spelling, and punctuation. Which errors does your spelling or grammar checker catch? Which errors does it miss? Does it flag as errors any words that are correct?

a. Answer to an Inquiry
   Enclosed are the tow copies you requested of our pamphlet, "Using the Internet to market Your products. The pamphelt walks you through the steps of planning the Home Page (The first page of the web cite, shows examples of other Web pages we have designed, and provide a questionaire that you can use to analyze audience the audience and purposes.

b. Performance Appraisal
   Most staff accountants complete three audits a month. Ellen has completed 21 audits in this past six months she is our most productive staff accountant. Her technical skills our very good however some clients feel that she could be more tactful in suggesting ways that the clients accounting practices courld be improved.

c. Brochure
   Are you finding that being your own boss crates it's own problems? Take the hassle out of working at home with a VoiceMail Answering System. Its almost as good as having your own secratery.

d. Presentation Slides
   How to Create a Web résumé
   - Omit home adress and phone number
   - Use other links only if they help an employer evalaute you.
     ☐ Be Professional.
     ☐ Carefully craft and proof read the phrase on the index apage.

   How to Create a Scannable Résumé
   - Create a "plain vanilla" document.
   - Use include a "Keywords" section. Include personality trait sas well as accomplishments.
   - Be specific and quantifyable.

6

Designing Documents, Slides, and Screens

Designing Documents, Slides, and Screens

Susan Kleimann
President, Kleimann Communication Group, LLC

Susan Kleimann, PhD, works with companies and government to improve their communication process and products, including designing and testing documents that work for their customers. She formerly directed the Document Design Center at the American Institutes for Research in Washington, DC. Kleimann Communication Group, LLC, is a woman-owned small business helping companies understand that clear writing is clear thinking.

www.kleimann.com

Good document design focuses on the reader. Imagine a particular reader trying to do something with your document.

Think about a credit card statement. Its purpose is partly to let you know what you owe, the due date, how much credit you have left. But the most basic purpose is to get you to pay your debt. The "what you owe" line is almost always surrounded by white space and set off so that you can easily find it. Document design is not about decoration but rather about guiding the reader through a task.

To test a document, ask people to do something with it, such as fill out a form. Ask them how well it worked; they'll tell you what they understand and what they don't. Observe them; they'll show you when the instructions are unclear or when they can't find the right information. The first kind is cognitive testing, which tells you what readers understand. The second is usability testing, which tells you what readers can do. Both let you know what works.

Good document design is good business. Good design saves money by preventing errors and reducing the number of phone calls from customers who don't understand what they're supposed to do. Employees can be freed up to do other work—including providing better customer service. Good design can ensure that important messages get heard. (See the stories in this chapter.) Good design shows customers that you care about their time and want to make tasks easier for them. Isn't that the best marketing a company can have?

Standards continue to evolve for online documents. The Nielsen Norman Group, founded by two pioneers of usability (Donald Norman and Jakob Nielsen), offers advice on what works and what online documents should be able to achieve. You can find their Web site at www.useit.com. Look at www.webpagesthatsuck.com for great examples of what doesn't work and a somewhat irreverent approach.

In an age when we all deal with too much information, people have a right to spend as little time as possible with a document or screen and still get the right result. That's what document design is about.

> "*Document design is not about decoration but rather about guiding the reader through a task.*"

Good Document Design Saves Money, I*

- Clearer forms and computer-screen prompts enable Motorola's Corporate Finance department to close its books in 4 days, down from 12. The savings: $20 million a year.

- After rewriting its rules for citizen band radios, the Federal Communications Commission was able to transfer to other jobs five employees who spent all day answering telephone questions about the rules.

- Revised forms cut training time for Citibank employees in half—while improving the accuracy of the information that employees give to customers.

- Simplifying its billing statement reduced customer inquiries at Southern Gas Company and is saving the company an estimated $252,000 a year.

*Based on Karen A. Schriver, "Quality in Document Design: Issues and Controversy," *Technical Communication* 40, no. 2 (1993): 250–51.

Good document design saves time and money, reduces legal problems, and builds goodwill. A well-designed document looks inviting, friendly, and easy to read. Effective design also groups ideas visually, making the structure of the document more obvious so the document is easier to read. Research shows that easy-to-read documents also enhance your credibility and build an image of you as a professional, competent person.[1] Good design is important not only for reports, Web pages, and newsletters but also for announcements and one-page letters and memos.

The Importance of Effective Design

When document design is poor, both organizations and society suffer.

The nuclear accident at Three Mile Island could have been prevented if safety guidelines recommended 17 months before the accident had been implemented.[2] But none of the 12 people who received the memo responded. The memo was ignored because the subject line was vague, the writing was ineffective, and the recommendations were on the second page. The *Challenger* space shuttle blew up because its O-rings failed in the excessive cold. Poor communication—including charts that hid, rather than emphasized, the data—contributed to the decision to launch. In 2000, the badly designed "butterfly ballot" confused enough voters to change the outcome of the US presidential election.[3] For links to the *Challenger* charts and the butterfly ballot, see the BAC Web site.

Design as Part of Your Writing Process(es)

Design isn't something to "tack on" when you've finished writing. Indeed, the best documents, slides, and screens are created when you think about design at each stage of your writing process(es).

- As you plan, think about your audience. Are they skilled readers? Are they busy? Will they read the document straight through or skip around in it?
- As you write, incorporate lists and headings. Use visuals to convey numerical data clearly and forcefully (➡ Chapter 15).
- Get feedback from people who will be using your document. What parts of the document do they think are hard to understand? Do they need additional information?
- As you revise, check your draft against the guidelines in this chapter.

Guidelines for Page Design

Use the eight guidelines in Figure 6.1 to create visually attractive documents.

1. Use White Space.

White space—the empty space on the page—makes material easier to read by emphasizing the material that it separates from the rest of the text. To create white space,

- Use headings.
- Use a mix of paragraph lengths (most no longer than seven typed lines). It's OK for a paragraph to be just one sentence. First and last paragraphs, in particular, should be short.
- Use lists.
    - Use tabs or indents—not spacing—to align items vertically.
    - Use numbered lists when the number or sequence of items is exact.

FIGURE 6.1   Guidelines for Page Design

1. Use white space to separate and emphasize points.
2. Use headings to group points and lead the reader through the document.
3. Limit the use of words set in all capital letters.
4. Use no more than two fonts in a single document.
5. Decide whether to justify margins based on the situation and the audience.
6. Put important elements in the top left and lower right quadrants of the page.
7. Use a grid of imaginary columns to unify visuals and other elements in a document.
8. Use highlighting, decorative devices, and color in moderation.

Good Document Design Saves Money, II*

- Rewriting its policy and procedure manuals saved FedEx $400,000 in the first year in increased productivity. More searches for information were successful, and more of them could be completed in less than three minutes.

- A Sabre computer reservation manual was cut from 100 pages to 20, saving $19,000 just in producing the document.

- Improving its documentation for its products saved Fisher Controls more than $100,000 and enabled the company to ship a major new product three months early.

*Based on Jay Mead, "Measuring the Value Added for Technical Documentation: A Review of Research and Practice," *Technical Communication* 45, no. 3 (August 1998): 353–79.

- Use **bullets** (large dots or squares like those in this list) when the number and sequence don't matter.

When you use a list, make sure that all of the items in it are parallel (◄ p. 101) and fit into the structure of the sentence that introduces the list.

Faulty: The following suggestions can help employers avoid bias in job interviews:
1. Base **questions on the job description.**
2. Questioning **techniques.**
3. Selection and training **of interviewers.**

Parallel: The following suggestions can help employers avoid bias in job interviews:
1. Base **questions on the job description.**
2. Ask **the same questions of all applicants.**
3. Select and train **interviewers carefully.**

Also parallel: Employers can avoid bias in job interviews by
1. Basing **questions on the job description.**
2. Asking **the same questions of all applicants.**
3. Selecting and training **interviewers carefully.**

Figure 6.2 shows an original typed document. In Figure 6.3, the same document has been improved by using shorter paragraphs, lists, and headings. These devices take space. When saving space is essential, it's better to cut the text and keep white space and headings. To see how to set up subheadings, see Figure 14.6 in Chapter 14.

2. Use Headings.

As George Miller has shown, our short-term memories can hold only seven plus or minus two bits of information.[4] Only after those bits are processed and put into long-term memory can we assimilate new information. Large amounts of information will be easier to process if they are grouped into three to seven chunks rather than presented as individual items.

Headings are words, short phrases, or short sentences that group points and divide your document into sections. Headings enable your reader to see at a glance how the document is organized, to turn quickly to sections of special interest, and to compare and contrast points more easily. Headings also break up the page, making it look less formidable and more interesting.

- Make headings specific.
- Make each heading cover all the material until the next heading.
- Keep headings at any one level parallel: all nouns, all complete sentences, or all questions.

How Big Is Your Short-Term Memory?

One way to test the capacity of your short-term memory is to think about phone numbers. Telephone numbers in the United States are seven digits. If you sometimes forget a phone number while you are dialing it and have to look back at the listing in order to finish dialing, your short-term memory holds only five or six bits of information. If you never have to look back at the book, your memory holds at least seven bits of information.

FIGURE 6.2 A Document with Poor Visual Impact

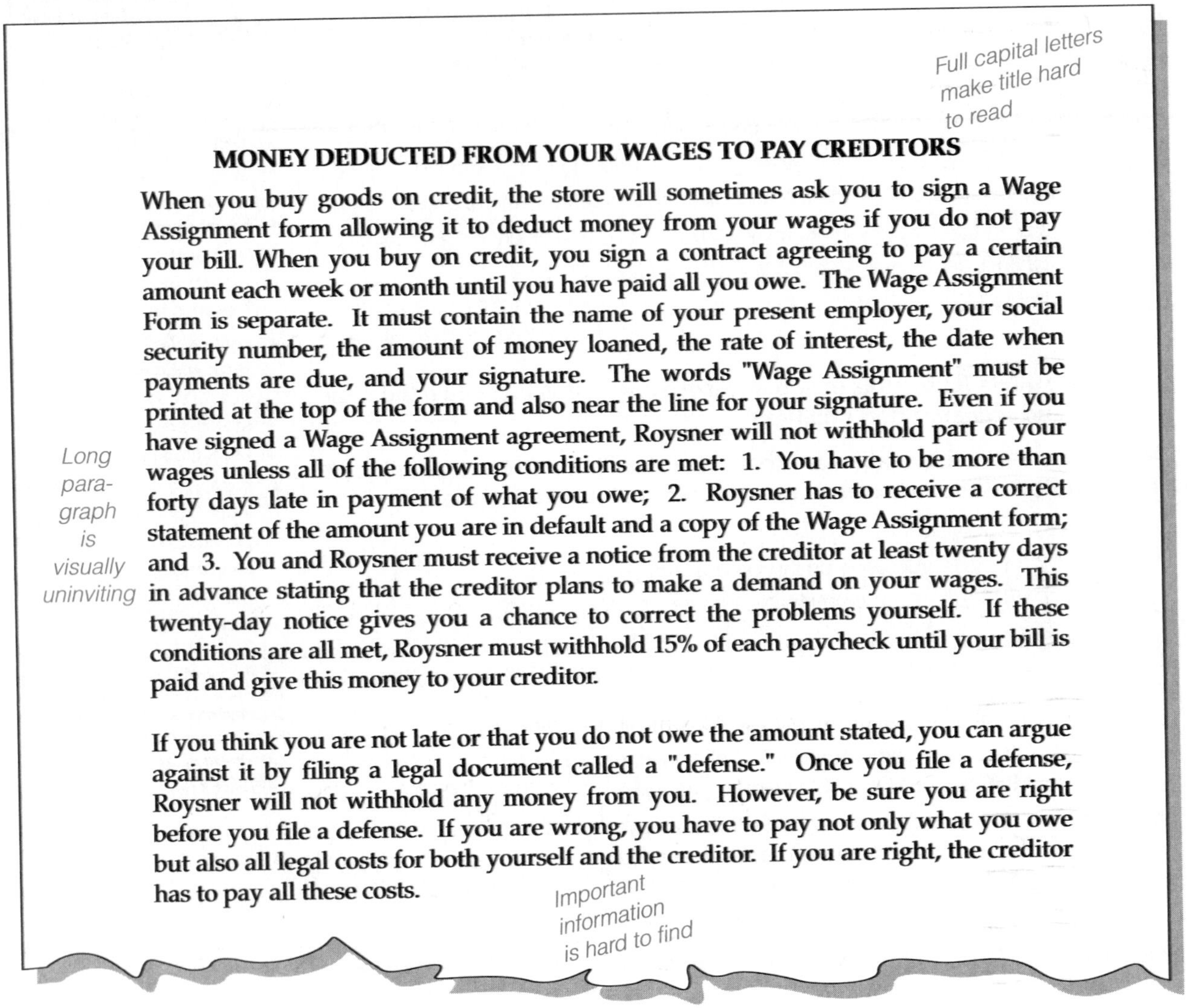

Full capital letters make title hard to read

MONEY DEDUCTED FROM YOUR WAGES TO PAY CREDITORS

When you buy goods on credit, the store will sometimes ask you to sign a Wage Assignment form allowing it to deduct money from your wages if you do not pay your bill. When you buy on credit, you sign a contract agreeing to pay a certain amount each week or month until you have paid all you owe. The Wage Assignment Form is separate. It must contain the name of your present employer, your social security number, the amount of money loaned, the rate of interest, the date when payments are due, and your signature. The words "Wage Assignment" must be printed at the top of the form and also near the line for your signature. Even if you have signed a Wage Assignment agreement, Roysner will not withhold part of your wages unless all of the following conditions are met: 1. You have to be more than forty days late in payment of what you owe; 2. Roysner has to receive a correct statement of the amount you are in default and a copy of the Wage Assignment form; and 3. You and Roysner must receive a notice from the creditor at least twenty days in advance stating that the creditor plans to make a demand on your wages. This twenty-day notice gives you a chance to correct the problems yourself. If these conditions are all met, Roysner must withhold 15% of each paycheck until your bill is paid and give this money to your creditor.

Long paragraph is visually uninviting

If you think you are not late or that you do not owe the amount stated, you can argue against it by filing a legal document called a "defense." Once you file a defense, Roysner will not withhold any money from you. However, be sure you are right before you file a defense. If you are wrong, you have to pay not only what you owe but also all legal costs for both yourself and the creditor. If you are right, the creditor has to pay all these costs.

Important information is hard to find

In a letter or memo, type main headings even with the left-hand margin in bold. Capitalize the first letters of the first word and of other major words; use lowercase for all other letters. (See Figure 6.3 for an example.) In single-spaced text, triple-space between the previous text and the heading; double-space between the heading and the text that follows.

If you need subdivisions within a head, use bold type and put a period after the subhead. Begin the paragraph on the same line. Use subheadings only when you have at least two subdivisions under a given main heading.

In a report, you may need more than two levels of headings. Figure 14.6 in Chapter 14 shows levels of headings for reports.

3. Limit the Use of Words Set in All Capital Letters.

We recognize words by their shapes.[5] (See Figure 6.4.) In capitals, all words are rectangular; letters lose the descenders and ascenders that make reading go 19% more quickly.[6] Use full capitals sparingly.

FIGURE 6.3   A Document Revised to Improve Visual Impact

Money Deducted from Your Wages to Pay Creditors

First letter of each main word capitalized— Title split onto two lines

When you buy goods on credit, the store will sometimes ask you to sign a Wage Assignment form allowing it to deduct money from your wages if you do not pay your bill.

Have You Signed a Wage Assignment Form?

Headings divide document into chunks

When you buy on credit, you sign a contract agreeing to pay a certain amount each week or month until you have paid all you owe. The Wage Assignment Form is separate. It must contain

- The name of your present employer,
- Your social security number,
- The amount of money loaned,
- The rate of interest,
- The date when payments are due, and
- Your signature.

List with bullets where order of items doesn't matter

Single-space list when items are short.

The words "Wage Assignment" must be printed at the top of the form and also near the line for your signature.

When Would Money Be Deducted from Your Wages to Pay a Creditor?

Headings must be parallel.

Here all are questions

Even if you have signed a Wage Assignment agreement, Roysner will not withhold part of your wages unless all of the following conditions are met:

White space between items emphasizes them

1. You have to be more than 40 days late in payment of what you owe;

2. Roysner has to receive a correct statement of the amount you are in default and a copy of the Wage Assignment form; and

Double-space between items in list when most items are two lines or longer.

Numbered list where number, order of items matter

3. You and Roysner must receive a notice from the creditor at least 20 days in advance stating that the creditor plans to make a demand on your wages. This 20-day notice gives you a chance to correct the problem yourself.

If these conditions are all met, Roysner must withhold fifteen percent (15%) of each paycheck until your bill is paid and give this money to your creditor.

What Should You Do If You Think the Wage Assignment Is Incorrect?

If you think you are not late or that you do not owe the amount stated, you can argue against it by filing a legal document called a "defense." Once you file a defense, Roysner will not withhold any money from you. However, be sure you are right before you file a defense. If you are wrong, you have to pay not only what you owe but also all legal costs for both yourself and the creditor. If you are right, the creditor has to pay all these costs.

Good Document Design Saves Money, III*

■ The British government began reviewing its forms in 1982. Since then, it has eliminated 27,000 forms, redesigned 41,000, and saved over $28 million.

■ Revising the British lost-baggage form for airline passengers cut a 55% error rate to 3%.

■ In Australia, rewriting one legal document saved the Victorian government the equivalent of $400,000 a year in staff salaries.

■ In the Netherlands, revising the form for educational grants reduced by two-thirds the number of forms applicants filled out incompletely or incorrectly. The government saved time and money; the applicants got decisions more quickly.

*Based on Karen A. Schriver, "Quality in Document Design: Issues and Controversy," *Technical Communication* 40, no. 2 (1993): 250–51.

4. Use No More Than Two Fonts in a Single Document.

Fonts are unified styles of type. Each font comes in several sizes and usually in several styles (bold, italic, etc.). Typewriter fonts are **fixed;** that is, every letter takes the same space. An *i* takes the same space as a *w*. Courier and Prestige Elite are fixed fonts. Computers usually offer **proportional** fonts as well, where wider letters take more space than narrower letters. Times Roman, Palatino, Helvetica, and Arial are proportional fonts.

Serif fonts have little extensions, called serifs, from the main strokes. (In Figure 6.5, look at the feet on the *r*'s in New Courier and the flick on the top of the *d* in Lucinda.) New Courier, Elite, Times Roman, Palatino, and Lucinda Calligraphy are serif fonts. Serif fonts are easier to read since the serifs help the eyes move from letter to letter. Helvetica, Arial, Geneva, and Technical are **sans serif** fonts since they lack serifs (*sans* is French for *without*). Sans serif fonts are good for titles and tables.

Most business documents use just one font—usually Times Roman, Palatino, Helvetica, or Arial. You can create emphasis and levels of headings by using bold, italics, and different sizes. Bold is easier to read than italics, so use bolding if you only need one method to emphasize text. In a complex document, use bigger type for main headings and slightly smaller type for subheadings and text. If you combine two fonts in one document, choose one serif and one sans serif typeface.

Eleven-point Times Roman is ideal for letters, memos, and reports. Twelve-point type is acceptable, especially for readers older than 40. Use 9- or 10-point type to get the effect of a printed book or brochure.

If your material will not fit in the available pages, cut one more time. Putting some sections in tiny type will save space but creates a negative response—a negative response that may extend to the organization that produced the document.

FIGURE 6.4   Full Capitals Hide the Shape of a Word

[Full] [capitals] [hide] [the] [shape] [of] [a] [word] [and] [slow] [reading] [19%].

[FULL] [CAPITALS] [HIDE] [THE] [SHAPE] [OF] [A] [WORD] [AND] [SLOW] [READING] [19%].

FIGURE 6.5   Examples of Different Fonts

This sentence is set in 12-point Times Roman.

This sentence is set in 12-point Arial.

This sentence is set in 12-point New Courier.

This sentence is set in 12-point Lucinda Calligraphy.

This sentence is set in 12-point Broadway.

This sentence is set in 12-point Technical.

5. Decide Whether to Justify Margins Based on the Situation and the Audience.

Computers often allow you to use **full justification** so that type on both sides of the page is evenly lined up. This paragraph justifies margins. Margins justified only on the left are sometimes called **ragged right margins.** Lines end in different places because words are of different lengths. The Sidebar columns in this book use ragged right margins.

Use full justification when you

■ Can use proportional fonts.

■ Want a more formal look.

■ Want to use as few pages as possible.

■ Write to skilled readers.[7]

Use ragged right margins when you

■ Cannot use a proportional font.

■ Want an informal look.

■ Want to be able to revise an individual page without reprinting the whole document.

■ Use very short line lengths.

■ Write to poor readers.

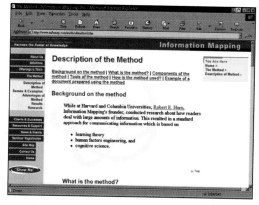

InSite

www.infomap.com/method/method.htm

Information Mapping uses grids and tables to present complex information in an easy-to-find format.

6. Put Important Elements in the Top Left and Lower Right Quadrants.

Readers of English start in the upper left-hand corner of the page and read to the right and down. The eye moves in a Z pattern.[8] (See Figure 6.6.) Therefore, as Philip M. Rubens notes, the four quadrants of the page carry different visual weights. The top left quadrant, where the eye starts, is the most important; the bottom right quadrant, where the eye ends, is next most important.[9] Titles

FIGURE 6.6 Put Important Elements in the Top Left and Bottom Right Quadrants

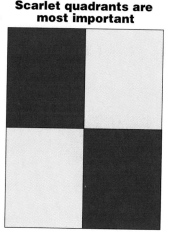

Eye movement on the page

Start

Stop

Scarlet quadrants are most important

Source: Based on Russel N. Baird, Arthur T. Turnbull, and Duncan McDonald, *The Graphics of Communication: Typography, Layout, Design, Production,* 5th ed. (New York: Holt, Rinehart, and Winston, 1987), 37.

Cultural Differences in Document Design*

Cultural differences in document design are based on reading practices and experiences with other documents. For example, one laundry detergent company printed ads in the Middle East showing soiled clothes on the left, its box of soap in the middle, and clean clothes on the right. But, because people in that part of the world read not from left to right but from right to left, many people thought the ads meant that the soap actually soiled the clothes.

People in the United States focus first on the left side of a Web site. However, Middle Eastern people focus first on the right side. Web sites in Arabic and Hebrew orient text, links, and graphics from right to left.

*Based on David A. Ricks, *Blunders in International Business* (Cambridge, MA: Blackwell, 1993), 53; and Albert N. Badre, "The Effects of Cross Cultural Interface Design Orientation on World Wide Web User Performance," GVU Technical Report GIT-GVU-01-03, August 31, 2000, 8, www.cc.gatech.edu/gvu/reports/2001, visited September 1, 2001.

should always start in the top left; reply coupons or another important element should be in the bottom right.

7. Use a Grid to Unify Graphic Elements.

For years, graphic designers have used a **grid system** to design pages. In its simplest form, a grid imposes two or three imaginary columns on the page. In more complex grids, these columns can be further subdivided. Then all the graphic elements—text indentations, headings, visuals, and so on—are lined up within the columns. The resulting symmetry creates a more pleasing page[10] and unifies long documents.

Figure 6.7 uses grids to organize a page with visuals and a résumé.

8. Use Highlighting, Decorative Devices, and Color in Moderation.

Many word-processing programs have arrows, pointing fingers, and a host of other **dingbats** that you can insert. Clip art packages and presentation software allow you to insert more and larger images into your text. The Document Design Center used icons as well as better page design when it revised Ford's warranty booklet. (See Figure 6.8.) Used in moderation, highlighting and decorative devices make pages more interesting. However, don't overdo them. A page or screen that uses every possible highlighting device just looks busy and hard to read.

Color works well to highlight points. Use color for overviews and main headings, not for small points. Blue, green, or violet type is most legible for younger readers, but perception of blue diminishes for readers over 50.[11] Red is appropriate for warnings in North America. Since the connotations of colors vary among cultures, check Chapter 11 before you use color with international or multicultural audiences.

When you use color,

- Use glossy paper to make colors more vivid.
- Be aware that colors on a computer screen always look brighter than the same colors on paper because the screen sends out light.

FIGURE 6.7   Examples of Grids to Design Pages

A page with visuals

Three-column grid.

A newsletter page

Six-column grid.

A résumé page

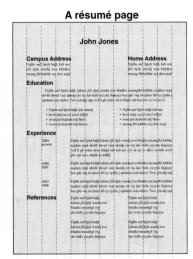

Twelve-column grid.

FIGURE 6.8   "Before" and "After" Pages from Ford's Warranty Booklet

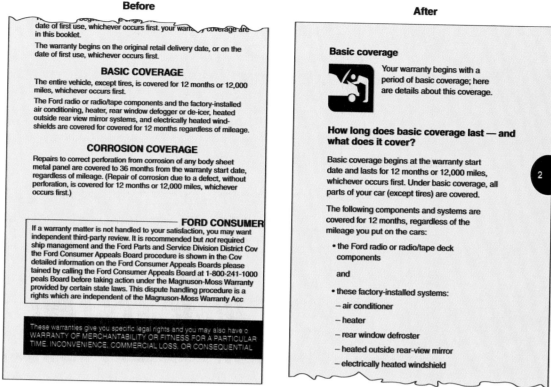

Source: Lee L. Gray, "Ford Offers a Readable Warranty Booklet," *Simply Stated . . . in Business,* no. 18 (March 1987): 12.

Designing Brochures

To design brochures and newsletters, first think about audience and purpose. An "image" brochure designed to promote awareness of your company will have a different look than an "information" brochure telling people how to do something and persuading them to do it.

Use this process to create effective brochures.

1. Determine your objective(s).
2. Identify your target audience(s).
3. Identify a **central selling point**: one overarching reader benefit the audience will get.
4. Choose the image you want to project. (Clean and clear? Postmodern and hip? Or what?)
5. Identify objections and brainstorm ways to deal with them (➡ Chapter 9).
6. When text is important, draft text to see how much room you need. Do tighten your writing (⬅ Chapter 4). But when you really need more room, use a bigger brochure layout or a series of brochures.
7. Experiment with different sizes of paper and layout. Consider how reader will get the brochure—must it fit in a standard rack? Use thumbnail sketches to test layouts.
8. Make every choice—color, font, layout, paper—a conscious one. The three-fold brochure shown in Figure 6.9 is the most common, but many other arrangements are possible. See the BAC Web site for other ways to fold brochures.
9. Polish the prose and graphics. Use you-attitude and positive emphasis.

FIGURE 6.9   Three-fold Brochure on 8½-by-11-inch Paper

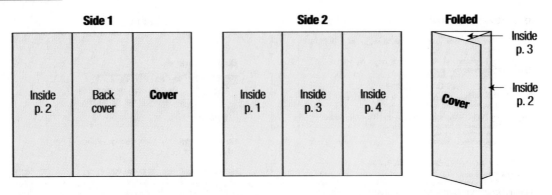

PaperDirect provides special stationery to use with your laser printer or photocopier to produce brochures.

Follow these design principles:

- Use the cover effectively.
    - Put your central selling point on the cover.
    - Use a photo that tells a story. Remember that the photo has to work for the audience. A photo of a campus landmark may not mean much to an audience thinking about attending a summer program on campus.
- Use a grid to align the elements within the panels. Make sure that the Z pattern emphasizes important points for each spread the reader sees. In a three-fold brochure, the Z pattern needs to work for the cover alone, for inside pages 1 and 2 (as the reader begins to unfold the brochure), and for inside pages 1, 3, and 4 (when the brochure is fully opened).
- Effective brochures not only repeat graphic elements (headings, small photos) across panels to create a unified look but also contain contrast (between text and images, between a larger font for headings and a smaller one for text).
- Use color effectively.
    - Restraint usually works best for informative brochures. To get the effect of color with the least expense, use black print on colored paper.
    - If you use four-color printing, use glossy paper.
    - Readers over 50 may have trouble reading text in some shades of blue.
- Make the text visually appealing.
    - Use no more than two fonts—just one may be better.
    - Use proportional fonts.
    - Avoid italic type and underlining, which make text hard to read. To emphasize text, use bold (sparingly).

- Most brochures use 8-, 9-, or 10-point type. Use 10-point rather than 8-point for readers over 40.
- Use small tab indents.
- Make sure that you have enough white space in your copy. Use lists and headings. Use short paragraphs with extra space between paragraphs.
- Ragged right margins generally work better with short line lengths.

- If you use a reply coupon, make sure its back side doesn't have crucial information the reader needs to keep.

To make the brochure worth keeping, provide useful information. Make the text candid, believable, and human.

For more information about designing brochures, see the BAC Web page.

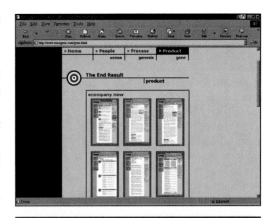

InSite

www.xenogene.com

Xenogene, a Web design company, outlines the process of Web design/redesign. Thumbnails show sample end products.

Designing Presentation Slides

As you design slides for PowerPoint and other presentation programs, keep the following guidelines in mind:

- Use a big font: 44- or 50-point for titles, 32-point for subheads, and 28-point for examples.
- Use bullet-point phrases rather than complete sentences.
- Use clear, concise language.
- Make only three to five points on each slide. If you have more, consider using two slides.
- Customize your slides with the company logo, charts, downloaded Web pages, and scanned-in photos and drawings.

Use clip art only if the art is really appropriate to your points and only if you are able to find nonsexist and nonracist images. (In 1997, Marilyn Dyrud has shown, the major clip art packages were biased.)[12]

Choose a consistent template, or background design, for the entire presentation. Make sure that the template is appropriate for your subject matter. For example, use a globe only if your topic is international business and palm trees only if you're talking about tropical vacations. One problem with PowerPoint is that the basic templates may seem repetitive to people who see lots of presentations made with the program. For a very important presentation, you may want to consider customizing the basic template.

Choose a light background if the lights will be off during the presentation and a dark background if the lights will be on. Slides will be easier to read if you use high contrast between the words and backgrounds. See Figure 6.10 for examples of effective and ineffective color combinations.

Designing Web Pages

Good Web pages have both good content and an interesting design.

Your opening screen is crucial. Jakob Nielsen claims that only 10% of users scroll beyond the first screen.[13] To make it more likely that visitors to your page will scroll down, on the first screen

- Provide an introductory statement or graphic orienting the surfing reader to the organization sponsoring the page.
- Offer an overview of the content of your page, with links to take readers to the parts that interest them.

Making Your Web Page Accessible

Users with hearing impairments need captions for audio material on the Web.

Blind users need words, not images. Words can be voiced by a screen reader or translated into Braille text. US screen reader programs go from left to right, then down line by line. Keystrokes can let users skip to a specific letter in a list. To make your Web page accessible for people with vision impairments,

- Put a link to a text-only version of the site in the upper-left-hand corner.
- Put navigation links, a site map, and search box at the top of the screen, preferably in the upper-left-hand corner.
- Arrange navigation links alphabetically so that blind users can jump to the links they want.
- Provide alternative text (an "Alt tag") for all images, applets, and submit buttons.
- Provide a static alternative to flash or animation.

For links to more information about Web accessibility, see the BAC Web site.

FIGURE 6.10   Effective and Ineffective Colors for Presentation Slides

Effective

Ineffective

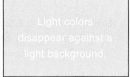

- Put information that will be most interesting and useful to most readers on the first screen.

  Make it clear what readers will get if they click on a link.

  Ineffective phrasing: Employment. Openings and skill levels are determined by each office.

  Better phrasing: Employment. Openings listed by skill level and by location.

As you design pages,

- Keep graphics small. Specify the width and height so that the text can load while the graphics are still coming in. Keep animation to a minimum.
- Provide visual variety. Use indentations, bulleted or numbered lists, and headings.
- Unify multiple pages with a small banner, graphic, or label so surfers know who sponsors each page.
- On each page, provide a link to the home page, the name and e-mail address of the person who maintains the page, and the date when the page was last revised.

  Appropriately enough, the Web has many Web pages on Web page design, as well as technical pages on HTML and Java. For links to some of the most useful pages, see the BAC Web site.

Testing the Design for Usability

A design that looks pretty may or may not work for the audience. To know whether your design is functional, test it with your audience.

For links to Web pages about testing documents for usability, see the BAC Web site.

Testing a draft with five users will reveal 85% of the problems with the document.[14] If time and money permit additional testing, revise the document and test the new version with another five users. Test the document with the people who are most likely to have trouble with it: very old or young readers, people with little education, people who read English as a second language.

Three kinds of tests yield useful information:

- Watch someone as he or she uses the document to do a task. Where does the reader pause, re-read, or seem confused? How long does it take? Does the document enable the reader to complete the task accurately?

- Ask the reader to "think aloud" while completing the task, interrupt the reader at key points to ask what he or she is thinking, or ask the reader to describe the thought process after completing the document and the task. Learning the reader's thought processes is important, since a reader may get the right answer for the wrong reasons. In such a case, the design still needs work.

- Ask readers to put a plus sign (+) in the margins by any part of the document they like or agree with, and a minus sign (−) by any part of the document that seems confusing or wrong. Then use interviews or focus groups to find out the reasons for the plus and minus judgments.

Summary of Key Points

- An attractive document looks inviting, friendly, and easy to read. The visual grouping of ideas also makes the structure of the document more obvious so it is easier to read.

- Good document design can save time and money, and can prevent legal problems.

- The best documents are created when you think about design at each stage of the writing process.
  - As you plan, think about the needs of your audience.
  - As you write, incorporate lists, headings, and visuals.
  - Get feedback from people who will be using your document.
  - As you revise, check your draft against the guidelines in this chapter.

- Eight guidelines help writers create visually attractive documents:
  1. Use white space.
  2. Use headings.
  3. Limit the use of words set in all capital letters.
  4. Use no more than two fonts in a single document.
  5. Decide whether to justify margins based on the situation and the audience.
  6. Put important elements in the top left and lower right quadrants.
  7. Use a grid to unify visuals and other graphic elements.
  8. Use highlighting, decorative devices, and color in moderation.

- To design brochures, first think about audience and purpose. Use a consistent design for a series of brochures or for issues of a newsletter.

- As you design slides for PowerPoint and other presentation programs,
  - Use a big font.
  - Use bullet-point phrases.
  - Make only three to five points on each slide.
  - Customize your slides.

- Good Web pages have both good content and an interesting design.
  - Orient the surfing reader to the organization sponsoring the page.
  - Offer an overview of the content of your page, with links to take readers to the parts that interest them.
  - Make it clear what readers will get if they click on a link.
  - Keep graphics small.
  - Provide visual variety.

- To test a document, observe readers, ask them to "think aloud" while completing the task, interrupt them at key points to ask what they are thinking, or ask them to describe the thought process after completing the document and the task.

Designing Documents for Mutual Funds*

Putnam Investments manages over $150 billion in mutual fund and retirement assets. Says its CEO, Lawrence Lasser, "Visually, we started with two objectives: First, we wanted to differentiate ourselves. . . . We wanted to break through the clutter . . . to get both the intermediary's and the investor's attention.

"Our second objective was to simplify. We wanted to simplify the language by getting rid of jargon, and make our literature visually inviting and user-friendly. In this industry, companies typically jam as much as they can into every piece, thinking more is better. We took the opposite approach, saying let's give people something they can comprehend and absorb. We used vivid colors and icons. . . . We added white space, . . . and key messages were highlighted, so that if you just read the headlines and subheads you got a story. . . .

"Design has provided a major way for us to communicate clearly and convincingly what is sometimes pretty archaic stuff."

*Quoted from "Putnam's Lawrence J. Lasser on Design," *@ Issue* 2, no. 2 (Fall 1996): 1–5.

Getting Started

6.1   Evaluating Page Designs

Use the guidelines in Chapter 6 to evaluate each of the following page designs. What are their strong points? What could be improved?

a.

b.

☞ RESIST the TEMPTATION to use **all the fonts** available on your COMPUTER. Too *many* fonts **create** *visual* clutter ☹ and **make a document HARD** to read!! **FONTS** that call *attention* to **themselves** are **NOT** *appropriate* for **BUSINESS** *letters*, memos, and reports.❦ *Even* in a **standard font,** avoid shadows, **outlines,** and ***OVERUSE OF* bold** and *italics.* ❧

6.2 Evaluating PowerPoint Slides

Evaluate the following drafts of PowerPoint slides.
- Are the slides' background appropriate for the topic?
- Do the slides use words or phrases rather than complete sentences?
- Is the font big enough to read from a distance?
- Is the art relevant and appropriate?
- Is each slide free from errors?

a(1)

a(2)

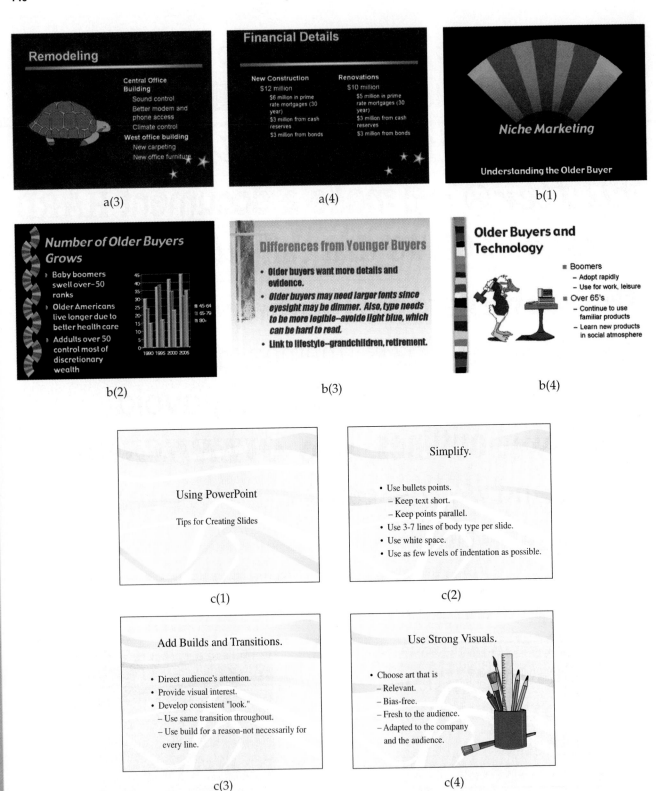

6.3   Recognizing Typefaces

Some companies commission a unique typeface, or wordmark, for their logos. Other companies use a standard font. When a logo is used consistently and frequently, it becomes associated with the organization. Can you name the brands that go with each letter of the alphabet below?

Source: "Alphabet Soup," *@Issue: The Journal of Business and Design* 3, no. 2 (Fall 1997): 24–25.

● ISSUE :

● ISSUE :

Alphabet Soup You don't always need to see the whole word to recognize the name of the brand. One letter will do. Used effectively, a distinctive logotype becomes the corporate signature. That is why many companies commission the design of a unique typeface, or wordmark, that incorporates clues to their line of business or operating philosophy. Other companies have adopted an off-the-shelf typeface that they have made their own through the use of designated corporate colors, upper or lower case styling, condensed or expanded leading and other techniques. As with any branding tool, a logotype must be used consistently and frequently to work. Test your familiarity with some of the best-known logotypes by naming the brand that goes with each letter in this alphabet.

WESTINGHOUSE, XEROX, YMCA, ZENITH.

CIRCLE K, LEGO, MAYTAG, NASA, OREO, PERRIER, REUTERS, SEARS, TWA, UNILEVER, VIRGIN,

NONSNHOL & NOSNHOL, IBM, JOHNSON & JOHNSON,

AUDI, BALL JARS, CHICAGO CUBS, CHIL, ETHAN ALLEN, FIRESTONE, GOODYEAR, HOLIDAY INN,

24

25

Source: "Alphabet Soup." Reprinted with permission from @Issue: The Journal of Business & Design, Vol. 1, No. 2 (Fall 1997) 24–25. Published by Corporate Design Foundation and sponsored by Potlatch Corporation.

6.4   Evaluating the Ethics of Design Choices

Indicate whether you consider each of the following actions ethical, unethical, or a gray area. Which of the actions would you do? Which would you feel uncomfortable doing? Which would you refuse to do?

1. Putting the advantages of a proposal in a bulleted list, while discussing the disadvantages in a paragraph.
2. Using a bigger type size so that a résumé visually fills a whole page.
3. Putting reasons to buy a product in the upper left and lower right quadrants, and the price in a part of the page that will get less emphasis.
4. Using a line at the bottom of the first page so it appears that the document is finished, and then putting the price and limitations on the back of that page.
5. Putting the services that are not covered by your health plan in full caps to make it less likely that people will read the page.

6.5   Using Headings

Reorganize the items in each of the following lists, using appropriate headings. Use bulleted or numbered lists as appropriate.

a. Rules and Procedures for a Tuition Reimbursement Plan

1. You are eligible to be reimbursed if you have been a full-time employee for at least three months.
2. You must apply before the first class meeting.
3. You must earn a "C" or better in the course.
4. You must submit a copy of the approved application, an official grade report, and a receipt for tuition paid to be reimbursed.
5. You can be reimbursed for courses related to your current position or another position in the

company, or for courses which are part of a degree related to a current or possible job.

6. Your supervisor must sign the application form.
7. Courses may be at any appropriate level (high school, college, or graduate school).

b. Activities in Starting a New Business
   - Getting a loan or venture capital
   - Getting any necessary city or state licenses
   - Determining what you will make, do, or sell
   - Identifying the market for your products or services
   - Pricing your products or services
   - Choosing a location
   - Checking zoning laws that may affect the location
   - Identifying government and university programs for small business development
   - Figuring cash flow
   - Ordering equipment and supplies
   - Selling
   - Advertising and marketing

Communicating at Work

6.6　Analyzing Documents at Work

1. Collect several documents: letters and memos, newsletters, ads and flyers, and reports. Use the guidelines in Chapter 6 to evaluate each of them.
2. Compare documents or pages produced by your competitors to those produced by your own organization in a specific category (for example, brochures, instructions, Web pages). Which documents are more effective? Why?

As Your Instructor Directs,

a. Discuss the documents with a small group of classmates.

b. Write a memo to your instructor evaluating three or more of the documents. Include originals or photocopies of the documents you discuss as an appendix to your memo.

c. Write a memo to your supervisor recommending ways the organization can improve its documents.

d. In an oral presentation to the class, explain what makes one document good and another one weak. If possible, use transparencies so that classmates can see the documents as you evaluate them.

Document Assignments

6.7　Evaluating Page Designs

Collect several documents that you receive as a consumer or a student: forms, letters, newsletters, announcements, ads, and flyers. Use the guidelines in Chapter 6 to evaluate each of them.

As Your Instructor Directs,

a. Discuss the documents with a small group of classmates.

b. Write a memo to your instructor evaluating three or more of the documents. Include originals or photocopies of the documents you discuss as an appendix to your memo.

c. Write a letter to an organization recommending ways it can improve the design of the documents.

d. In an oral presentation to the class, explain what makes one document good and another one weak. If possible, use transparencies so that classmates can see the documents as you evaluate them.

6.8　Evaluating Web Pages

Compare three Web pages in the same category (for example, helping the homeless, organizations, car companies, university departments, sports information). Which page(s) are most effective? Why? What weaknesses do the pages have?

As Your Instructor Directs,

a. Discuss the pages with a small group of classmates.

b. Write a memo to your instructor evaluating the pages. Include URLs of the pages in your memo.

c. In an oral presentation to the class, explain what makes one page good and another one weak. If possible, put the pages on screen so that classmates can see the pages as you evaluate them.

d. Post your evaluation in an e-mail message to the class. Include the URLs so classmates can click to the pages you discuss.

6.9   Creating a Brochure

Create a brochure for a campus, nonprofit, government, or business organization. Write a memo to your instructor explaining your choices for content and design.

6.10   Creating a Web Page

Create a Web page for an organization that does not yet have one. Write a memo to your instructor explaining your choices for content and design.

6.11   Testing a Document

Ask someone to follow a set of instructions or to fill out a form. (Consider consumer instructions, forms for financial aid, and so forth.)

- Time the person. How long does it take? Is the person able to complete the task?
- Observe the person. Where does he or she pause, reread, seem confused?
- Interview the person. What parts of the document were confusing?

As Your Instructor Directs,

a. Discuss the changes needed with a small group of classmates.

b. Write a memo to your instructor evaluating the document and explaining the changes that are needed. Include the document as an appendix to your memo.

c. Write to the organization that produced the document recommending necessary improvements.

d. In an oral presentation to the class, evaluate the document and explain what changes are needed. If possible, use a transparency of the document so that classmates can see it.

6.12   Improving a Financial Aid Form

You've just joined the financial aid office at your school. The director gives you the following form and asks you to redesign it. The director says:

> We need this form to see whether parents have other students in college besides the one requesting aid. Parents are supposed to list all family members that the parents support—themselves, the person here, any other kids in college, and any younger dependent kids.
>
> Half of these forms are filled out incorrectly. Most people just list the student going here; they leave out everyone else.
>
> If something is missing, the computer sends out a letter and a second copy of this form. The whole process starts over. Sometimes we send this form back two or three times before it's right. In the meantime, students' financial aid is delayed—maybe for months. Sometimes things are so late that they can't register for classes, or they have to pay tuition themselves and get reimbursed later.
>
> If so many people are filling out the form wrong, the form itself must be the problem. See what you can do with it. But keep it to a page.

As Your Instructor Directs,

a. Analyze the current form and identify its problems.

b. Revise the form. Add necessary information; reorder information; change the chart to make it easier to fill out.

Hints:

- Where are people supposed to send the form? What is the phone number of the financial aid office? Should they need to call the office if the form is clear?
- Does the definition of *half-time* apply to all students or just those taking courses beyond high school?
- Should capital or lowercase letters be used?
- Are the lines big enough to write in?
- What headings or subdivisions within the form would remind people to list all family members whom they support?
- How can you encourage people to return the form promptly?

Please complete the chart below by listing all family members for whom you (the parents) will provide more than half support during the academic year (July 1 through June 30). Include yourselves (the parents), the student, and your dependent children, even if they are not attending college.

EDUCATIONAL INFORMATION, 200_ - 200_						
FULL NAME OF FAMILY MEMBER	AGE	RELATIONSHIP OF FAMILY MEMBER TO STUDENT	NAME OF SCHOOL OR COLLEGE THIS SCHOOL YEAR	FULL-TIME	HALF-TIME* OR MORE	LESS THAN HALF-TIME
STUDENT APPLICANT						

*Half-time is defined as 6 credit hours or 12 clock hours a term.

When the information requested is received by our office, processing of your financial aid application will resume.

Please sign and mail this form to the above address as soon as possible. Your signature certifies that this information and the information on the FAF is true and complete to the best of your knowledge. If you have any questions, please contact a member of the need analysis staff.

_____   _____
        Signature of Parent(s)   Date

Letters, Memos, and E-Mail Messages

PART

TWO

7

Informative and Positive Messages

Informative and Positive Messages

Diana Sun
Director, Consumer Affairs, Capital One

Diana Sun manages Capital One's Consumer Affairs group. Using its proprietary Information-Based Strategy, Capital One has quickly become one of the world's largest issuers of credit cards, a direct marketer of consumer lending products, and a leader in the financial services industry.

www.capitalone.com

As one of the nation's fastest-growing companies, we attribute our success to our proprietary Information-Based Strategy, which is enormously complex to execute. It's critical that our more than 10,000 associates around the world have a good understanding of our company's business strategies. And that's where our intensive internal communications come in.

We "layer" our communications, sending messages through a variety of channels: our intranet (The One Place) and e-mail for urgent messages and key strategic initiatives; printed materials for in-depth discussions; and events to celebrate successes. For example, we recently announced the opening of a new office in Paris. The celebration included an e-mail to executives and an announcement on The One Place intranet site. We also celebrated with posters, a special menu in cafeterias, and mouse pads featuring the Arc de Triomphe.

Another big part of our culture is the incredible access that our associates have to senior management, including our CEO and our president. These executives make comments and answer questions during town hall events at most business units. An annual "roadshow" celebration gives associates at all levels insight into the past year and upcoming initiatives.

> "*Remember that your communication has a lot of competition out there.*"

We always keep in mind that it is vital to listen to our associates. By using continual feedback loops, we're able to make sure we're delivering the right information to the right person at the right time, using the right channels. Our twice-yearly survey of all associates tells the story: 94% are proud to work for Capital One, and 92% would highly recommend Capital One to a friend seeking employment. The right messages are clearly reaching our associates. In fact, 45% of all new hires are referred by existing employees!

Remember that your communication has a lot of competition out there. People forget two-thirds of what they've heard or read in 24 hours and 98% in 30 days! So build your communication around the two or three points you want folks to remember. Research tells us that most people can remember no more than three different points. You want to select which three they remember!

The Power of Good Writing*

Darlene was an entry-level auditor for a state government auditing bureau that audited organizations that provided services to citizens of the state. Her audit reports were noticeably superior to those written by everyone else in the bureau. She thought about the multiple audiences for the reports, questioned organizational norms that seemed counterproductive, and chose words consciously to achieve the multiple purposes that even simple reports had.

As a result of her good writing, Darlene was promoted. In her new position, she changed the composing process for reports and the ways that managers worked with staff auditors. She created a database of the various providers and identified whom the bureau was—and was not—auditing. This information will enable the bureau to conduct more and more focused audits.

In her new position, Darlene had less travel and more power. She was allowed to choose and define her own projects. At the end of her first year in the organization, she had gained real power in it.

*Based on Susan M. Katz, "A Newcomer Gains Power: An Analysis of the Role of Rhetorical Expertise," *The Journal of Business Communication* 35, no. 4 (October 1998): 419–42.

Business messages must meet the needs of the writer (and the writer's organization), be sensitive to the audience, and accurately reflect the topic being written about. Informative and positive messages are the bread-and-butter correspondence in organizations.

When we need to convey information to which the reader's basic reaction will be neutral, the message is **informative.** If we convey information to which the reader's reaction will be positive, the message is a **positive** or **good news message.** Neither message immediately asks the reader to do anything. You usually do want to build positive attitudes toward the information you are presenting, so in that sense, even an informative message has a persuasive element. Chapter 8 will discuss messages where the reader will respond negatively; Chapters 9 and 10 discuss messages where you want the reader to act.

Informative and positive messages include acceptances; positive answers to reader requests; information about procedures, products, services, or options; announcements of policy changes that are neutral or positive; and changes that are to the reader's advantage.

Even a simple informative or good news message usually has several purposes:

Primary purposes:

To give information or good news to the reader or to reassure the reader.

To have the reader read the message, understand it, and view the information positively.

To deemphasize any negative elements.

Secondary purposes:

To build a good image of the writer.

To build a good image of the writer's organization.

To cement a good relationship between the writer and reader.

To reduce or eliminate future correspondence on the same subject so the message doesn't create more work for the writer.

Informative and positive messages are not necessarily short. Instead, the length of a message depends on your purposes, the audience's needs, and the complexity of the situation. A public health inspector got a lot of teasing from his colleagues because he wrote 10-page inspection reports; the other inspectors rarely wrote more than 4 pages. He got the last laugh, however, when the lawyers in the enforcement division complimented him on his reports. For the first time, they were getting enough information to win cases against companies and individuals charged with violating the public health statutes. The shorter reports didn't give enough information.

Writing Letters and Memos

Letters go to someone outside your organization; **memos** go to someone in your own organization.

In large organizations where each unit is autonomous, the organization's culture determines whether people in different units send letters or memos to each other. In some universities, for example, faculty send letters if they need to write to faculty in other departments.

Letters and memos use different formats. The most common formats are illustrated in Appendix A. The AMS Simplified letter format is very similar to memo format: it uses a subject line and omits the salutation and the complimentary close. Thus, it is a good choice when you don't know the reader's name.

The differences in audience and format are the only differences between letters and memos. Both kinds of messages can be long or short, depending on how much you have to say and how complicated the situation is. Both kinds of messages can be informal when you write to someone you know well, or more formal when you write to someone you don't know, to several audiences, or for the record. Both kinds of messages can be simple responses that you can dash off in 15 minutes; both can take hours of analysis and revision when you've never faced that situation before or when the stakes are high.

Organizing Informative and Positive Messages

The patterns of organization in this chapter and the chapters that follow will work for 70 to 90% of the writing situations most people in business and government face. Using the appropriate pattern can help you compose more quickly and create a better final product.

- Be sure you understand the rationale behind each pattern so that you can modify the pattern if necessary. (For example, if you write instructions, any warnings should go up front, not in the middle of the message.)
- Not every message that uses the basic pattern will have all the elements listed. The elements you do have will go in the order presented in the pattern.
- Sometimes you can present several elements in one paragraph. Sometimes you'll need several paragraphs for just one element.

In real life, writing problems don't come with labels that tell you which pattern to use. Chapters 7, 8, and 9 offer advice about when to use each pattern.

Figure 7.1 shows how to organize informative and positive messages.

Figures 7.2 and 7.3 illustrate two ways that the basic pattern can be applied.

The letter in 7.2 authorizes a one-year appointment that the reader and writer have already discussed and describes the organization's priorities. Since the writer knows that the reader wants to accept the job, the letter doesn't need

Information, Please*

[Old-style managers believed in] keeping information tightly controlled. [But new-style managers disagree.] "It's better to over communicate," says [Anu] Shukla, whose Web startup, Rubric, made 65 of her 85 employees millionaires. Rather than dispensing information on a need-to-know basis, she made sure information was shared with all of her employees. She also created the CEO lunch, inviting six to eight employees at a time to discuss the business with her.

*Quoted from Rochelle Sharpe, "As Leaders, Women Rule," *BusinessWeek*, November 20, 2000, 80.

 How to Organize Informative and Positive Messages

1. **Give any good news and summarize the main points.** Include the date policies begin, the percent of a discount, etc. If the reader has already raised the issue, make it clear that you're responding.

    Share good news immediately.

2. **Give details, clarification, background.** Don't repeat information you've already given. Do answer all the questions your reader is likely to have; provide all the information necessary to achieve your purposes. Present details in the order of importance to the reader.

3. **Present any negative elements—as positively as possible.** A policy may have limits; information may be incomplete; the reader may have to satisfy requirements to get a discount or benefit. Make these negatives clear, but present them as positively as possible.

4. **Explain any reader benefits.** Most informative memos need reader benefits. Show that the policy or procedure helps readers, not just the company. Give enough detail to make the benefits clear and convincing. In letters, you may want to give benefits of dealing with your company as well as benefits of the product or policy.

    In a good news message, it's often possible to combine a short reader benefit with a goodwill ending in the last paragraph.

5. **Use a goodwill ending: positive, personal, and forward-looking.** Shifting your emphasis away from the message to the specific reader suggests that serving the reader is your real concern.

FIGURE 7.2 A Positive Letter

**INTERSTATE
FIDELITY
INSURANCE COMPANY**

100 Interstate Plaza
Atlanta, GA 30301
404-555-5000
Fax: 404-555-5270

March 7, 2003

Professor Adrienne Prinz
Department of History
Duke University
Durham, NC 27000

Dear Professor Prinz:

Good news — Your appointment as archivist for Interstate Fidelity Insurance has been approved. When you were in Atlanta in December, you said that you could begin work June 2. We'd like you to start then if that date is still good for you. *Tactful*

The Board has outlined the following priorities for your work: *Assumes reader's primary interest is the job*

Negative about lighting and security presented impersonally

1. **Organize and catalogue the archives.** You'll have the basement of the Palmer Building for the archives and can requisition the supplies you need. You'll be able to control heat and humidity; the budget doesn't allow special lighting or security measures.

Details

2. **Prepare materials for a 4-hour training session in October** for senior-level managers. We'd like you to cover how to decide what to send to the archives. If your first four months of research uncover any pragmatic uses for our archives (like Wells Fargo's use of archives to teach managers about past pitfalls), include those in the session.

3. **Write an article each month for the employee newsletter** describing the uses of the archives. When we're cutting costs in other departments, it's important to justify committing funds to start an archive program.

4. **Study the IFI archives to compile** information that (a) can help solve current management problems, (b) could be included in a history of the company, and (c) might be useful to scholars of business history.

These provisions will appeal to the reader

5. **Begin work on a corporate history of IFI.** IFI will help you find a publisher and support the book financially. You'll have full control over the content.

Negative that reader will have to reapply presented as normal procedure

Your salary will be $34,000 for six months; your contract can be renewed twice for a total of 18 months. You're authorized to hire a full-time research assistant for $10,000 for six months; you'll need to go through the normal personnel request process to request that that money be continued next year. A file clerk will be assigned full-time to your project. You'll report to me. At least for the rest of this calendar year, the budget for the Archives Project will come from my department.

Salary is deemphasized to avoid implying that reader is "just taking the job for the money"

FIGURE 7.2   A Positive Letter *(continued)*

Professor Adrienne Prinz
March 7, 2003
Page 2

IFI offices are equipped with Pentium computers with Access, WordPerfect, and Excel. Is there any software that we should buy for cataloguing or research? Are there any office supplies that we need to have on hand June 2 so that you can work efficiently?

In the meantime,

1.   Please send your written acceptance right away.

2.   Let me know if you need any software or supplies.

3.   Send me the name, address, and Social Security number of your research assistant by May 1 so that I can process his or her employment papers.

4.   If you'd like help finding a house or apartment in Atlanta, let me know. I can give you the name of a real estate agent.

Goodwill ending

On June 2, you'll spend the morning in Personnel. Stop by my office at noon. We'll go out for lunch and then I'll take you to the office you'll have while you're at IFI.

Welcome to IFI!

Cordially,

Cynthia Yen

Cynthia Yen
Director of Education and Training

to persuade. The opportunity for the professor to study records that aren't available to the public is an implicit reader benefit; the concern for the reader's needs builds goodwill.

The memo in Figure 7.3 announces a new employee benefit. The first paragraph summarizes the policy. Paragraphs 2–5 give details. Negative elements are in paragraphs 3–5, stated as positively as possible. The last section of the memo gives reader benefits and a goodwill ending.

Subject Lines for Informative and Positive Messages

A **subject line** is the title of a document. It aids in filing and retrieving the document, tells readers why they need to read the document, and provides a framework in which to set what you're about to say.

Subject lines are standard in memos. Letters are not required to have subject lines (see Appendix A, Formats for Letters, Memos, and E-mail Messages). However, a survey of business people in the southwest United States found that 68% of them considered a subject line in a letter to be important, very

FIGURE 7.3   A Positive Memo

March 1, 2003

To: All Chamber Employees and Members of the Chamber Insurance Group

From: Lee Ann Rabe, Vice President for Human Resources   *LAR*

Subject: Health Care Benefits for Same-Sex Longterm Partners

Good news in subject line and first paragraph

Beginning May 1, same-sex longterm partners of employees covered by the Chamber Health Plan will be eligible for the same coverage as spouses.

Details   In order to have a longterm partner covered, an employee must sign an affidavit in the Human Resources Department stating that the employee and his or her partner (1) live together, (2) intend to stay together, and (3) are responsible for each other. If the relationship ends, employees must notify the Human Resources Department within 30 days, just as do married couples who divorce.

Negatives presented as positively as possible

Costs and coverage of the Chamber of Health plan remain the same. Dental and vision coverage are also available for a fee; limitations apply and remain the same. For information about the specifics of the Chamber's Health Plan, pick up a brochure in the Human Resources Department.

Opposite-sex couples must still marry to receive the spousal coverage. As same-sex couples cannot legally marry, the affidavit option has been made available to them.

Extending coverage to same-sex longterm partners of employees shows the Chamber as a progressive, open-minded organization. This in turn portrays Columbus in a positive light.

The new policy will affect not only Chamber employees but also the small businesses that are a part of the Chamber's Health Plan. New businesses may see the change as a reason to join the Chamber–and the Health Plan. Growth in the Health Plan creates a wider base for insurance premiums and helps keep costs as low as possible. Additional Chamber members give us the funds and resources to plan more conferences for members. These conferences, such as the recent "R&D in Ohio's Small Businesses," help Chamber members do business successfully.

Reader Benefits

Making the Health Plan more comprehensive keeps us competitive with other major US cities. As we move out of the recession, businesses are carefully considering possible moves. The anti-homosexual ballots in Oregon and Colorado in the last few years will influence businesses that either have gay employees or who deal with companies that do. A policy change like this one shows Columbus' continued goodwill toward minorities in general and will make convincing businesses to relocate here that much easier.

Selling Columbus as a good place to live and do business has never been easier.

Goodwill ending

important, or essential; only 32% considered subject lines to be unimportant or only somewhat important.[1]

A good subject line meets three criteria: it is specific, concise, and appropriate to the kind of message (positive, negative, persuasive).

Making Subject Lines Specific

The subject line needs to be specific enough to differentiate that message from others on the same subject, but broad enough to cover everything in the message.

Too general:	Training Sessions
Better:	Dates for 2004 Training Sessions
or:	Evaluation of Training Sessions on Conducting Interviews
or:	Should We Schedule a Short Course on Proposal Writing?

Making Subject Lines Concise

Most subject lines are relatively short—usually no more than 10 words, often only 3 to 7 words.[2]

Wordy:	Survey of Student Preferences in Regards to Various Pizza Factors
Better:	Students' Pizza Preferences
or:	The Feasibility of a Cassano's Branch on Campus
or:	What Students Like and Dislike about Giovanni Pizza

If you can't make the subject both specific and short, be specific.

Making Subject Lines Appropriate for the Pattern of Organization

Since your subject line introduces your reader to your message, it must satisfy the psychological demands of the situation; it must be appropriate to your purposes and to the immediate response you expect from your reader. In general, do the same thing in your subject line that you would do in the first paragraph.

When you have good news for the reader, build goodwill by highlighting it in the subject line. When your information is neutral, summarize it concisely for the subject line.

Subject: Discount on Rental Cars Effective January 2

Starting January 2, as an employee of Amalgamated Industries you can get a 15% discount on cars you rent for business or personal use from Roadway Rent-a-Car.

Subject: Update on Arrangements for Videoconference with France

In the last month, we have chosen the participants and developed a tentative agenda for the videoconference with France scheduled for March 21.

Subject Lines for E-Mail Messages

Subject lines in e-mail are even more important than those in letters and memos. Subject lines must be specific, concise, and catchy. Some e-mail users get so many messages that they don't bother reading messages if they don't recognize the sender or if the subject doesn't catch their interest. If you have

Data, Data*

454 Number of documents added to Lexis-Nexis each minute . . .

50% Percentage of US professionals who repeatedly receive messages that say the same thing . . .

190 Number of messages in all media sent and received daily by the average Fortune 1000 office worker

80% Percentage of information that is filed but never used

150 Hours that the average person spends looking for lost information each year

71% Percentage of workers who say their main job is tracking down information . . .

7,349,000 Projected increase in the number of URLs between 1997 and 2002

$25,000 Amount that an executive earning $60,000 a year is being paid just to read

*Quoted from "Data, Data," *Inc.*, January 1999, 70.

good news to convey, put it in the subject line. Be as brief as you can. The following subject lines would be acceptable for informative and good news e-mail messages:

> Travel Plans for Sales Meeting
> Your Proposal Accepted
> Reduced Prices During February
> Your Funding Request Approved

When you reply to a message, the e-mail system automatically creates a subject line "Re: [subject line of message to which you are responding]." If the subject line is good, that's fine. If it isn't, you may want to create a new subject line. And if a series of messages arises, create a new subject line. "Re: Re: Re: Re: Question" is not an effective subject line.

Using Reader Benefits in Informative and Positive Messages

Not all informative and positive messages need reader benefits (◀▥ p. 70). You don't need reader benefits when

- You're presenting factual information only.
- The reader's attitude toward the information doesn't matter.
- Stressing benefits may make the reader sound selfish.
- The benefits are so obvious that to restate them insults the reader's intelligence.

You do need reader benefits when

- You are presenting policies.
- You want to shape readers' attitudes toward the information or toward your organization.
- Stressing benefits presents readers' motives positively.
- Some of the benefits may not be obvious to readers.

Messages to customers or potential customers sometimes include a sales paragraph promoting products or services you offer in addition to the product or service that the reader has asked about. Sales promotion in an informative or positive message should be low-key, not "hard sell."

Reader benefits are hardest to develop when you are announcing policies. The organization probably decided to adopt the policy because it appeared to help the organization; the people who made the decision may not have thought at all about whether it would help or hurt employees. Yet reader benefits are most essential in this kind of message so readers see the reason for the change and support it.

When you present reader benefits, be sure to present advantages *to the reader*. Most new policies help the organization in some way, but few workers will see their own interests as identical with the organization's. Even if the organization saves money or increases its profits, workers will benefit directly only if they own stock in the company, if they're high up enough to receive bonuses, if the savings enables a failing company to avoid layoffs, or if all of the savings goes directly to employee benefits. In many companies, any money saved will go to executive bonuses, shareholder profits, or research and development.

To develop reader benefits for informative and positive messages, use the steps suggested in Chapter 2. Be sure to think about benefits that come from the activity or policy itself, apart from any financial benefits. Does a policy improve the eight hours people spend at work?

Writing the One-Page Memo

Some organizations force writers to be concise by requiring or encouraging one-page memos. In simple situations, a page may be more than you need. Sometimes, careful revising and editing may enable you to cut your memo to a page. When you can't get everything on one page even with careful revision, put the key points on one well-designed page and attach appendices for readers who need more information.

Ending Informative and Positive Messages

Ending a letter or memo gracefully can be a problem in short informative and positive messages. In a one-page memo where you have omitted details and proof, you can tell readers where to get more information. In long messages, you can summarize your basic point. In persuasive messages, as you'll learn in Chapter 9, you can tell readers what you want them to do. In a short message containing all the information readers need, either write a goodwill paragraph that refers directly to the reader or the reader's organization, or just stop.

Goodwill endings should focus on the business relationship you share with your reader rather than on the reader's hobbies, family, or personal life. When you write to one person, a good last paragraph fits that person so specifically that it would not work if you sent the same basic message to someone else or to a person with the same title in another organization. When you write to someone who represents an organization, the last paragraph can refer to your company's relationship to the reader's organization. When you write to a group (for example, to "All Employees") your ending should apply to the whole group.

Use a paragraph that shows you see your reader as an individual. Possibilities include complimenting the reader for a job well done, describing a reader benefit, or looking forward to something positive that relates to the subject of the message.

In the following examples, a letter answers the question "When a patient leaves the hospital and returns, should we count it as a new stay?" For one company the answer was that if a patient was gone from the hospital overnight or longer, the hospital should start a new claim when the patient was readmitted.

Weak closing paragraph:	Should you have any questions regarding this matter, please feel free to call me.
Goodwill paragraph:	Many employee-patients appreciate the freedom to leave the hospital for a few hours. It's nice working with a hospital which is flexible enough to offer that option.
Also acceptable:	Omit the paragraph; stop after the explanation.

Some writers end every message with a standard invitation:

If you have questions, please do not hesitate to ask.

That sentence lacks positive emphasis. But revising it to say "feel free to call" is rarely a good idea. Most of the time, the writer should omit the sentence entirely.

Inviting readers to call suggests that you have not answered the question fully. In very complicated situations, it may be simpler to let people call with individual questions. But in simple situations, you can answer the question clearly.

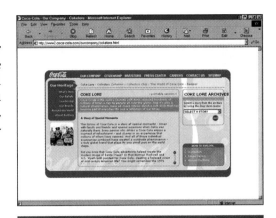

InSite

www2.coca-cola.com/ourcompany/cokelore.html

Stories are powerful ways to inform, teach, and persuade. Coca-Cola is one of several companies posting customer stories on its Web site.

It's News to Me*

Sometimes, information that's old to you can be new to someone else. During a company retreat of senior executives, Boeing's new chief financial officer, Deborah Hopkins, went to the blackboard to explain some financial basics: profit margins, return on net assets, and inventory turnover. Afterward, she got dozens of compliments. Some of the senior executives said it was the first time they had understood the concepts.

*Based on Jeff Cole, "New Boeing CFO's Assignment: Signal a Turnaround," *The Wall Street Journal*, January 26, 1999, B1.

A state agency sent out a memo explaining when the state would pay for the cost of lunch that was included in a conference registration fee. The state would pay for lunch if the conference was out of town. If the conference was in the same town as the employee's office, the employee had to pay for lunch. Either the conference is in the same town or a different town. The answer is simple; no further explanation is necessary.

One of the reasons you write is to save the time needed to tell everyone individually. People in business aren't shrinking violets; they will call if they need help. Don't make more work for yourself by inviting calls to clarify simple messages.

Varieties of Informative and Positive Messages

Many messages can be informative, negative, or persuasive depending on what you have to say. A transmittal, for example, can be positive when you're sending glowing sales figures or persuasive when you want the reader to act on the information. A performance appraisal is positive when you evaluate someone who's doing superbly, negative when you want to compile a record to justify firing someone, and persuasive when you want to motivate a satisfactory worker to continue to improve. A collection letter is persuasive; it becomes negative in the last stage when you threaten legal action. Each of these messages is discussed in the chapter of the pattern it uses most frequently. However, in some cases you will need to use a pattern from a different chapter.

See the BAC Web site for links to electronic greeting cards.

Transmittals

When you send someone something in an organization, attach a memo or letter of transmittal explaining what you're sending. A transmittal can be as simple as a small yellow Post-it™ note with "FYI" ("for your information") written on it, or it can be a separate typed document.

Organize a memo or letter of transmittal in this order:

1. Tell the reader what you're sending.
2. Summarize the main point(s) of the document.
3. Indicate any special circumstances or information that would help the reader understand the document. Is it a draft? Is it a partial document that will be completed later?
4. Tell the reader what will happen next. Will you do something? Do you want a response? If you do want the reader to act, specify exactly what you want the reader to do and give a deadline.

Frequently transmittals have important secondary purposes. Consider the writer's purpose in Figure 7.4, a transmittal from a lawyer to her client. The primary purpose of this transmittal is to give the client a chance to affirm that his story and the lawyer's understanding of it are correct. If there's anything wrong, the lawyer wants to know *before* she files the brief. But an important secondary purpose is to build goodwill: "I'm working on your case; I'm earning my fee." The greatest number of complaints officially lodged against lawyers are for the lawyer's neglect—or what the client perceives as neglect—of the client's case.

Confirmations

Many informative messages record oral conversations. These messages are generally short and give only the information shared orally; they go to the

FIGURE 7.4   A Transmittal

DREW & Associates

100 Barkley Plaza • Denver, CO 80210 • 303.555.4783 • Fax 303.555.4784

October 8, 2004

Mr. Charles Gibney
Personnel Manager
Roydon Interiors
146 East State Street
Denver, CO   80202

Dear Mr. Gibney:

Paragraph one tells reader what is enclosed and summarizes main points.

Here is a copy of the brief we intend to file with the Tenth Circuit Court in support of our position that the sex discrimination charge against Roydon Interiors should be dropped.

Will you please examine it carefully to make sure that the facts it contains are correct? If you have changes to suggest, please call my office by October 22nd, so that we can file the brief by October 24th.

Sincerely,

Last paragraph asks for action by a specific date.

Diana Drew

Diana Drew

other party in the conversation. Start the message by indicating that it is a confirmation, not a new message:

As we discussed on the phone today, . . .

As I told you yesterday, . . .

Attached is the meeting schedule we discussed earlier today.

Be sure to avoid dangling modifiers.

Voice-Mail Information

Before you make a phone call, think of the information you'll need if you must leave a voice-mail message.

- Summarize the purpose of your message in a sentence or two.
- Give your name and phone number early in the message. Speak slowly and distinctly.
- Give the recipient enough information to act.
- Tell when you'll be at your desk to receive a return call.

Saving Money Answering Customer Complaints*

Ed Hurston of Wonderwood Corp. says he used to spend an average of $50,000 annually addressing customers' complaints. Then he started asking grumblers this simple question: "How would you like us to handle the situation?" "It's unbelievable what happened when we put it in their hands," says Hurston, the president of the $12 million wood-products manufacturer. "They always tell us something that costs far less than what we'd do." Here's an example: After Wonderwood spent $2,000 replacing an entire picket fence twice for an unhappy customer, the customer still wasn't satisfied. When he was finally asked how he'd like the situation handled, he suggested a $100 solution. Hurston estimates that the company, based in Deland, Fla., now spends less than $2,000 a year addressing customers' complaints.

*Quoted from Stephanie Gruner, "Can We Reduce the Cost of Handling Customers' Complaints?" *Inc.*, December 1997, 148.

Dangling modifier:	Confirming our conversation, your Hot Springs Hot Tub Spa is scheduled for delivery April 12. (This sentence says that the Spa is doing the confirming.)
Correct:	As I told you yesterday, your Hot Springs Hot Tub Spa is scheduled for delivery April 12.

Summaries

You may be asked to summarize a conversation, document, or an outside meeting for colleagues or superiors. (Minutes of an internal meeting are usually more detailed. See Chapter 12 for advice on writing minutes of meetings.)

In a summary of a conversation for internal use, identify the people who were present, the topic of discussion, decisions made, and who does what next.

To summarize a document, start with the main point. Then go on to give supporting evidence or details. In some cases, your audience may also want you to evaluate the document. Should others in the company read this book? Should someone in the company write a letter to the editor responding to this newspaper article?

When you visit a client or go to a conference, you may be asked to share your findings and impressions with other people in your organization. Chronological accounts are the easiest to write but the least useful for the reader. Your company doesn't need a blow-by-blow account of what you did; it needs to know what *it* should do as a result of the meeting.

Summarize a visit with a client or customer in this way:

1. Put the main point from your organization's point of view—the action to be taken, the perceptions to be changed—in the first paragraph.
2. Provide an **umbrella paragraph** to cover and foreshadow the points you will make in the report.
3. Provide necessary detail to support your conclusions and cover each point. Use lists and headings to make the structure of the document clear.

In the following example, the revised first paragraph summarizes the sales representative's conclusions after a call on a prospective client:
Original:

> On October 10th, Rick Patel and I made a joint call on Consolidated Tool Works. The discussion was held in a conference room, with the following people present:
> 1. Kyle McCloskey (Vice President and General Manager)
> 2. Bill Petrakis (Manufacturing Engineer)
> 3. Garett Lee (Process Engineering Supervisor)
> 4. Courtney Mansor-Green (Project Engineer)

Revised:

> Consolidated Tool Works is an excellent prospect for purchasing a Matrix-Churchill grinding machine. To get the order, we should
> 1. Set up a visit for CTW personnel to see the Matrix-Churchill machine in Kansas City;
> 2. Guarantee 60-day delivery if the order is placed by the end of the quarter; and
> 3. Extend credit terms to CTW.

 See the BAC Web site for links to postings for intranets.

Thank-you notes can be written on standard business stationery, using standard formats. But one student noticed that his adviser really liked cats and had pictures of them in her office. So he found a cat card for his thank-you note.

Thank-You and Congratulatory Notes

Sending a **thank-you note** will make people more willing to help you again in the future. Thank-you letters can be short but must be prompt. They need to be specific to sound sincere.

Congratulating someone can cement good feelings between you and the reader and enhance your own visibility. Again, specifics help.

Avoid language that may seem condescending or patronizing. A journalism professor was offended when a former student wrote to congratulate her for a feature article that appeared in a major newspaper. As the professor pointed out, the letter's language implied that the writer had more status than the person being praised. The praiser was "quite impressed," congratulated the professor on reaching a conclusion that she had already reached, and assumed that the professor would have wanted to discuss matters with the praiser. To the professor, "Keep up the good work!" implied that the one cheering her on had been waiting for ages at the finish line.[3]

See the BAC Web site for links on writing thank-you notes.

Adjustments and Responses to Complaints

A study sponsored by Travelers Insurance showed that when people had gripes but didn't complain, only 9% would buy from the company again. But when people did complain—and their problems were resolved quickly—82% would buy again.[4]

When you grant a customer's request for an adjusted price, discount, replacement, or other benefit to resolve a complaint, do so in the very first sentence.

Your Visa bill for a night's lodging has been adjusted to $63. Next month a credit of $37 will appear on your bill to reimburse you for the extra amount you were originally asked to pay.

A policy of asking for and responding to customer complaints has helped Applebee's restaurants grow, according to Lloyd Hill, CEO (pictured left, with Lou Kaucic, Senior Vice President of human resources). Randomly selected guests receive coupons they can redeem by calling a toll-free phone number and evaluating the food and service they've received. If a customer rates a particular restaurant as "very poor," a live operator comes on the line and offers to connect the customer with either a customer service representative or the manager of that restaurant. Fixing the problem and pleasing the customer create loyal guests.

Don't talk about your own process in making the decision. Don't say anything that sounds grudging. Give the reason for the original mistake only if it reflects credit on the company. (In most cases, it doesn't, so the reason should be omitted.)

Solving a Sample Problem

Real-life problems are richer and less well defined than textbook problems and cases. But even textbook problems require analysis before you begin to write. Before you tackle the assignments for this chapter, examine the following problem. See how the analysis questions probe the basic points required for a solution. Study the two sample solutions to see what makes one unacceptable and the other one good. Note the recommendations for revision that could make the good solution excellent.[5] The checklist at the end of the chapter (p. 164) can help you evaluate a draft.

Problem

Interstate Fidelity Insurance (IFI) uses computers to handle its payments and billings. There is often a time lag between receiving a payment from a customer and recording it on the computer. Sometimes, while the payment is in line to be processed, the computer sends out additional notices: past-due notices, collection letters, even threats to sue. Customers are frightened or angry and write asking for an explanation. In most cases, if they just waited a little while, the situation would be straightened out. But policyholders are afraid that they'll be without insurance because the company thinks the bill has not been paid.

IFI doesn't have the time to check each individual situation to see if the check did arrive and has been processed. It wants you to write a letter that will per-

Sharing information is crucial to business success. To drive home that point, Siemens deposited 60 managers from around the world on the shores of a lake south of Munich, Germany, and told them to build rafts. They weren't allowed to talk: They had to write messages and diagrams on flip charts. Back in the office, ShareNet lets employees around the world ask questions and share answers.

suade customers to wait. If something is wrong and the payment never reached IFI, IFI would send a legal notice to that effect saying the policy would be canceled by a certain date (which the notice would specify) at least 30 days after the date on the original premium bill. Continuing customers always get this legal notice as a third chance (after the original bill and the past-due notice).

Prepare a form letter that can go out to every policyholder who claims to have paid a premium for automobile insurance and resents getting a past-due notice. The letter should reassure readers and build goodwill for IFI.

Analysis of the Problem

1. Who is (are) your audience(s)? What characteristics are relevant to this particular message? If you are writing to more than one reader, how do the readers differ?

    Automobile insurance customers who say they've paid but have still received a past-due notice. They're afraid they're no longer insured. Since it's a form letter, different readers will have different situations: in some cases payments did arrive late, in some cases the company made a mistake, in some the reader never paid (check was lost in mail, unsigned, bounced, etc.).

2. What are your purposes in writing?

    To reassure readers that they're covered for 30 days. To inform them that they can assume everything is OK *unless* they receive a second notice. To avoid further correspondence on this subject. To build goodwill for IFI: (a) we don't want to suggest IFI is error-prone or too cheap to hire enough people to do the necessary work; (b) we don't want readers to switch companies; (c) we do want readers to buy from IFI when they're ready for more insurance.

3. What information must your message include?

    Readers are still insured. We cannot say whether their checks have now been processed (company doesn't want to check individual accounts). Their insurance will be canceled if they do not pay after receiving the second past-due notice (the legal notice).

4. How can you build support for your position? What reasons or reader benefits will your reader find convincing?

    Computers help us provide personal service to policyholders. We offer policies to meet all their needs. Both of these points would need specifics to be interesting and convincing.

Good Communication Leads to Corporate Success*

Emerson Electronics is a world-class competitor. One way it achieved that status was using effective communication to outline corporate economic goals for employees and to explain why those goals affect jobs, salaries, and survival. Sharing information and shaping attitudes toward it enabled Emerson to excel.

Martin Marietta Government Electronic Systems, a union shop, speeded up information so that changes were communicated within 48 hours of any decision. Once everyone knew what was going on at all times, grievances dropped from 281 a year to just 12. Information creates openness and a sense of trust.

*Based on James L. Gibson, John M. Ivancevich, and James H. Donnelly, *Organizations: Behavior, Structure, Processes* (Burr Ridge, IL: Richard D. Irwin, 1995), 408.

5. What objection(s) can you expect your reader(s) to have? What negative elements of your message must you deemphasize or overcome?

> Computers appear to cause errors. We don't know if the checks have been processed. We will cancel policies if their checks don't arrive.

6. What aspects of the total situation may affect reader response? The economy? The time of year? Morale in the organization? The relationship between the reader and writer? Any special circumstances?

> The insurance business is highly competitive—other companies offer similar rates and policies. The customer could get a similar policy for about the same money from someone else. Most people find that money is tight, so they'll want to keep insurance costs low. Yet the fact that prices are steady or rising means that the value of what they own is higher—they need insurance more than ever.
>
> Many insurance companies are refusing to renew policies (car, liability, malpractice insurance). These refusals to renew have gotten lots of publicity, and many people have heard horror stories about companies and individuals whose insurance has been canceled or not renewed after a small number of claims. Readers don't feel very kindly toward insurance companies.
>
> People need car insurance. If they have an accident and aren't covered, they not only have to bear the costs of that accident alone but also (depending on state law) may need to place as much as $50,000 in a state escrow account to cover future accidents. They have a legitimate worry.

Discussion of the Sample Solutions

The solution in Figure 7.5 is unacceptable. The red marginal comments show problem spots. Since this is a form letter, we cannot tell customers we have their checks; in some cases, we may not. The letter is far too negative. The ex-

---

FIGURE 7.5   An Unacceptable Solution to the Sample Problem

Need date

Dear Customer:

Relax. We got your check.   *Not necessarily true. Reread problem.*

This explanation makes company look bad.   There is always a (time lag) between the time payments come in and the time they are processed. While payments are waiting to be processed, the computer with super-human quickness is sending out past-due notices and (threats) of (cancellation).

Too negative

Need to present this positively   Cancellation is not something you should (worry) about. No policy would be (canceled) without a (legal notice) to that effect giving a specific date for (cancellation) which would be at least 30 days after the date on the original premium notice.

If you want to buy more insurance, just contact your local Interstate Fidelity agent. We will be happy to help you.

This paragraph isn't specific enough to work as a reader benefit. It lacks you-attitude and positive emphasis.

Sincerely,

planation in paragraph 2 makes IFI look irresponsible and uncaring. Paragraph 3 is far too negative. Paragraph 4 is too vague; there are no reader benefits; the ending sounds selfish. A major weakness with the solution is that it lifts phrases straight out of the problem; the writer does not seem to have thought about the problem or about the words he or she is using. Measuring the draft against the answers to the questions for analysis suggests that this writer should start over.

The solution in Figure 7.6 is much better. The blue marginal comments show the letter's strong points. The message opens with the good news that is true for all readers. (Whenever possible, one should use the good news pattern of organization.) Paragraph 2 explains IFI's policy. It avoids assigning blame and ends on a positive note. The negative information is buried in paragraph 3 and is presented positively: the notice is information, not a threat; the 30-day extension is a "grace period." Telling the reader now what to do if a second notice arrives eliminates the need for a second exchange of letters. Paragraph 4 offers benefits for using computers, since some readers may blame the notice on computers, and offers benefits for being insured by IFI. Paragraph 5 promotes other policies the company sells and prepares for the last paragraph.

FIGURE 7.6   A Good Solution to the Sample Problem

Need date

Dear Customer: *Better: use computer to personalize. Put in name and address of a specific reader*

Your auto insurance is still in effect.   *Good ¶ 1. True for all readers*

Good to treat notice as information, tell reader what to do if it arrives   Past-due notices are mailed out if the payment has not been processed within three days after the due date. This may happen if a check is delayed in the mail or arrives without a signature or account number. When your check arrives with all the necessary information, it is promptly credited to your account.   *Good you-attitude*

Even if a check is lost in the mail and never reaches us, you still have a 30-day grace period. If you do get a second notice, you'll know that we still have not received your check. To keep your insurance in force, just stop payment on the first check and send a second one.

Benefits of using computers   Computer processing of your account guarantees that you get any discounts you're eligible for: multicar, accident-free record, good student. If you have a claim, your agent uses computer tracking to find matching parts quickly, whatever car you drive. You get a check quickly—usually within 3 working days—without having to visit dealer after dealer for time-consuming estimates.   *Better to put in agent's name, phone number*

Too negative

Need to add benefits of insuring with IFI   Today, your home and possessions are worth more than ever. You can protect them with Interstate Fidelity's homeowners' and renters' policies. Let your local agent show you how easy it is to give yourself full protection. If you need a special rider to insure a personal computer, a coin or gun collection, or a fine antique, you can get that from IFI, too.   *Good specifics*

Whatever your insurance needs—auto, home, life, or health—one call to IFI can do it all.   *Acceptable ending*

Sincerely,

☑ **CHECKLIST**   Checklist for Informative and Positive Messages

☐ In positive messages, does the subject line give the good news? In either message, is the subject line specific enough to differentiate this message from others on the same subject?

☐ Does the first paragraph summarize the information or good news? If the information is too complex to fit into a single paragraph, does the paragraph list the basic parts of the policy or information in the order in which the memo discusses them?

☐ Is all the information given in the message? [What information is needed will vary depending on the message, but information about dates, places, times, and anything related to money usually needs to be included. When in doubt, ask!]

☐ In messages announcing policies, is there at least one reader benefit for each segment of the audience? Are all reader benefits ones that seem likely to occur in this organization?

☐ Is each reader benefit developed, showing that the benefit will come from the policy and why the benefit matters to this organization? Do the benefits build on the job duties of people at this organization and the specific circumstances of the organization?

☐ Does the message end with a positive paragraph—preferably one that is specific to the readers, not a general one that could fit any organization or policy?

And, for all messages, not just informative and positive ones,

☐ Does the message use you-attitude and positive emphasis?

☐ Is the style easy to read and friendly?

☐ Is the visual design of the message inviting?

☐ Is the format correct?

☐ Does the message use standard grammar? Is it free from typos?

Originality in a positive or informative message may come from

- Creating good headings, lists, and visual impact.
- Developing reader benefits.
- Thinking about readers and giving details that answer their questions and make it easier for them to understand and follow the policy.

As the red comments indicate, this good solution could be improved by personalizing the salutation and by including the name and number of the local agent. Computers could make both of those insertions easily. This good letter could be made excellent by revising paragraph 4 so that it doesn't end on a negative note and by using more reader benefits. For instance, do computers help agents advise clients of the best policies for them? Does IFI offer good service—quick, friendly, nonpressured—that could be stressed? Are agents well trained? All of these might yield ideas for additional reader benefits.

Summary of Key Points

■ Informative and positive messages normally use the following pattern of organization:

1. Give any good news and summarize the main points.
2. Give details, clarification, background.
3. Present any negative elements—as positively as possible.
4. Explain any reader benefits.
5. Use a goodwill ending: positive, personal, and forward-looking.

■ **Letters** go to people in other organizations. **Memos** go to people within your own organization.

■ A **subject line** is the title of a document. A good subject line meets three criteria: it's specific; it's reasonably short; and it's adapted to the kind of message (positive, negative, persuasive). If you can't make the subject both specific and short, be specific.

- The subject line for an informative or positive message should highlight any good news and summarize the information concisely.
- Use reader benefits in informative and positive messages when
  - You are presenting policies.
  - You want to shape readers' attitudes toward the information or toward your organization.
  - Stressing benefits presents readers' motives positively.
  - Some of the benefits may not be obvious to readers.
- **Goodwill endings** should focus on the business relationship you share with your reader or the reader's organization. The last paragraph of a message to a group should apply to the whole group.
- Use the analysis questions listed in Chapter 1 to probe the basic points needed for successful informative and positive messages.

CHAPTER 7   Exercises and Problems

Getting Started

7.1   Memos for Discussion—Introducing a Suggestion System

Your organization has decided to institute a suggestion system. Employees on hourly pay scales will be asked to submit suggestions. (Managers and other employees on salary are not eligible for this program; they are supposed to be continually suggesting ways to improve things as part of their regular jobs.) If the evaluating committee thinks that the suggestion would save money, the em-

ployee will receive 10% of the first year's estimated annual savings. If the suggestion won't save money but will improve work conditions, service, or morale, the employee will get a check for $50.

The following memos are possible approaches. How well does each message meet the criteria in the checklist for informative and positive messages?

1.
Subject: Suggestion System (SS)

I want to introduce you to the Suggestion System (SS). This program enables the production worker to offer ideas about improving his job description, working conditions, and general company procedures. The plan can operate as a finely tuned machine, with great ideas as its product.

Operation will begin November 1. Once a week, a designate of SS will collect the ideas and turn them over to the SS Committee. This committee will evaluate and judge the proposed changes.

Only employees listed as factory workers are eligible. This excludes foremen and the rest of supervisory personnel. Awards are as follows:

1. $50 awards will be given to those ideas judged operational. These are awarded monthly.

2. There will be grand prizes given for the best suggestions over the six-month span.

Ideas are judged on feasibility, originality, operational simplicity, and degree of benefit to the worker and company. Evaluation made by the SS Committee is final. Your questions should be channeled to my office.

2.   Subject: Establishment of Suggestion System

We announce the establishment of a Suggestion System. This new program is designed to provide a means for hourly employees to submit suggestions to company management concerning operations and safety. The program will also provide an award system to compensate nonmanagement employees for implemented suggestions.

Here is how the program will work: beginning October 1, suggestions can be submitted by hourly workers to the company on Form 292, which will be furnished to all plants and their departments by October 1st. On the form, the submitting employee should include the suggestion, his or her name, and the department number. The form can be deposited in a suggestion drop box, which will be located near the personnel office in each plant.

Any suggestion dealing with the improvement of operations, safety, working conditions, or morale is eligible for consideration. The award structure for the program will be as follows:

1.   For an implemented suggestion which improves safety or efficiency with no associated monetary benefits or cost reduction: $50.00.

2.   For an implemented suggestion which makes or saves the company money: 10% of the first year's estimated annual savings or additional revenue.

It is hoped that we will have a good initial and continuous response from all hourly employees. This year, we are out to try to cut production costs, and this program may be the vehicle through which we will realize new savings and increased revenues. New ideas which can truly increase operational efficiency or cut safety problems will make the company a nicer place for all employees. A safer work environment is a better work environment. If department operations can be made more efficient, this will eventually make everyone's job just a little easier, and give that department and its employees a sense of pride.

3.　Subject: New Employee Suggestion System

Beginning October 1, all of you who are hourly employees of Video Adventures will be able to get cash awards when your suggestions for improving the company are implemented.

Ideas about any aspect of Video Adventures are eligible: streamlining behind-the-counter operations, handling schedule problems, increasing the life of videotapes.

- If your idea cuts costs or increases income (e.g., increasing membership sales, increasing the number of movie rentals per customer), you'll receive 10% of the first year's estimated annual savings.

- If the idea doesn't save money but does improve service, work conditions, or morale, you'll receive a check for $50.

To submit a suggestion, just pick up a form from your manager. On the form, explain your suggestion, describe briefly how it could be implemented, and show how it will affect Video Adventures. Return the completed form in the new suggestion box behind the back counter. Suggestions will be evaluated at the end of each month. Turn in as many ideas as you like!

Think about ways to solve the problems you face every day. Can we speed up the check-in process? Cut paperwork? Give customers faster service? Increase the percentage of customers who bring back their tapes on time? As you serve people at the counter, ask them what they'd like to see at Video Adventures.

Your ideas will keep Video Adventures competitive. Ten years ago, Video Adventures was the only video store on the west side of town. Now there are six other video stores within a two-mile radius, and even the grocery stores rent videotapes. Efficiency, creativity, and service can keep Video Adventures ahead.

Employees whose ideas are implemented will be recognized in the regional Video Adventures newsletter. The award will also be a nice accomplishment to add to any college application or résumé. By suggesting ways to improve Video Adventures, you'll demonstrate your creativity and problem-solving abilities. And you'll be able to share the credit for keeping Video Adventures' reputation as the best video store in town.

7.2　E-Mails for Discussion—Saying Yes to a Subordinate

Today, you get this request from a subordinate.

Subject: Request for Leave

You know that I've been feeling burned out. I've decided that I want to take a three-month leave of absence this summer to travel abroad. I've got five weeks of vacation time saved up; I would take the rest as unpaid leave. Just guarantee that my job will be waiting when I come back!

You decide to grant the request. The following messages are possible responses. How well does each message meet the criteria in the checklist for informative and positive messages?

1.   Subject: Re: Request for Leave

I highly recommend Italy. Spend a full week in Florence, if you can. Be sure to visit the Brancacci Chapel—it's been restored, and the frescoes are breathtaking. And I can give you the names of some great restaurants. You may never want to come back!

2.   Subject: Your Request for Leave

As you know, we are in a very competitive position right now. Your job is important, and there is no one who can easily replace you. However, because you are a valued employee, I will permit you to take the leave you request, as long as you train a replacement before you leave.

3.   Subject: Your Request for Leave Granted

Yes, you may take a three-month leave of absence next summer using your five weeks of accumulated vacation time and taking the rest as unpaid leave. And yes, your job will be waiting for you when you return!

I'm appointing Garrick to take over your duties while you're gone. Talk with him to determine how much training time he'll need, and let me know when the training is scheduled.

Have a great summer! Let us know every now and then how you're doing!

7.3 Revising a Letter

Your assistant gives you the following letter to sign:

Dear Ms. Hebbar:

I received your request to send a speaker to participate in "Career Day" at King Elementary School next month. I am pleased to be able to send Audrey Lindstrom to speak at your school about her job at the child care center.

Audrey has been working in the child care center for over five years. She trains contracted center personnel on policies and procedures of the department.

Another commitment later that day will make it impossible for her to spend the whole day at your school. She will be happy to spend two hours with your class participating in the event.

Call Audrey to coordinate the time of the program, the expected content, and the age group of the audience.

Your students will see the importance of trained day care providers in our neighborhoods.

Thank you for asking our agency to be part of your school's special event. Our future lies in the hands of today's students.

Sincerely,

This draft definitely needs some work. It lacks you-attitude and positive emphasis, it isn't well organized, and it doesn't have enough details. Though employees in your office call each other by their first names, in a letter to another group, "Ms. Lindstrom" would be more professional than "Audrey." And more information is needed. Exactly when should she show up? Will she be giving a speech (how long?), speaking as a member of a panel, or sitting at a table to answer questions? Will all grade levels be together, or will she be speaking to specific grades? Will all students hear each speaker, or will there be several concurrent speakers from which to choose?

As Your Instructor Directs,

a. Write a memo to your subordinate, explaining what revisions are necessary.

b. Revise the letter.

E-Mail Messages

7.4   Announcing Holiday Diversity

Your organization has traditionally given employees several holidays off: New Year's, Martin Luther King, Jr., Day, Independence Day, Veterans' Day, Thanksgiving, and Christmas. Employees who celebrate other holidays (e.g., Good Friday, Yom Kippur, Ramadan, Chinese New Year, the Hindu holiday Diwali) have been able to take those days off with the consent of their supervisors. But some employees have complained that it is unfair to depend on the goodwill of supervisors. And now a few other employees have complained that people who honor other holidays are getting "extra" days off, since they take those days in addition to the standard holidays.

Therefore, the Executive Committee of your organization has decided to allow employees any 10 days off for holidays; they will have to tell their supervisors which days they plan to take off. People will be asked in December which holidays they want to take off in the following year. People can change their minds during the year as long as they have not yet taken off the full 10 holidays. Any religious, ethnic, or cultural holiday is acceptable. (Someone who wants to take off Cinco de Mayo or

Bastille Day can do so.) Vacations, personal days, and sick days are not affected by this policy.

As Vice President for Human Resources, write an e-mail to all employees, announcing the new policy.

Hints:

- Pick a business, government, or nonprofit organization that you know something about.
- Will the building be "open" every day? If not, do all employees already have keys, or will they need to pick them up when they work days that few other people work?
- Will people know what work to do if they're working alone? Suggest activities for people who cannot do their normal work if the building is closed.
- See Chapter 11 for a list of sample holidays in various countries.
- Use your analysis from Chapter 3, problem 3.6.

7.5   Responding to a Supervisor's Request

You've received this e-mail message from your supervisor:

> Subject: Need "Best Practices"
>
> Please describe something our unit does well—ideally something that could be copied by or at least applied to other units. Our organization is putting together something on "Best Practices" so that good ideas can be shared as widely as possible.
>
> Be specific. For example, don't just say "serve customers"—explain exactly what you do and how you do it to be effective. Anecdotes and examples would be helpful.
>
> Also indicate whether a document, a videotape, or some other format would be the best way to share your practice. We may use more than one format, depending on the response.
>
> I need your answer ASAP so that I can send it on to my boss.

Answer the message, describing something that you or others in your unit do well.

7.6   Making Personal Time More Flexible

You're manager of Human Resources at your company. Two weeks ago, you got this e-mail message:

> Subject: Flexibility Needed
>
> Higher-up people routinely take time off from work to play golf, coach soccer, or go to school plays. We peons have to fight to stay home with a sick child. It isn't fair. Can you do something about it?

Yesterday, the Executive Committee voted that a change was in order. As long as people tell their supervisors, get their own work done, and aren't out of the office more than a couple of hours a day a couple of times a week, requests for time off will be granted and will be "free"—that is, they won't be deducted from personal or vacation time. But someone who is going to be out all day does have to use sick, personal, or vacation time.

Write an e-mail message to all employees, telling them about the new policy.

7.7   Changing a Deadline

You offer employees a choice of three health maintenance organizations (HMOs) and several optional benefits, such as spending accounts for dependent care or medical expenses. Normally, employees must sign up for the following year by October 30 (or April 30). However, due to a printing problem, the booklets explaining the various options arrived late. So you're extending the deadline for people to register for an HMO, change any dependent information, and select any of the optional benefits until the second Friday of November (or May). In addition, you will have two information sessions next week. You would prefer that people attend those information sessions instead of e-mailing you to ask individual questions, but you will answer questions if necessary.

As Your Instructor Directs,

a. Write an e-mail to all employees changing the deadline and announcing the information sessions. (Pick times and locations that work for the employees of the organization you select.)

b. Write an e-mail reminder to go out the day before the first information session.

c. Write an e-mail reminder to go out the day before the last information session.

d. Write an e-mail to go out the Monday of the last week before the changed deadline.

Web Pages

7.8   Creating a Human Resources Web Page

As firms attempt to help employees balance work and family life (and as employers become aware that personal and family stresses affect performance at work), Human Resource departments sponsor an array of programs and provide information on myriad subjects. However, some people might be uncomfortable asking for help, either because the problem is embarrassing (who wants to admit needing help to deal with drug abuse, domestic violence, or addiction to gambling?) or because focusing on non-work issues (e.g., child care) might lead others to think they aren't serious about their jobs. The World Wide Web allows organizations to post information that employees can access privately—even from home.

Create a Web page that could be posted by Human Resources to help employees with one of the challenges they face. Possible topics include

- Appreciating an ethnic heritage.
- Buying a house.
- Caring for dependents: child care, helping a child learn to read, living with teenagers, elder care, and so forth.
- Dealing with a health issue: exercising, having a healthy diet, and so forth.
- Dealing with a health problem: alcoholism, cancer, diabetes, heart disease, obesity, and so forth.
- Dressing for success or dressing for casual days.
- Financial management: basic budgeting, deciding how much to save, choosing investments, and so forth.
- Nourishing the spirit: meditation, religion.
- Getting out of debt.
- Planning for retirement.
- Planning vacations.
- Reducing stress.
- Resolving conflicts on the job or in families.

Assume that this page can be accessed from another of the organization's pages. Offer at least seven links. (More is better.) You may offer information as well as links to other pages with information. At the top of the page, offer an overview of what the page covers. At the bottom of the page, put the creation/update date and your name and e-mail address.

As Your Instructor Directs,

a. Turn in two laser copies of your page(s). On another page, give the URLs for each link.

b. Turn in one laser copy of your page(s) and a disk with the HTML code and .gif files.

c. Write a memo to your instructor identifying the audience for which the page is designed and explaining (a) the search strategies you used to find material on this topic, (b) why you chose the pages and information you've included, and (c) why you chose the layout and graphics you've used.

d. Present your page orally to the class.

Hints:

- Pick a topic you know something about.
- Realize that audience members will have different needs. You could explain the basics of choosing day care or stocks, but don't recommend a specific day care center or a specific stock.
- If you have more than nine links, chunk them in small groups under headings.
- Create a good image of the organization.

Communicating at Work

7.9 Praising Work Done Well

Write a memo to a co-worker (with a copy to the person's supervisor) thanking him or her for helping you or complimenting him or her on a job well done.

7.10 Giving Good News

Write to a customer or client, to a vendor or supplier, or to your boss announcing good news. Possibilities include a product improvement, a price cut or special, an addition to your management team, a new contract, and so forth.

7.11 Recording Information for Other Workers

You have a lot of information in your head. Perhaps you've figured out a machine's quirks; you know a customer's idiosyncrasies; you understand the history of a situation. Write a memo that could be used by a vacation replacement or a new hire who might be asked to fill in for you.

7.12 Easing New Hires' Transition into Your Unit

Prepare a document to help new hires adjust quickly to your unit. You may want to focus solely on work procedures; you may also want to discuss aspects of the corporate culture.

Letter and Memo Assignments

7.13 Correcting a Misconception

You're an assistant in the Governor's office. Today, the Press Secretary gives you this letter and asks you to answer it.

> I see state employees driving BMWs and sports cars. These cars are a waste of taxpayer money!
>
> Sincerely,
>
> *Rick Shipley*
>
> Rick Shipley

After checking with the Department of Public Safety, you find that some state employees do drive luxury cars. The vehicles were confiscated in criminal investigations, and the state uses them instead of buying other vehicles. In the 10 years the policy has been in effect, the state has confiscated 43 vehicles—and thus bought 43 fewer vehicles than it would have otherwise needed.

Write to Mr. Shipley, responding to his criticism.

7.14 Reminding Guests about the Time Change

Twice a year in the United States, cities switch to daylight saving time and back again. The time change can be disruptive for hotel guests, who may lose track of the date, forget to change the clocks in their rooms, and miss appointments as a result.

Prepare a form letter to leave in each hotel room reminding guests of the impending time change. What should guests do?

Write the letter.

Hints:

■ Use an attention-getting page layout so readers don't ignore the message.

■ Pick a specific hotel or motel chain you know something about.

■ Use the letter to build goodwill for your hotel or motel chain. Use specific references to services or features the hotel offers, focusing not on what the hotel does for the reader, but on what the reader can do at the hotel.

7.15 Announcing a New Employee Benefit

Your company has decided to allow employees to spend one hour of "charity" time for every 40 they work (one hour a week for people who are on salary rather than paid by the hour). Employees will be paid for this hour, so their salaries will not fall. People who choose not to participate will work and be paid for the same number of hours as before. Supervisors are responsible for ensuring that essential business services are covered during business hours. Any employee who will be away during regular business hours (either to volunteer or to take off an hour in compensation for volunteering off-shift or on a weekend) will need to clear the planned absence with his or her supervisor. Your office is collecting a list of organizations that would welcome volunteers. People can work with an organized group or do something informal (such as tutoring at a local school or coaching kids at a local playground). People can volunteer one hour every week, two hours every other week, or a half-day each month. Volunteer hours cannot be banked from one month to the next; they must be used each month. The program starts January 1 (or June 1). The various groups that people work with will be featured in company publications.

As Vice President of Human Resources, write a memo to all employees announcing this new program.

Hints:

■ Pick a business, government, or nonprofit organization that you know something about.

■ What proportion of your employees are already involved in volunteer work?

■ Is community service or "giving back" consistent with your corporate mission?

- Some employees won't be able or won't want to participate. What is the benefit for them in working for a company that has such a program?

- Will promoting community participation help your organization attract and retain workers?
- Use your analysis from Chapter 3, problem 3.7.

7.16　Announcing an Additional Employee Benefit

Your organization has just created a benefit to help employees who are caring for elderly relatives. Now the Human Resources office will provide information and referral services for elder day care and long-term assisted-living or nursing care, and names and addresses of people willing to work part- or full-time as caregivers. Your organization will not pay for any of the actual cost of hiring a caregiver or paying for a nursing home. In addition, you will sponsor seminars on a number of topics about dealing with elderly parents, ranging from choosing a nursing facility, deciding when to stop driving, and filling out medical forms.

As part of the new policy, the organization will allow employees to use personal time off and sick time to care for any family member. You will also allow employees to take time off during the workday to stay until a nurse arrives or to drive a parent to a doctor's appointment. Employees must notify their supervisors in advance that they will be away and must make up the time sometime during the next 30 days. Employees who need more time can take unpaid leaves of up to 15 months and can return to their present jobs and current salaries.

The policy takes effect the first of next month.

Nationally, one in four workers over 40 provides care for an aging parent or other relative; in some organizations, the figure is higher. People who care for aging parents without assistance often make more mistakes on the job and have higher absenteeism and higher medical claims due to increased stress. Even greater than the loss of time (9.3 hours a month, according to one study) may be the inability of caregivers to accept promotions and more responsibility in their jobs. Some of them even quit their jobs to care for their parents; thus, their skills are no longer available to the organization at all.

Assume that you're Director of Human Resources, and write a memo to all employees announcing the benefit.

Hints:

- Pick a business, government, or nonprofit organization you know well.
- What age groups do employees represent? How many of them are caring for elderly parents now?
- Specify the topic, date, and place of the first seminar you'll sponsor. If possible, give the schedule for the first three months.
- Be sure to provide reader benefits for employees who do not care for elderly parents as well as those who do.
- How easy is it for your organization to attract and retain skilled workers? Why is it important to your organization that people be alert and be willing to take more responsibility?

7.17　Announcing an Employee Fitness Center

Your company is ready to open an employee fitness center with on-site aerobics classes, a swimming pool, and weight machines. The center will be open 6 AM to 10 PM daily; at least one qualified instructor will be on duty at all times. Employees get first preference; if there is extra room, clients, spouses, and children may also use the facilities. Locker rooms and showers will also be available.

Your company hopes that the fitness center will help out-of-shape employees get the exercise they need to be more productive. Other companies have gained as many as 762 workdays from shorter hospital stays by fitness center members. People who exercise have medical bills that are 35% lower than people who do not get enough exercise.

Write the memo announcing the center.

Hints:

- Who pays the medical insurance for employees? If the employer pays, then savings from healthier employees will pay for the center. If another payment plan is in effect, you'll need a different explanation for the company's decision to open the fitness center.
- Stress benefits apart from the company's saving money. How can easier access to exercise help employees? What do they do? How can exercise reduce stress, improve strength, and increase productivity at work?
- What kind of record does the company have of helping employees be healthy? Is the fitness center a departure for the company, or does the company have a history of company sports teams, stop-smoking clinics, and the like?
- What is the company's competitive position? If the company is struggling, you'll need to convince readers that the fitness center is a good use of scarce funds. If the company is doing well, show how having fit employees can make people even more productive.
- Stress fun as a benefit. How can access to the center make employees' lives more enjoyable?

7.18   Lining up a Consultant to Improve Teamwork

As Director of Education and Training you oversee all in-house training programs. Five weeks ago, Pat Dyrud, Vice President for Human Resources, asked you to set up a training course on teams. After making some phone calls, you tracked down Sarah Reed, a business communication professor at a nearby college.

"Yes, I do workshops on teamwork," she told you on the phone. "I would want at least a day and a half with participants—two full days would be better. They need time to practice the skills they'll be learning. I'm free Mondays and Tuesdays. I'm willing to work with up to five teams at a time, as long as the total number of people is 30 or less. Tell me what kinds of teams they work in, what they already know, and what kinds of things you want me to emphasize. My fee is $2,500 a day. Of course, you'd reimburse me for expenses."

You told her you thought a two-day session would be feasible, but you'd have to get back to her after you got budget approval. You wrote a quick memo to Pat Dyrud explaining the situation and asking about what the session should cover.

Two weeks ago, you received this memo:

> I've asked the Veep for budget approval for $5,000 for a two-day session plus no more than $750 for all expenses. I don't think there will be a problem.
>
> We need some of the basics: strategies for working in groups, making decisions, budgeting time, and so forth. We especially need work on dealing with problem group members and on handling conflict—I think some of our people are so afraid that they won't seem to be "team players" that they agree too readily.
>
> I don't want someone to lecture. We've already had a lecture and frankly, it didn't do much good. Our people have even read some articles on teamwork, but somehow even with teams people are using old work habits. I don't want some ivory tower theorist. We need practical exercises that can help us acquire skills that we can put into effect immediately.
>
> Attached is a list of 24 people who are free Monday and Tuesday of the second week of next month. Note that we've got a good mix of people. If the session goes well, I may want you to schedule additional sessions.

Today, you got approval from the Vice President to schedule the session, pay Professor Reed the fee, and reimburse her for expenses to a maximum of $750. She will have to keep all receipts and turn in an itemized list of expenses to be reimbursed; you cannot reimburse her if she does not have receipts.

You also need to explain the mechanics of the session. You'll meet in the Conference Room, which has a screen and flip charts. You have an overhead projector, a slide projector, a laptop computer for showing PowerPoint slides, a video camera, a VCR, and a TV, but you need to reserve these if she wants to use them.

Write to Professor Reed. You don't have to persuade her to come since she's already informally agreed, but you do want her to look forward to the job and to do her best work.

Hints:

- Choose an organization you know something about.
- What do teams do in this organization? What challenges do they face?
- Will most participants have experience working in teams? Will they have bad habits to overcome? What attitudes toward teams are they likely to have?
- Check the calendar to get the dates. If there's any ambiguity about what "the second week of next month" is, call Pat Dyrud to check.

7.19   Agreeing to Waive a Fee

You're a customer service representative for a major credit card company. Last week, Naomi Neyens called asking that you waive the annual fee on her account. "I'm getting offers from other companies with no annual fee. I'd like to keep my account, but only if you waive the fee for the life of the account." You agreed to do as she asked, effective immediately.

Write to Ms. Neyens, confirming the conversation (and specifying her 16-digit account number).

7.20   Answering an International Inquiry

Your business, government, or nonprofit organization has received the following inquiries from international correspondents. (You choose the country the inquiry is from.)

1. Please tell us about a new product, service, or trend so that we can decide whether we want to buy, license, or imitate it in our country.

2. We have heard about a problem [technical, social, political, or ethical] that occurred in your organization. Could you please tell us what really happened and estimate how it is likely to affect the long-term success of the organization?

3. Please tell us about college programs in this field. We are interested in sending some of our managers to your country to complete a college degree.

4. We are considering setting up a plant in your city. We have already received adequate business information. However, we would also like to know how comfortable our nationals will feel. Do people in your city speak our language? How many? What opportunities exist for our nationals to improve their English? Does your town already have people from a wide mix of nations? Which are the largest groups?

5. Our organization would like to subscribe to an English-language trade journal. Which one would you recommend? Why? How much does it cost? How can we order it?

As Your Instructor Directs,

a. Answer one or more of the inquiries. Assume that your reader either reads English or can have your message translated.

b. Write a memo to your instructor explaining how you've adapted the message for your audience.

Hints:

■ Even though you can write in English, English may not be your reader's native language. Write a letter that can be translated easily.

■ In some cases, you may need to spell out background information that might not be clear to someone from another country.

7.21   Providing Information to Job Applicants

Your company is in a prime vacation spot, and as Personnel Manager you get many letters from students asking about summer jobs. Company policy is to send everyone an application for employment, a list of the jobs you expect to have open that summer with the rate of pay for each, a description of benefits for seasonal employees, and an interview schedule. Candidates must come for an interview at their own expense and should call to sched-ule a time in advance. Competition is keen: only a small percentage of those interviewed will be hired.

Write a form letter to students who've written to you asking about summer jobs. Give them the basic information about the hiring procedure and tell them what to do next. Be realistic about their chances, but maintain their interest in working for you.

7.22   Announcing a Premium Holiday

Rather than paying fees to an insurer, your company is self-insured. That is, you set aside corporate funds to pay for medical bills. If claims are light, the company saves money.

Employees pay a monthly fee for part of the amount of their health insurance. However, with one month to go in the fiscal year, you have more than enough set aside to cover possible costs. You're going to pass along some of the savings to employees (who, by staying healthy, have kept medical costs down). Next month will be a "premium holiday." You will not deduct the monthly premium from employees' checks. As a result, they will have a slightly higher take-home pay next month. The holiday is just for one month; after it, the premium for health insurance will again be deducted each month.

Write a memo to all employees.

7.23   Announcing a Tuition Reimbursement Program

Your organization has decided to encourage employees to take courses by reimbursing each eligible employee a maximum of $3,500 in tuition and fees during any one calendar year. Anyone who wants to participate in the program must apply before the first class meeting; the application must be signed by the employee's immediate supervisor. The Office of Human Resources will evaluate applications. That office has application forms; it also has catalogs from nearby schools and colleges.

The only courses employees may choose are those either related to the employee's current position (or to a position in the company that the employee might hold someday) or part of a job-related degree program. Again, the degree may be one that would help the employee's current position or that would qualify him or her for a promotion or transfer in the organization.

Only tuition and fees are covered, not books or supplies. People whose applications are approved will be reimbursed when they have completed the course with a grade of C or better. An employee cannot be reimbursed until he or she submits a copy of the approved application, an official grade report, and a statement of the tuition paid. If someone is eligible for other financial aid (scholarship, veterans benefits), the company will pay tuition costs not covered by that aid as long as the employee does not receive more than $3,500 and as long as the total tuition reimbursement does not exceed the actual cost of tuition and fees.

Part-time employees are not eligible; full-time employees must work at the company three months before they can apply to participate in the program. Courses may be at any appropriate level (high school, college, or graduate). However, the Internal Revenue Service currently requires workers to pay tax on any reimbursement for graduate programs. Undergraduate and basic education reimbursements of $5,250 a year are not taxed.

7.24 Sending Tapes to a Customer

Two months ago, your business school sponsored a colloquium with many local and out-of-town business people. A highlight of the colloquium was small group discussions. The discussions were taped, and people could order tapes and transcripts.

Some of the tapes turned out well: "Ethics in Small Business," "How the Internet Is Changing Business," and "When Your Business Partner Is Your Spouse." But the audiotapes of "Valuing Diversity" and "Small Businesses

As Director of Human Resources, write a memo to all employees explaining this new benefit.

Hints:

■ Pick an organization you know something about. What do its employees do? What courses or degrees might help them do their jobs better?

■ How much education do employees already have? How do they feel about formal schooling?

■ The information in the problem is presented in a confusing order. Put related items together.

■ The problem stresses the limits of the policy. Without changing the provision, present them positively.

■ How will having a better educated workforce help the organization? Think about the challenges the organization faces, its competitive environment, and so forth.

Can Be Exporters Too" didn't turn out well. You haven't been able to transcribe them, and the quality isn't good enough to distribute.

Write to Paul Cambiaso. You're enclosing the tape on the Internet that he ordered. But he also ordered the tape on diversity. Since it isn't available, you're sending him a check of $12.62 to reimburse him. He's one of several people you have to write. He has a local address, but you don't know him.

7.25 Summarizing *The Wall Street Journal*

Today, your in-basket contains this message from your boss:

As you know, I'm leaving tomorrow for a vacation in Egypt. While I'm gone, will you please scan *The Wall Street Journal* every day and summarize any articles that are relevant to our business? I'd like your summary in hard copy on my desk when I return.

As Your Instructor Directs,

a. Scan *The Wall Street Journal* for one week, two weeks, or until you find three to five relevant articles for the company you have chosen.

b. Summarize the articles in a memo.

c. Compare summaries with a small group of students. Do summaries of the same article for different organizations focus on different points?

d. Present one of your summaries to the class.

Hints:

■ Pick an organization you know something about. If the organization is large, focus on one division or department.

■ Provide an overview to let your boss know whether the articles you've summarized are on a single topic or on several topics.

■ Show how each article relates to the organization.

■ Give the full citation (see Chapter 13) so that it's easy to track down articles if the boss wants to see the original.

7.26   Summarizing Information

Summarize one or more of the following:

1. Richard B. Chase and Sriram Dasu, "Want to Perfect Your Company's Service? Use Behavioral Science," *Harvard Business Review,* June 2001, 79–84; reprint R0106D.

2. One of Jakob Nielsen's Alertboxes <www.useit.com/alertbox>.

3. Benefits and programs offered by one of *Fortune's* "Best Companies to Work For." (On <www.fortune.com>, go to "Lists" and then to "Best Companies.")

4. The criticisms of a company on an "anticorporate activism" Web site (in a search engine, key in the company name and "customer opinion").

5. An article assigned by your instructor.

6. An article or Web page of your choice.

As Your Instructor Directs,

a. Write a summary of no more than 100 words.

b. Write a 250- to 300-word summary.

c. Write a one-page summary.

d. Compare your summary to those of a small group of students. Did everyone agree on what information to include? How do you account for any differences?

7.27   Evaluating Web Pages

Today you get this e-mail from your boss:

> Subject: Evaluating Our Web Page
>
> Our CEO wants to know how our Web page compares to those of our competitors. I'd like you to do this in two steps. First, send me a list of your criteria. Then give me an evaluation of two of our competitors' and of our own pages. I'll combine your memo with others on other Web pages to put together a comprehensive evaluation for the next Executive Meeting.

As Your Instructor Directs,

a. List the generic criteria for evaluating a Web page. Think about the various audiences for the page and the content that will keep them coming back, the way the page is organized, how easy it is to find something, the visual design, and the details, such as a creation/update date.

b. List criteria for pages of specific kinds of organizations. For example, a nonprofit organization might want information for potential and current donors, volunteers, and clients. A financial institution might want to project an image both of trustworthiness and as a good place to work.

c. Evaluate three Web pages of similar organizations. Which is best? Why?

7.28   Writing a Thank-You Letter

Write a thank-you letter to someone who has helped you achieve your goals.

As Your Instructor Directs,

a. Turn in a copy of the letter.

b. Mail the letter to the person who helped you.

c. Write a memo to your instructor explaining the choices you made in writing the thank-you letter.

7.29   Writing a Job Description

Your unit has more business than it can handle, and you're authorized to hire additional staff. Previous searches at advanced levels have rarely been successful, but you've had good luck bringing in entry-level people and teaching them what they need to know. Three groups in your town have higher-than-average unemployment: Russian immigrants, African Americans, and Hispanics.

The Russian immigrants are quite recent; few of them speak English. But their sponsors say that they are very willing to learn. The unemployed African Americans and Hispanics may not have had experience with computers. You could write the job description so that members of all three of these groups could compete equally, and people in all three groups need jobs. You also know some specific individuals you'd like to hire: Last summer you had two excellent interns, both of whom have good communication skills and both of whom (after a summer of training) have relevant computer experience. And you know that your supervisor's nephew is finishing college and looking for a job. He's majored in marketing and has been a member of the school's basketball team. Interviews on TV and in the local paper suggest he isn't articulate. Your supervisor hasn't put any explicit pressure on you to hire him, but you do get regular updates on his job hunt when you see your supervisor.

As Your Instructor Directs,

a. Write a job description for an entry-level job. Pick an organization you know something about.

b. Write a memo to your instructor explaining the ethical choices you made.

7.30 Announcing a Corporate Chaplain

To provide emotional support to employees, your company has hired a part-time corporate chaplain. Elizabeth Singleton is an ordained Methodist minister, but her work will be nondenominational. She'll come to your company four afternoons a week to be available to talk with employees about personal and professional problems. She will offer caring and confidentiality; nothing anyone says to her will be passed on to anyone else in the company without explicit permission. Employees will not have to pay for conversations with her.

Write a memo to all employees.

Hints:

- Choose an organization you know something about.
- Think about the ages of your employees and the kinds of problems they're likely to face.

- What percentage of your employees participate in organized religion?
- What is the general attitude in the community and in your workplace to personal problems and crises?
- How can you show all employees that this appointment is a good use of company funds?

Source: Problem inspired by Edward O. Welles, "Chaplain for a New Economy," *Inc.*, November 1997, 68–77; and Emma Jean Ghee Leche, "Organizational Spirituality: A New Construct for Organizational Communication," Association for Business Communication Annual Conference, San Antonio, TX, November 11–14, 1998.

8

Negative Messages

Apologies

Subject Lines for Negative Messages

Organizing Negative Letters

Organizing Negative Memos

- Giving Bad News to Superiors
- Giving Bad News to Peers and Subordinates

The Parts of a Negative Message

- Buffers
- Reasons
- Refusals
- Alternatives
- Endings

Tone in Negative Messages

Alternate Strategies for Negative Messages

- Recasting the Situation as a Positive Message
- Recasting the Situation as a Persuasive Message
- Humor in Negative Messages

Writing Negative E-Mail Messages

Varieties of Negative Messages

- Rejections and Refusals
- Disciplinary Notices and Negative Performance Appraisals
- Layoffs and Firings

Solving a Sample Problem

- Problem
- Analysis of the Problem
- Discussion of the Sample Solutions

Summary of Key Points

Negative Messages

Rajani J. Kamath
Communications and Organizational Effectiveness Consultant

A Communications and Organizational Effectiveness Consultant, Rajani Kamath formerly led the leadership effectiveness and communication efforts for the Card Operations business at Amex Canada Inc., a wholly owned subsidiary of American Express Travel Related Services Company.

Delivering bad news is one of the most difficult tasks a leader may be asked to perform. When employee expectations do not match reality, dysfunctional behavior may result. To reduce the potential for dysfunctional behavior, bad news should be communicated openly and honestly, despite how difficult the news may be for the employees to hear.

Preparation is required to effectively communicate bad news to employees so they understand the reasons for a decision and how it affects them. Be able to answer the following key questions:

- What is the big picture? Why is the change needed?
- What is the purpose of the change?
- How does the bad news relate to corporate/business objectives?
- How will the bad news affect employees, customers, and shareholders?

In 1998, a decision was made to eliminate the third shift (12 AM to 8 AM) in one of our departments at Amex due to a reduction in workflow. We needed to communicate these layoffs not only to the nearly 80 employees who would be directly affected but also to people who would be indirectly affected. Otherwise, rumors would run rampant. Everyone needed to hear the bad news at about the same time.

The department leaders met face-to-face with the third-shift employees to inform them of the organizational decision. The leaders communicated the bad news openly and honestly. The face-to-face format allowed employees to ask questions and voice their concerns immediately. Whenever possible, third-shift employees were reassigned to positions in other departments.

Management teams in other departments then sent a memo about the reorganization to all other employees.

Well-planned, honest communication paid dividends because the employees had a clear understanding for the reasons behind the decision and how the decision would affect them.

Open and honest communication, whether the news is good or bad, is the key to business integrity and success.

> "*Bad news should be communicated openly and honestly, despite how difficult the news may be for the employees to hear.*"

The Awful News*

Sharing the bad news, all the news, may be the only way to save a company.

After six years of dot-com success, the bubble burst. And suddenly Logical Net, an $8 million Internet service provider based in Albany, New York, couldn't collect its accounts receivable from its customers. In six months, the company went from earning money to losing $130,000 a month. Bankruptcy loomed.

The CEO decided to share all of the company's financial information with his managers. To avoid bankruptcy, he needed help from everyone in the company. He hoped that opening the books would create buy-in.

It worked.

Employees found ways to eliminate waste and save money. Salespeople focused on bringing in recurring revenues and nudged customers to pay their bills. The company was saved. And the corporate culture changed. Now all employees think about the financial implications of everything they do.

*Based on Ilan Mochari, "The Talking Cure," *Inc.*, November 2001, 122–23.

In a **negative message,** the basic information we have to convey is negative; we expect the reader to be disappointed or angry.

Negative messages include rejections and refusals, announcements of policy changes that do not benefit customers or consumers, requests the reader will see as insulting or intrusive, negative performance appraisals, disciplinary notices, and product recalls or notices of defects.

A negative message always has several purposes:

Primary purposes:

To give the reader the bad news.

To have the reader read, understand, and accept the message.

To maintain as much goodwill as possible.

Secondary purposes:

To build a good image of the writer.

To build a good image of the writer's organization.

To reduce or eliminate future correspondence on the same subject so the message doesn't create more work for the writer.

In many negative situations, the writer and reader will continue to deal with each other. Even when further interaction is unlikely (for example, when a company rejects a job applicant or refuses to renew a customer's insurance), the firm wants anything the reader may say about the company to be positive or neutral rather than negative.

Some messages that at first appear to be negative can be structured to create a positive feeling. Even when it is not possible to make the reader happy with the news we must convey, we still want readers to feel that

- They have been taken seriously.
- Our decision is fair and reasonable.
- If they were in our shoes, they would make the same decision.

Apologies

Not all negative messages need to include apologies.

- **No explicit apology is necessary if the error is small and if you are correcting the mistake.**

    Negative: I'm sorry the clerk did not credit your account properly.

    Better: Your statement has been corrected to include your payment of $263.75.

- **Do not apologize when you are not at fault.** When you have done everything you can and when a delay or problem is due to circumstances beyond your control, you aren't at fault and don't need to apologize. It may be appropriate to include an explanation so the reader knows you weren't negligent. If the news is bad, put the explanation first. If you have good news for the reader, put it before your explanation.

    Negative: I'm sorry that I could not answer your question sooner. I had to wait until the sales figures for the second quarter were in.

    Better (neutral or bad news):   We needed the sales figures for the second quarter to answer your question. Now that they're in, I can tell you that . . .

    Better (good news):   The new advertising campaign is a success. The sales figures for the second quarter are finally in, and they show that . . .

If the delay or problem is long or large, it is good you-attitude to ask the reader whether he or she wants to confirm the original plan or make different arrangements.

Negative: I'm sorry that the chairs will not be ready by August 25 as promised.

Better: Due to a strike against the manufacturer, the desk chairs you ordered will not be ready until November. Do you want to keep that order, or would you like to look at the models available from other suppliers?

■ **When you apologize, do it early, briefly, and sincerely.** Apologize only once, early in the message. Let the reader move on to other, more positive information.

Even if major trouble or inconvenience has resulted from your error, you don't need to go on about all the horrible things that happened. The reader already knows this negative information, and you can omit it. Instead, focus on what you have done to correct the situation.

If you don't know whether or not any inconvenience has resulted, don't raise the issue at all.

Negative: I'm sorry I didn't answer your letter sooner. I hope that my delay hasn't inconvenienced you.

Better: I'm sorry I didn't answer your letter sooner.

In business documents, apologize only when you are at fault. According to linguist Deborah Tannen, US women use "I'm sorry" both to mean "I'm responsible for the error or problem" and "It's too bad that this situation happened." She claims that US men interpret "I'm sorry" as admitting guilt and avoid using the words to avoid being put down in a conversation.[1] Certainly not all women or all men fit these generalizations. Nevertheless, be aware that "I'm sorry" may be interpreted as an admission of error, and avoid overusing the phrase. Refer to Chapter 2, Figure 2.3, for examples of other negative words to avoid.

Subject Lines for Negative Messages

When you write to superiors, use a subject line (◂ p. 151) that focuses on solving the problem.

Subject: Improving Our Subscription Letter

When you write to peers and subordinates, put the topic (but not your action on it) in the subject line.

Subject: Status of Conversion Table Program

Due to heavy demands on our time, we have not yet been able to write programs for the conversion tables you asked for.

Use a negative subject line in e-mail messages.

Subject: Delay in Converting Tables

Use a negative subject line in letters when you think readers may ignore what they think is a routine message.

The best subject line for negative e-mail messages depends on whether you're refusing a request or initiating the negative. When you say *no* to an

Admit Guilt and Fix the Problem*

When a company makes a major mistake, it needs to admit guilt and fix the problem.

NCS (formerly National Computer Systems) grades standardized tests from around the world. Somehow, the company used the wrong "correct" answer to score the eighth-grade math test Minnesota requires for high school graduation. The misscoring mistakenly failed 8,000 students, including 300 seniors who were denied the right to graduate.

The reason for the mistake didn't really matter, and the company didn't try to blame the error on tight deadlines or unreliable help. Instead, the company president announced baldly, "We screwed up."

And the company moved to undo the damage it had done. It reimbursed students for math tutors, summer school courses, and lost wages. It created and paid for a special graduation ceremony where students could have pictures taken with Governor Jesse Ventura.

NCS's proactive work kept the criticism and bad press to a minimum and reestablished goodwill.

*Based on " 'We Screwed Up,' " *Presentations,* February 2001, 42.

Never Say No*

e-mail request, just hit "reply" and use "Re:" plus whatever the original subject line was for your response. When you write a new message, you will have to decide whether to use the negative in the subject line. The subject line should contain the negative when

- ▪ The negative is serious. Many people do not read all their e-mail messages. A neutral subject line may lead the reader to ignore the message.
- ▪ The reader needs the information to make a decision or act.
- ▪ You report your own errors (as opposed to the reader's).

Thus the following would be acceptable subject lines in e-mail messages:

Subject: We Lost McDonald's Account

Subject: Power to Be Out Sunday, March 8

Subject: Error in Survey Data Summary

When you write to people whom you know well, exaggerated subject lines are acceptable:

Subject: Gloom, Despair, and Agony

In other situations, a neutral subject line is acceptable.

Subject: Results of 360° Performance Appraisals

Organizing Negative Letters

The first pattern in Figure 8.1 helps writers maintain goodwill.

Figure 8.2 illustrates how the basic pattern for negative messages can be used. This letter omits the reason, probably because the change benefits the company, not the customer. Putting the bad news first (though pairing it immediately with an alternative) makes it more likely that the recipient will read the letter. If this letter seemed to be just a routine renewal, or if it opened with the good news that the premium was lower, few recipients would read the letter carefully, and many would not read it at all. Then, if they had accidents and found that their coverage was reduced, they'd blame the company for not communicating clearly. Emphasizing the negative here is both good ethics and good business.

Organizing Negative Memos

The best way to organize a negative memo depends on whether you're writing to a superior or to a peer or subordinate and on the severity of the negative information.

Giving Bad News to Superiors

Your superior expects you to solve minor problems by yourself. But sometimes, solving a problem requires more authority or resources than you have. When you give bad news to a superior, also recommend a way to deal with the problem. Turn the negative message into a persuasive one. See the middle column in Figure 8.1.

Giving Bad News to Peers and Subordinates

When you must pass along serious bad news to peers and subordinates, use the variation in the last column in Figure 8.1.

No serious negative (such as being downsized or laid off) should come as a complete surprise. Managers can prepare for possible negatives by giving full

FIGURE 8.1   How to Organize Negative Messages

Negative letters	Negative memos to superiors	Negative memos to peers and subordinates
1. **When you have a reason that readers will understand and accept, give the reason before the refusal.** A good reason prepares the reader to expect the refusal.	1. **Describe the problem.** Tell what's wrong, clearly and unemotionally.	1. **Describe the problem.** Tell what's wrong, clearly and unemotionally.
2. **Give the negative information or refusal just once, clearly.** Inconspicuous refusals can be missed altogether, making it necessary to say *no* a second time.	2. **Tell how it happened.** Provide the background. What underlying factors led to this specific problem?	2. **Present an alternative or compromise, if one is available.** An alternative not only gives readers another way to get what they want but also suggests that you care about readers and helping them meet their needs.
3. **Present an alternative or compromise, if one is available.** An alternative not only gives readers another way to get what they want but also suggests that you care about readers and helping them meet their needs.	3. **Describe the options for fixing it.** If one option is clearly best, you may need to discuss only one. But if the reader will think of other options, or if different people will judge the options differently, describe all the options, giving their advantages and disadvantages.	3. **If possible, ask for input or action.** People in the audience may be able to suggest solutions. And workers who help make a decision are far more likely to accept the consequences.
4. **End with a positive, forward-looking statement.**	4. **Recommend a solution and ask for action.** Ask for approval so that you can go ahead to make the necessary changes to fix the problem.	

information as it becomes available. It is also possible to let the people who will be affected by a decision participate in setting the criteria. Someone who has bought into the criteria for awarding cash for suggestions or retaining workers is more likely to accept decisions using such criteria. And in some cases, the synergism of groups may make possible ideas that management didn't think of or rejected as "unacceptable." Some workplaces, for example, might decide to reduce everyone's pay slightly rather than laying off some individuals. Employee suggestions enabled Mentor Training, a San Jose company providing software training, to cut its payroll by 30% without laying off any full-time employees.[2]

When the bad news is less serious, as in Figure 8.3, use the pattern for negative letters unless your knowledge of the reader(s) suggests that another pattern will be more effective. For example, in some organizations each person takes the Myers-Briggs Personality Inventory and puts a sign up indicating his or her "type." In such an organization, someone sending a negative message to a "feeling type" might want to delay the negative by using a buffer (a neutral or positive sentence) even though the organization's discourse community (◄ p. 59) as a whole favored directness.

For memos, the context of communication is crucial. The reader's reaction is influenced by the following factors:

- Do you and the reader have a good relationship?
- Does the organization treat people well?
- Have readers been warned of possible negatives?
- Have readers bought into the criteria for the decision?
- Do communications after the negative build goodwill?

For example, Tiburon, a company that provides public safety systems and services, used "open book management"—sharing all its financial information

FIGURE 8.2   A Negative Letter

Vickers
Insurance Company

3373 Forbes Avenue
Rosemont, PA 19010
(215) 572-0100

Negative information highlighted so reader won't ignore message

Liability Coverage Is Being Discontinued— Here's How to Replace It!

Negative

Alternative

Dear Policyholder:

Negative

When your auto insurance is renewed, it will no longer include liability coverage unless you select the new Assurance Plan. Here's why.

Positive information underlined for emphasis

Liability coverage is being discontinued. It, and the part of the premium which paid for it, will be dropped from all policies when they are renewed.

This change could leave a gap in your protection. But you can replace the old Liability Coverage with Vickers' new Assurance Plan.

No reason is given. The change probably benefits the company rather than the reader, so it is omitted.

Alternative

With the new Assurance Plan, you receive benefits for litigation or awards arising from an accident—regardless of who's at fault. The cost for the Assurance Plan at any level is based on the ages of drivers, where you live, your driving record, and other factors. If these change before your policy is renewed, the cost of your Assurance Plan may also change. The actual cost will be listed in your renewal statement.

To sign up for the Assurance Plan, just check the level of coverage you want on the enclosed form and return it in the postage-paid envelope within 14 days. You'll be assured of the coverage you select.

Forward-looking ending emphasizes reader's choice

Sincerely,

C. J. Morgan

C. J. Morgan
President

Alternative

P.S. The Assurance Plan protects you against possible legal costs arising from an accident. Sign up for the Plan today and receive full coverage from Vickers.

with employees. When the company had to lay off 80 of its 320 employees, the layoffs weren't a surprise, and people understood that the layoffs were necessary. Says founder and CEO Bruce Kelling, "I even received calls and in one case a letter from terminated employees, offering condolences, knowing how difficult it was for the company and that we did the right thing." Cuts to the rank-and-file hurt less when it's clear that senior managers are also taking cuts.[3]

FIGURE 8.3   A Negative Memo to Subordinates

Memo

Board of County Commissioners
Olentangy County, Nebraska

Date: January 10, 2003

To: All Employees

From: Floyd E. Loer, Dorothy A. Walters, and Stewart Mattson

Subject: Accounting for Work Missed Due to Bad Weather

Reason   As you know, Olentangy County Services are always open for our customers, whatever the weather. Employees who missed work during the snowstorm last week may count the absence as vacation, sick day(s), or personal day(s).

Refusal, stated as positively as possible   Hourly workers who missed less than a day have the option of taking the missed time as vacation, sick, or personal hours or of being paid only for the hours they worked.

One small positive   Approval of vacation or personal days will be automatic; the normal requirement of giving at least 24 hours' notice is waived.

Goodwill ending   Thanks for all the efforts you have made to continue giving our customers the best possible service during one of the snowiest winters on record.

The Parts of a Negative Message

This section provides more information about wording each part of a negative message.

Buffers

Traditionally, textbooks recommended that negative messages open with buffers. A **buffer** is a neutral or positive statement that allows you to delay the negative. Recent research suggests that buffers do not make readers respond more positively,[4] and good buffers are very hard to write. However, in special situations, you may want to use a buffer.

To be effective, a buffer must put the reader in a good frame of mind, not give the bad news but not imply a positive answer either, and provide a natural transition to the body of the letter. The kinds of statements most often used as buffers are good news, facts and chronologies of events, references to enclosures, thanks, and statements of principle.

Negative Messages to Customers*

I only use buffers when they mean something. Let's face it, most people see right through buffers. The real reason to use one is to save face, to be nice, or for other cultural reasons—important, but issues of style, not substance.

I'm a firm believer in giving the real reason for doing something, unless the reason is too technical or creates liabilities for the business. Sometimes it's enough to give the facts and let the reader draw the conclusions.

If disclosure creates potential liabilities, or is too complex, or will create a firestorm of negative reaction, you've got to think hard. Fortunately, only the rare negative message falls into those categories. Most negative events are temporary, and very few, if any, mean a meltdown of your business or your career. Most customers and employees know you have a business to run and that you need to make and implement business decisions.

*Quoted from statement by Karl P. Keller, Vice President, First Chicago NBD Investments, to Kitty Locker, April 8, 1997.

1. **Start with any good news or positive elements the letter contains.**

> Starting Thursday, June 26, you'll have access to your money 24 hours a day at First National Bank.

Letter announcing that the drive-up windows will be closed for two days while automatic teller machines are installed

2. **State a fact or provide a chronology of events.**

> As a result of the new graduated dues schedule—determined by vote of the Delegate Assembly last December and subsequently endorsed by the Executive Council—members are now asked to establish their own dues rate and to calculate the total amount of their remittance.

Announcement of a new dues structure that will raise most members' dues

3. **Refer to enclosures in the letter.**

> Enclosed is a new sticker for your car. You may pick up additional ones in the office if needed. Please *destroy* old stickers bearing the signature of "L.S. LaVoie."

Letter announcing increase in parking rental rates

4. **Thank the reader for something he or she has done.**

> Thank you for scheduling appointments for me with so many senior people at First National Bank. My visit there March 14 was very informative.

Letter refusing a job offer

5. **State a general principle.**

> Good drivers should pay substantially less for their auto insurance. The Good Driver Plan was created to reward good drivers (those with five-year accident-free records) with our lowest available rates. A change in the plan, effective January 1, will help keep those rates low.

Letter announcing that the company will now count traffic tickets, not just accidents, in calculating insurance rates—a change that will raise many people's premiums

Some readers will feel betrayed by messages whose positive openers delay the central negative point. Therefore, use a buffer only when the reader (individually or culturally) values harmony or when the buffer serves another purpose. For example, when you must thank the reader somewhere in the letter, putting the "thank you" in the first paragraph allows you to start on a positive note.

Buffers are hard to write. Even if you think the reader would prefer to be let down easily, use a buffer only when you can write a good one.

Reasons

Research shows that readers who described themselves as "totally surprised" had much more negative feelings and described their feelings as being stronger than did those who expected the refusal.[5] A clear and convincing reason prepares the reader for the refusal, resulting in readers who find it easier to accept the negative.

The following reason is inadequate.

> Weak reason: The goal of the Knoxville CHARGE-ALL Center is to provide our customers faster, more personalized service. Since you now live outside the Knoxville CHARGE-ALL service area, we can no longer offer you the advantages of a local CHARGE-ALL Center.

If the reader says, "I don't care if my bills are slow and impersonal," will the company let the reader keep the card? No. The real reason for the negative is that the bank's franchise allows it to have cardholders only in a given geographical region.

Real reason:	Each local CHARGE-ALL center is permitted to offer accounts to customers in a several-state area. The Knoxville CHARGE-ALL center serves customers east of the Mississippi. You can continue to use your current card until it expires. When that happens, you'll need to open an account with a CHARGE-ALL center that serves Texas.

Don't hide behind "company policy": readers will assume the policy is designed to benefit you at their expense. If possible, show how readers benefit from the policy. If they do not benefit, don't mention policy at all.

Weak reason:	I cannot write an insurance policy for you because company policy does not allow me to do so.
Better reason:	Gorham insures cars only when they are normally garaged at night. Standard insurance policies cover a wider variety of risks and charge higher fees. Limiting the policies we write gives Gorham customers the lowest possible rates for auto insurance.

Avoid saying that you *cannot* do something. Most negative messages exist because the writer or company has chosen certain policies or cutoff points. In the example above, the company could choose to insure a wider variety of customers if it wanted to do so.

Often you as a middle manager will enforce policies that you did not design and announce decisions that you did not make. Don't pass the buck by saying, "This was a terrible decision." In the first place, carelessly criticizing your superiors is never a good idea. In the second place, if you really think a policy is bad, try to persuade your superiors to change it. If you can't think of convincing reasons to change the policy, maybe it isn't so bad after all.

If you have several reasons for saying *no,* use only those that are strong and watertight. If you give five reasons and readers dismiss two of them, readers may feel that they've won and should get the request.

Weak reason:	You cannot store large bulky items in the dormitory over the summer because moving them into and out of storage would tie up the stairs and the elevators just at the busiest times when people are moving in and out.
Way to dismiss the reason:	We'll move large items before or after the two days when most people are moving in or out.

If you do not have a good reason, omit the reason rather than use a weak one. Even if you have a strong reason, omit it if it makes the company look bad.

Reason that hurts company:	Our company is not hiring at the present time because profits are down. In fact, the downturn has prompted top management to reduce the salaried staff by 5% just this month, with perhaps more reductions to come.
Better:	Our company does not have any openings now.

The Best Negative Is No Surprise*

In the 1990s, Ford Motor Co. downsized, closing the venerable Thunderbird factory and laying off thousands of workers. Ford was able to do this without union strife—by talking about plans far in advance.

Ford's CEO and the United Autoworkers' vice president met for breakfast every other month. Ford shared sensitive information and sought union input. When the Thunderbird factory closed, the union knew six months ahead of time (not the mere 60 days required by law). The union negotiated a hefty bonus for workers who moved to a Ford truck plant in another state.

According to industry analysts, Ford's honesty about upcoming negatives not only averts costly strikes but also contributes to its workers' high productivity.

*Based on "If Ford Can Do It, Why Can't GM?" *Business Week,* June 29, 1998, p. 36.

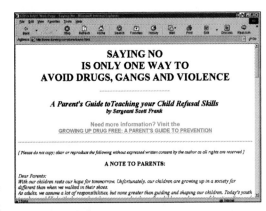

InSite

www.dareing.com/dare/sayno.html

Being able to say *no* is a necessary skill in life as well as in business. Some of the techniques offered by Drug Abuse Resistance Education (D.A.R.E.) may be more appropriate for saying *no* to friends than to co-workers or customers. However, even in business, simply not answering—similar to walking away—is one of the most common ways to refuse a request.

Refusals

Deemphasize the refusal by putting it in the same paragraph as the reason, rather than in a paragraph by itself.

Sometimes you may be able to imply the refusal rather than stating it directly.

Direct refusal: You cannot get insurance for just one month.

Implied refusal: The shortest term for an insurance policy is six months.

Be sure the implication is crystal clear. Any message can be misunderstood, but an optimistic or desperate reader is particularly unlikely to understand a negative message. One of your purposes in a negative message is to close the door on the subject. You do not want to have to write a second letter saying that the real answer is *no*.

Alternatives

Giving the reader an alternative or a compromise, if one is available, is a good idea for several reasons:

- It offers the reader another way to get what he or she wants.
- It suggests that you really care about the reader and about helping to meet his or her needs.
- It enables the reader to reestablish the psychological freedom you limited when you said *no*.
- It allows you to end on a positive note and to present yourself and your organization as positive, friendly, and helpful.

When you give an alternative, give readers all the information they need to act on it, but don't take the necessary steps. Let readers decide whether to try the alternative.

Negative messages limit the reader's freedom. People may respond to a limitation of freedom by asserting their freedom in some other arena. Jack W. Brehm calls this phenomenon **psychological reactance.**[6] Psychological reactance is at work when a customer who has been denied credit no longer buys even on a cash basis, a subordinate who has been passed over for a promotion gets back at the company by deliberately doing a poor job, or someone who has been laid off sabotages the company's computers.

An alternative allows the reader to react in a way that doesn't hurt you. By letting readers decide for themselves whether they want the alternative, you allow them to reestablish their sense of psychological freedom.

The specific alternative will vary depending on the circumstances. In Figure 8.4, the company is unwilling to quote a price on an item on which it cannot be competitive. In different circumstances, the writer might offer different alternatives.

Endings

If you have a good alternative, refer to it in your ending: "Let me know if you can use A515 grade 70."

The best endings look to the future.

> Wherever you have your account, you'll continue to get all the service you've learned to expect from CHARGE-ALL, and the convenience of charging items at over a million stores, restaurants, and hotels in the United States and abroad—and in Knoxville, too, whenever you come back to visit!

Letter refusing to continue charge account for a customer who has moved

FIGURE 8.4 A Refusal with an Alternative

Steel Fabrication

"Serving the needs of America since 1890"
1800 Olney Avenue • Philadelphia, PA 19140 • 215•555•7800 • Fax: 215•555•9803

April 27, 2004

Mr. H. J. Moody
Canton Corporation
2407 North Avenue
Kearney, NE 68847

Subject: Bid Number 5853, Part Number D-40040

Dear Mr. Moody:

Buffer Thank you for requesting our quotation on your Part No. D-40040.

Reason Your blueprints call for flame-cut rings 1/2" thick A516 grade 70. To use that grade, we'd have to grind down from 1" thick material. However, if you can use A515 grade 70, which we stock in 1/2" thick, you can cut the price by more than half.

Quantity	Description	Gross Weight	Price/Each
75	Rings Drawing D-40040, A516 Grade 70 1" thick x 6" O.D. x 2.8" I.D. ground to .5" thick.	12 lbs.	$15.08
75	Rings Drawing D-40040, A515 Grade 70 1/2" thick x 6" O.D. x 2.8" I.D.	6 lbs.	$6.91

Alternative (Depending on circumstances, different alternatives may exist.)

If you can use A515 grade 70, let me know.   *Leaves decision up to reader to re-establish psychological freedom*

Sincerely,

Valerie Prynne
Valerie Prynne

VP:wc

Avoid endings that seem insincere.

We are happy to have been of service, and should we be able to assist you in the future, please contact us.

This ending lacks you-attitude and would not be good even in a positive message. In a situation where the company has just refused to help, it's likely to sound sarcastic or sadistic.

Workplace Violence*

An increasing number of people respond violently to bad news.

In a national survey, 10% of workers said that physical violence had happened in their workplaces. Too often, the violence is deadly. Murder is now second only to highway accidents as the leading cause of death on the job. Convenience store clerks and taxicab drivers aren't the only targets. Navistar International in suburban Chicago; Edgewater Technology in Wakefield, Massachusetts; and Xerox in Honolulu are among the many companies where disgruntled former employees, employees, or service people have killed. After three shootings at factories in Michigan, Ford developed a multidisciplinary workplace violence response team.

*Based on Ann Brown, "When Your Work Is All the Rage—Literally," *Black Enterprise*, November 2001, 64; and Mike France and Michael Arndt, "When the Shooting Stops," *BusinessWeek*, March 12, 2001, 100.

| **FIGURE 8.5** | Avoid These Phrases in Negative Messages |

Phrase	Because
I am afraid that we cannot	You aren't fearful. Don't hide behind empty phrases.
I am sorry that we are unable	You probably are *able* to grant the request; you simply choose not to. If you are so sorry about saying *no*, why don't you change your policy and say *yes*?
I am sure you will agree that	Don't assume that you can read the reader's mind.
Unfortunately	*Unfortunately* is negative in itself. It also signals that a refusal is coming.

Tone in Negative Messages

Tone—the implied attitude of the author toward the reader and the subject—is particularly important when you want readers to feel that you have taken their requests seriously. Check your draft carefully for positive emphasis (◄ p. 37) and you-attitude (◄ p. 34), both at the level of individual words and at the level of ideas.

Figure 8.5 lists some of the phrases to avoid in negative messages.

Even the physical appearance and timing of a letter can convey tone. An obvious form rejection letter suggests that the writer has not given much consideration to the reader's application. An immediate negative suggests that the rejection didn't need any thought. A negative delivered just before a major holiday seems especially unfeeling. AT&T was widely criticized for telling a man that he had been fired when he arrived at work with his daughter on "Take Your Daughter to Work" Day. AT&T later found another job for him, but the cost to the company's image was high.

Alternate Strategies for Negative Situations

Whenever you face a negative situation, consider recasting it as a positive or persuasive message.

Recasting the Situation as a Positive Message

If the negative information will directly lead to a benefit that you know readers want, use the pattern of organization for informative and positive messages:

Situation:	You're raising parking rates to pay for lot maintenance, ice and snow removal, and signs so renters can have cars towed away that park in their spots—all services renters have asked for.
Negative:	Effective May 1, parking rentals will go up $5 a month.
Positive emphasis:	Effective May 1, if someone parks in your spot, you can have the car towed away. Signs are being put up announcing that all spaces in the lot are rented. Lot maintenance is also being improved. The lot will be resurfaced this summer, and arrangements have been made for ice and snow removal next winter.

Recasting the Situation as a Persuasive Message

Often a negative situation can be recast as a persuasive message. If your organization has a problem, ask readers to help solve it. A solution that workers have created will be much easier to implement.

When the Association for Business Communication raised dues in 1987, the Executive Director wrote a persuasive letter urging members to send in renewals early so they could beat the increase. The letter shared some of the qualities of any persuasive letter: using an attention-getting opener, offsetting the negative by setting it against the benefits of membership, telling the reader what to do, and ending with a picture of the benefit the reader received by acting. More recent increases, however, have been announced directly.

If you are criticizing someone, your real purpose may be to persuade the reader to act differently.[7] Chapter 9 offers patterns for direct requests and problem-solving persuasive messages.

Humor in Negative Messages

Humor can defuse negative messages.

Kathryn McGrath, head of the Securities and Exchange Commission's division of investment management, needed to tell an investment firm that its ad was illegal. The ad showed an index finger pointing up and large bold letters saying that performance was "up," too. Tiny print at the bottom of the page admitted that performance figures hadn't been adjusted to include front-end sales charges. Rather than writing a heavy-handed letter, McGrath sent the firm a photocopy of a thumb pointing down. The ad never ran again.[8]

Humor works best when it's closely related to the specific situation and the message. Humor that seems tacked on is less likely to work. Never use humor that belittles readers.

 See the BAC Web site for more examples of humor—successful and unsuccessful.

Writing Negative E-Mail Messages

Major negatives, like firing someone, should be delivered in person, not by e-mail. But e-mail is appropriate for many less serious negatives.

Schwinn needed a new product line to attract sophisticated cyclists. This apology for its old, boring line moves quickly to a discussion of its new technology. By evoking an experience every cyclist has had, the headline also suggests that falling is a minor event.

Never write e-mail messages when you're angry. If a message infuriates you, wait until you're calmer before you reply—and even then, reply only if you must. Flaming does not make you look like a mature, level-headed professional who is a candidate for bigger things. And since employers have the right to read all e-mail, flaming—particularly if directed at co-workers, regulators, suppliers, or customers—may cause an employee to be fired.

Use a friendly, conversational tone. Keep the message short. Edit and proofread your message carefully. An easy way for an angry reader to strike back is to attack typos or other errors.

Remember that e-mail messages, like any other documents, can become documents in lawsuits. When a negative e-mail is hard to write, compose it offline so that you can revise and even get feedback before you send the message.

Varieties of Negative Messages

Three of the most difficult kinds of negative messages to write are rejections and refusals, disciplinary notices and negative performance appraisals, and layoffs and firings.

Rejections and Refusals

When you refuse requests from people outside your organization, try to use a buffer. Give an alternative if one is available. For example, if you are denying credit, it may still be possible for the reader to put an expensive item on layaway.

Politeness and length help. In two studies, job applicants preferred rejection letters that addressed them as *Mr./Ms.* rather than calling them by their first names, that said something specific about their good qualities, that phrased the refusal itself indirectly, that offered alternatives (such as another position the applicant might be qualified for), and that were longer.[9] An experiment using a denial of additional insurance found that subjects preferred a rejection letter that was longer, more tactful, and more personal. The preferred letter started with a buffer, used a good reason for the refusal, and offered sales promotion in the last paragraph. The finding held both for English-speaking US subjects and for Spanish-speaking Mexican subjects.[10]

Double-check the words in the draft to be sure the reason can't backfire if it is applied to other contexts. As Elizabeth McCord has shown, the statement that a plant is "too noisy and dangerous" for a group tour could be used as evidence against the company in a worker's compensation claim.[11]

When you refuse requests within your organization, use your knowledge of the organization's culture and of the specific individual to craft your message. In some organizations, it may be appropriate to use company slogans, offer whatever help already-established departments can give, and refer to the individual's good work (if you indeed know that it is good). In other, less personal organizations, a simple negative without embellishment may be more appropriate.

Disciplinary Notices and Negative Performance Appraisals

Performance appraisals are discussed in detail in Chapter 9. Performance appraisals will be positive when they are designed to help a basically good employee improve. But when an employee violates a company rule or fails to improve after repeated negative appraisals, the company may discipline the employee or build a dossier to support firing him or her.

Present disciplinary notices and negative performance appraisals directly, with no buffer. A buffer might encourage the recipient to minimize the message's importance—and might even become evidence in a court case that the employee had not been told to shape up "or else." Cite quantifiable observations of the employee's behavior, rather than generalizations or inferences based on it. If an employee is disciplined by being laid off without pay, specify when the employee is to return.

Layoffs and Firings

If a company is in financial trouble, management needs to communicate the problem clearly. Sharing information and enlisting everyone's help in finding solutions may make it possible to save jobs. Sharing information also means that layoff notices, if they become necessary, will be a formality; they should not be new information to employees.

Give the employee the real reason for the firing. Offering a face-saving reason unrelated to poor performance can create legal liabilities. But avoid broadcasting the reason: to do so can leave the company liable to a defamation suit.[12]

Information about layoffs and firings is normally delivered orally but accompanied by a written statement explaining severance pay or unemployment benefits that may be available.

Solving a Sample Problem

Solving negative problems requires careful analysis. The checklist at the end of the chapter on p. 199 can help you evaluate your draft.

Problem

You're Director of Employee Benefits for a Fortune 500 company. Today, you received the following memo:

> From: Michelle Jagtiani
> Subject: Getting My Retirement Benefits
>
> Next Friday will be my last day here. I am leaving [name of company] to take a position at another firm.
>
> Please process a check for my retirement benefits, including both the deductions from my salary and the company's contributions for the last six and a half years. I would like to receive the check by next Friday if possible.

You have bad news for Michelle. Although the company does contribute an amount to the retirement fund equal to the amount deducted for retirement from the employee's paycheck, employees who leave with less than seven years of employment get only their own contributions. Michelle will get back only the money that has been deducted from her own pay, plus 4½% interest compounded quarterly. Her payments and interest come to just over $17,200; the amount could be higher depending on the amount of her last paycheck, which will include compensation for any unused vacation days and sick leave. Furthermore, since the amounts deducted were not considered taxable income, she will have to pay income tax on the money she will receive.

You cannot process the check until after her resignation is effective, so you will mail it to her. You have her home address on file; if she's moving, she needs to let you know where to send the check. Processing the check may take two to three weeks.

Write a memo to Michelle.

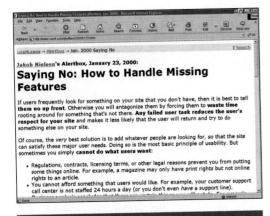

InSite

www.useit.com/alertbox/20000123.html

General guidelines for saying *no* can be applied to specific situations. Computer expert Jakob Neilsen explains how to tell users that your Web site can't do what they want.

Effective Negative Letters*

Researcher Catherine Schryer asked writers at an insurance company to evaluate the firm's letters denying claims. She found four differences between the letters judged effective and the letters judged ineffective:

- Good letters were easier to read. Poor letters contained more jargon; longer words and sentences; and stiff, awkward phrasing.

- Good letters gave fuller reasons for the rejection. Poor letters often used boilerplate and did not explain terms.

- Good letters were less likely to talk about the reader's emotions ("angry," "disappointed").

- Good letters were more likely to portray the writer and reader as active agents.

*Based on Catherine Schryer, "Walking a Fine Line: Writing Negative Letters in an Insurance Company," *Journal of Business and Technical Communication* 14 (October 2000): 445–97.

Analysis of the Problem

1. **Who is (are) your audience(s)? What characteristics are relevant to this particular message? If you are writing to more than one reader, how do the readers differ?**

    Michelle Jagtiani. Unless she's a personal friend, I probably wouldn't know why she's leaving and where she's going.

    There's a lot I don't know. She may or may not know much about taxes; she may or may not be able to take advantage of tax-reduction strategies. I can't assume the answers because I wouldn't have them in real life.

2. **What are your purposes in writing?**

    To tell her that she will get only her own contributions, plus 4½% interest compounded quarterly; that the check will be mailed to her home address two to three weeks after her last day on the job; and that the money will be taxable as income.

    To build goodwill so that she feels that she has been treated fairly and consistently. To minimize negative feelings she may have.

    To close the door on this subject.

3. **What information must your message include?**

    When the check will come. The facts that her check will be based on her contributions, not the employer's, and that the money will be taxable income. How lump-sum retirement benefits are calculated. The fact that we have her current address on file but need a new address if she's moving.

4. **How can you build support for your position? What reasons or reader benefits will your reader find convincing?**

    Giving the amount currently in her account may make her feel that she is getting a significant sum of money. Suggesting someone who can give free tax advice (if the company offers this as a fringe benefit) reminds her of the benefits of working with the company. Wishing her luck with her new job is a nice touch.

5. **What objection(s) can you expect your reader(s) to have? What negative elements of your message must you deemphasize or overcome?**

    She is getting about half the amount she expected, since she gets no matching funds. She might have been able to earn more than 4 1/2% interest if she had invested the money in the stock market. Depending on her personal tax situation she may pay more tax on the money as a lump sum than would have been due had she paid it each year as she earned the money.

Discussion of the Sample Solutions

The solution in Figure 8.6 is not acceptable. The subject line gives a bald negative with no reason or alternative. The first sentence has a condescending tone that is particularly offensive in negative messages. The last sentence focuses on what is being taken away rather than what remains. Paragraph 2 lacks you-

FIGURE 8.6   An Unacceptable Solution to the Sample Problem

April 21, 2003

To: Michelle Jagtiani

From: Lisa Niaz   *LN*

Subject: Denial of Matching Funds

Give reason before refusal — You cannot receive a check the last day of work and you will get only your own contributions, not a matching sum from the company, because you have not worked for the company for at least seven full years.

Better to be specific

This is lifted straight from the problem. The language in problems is often negative and stuffy; information is disorganized. — Your payments and interest come to just over $17,200; the amount could be higher depending on the amount of your last paycheck, which will include compensation for any unused vacation days and sick leave. Furthermore, since the amounts deducted were not considered taxable income, you will have to pay income tax on the money you receive.

The check will be sent to your home address. If the address we have on file is incorrect, please correct it so that your check is not delayed. — *Negative*

How will reader know what you have on file? Better to give current address as you have it.

Think about the situation and use your own words to create a satisfactory message.

attitude and is vague. The memo ends with a negative. There is nothing anywhere in the memo to build goodwill.

The solution in Figure 8.7, in contrast, is very good. The policy serves as a buffer and explanation. The negative is stated clearly but is buried in the paragraph to avoid overemphasizing it. The paragraph ends on a positive note by specifying the amount in the account and the fact that the sum might be even higher.

Paragraph 2 contains the additional negative information that the amount will be taxable but offers the alternative that it may be possible to reduce taxes. The writer builds goodwill by suggesting a specific person the reader could contact.

Paragraph 3 tells the reader what address is in the company files (Michelle may not know whether the files are up-to-date), asks that she update it if necessary, and ends with the reader's concern: getting her check promptly.

The final paragraph ends on a positive note. This generalized goodwill is appropriate when the writer does not know the reader well.

FIGURE 8.7   A Good Solution to the Sample Problem

April 21, 2003

To: Michelle Jagtiani

From: Lisa Niaz *LN*

Subject: Receiving Employee Contributions from Retirement Accounts

Good to state reason in third-person to deemphasize negative.

Employees who leave the company with at least seven full years of employment are entitled both to the company contributions and the retirement benefit paycheck deductions contributed to retirement accounts. Those employees who leave the company with less than seven years of employment will receive the employee paycheck contributions made to their retirement accounts.

Good to be specific

You now have $17,240.62 in your account which includes 4.5% interest compounded quarterly. The amount you receive could be even higher since you will also receive payment for any unused leave and vacation days.

Good to show how company can help

Because you now have access to the account, the amount you receive will be considered income. Beth Jordan in Employee Financial Services can give you information about possible tax deductions and financial investments which can reduce your income taxes.

Good to be specific

The check will be sent to your home address on May 16. The address we have on file is 2724 Merriman Road, Akron, Ohio 44313. If your address changes, please let us know so you can receive your check promptly.

Positive

Good luck with your new job!

Forward-looking

Summary of Key Points

- In a negative message, the basic information is negative; we expect the reader to be disappointed or angry.
- A good negative message conveys the negative information clearly while maintaining as much goodwill as possible. The goal is to make readers feel that they have been taken seriously, that the decision is fair and reasonable, and that they would have made the same decision. A secondary purpose is to reduce or eliminate future correspondence on the same subject so that the message doesn't create more work for the writer.
- In memos to superiors, the subject line should focus on solving the problem. In memos to peers and subordinates, state the topic but not your action. Use a negative subject line in e-mail messages.
- Organize negative letters in this way:
    1. Give the reason for the refusal before the refusal itself when you have a reason that readers will understand and accept.

✓ **CHECKLIST** Negative Messages

☐ Is the subject line appropriate?

☐ If a buffer is used, does it avoid suggesting either a positive or a negative response?

☐ Is the reason, if it is given, presented before the refusal? Is the reason watertight, with no loopholes?

☐ Is the negative information clear?

☐ Is an alternative given if a good one is available? Does the message provide all the information needed to act on the alternative but leave the choice up to the reader?

☐ Does the last paragraph avoid repeating the negative information?

☐ Is tone acceptable—not defensive, but not cold, preachy, or arrogant either?

And, for all messages, not just negative ones,

☐ Does the message use you-attitude and positive emphasis?

☐ Is the style easy to read and friendly?

☐ Is the visual design of the message inviting?

☐ Is the format correct?

☐ Does the message use standard grammar? Is it free from typos?

Originality in a negative message may come from

☐ An effective buffer, if one is appropriate.

☐ A clear, complete statement of the reason for the refusal.

☐ A good alternative, clearly presented, which shows that you're thinking about what the reader really needs.

☐ Adding details that show you're thinking about a specific organization and the specific people in that organization.

---

2. Give the negative just once, clearly.
3. Present an alternative or compromise, if one is available.
4. End with a positive, forward-looking statement.

▪ Organize negative memos to superiors in this way:
1. Describe the problem.
2. Tell how it happened.
3. Describe the options for fixing it.
4. Recommend a solution and ask for action.

▪ When you must pass along serious bad news to peers and subordinates, use a variation of the pattern to superiors:
1. Describe the problem.
2. Present an alternative or compromise, if one is available.
3. If possible, ask for input or action.

▪ When the bad news is less serious, use the pattern for negative letters unless your knowledge of the reader(s) suggests that another pattern will be more effective.

▪ A **buffer** is a neutral or positive statement that allows you to bury the negative message. Buffers must put the reader in a good frame of mind, not give the bad news but not imply a positive answer either, and provide a natural transition to the body of the letter. Use a buffer only when the reader values harmony or when the buffer serves a purpose in addition to simply delaying the negative.

- The kinds of statements most often used as buffers are (1) good news, (2) facts and chronologies of events, (3) references to enclosures, (4) thanks, and (5) statements of principle.

- A good reason must be watertight. Give several reasons only if all are watertight and are of comparable importance. Omit the reason for the refusal entirely if it is weak or if it makes your organization look bad.

- Make the refusal crystal clear.

- Giving the reader an alternative or a compromise

   - Offers the reader another way to get what he or she wants.

   - Suggests that you really care about the reader and about helping to meet his or her needs.

   - Enables the reader to reestablish the psychological freedom you limited when you said *no.*

   - Allows you to end on a positive note and to present yourself and your organization as positive, friendly, and helpful.

- People may respond to limits by striking out in ways that are unacceptable. This effort to reestablish freedom is called **psychological reactance.**

- When you give an alternative, give the reader all the information he or she needs to act on it, but don't take the necessary steps for the reader. Letting the reader decide whether to try the alternative allows the reader to reestablish a sense of psychological freedom.

- Many negative situations can be redefined to use the patterns of organization for informative and positive or for persuasive messages. Humor sometimes works to defuse negative situations.

- Use the analysis questions in Chapter 1 to solve negative problems.

| CHAPTER 8 | Exercises and Problems |

Getting Started

8.1   Letters for Discussion—Credit Refusal

As director of customer service at C'est Bon, an upscale furniture store, you manage the store's credit. Today you are going to reject an application from Frank Steele. Although his income is fairly high, his last two payments on his college loans were late, and he has three bank credit cards, all charged to the upper limit, on which he's made just the minimum payment for the last three months.

The following letters are possible approaches to giving him the news. How well does each message meet the criteria in the checklist for negative messages?

1.   Dear Mr. Steele:

Your request to have a C'est Bon charge account shows that you are a discriminating shopper. C'est Bon sells the finest merchandise available.

Although your income is acceptable, records indicate that you carry the maximum allowable balances on three bank credit cards. Moreover, two recent payments on your student loans have not been made in a timely fashion. If you were given a C'est Bon charge account, and if you charged a large amount on it, you might have difficulty paying the bill, particularly if you had other unforeseen expenses (car repair, moving, medical emergency) or if your income dropped suddenly. If you were unable to repay, with your other debt you would be in serious difficulty. We would not want you to be in such a situation, nor would you yourself desire it.

Please reapply in six months.

Sincerely,

2.   Dear Frank:

No, you can't have a C'est Bon credit card—at least not right now. Get your financial house in order and try again.

Fortunately for you, there's an alternative. Put what you want on layaway. The furniture you want will be held for you, and paying a bit each week or month will be good self-discipline.

Enjoy your C'est Bon furniture!

Sincerely,

3.   Dear Mr. Steele:

Over the years, we've found that the best credit risks are people who pay their bills promptly. Since two of your student loan payments have been late, we won't extend store credit to you right now. Come back with a record of six months of on-time payments of all bills, and you'll get a different answer.

You might like to put the furniture you want on layaway. A $50 deposit holds any item you want. You have six months to pay, and you save interest charges.

You might also want to take advantage of one of our Saturday Seminars. On the first Saturday of each month at 11 AM, our associates explain one topic related to furniture and interior decorating. Upcoming topics are

How to Wallpaper a Room   February 5
Drapery Options   March 6
Persian Carpets   April 1

Sincerely,

8.2   E-Mails for Discussion—Saying *No* to a Colleague

A colleague in another state agency has e-mailed you asking if you would like to use the payroll software her agency developed. You wouldn't. Switching to a new program would take a lot of time, and what you have works well for you.

The following messages are possible approaches to giving her the news. How well does each message meet the criteria in the checklist for negative messages?

1.   Subject: Re: Use Our Software?

No.

2.   Subject: Re: Use Our Software?

Thanks for telling me about the payroll software your team developed. What we have works well for us. Like every other agency, we're operating on a bare-bones budget, and no one here wants to put time (that we really don't have) into learning a new program. So we'll say, no, thanks!

3.   Subject: Re: Use Our Software?

The payroll software your team developed sounds very good.

I might like to use it, but the people here are computer phobic. They HATE learning new programs. So, being a good little computer support person, I soldier on with the current stuff. (And people wonder why state government is SO INEFFICIENT! Boy, the stories I could tell!)

Anyway, thanks for the offer. Keep me posted on the next development—maybe it will be something so obviously superior that even the Neanderthals here can see its advantages!

8.3   Revising a Negative Message

Rewrite and reorganize the following negative message to make it more positive. Eliminate any sentences that are not needed.

> Dear Renter:
>
> Effective March 1, the rent for your parking space will go up $10 a month. However, our parking lot is still not the most expensive in town.
>
> Many of you have asked us to provide better snow and ice removal and to post signs saying that all spaces are rented so that a car can be towed if it parks in your space. Signs will be posted by March 1, and, if we get any more snow, Acme Company has contracted to have the lot cleared by 7 AM.
>
> Enclosed is a new parking sticker. Please hang it on your rearview mirror.
>
> Sincerely,
>
> A. E. Jackson

E-Mail Messages

8.4   Notifying Seniors That They May Not Graduate

State University asks students to file an application to graduate one term before they actually plan to graduate. The application lists the courses the student has already had and those he or she will take in the last two terms. Your office reviews the lists to see that the student will meet the requirements for total number of hours, hours in the major, and general education requirements. Some students have forgotten a requirement or not taken enough courses and cannot graduate unless they take more courses than those they have listed.

a. Students who have not taken enough total hours.
b. Students who have not fulfilled all the requirements for their majors.
c. Students who are missing one or more general education courses.
d. Advisers of students who do not meet the requirements for graduation.

As Your Instructor Directs,
Write form e-mail messages to the following audiences. Leave blanks for the proposed date of graduation and specific information that must be merged into the message:

8.5   Correcting a Mistake

Today, as you reviewed some cost figures, you realized they didn't fit with the last monthly report you filed. You had pulled the numbers together from several sources, and you're not sure what happened. Maybe you miscopied, or didn't save the final version after you'd checked all the numbers. But whatever the cause, you've found errors in three categories. You gave your boss the following totals:

Personnel	$2,843,490
Office supplies	$43,500
Telephone	$186,240

E-mail your boss to correct the information.

As Your Instructor Directs,
Write e-mail messages for the following situations:

a. The correct numbers are

Personnel	$2,845,490
Office supplies	$34,500
Telephone	$186,420

b. The correct numbers are

Personnel	$2,845,490
Office supplies	$84,500
Telephone	$468,240

Variations for each situation:

(1) Your boss has been out of the office; you know she hasn't seen the data yet.

(2) Your boss gave a report to the executive committee this morning using your data.

Hints:

- How serious is the mistake in each situation?
- In which situations, if any, should you apologize?
- Should you give the reason for the mistake? Why or why not?
- How do your options vary depending on whether your job title gives you responsibility for numbers and accounting?

8.6   Refusing to Pay an Out-of-Network Bill

Your employees' health insurance allows them to choose from one of three health maintenance organizations (HMOs). Once the employee has selected an HMO, he or she must get all medical care (except for out-of-state emergency care) from the HMO. Employees receive a listing of the doctors and hospitals affiliated with each HMO when they join the company and pick an HMO and again each October when they have a one-month "open enrollment period" to change to another of the three HMOs if they choose.

As Director of Employee Benefits, you've received an angry e-mail from Alvin Reineke. Alvin had just received a statement from his HMO stating that it would not pay for the costs of his hernia operation two months ago at St. Catherine's Hospital in your city. Alvin is furious: one of the reasons he accepted a job with your company six months ago was its excellent health care coverage. He feels the company lied to him and should pay for his (rather large) hospital bill since the HMO refuses to do so.

The HMO which Alvin had selected uses two hospitals, but not St. Catherine's. When Alvin joined the company six months ago, he (like all new employees) received a thick booklet explaining the HMO options. Perhaps he did not take the time to read it carefully. But that's not your fault. Alvin can change plans during the next open enrollment, but even if he switched to an HMO that included St. Catherine's, that HMO wouldn't pay for surgery performed before he joined that HMO.

Write an e-mail message to Alvin giving him the bad news.

Hints:

- What tone should you use? Should you be sympathetic? Should you remind him that this is his own fault?
- Is there any help you can give Alvin (e.g., information about credit-union short-term loans or even information about negotiating payment terms with the hospital)?
- What can you do to make Alvin feel that the company has not lied to him?

8.7   Announcing a Smaller Holiday Party

In years past, your company has had impressive corporate parties for employees and their guests in late December. But this year, the celebration will be more modest: a two-hour open house with food and drink rather than a four-hour evening bash complete with dinner and a dance band. This year, the open house will be from 3 to 5 PM on the Friday before Christmas, and employees are encouraged to bring children as well as partners. Santa will appear.

As Your Instructor Directs,

Write an e-mail message to the employees of

a. A large advertising agency in a big city. The agency's billings have fallen 30% in the last six months, and 10% of the staff has already been laid off.

b. A manufacturing company. The company is still making a profit, but just barely. Unless the company saves money, layoffs may be necessary.

c. A successful small business. The business is doing well, but most of the employees earn only the minimum wage. They do not own stock in the company.

8.8   Rejecting a Suggestion

Your company has a suggestion system that encourages workers to submit suggestions that will save the organization money or improve safety, customer service, or morale. If a suggestion is accepted that will save the company money, its proposer gets 10% of the estimated first year's savings. If a suggestion is accepted but will not save money, the proposer gets $25. You chair the committee which makes the decisions.

Today, you must tell Wayne Andersen that the committee has rejected his suggestion to buy a second photocopying machine for the sales department. Wayne pointed out that the sales department occupies a whole floor yet has only one copier. Although the copier is in the center of the room (by the coffee and vending machines), some people have to walk quite a distance to get to it. Of course, they often stop to talk to the people they pass.

Wayne calculated how much time people waste walking to the copier and talking to co-workers multiplied by annual salaries compared to the shorter time needed to walk to one of two copiers, each located to serve half the floor. He calculated that the company could save the cost of a $10,000 machine in just six months, with a further $10,000 savings by the end of the first year.

No one on the committee liked Wayne's idea:

"I don't trust his numbers. After all, lots of people combine trips to the copier with a trip to get a cup of coffee or a cola. They'd do even more walking if they had to make two trips."

"He talks about people waiting in line to use the copier, but I'm in sales, and I know the copier really isn't used that much. Sure, there are some bottlenecks—especially when reports are due—but lots of the time the machine just sits there."

"I'm worried about the economy. I don't think this is the time to spend money we don't have to spend."

"I guess his system would be more efficient. But the real savings comes not from less walking but from less talking. And I think we *want* people to talk to each other. Informal conversations are great for relieving stress, sharing ideas, and strengthening our loyalty to each other and to the company."

"I agree. I think our company is built on informal interchange and a sense that you don't have to

account for every single minute. Our people are almost all on salary; they stay overtime without any extra pay. If someone wants to take a break and talk to someone, I think that's OK."

"Well, sometimes we do waste time talking. But his idea isn't really new. Lots of people think we could save money by buying more of every kind of equipment. Even if we get a copier, I don't think he should get any money."

You pointed out that even if a new copier didn't save as much money as Wayne predicted, it would shorten the lines when lots of people have copying to do. You suggested adopting his suggestion but reducing the estimated savings and therefore the award. But the committee rejected your compromise and the suggestion. As chair of the committee, you vote only to break a tie.

Write an e-mail message to Wayne, reporting the committee's decision.

Hints:
- What reason(s) should you give for the committee's decision?
- Should you tell Wayne that you disagreed with the majority?
- How can you encourage Wayne to continue to submit suggestions?

8.9 Refusing to Post E-Mail Addresses

You're the Web Weaver for a major organization. Today, you get this e-mail:

> Subject: Want E-Mail Addresses
>
> Your "contact us" page does not give the e-mail addresses of your executives and managers. Could you please list them?

You could, but the company isn't willing to. Some time ago, you *did* list them, and some slightly twisted individual from outside the company flooded the addresses with spam, viruses, and hate mail. To protect your employees and your system, you removed them.

Answer the e-mail message.

8.10 Telling Employees to Remove Personal Web Sites

You're Director of Management and Information Systems (MIS) in your organization. At your monthly briefing for management, a vice president complained that some employees have posted personal Web pages on the company's Web server.

"It looks really unprofessional to have stuff about cats and children and musical instruments. How can people do this?"

You took the question literally. "Well, some people have authorization to post material—price changes, job listings, marketing information. Someone who has authorization could put up anything."

Another manager said, "I don't think it's so terrible—after all, there aren't any links from our official pages to these personal pages."

A third person said, "But we're paying for what's posted—so we pay for server space and connect time. Maybe it's not much right now, but as more and more people become Web-literate, the number of people putting up unauthorized pages could spread. We should put a stop to this now."

The vice president agreed. "The Web site is carefully designed to present an image of our organization. Personal pages are dangerous. Can you imagine the flak we'd get if someone posted links to pornography?"

You said, "I don't think that's very likely. If it did happen, as system administrator, I could remove the page."

The third speaker said, "I think we should remove all the pages. Having any at all suggests that our people have so much extra time that they're playing on the Web. That suggests that our prices are too high and may make some people worry about quality. In fact, I think that we need a new policy prohibiting personal pages on the company's Web server. And any pages that are already up should be removed."

A majority of the managers agreed and told you to write a message to all employees. Create an e-mail message to tell employees that you will remove the personal pages already posted and that no more will be allowed.

Hint:

- Suggest other ways that people can post personal Web pages. Commercial services such as America Online are possibilities. Students at Plugged In (www.pluggedin.org) can also provide Web access for a fee. (Check to be sure that the groups you recommend are still offering Web sites. If possible, get current prices.)
- Give only reasons that are watertight and make the company look good.

Communicating at Work

As Your Instructor Directs in 8.11 and 8.12,

a. Prepare notes for a meeting with or phone call to the person to whom you must give the bad news.

b. Write a paper or e-mail document to achieve the goal.

c. Write a memo to your instructor describing the situation and culture at your workplace and explaining your rhetorical choices (medium, strategy, tone, wording, graphics or document design, and so forth).

d. Examine your organization's files for messages responding to similar situations in the past. Are the messages effective? Why or why not? Write a memo to your instructor analyzing the messages, including copies of them, or make a presentation to the class, using the messages as handouts, transparencies, or slides.

8.11   Telling the Boss about a Problem

In any organization, things sometimes go wrong. Tell your supervisor about a problem in your unit and recommend what should be done.

8.12   Refusing a Customer Request

The customer isn't always right. Sometimes customers ask for things you're truly unable to provide. Even more frequently, you say *no* because the refusal serves your organization's needs. Think of a situation where a customer asked for something your organization could not provide or felt was unreasonable. Write a response refusing the request.

Letter and Memo Assignments

8.13   Refusing to Waive a Fee

As the Licensing Program Coordinator for your school, you evaluate proposals from vendors who want to make or sell merchandise with the school's name, logo, or mascot. If you find the product acceptable, the vendor pays a $250 licensing fee and then 6.5% of the wholesale cost of the merchandise manufactured (whether or not it is sold). The licensing fee helps to support the cost of your office; the 6.5% royalty goes into a student scholarship fund. At well-known universities or those with loyal students and alumni, the funds from such a program can add up to hundreds of thousands of dollars a year.

On your desk today is a proposal from a current student, Meg Winston.

> I want to silk-screen and sell T-shirts printed with the name of the school, the mascot, and the words "We're Number One!" (A copy of the design I propose is enclosed.) I ask that you waive the $250 licensing fee you normally require and limit the 6.5% royalty only to those T-shirts actually sold, not to all those made.
>
> I am putting myself through school by using student loans and working 30 hours a week. I just don't have $250. In my marketing class, we've done feasibility analyses, and I've determined that the shirts can be sold if the price is low enough. I hope to market these shirts in an independent study project with Professor Doulin, building on my marketing project earlier this term. However, my calculations show that I cannot price the shirts competitively if just one shirt must bear the 6.5% royalty for all the shirts produced in a batch. I will of course pay the 6.5% royalty on all shirts sold and not returned. I will produce the shirts in small batches (50–100 at a time). I am willing to donate any manufactured but unsold shirts to the athletic program so that you will know I'm not holding out on you.
>
> By waiving this fee, you will show that this school really wants to help students get practical experience in business, as the catalog states. I will work hard to promote these shirts by getting the school president, the coaches, and campus leaders to endorse them, pointing out that the money goes to the scholarship fund. The shirts themselves will promote school loyalty, both now and later when we're alumni who can contribute to our alma mater.
>
> I look forward to receiving the "go-ahead" to market these shirts.

The design and product are acceptable under your guidelines. However, you've always enforced the fee structure across the board, and you see no reason to make an exception now. Whether the person trying to sell merchandise is a student or not doesn't matter; your policy is designed to see that the school benefits whenever it is used to sell something. Students aren't the only ones whose cash flow is limited; many businesses would find it easier to get into the potentially lucrative business of selling clothing, school supplies, and other items with the school name or logo if they got the same deal Meg is asking for. (The policy also lets the school control the kind of items on which its name appears.) Just last week, your office confiscated about 400 T-shirts and shorts made by a company that had used the school name on them without permission; the company has paid the school $7,500 in damages.

Write a letter to Meg rejecting her special requests. She can get a license to produce the T-shirts, but only if she pays the $250 licensing fee and the royalty on all shirts made.

8.14   Correcting Misinformation

You're the director of the city's Division of Water. Your mail today contains this letter:

> When we bought our pool, the salesman told us that you would give us a discount on the water bill when we fill the pool. Please start the discount immediately. I tried to call you three times and got nothing but busy signals.
>
> Sincerely,
>
> *Larry Shadburn-Butler*
>
> Larry Shadburn-Butler

The salesperson was wrong. You don't provide discounts for pools (or anything else). At current rates, filling a pool with a garden hose costs from $8.83 (for a 1,800-gallon pool) to $124.67 (for 26,000 gallons) in the city. Filling a pool from any other water source would cost more. Rates are 30% higher in the suburbs and 50% higher in unincorporated rural areas. And you don't have enough people to answer phones. You tried a voice-mail system but eliminated it when you found people didn't have time to process all the messages that were left. But the city budget doesn't allow you to hire more people.

As Your Instructor Directs,

a.   Write a letter to Mr. Shadburn-Butler.

b. Write a letter to all the stores that sell swimming pools, urging them to stop giving customers misinformation.

c. Write a notice for the one-page newsletter that you include with quarterly water bills. Assume that you can have half a page for your information.

8.15   Sending Canceled Checks

Your bank returns customers' canceled checks to them when you send the statement. However, you have discovered several customers' canceled checks that were not included with last month's statements.

As Customer Service Manager, write a letter to go with the canceled checks.

As Your Instructor Directs,
Write letters for one or more of the following situations:

a. Two days have passed since the statements went out. Write a form letter to people who have not complained.

b. A week has passed since the statements went out. You discovered the mistake after two different customers called to ask where the checks were. A search for their checks discovered several other checks as well.

8.16   Analyzing Job Rejection Letters

Collect job rejection letters mailed to seniors on your campus. Analyze the letters, answering the following questions:

- What percentage of the letters use a buffer?
- What reasons do the letters give, if any?
- Does the format build goodwill?
- How do the recipients feel about the letters? Which (if any) do they like best?

As Your Instructor Directs,
a. Discuss your findings in a small group.
b. Present your findings orally to the class.
c. Present your findings in a memo to your instructor.
d. Join with other students to write a report based on your findings.

8.17   Turning Down a Faithful Client

You are Midas Investment Services' specialist in estate planning. You give talks to various groups during the year about estate planning. You ask nonprofit groups (churches, etc.) just to reimburse your expenses; you charge for-profit groups a fee plus expenses. These fees augment your income nicely, and the talks also are marvelous exposure for you and your company.

Every February for the last five years, Gardner Manufacturing Company has hired you to conduct an eight-hour workshop (two hours every Monday night for four weeks) on retirement and estate planning for its employees who are over 60 or who are thinking of taking early retirement. These workshops are popular and have generated clients for your company. The session last February went smoothly, as you have come to expect.

Today, out of the blue, you got a letter from Hope Goldberger, Director of Employee Benefits at Gardner, asking you to conduct the workshops every Tuesday evening *next* month at your usual fee. She didn't say whether this is an extra series or whether this will replace next February's series.

You can't do it. Your spouse, a microbiologist, is giving an invited paper at an international conference in Paris next month and the two of you are taking your children, ages 13 and 9, on a three-week trip to Europe. (You've made arrangements with school authorities to have the kids miss three weeks of classes.) Your spouse's trip will be tax-deductible, and you've been looking forward to and planning the trip for the last eight months.

Unfortunately, Midas Investment Services is a small group, and the only other person who knows anything about estate planning is a terrible speaker. You could suggest a friend at another financial management company, but you don't want Gardner to turn to someone else permanently; you enjoy doing the workshops and find them a good way to get leads.

Write the letter to Ms. Goldberger.

8.18   Dropping Clients

Your bank's software allows you to calculate how profitable each client is. You've discovered that you lose money on corporate loans when the company has no other banking relationship with you. The bank's Lending Committee has decided to notify the corporate customers in this category—nearly 20% of your corporate customers—that it will drop them or extend less credit. If a customer's loan is due, you won't renew it. If the due date is some time away, you are asking companies to find other lenders in the next six months. Of course, you will continue to fund the loan if a company makes significant use of your other services, such as checking, cash management, asset management, investment banking, and securities underwriting.

Prepare a form letter to go to the customers whom you plan to drop.

8.19 Rejecting a Would-Be Client

You've just joined Sportstars Inc., a company that represents athletes who want to increase their incomes by doing commercials, making speeches and personal appearances, and endorsing products. Sportstars persuades the sponsor to hire the athlete and helps to negotiate the contract. In addition, a considerable amount of hand-holding is necessary to see the client through rough times. For these services, Sportstars receives 20% of the fees paid to the athlete.

As part of your orientation, your boss points out what you know already: a well-known athlete can command much higher fees than someone who's less well known; normally, people who win championships net much higher fees than someone who is consistently good but who has not caught the public eye. "The big problem," your boss says, "is what to do about young athletes. We can't afford to represent the also-rans; we'd go broke spending time on them. But some rookies will eventually make it big, and we want to represent them when they get to the top. We've evolved a foolproof way to do this. When an unknown comes to us and asks to hire us as his or her personal representative, we decline but suggest a competing firm that we know does a terrible job representing its clients. Then, when the winner emerges from the pack, we approach that person and offer to represent him or her. We know we'll do a better job—and we can prove it. We've signed everyone we've approached this way."

Today you have a letter from Lisa Walton. She won the NCAA Women's Division II championship and has just joined the Ladies Professional Golf Association tour. She's a very good athlete, but she isn't yet a star—and may never be. Under Sportstars' policy, you can't grant her request.

As Your Instructor Directs,

a. Write a letter to Lisa.

b. Write a memo to your boss at Sportstars suggesting that the company's policy be modified.

c. Write a memo to your instructor listing the choices you made and giving the reasons for your choices.

Hints:

- You have no obligation to give a contract to everyone who asks for one, but is it ethical to deliberately recommend the worst of your competitors? At a minimum, you're depriving Lisa of income, since you know that the competitor doesn't seek commercials and endorsements aggressively for athletes and doesn't get them nearly as favorable terms as Sportstars has been able to do.
- What will happen to you if you disobey your boss and recommend a competent competitor, several competitors, or no competitor at all?
- How can you build goodwill so that Lisa will have a positive image of Sportstars?

Based on Mark H. McCormack, *What They Don't Teach You at Harvard Business School* (New York: Bantam, 1984).

8.20 Rejecting a Member's Request

All nonsupervisory workers employed by your state government are union members. As a paid staff person for the union, you spend about a third of your time writing and editing the monthly magazine, *Public [Your State] Employee.* You receive this letter:

Dear Editor:

Every month, we get two copies of the union magazine—one addressed to me, one to my husband. We have different last names, so your computer may not realize that we're connected, but we are, and we don't need two copies. Sending just one copy will save printing and postage costs and reduce environmental waste. My name is Dorothy Livingston; my husband is Eric Beamer. Please combine our listings to send just one copy.

Sincerely,

Dorothy Livingston

Dorothy Livingston

As it happens, a couple of years ago you investigated possible savings of sending just one mailing to couples who both work for the state. Sophisticated computerized merge/purge programs to eliminate duplicates are far too expensive for the union's tight budget. And going through the mailing list manually to locate and change duplications would cost more than would be saved in postage. Printing costs wouldn't necessarily drop either, since it actually costs less for each copy to print big runs.

But you want to build goodwill—both to this writer, and for the union in general. Extra copies of the magazine (whether a double mailing or simply a copy someone is finished with) could be given to a nonmember or taken to a doctor's or dentist's waiting room or a barber or beauty shop. Such sharing would help spread public support for the union and state workers.

Write a letter to Ms. Livingston, explaining why you can't combine mailings.

9

Persuasive Messages

Persuasive Messages

James Davis, CEO
Davis Safety Supply Inc.

James Davis founded Davis Safety Supply with an initial investment of $500 in 1993. In six years, the company was worth $3 million. Davis Safety provides safety and environmental equipment to Fortune 500 and smaller businesses.

www.davissafety.com

I built my business by persuading customers to buy equipment that they need to comply with OSHA regulations, protect their employees, and prevent or clean up environmental problems. For me, the most important parts of persuasion are logical reasons, emotional appeal, and credibility.

Most of my customers were already buying the supplies I sell (such as goggles, boots, and gloves) from someone else. I had to give them a reason to change. I decided to offer free shipping—even for next-day or same-day delivery out-of-state. So saving money offers a logical reason for the customer to buy from us.

I build relationships with my customers. Even on a first visit, I get to know people. I look around in their offices. If I see pictures of racing cars or baseball players, I can pick up on the customer's interests. That's one way to build a common foundation.

You have to overcome objections. When I started my business, I learned that many people didn't want to deal with a black business owner. I said, I've got to think of another way. So I went in as a sales representative for the company rather than CEO—and made sales. Prejudice is an obstacle that you have to overcome like any other objection.

Credibility is very important. Look the customer in the eye and tell what you can provide. Then deliver what you've promised! Knowledge is another way to build credibility. I know the regulations, so I can tell a customer ways to use products more efficiently to save money. For example, Marriott was using expensive solvent gloves for washing dishes. These gloves are used when working with gasoline; a less expensive glove is fine for washing dishes. Helping customers solve their problems builds my credibility, builds our relationship, and gives them another reason to buy from me.

> "*The most important parts of persuasion are logical reasons, emotional appeal, and credibility.*"

Persuasion and Emotional Intelligence*

Emotional intelligence is the buzzword for what enables people to succeed in the workplace. Psychologist Daniel Goleman studied 181 jobs in 121 companies worldwide. He separated technical skills from emotional competencies. The latter were twice as important: "The abilities considered vital for success were emotional competencies like trustworthiness, adaptability, and a talent for collaboration."

For high-level executive jobs, says Goleman, perhaps the most important characteristic is "How persuasive are you? Can you get 'buy-in' for your ideas from the people around you? . . . [Can you] articulat[e] a mission or a goal and . . . bring everyone on board to get it accomplished [?] Can you take the pulse of a group, understand its unspoken currents of thought and concerns, and communicate with people in terms they can understand and embrace? That is great leadership. And it takes huge social intelligence, including a strongly developed sense of empathy."

*Based on and quotations taken from Anne Fisher, "Success Secret: A High Emotional IQ," *Fortune,* October 26, 1998, 293–94.

Whether you're selling safety equipment or ideas, effective persuasion is based on accurate logic, effective emotional appeal, and credibility or trust. Reasons have to be reasons the audience finds important; emotional appeal is based on values the audience cares about; credibility is in the eye of the beholder.

In the 21st century, businesses and other administrative agencies depend more and more on persuasion and buy-in to get quality work done. You can command people to make widgets. You can't command people to be creative. And even if you're making widgets, just going through the motions isn't enough. You want people to make high-quality widgets, while reducing scrap and other costs. Internal commitment is needed to make that happen.

External motivation doesn't last. Some people will buy a certain brand of pizza if they have a "2 for the price of 1" coupon. But if the coupon expires, or if another company offers the same deal, customers may leave. In contrast, if customers like your pizza better, if they are motivated internally to choose it, then you may keep your customers even if another company comes in with a lower price.

Persuasive messages include orders and requests, proposals and recommendations, sales and fund-raising letters, job application letters, and efforts to change people's behavior, such as collection letters, criticisms or performance appraisals where you want the subordinate to improve behavior, and public-service ads designed to reduce drunk driving, drug use, and so on. Reports are persuasive messages if they recommend action.

This chapter gives general guidelines for persuasive messages. Chapter 10 discusses sales, fund-raising, and promotional materials. Chapter 13 discusses grants and proposals; reports are the subject of Chapter 14. Chapter 18 covers job application letters.

All persuasive messages have several purposes:

Primary purposes:

To have the reader act.

To provide enough information so that the reader knows exactly what to do.

To overcome any objections that might prevent or delay action.

Secondary purposes:

To build a good image of the writer.

To build a good image of the writer's organization.

To cement a good relationship between the writer and reader.

To reduce or eliminate future correspondence on the same subject so the message doesn't create more work for the writer.

Choosing a Persuasive Strategy

Choose a persuasive strategy based on your answers to four questions:

1. What do you want people to do?
2. What objections, if any, will the audience have?
3. How strong a case can you make?
4. What kind of persuasion is best for the organization and the culture?

1. What Do You Want People to Do?

Identify the specific action you want and the person who has the power to do it. If your goal requires several steps, specify what you want your audience to do *now.* For instance, your immediate goal may be to have people come to a meeting or let you make a presentation, even though your long-term goal is a major sale or a change in policy.

2. What Objections, If Any, Will the Audience Have?

If you're asking for something that requires little time, money, or physical effort and for an action that's part of the person's regular duties, the audience is likely to have few objections. For example, when you order a product, the firm is happy to supply it.

Often, however, you'll encounter some resistance. People may be busy and have what they feel are more important things to do. They may have other uses for their time and money. To be persuasive, you need to show your audience that your proposal meets their needs; you need to overcome any objections.

The easiest way to learn about objections your audience may have is to ask. Particularly when you want to persuade people in your own organization or your own town, talk to knowledgeable people. Phrase your questions nondefensively, in a way that doesn't lock people into taking a stand on an issue: "What concerns would you have about a proposal to do *x*?" "Who makes a decision about *y*?" "What do you like best about [the supplier or practice you want to change]?" Ask follow-up questions to be sure you understand: "Would you be likely to stay with your current supplier if you could get a lower price from someone else? Why?"

People are likely to be most aware of and willing to share objective concerns such as time and money. They will be less willing to tell you that their real objection is emotional. Readers have a **vested interest** in something if they benefit directly from keeping things as they are. People who are in power have a vested interest in retaining the system that gives them their power. Someone who designed a system has a vested interest in protecting that system from criticism. To admit that the system has faults is to admit that the designer made mistakes. In such cases, you'll need to probe to find out what the real reasons are.

Both individuals and organizations have self-images. It's easier for readers to say *yes* when you ask for something that is consistent with that self-image. For example, a marine biologist used a financial argument to persuade Phillips Petroleum to let him harvest the mussels that grow on oil platforms: "I hear you've just written a check for $100,000 to a hydro-blasting company. I could remove those mussels for free." (The biologist sells the mussels to restaurants.)[1] Aramis persuaded men to buy its over-the-counter skin peel, Lift Off, by linking it to shaving: men who exfoliated with the product could reduce their shaving time by one-third.[2]

3. How Strong Is Your Case?

The strength of your case is based on three aspects of persuasion: argument, credibility, and emotional appeal.

Argument refers to the reasons or logic you offer. Sometimes you may be able to prove conclusively that your solution is best. Sometimes your reasons may not be as strong, the benefits may not be as certain, and obstacles may be difficult or impossible to overcome. For example, suppose that you wanted to persuade your organization to offer a tuition reimbursement plan for employees. You'd have a strong argument if you could show that tuition reimbursement would improve the performance of marginal workers or that reimbursement would be an attractive recruiting tool in a tight job market. However, if dozens of fully qualified workers apply for every opening you have, your argument would be weaker. The program might be nice for workers, but you'd have a hard job proving that it would help the company.

Credibility is the audience's response to you as the source of the message. Credibility in the workplace has three sources: knowledge, image, and relationships.[3] Citing experts can make your argument more credible. In some organizations, workers build credibility by getting assigned to high-profile

What Do Lawyers Want?*

Sales at Tom Carns's PDQ Printing in Las Vegas are 19 times the average for small print shops. He succeeds by analyzing his audience, identifying decision makers, and meeting their needs.

To enter the market for law-firm photocopying, Tom identified the head of the professional association of paralegals in Las Vegas. He met with her for two hours twice a month for three months to learn about the market, paying $500 for each consultation.

The meetings taught him that price didn't really matter when a legal firm needed photocopying. Quality, timeliness, and confidentiality were crucial. So he made some small changes in his procedures to meet those needs and then advertised the changes in a brochure with "Confidential" on the cover in bright red letters. Inside, his employees promised to treat documents confidentially and to shred any flawed copies. PDQ Printing itself would be liable for any breach of confidentiality.

In the first year of the promotion, law-firm copying generated $600,000 in revenues.

*Based on Edward O. Welles, "Quick Study," *Inc.*, April 1992, 67–76.

Target's tongue-in-cheek "Fashion and Housewares" ads create subtle emotional appeal and help position "Tar-zhay" (to use the faux-French pronunciation) as the upscale discount store. The quality of Target's brands builds credibility and logically supports buying decisions.

teams. You build credibility by your track record. The more reliable you've been in the past, the more likely people are to trust you now.

We are also more likely to trust people we know. That's one reason that new CEOs make a point of visiting as many branch offices as they can. Building a relationship with someone—even if the relationship is based on an outside interest, like sports or children—makes it easier for that person to see you as an individual and to trust you.

When you don't yet have the credibility that comes from being an expert or being powerful, build credibility by the language and strategy you use:

- **Be factual.** Don't exaggerate.
- **Be specific.** If you say "X is better," show in detail *how* it is better. Show the reader exactly where the savings or other benefits come from so that it's clear that the proposal really is as good as you say it is.
- **Be reliable.** If you suspect that a project will take longer to complete, cost more money, or be less effective than you originally thought, tell your audience *immediately.* Negotiate a new schedule that you can meet.

Emotional appeal means making the reader *want* to do what you ask. People don't make decisions—even business decisions—based on logic alone. J. C. Mathes and Dwight W. Stevenson cite the following example. During his summer job, an engineering student who was asked to evaluate his company's waste treatment system saw a way that the system could be redesigned to save the company over $200,000 a year. He wrote a report recommending the change and gave it to his boss. Nothing happened. Why not? His supervisor wasn't about to send up a report that would require him to explain why *he'd* been wasting over $200,000 a year of the company's money.[4]

4. What Kind of Persuasion Is Best for the Organization and the Culture?

A strategy that works in one organization may not work somewhere else. James Suchan and Ron Dulek point out that DEC's corporate culture values no-holds-barred aggressiveness. "Even if opposition is expected, a subordinate should write a proposal in a forceful, direct manner."[5] In another organization with different cultural values, an employee who used a hard-sell strategy for a request antagonized the boss.[6]

Corporate culture (◄▬ p. 59) isn't written down; it's learned by imitation and observation. What style do high-level people in your organization use? When you show a draft to your boss, are you told to tone down your statements or to make them stronger? Role models and advice are two ways organizations communicate their culture to newcomers.

Different cultures also have different preferences for gaining compliance. In one study, students who were native speakers of American English judged direct statements ("Do this"; "I want you to do this") clearer and more effective than questions ("Could you do this?") or hints ("This is needed"). Students who were native speakers of Korean, in contrast, judged direct statements to be *least* effective. In the Korean culture, the clearer a request is, the ruder and therefore less effective it is.[7]

Using Your Analysis to Choose a Persuasive Strategy

If your organization prefers a specific approach, use it. If your organization has no preference, or if you do not know your readers' preference, use the following guidelines to choose a strategy:

- Use the **direct request pattern** when
    - The audience will do as you ask without any resistance,
    - You need responses only from people who will find it easy to do as you ask, or
    - Busy readers may not read all the messages they receive.
- Use the **problem-solving pattern** when the audience may resist doing as you ask and you expect logic to be more important than emotion in the decision.
- Use the **star-chain-knot pattern** presented in Chapter 10 when the audience may resist doing as you ask and you expect emotion to be more important than logic in the decision.

Why Threats Are Less Effective than Persuasion

Sometimes people think they will be able to mandate change by ordering or threatening subordinates. Real managers disagree. Research shows that managers use threats only for obligatory duties such as coming to work on time. For more creative duties—like being part of a team or thinking of ways to save the company money—managers give reasons.[8] A survey showed that sales representatives were motivated by selling a good product; getting backup, support, training, and commissions; and being affiliated with a good company. Threats ("perform or else") were rated dead last, with 86% saying threats offered little or no motivation.[9] And threats are even less effective in trying to persuade people whose salaries you don't pay.

A **threat** is a statement—explicit or implied—that someone will be punished if he or she does (or doesn't do) something. Six reasons explain why punishment and threats don't work:[10]

1. **Threats don't produce permanent change.** Many people obey the speed limit only when a marked police car is in sight.
2. **Threats won't necessarily produce the action you want.** If you embarrass or punish people who take too many felt-tip pens or too much paper, they might write fewer reports—hardly the response you'd want!

Responding to Criticism*

By definition, your boss criticizes you during a performance appraisal. Criticism often feels like an attack, and when we are attacked, most of us try to defend ourselves. But doing that in a performance appraisal just makes us look like we can't take criticism.

Fernando Flores, former Chilean minister of finance and current consultant, recommends the following script to respond to criticism: "[Name,] thank you for your assessment. I appreciate your sincerity. I would like to have further conversations with you about the topic."

This script does three things. First it is nondefensive and avoids escalating the conflict. Second, it recognizes that the boss means what he or she says (whether or not the criticism is on target). Third, it asks for further discussion. This discussion might involve probing the meaning of the criticism more fully or discussing ways to improve or even discussing competing agendas that create a double bind for you.

*Based on Harriet Rubin, "The Power of Words," *Fast Company,* January 1999, 144.

FIGURE 9.1   How to Organize a Persuasive Direct Request

1. **Consider asking immediately for the information or service you want.** Delay the request if it seems too abrupt or if you have several purposes in the message.

2. **Give readers all the information they will need to act on your request.** Number your questions or set them off with bullets so the reader can check to see that all of them have been answered.

   In a claim (where a product is under warranty or a shipment was defective), explain the circumstances so that the reader knows what happened. Be sure to include all the relevant details: date of purchase, model or invoice number, and so on.

   In more complicated direct requests, anticipate possible responses. Suppose you're asking for information about equipment meeting certain specifications. Explain which criteria are most important so that the reader can recommend an alternative if no single product meets all your needs. You may also want to tell the reader what your price constraints are and ask whether the item is in stock or must be special-ordered.

3. **Ask for the action you want.** Do you want a check? A replacement? A catalog? Answers to your questions? If you need an answer by a certain time, say so. If possible, show the reader why the time limit is necessary.

Direct Requests Don't Translate*

Making a direct request may not be the most direct way to get what you want in all cultures.

In Saudi Arabia, it's rude to say to a taxi driver, "Take me to the airport." Instead say that a ride to the airport might be pleasant. Instead of ordering, suggest.

If you have a problem in China, start by thanking your hosts for all the things that make the experience a good one, praising the people, the accommodations and food, and even the scenery. Only after that should you mention "one little problem." Express confidence that your hosts will fix it. Instead of asking for immediate action, indicate that you'll check back in a few days. And leave behind a small gift.

*Based on Myron W. Lustig and Jolene Koester, *Intercultural Competence* (New York: HarperCollins, 1993), 228; and Linda Beamer and Iris Varner, *Intercultural Communication in the Global Workplace,* 2nd ed. (Burr Ridge, IL: Irwin/McGraw-Hill, 2001), 123–24.

3. **Threats may make people abandon an action—even in situations where it would be appropriate.** Criticizing workers for talking about nonbusiness topics such as sports may reduce communication about business topics as well.

4. **Threats produce tension.** People who feel threatened put their energies into ego defense rather than into productive work.

5. **People dislike and avoid anyone who threatens them.** A supervisor who is disliked will find it harder to enlist cooperation and support on the next issue that arises.

6. **Threats can provoke counteraggression.** Getting back at a boss can run the gamut from complaints to work slowdowns to sabotage.

Writing Persuasive Direct Requests

When you expect quick agreement, save the reader's time by presenting the request directly (see Figure 9.1). Also use the direct request pattern for busy people who do not read all the messages they receive and in organizations whose cultures favor putting the request first.

Figure 9.2 illustrates a direct request. Note that a direct request does not contain reader benefits and does not need to overcome objections: it simply asks for what is needed.

Direct requests should be direct. Don't make the reader guess what you want.

Indirect request: Is there a newer version of the 1995 *Accounting Reference Manual?*

Direct request: If there is a newer version of the 1995 *Accounting Reference Manual,* please send it to me.

Subject Lines for Direct Requests

In a direct request, put the request, the topic of the request, or a question in the subject line.

Subject: Request for Updated Software

My copy of HomeNet does not accept the nicknames for Eudora accounts.

Subject: Status of Account #3548-003

Please get me the following information about account #3548-003.

FIGURE 9.2 A Direct Request

BCS Interoffice Memo
Keep each message to one topic.

Date: May 15, 2003

To: Michael Antonucci

DA

From: David Anthony, Chair, BCS Suggestion Committee

Subject: Suggestion #97204 *Topic of request in subject line*

Please evaluate the attached suggestion by May 29. *Put request in ¶ 1.*

Spell out subquestions

- Should BCS adopt it? Why or why not?
- Will it save the company money? If so, how much a year?
- If the suggestion is adopted, how large an award should be given?

Make action easy

You may put your answers and brief reasons for them at the bottom of this page or send them to me by e-mail (anthony.37@bcs.com). Please get your response in by May 29 as the suggestion committee is meeting on May 30. *Ask for the action you want.*

Thanks! *Reason to act promptly*

Subject: Do We Need an Additional Training Session in October?

The two training sessions scheduled for October will accommodate 40 people. Last month, you said that 57 new staff accountants had been hired. Should we schedule an additional training session in October? Or can the new hires wait until the next regularly scheduled session in February?

Direct Requests with Multiple Purposes

In some direct requests, your combination of purposes may suggest a different pattern of organization. For example, in a letter asking an employer to reimburse you for expenses after a job interview, you'd want to thank your hosts for their hospitality and cement the good impression you made at the interview. To do that, you'd spend the first several paragraphs talking about the trip and the interview. Only in the last third of the letter (or even in the P.S.) would you put your request for reimbursement.

Similarly, in a letter asking about transferring to a four-year school or entering a graduate program, a major purpose might be to build a good image of yourself so that your application for financial aid would be viewed positively. To achieve that goal, provide information about your qualifications and interest in the field as well as asking questions.

Writing Persuasive Problem-Solving Messages

Use an indirect approach and the problem-solving pattern of organization when you expect resistance from your reader but can show that doing what

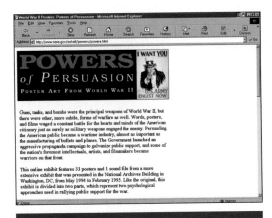

Persuasion can be based on positive or negative appeals. Part I of this exhibition of World War II poster art presents positive appeals focusing on confidence, patriotism, and strength. Part II presents negative appeals: suspicion, fear, and hate.

you want will solve a problem you and your reader share. The pattern in Figure 9.3 allows you to disarm opposition by showing all the reasons in favor of your position before you give your readers a chance to say *no*.

Figure 9.4 uses the problem-solving pattern of organization. Reader benefits can be brief in this kind of message since the biggest benefit comes from solving the problem.

Subject Lines for Problem-Solving Messages

When you have a reluctant reader, putting the request in the subject line just gets a quick *no* before you've had a chance to give all your arguments. One option is to use a **directed subject line** that makes your stance on the issue clear.[11] In the following examples, the first is the most neutral. The remaining two increasingly reveal the writer's preference.

Subject: A Proposal to Change the Formula for Calculating Retirees' Benefits

Subject: Arguments for Expanding the Marysville Plant

Subject: Why Cassano's Should Close Its West Side Store

Another option is to use common ground or a reader benefit—something that shows readers that this message will help them.

Subject: Reducing Energy Costs in the New Orleans Office

Energy costs in our New Orleans office have risen 12% in the last three years, even though the cost of gas has fallen and the cost of electricity has risen only 5%.

Although your first paragraph may be negative in a problem-solving message, your subject line should be neutral or positive.

Both directed subject lines and benefit subject lines can also be used as report titles.

FIGURE 9.3   How to Organize a Persuasive Problem-Solving Message

1. **Catch the reader's interest by mentioning a common ground.** Show that your message will be interesting or beneficial. You may want to catch attention with a negative (which you will go on to show can be solved).

2. **Define the problem you both share (which your request will solve).** Present the problem objectively: don't assign blame or mention personalities. Be specific about the cost in money, time, lost goodwill, and so on. You have to convince readers that *something* has to be done before you can convince them that your solution is the best one.

3. **Explain the solution to the problem.** If you know that the reader will favor another solution, start with that solution and show why it won't work before you present your solution.

   Present your solution without using the words *I* or *my*. Don't let personalities enter the picture; don't let the reader think he or she should say *no* just because you've had other requests accepted recently.

4. **Show that any negative elements (cost, time, etc.) are outweighed by the advantages.**

5. **Summarize any additional benefits of the solution.** The main benefit—solving the problem—can be presented briefly since you described the problem in detail. However, if there are any additional benefits, mention them.

6. **Ask for the action you want.** Often your reader will authorize or approve something; other people will implement the action. Give your reader a reason to act promptly, perhaps offering a new reader benefit. ("By buying now, we can avoid the next quarter's price hikes.")

FIGURE 9.4 A Problem-Solving Persuasive Message

Memorandum

February 16, 2004

To: All Staff Members

From: Melissa J. Gutridge *MJG*

Subject: Why We Are Implementing a New Sign-Out System *Directed subject line indicates writer's position*

Common ground
Successfully mainstreaming our clients into the community is very important and daily interaction with the public is necessary. Our clients enjoy the times they get to go to the mall or out to lunch instead of remaining here all day. Recently, however, clients
Problem
have been taken out on activities without a staff member's knowing where the client is and whom the client is with.

Specific example of problem
We need to know where all clients are at all times because social workers, psychologists, and relatives constantly stop by unannounced. Last week Janet's father stopped by to pick her up for a doctor's appointment and she was not here. No one knew where she was or whom she was with. Naturally her father was very upset and wanted to know what kind of program we were running. Staff members' not knowing where our clients are and whom they are with is damaging to the good reputation of our staff and program.

Solution presented impersonally
Starting Monday, February 23, a sign-out board will be located by Betty's desk. Please write down where you and the client are going and when you expect to be back. When signing out, help clients sign themselves out. We can turn this into a learning experience for our clients. Then when a social worker stops by to see
Additional reader benefit
someone who isn't here, we can simply look at the sign-out board to tell where the client is and when he or she will return.

Ask for action
Please help keep up the superb reputation you have helped Weststar earn as a quality center for adults with handicaps. Sign out yourself and clients at all times.

Developing a Common Ground

A common ground avoids the me-against-you of some persuasive situations and suggests that both you and your audience have a mutual interest in solving the problems you face. To find a common ground, we analyze the audience, understand their biases, objections, and needs, and identify with them so that we can make them identify with us. This analysis can be carried out in a cold, manipulative way. It can also be based on a respect for and sensitivity to the audience's position.

Readers are highly sensitive to manipulation. No matter how much you disagree with your audience, respect their intelligence. Try to understand why they believe or do something and why they may object to your position. If you

Read This*

Busy executives get so many messages a day that they can't pay attention to all of them. One study found that executives were most likely to pay attention to messages that

- Were personalized.
- Evoked an emotional response.
- Came from a credible sender.
- Were concise.

*Based on Thomas H. Davenport and John C. Beck, "Getting the Attention You Need," *Harvard Business Review*, September–October 2000, 124.

Say What?*

The following "benefits" appeared in classified ads. Did the writers think readers are that gullible? Or did they just not realize what they were really saying?

- The Macon County Humane Society offers free spaying/neutering to senior citizens if they adopt an animal out of the animal shelter.
- Remember, you get what you pay for. And at Hub Furniture Store, you pay less.
- Home, $199,500. Great location. . . . Built the way they used to. Won't last.
- Try our cough syrup. You will never get any better.
- Artle's Restaurant and Yogurt Parlor: "An Alternative to Good Eating."
- FOR SALE: Braille dictionary. Must see to appreciate.
- Now you can borrow enough money to get completely out of debt.

*Examples quoted from Richard Lederer, *More Anguished English* (New York: Delacorte, 1993), 107–12.

can understand your readers' initial positions, you'll be more effective—and you won't alienate your readers by talking down to them.

The best common grounds are specific. Often a negative—a problem the reader will want to solve—makes a good common ground.

Weak common ground:	This program has had some difficulty finding enough individuals to volunteer their services for the children. As a result, we are sometimes unable to provide the one-on-one mentoring that is our goal.
Improved common ground:	On five Sundays in the last three months, we've had too few volunteers to provide one-on-one mentoring. Last Sunday, we had just two college students to take eight children to the Museum of Science and Industry.

Generalizations are likely to bore the reader. Instead, use the idea behind the generalization to focus on something the reader cares about.

Weak common ground:	We all want this plant to be profitable.
Improved common ground:	We forfeited a possible $186,000 in profits last summer due to a 17% drop in productivity.

In your common ground, emphasize the parts of your proposal that fit with what your audience already does or believes. An employee of 3M wanted to develop laser disks. He realized that 3M's previous products were thin and flat: Scotch tape, Post-it Notes, magnetic tape. When he made his presentation to the group that chose new products for development, he held his prototype disk horizontally, so his audience saw a flat, thin object rather than a large, round, record-like object. Making his project fit with the audience's previous experience was a subtle and effective emotional tool to make it easier for the audience to say *yes*.[12]

Use audience analysis to evaluate possible common grounds. Suppose you want to install a system to play background music in a factory. To persuade management to pay for the system, a possible common ground would be increasing productivity. However, to persuade the union to pay for the system, you'd need a different common ground. Workers would see productivity as a way to get them to do more work for the same pay. A better common ground would be that the music would make the factory environment more pleasant.

Dealing with Objections

If you know that your readers will hear other points of view, or if your audience's initial position is negative, you have to deal with their objections to persuade them. The stronger the objection is, the earlier in your message you should deal with it.

The best way to deal with an objection is to eliminate it. James Davis keeps frequently ordered items in stock to eliminate the objection "I don't want to wait." To sell Jeep Cherokees in Japan, Mitsuru Sato convinced Chrysler to put the driver's seat on the right side, to make an extra preshipment quality check, and to rewrite the instruction booklet in Japanese style, with big diagrams and cartoons.[13]

If an objection is false and is based on misinformation, give the response to the objection without naming the objection. In a brochure, you can present responses with a "question/answer" format. When objections have already been voiced, you may want to name the objection so that your audience realizes that you are responding to that specific objection. However, to avoid solidifying the opposition, don't attribute the objection to your audience. Instead, use a less personal attribution: "Some people wonder . . ."; "Some citizens are afraid that . . ."

If you can't overcome an objection, admit it. A potential client asked Evonne Weinhaus, "Do you really do anything new in your training?" She looked him in the eye and said, "No, I don't. I just add a twist." After a moment of silence, he said, "That's good. There is nothing new out there, and if you had said yes this lunch would have been over immediately!" They talked about her approach and her "twist" on sales training. The potential client became a real client, signing up for 26 workshops.

If real objections remain, try one or more of the following strategies to counter objections:

1. Specify how much time and/or money is required—it may not be as much as the reader fears.

> Distributing flyers to each house or apartment in your neighborhood will probably take two afternoons.

2. Put the time and/or money in the context of the benefits they bring.

> The additional $152,500 will (1) allow the Open Shelter to remain open 24 rather than 16 hours a day, (2) pay for three social workers to help men find work and homes, and (3) keep the Neighborhood Bank open, so that men don't have to cash Social Security checks in bars and so that they can save up the $800 they need to have up front to rent an apartment.

3. Show that money spent now will save money in the long run.

> By buying a $100 safety product, you can avoid $500 in OSHA fines.

Persuading the Boss*

When a close friend confided his HIV-positive status to her, [Lynn Kutner decided to become] a Spokebuster—someone who does all five [bicycle] rides [to raise funds for AIDS] in a year. . . .

Although Kutner, . . . who supervises a team of four people, was entitled to some vacation time, she knew that requesting 20 days off was unusual. So she submitted a formal request nine months in advance and talked at length with her boss about why doing all five rides was so important to her. She also explained that at the most she'd be out of the office for a week and a half at a time.

"I was able to demonstrate that I was going to be in the office enough to follow through with my commitments," she says. . . . "Initially people were concerned, but it was clearly something that I thought through. And it meant a lot to me; my level of commitment carried a lot of weight."

Kutner's participation had a clear work benefit: She says she's now less intimidated by new tasks and [is] more efficient. . . . Nobody was surprised when she asked to go this year, she says, and nobody objected.

*Quoted from Erica Rasmusson, "Doing Well, Doing Good," *Working Woman,* December/January 2001, 42.

4. Show that doing as you ask will benefit some group or cause the reader supports, even though the action may not help the reader directly. This is the strategy used in fund-raising letters, discussed in detail in Chapter 10.

> By being a Big Brother or a Big Sister, you'll give a child the adult attention he or she needs to become a well-adjusted, productive adult.

5. Show the reader that the sacrifice is necessary to achieve a larger, more important goal to which he or she is committed.

> These changes will mean more work for all of us. But we've got to cut our costs 25% to keep the plant open and to keep our jobs.

6. Show that the advantages as a group outnumber or outweigh the disadvantages as a group.

> None of the locations is perfect. But the Backbay location gives us the most advantages and the fewest disadvantages.

7. Turn a disadvantage into an opportunity.

> With the hiring freeze, every department will need more lead time to complete its own work. By hiring another person, the Planning Department could provide that lead time.

Use the following five steps when you face major objections:

1. **Find out why your audience members resist what you want them to do.** Sit down one-on-one with people and listen. Don't try to persuade them; just try to understand.

2. **Try to find a win–win solution.** People will be much more readily persuaded if they see benefits for themselves. Sometimes your original proposal may have benefits that the audience had not thought of, and explaining the benefits will help. Sometimes you'll need to modify your original proposal to find a solution that solves the real problem and meets everyone's needs (➡ Chapter 12).

3. **Let your audience save face.** Don't ask people to admit that they have been wrong all along. If possible, admit that the behavior may have been appropriate in the past. Whether you can do that or not, always show how changed circumstances or new data call for new action.

4. **Ask for something small.** When you face great resistance, you won't get everything at once. Ask for a month's trial. Ask for one step that will move toward your larger goal. For example, if your ultimate goal is to eliminate prejudice in your organization, a step toward that goal might be to convince managers to make a special effort for one month to recognize the contributions of women or members of minorities in group meetings.

5. **Present your arguments from your audience's point of view.** Offer benefits that help the reader, not just you. Take special care to avoid words that attack or belittle readers. Present yourself as someone helping readers achieve their goals, not someone criticizing or giving orders from above.

The draft in Figure 9.5 makes the mistake of attacking readers in a negative message. Making the memo less accusatory would help, but the message doesn't need to be negative at all. Instead, the writer can take the information in paragraph 3 and use it as the attention-getter and common ground for a problem-solving persuasive message. Figure 9.6 shows a possible revision.

FIGURE 9.5 Original Unprofessional Memo Attacking Readers

Inter-office Memorandum

October 24, 2003

To: Todd Neumann

From: Heather Johnson

Subject: Problems with Instrument Lab Results

Accusatory tone makes this writer look unprofessional

Negative

Makes reader feel incompetent

Accusatory tone

The Instrument Technicians Lab again seems to believe that if a result is printed out, it is the correct answer. It doesn't seem to matter that the chromatogram is terribly noisy, the calibration standards are over a month old, or the area of the internal standards is about half what it should be. What does it matter if the correction factor is 1286 and at the very minimum it should be 1300? That's an average of two results—so what if the calibration standard is six weeks old? I'm aware that the conditions in the lab have contributed to the discouraged atmosphere, but I don't feel it's an excuse for the shape of the lab and the equipment. The G.C. columns are in bad shape just from abuse. I've lost count of the number of 10 ml. syringes the lab has buried (at least $20 each) mainly because they were not properly rinsed and the plungers were lost trying to push through dried protein material. When was the last time the glass insert in the B column was changed or even looked at? Has anyone checked the filter on the Autolab I?

Attacks reader

Insults and attacks reader

Lacks YA

During the last six months, I have either reminded the technician of such things or written reminders in the log book. Isn't it time for our responsible lab technicians to take on this responsibility? Shouldn't they have fresh standards made up, especially when they know a run is coming? Granted, we've had many false starts, but I am still uncomfortable that the technicians will be ready when the time comes.

Lacks YA

Problem presented as reader's fault, not a common problem that both share

I don't feel that I should have to go over the chromatograms, printouts, and G.C. book every time we submit samples for analysis. However, just two weeks ago I sent out results without doing this and immediately received a call that the results were impossible—and they were because unacceptable KF was used, the result of an old calibration standard.

Lacks YA

One other item bothers me. I don't know how to get the technicians interested in the way the Autolab integrates each peak when they don't seem to look at anything other than the answer. I feel it's very important they learn this so they will know when a peak has been incorrectly integrated.

Attacks and insults reader

I think it's time they either take hold and run the lab themselves or they be treated as if they were children and told what to do which means they'll need a baby-sitter. I also would like to see them read the Autolab I Instruction Manual and take the tape courses on the gas chromatograph and the Autolab I. I really think the above should be a mandatory part of their training.

Whole ¶ lacks YA

The overall attitude and morale of the lab must be raised and a step in that direction is to give them the responsibility which they were supposed to have in the first place and expect them to accept it. These people are being called technicians but they are actually classed as chemists and should be assuming more initative and responsibility.

Attacks reader

FIGURE 9.6   Revised Memo Creating a Common Ground and a Professional Image

Straightforward problem-solving approach is the mark of a professional manager   *Inter-office Memorandum*

October 24, 2003

To: Todd Neumann

From: Heather Johnson

Subject: Cutting Requests for Re-Work   *Positive Subject Line*

Common ground:

Problem writer and reader share

Two weeks ago a customer called to tell me that the results we'd sent out were impossible. I checked, and the results were wrong because we'd used an old calibration standard.

Redoing work for outside customers and for in-house projects doubles our workload. Yet because people don't trust our results, we're getting an increasing number of requests for re-work.

Writer shows understanding of reader's problems

Part of the problem is that we've had so many false starts. Customers and especially in-house engineers say they'll need a run but then don't have the materials for another day or even a week. Paul Liu has told me that these schedule glitches are inevitable. We'll just have to prepare fresh calibration standards every time a run is scheduled—and prepare them again when the run actually is ready.

You've told me that the equipment in the lab is unreliable. The Capital Expenditures Request includes a line item for G.C. columns and a new gas chromatograph. We'll be able to be more persuasive at the Board meeting if we can show that we're taking good care of the equipment we have. Please remind your staff to

- Rinse the 10-ml. syringes every day.

- Check the glass insert in the B column every week.   *List emphasizes what reader needs to do*

- Check the filter on the Autolab I every week.

Treats reader as an equal who can help solve the problem

Do workers find the Autolab I instruction manual and the tape courses on the gas chromatograph and the Autolab I helpful? If the manual is hard to use or the tape course is boring, perhaps we should ask the manufacturer to redo them and, in the meantime, to send a service worker to offer a short course for our workers. What do you think would be the best way to increase the technical expertise of our staff?

By getting our results right the first time, we can eliminate the re-work and give both customers and in-house clients better service.

Links desired action to benefit and picture of the problem being solved

Organizational changes work best when the audience buys into the solution. And that happens most easily when they themselves find it. Management can

1. Help people see and own the problem.
2. Identify values and cultures that need to change.
3. Let people discover solutions.
4. Support change tangibly and symbolically.

 See the BAC Web site for links on persuasion.

Offering a Reason for the Reader to Act Promptly

The longer people delay, the less likely they are to carry through with the action they had decided to take. In addition, you want a fast response so you can go ahead with your own plans.

Request action by a specific date. Try to give people at least a week or two: they have other things to do besides respond to your requests. Set deadlines in the middle of the month, if possible. If you say, "Please return this by March 1," people will think, "I don't need to do this till March." Ask for the response by February 28 instead. If you can use a response even after the deadline, say so. Otherwise, people who can't make the deadline may not respond at all.

Readers may ignore deadlines that seem arbitrary. Show why you need a quick response:

■ **Show that the time limit is real.** Perhaps you need information quickly to use it in a report that has a due date. Perhaps a decision must be made by a certain date to catch the start of the school year, the Christmas selling season, or an election campaign. Perhaps you need to be ready for a visit from out-of-town or international colleagues.

■ **Show that acting now will save time or money.** If business is slow and your industry isn't doing well, then your company needs to act now (to economize, to better serve customers) in order to be competitive. If business is booming and everyone is making a profit, then your company needs to act now to get its fair share of the available profits.

■ **Show the cost of delaying action.** Will labor or material costs be higher in the future? Will delay mean more money spent on repairing something that will still need to be replaced?

Building Emotional Appeal

Stories and psychological description are effective ways of building emotional appeal. Emotional appeal works best when people want to be persuaded.

Even when you need to provide statistics or numbers to convince the careful reader that your anecdote is a representative example, telling a story first makes your message more persuasive. Experiments with both high school teachers and quantitatively trained MBA students show that people are more likely to believe a point and more likely to be committed to it when points were made by examples, stories, and case studies. Stories alone were more effective than a combination of stories and statistics; the combination was more effective than statistics alone. In another experiment, attitude changes lasted longer when the audience had read stories than when they had only read numbers. Recent research suggests that stories are more persuasive because people remember them.[14]

Creative Response to an Objection, I*

To cut costs, banks want customers to use automated teller machines (ATMs) rather than expensive tellers. But older customers prefer talking to a person. And retirees want their errands to provide social contact.

Canada's second-largest bank, CIBC, hires greeters to train people how to use the ATMs and to provide human contact at tellerless branches.

And humor helps. Victoria Brink Guillot, manager of a Citibank branch in San Mateo, California, tells her mature customers, "ATMs are just like slot machines, only you never lose."

*Based on Paco Underbill, "Seniors in Stores," *American Demographics*, April 1996, 48.

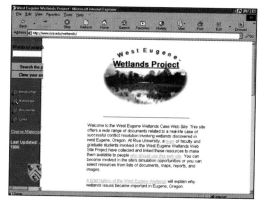

InSite

www.rice.edu/wetlands

Difficult situations arise when multiple stakeholders in an issue have different—perhaps contradictory—points of view. This Web site, created by faculty and graduate students at Rice University, presents documents, maps, and reports that led to a successful resolution.

Let the Audience Find a Solution*

When Carol Roberts joined International Paper as Vice President of People Development, she quickly realized that people were not in fact being developed. How could someone new talk about a major problem?

She realized that she needed to win top managers' hearts and minds to make a change. She scheduled a two-day off-site meeting (led by an outside consultant to build credibility). During the meeting, the managers themselves saw that a problem existed.

The managers came up with some solutions, but they needed backing from the top to implement them. After the off-site meeting, Roberts met with top management to get the needed support.

Less than a year later, the company had a new policy of twice-yearly meetings between employees and managers to discuss career development and "people champions" to make sure that workers got the help they needed to grow.

*Based on Michael Warshaw, "Open Mouth, Close Career?" *Fast Company*, December 1998, 241–51.

Sometimes a visual image communicates even more powerfully than words. Don Winkler was managing a Citibank branch in Italy when a change in the tax law seemed to threaten bank deposits. To forestall a run of people withdrawing their money, Winkler took all the cash out of the vaults and piled it high at every teller station. The visual message that the bank had plenty of money was so strong that deposits actually grew.[15]

Difficult situations sometimes have ethical implications. Figure 9.7 lists some of the Web resources that deal with business ethics. You can find links to these sites on the BAC Web page.

Sense impressions—what the reader sees, hears, smells, tastes, feels—evoke a strong emotional response. **Psychological description** means creating a scenario rich with sense impressions so readers can picture themselves using your product or service and enjoying its benefits. You can also use psychological description to describe the problem your product will solve. Psychological description works best early in the message to catch readers' attention.

Feature:	Snooze alarm
Benefit:	If the snooze button is pressed, the alarm goes off and comes on again nine minutes later.
Psychological description:	Some mornings, you really want to stay in bed just a few more minutes. With the Sleepytime Snooze Alarm, you can snuggle under the covers for a few extra winks, secure in the knowledge that the alarm will come on again to get you up for that breakfast meeting with an important client. If you don't have to be anywhere soon, you can keep hitting the snooze alarm for up to an additional 63 minutes of sleep. With Sleepytime, you're in control of your mornings.
Feature:	Tilt windows
Benefit:	Easier to clean
Psychological description:	It's no wonder so many cleaners "don't do windows." Balancing precariously on a rickety ladder to clean upper-story windows . . . shivering outside in the winter winds and broiling in the summer sun as you scrub away . . . running inside, then outside, then inside again to try to get the spot that always seems to be on the other side. Cleaning traditional windows really is awful.
	In contrast, cleaning is a breeze with Tilt-in Windows. Just pull the inner window down and pull the bottom toward you. The whole window lifts out! Repeat for the outer window. Clean them inside in comfort (sitting down or even watching TV if you choose). Then replace the top of the outer window in its track, slide up, and repeat with the inner window. Presto! Clean windows!

Someone who's already looking for a product may need only the feature or the benefit. Good psychological description uses vivid details and sensory imagery to motivate uncommitted readers. The flyer for a university's food services in Figure 9.8 gets your gastric juices flowing.

In psychological description, you're putting your reader in a picture. If the reader doesn't feel that the picture fits him or her, the technique backfires. To prevent this, psychological description often uses subjunctive verbs ("if you like . . ." "if you were . . .") or the words *maybe* and *perhaps*.

FIGURE 9.7 Business Ethics Resources on the Web

- **Business ethics resources on the Internet**
  www.ethics.ubc.ca/resources/business
- **Defense Industry Initiative on Business Ethics and Conduct**
  www.dii.org
- **DePaul University's Institute for Business and Professional Ethics**
  www.condor.depaul.edu/ethics
- **Ethics Effectiveness Quick Test**
  www.ethics.org/quicktest/quicktest.cfm

- **Ethics in International Business**
  library.lib.binghamton.edu/subjects/business/intbuseth.html
- **E-Business Ethics**
  www.e-businessethics.com
- **Various codes of conduct**
  www.ethics.ubc.ca/resources/business/codes.html

You're hungry but you don't want to bother with cooking. Perhaps you have guests to take to dinner. Or it's 12 noon and you only have an hour for lunch. Whatever the situation, the Illini Union has a food service to fit your needs. If you want convenience, we have it. If it's atmosphere you're seeking, it's here too. And if you're concerned about the price, don't be. When you're looking for a great meal, the Illini Union is the place to find it.

Illini Union brochure

Tone in Persuasive Messages

The best phrasing depends on your relationship to the reader. When you ask for action from people who report directly to you, orders ("Get me the Ervin file") and questions ("Do we have the third-quarter numbers yet?") will work. When you need action from co-workers, superiors, or people outside the organization, you need to be more forceful but also more polite.

How you ask for action affects whether you build or destroy positive relationships with other employees, customers, and suppliers. Professor and consultant Dan Dieterich notes that the calls to action in many messages are

- Buried somewhere deep in the middle of the correspondence.
- Disguised as either statements or questions.
- Insulting because they use "parental language."

Such messages, Dieterich points out, "lower productivity within the organization and reduce or eliminate the goodwill customers have toward the organization. . . . [T]hose two things . . . can put the organization out of business."[16]

Avoiding messages that sound parental or preachy is often a matter of tone. Saying "Please" is a nice touch, especially to people on your level or outside the organization. Tone will also be better when you give reasons for your request or reasons to act promptly.

Parental: Everyone is expected to comply with these regulations. I'm sure you can see that they are commonsense rules needed for our business.

Better: Even on casual days, visitors expect us to be professional. So leave the gym clothes at home!

When you write to people you know well, humor can work. Just make sure that the message isn't insulting to anyone who doesn't find the humor funny.

Writing to superiors is trickier. You may want to tone down your request by using subjunctive verbs and explicit disclaimers that show you aren't taking a *yes* for granted.

Arrogant: Based on this evidence, I expect you to give me a new computer.

Better: If department funds permit, I would like a new computer.

Creative Response to an Objection, II*

Jim Young sold apples by direct mail order. One year, a hailstorm just before the harvest bruised the apples.

At first, the obstacle appeared insurmountable. For years, his selling point had been that his apples looked as good as they tasted.

But Jim was able to turn the disadvantage into an advantage.

He knew that cold weather (partially responsible for the hailstorm) improves the flavor of ripening apples. So he filled the orders, inserting a note in each box:

Note the hail marks which have caused minor skin blemishes in some of these apples. They are proof of their growth at a high mountain altitude where the sudden chills from hailstorms help firm the flesh, develop the natural sugars, and give these apples their incomparable flavor.

Not one customer asked for a refund. In fact, the next year, some people wrote on their orders, "Send the hail-marked apples if possible."

*Based on Ray Considine and Murray Raphael, *The Great Brain Robbery* (Pasadena, CA: The Great Brain Robbery, 1981), 95–96.

FIGURE 9.8   Using Psychological Description to Develop Reader Benefits

You–attitude psychological description

The Colonial Room

When you dine in the Illini Union Colonial Room, it's easy to imagine yourself a guest in a fine Virginian mansion. Light from the gleaming chandeliers reflects from a hand-carved mirror hanging over the dark, polished buffet. Here you can dine in quiet elegance amid furnishings adapted from 18th century Williamsburg and the Georgian homes of the James River Valley in Virginia.

Perhaps you'd like a dinner of stuffed rainbow trout. Or the pork fricassee. The menu features a variety of complete meals which are changed daily, as well as the regular a la carte service. Whatever your choice, you'll enjoy an evening of fine dining at very reasonable prices.

The Illini Union Colonial Room is located on the northeast corner of the first floor. Dinners are served Monday through Friday from 5:30 to 7:30 p.m. Please call 333-0690 for reservations, and enjoy the flavor of the Colonies tonight.

Visual details

Details appeal to sight, taste, smell

Emphasis on reader's choice– Not every reader will want the same thing

The Cafeteria

In the Illini Union Cafeteria, you start out with an empty tray and silverware. Then comes the food, several yards of it, all yours for the choosing. By the time you've finished, your empty tray has become a delicious meal.

In the morning, the warm aroma of breakfast fills the air. Feast your eyes and then your appetite on the array of eggs, bacon, pancakes, toast, sausage, rolls, juices, and coffee . . . They're all waiting to wake you up with good taste. Have a hearty breakfast or make it quick and tasty. The warm, freshly baked sweet rolls and coffeecakes practically beg to be smothered in butter and savored with a cup of hot coffee.

By 11 a.m. the breakfast menu has made way for lunch. Here come the plump Reuben sandwiches and the toasty grilled cheese. Soups and salads make their appearance. A variety of vegetables are dressed up to entice you and several main dishes lead the luncheon parade. Any number of complete meals can take shape as you move along.

What? Back for dinner? Well, no wonder! The Cafeteria sets out a wide selection of entrees and side dishes. Veal parmigiana steams for your attention but the roast beef right next to it is rough competition. Tomorrow the fried chicken might be up for selection. Choose the dinner combination that best fits your appetite and your pocket.

The newly remodeled Cafeteria is on the ground floor and is open for breakfast from 7 to 11 a.m. Monday through Saturday and 8 to 11 a.m. on Sunday. Lunch is served from 11 a.m. to 1:15 p.m. Monday through Saturday and 11 a.m. to 2 p.m. on Sunday. Dinner is served from 4:45 to 7 p.m. Monday through Friday.

A meal in a restaurant is expensive. A meal at home is a chore. But a meal at the Cafeteria combines good food and reasonable prices to make dining a pleasure.

Passive verbs and jargon sound stuffy. Use active imperatives—perhaps with "Please" to create a friendlier tone.

Stuffy: It is requested that you approve the above-mentioned action.

Better: Please authorize us to create a new subscription letter.

Writing Persuasive E-Mail Messages

It can be particularly tricky to control tone in e-mail messages, which always tend to sound less friendly than paper documents or conversations. For important requests, compose your message offline and revise it carefully before you send it.

E-mail messages have to catch the reader's eye in the subject line. If the message is longer than one screen, the first screen must interest the reader enough to make him or her continue.

The subject line of a persuasive e-mail message should make it clear that you're asking for something. If you're sure that the reader will read the message, something as vague as "Request" may work. Most of the time, it's better to be more specific.

Subject: Move Meeting to Tuesday?

Subject: Need Your Advice

Subject: Provide Story for Newsletter?

Subject: Want You for United Way Campaign

Try to keep the subject line short. If that's difficult, put the most important part into the first few words since many e-mail programs only show the first 28 characters of the subject line.

When you ask for something small or for something that it is part of the reader's job duties to provide, your request can be straightforward. In the body of the message, give people all the information they need to act. At the end of the message, ask for the action you want. Make the action as easy as possible, and specify when you need a response. You may want an immediate response now ("Let me know ASAP whether you can write a story for the newsletter so that I can save the space") and a fuller one later ("We'll need the text by March 4").

When you ask for something big or something that is not a regular part of a person's duties, the first paragraph must not only specify the request but also make the reader view it positively. Use the second paragraph to provide an overview of the evidence that the rest of the message will provide: "Here's why we should do this." "Let me describe the project. Then, if you're willing to be part of it, I'll send you a copy of the proposal." Use audience analysis to find a reason to do as you ask that the reader will find convincing. Everyone is busy, so you need to make the reader *want* to do as you ask. Be sure to provide complete information that the reader will need to act on your request. Ask for the action you want.

Major requests that require changes in values, culture, or lifestyles should not be made in e-mail messages.

Varieties of Persuasive Messages

Collection letters, performance appraisals, and letters of recommendation are among the most common varieties of persuasive messages.

Collection Letters

Most businesses find that phoning rather than writing results in faster payment. But as more and more companies install voice-mail systems, you will need to write letters when leaving messages doesn't work.

Collection letters ask customers to pay (as they have already agreed to do) for the goods and services they have already received. Good credit departments send a **series** of letters a week apart.

Early letters are gentle, assuming that the reader intends to pay but has forgotten or has met with temporary reverses. Early letters can be obvious form letters or even just a second copy of the bill with the words "Second Notice" or "Past Due" stamped on it.

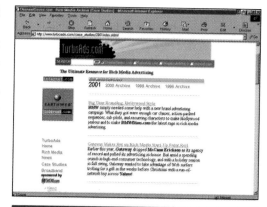

InSite

www.turboads.com/case_studies/ 2001index.shtml

Channelseven.com provides case studies of e-advertisements.

Creative Response to a Problem, III*

Moving raw ingredients in and food items out to buyers—500 types of cookies alone—costs Nabisco more than $200 million a year in trucking expenses. The worst of it was that during much of the journey, the truck wasn't full.

To solve the problem, Nabisco joined forces with other retailers—even competitors—to share truck and warehouse space. A Web site lets companies coordinate loads, so that a half-full truck can fill up with a second load. In spite of a few extra miles to fill up trucks, the process is a success. Just in southern California, Nabisco saved $78,000 in shipping costs, and all manufacturers combined saved almost $900,000. Lucky Stores, Inc., saved $4.8 million in inventory costs because the more flexible trucking let it more closely match orders and deliveries to customer needs. And some items were less expensive because suppliers didn't have to pay for half-empty trucks.

*Based on Faith Keenan, "One Smart Cookie," *Business Week E.BIZ*, November 20, 2000, EB 120.

A student who had not yet been reimbursed by a company for a visit to the company's office put the second request in the P.S. of a letter refusing a job offer:

> P.S. The check to cover my expenses when I visited your office in March hasn't come yet. Could you check to see whether you can find a record of it? The amount was $490 (airfare $290, hotel room $185, taxi $15).

Early collection letters sometimes use humor to defuse negative feelings and to set themselves apart from other mail. Since readers' senses of humor differ, the real test of a collection letter using humor should be: Does it enrage readers who think they have already paid? Does it make the request seem trivial, as though the bill is a joke? If the answer to either of these questions is *yes*, don't use the humor.

If one or two early letters don't result in payment, call the customer to ask if your company has created a problem. It's possible that you shipped something the customer didn't want or sent the wrong quantity. It's possible that the invoice arrived before the product and was filed and forgotten. It's possible that the invoice document is poorly designed, so customers set it aside until they could figure it out. If any of these situations apply, you'll build goodwill by solving the problem rather than arrogantly asking for payment.[17]

Middle letters are more assertive in asking for payment. Figure 9.9 gives an example of a middle letter. This form letter is merged with database information about the customer's name, the amount due, and the magazine the customer is receiving. Other middle letters offer to negotiate a schedule for repayment if the reader is not able to pay the whole bill immediately, may remind the reader of the importance of a good credit rating (which will be endangered if the bill remains unpaid), educate the reader about credit, and explain why the creditor must have prompt payment.

Unless you have firm evidence to the contrary, middle letters should assume that readers have some legitimate reason for not yet paying. Perhaps they've been out of town. Perhaps their checks were lost in the mail. Perhaps they're waiting to receive payments due them so that they can pay their own creditors. Even people who are "juggling" payments because they do not have enough money to pay all their bills or people who will put payment off as long as possible will respond more quickly if you do not accuse them. If a reader is offended by your assumption that he or she is dishonest, that anger can become an excuse to continue delaying payment.

Late letters threaten legal action if the bill is not paid. Under federal law, the writer cannot threaten legal action unless he or she actually intends to sue. Other regulations also spell out what a writer may and may not do in a late letter.

Many small businesses find that establishing personal relationships with customers is the best way to speed payment.

Performance Appraisals

At regular intervals, supervisors evaluate, or appraise, the performance of their subordinates. In most organizations, employees have access to their files; sometimes they must sign the appraisal to show that they've read it. The superior normally meets with the subordinate to discuss the appraisal.

As a subordinate, you should prepare for the appraisal interview by listing your achievements and goals. Where do you want to be in a year or five years? What training and experience do you need to reach your goals? Also think about any weaknesses. If you need training, advice, or support from the organization to improve, the appraisal interview is a good time to ask for this help.

Appraisals need to both protect the organization and motivate the employee. These two purposes conflict. Most of us will see a candid appraisal as negative; we need praise and reassurance to believe that we're valued and can do better. But the praise that motivates someone to improve can come back to haunt the company if the person does not eventually do acceptable work. An organization is in trouble if it tries to fire someone whose evaluations never mention mistakes.

Avoid labels (*wrong, bad*) and inferences (➡ Appendix C). Instead, cite specific observations that describe behavior.

Inference:	Sam is an alcoholic.
Vague observation:	Sam calls in sick a lot. Subordinates complain about his behavior.
Specific observation:	Sam called in sick a total of 12 days in the last two months. After a business lunch with a customer last week, Sam was walking unsteadily. Two of his subordinates have said that they would prefer not to make sales trips with him because they find his behavior embarrassing.

Sam might be an alcoholic. He might also be having a reaction to a physician-prescribed drug; he might have a mental illness; he might be showing symptoms of a physical illness other than alcoholism. A supervisor who jumps to conclusions creates ill will, closes the door to solving the problem, and may provide grounds for legal action against the organization.

Be specific in an appraisal.

Too vague:	Sue does not manage her time as well as she could.
Specific:	Sue's first three weekly sales reports have been three, two, and four days late, respectively; the last weekly sales report for the month is not yet in.

Without specifics, Sue won't know that her boss objects to late reports. She may think that she is being criticized for spending too much time on sales calls or for not working 80 hours a week. Without specifics, she might change the wrong things in a futile effort to please her boss.

Good supervisors try not only to identify the specific problems in subordinates' behavior but also in conversation to discover the causes of the problem. Does the employee need more training? Perhaps a training course or a mentor will help. Does he or she need to work harder? Then the supervisor needs to motivate the worker and help him or her manage distractions. Is a difficult situation causing the problem? Perhaps the situation can be changed. If it can't be changed, the supervisor and the company should realize that the worker is not at fault.

Sometimes a performance appraisal reflects mostly the month or week right before the appraisal, even though it is supposed to cover six months or a year. Many managers record specific observations of subordinates' behavior two or three times a month. These notes jog the memory so that the appraisal doesn't focus unduly on recent behavior.

Appraisals are more useful to subordinates if they make clear which areas are most important and contain specific recommendations for improvement. No one can improve 17 weaknesses at once. Which two should the employee work on this month? Is getting in reports on time more important than increasing sales?

Phrase goals in specific, concrete terms. The subordinate may think that "considerable progress toward completing" a report may mean that the project should be 15% finished. The boss may think that "considerable progress" means 50% or 85% of the total work.

Figure 9.10 shows a performance appraisal for a member of a collaborative business communication group who is doing good work.

Saving Face Saves Money*

Helping people save face can help them act in ways that can help your company. To customers who had fallen behind with their payments, a credit card company sent not the expected stern collection letter but a hand-addressed, hand-signed greeting card. The front of the card pictured a stream running through a forest. The text inside noted that sometimes life takes unexpected turns and asked people to call the company to find a collaborative solution. When people called the 800 number, they got credit counseling and help in creating a payment plan.

The project was successful. Instead of having to write off bad debts, the company received payments—and created goodwill.

*Based on Scott Robinette, "Get Emotional," *Harvard Business Review*, May 2001, 25.

Getting Action with Voice Mail

If your action is small and easy, you can ask for it in a voice-mail message: "Please fax me a copy of your price list."

When you want something more complicated or that the other person may be less willing to give, prepare a 30-second summary of your request, including the benefit to the person whose action you want. Put energy into your voice, so that you sound interesting to talk to.

As in any voice-mail message, state your name and phone number slowly and clearly. If you want something sent by e-mail, fax, or mail, give the appropriate number or address clearly. Specify when you'll be available to take return calls. If possible, give the person several options.

Negotiating a Raise*

- Seek assignments where you can implement ideas and be accountable for results. Tangible accomplishments increase your worth.

- Be able to show how your work helps the whole organization, not just your own unit.

- Know what your job is worth. See www.wageweb.com, www.execunet.com, and jobsmart.org/tools/salary/index.htm for salary information.

- Prepare your boss for the discussion. Perhaps even write out a proposal explaining what comparable jobs pay, what you want, and why you think you deserve a raise. Base your argument not on what you need the money for, but on your contribution to the organization's bottom line.

- Consider alternatives. If a raise isn't possible, what about an extra week of vacation?

*Based on Michael O'Malley, "How to Get the Raise You Deserve," *Fortune*, September 7, 1998, 169–70; Hal Lancaster, "Managing Your Career," *The Wall Street Journal*, September 1, 1998, B1; and *American Demographics*, "For the Bookmark," November 1998, 21.

FIGURE 9.9   A Middle Collection Letter

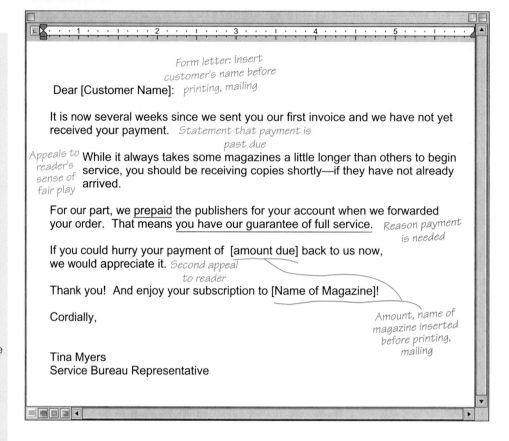

Letters of Recommendation

In an effort to protect themselves against lawsuits, some companies state only how long they employed someone and the position that person held. Such bare-bones letters have themselves been the target of lawsuits when employers did not reveal relevant negatives. Whatever the legal climate, there may be times when you want to recommend someone for an award or for a job.

Letters of recommendation must be specific. General positives that are not backed up with specific examples and evidence are seen as weak recommendations. Letters of recommendation that focus on minor points also suggest that the person is weak.

Either in the first or the last paragraph, summarize your overall evaluation of the person. Early in the letter, perhaps in the first paragraph, show how well and how long you've known the person. In the middle of the letter, offer specific details about the person's performance. At the end of the letter, indicate whether you would be willing to rehire the person and repeat your overall evaluation. Figure A.3 in Appendix A ➠ shows a sample letter of recommendation.

Experts are divided on whether you should include negatives. Some people feel that any negative weakens the letter. Other people feel that presenting but not emphasizing honest negatives makes the letter more convincing.

In many discourse communities, the words "Call me if you need more information" in a letter of recommendation mean "I have negative information that I am unwilling to put on paper. Call me and I'll tell you what I really think."

FIGURE 9.10 A Performance Appraisal

February 13, 2004

To: Barbara Buchanan

From: Brittany Papper BAP

Subject: Your Performance Thus Far in Our Collaborative Group

Overall evaluation — You have been a big asset to our group. Overall, our business communication group has been one of the best groups I have ever worked with, and I think that only minor improvements are needed to make our group even better.

What You're Doing Well

These headings would need to be changed in a negative performance appraisal.

Specific observations provide dates, details of performance — You demonstrated flexibility and compatibility at our last meeting before we turned in our proposal on February 12 by offering to type the proposal since I had to study for an exam in one of my other classes. I really appreciated this because I really did not have the time to do it. I will definitely remember this if you are ever too busy with your other classes and cannot type the final report.

Another positive critical incident occurred February 5. We had discussed researching the topic of sexual discrimination in hiring and promotion at Midstate Insurance. As we read more about what we had to do, we became uneasy about reporting the information from our source who works at Midstate. I called you later that evening to talk about changing our topic to a less personal one. You were very understanding and said that you agreed that the original topic was a touchy one. You offered suggestions for other topics and had a positive attitude about the adjustment. Your suggestions ended my worries and made me realize that you are a positive and supportive person.

Other strengths — Your ideas are a strength that you definitely contribute to our group. You're good at brainstorming ideas, yet you're willing to go with whatever the group decides. That's a nice combination of creativity and flexibility.

Areas for Improvement

Two minor improvements could make you an even better member.

Specific recommendations for improvement — The first improvement is to be more punctual to meetings. On February 5 and February 8 you were about 10 minutes late. This makes the meetings last longer. Your ideas are valuable to the group, and the sooner you arrive the sooner we can share in your suggestions.

Specific behavior to be changed — The second suggestion is one we all need to work on. We need to keep our meetings positive and productive. I think that our negative attitudes were worst at our first group meeting February 5. We spent about half an hour complaining about all the work we had to do and about our busy schedules in other classes. In the future if this happens, maybe you could offer some positive things about the assignment to get the group motivated again.

Overall Compatibility

Positive, forward-looking ending — I feel that this group has gotten along very well together. You have been very flexible in finding times to meet and have always been willing to do your share of the work. I have never had this kind of luck with a group in the past and you have been a welcome breath of fresh air. I don't hate doing group projects any more!

Rebuilding a brand, like any major persuasive campaign, takes many messages. When Mannie Jackson bought the Harlem Globetrotters in 1992, he showed how good the Globetrotters were by scheduling matches with top college teams. He focused on his audiences—from gatekeeper audiences such as the arena owners to customers who bought tickets for the shows. Charitable work and public appearances cement the team's family-friendly image and keep it in the news.

Solving a Sample Problem[18]

Problem

In one room in the production department of Nakamura Electronics Company, employees work on TV picture tubes under conditions that are scarcely bearable due to the heat. Even when the temperature outside is only 75°, it is over 100° in the "tube room." In June, July, and August, 24 out of 36 workers quit because they couldn't stand the heat. This turnover happens every summer.

In a far corner of the room sits a quality control inspector in front of a small fan (the only one in the room). The production workers, in contrast, are carrying 20-pound TV tubes. As Production Supervisor, you tried to get air-conditioning two years ago, before Nakamura acquired the company, but management was horrified at the idea of spending $300,000 to insulate and air-condition the warehouse (it is impractical to air-condition the tube room alone).

Inflation has pushed the price of insulation and air-conditioning up to $500,000, but with such high turnover, you're losing money every summer.

Write a memo to Jennifer M. Kirkland, Operations Vice President, renewing your request.

Analysis of the Problem

1. Who is (are) your audience(s)? What characteristics are relevant to this particular message? If you are writing to more than one reader, how do the readers differ?

   The Operations Vice President will be concerned about keeping costs low and keeping production running smoothly. Kirkland may know that the request was denied two years ago, but another person was Vice President then; Kirkland wasn't the one who said *no*.

2. What are your purposes in writing?

   To persuade Kirkland to authorize insulation and air-conditioning. To build a good image of myself.

3. What information must your message include?

   The cost of the proposal. The effects of the present situation.

4. How can you build support for your position? What reasons or reader benefits will your reader find convincing?

   Cutting turnover may save money and keep the assembly line running smoothly. Experienced employees may produce higher-quality parts. Putting in air-conditioning would relieve one of the workers' main complaints; it might make the union happier.

5. What objection(s) can you expect your reader(s) to have? What negative elements of your message must you deemphasize or overcome?

   The cost. The time operations will be shut down while installation is taking place.

6. What aspects of the total situation may affect reader response? The economy? The time of year? Morale in the organization? The relationship between the reader and writer? Any special circumstances?

   The electronics industry is having a shakeout; money is tight; the company will be reluctant to make a major expenditure. Filling vacancies in the tube room is hard—we are getting a reputation as a bad place to work. Summer is over, and the problem is over until next year.

Discussion of the Sample Solutions

Solution 1, shown in Figure 9.11, is unacceptable. By making the request in the subject line and the first paragraph, the writer invites a *no* before giving all the arguments. The writer does nothing to counter the objections that any manager will have to spending a great deal of money. By presenting the issue in terms of fairness, the writer produces defensiveness rather than creating a common ground. The writer doesn't use details or emotional appeal to show that the problem is indeed serious. The writer asks for fast action but doesn't show why the reader should act now to solve a problem that won't occur again for eight months.

Solution 2, shown in Figure 9.12, is an effective persuasive message. The writer chooses a positive subject line. The opening sentence is negative, catching the reader's attention. However, the paragraph makes it clear that the memo offers a solution to the problem. The problem is spelled out in detail. Emotional impact is created by taking the reader through the day as the temperature rises. The solution is presented impersonally. There are no *I*'s in the memo.

The memo stresses reader benefits: the savings that will result once the investment is recovered. The last paragraph tells the reader exactly what to do and links prompt action to a reader benefit. The memo ends with a positive picture of the problem solved.

Small Victories*

You can change the culture of a company to make it more ethical and more inclusive. And you don't have to wait till you're the CEO. Do it by making small changes.

One man wanted to coach his kids' soccer teams—so he left work before his colleagues did. He didn't want phone calls about work between 6 and 8 P.M. As people stopped calling him, it became clear that others felt the same way. Gradually, the company culture changed to reserve early-evening hours for family time.

At PricewaterhouseCoopers, a woman partner changed pronouns. When she created example scenarios for other partners, she populated them with *she*'s. It was a step in creating a cultural shift.

At still another company, a superior asked an African American woman to unbraid her hair before a meeting with a client. She refused. Her immediate boss praised her courage and congratulated the organization on expanding its understanding of professionalism.

Successful radicals have allies, both inside the company and outside it. Networks of supporters provide emotional support, information, resources, and sounding boards. Small victories, over time, lead to worthwhile change.

*Based on Keith H. Hammonds, "Practical Radicals," *Fast Company*, September 2000, 162–74.

FIGURE 9.11 An Unacceptable Solution to the Sample Problem

Date: October 10, 2003

To: Jennifer M. Kirkland, Operations Vice President

From: Arnold M. Morgan, Production Supervisor *AMM*

Subject: Request for Air-Conditioning the Tube Room

Request in subject line stiffens resistance when reader is reluctant

Please put air-conditioning in the tube room. This past summer, 2/3 of our employees quit because it was so hot. It's not fair that they should work in unbearable temperatures when management sits in air-conditioned comfort.

attacks reader

Inappropriate emphasis on writer

I propose that we solve this problem by air-conditioning the tube room to bring down the temperature to 78°.

Insulating and air-conditioning the tube room would cost $500,000.

Cost sounds enormous without a context

Please approve this request promptly.

Memo sounds arrogant.
Logic isn't developed.
This attacks reader instead of enlisting reader's support.

✓ **CHECKLIST**   Checklist for Direct Requests

- ☐ If the message is a memo, does the subject line indicate the request? Is the subject line specific enough to differentiate this message from others on the same subject?
- ☐ Does the first paragraph summarize the request or the specific topic of the message?
- ☐ Does the message give all of the relevant information? Is there enough detail?
- ☐ Does the message answer questions or overcome objections that readers may have without introducing unnecessary negatives?
- ☐ Does the last paragraph tell the reader exactly what to do? Does it give a deadline if one exists and a reason for acting promptly?

And, for all messages, not just direct requests,
- ☐ Does the message use you-attitude and positive emphasis?
- ☐ Is the style easy to read and friendly?
- ☐ Is the visual design of the message inviting?
- ☐ Is the format correct?
- ☐ Does the message use standard grammar? Is it free from typos?

Originality in a direct request may come from
- ☐ Good lists and visual impact.
- ☐ Thinking about readers and giving details that answer their questions, overcome any objections, and make it easier for them to do as you ask.
- ☐ Adding details that show you're thinking about a specific organization and the specific people in that organization.

FIGURE 9.12   A Good Solution to the Sample Problem

Date: October 10, 2003

To: Jennifer M. Kirkland, Operations Vice President

From: Arnold M. Morgan, Production Supervisor   *AMM*

Subject: Improving Summer Productivity

*Reader benefit
in subject line*

*Problem
creates a
common
ground*

Nakamura forfeited a possible $186,000 in profits last summer due to a 17% drop
in productivity. That's not unusual: Nakamura has a history of low summer
productivity. But we can reverse the trend and bring summer productivity in line
with the rest of the year's.

*Good to show
problem can be
resolved*

*Cause of
problem*

The problem starts in the tube room. Due to high turnover and reduced efficiency
from workers who are on the job, we just don't make as many TV tubes as we do
during the rest of the year. And when we don't have tubes, we can't make TV sets.

Both the high turnover and reduced efficiency are due to the unbearable heat in
the tube room. Temperatures in the tube room average 25° over the outside
temperature. During the summer, when work starts at 8, it's already 85° in the
tube room. By 11:30, it's at least 105°. On six days last summer, it hit 120°. When
the temperatures are that high, we may be violating OSHA regulations.

*Additional
reason to
solve problem*

Production workers are always standing, moving, or carrying 20-lb. TV tubes.
When temperatures hit 90°, they slow down. When no relief is in sight, many of
them quit.

We replaced 24 of the 36 employees in the tube room this summer. When
someone quits, it takes an average of five days to find and train a replacement;
during that time, the trainee produces nothing. For another five days, the new
person can work at only half speed. And even "full speed" in the summer is only
90% of what we expect the rest of the year.

*More
details
about
problem*

Here's where our losses come from:

Normal production = 50 units a person each day (upd)

Loss due to turnover:
    loss of 24 workers for 5 days =   6,000 units
    24 at $^1/_2$ pace for 5 days =   3,000 units
        Total loss due to turnover =   9,000 units

*Shows detail—
Set up like an
arithmetic
problem*

Loss due to reduced efficiency:
    loss of 5 upd x 12 workers x 10 days =   600 units
    loss of 5 upd x 36 x 50 days =   9,000 units
        Total loss due to reduced efficiency =   9,600 units

Total Loss =   18,600 units

FIGURE 9.12   A Good Solution to the Sample Problem

Jennifer M. Kirkland   2   October 10, 2003

According to the accounting department, Nakamura makes a net profit of $10 on every TV set we sell. And, as you know, with the boom in TV sales, we sell every set we make. Those 18,600 units we don't produce are costing us $186,000 a year.

Shows where numbers in paragraph 1 come from

Additional benefit

Bringing down the temperature to 78° (the minimum allowed under federal guidelines) from the present summer average of 112° will require an investment of $500,000 to insulate and air-condition the tube room. Extra energy costs for the air-conditioning will run about $30,000 a year. We'll get our investment back in less than three years. Once the investment is recouped, we'll be making an additional $150,000 a year—all without buying additional equipment or hiring additional workers.

Tells reader what to do

By installing the insulation and air-conditioning this fall, we can take advantage of lower off-season rates. Please authorize the Purchasing Department to request bids for the system. Then, next summer, our productivity can be at an all-time high.

Reason to act promptly

Ends on positive note of problem solved, reader enjoying benefit

---

✓ CHECKLIST   Checklist for Problem-Solving Persuasive Messages

☐ If the message is a memo, does the subject line indicate the writer's purpose or offer a reader benefit? Does the subject line avoid making the request?

☐ Does the first sentence interest the reader?

☐ Is the problem presented as a joint problem both writer and reader have an interest in solving, rather than as something the reader is being asked to do for the writer?

☐ Does the message give all of the relevant information? Is there enough detail?

☐ Does the message overcome objections that readers may have?

☐ Does the message avoid phrases that sound dictatorial, condescending, or arrogant?

☐ Does the last paragraph tell the reader exactly what to do? Does it give a deadline if one exists and a reason for acting promptly?

And, for all messages, not just persuasive ones,

☐ Does the message use you-attitude and positive emphasis?

☐ Is the style easy to read and friendly?

☐ Is the visual design of the message inviting?

☐ Is the format correct?

☐ Does the message use standard grammar? Is it free from typos?

Originality in a problem-solving persuasive message may come from

☐ A good subject line and common ground.

☐ A clear and convincing description of the problem.

☐ Thinking about readers and giving details that answer their questions, overcome objections, and make it easier for them to do as you ask.

☐ Adding details that show you're thinking about a specific organization and the specific people in that organization.

Summary of Key Points

- The primary purposes in a persuasive message are to have the reader act, to provide enough information so that the reader knows exactly what to do, and to overcome any objections that might prevent or delay action. Secondary purposes are to build a good image of the writer and the writer's organization, to cement a good relationship between the writer and reader, and to reduce or eliminate future correspondence on the same subject.

- Readers have a vested interest in something if they benefit directly from keeping things as they are.

- **Credibility** is the audience's response to you as the source of the message. You can build credibility by being factual, specific, and reliable.

- Use the persuasive strategy your organization prefers.

- Use the **direct request pattern** when the audience will do as you ask without any resistance. Also use the direct request pattern for busy readers in your own organization who do not read all the messages they receive.

- Use the **problem-solving pattern** when the audience may resist doing what you ask and you expect logic to be more important than emotion in the decision.

- In a direct request, consider asking in the first paragraph for the information or service you want. Give readers all the information they will need to act on your request. In the last paragraph, ask for the action you want.

- Organize a problem-solving persuasive message in this way:
  1. Catch the reader's interest by mentioning a common ground.
  2. Define the problem you both share (which your request will solve).
  3. Explain the solution to the problem.
  4. Show that any negative elements (cost, time, etc.) are outweighed by the advantages.
  5. Summarize any additional benefits of the solution.
  6. Ask for the action you want.

- In a direct request, put the request, the topic of the request, or a question in the subject line. Do not put the request in the subject line of a problem-solving persuasive message. Instead, use a **directed subject line** that reveals your position on the issue or a reader benefit. Use a positive or neutral subject line even when the first paragraph will be negative.

- Use one or more of the following strategies to counter objections that you cannot eliminate:

  - Specify how much time and/or money is required.

  - Put the time and/or money in the context of the benefits they bring.

  - Show that money spent now will save money in the long run.

  - Show that doing as you ask will benefit some group the reader identifies with or some cause the reader supports.

  - Show the reader that the sacrifice is necessary to achieve a larger, more important goal to which he or she is committed.

  - Show that the advantages as a group outnumber or outweigh the disadvantages as a group.

  - Turn the disadvantage into an opportunity.

- Threats don't produce permanent change. They won't necessarily produce the action you want, they may make people abandon an action entirely (even in situations where it would be appropriate), and they produce tension. People dislike and avoid anyone who threatens them. Threats can provoke counteraggression.

Creative Response to a Problem, V*

Demand is high when a hot movie comes out on video. The 10–12 copies that each Blockbuster Video store had for rental went quickly and left many potential customers unsatisfied. But each video cost $60. If it charged $3 a rental, Blockbuster began to make a profit only if it rented the tape 21 times or more. Peak demand doesn't last very long, and Blockbuster couldn't justify buying enough tapes to meet initial demand.

Blockbuster solved the problem by changing the way it paid its suppliers. It received a much lower price on each video—only $9—in exchange for giving the studio half of the rental income. Even though it keeps only $1.50 for each rental, Blockbuster makes a profit when it rents the video just seven times. And it can afford to buy many more copies of each movie, generating more income and satisfying customers. Blockbuster increased its market share 5% in the first year after the change. The movie studios also make more money. It's a win–win solution.

*Based on Gérard P. Cachon and Martin A. Lariviere, "Turning the Supply Chain into a Revenue Chain," *Harvard Business Review*, March 2001, 20.

■ Base persuasion in difficult persuasive situations on the following five steps:
1. Find out why your audience members resist what you want them to do.
2. Try to find a win–win solution.
3. Find a way to let your audience save face.
4. Ask for something small.
5. Present your argument from your audience's point of view.

■ When you want people to change their behavior, don't criticize them. Instead, show that you're on their side, that you and they have a mutual interest in solving a problem.

■ To encourage readers to act promptly, set a deadline. Show that the time limit is real, that acting now will save time or money, or that delaying action will cost more.

■ Build emotional appeal with stories and psychological description.

■ Performance appraisals should cite specific observations, not inferences. They should contain specific suggestions for improvement and identify the two or three areas that the worker should emphasize in the next month or quarter.

■ Letters of recommendation must be specific and tell how well and how long you've known the person.

■ Early in the collection series, remind the reader about the debt matter-of-factly. In middle letters, be more assertive. Try to negotiate for partial payment if the reader is not able to pay the full amount.

■ Use the analysis questions from Chapter 1 to analyze persuasive situations.

CHAPTER 9   Exercises and Problems

Getting Started

9.1   Writing Psychological Description

For one or more of the following groups, write two or three paragraphs of psychological description that could be used in a brochure, news release, or direct mail letter directed to members of that group.

1. Having a personal trainer.
   Audiences: Professional athletes.
   Busy managers.
   Someone trying to lose weight.
   Someone making a major lifestyle change after a heart attack.

2. Buying a cellular phone.
   Audiences: People who do a lot of big-city driving.
   People who do a lot of driving in rural areas.
   People who do a lot of flying.

3. Buying a laptop computer.
   Audiences: College students.
   Financial planners who visit clients at home.
   Sales representatives who travel constantly.
   People who make PowerPoint presentations.

4. Attending a fantasy sports camp (you pick the sport), playing with and against retired players who provide coaching and advice.

5. Attending a health spa where clients get low-fat and low-calorie meals, massages, beauty treatments, and guidance in nutrition and exercise.

Hints:

■ For this assignment, you can combine benefits or programs as if a single source offered them all.

■ Add specific details about particular sports, activities, and so on, as material for your description.

■ Be sure to move beyond reader benefits to vivid details and sense impressions.

■ Put your benefits in you-attitude.

9.2 Evaluating Subject Lines

Evaluate the following subject lines. Is one subject line in each group clearly best? Or does the "best" line depend on company culture, whether the message is a paper memo or an e-mail message, or on some other factor?

1. Subject: Request
   Subject: Why I Need a New Computer
   Subject: Increasing My Productivity
2. Subject: Who Wants Extra Hours?
   Subject: Holiday Work Schedule
   Subject: Working Extra Hours During the Holiday Season
3. Subject: Student Mentors
   Subject: Can You Be an E-Mail Mentor?
   Subject: Volunteers Needed

4. Subject: More Wine and Cheese
   Subject: Today's Reception for Japanese Visitors
   Subject: Reminder
5. Subject: Reducing Absenteeism
   Subject: Opening a Day Care Center for Sick Children of Employees
   Subject: Why We Need Expanded Day Care Facilities

9.3 Brainstorming Reasons to Act Promptly

Brainstorm one or more reasons that readers should act promptly in each of the following situations:

1. Persuading CPAs to take a continuing education course about changes in the tax law
   a. In May.
   b. In October.
   c. In December.
2. Persuading customers to install storm windows and insulation
   a. In March.
   b. In June.
   c. In October.

3. Persuading your office to make a major change in its computer hardware and software
   a. Just before the end of the fiscal year.
   b. Right before the busiest season of the year.
   c. During the least busy time of the year.

9.4 Identifying Observations

Susan has taken the following notes about her group's meetings. Which of the following are specific observations that she could use in a performance appraisal of group members? If she had it to do over again, what kinds of details would turn the inferences into observations?

1. Feb. 22: Today was very frustrating. Sam was totally out of it—I wonder if he's on something. Jim was dictatorial. I argued, but nobody backed me up. Masayo might just as well have stayed home. We didn't get anything done. Two hours, totally wasted.
2. February 24: Jim seems to be making a real effort to be less domineering. Today he asked Sam and me for our opinions before proposing his own. And he noticed that Masayo wasn't talking much and brought her into the conversation. She suggested some good ideas.
3. February 28: Today's meeting was OK. I thought Masayo wasn't really focusing on the work at hand. She needs to work on communicating her ideas to others. Sam was doing some active listening, but he needs to work at being on time. Jim was involved in the project. He has strong leadership skills. There were some tense moments, but we got a lot done,

and we all contributed. I got to say what I wanted to say, and the group decided to use my idea for the report.

4. March 5: This week most of us had midterms, and Masayo had an out-of-town gymnastics trip. We couldn't find a time to meet. So we did stuff by e-mail. Sam and Jim found some great stuff at the library and on the Web. Jim created a tentative schedule that he sent to all of us and then revised. I wrote up a draft of the description of the problem. Then Masayo and I put everything together. I sent my draft to her; she suggested revisions (in full caps so I could find them in the e-mail message). Then I sent the message to everyone. Masayo and Jim both suggested changes, which I made before we handed the draft in.
5. March 15: We were revising the proposal, using Prof. Jones's comments. When we thought we were basically done, Masayo noticed that we had not responded to all of the specific comments about our introductory paragraph. We then went back and thought of some examples to use. This made our proposal better and more complete.

9.5   Revising a Form Memo

You've been hired as a staff accountant; one of your major duties will be processing expense reimbursements. Going through the files, you find this form memo:

> Subject: Reimbursements
>
> Enclosed are either receipts that we could not match with the items in your request for reimbursement or a list of items for which we found no receipts or both. Please be advised that the Accounting Department issues reimbursement checks only with full documentation. You cannot be reimbursed until you give us a receipt for each item for which you desire reimbursement. We must ask that you provide this information. This process may be easier if you use the Expense Report Form, which is available in your department.
>
> Thank you for your attention to this matter. Please do not hesitate to contact us with questions.

You know this memo is horrible. In addition to wordiness, a total lack of positive emphasis and you-attitude, and a vague subject line, the document design and organization of information bury the request.

Create a new memo that could be sent to people who do not provide all the documentation they need in order to be reimbursed.

E-Mail Messages

9.6   Suggesting a Change in Your Organization's Communication Materials

Your organization has a Web page, but its address isn't on all your business communication materials (stationery, business cards, invoices, product packaging, brochures, catalogs, voice-mail announcements, e-mail signatures, and promotional items such as pens, coffee cups, and mouse pads). Adding the URL would promote the Web site (and suggest that your organization is up-to-date).

As Your Instructor Directs,

a. Identify the person in your organization with the power to authorize adding the URL to physical materials, and e-mail that person asking him or her to authorize this change.

b. Write an e-mail to all employees, asking them to add the URL and a brief message promoting the organization to their e-mail signature blocks.

Hints:

- Pick a business, nonprofit, or government organization you know something about. What materials does it produce? Which lack the URL?
- Will the reader know you? Has your organization asked for suggestions, or will this come out of the blue?
- What should be done with materials already printed or manufactured that lack the Web address? Should they be discarded, or should they be used until they run out?
- Who in your organization has the authority to authorize this change?
- What exactly do you want your reader to do? What information does your reader need?

9.7   Asking for a Job Description

Your organization has gone through a lot of changes, and you suspect that the original job descriptions people were hired into are no longer accurate. So you'd like all employees to list their current job duties. You'd also like them to indicate which parts of their jobs they see as most important, and to indicate how much time they spend on each part of the job.

    E-mail all employees, asking for the descriptions.

Hints:

- Pick a real business, government, or nonprofit group you know about.
- When is the next cycle of performance appraisals? Will these descriptions be used then?
- People will be reluctant to tell you they're spending lots of time on things that aren't important, and

some people may honestly not know how they spend their time. How can you encourage accurate reporting? (If you ask people to keep logs for a week, be sure also to ask them if that week was typical—it may or may not be.)

■ Some people will want to change their job descriptions—that is, to change their duties or the

proportion of time they spend on each. Is that an option in your organization right now? If it isn't (or if it is an option for very few people), how can you make that clear to readers?

9.8 Asking for More Time and/or Resources

Today, this message shows up in your e-mail inbox from your boss:

> Subject: Want Climate Report
>
> This request has come down from the CEO. I'm delegating it to you. See me a couple of days before the board meeting—the 4th of next month—so we can go over your presentation.
>
> I want a report on the climate for underrepresented groups in our organization. A presentation at the last board of directors' meeting showed that while we do a good job of hiring women and minorities, few of them rise to the top. The directors suspect that our climate may not be supportive and want information on it. Please prepare a presentation for the next meeting. You'll have 15 minutes.

Making a presentation to the company's board of directors can really help your career. But preparing a good presentation and report will take time. You can look at exit reports filed by Human Resources when people leave the company, but you'll also need to interview people—lots of people. And you're already working 60 hours a week

on three major projects, one of which is behind schedule. Can one of the projects wait? Can someone else take one of the projects? Can you get some help? Should you do just enough to get by? Ask your boss for advice—in a way that makes you look like a committed employee, not a shirker.

9.9 Persuading People to Use Better Passwords

Your computer system requires each employee to change his or her password every three months. But many people choose passwords that are easy to guess. According to Deloitte & Touche's fraud unit, the 10 most commonly used passwords are (1) the employee's name or child's name, (2) "secret," (3) stress-related words ("deadline," "work"), (4) sports teams or terms, (5) "payday," (6) "bonkers," (7) the current season ("autumn," "spring"), (8) the employee's ethnic group, (9) repeated characters ("AAAAA"), (10) obscenities and sexual terms ("Hackers' Delight," *BusinessWeek*, February 10, 1997, 4).

As Director of Management Information Systems (MIS), you want employees to choose passwords that hackers can't guess based on knowing an employee's background. The best passwords contain numbers as well as letters, use more characters (at least five; eight possible), and aren't real words.

Write an e-mail message to all employees, urging them to choose better passwords.

9.10 Sending a Question to a Web Site

Send a question or other message that calls for a response to a Web site. You could

■ Ask a question about a product.

■ Apply for an internship or a job (assuming you'd really like to work there).

■ Ask for information about an internship or a job.

■ Ask a question about an organization or a candidate before you donate money or volunteer.

■ Offer to volunteer for an organization or a candidate. You can either offer to do so something small and one-time (e.g., spend an afternoon stuffing envelopes, put up a yard sign) or offer to do something more time-consuming or even ongoing.

As Your Instructor Directs,

a. Turn in a copy of your e-mail message and the response you received.

b. Critique messages written by other students in your class. Suggest ways the messages could be clearer and more persuasive.

c. Write a memo evaluating your message and the response, using the checklists for Chapters 9 and 7. If you did not receive a response, did the fault lie with your message?

d. Make an oral presentation to the class, evaluating your message and the response, using the checklists for Chapters 9 and 7. If you did not receive a response, did the fault lie with your message?

Hints:

- Does the organization ask for questions or offers? Or will yours come out of the blue?

- How difficult will it be for the organization to supply the information you're asking for or to do what you're asking it to do? If you're applying for an internship or offering to volunteer, what skills can you offer? How much competition do you have?

- What can you do to build your own credibility so that the organization takes your question or request seriously?

9.11   Not Doing What the Boss Asked

Today, you get this e-mail message:

To:	All Unit Managers
Subject:	Cutting Costs

Please submit five ideas for cutting costs in your unit. I will choose the best ideas and implement them immediately.

You think your boss's strategy is wrong. Cutting costs will be easier if people buy into the decision rather than being handed orders. Instead of gathering ideas by e-mail, the boss should call a meeting so that people can brainstorm, teaching each other why specific strategies will or won't be easy for their units to implement.

Reply to your boss's e-mail request. Instead of suggesting specific ways to cut costs, persuade the boss to have a meeting where everyone can have input and be part of the decision.

9.12   Asking for Volunteers

You have an executive position with one of the major employers in town. (Pick a business, nonprofit organization, or government office you know something about.) Two years ago, your company "adopted" a local school. You've provided computers and paid for Internet access; a small number of workers have signed up to be mentors. Today you get a call from the school's principal, a friend of yours.

Principal: I'd like to talk to you about the mentoring program. You're providing some mentors, and we're grateful for them, but we need ten times that number.

You: [You wince. This program has not been one of your successes.] I know that part of the program hasn't worked out as well as we hoped it would. But people are really busy here. Not all that many people have two or three hours a week to spend with a kid.

Principal: So you think the time it takes is really the problem.

You: [Maybe your friend will appreciate that you can't force people to do this.] Pretty much.

Principal: Do you think people would be willing to be mentors if we could find a way for it to take less time?

You: Maybe. [You sense that a hook is coming, and you're wary.]

Principal: Your people spend a lot of time on e-mail, don't they?

You: Yes. Two to three hours a day, for most of them.

Principal: What if we created a new mentoring structure, where people just e-mailed their mentees instead of meeting with them? That way they could still provide advice and support, but they could do it at any time of the day. And it wouldn't have to take long.

You: [This sounds interesting.] So people would just have e-mail conversations. That would be a lot easier, and we'd get more people. But can they really have a relationship if they don't meet the kids?

Principal: Maybe we could have a picnic or go to a game a couple of times a year so people could meet face-to-face.

You:	And all the kids have computers?
Principal:	Not necessarily at home. But they all have access to e-mail at school. Writing e-mail to professionals will also give them more practice and more confidence. People like to get e-mail.
You:	Not when they get 200 messages a day, they don't.
Principal:	Well, our kids aren't in that category. What do you say?

You:	I think it will work. Let's try it.
Principal:	Great. Just send me a list of the people who are willing to do this, and we'll match them up with the kids. We'd like to get this started as soon as possible.

Write an e-mail message to all employees asking them to volunteer, while you're thinking about it right now.

Check the BAC Web site to learn more about e-mail mentoring.

9.13 Persuading the CEO to Attend Orientation

As the Director of Education and Training of your organization, you run orientation sessions for new hires. You're planning next quarter's session (new quarters start in January, April, July, and October) for a big group of new college graduates. You'd really like the organization's president and CEO to come in and talk to the group for at least 15 minutes. Probably most of the employees have seen the CEO, but they haven't had any direct contact. The CEO could come any time during the three-day session. Speaking just before or after lunch would be ideal, because then the CEO could also come to lunch and talk informally with at least a few people. Next best would be speaking just before or after the midmorning or midafternoon breaks. But the CEO is busy, and you'll take what you can get.

As Your Instructor Directs,

a. Assume that your instructor is your CEO, and send an e-mail message persuading him or her to come to orientation.

b. Send an e-mail message to your instructor, asking him or her to address new members of a campus organization.

c. Address the CEO of your college or your workplace, asking him or her to speak to new employees.

Communicating at Work

As Your Instructor Directs,

In 9.14 through 9.18,

a. Create a document or presentation to achieve the goal.

b. Write a memo to your instructor describing the situation at your workplace and explaining your rhetorical choices (medium, strategy, tone, wording, graphics or document design, and so forth).

9.14 Recommending a Co-Worker for a Bonus or an Award

Recommend someone at your workplace for a bonus or an award. The award can be something bestowed by the organization itself ("Employee of the Month," "Dealership of the Year," and so forth), or it can be a community or campus award ("Business Person of the Year," "Volunteer of the Year," an honorary degree, and so forth).

9.15 Justifying Your Position

Organizations facing downsizing have to decide which positions to keep and which to cut. Imagine that your organization is facing financial problems and that your supervisor, who wants to keep you, has asked you to draft something explaining why your position should be retained and why you are the best person to keep in the position. Create a memo or presentation to do the job.

Hints:

■ Show how you contribute to the unit's and the organization's goals.

■ Write your memo in the third person, so that your supervisor can send it upward without having to revise it.

9.16 Requesting Information from a Co-Worker

Often, you need information from other people to do your own work. Write to a co-worker, asking for the information you need.

9.17   Changing What's Wrong

No workplace is perfect. Pick one of the things you'd like to change about your workplace, identify the decision maker(s), and create a memo or presentation to start the persuasion process.

9.18   Asking for More Resources for Your Unit

Write a memo or prepare a presentation to persuade your organization to give more resources to your unit.

Hints:

- Who in the organization decides the level of resources your unit receives? What are the values of that person or group?

- How much do the decision makers know about your unit? How much evidence do you need to provide about your contribution to organization goals?

- What kind of evidence is most persuasive in your organization? Should you talk about customers or clients? About internal clients? Give numbers?

- Will you be more persuasive if you ask for funds to take on new tasks, or argue that additional resources will help you do current tasks better?

Memo and Letter Assignments

9.19   Writing Collection Letters

You have a small desktop publishing firm. Unfortunately, not all your clients pay promptly.

As Your Instructor Directs,

Write letters for one or more of the following situations:

a. A $450 bill for designing and printing a brochure for Juggles, Inc., a company that provides clowns and jugglers for parties, is now five weeks overdue. You've phoned twice, and each time the person who answered the phone promised to send you a check, but nothing has happened.

b. A $2,000 bill for creating a series of handouts for a veterinarian to distribute to clients. This one is really embarrassing: somehow you lost track of the invoice, so you never followed up on the original (and only) bill. The bill is now 72 days overdue.

c. A $3,750 bill for designing and printing a series of 10 brochures for Creative Interiors, a local interior decorating shop, is three weeks past due. When you billed Creative Interiors, you got a note saying that the design was not acceptable and that you would not be paid until you redesigned it (at no extra charge) to the owner's satisfaction. The owner had approved the preliminary design on which the brochures were based; she did not explain in the note what was wrong with the final product. She's never free when you are; indeed, when you call to try to schedule an appointment, you're told the owner will call you back—but she never does. At this point, the delay is not your fault; you want to be paid.

d. A $100 bill for designing (but not actually creating) a brochure for a cleaning company that, according to its owner, planned to expand into your city. You got the order and instructions by mail and talked to the person on the phone but never met him. You tried to call once since then (as much to try to talk him into having the brochures printed as to collect the $100); the number was no longer in service. You suspect the owner may no longer be in business, but you'd like to get your money if possible.

9.20   Persuading Guests to Allow Extra Time for Checkout

Your hotel has been the headquarters for a convention, and on Sunday morning you're expecting 5,000 people to check out before noon. You're staffing the checkout desk to capacity, but if everyone waits till 11:30 to check out, things will be a disaster.

So you want to encourage people to allow extra time. And they don't have to stand in line at all: by 4 A.M., you'll put a statement of current charges under each guest's door. If that statement is correct and the guest is leaving the bill on the credit card used at check-in, the guest can just leave the key in the room and leave. You'll mail a copy of the final bill together with any morning charges by the end of the week.

Write a one-page message that can be put on pillows when the rooms are made up Friday and Saturday night.

9.21 Asking for Sick-Child Care

Day care is a fact of life for working parents in the United States. But day care centers won't accept sick children. So when their kids are sick, parents may have to call in sick themselves. The problem wreaks havoc on schedules for production, travel, meetings, and presentations.

Write a memo to the upper management of your organization, urging that it provide sick care service. One model is to create a site in a central area. An organization big enough to need a site just for its employees' children may be able to create one on-site. Small companies will want to team up with several other small businesses and split the cost. Another option is to have a visiting caregiver stay with the child in the employee's home.

Hints:

- Pick a business, government office, nonprofit agency, or educational institution that you know something about.
- Use your analysis from Chapter 3, problems 3.11 and 3.12. How will this program help individuals? And how will that help the organization?
- Will your organization be more persuaded by a dollars-and-cents comparison showing how much this benefit could save the company? Or would stories be more persuasive?

9.22 Convincing a Member to Become Active Again

In every organization, one of the ongoing problems is convincing inactive members to become active again. Sometimes members become inactive because of short-term pressures. Sometimes they are offended by something the organization has done or not done. Sometimes they fall through the cracks and are not included in events. Whatever the reason, once they've become less active, it's psychologically easy for them to drop out entirely. Persuading these members to become active again is important. Because they once supported the organization, it may be easier to persuade them than to seek new members. And if they remain disenchanted with the organization, they may convince other people that the organization has little to offer.

As Your Instructor Directs,

a. Write to someone you know well, urging him or her to become active in the organization again.

b. Write notes for a phone conversation or meeting with your friend.

c. Join with a small group of students to write a form letter to go to inactive members in an organization.

d. Write a memo to your instructor explaining your audience analysis and your choice of strategy and appeals.

Hints:

- Pick a campus, professional, civic, social, or religious organization you know well.
- Be specific about what the organization is doing now, how readers can benefit from it, and why the organization needs them.
- If your audience objects to specific things the organization has done or not done, respond to these concerns in your message. Did a misunderstanding occur? Is change already under way? Is change possible if enough people (like your audience, perhaps) work for it?
- What are your audience's priorities? Can you show that this organization will help your audience meet its needs?

9.23 Requesting More Funds for the Writing Center

State University is facing major budget cuts. A popular idea is to reduce or eliminate funding for the Writing Center. As the Center's director, you're horrified by these ideas.

The Writing Center offers free tutoring in writing to any student or faculty member on campus. Your emphasis is not on fixing an individual paper, but on helping the writer develop strategies that he or she can use not only in this paper but in everything he or she writes.

The services you offer help students do better in classes. Your help is particularly important when budget cuts are leading to larger classes, so that faculty spend less time with each student. Furthermore, your operation is really quite efficient. You only have one paid regular faculty member on your staff; the rest are graduate teaching assistants (who are paid much less than faculty receive) or undergraduate peer tutors. Finally, the dollars involved aren't that great. Cutting the Center's budget in half would mean you would have to turn away most students. Yet the dollars are small in comparison with the budgets of large departments.

As Your Instructor Directs,

a. Write a memo to all faculty urging them to support full funding for the Writing Center.

b. Write a news release for the campus newspaper about the problem.

c. Identify the person or group on your campus with the power to make budget decisions, and write to that group urging that it support a Writing Center on your campus. Use information about the center and the fiscal situation that fits your community college, college, or university.

Hints:

- Visit the Writing Center on campus to get information about its hours and policies. Sign up for an appointment. What happens in a session? What parts are especially helpful?

- Be sure to prove and limit your claims. Even if the Center is fully funded, some students will be turned away. Even if its funding is increased, not everyone will write well.

- Be sure to use you-attitude and to make sure that the writing in your message is a good advertisement for your own writing skills.

9.24   Handling a Sticky Recommendation

As a supervisor in a state agency, you have a dilemma. You received this e-mail message today:

> From: John Inoye, Director of Personnel, Department of Taxation
>
> Subject: Need Recommendation for Peggy Chafez
>
> Peggy Chafez has applied for a position in the Department of Taxation. On the basis of her application and interview, she is the leading candidate. However, before I offer the job to her, I need a letter of recommendation from her current supervisor.
>
> Could you please let me have your evaluation within a week? We want to fill the position as quickly as possible.

Peggy has worked in your office for 10 years. She designed, writes, and edits a monthly statewide newsletter that your office puts out; she designed and maintains the department Web site. Her designs are creative; she's a very hard worker; she seems to know a lot about computers.

However, Peggy is in many ways an unsatisfactory staff member. Her standards are so high that most people find her intimidating. Some find her abrasive. People have complained to you that she's only interested in her own work; she seems to resent requests to help other people with projects. And yet both the newsletter and the Web page are projects that need frequent interaction. She's out of the office a lot. Some of that is required by her job (she takes the newsletters to the post office, for example), but some people don't like the fact that she's out of the office so much. They also complain that she doesn't return voice mail and e-mail messages.

You think managing your office would be a lot smoother if Peggy weren't there. You can't fire her: state employees' jobs are secure once they get past the initial six-month probationary period. Because of budget constraints, you can hire new employees only if vacancies are created by resignations. You feel that it would be pretty easy to find someone better.

If you recommend that John Inoye hire Peggy, you will be able to hire someone you want. If you recommend that John hire someone else, you may be stuck with Peggy for a long time.

As Your Instructor Directs,

a.   Write an e-mail message to John Inoye.

b.   Write a memo to your instructor listing the choices you've made and justifying your approach.

Hints:

- Polarization may make this dilemma more difficult than it needs to be. What are your options? Consciously look for more than two.

- Is it possible to select facts or to use connotations so that you are truthful but still encourage John to hire Peggy? Is it ethical? Is it certain that John would find Peggy's work as unsatisfactory as you do? If you write a strong recommendation and Peggy doesn't do well at the new job, will your credibility suffer? Why is your credibility important?

9.25   Persuading Tenants to Follow the Rules

As resident manager of a large apartment complex, you receive free rent in return for collecting rents, doing simple maintenance, and enforcing the complex's rules. You find the following notice in the files:

> Some of you are failing to keep any kind of standard of sanitation code, resulting in the unnecessary cost on our part to hire exterminators to rid the building of roaches.
>
> Our leases state breach of contract in the event that you are not observing your responsibility to keep your apartment clean.
>
> We are in the process of making arrangements for an extermination company to rid those apartments that are experiencing problems. Get in touch with the manager no later than 10 P.M. Monday to make arrangements for your apartment to be sprayed. It is a fast, odorless operation. You are also required to put your garbage in plastic bags. Do not put loose garbage or garbage in paper bags in the dumpster, as this leads to rodent or roach problems.
>
> Should we in the course of providing extermination service to the building find that your apartment is a source of roaches, then you will be held liable for the cost incurred to rid your apartment of them.

The message is horrible. The notice lacks you-attitude, and it seems to threaten anyone who asks to have his or her apartment sprayed.

The annual spraying scheduled for your complex is coming up. Under the lease, you have the right to enter apartments once a year to spray. However, for spraying to be fully effective, residents must empty the cabinets, remove kitchen drawers, and put all food in the refrigerator. People and pets need to leave the apartment for about 15 minutes while the exterminator sprays.

Tell residents about the spraying. Persuade them to prepare their apartments to get the most benefit from it, and persuade them to dispose of food waste quickly and properly so that the bugs don't come back.

Hints:

- What objections may people have to having their apartments sprayed for bugs?
- Why don't people already take garbage out promptly and wrap it in plastic? How can you persuade them to change their behavior?
- Analyze your audience. Are most tenants students, working people, or retirees? What tone would be most effective for this group?

9.26   Helping Students Use Debt Responsibly

Your college, community college, or university is concerned that some students have high levels of credit card debt and may be using credit cards irresponsibly. Many students—especially those without full-time jobs—pay only part of the bill each month, thus compounding the original amount charged with interest rates that can be 18% annually, or even higher. Nationwide, 20% of students have credit card debt of more than $10,000—and that doesn't count amounts owed for student loans. Excessive credit card debt makes it harder for a student to become financially independent; in extreme cases, students may have to drop out just to pay off the credit card debt.

As Your Instructor Directs,

a. Create a message to urge students on your campus to use credit cards responsibly. Create a document that has the greatest chance of being read and heeded (not just dropped on the ground or in a trash can).

b. Write a memo to your instructor explaining how and when the document would be distributed and why you've chosen the design you have. Show how your decisions fit the students on your campus.

Hints:

- Suggest guidelines for responsible use of credit (limiting the number of credit cards, charging only what one can repay each month except in the case of an emergency, shopping around for a card with the lowest interest rate, and so forth). Suggest a way to test one's own credit savvy.
- Remind students that for continuing expenses, a loan will have a lower interest rate (and may not have to be repaid until after graduation).
- Some students may like the freebies they get with some credit cards (e.g., frequent flyer miles). How can you persuade these students that the freebies aren't worth charging more than they can pay off each month?
- Part of your audience already uses credit responsibly. Be sure the message doesn't offend these people.
- Some students in your audience may already know that they owe too much. What can students do if they already have too much debt?

9.27   Persuading Your Company to Change Its Collection Practices

You've been hired in the credit department of a major retail chain. In your third week on the job, you get this note
from your boss:

> Here's a list of customers with open accounts. All of them passed our credit require-
> ments at one time, but now they're late. As is our practice, when they didn't pay their
> bills we sent a second bill a month later and a third bill the month after that. Now it's
> time for a letter. Since the list is long, write a form letter, but make it sound like an in-
> dividual letter. Merge the letter with this list of names and addresses and sign each
> one individually.

As Your Instructor Directs,

a. Write a form letter, putting in the name, address, and
    amount owed of one customer.

b. Write a memo to your boss recommending that the
    company policy be changed to send a second bill a

week or two after the due date for the first and to
send a first letter one month—rather than three
months—after the original due date if the bill still
hasn't been paid.

9.28   Getting Permission from Parents for a School Project

As part of a community cleanup program, all public-
school students will spend the afternoon of the second
Friday of April picking up trash. Younger students will
pick up trash on school grounds, in parks, and in parking
lots; older students will pick up trash downtown. School-
teachers will supervise the students; where necessary,
school buses will transport them. After students are finished, they'll return to their school's playground, where
they'll be supervised until the end of the school day. Each
school will maintain a study hall for any students whose
parents do not give them permission to participate. Trash
bags and snacks have been donated by local merchants.

   Write a one-page cover letter that students can take
home to their parents telling them about the project and

persuading them to sign the necessary permission form.
You do *not* need to create the permission form, but do refer to it in your letter.

Hints:

- What objections may parents have? How can you
  overcome these?
- Where should parents who drive their kids to school
  pick them up?
- Should students wear their normal school clothing?
- When must the form be returned? Who gets it?
  Whom can parents call if they have questions before
  they sign the form?

9.29   Asking an Instructor for a Letter of Recommendation

You're ready for the job market, transfer to a four-year
college, or graduate school, and you need letters of recommendation.

As Your Instructor Directs,

a. Assume that you've orally asked an instructor for a
    recommendation, and he or she has agreed to write
    one. "Why don't you write up something to remind
    me of what you've done in the class? Tell me what
    else you've done, too. And tell me what they're look-
    ing for. Be sure to tell me when the letter needs to be
    in and whom it goes to."

b. Assume that you've been unable to talk with the in-
    structor whose recommendation you want. When
    you call, no one answers the phone; you stopped by
    once and no one was in. Write asking for a letter of
    recommendation.

c. Assume that the instructor is no longer on campus.
    Write him or her a letter asking for a recommendation.

Hints:

- Be detailed about the points you'd like the instructor
  to mention.
- How well will this instructor remember you? How
  much detail about your performance in his or her
  class do you need to provide?
- Specify the name and address of the person to
  whom the letter should be written; specify when the
  letter is due. If there's an intermediate due date (for
  example, if you must sign the outside of the
  envelope to submit the recommendation to law
  school), say so.

9.30 Writing a Performance Appraisal for a Member of a Collaborative Group

During your collaborative writing group meetings, keep a log of events. Record specific observations of both effective and ineffective things that group members do. Then evaluate the performance of the other members of your group. (If there are two or more other people, write a separate appraisal for each of them.)

In your first paragraph, summarize your evaluation. Then in the body of your memo, give the specific details that led to your evaluation by answering the following questions:

- What specifically did the person do in terms of the task? Brainstorm ideas? Analyze the information? Draft the text? Suggest revisions in parts drafted by others? Format the document or create visuals? Revise? Edit? Proofread? (In most cases, several people will have done each of these activities together. Don't overstate what any one person did.) What was the quality of the person's work?

- What did the person contribute to the group process? Did he or she help schedule the work? Raise or resolve conflicts? Make other group

members feel valued and included? Promote group cohesion? What roles did the person play in the group?

Support your generalizations with specific observations. The more observations you have and the more detailed they are, the better your appraisal will be.

As Your Instructor Directs,

a. Writing a midterm performance appraisal for one or more members of your collaborative group. In each appraisal, identify the two or three things the person should try to improve during the second half of the term.

b. Write a performance appraisal for one or more members of your collaborative group at the end of the term. Identify and justify the grade you think each person should receive for the portion of the grade based on group process.

c. Give a copy of your appraisal to the person about whom it is written.

10

Sales, Fund-Raising, and Promotional Messages

Components of Good Direct Mail

Is It "Junk" Mail?

Basic Direct Mail Strategy

1. Understand Your Product, Service, or Organization.
2. Identify and Analyze Your Target Audience.
3. Choose a Central Selling Point.

How to Organize a Sales or Fund-Raising Letter

- Opener (Star)
- Body (Chain)
- Action Close (Knot)
- Using a P.S.

Strategy in Sales Letters

- Dealing with Price
- Sample Sales Letter

Strategy in Fund-Raising Appeals

- Deciding How Much to Ask For
- Logical Proof in Fund-Raising Letters
- Emotional Appeal in Fund-Raising Letters
- Sample Fund-Raising Letter

Strategy in Contact Letters

Strategy in Brochures

Writing Style

1. Make Your Writing Interesting.
2. Use Sound Patterns to Emphasize Words.
3. Use Psychological Description.
4. Make Your Letter Sound Like a Letter, Not an Ad.

Parts of a Direct Mail Package

Summary of Key Points

Sales, Fund-Raising, and Promotional Messages

Linda Westphal
Freelance Copywriter

Linda Westphal works with advertising agency creative professionals, business owners, and other marketing professionals from her office in Sacramento, California. She also writes a column for *Direct Marketing* magazine on writing copy.

www.lindawestphal.com

Good sales letters are as intimate as a one-on-one conversation. Imagine you're talking with a friend sitting across the table from you. You can see her facial expressions and whether you're holding her attention as you talk (write).

A powerful opening paragraph is one or two sentences long (on occasion, three). Offer information, tell a tale or story, or hit your readers with interesting facts.

- **Offer Information.** "Why should you . . . Buy Parmesan cheese with the rind attached? (It will help keep the cheese fresh.) Coat batter-fried chicken or fish a good hour before cooking? (The batter will stay on better!)" [*Reader's Digest*]

- **Tell a Tale.** "On an autumn day, not too long ago, sociologist Robert Harner visited the Great Serpent Mound of Ohio. As he stood on this sacred Indian ground, the air was oddly still—not even a breeze." [Time-Life Books]

- **Offer Facts.** "The Greenland Eskimos ate more fat than anyone in the world. And yet . . . they had virtually no heart disease." [Rodale Press]

> *"Get your message in front of the people who are interested in your product or service. Then . . . give them the details they crave."*

Serious buyers want information. Information-gathering is the first phase in considering a product you know nothing about—such as a digital camera. You want to know, *How easy is it to use? What "extras" must I also purchase? Is it better than a new 35mm camera? Would it be a good investment for me?* In your search for information, you'll be attracted to any article or advertisement about digital cameras. In contrast, folks who are not considering a digital camera purchase probably won't even notice the ads. You need to get your message in front of the people who are interested in your product or service. Then, once you're there, give them the details they crave.

Use examples: "In the time it takes you to watch one episode of *Friends,* you can get your oil changed and be back on the road." Identify the areas that most people tune into, such as the opening headline and paragraph, photo captions, postscripts, call-outs, the order card or coupon, and brief paragraphs, and emphasize your key ideas there.

Time-Life Books, Buick, FedEx—these are only a few of the companies that use letters to persuade customers to buy their products, visit their showrooms, and use their services. The American Cancer Society, the Republican National Committee, Gallaudet University—these are only a few of the organizations that use letters to persuade people to donate time or money to their causes.

Sales and fund-raising letters are a special category of persuasive messages. They are known as **direct mail** because they ask for an order, inquiry, or contribution directly from the reader. In 2000, direct mail sold $289 billion worth of products in the United States and raised nearly $70 billion for charities.[1] For more statistics on direct mail, see the BAC Web site.

Organizations also use a variety of promotional materials. This chapter discusses two of the most common types: contact letters and brochures.

Fortune 500 companies and well-endowed charitable or political organizations hire professionals to write their direct mail. Professionals charge $5,000 to $25,000 to create a package. And that's just the creative cost: you still have to pay for printing and postage. If you own your own business, you can save money by doing your firm's own direct mail. If you are active in a local group that needs to raise money, writing the letter yourself is likely to be the only way your group can afford to use direct mail. The principles in this chapter will help you write solid, serviceable letters and brochures that will build your business and help fund your group.

Sales, fund-raising, and promotional messages have several purposes.

Primary purposes:

To motivate the reader to read the message.

To have the reader act (order the product, schedule a demonstration, send a donation).

To provide enough information so that the reader knows exactly what to do (even if he or she keeps only the reply coupon).

To overcome any objections that might prevent or delay action.

Secondary purpose:

To build a good image of the writer's organization (to strengthen the commitment of readers who act, and make readers who do not act more likely to respond positively next time).

Components of Good Direct Mail

Good direct mail has three components: a good product, service, or cause; a good mailing list; and a good appeal. A **good product** appeals to a specific segment of people, can be mailed, and provides an adequate profit margin. A **good service or cause** fills an identifiable need. A **good mailing list** has accurate addresses and is a good match to the product. Most professional direct mailers rent their lists from companies that specialize in compiling and maintaining lists. Small businesses and charities can use in-house lists of their customers or members and can compile lists of prospects from city directories or other local sources. A **good appeal** offers a believable description of benefits, links the benefits of the product or service to a need or desire that motivates the reader, makes the reader want to read the letter, and motivates the reader to act. The appeal is made up of the words in the letter, the pictures in the brochure, and all the parts of the package, from outer envelope to reply card.

All three elements are crucial: the best letter in the world won't persuade someone who doesn't have room for a garden to buy a Rototiller. However, this chapter will examine only the elements of a good appeal: how to create a message that will motivate a reader to act, assuming that you already have a good product to sell or a worthy cause to raise funds for, and that you already have a good list of people who might be interested in that product or organization.

Industry wisdom is that a **cold list**—a list of people with no prior connection to your group—will have a 2% response rate. Good timing, a good list, and a good appeal can double or even triple that percentage.

You can raise the response rate 1% or 2% by including an 800 number as another way for people to respond. Following up the mailing with a phone call 24 to 72 hours after the reader receives the mailing can bring in another 2% to 14%. If people on your list have some connection with your organization (e.g., have been patients at the hospital or have visited the museum you're raising money for), you can expect a higher response rate. From a list of people who have bought from or given *to your organization* before, the response rate can be well over 50% and for some groups can approach 90%.[2]

Is It "Junk" Mail?

Industry expert and critic James P. Rosenfield defines *junk mail* as mail that is "(1) Irrelevant; (2) Sleazy, dishonest, deceptive; (3) Discarded immediately because of one or both of the above."[3] Well-written, ethical mailings sent to people who are interested in the product or organization aren't junk. Using that term can cause us to respond to the symbol rather than to the reality.

In 2001, some people automatically threw direct mail away. But, according to one survey, 77% of adults regularly read their direct mail, and 59% read it in the week before the survey. For people who open some of their mail, the three most important factors in deciding whether to open a specific envelope were timing, personalization, and an attractive appearance.[4]

Lists, Lists, and More Lists*

Nearly 40,000 mailing lists are available commercially. Among the lists available from one company are

130,310	Women accountants
3,953	Owners of balloon aircraft
171,983	High school athletic directors
6,195,311	Dog owners
263,877	Republican contributors
59,641	Highest salaried executives (home addresses)
2,450	Rabbis
4,600,000	Hispanic families
204,443	Heads of households ages 18–34 in Utah
2,046	Yacht owners in Illinois
62,301	Californians with annual income over $100,000

*Based on Best Mailing Lists, Inc., 1996 Catalog.

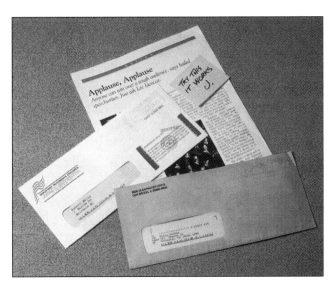

These three documents are unethical attempts to mislead the reader. The top contains a page apparently torn out of a magazine with a personalized Post-it: "Try this. It works." Almost everyone knows someone whose name starts with *J*, and people may not realize that this is a scam. The middle document says "Important Documents Enclosed," repeats in small print the US Postal Service statute about tampering with mail, and in the lower right-hand corner has an imprint designed to look like a registered mail sticker (though it is only fluff, saying nothing). The bottom envelope is designed to look like an official check. In fact it can be cashed only as a "discount" on a product the mailer is trying to sell.

Ethics and Direct Mail, I

Deception in direct mail is all too easy to find.

Some mailers have sent "checks" to readers. But the "check" can only be applied toward the purchase of the item the letter is selling.

Some mailings now have yellow Post-it notes with "handwritten" notes signed with initials or a first name only—to suggest that the mailing is from a personal friend.

One letter offers a "free" membership "valued at $675" (note the passive—who's doing the valuing?) but charges—up front—$157 for "maintenance fees."

Such deception has no place in well-written direct mail.

The Name Change*

If you have a sizable customer file, you can bet that at least 10% of the names are incorrect. As the U.S. becomes more multicultural, this percentage is beginning to veer in the direction of 15%. For centuries now (it seems) I've been suggesting that direct marketers prominently display a self-correction device anytime they send out direct mail, particularly to customers: "If your name or any other information is incorrect, please call 1-800-123-4567 and we'll fix things immediately."

*Quoted from James R. Rosenfield, "Personalization and Authenticity," *Direct Marketing*, July 1998, 40.

Basic Direct Mail Strategy

Direct mail strategies start with three basic steps: (1) learn about the product, service, or organization; (2) choose and analyze the target audience; and (3) choose a central selling point. These steps interact. An understanding of your target audience may suggest questions to ask about your product. Information you find in researching the product may suggest an idea for a possible central selling point.

1. Understand Your Product, Service, or Organization.

Try to use the product or service. Talk to volunteers who work for your charitable organization; if possible, visit the site where the good work is done.

To sell a product, ask

- What needs does the product meet? What benefits does it provide? What problems does it remove?
- What are the product's objective features? Size? Color? Materials? How does it work? What options are available?
- How much does it cost? What does the buyer get for the money?
- How is it different from or better than competing products? (If the *details* of differences or superiority are interesting, jot them down. They may work well in a letter.)
- How easy is it to install? To use? To maintain?

To raise money, ask

- What is the problem your group is helping to solve? (If possible, collect examples to illustrate the need.)
- How, specifically, is your group helping? (Collect stories about specific people who have been helped, specific gains that have been achieved. Also get overall figures.)
- What support does your group already get from tax dollars, user fees, ticket sales, and so on? Why are private funds necessary?
- What are the group's immediate goals? How much will it cost to achieve them? (Try to get costs for some of the specific subgoals as well as the total budget needed.)

If you're writing a document for a local organization, visit its office or center and talk to the people who work there, or visit its Web site. If you're writing a letter for a national group, check the phone book to see if there's a local chapter where you can get brochures, flyers, and information. The library may also have information. For fund-raising letters, you can learn about the problem the group is working to solve by checking *The Reader's Guide to Periodical Literature* or the *Business Periodicals Index*. Magazine articles about the problem may have anecdotes and specifics you can use. Also check the Web.

2. Identify and Analyze Your Target Audience.

The **target audience** is all of the people who are likely to be interested in buying the product, using the service, or contributing to the cause. In direct mail, you do not try to sell a subscription to *Sports Illustrated* to someone who loathes sports; you do not ask Republicans to contribute to a Democratic candidate's campaign. In the latter case you might, however, include Independents or people who had never indicated a party preference. In addition to the small number of people who are already interested in your product or committed to your cause, the audience always includes people who could be persuaded if you gave them enough evidence.

As Chapter 3 explains, you can analyze your audience in terms of demographics (◀▥ p. 63)—objective, measurable features: "This letter is going to homeowners who have children between the ages of 4 and 10." You can also use **psychographic characteristics** (◀▥ p. 63)—values, beliefs, goals, and lifestyles: "I'm writing to people who care about protecting the environment." Often a combination of demographic and psychographic characteristics works best: 21-year-old college students may have different reasons for using a health club than do 45-year-old executives, even though both groups want to look good and deal with stress.

Whenever possible, think of specific people you know while you write the letter. What do they care about? What would motivate *them?*

3. Choose a Central Selling Point.

Since even a well-defined audience will have people with different motivations and different objections to buying or giving, a direct mail letter needs several selling points. To unify the letter, use a central selling point. A **central selling point** is a reader benefit that by itself could motivate your readers to act and that can serve as an umbrella under which all the other benefits can fit.

Suppose you want to sell copies of a book that explains how to grow vegetables in home gardens. Whenever you try to sell a book or magazine by mail, you are really selling the activity; the book helps readers do the activity successfully. Any of the following statements could be used as central selling points:

▥ Fresh vegetables from your own garden taste better than store-bought vegetables that are ripened with chemicals.

▥ Vegetables from your own garden are healthier. You control the chemicals you put on them; you can avoid any insecticides and wax that you don't want.

▥ It's cheaper to grow your own vegetables than to buy them in a grocery store.

▥ Growing vegetables is fun for the whole family. Children will be fascinated by growing plants.

▥ Growing your own vegetables is a way to get back to nature, to have a simpler, more natural lifestyle.

A professional direct mailer might test two or more different approaches with samples of the target market, then send the best letter to the whole list. When you can't run a test, how do you choose? First, eliminate any central selling points that don't fit your target audience. Next, use your own understanding of people to decide whether to stress taste or health or economy or fun or working with nature. If two or more appeals seem equally effective, try writing each of them. In your assignment, use the one that you can develop most effectively.

In a fund-raising letter, you must also choose the appeal that will be most powerful for the target audience. A fund-raising letter to college alumni could use nostalgia, the obligation to repay the college, the feeling of making an investment in young people, or a sense of social responsibility. To create a sense

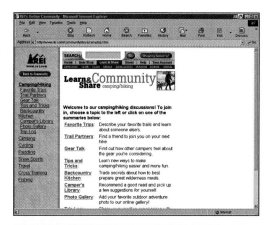

InSite

www.rei.com/community/docso/
camptop.html

Analyze your target audience. What information will they find useful or interesting? The Camping/Hiking page on the REI site allows hikers to find a partner, announce hikes, and trade tips.

Recruiting Students*

Sending mail to prospective students helps strengthen their interest in enrolling in a college or university. In the early 1990s, the University of Detroit Mercy was able to print out only one or two letters for each prospective student. Most of these letters were mailed without a signature—hardly a way to build goodwill.

In the mid-1990s, the university installed a system that allows it to create personalized letters triggered by database information. A series of letters could now go out from the admissions counselor, the dean of the college the prospective student might enter, the director of financial aid, and the director of the cooperative education program. Best of all, signatures could be saved as graphic images and printed automatically with the appropriate letter.

By 1997, the university was mailing 250,000 personalized letters a year. The admissions office credits the letters for a 25% increase in enrollment in five years, during a period when the pool of college-age students was growing smaller.

*Based on Janet Kuras, "Personalized Correspondence Contributes to 25% Increase in Student Enrollment at University of Detroit Mercy," *Direct Marketing*, October 1997, 62–63.

FIGURE 10.1   How to Organize a Sales or Fund-Raising Letter

1. Open your letter with a **star** designed to catch the reader's attention.
2. In the body, provide a **chain** of reasons and logic.
3. End by telling the reader what to do and providing a reason to act promptly. Tie up **(knot)** the motivation you have created and turn it into action.

---

of nostalgia, refer to events that happened when readers were in school. (Check back issues of the college newspaper or yearbook for ideas.) If you're writing to members of a sorority or fraternity, refer to events the house is proud of, and use a salutation and complimentary close that will remind readers of their membership. If you are writing to a group that sees the Bible as an authority, use appropriate biblical quotes and allusions.

When you hope to raise funds from two different target audiences, you may need two separate mailing pieces with different central selling points. Ducks Unlimited can appeal to both hunters and nonhunting environmentalists. Its letters remind hunters that preserving wetlands is essential to maintain the duck populations that hunters need. Environmentalists will be interested in saving the wetlands because of the importance of wetlands as ecosystems.

How to Organize a Sales or Fund-Raising Letter

Use the star-chain-knot pattern[5] to organize your letter (see Figure 10.1).

Opener (Star)

The opener, or **star,** of your letter gives you 30 to 60 seconds to motivate readers to read the rest of the letter.

A good star opener will make readers want to read the letter and provide a reasonable transition to the body of the letter. A very successful subscription letter for *Psychology Today* started out,

> Do you still close the bathroom door when there's no one in the house?

The question is both intriguing in itself and a good transition into the content of *Psychology Today:* practical psychology applied to the quirks and questions we come across in everyday life.

It's essential that the opener not only get the reader's attention but also be something that can be linked logically to the body of the letter. A sales letter started,

> Can You Use $50 This Week?

Certainly that gets attention. But the letter only offered the reader the chance to save $50 on a product. Readers may feel disappointed or even cheated when they learn that instead of getting $50, they have to spend money to save $50.

It's hard to write a brilliant opener the minute you sit down. Two reliable strategies are (1) write four or five openers, and pick the best; (2) just start writing. A good opener may in fact appear on your second or third page; sometimes you can throw away much of the prose that preceded it.

To brainstorm possible openers, use the four basic modes: questions, narration, startling statements, and quotations.

The Web is an effective direct marketing channel. The Italian motorcycle company Ducati launched its 2000 and 2001 models on the Web—and sold out the whole production planned for each year. One $15,000 limited-production vehicle sold out in 31 minutes.

1. Questions

> Dear Writer:
>
>   What is the best way to start writing?

This letter selling subscriptions to *Writer's Digest* goes on to discuss Hemingway's strategy for getting started on his novels and short stories. *Writer's Digest* offers practical advice to writers who want to be published. The information in the letter is useful to any writer, so the recipient keeps reading; the information also helps to prove the claim that the magazine will be useful.

Good questions are interesting enough that readers want the answers, so they read the letter.

Poor question: Do you want to make extra money?

Better question: How *much* extra money do you want to make next year?

A series of questions (as in Figure 10.2 later in the chapter) can be an effective opener. Answer the questions in the body of the letter.

2. Narration, stories, anecdotes

> Dear Reader:
>
>   She hoisted herself up noiselessly so as not to disturb the rattlesnakes snoozing there in the sun.
>
>   To her left, the high desert of New Mexico. Indian country. To her right, the rock carvings she had photographed the day before. Stick people. Primitive animals.
>
>   Up ahead, three sandstone slabs stood stacked against the face of the cliff. In their shadow, another carving. A spiral consisting of rings. Curious, the young woman drew closer. Instinctively, she glanced at her watch. It was almost noon. Then just at that moment, a most unusual thing happened.

Long, Longer, Longest

Some tests show that six- or even eight-page letters outpull shorter letters. Many political fund-raising letters are six pages (particularly during the primary seasons when candidates are not yet well known).

Long letters are especially good for publications, high-involvement categories like health and investing, or expensive items. Liberty Mint used an eight-page letter to sell 100 castings of Remington's "The Bronco Buster" made of pure silver for $25,000 each.

Even long letters should look easy to read. Many long letters use short paragraphs (just a sentence or two), headings, and highlighted or underlined sections to encourage skimming.

> Suddenly, as if out of nowhere, an eerie dagger of light appeared to stab at the topmost ring of the spiral. It next began to plunge downwards—shimmering, laser-like.
>
> It pierced the eighth ring. The seventh. The sixth. It punctured the innermost and last. Then just as suddenly as it had appeared, the dagger of light was gone. The young woman glanced at her watch again. Exactly twelve minutes had elapsed.
>
> Coincidence? Accident? Fluke? No. What she may have stumbled across that midsummer morning three years ago is an ancient solar calendar. . . .

This subscription letter for *Science84* argues that it reports interesting and significant discoveries in all fields of science—all in far more detail than do other media. The opener both builds suspense so that the reader reads the subscription letter and suggests that the magazine will be as interesting as the letter and as easy to read.

3. Startling statements

> Dear Membership Candidate:
>
> I'm writing to offer you a job.
>
> It's not a permanent job, understand. You'll be working for only as much time as you find it rewarding and fun.
>
> It's not even a paying job. On the contrary, it will cost *you* money.

This fund-raising letter from Earthwatch invites readers to participate in its expeditions, subscribe to its journal, and donate to its programs. Earthwatch's volunteers help scientists and scholars dig for ruins, count bighorns, and monitor changes in water; they can work as long as they like; they pay their own (tax-deductible) expenses.

Variations of this mode include special opportunities, twists, and challenges.

4. Quotations

> "I never tell my partner that my ankle is sore or my back hurts. You can't give in to pain and still perform."
>
> —Jill Murphy
> Soloist

The series of which this letter is a part sells season tickets to the Atlanta Ballet by focusing on the people who work to create the season. Each letter quotes a different member of the company. The opening quote is used on the envelope over a picture of the ballerina and as an opener for the letter. The letters encourage readers to see the artists as individuals, to appreciate their hard work, and to share their excitement about each performance.

Body (Chain)

The **chain** is the body of the letter. It provides the logical and emotional links that move readers from their first flicker of interest to the action that is wanted. A good chain answers readers' questions, overcomes their objections, and involves them emotionally.

All this takes space. One of the industry truisms is "The more you tell, the more you sell." Tests show that longer letters bring in more new customers or new donors than do shorter letters. A four-page letter is considered ideal for mailings to new customers or donors.

To get that length, some letters use large type and margins. Expensive mailings sometimes use one uncut, folded 11-by-17-inch sheet, printed on the first and third sides, to give a two-page letter the psychological weight of four pages. And many letters now use bullet points or graphics to make the page easy to read.

Can short letters work? Yes, when you're writing to old customers or when the mailing is supported by other media. One study showed that a one-page letter was just as effective as a two-page letter in persuading recent purchasers of a product to buy a service contract.[6] E-mail direct mail is also short—generally just one screen. The shortest letter on record may be the two-word postcard that a fishing lake resort sent its customers: "They're biting!"

Content for the body of the letter can include

- Information readers will find useful even if they do not buy or give.
- Stories about how the product was developed or what the organization has done.
- Stories about people who have used the product or who need the organization's help.
- Word pictures of readers using the product and enjoying its benefits.

Action Close (Knot)

The action close, or **knot,** in the letter must do four things:

1. **Tell the reader what to do:** Respond. Avoid *if* ("If you'd like to try . . .") and *why not* ("Why not send in a check?"). They lack positive emphasis and encourage your reader to say *no.*
2. **Make the action sound easy:** Fill in the information on the reply card, sign the card (for credit sales), put the card and check (if payment is to accompany the order) in the envelope, and mail the envelope. If you provide an envelope and pay postage, stress those facts.
3. **Offer a reason for acting promptly.** Readers who think they are convinced but wait to act are less likely to buy or contribute. Reasons for acting promptly are easy to identify when a product is seasonal or there is a genuine limit on the offer—time limit, price rise scheduled, limited supply, and so on. Sometimes you can offer a premium or a discount if the reader acts quickly. When these conditions do not exist, remind readers that the sooner they get the product, the sooner they can benefit from it; the sooner they contribute funds, the sooner their dollars can go to work to solve the problem.
4. **End with a positive picture** of the reader enjoying the product (in a sales letter) or of the reader's money working to solve the problem (in a fund-raising letter). The last sentence should never be a selfish request for money.

The action close can also remind readers of the central selling point, stress the guarantee, and mention when the customer will get the product.

Using a P.S.

Studies of eye movement show that people often look to see who a letter is from before they read the letter. Ray Jutkins cites a study showing that 79% of the people who open direct mail read the P.S. first.[7] Therefore, direct mail often uses a deliberate P.S. after the signature block. It may restate the central selling point or some other point the letter makes, preferably in different words so that it won't sound repetitive when the reader reads the letter through from start to finish.

Here are four of the many kinds of effective P.S.'s.

■ Reason to act promptly:

> P.S. Once I finish the limited harvest, that's it! I do not store any SpringSweet Onions for late orders. I will ship all orders on a first-come, first-served basis and when they are gone they are gone. Drop your order in the mail today . . . or give me a call toll free at 800-531-7470! (In Texas: 800-292-5437)

Sales letter for Frank Lewis Alamo Fruit

■ Description of a premium the reader receives for giving:

> P.S. And . . . we'll be pleased to send you—as a *new* member—the exquisite, full-color Sierra Club Wilderness Calendar. It's our gift . . . absolutely FREE to you . . . to show our thanks for your membership at this critical time.

Fund-raising letter for Sierra Club

■ Reference to another part of the package:

> P.S. Photographs may be better than words, but they still don't do justice to this model. Please keep in mind as you review the enclosed brochure that your SSJ will look even better when you can see it firsthand in your own home.

Sales letter for the Danbury Mint's model of the Duesenberg SSJ

■ Restatement of central selling point:

> P.S. It is not easy to be a hungry child in the Third World. If your parents' crops fail or if your parents cannot find work, there are no food stamps . . . no free government-provided cafeteria lunches.
>
> Millions of hungry schoolchildren will be depending on CARE this fall. Your gift today will ensure that we will be there—that CARE won't let them down.

Fund-raising letter for CARE

Strategy in Sales Letters

The basic strategy in sales letters is satisfying a need. People buy to get something or to get rid of something. Your letter must remind people of the need your product meets, prove that the product will satisfy that need, show why your product is better than similar products, and make readers *want* to have the product. Use psychological description (◄ p. 226) to show readers how the product will help them. Testimonials from other buyers can help persuade them that the product works; details about how the product is made can carry the message of quality.

For Web links on sales letters, see the BAC Web site.

Dealing with Price

Many sales letters make the offer early in the letter—even on the envelope. The exact price, however, is not mentioned until the last fourth of the letter, after the copy makes the reader *want* the product. The only exception is when you're selling something that has a reputation for being expensive (a luxury car, *Encyclopaedia Britannica*). Then you may want to deal with the price issue early in the letter, especially if your readers want the product but think they can't afford it.

You can make the price more palatable with the following techniques:

1. **Link the price to the benefit the product provides.** "Your piece of history is just $39.95."
2. **Show how much the product costs each day, each week, or each month.** "You can have all this for less than the cost of a cup of coffee a day." Make sure that the amount seems small and that you've convinced people that they'll use this product all year long.
3. **Allow customers to charge sales or pay in installments.** Your bookkeeping costs will rise, and some sales may be uncollectible, but the total number of sales will increase.

Always offer a guarantee, usually right after the price. The best guarantees are short, convincing, and positive.

Negative: If the magazine fails to meet your expectations, you can cancel at any time and receive a refund on any unmailed copies.

Better: You'll be satisfied or we'll refund your money. I guarantee that.

Sample Sales Letter

The sample letter in Figure 10.2 is a subscription letter for *3-2-1 Contact*, a magazine for children ages 8–14. The letter uses an elite typeface on white paper with color in the logo, the "ABSOLUTELY FREE!" and the signature. The folded, uncut 11-by-17-inch paper is printed on four sides.

The letter opens with its central selling point: *3-2-1 Contact* educates kids in a fun way. Since the letter is addressed to parents, the opening questions are designed to be ones that will interest adults so that they'll read to find the answers. The body of the letter builds credibility by pointing out that the magazine is published by a nonprofit group. Material from the magazine itself helps to prove the claim that it teaches in an interesting way. The action close asks the reader to send in the reply card to subscribe.

Strategy in Fund-Raising Appeals

In a fund-raising letter, the basic emotional strategy is **vicarious participation.** By donating money, readers participate vicariously in work they are not able to do personally. This strategy affects the pronouns you use. Throughout the letter, use *we* to talk about your group. However, at the end, talk about what *you* the reader will be doing. End positively, with a picture of the reader's dollars helping to solve the problem.

To achieve both your primary and secondary purposes in fund-raising letters, you must give a great deal of information. This information (1) helps to persuade readers; (2) gives supporters evidence to use in conversations with others; and (3) gives readers who are not yet supporters evidence that may make them see the group as worthwhile, even if they do not give money now.

In your close, in addition to asking for money, suggest other ways the reader can help: doing volunteer work, scheduling a meeting on the subject, writing letters to Congress or the leaders of other countries, and so on. By suggesting other ways to participate, you not only involve readers but also avoid one of the traps of fund-raising letters: sounding as though you are selfish, only interested in readers for the money they can give.

For more information on fund-raising, see the BAC Web site.

Deciding How Much to Ask For

Most letters to new donors suggest a range of amounts, from $25 or $50 (for employed people) up to perhaps double what you *really* expect to get from a single donor. A second strategy is to ask for a small, set amount that nearly everyone can afford ($10 or $15).

Canadian Culture and Direct Mail*

In the United States, direct mail letters to total strangers often begin "Dear Friend." Canadian letters, in contrast, are more formal and less likely to imply any relationship other than business to be transacted.

US letters often offer some external reward for responding: a cash rebate, a credit on a bank card, a tote bag. Canadian letters avoid such rewards, perhaps because they suggest that if the product itself is not worth purchasing, the cause is not worth supporting.

*Based on Roger Graves, "'Dear Friend' (?): Culture and Genre in American and Canadian Direct Marketing Letters," *The Journal of Business Communication* 34, no. 3 (July 1997), 235–52.

FIGURE 10.2   A Magazine Subscription Letter

PL-CN1

Openers work when they are unusual. Avoid strategies that "everyone" is using.

Children's Television Workshop ▪ One Lincoln Plaza, New York, NY 10023

*   *   *   *   *   *   *   *   *   *   *   *

This letter is not for everyone. But if you're the parent of a youngster between the ages of 8 and 14 . . .

Identifies target audience

. . . then I invite you to send for a free copy of 3-2-1 CONTACT, the <u>award-winning</u> magazine of science, nature and math for the middle grades.

Statement of central selling point

Like the other Children's Television Workshop publications -- <u>Sesame Street</u> and <u>Kid City</u> -- 3-2-1 CONTACT is so spirited, so entertaining, so amusing that its readers seldom notice the fact that it's "educational."

Yet every issue is chock-full of mind-stretching puzzles, mazes, games and mysteries . . . amazing facts . . . and articles and features that promote analytical thinking, encourage patience and concentration, and generally help prepare your child for the world of tomorrow.

Keeps door open for reluctant reader

Don't worry -- I'm not asking you to <u>subscribe</u> to this magazine, at least not yet. All I'm asking is your permission to send an issue of 3-2-1 CONTACT to your home,

ABSOLUTELY FREE!

Repeats powerful word "Free"

*   *   *   *   *   *   *   *   *   *   *

Dear Fellow Parent,

"Why is the ocean salty?"

Attention-getting questions

"When you take an aspirin, how does it know where you hurt?"

Ideally, answer later in letter

"What are eyelashes for?"

"How does a magnifying glass work?"

(over, please . . .)

(continued)

FIGURE 10.2 A Magazine Subscription Letter *(continued)*

"Why is my image upside down when I see myself in a spoon?"

"How do fireworks work?"

"Why do some objects glow in the dark?"

"Why is the sky blue?"

                    *   *   *   *   *   *

Good you-attitude— avoids making reader feel inferior

I don't know about you, but I'm often stumped by the science questions my kids throw at me. I have no trouble helping them with spelling, or simple arithmetic, or even state capitals . . . but when it comes to explaining why teeth chatter, or how roosters know what time it is -- I guess I'm not as well-educated as I should be!

And yet our children are growing up into a world that is more technological than ever . . .

. . . a world where familiarity with computers is becoming essential, not just for scientists but for office workers, farmers, teachers, doctors, librarians, almost everyone . . .

Paragraphs indented for emphasis, visual appeal

. . . a world in which many of the most interesting, most challenging career opportunities call for a background in science and technology.

That's why I'm pleased that my children read 3-2-1 CONTACT, a magazine for 3rd through 8th graders that does for them what <u>Sesame Street</u> does for younger children: It educates without tears, using cartoons, games, jokes, and the attention-getting tricks of television to stimulate, enrich, and enlighten.

3-2-1 CONTACT is published by the non-profit Children's Television Workshop. It is a glossy, colorful magazine, loosely based on the television show of the same name. Like the show, the magazine has high production values: lively graphics, good writing, clear, full-color photographs and amusing illustrations throughout. Issue after issue, your youngsters will be entertained and challenged by such features as . . .

Builds credibility

<u>EXTRA!</u> The puzzles-and-games pages of the magazine, and the section most readers turn to first. Perhaps there'll be a "what's wrong with this picture" game, designed to promote logic and attention to detail. Sometimes there's a maze to get through, or a simple hands-on experiment, or a word-search puzzle.

There's often something to write away for -- for example, a free booklet from Kodak on how to make a pin-hole camera. Sometimes there's a riddle your child can solve by doing a series of math problems. (Can you imagine? Fun math!)

<u>TNT: Tomorrow's News Today</u> -- is a popular monthly column that brings our readers interesting news, often before their parents know of it. Have you heard about pop rice? (It tastes like pop corn, but is made from rice.) Did you know that the planet Pluto is a lot smaller than previously thought, and may be downgraded to a "minor planet"? Have

(continued)

FIGURE 10.2   A Magazine Subscription Letter *(continued)*

you heard about the plans for a two-mile-long elevated freeway in Los
Angeles -- for bicycles only? Do you know about the new aerosol spray
that protects against poison ivy? 3-2-1 CONTACT readers know about
all these, and more!

The famous magician Blackstone is a contributor to 3-2-1 CONTACT, usually with
a remarkable math trick, such as this one:

> Using a calculator, punch in any three-digit
> number. (Example: 627.) Then punch it in again,
> so you have a six-digit number. (Example: 627,627.)
> Then divide the six-digit number by seven, divide
> the answer by 11, and divide that answer by 13.
> Amazingly, you'll always end up with the original
> three-digit number! Try it!

Example of material in magazine — helps to prove claims

THE TIME TEAM is another popular feature of 3-2-1 CONTACT. In each
month's story, two teenagers -- with the help of a science fair
project gone awry -- travel into the past or the future. Transported
to different eras and cultures, the heroes become caught up in
exciting historical moments, and have adventures with people both
famous and ordinary. In one episode, set in the 1920s, they use their
mental agility to help Walt Disney solve a mystery involving the
original Mickey Mouse cartoon. In another, they find themselves in
the middle of the Civil War. An entertaining blend of fact and
fiction, the stories make history and science come alive!

FACTOIDS, too, is a popular monthly column, one that provides our
readers with curious little facts which they can share with their
friends. For example, did you know that . . .

Facts to interest parents as well as kids

* In one day, Americans eat enough pizza to cover 75 football
  fields.

* A codfish lays up to four million eggs at one time, but on
  average only two will become fish.

* Lions sleep about 18 hours a day.

* One hundred years ago, the average 9-year-old was about six
  inches shorter than a 9-year-old today.

* In one year, your heart beats about 36,000,000 times.

And of course, every issue of 3-2-1 CONTACT contains several major articles
spanning the depth and breadth of science today. For example, recently we had
a special issue on Water, with articles on Rescuing a Coral Reef . . . River
Rafting Catches On . . . and Are We Running Out of Water?

We've also had cover stories on Why Baby Animals Are Cute (in some species,
it's what makes adults take care of their young!) . . . on Finding Homes for
Wild Horses . . . and on Memory, including an article on how memory works,
with tricks and techniques for greatly improving your own memory!

                    *   *   *   *   *   *

(continued)

FIGURE 10.2 A Magazine Subscription Letter *(concluded)*

Need to improve positive emphasis here

If these examples of what you'll find in 3-2-1 CONTACT have convinced you to subscribe for your family, then indicate "I ACCEPT" on the enclosed Free Issue Request Card. Send no money now -- we'll send you your first issue, enter your subscription, and bill you later.

Lacks you-attitude

If you'd like to see the magazine before making up your mind, indicate "I'M NOT SURE" on the Free Issue Request Card. We'll send you an issue at no cost and with no obligation to subscribe.

When you receive your first issue, show it to your children. Look through it together, and decide if becoming a subscriber is a good idea for you.

Action close

If not, write "cancel" on our invoice, return it, and owe nothing. The first issue will be yours to keep, free. But if you like 3-2-1 CONTACT -- the only children's magazine ever to receive the National Magazine Award for General Excellence -- and wish to continue receiving it, we'll send you 9 more issues (10 issues in all) for the low price of $1.59 per issue.

Should use you-attitude

There's really nothing to lose -- and the exciting world of science and technology to gain. Say "I ACCEPT" or "I'M NOT SURE," but please -- return your Free Issue Card today!

Sincerely,

Nina B. Link

Nina B. Link
Publisher
3-2-1 CONTACT

Lacks you-attitude

P.S. If yours is one of the first fifty request cards to be processed, we'll send you -- absolutely FREE -- a NINTENDO Entertainment System Control Deck. The system includes the Control Deck and two precision-engineered controls designed for instant reflex action! You can play the complete library of NINTENDO games on this system. And its exclusive microchips give you brilliant color, 3-D images and actual shadows -- the most advanced graphics ever! To be considered for this state-of-the-art home entertainment system, remove the "FREE NINTENDO" sticker from the outer envelope and affix it to the postpaid reply envelope provided. Then enclose your request card and mail it immediately!

Split long P.S. into two paragraphs for better visual impact

As part of our promotion, we're giving away fifty (50) NINTENDO™ Entertainment System Control Decks, with a retail value of $100.00 each, to the first 50 people who respond to our offer. To assure equal opportunity for all, one system will be awarded to each of the first fifty respondents on a geographical basis proportionate to the geographical distribution of this offer. No purchase necessary. One entry per person. Only entries received by First Class mail are eligible. If you are a winner, you will be notified by mail. For a list of the winners, please send a self-addressed stamped envelope to: Children's Television Workshop, One Lincoln Plaza, New York, NY 10023. Attn: Magazine Circulation Department. Employees of Children's Television Workshop and its suppliers are not eligible. Void where prohibited by law. LIMIT—ONE SYSTEM PER HOUSEHOLD.

A Chill for Local Charities*

In the first five weeks after September 11, Americans contributed almost $1 billion to the victims of the terrorist attacks. But donations to local charities were down.

For the last three decades, Americans as a nation have given just 2% of their income to charity each year. Rich people actually give less as a percentage of their incomes than do poorer people. The 2% figure has held steady as the number of charitable organizations has mushroomed. In the past, giving to new causes like AIDS research has reduced giving to older causes like cancer research.

The fear is that giving to September 11 causes will leave other worthy groups in need. Optimists might say that the generosity after September 11 shows that Americans will give when they know about a need and are emotionally involved. Time will tell which view is right.

*Based on Nanette Byrnes and Ushma Patel, "Online Extra: A Chill for Local Charities," *BusinessWeek Online* (www.businessweek.com/magazine/content/01_44/b3755080.htm?mainwindow), October 29, 2001.

InSite

www.habitat.org

Habitat for Humanity's Web page provides information for potential and current donors, volunteers, and clients.

One of the several reasons people give for not contributing is that a gift of $25 or $100 seems too small to matter. It's not. Small gifts are important both in themselves and to establish a habit of giving. Some of the people who can only give $25 or even $5 today will someday have more money.[8]

You can increase the size of gifts by using the following techniques:

1. **Suggest amounts in descending order.** Both in your close and on the reply card, say "$100, $50, $25, or whatever amount you prefer" rather than starting with the smallest and going up.

2. **Ask for gifts slightly higher than the normal cut-off points.** Most people think in terms of a gift of $10, $25, $50, and so on, even though they could afford to give slightly more. You can increase the average gift by asking for $12, $30, $60, and so on.

3. **Link the gift to what it will buy.** Tell how much money it costs to buy a brick, a hymnal, or a stained glass window for a church; a book or journal subscription for a college library; a meal for a hungry child. Linking amounts to specific gifts helps readers feel involved and often motivates them to give more: instead of saying, "I'll write a check for $25," the reader may say, "I'd like to give a _____" and write a check to cover it.

4. **Offer a premium for giving.** Public TV and radio stations have used this ploy with great success, offering books, umbrellas, and carryall bags for gifts at a certain level. The best premiums are things that people both want and will use or display, so that the organization will get further publicity when other people see the premium.

5. **Ask for a monthly pledge.** People on tight budgets could give $5 or $10 a month; more prosperous people could give $100 a month or more. These repeat gifts not only bring in more money than the donors could give in a single check but also become part of the base of loyal supporters, which is essential to the continued success of any organization that raises funds.

Annual letters to past donors often use the amount of the last donation as the lowest suggested gift, with other gifts 25%, 50%, or even 100% higher.

Always send a thank-you letter to people who respond to your letter, whatever the size of their gifts. By telling about the group's recent work, a thank-you letter can help reinforce donors' commitment to your cause.

Logical Proof in Fund-Raising Letters

The body of a fund-raising letter must prove that (1) the problem deserves the reader's attention, (2) the problem can be solved or at least alleviated, (3) your organization is helping to solve it, (4) private funds are needed, and (5) your organization will use the funds wisely.

1. The problem deserves the reader's attention.

No reader can support every cause. Show why the reader should care about solving this problem.

If your problem is life-threatening, give some statistics: Tell how many people are killed in the United States every year by drunk drivers, or how many children in the world go to bed hungry every night. Also tell about one individual who is affected.

If your problem is not life-threatening, show that the problem threatens some goal or principle your readers find important. For example, a fund-raising letter to boosters of a high school swim team showed that team members' chances of setting records were reduced because timers relied on stopwatches. The letter showed that automatic timing equipment was accurate and produced faster times, since the timer's reaction time was no longer included in the time recorded.

2. The problem can be solved or alleviated.

People will not give money if they see the problem as hopeless—why throw money away? Sometimes you can reason by analogy. Cures have been found for other deadly diseases, so it's reasonable to hope that research can find a cure for cancer and AIDS. Sometimes you can show that short-term or partial solutions exist. For example, a UNICEF letter showed that four simple changes could save the lives of millions of children: oral rehydration, immunization, promoting breast feeding, and giving mothers cardboard growth charts so they'll know if their children are malnourished. Those solutions don't affect the underlying causes of poverty, but they do keep children alive while we work on long-term solutions.

3. Your organization is helping to solve or alleviate the problem.

Prove that your organization is effective. Be specific. Talk about your successes in the past. Your past success helps readers believe that you can accomplish your goals.

4. Private funds are needed to accomplish your group's goals.

We all have the tendency to think that taxes, or foundations, or church collections yield enough to pay for medical research or basic human aid. If your group does get some tax or foundation money, show why more money is needed. If the organization helps people who might be expected to pay for the service, show why they cannot pay, or why they cannot pay enough to cover the full cost. If some of the funds have been raised by the people who will benefit, make that clear.

5. Your organization will use the funds wisely.

Prove that the money goes to the cause, not just to the cost of fund-raising.

@   See the BAC Web site for sites that evaluate charities.

Emotional Appeal in Fund-Raising Letters

Emotional appeal is needed to make people pull out their checkbooks. How strong should emotional appeal be? A mild appeal is unlikely to sway any reader who is not already committed, but readers will feel manipulated by appeals they find too strong and reject them. Audience analysis may help you decide how much emotional appeal to use. If you don't know your audience well, use the strongest emotional appeal *you* feel comfortable with.

Emotional appeal is created by specifics. It is hard to care about, or even to imagine, a million people; it is easier to care about one specific person. Details and quotes help us see that person as real. A letter for a New York hospital talked about four people who owed their lives to the hospital: a baby, a young girl, a businessman, and an elderly woman. The letter brought in a greater response than previous mailings that simply used statistics.[9]

Sample Fund-Raising Letter

The letter from The Gorilla Foundation shown in Figure 10.3 uses interesting details and color photos to lead the reader through the document.

Enclosures In Fund-Raising Letters

Fund-raising letters sometimes use inexpensive enclosures to add interest and help carry the message.

Brochures are inexpensive, particularly if you photocopy them. Mailings to alumni have included "Why I Teach at Earlham" (featuring three professors) and letters from students who have received scholarships.

Seeds don't cost much. Mailings from both Care and the New Forests Fund include four or five seeds of the leucaena, a subtropical tree that can grow 20 feet in a year. Its leaves feed cattle; its wood provides firewood or building materials; its roots reduce soil erosion. (Indeed, the enclosure easily becomes the theme for the letter.)

Reprints of newspaper or magazine articles about the organization or the problem it is working to solve add interest and credibility. Pictures of people the organization is helping build emotional appeal.

Major campaigns may budget for enclosures: pictures of buildings, tapes of oral history interviews, even sea shells and Mason jars.

FIGURE 10.3   A Fund-Raising Letter

THE GORILLA FOUNDATION
BOX 620-640 WOODSIDE, CA 94062
INTERNET SITE: www.gorilla.org

Photos break up the text and provide visual interest.

Dear Friend of Animals,

Not you-attitude I'm writing to share with you an astonishing breakthrough in our understanding of the world. The news is that a very remarkable gorilla named Koko has changed myth into fact ... by speaking to humans!

First paragraph is weak. It isn't really news (as paragraph 3 admits); the allusion to a "myth" doesn't work; the paragraph lacks specifics.

Underlining is meant to look as though person had marked key points

Slightly revised, this ¶ would make an acceptable opener

It's true. After years of dedicated teaching, Koko has learned to use sign language--the gestural language used by the deaf. With her newfound vocabulary, Koko is now providing us with an astounding wealth of knowledge about the way animals view the world. *A detail would be nice.*

Builds credibility

If you read magazines such as *National Geographic*, *People*, and *Life*, or watch television programs like "I Witness Video, Day One and 20/20," then you already know about Koko and the fascinating things she is telling us. Through the media, more than 40 million Americans have discovered what this young female gorilla can teach you and me about *homo sapiens'* closest living relatives.

Builds credibility

My name is Penny Patterson, and I have been Koko's teacher since 1972. In this letter Koko and I would like to share with you what we are learning together. And, perhaps most importantly, we'd like to invite you to become a member of the amazing world of speaking with animals by joining the Gorilla Foundation as part of Koko's extended family.

Emotional appeal

Dangerous to assume reader's reaction

As you read this, I think you'll be astonished at what more than two decades of study here at the Gorilla Foundation have revealed. By using sign language, Koko has confirmed humanity's timeless intuitions about the nature of animal intelligence.

Indeed, I constantly marvel at the complex and all-encompassing spectrum of this gentle animal's emotions: joy and grief, hope and

Talking about your own responses, however, is OK.

(continued)

FIGURE 10.3 A Fund-Raising Letter *(continued)*

despair, patience and frustration, greed and generosity, guilt and remorse, confidence and fear, pride and shame, empathy and jealousy, love and hate ... all the emotions that you and I experience.

Let me tell you a particularly poignant story to illustrate what I mean.

For years, Koko had expressed an interest in the cats she saw through her windows or in the pages of her magazines. Her dreams came true when she selected a tailless manx kitten from a litter to be her very own.

I was moved by the relationship that developed between the 230-pound gorilla and the roly-poly kitten she named "All Ball." On occasion we would witness the tragicomical scene of Koko pouting when tiny All Ball had bitten or scratched her.

Interesting details keep the reader reading.

This photo is on the poster included in the package.

But far more frequently the then 13-year-old Koko would tell us how much she adored her tiny kitten. Certainly there's no better example of the old maxim "A picture is worth 1,000 words" than the cover of the January 1985 *National Geographic* that showed Koko softly cradling the diminutive kitten in her arms.

Koko is not alone in teaching us about the remarkable intelligence of these gentle primates. Her gorilla companion Michael has his own stories to tell. Unlike Koko, who was born in the San Francisco Zoo, Michael was orphaned in his birthplace in Cameroon, Africa.

Using sign language, the 400-pound gorilla can relate how he was captured--"big trouble"-- when he was only two years old. He and his mother were "chased" by native gorilla hunters, who then killed his mother. He uses startingly violent gestures to explain how the men "hit" him and his mother. (There are verified stories of the centuries-old native practice of butchering and eating adult gorillas in front of their young.)

Whether they're telling us about their cats or providing us with a great ape's ideas about life and death, the gorillas are doing something more remarkable and profound than "just" communicating with humans.

Koko and Michael are changing the way we view our world; they're forcing us to reexamine everything we've ever thought about animals.

(continued)

FIGURE 10.3 A Fund-Raising Letter *(continued)*

The effects of our studies are nothing less than revolutionary. Just as Copernicus proved that the universe doesn't revolve around the earth, we're proving that all life on this planet doesn't revolve around humans.

Imagine what could happen when people realize that animals have memories ... thought processes ... even hopes and dreams. The fight to end cruelty to animals will gain new momentum; the efforts to preserve animals from extinction will take on even greater importance when humanity realizes what the real stakes are.

links this project to larger environmental concerns

Humans are already reaping the benefits of our work as well. I have received thousands of letters from parents and educators who cite Koko and Michael as inspirations to young children to learn all kinds of skills--from reading to toilet training. (Yes, Koko uses a bathroom just as we do ... and even likes to use that time to leaf through magazines!)

Details are both interesting in themselves and help answer question, "Why does this matter?"

The breakthroughs in non-verbal communication we've pioneered and the teaching methods we've developed with Koko and Michael have exciting and promising applications for reaching autistic children, the severely retarded, and other handicapped people who have difficulty communicating. The possibilities are endless.

More breakthroughs will surely come, for the work we're doing with Koko and Michael is a lifetime project. That's right: A gorilla's life expectancy is over 50 years ... and my colleagues and I have committed the rest of our lives to learning everything these gorillas have to tell us.

This commitment overrides everything else. If we fail, such a long-term project may never happen again.

But our greatest fear--the one grim possibility that lends the greatest urgency to our work--is one simple fact: one day there simply may be no more gorillas.

The fact is that all sub-species of these wonderful animals are in trouble. Only about 600 mountain gorillas survive today in Uganda, Zaire and war-torn Rwanda. It's all too likely that these magnificent primates--all of whom live in a total of 113 square miles--will be extinct within 15 years.

Wouldn't it be tragic if--just as we are learning to talk with these beautiful animals--there were no more to talk with?

general goal
Some day, if you and hundreds of others help us, Koko and Michael will live in a large preserve with other gorillas where they will thrive in a natural setting, communicate with humans, and reproduce future generations.

Specific needs But many obstacles must be overcome before our dream can become reality. Just Koko and Michael's basics--housing, food, and staff to meet their basic needs--require the average income of two adults. And then there are the unique expenses of our revolutionary project: custom

(continued)

FIGURE 10.3 A Fund-Raising Letter *(concluded)*

educational tools, a well-trained teaching staff, special data collection and analysis hardware, custom-written computer programs and the weeks of computer time needed to run them, miles of videotape, and thousands of pieces of mail to answer every month from fascinated children and interested colleagues. Add to that the professional administrative support required to keep everything running efficiently and economically, and you can see that our breakthroughs have cost a great deal.

better to continue focus on new need that could be met with contributions

In fact, our work has cost much, much more than we've been able to afford--and so much needs to be done.

That's why we're making this appeal to the general public: We want to invite you to become part of Koko and Michael's extended family as a member of the Gorilla Foundation.

builds emotional appeal

When you do, you'll share in the excitement only "talking gorillas" can generate. As a member, you'll receive special updates on the latest developments in Koko and Michael's education. In addition, we'll send you our special reports--*The Gorilla Foundation Journal*--featuring transcriptions of our conversations with the gorillas; the latest reports on the state of the world's gorillas; and amazing, amusing photographs you'll find nowhere else.

largest amount mentioned is underlined

When I asked Koko "What do gorillas like to do most?" she replied "Gorilla love eat good." Your $50 contribution could buy the approximately 60 pounds of food Koko, Michael and their friend Ndume eat every day.

Good specifics

And you can help establish a sanctuary for gorillas. Your $35 donation could help pay for about two square feet of outdoor habitat in a new tropical preserve.

Amounts are both presented in descending order and linked to what they will buy

A $20 gift could help pay for an hour of videotaped documentation of our research, and $100 will help pay for a mailing to share vital information with every zoo in the world where gorillas are housed.

Highest amount should be first--but linked to something that will seem more important.

You know our work, how we've worked tirelessly for almost two decades to reveal some of nature's greatest secrets. Now we call on your dedication, too: Won't you please join the Gorilla Foundation?

Or, as Koko says, "Love gorilla."

Sincerely,

Penny Patterson

Penny Patterson, Ph.D.
President

Love,

The double signature is a nice touch.

Koko
"Fine Animal Gorilla"

P.S. Please don't put this letter aside with the intention of responding later. We need your help today. Just make your check payable to Koko, and return it in the convenient postage-paid envelope we have enclosed. Our heartfelt thanks.

The letter is printed in Courier on an 11-by-17-inch page folded into 8½ by 11 inches. The letter is a bit text-heavy. Using bigger margins, bigger paragraph indentations, and an occasional list would provide visual variety.

The opening paragraph is weak. The second paragraph offers several possibilities: "Sign language isn't just for Deaf people. A gorilla named Koko can use it too." However, the photo draws the reader's eye down the page. The letter would benefit from more specific supporting details. Much of the appeal of this letter is its novelty: this isn't the standard environmental fund-raising letter. The poster of Koko and her kitten included in the package is cute and involves the reader with the package.

Strategy in Contact Letters

Contact letters do not ask directly for action; instead, they keep in touch with customers or donors.

Contact letters are low key and short—often less than a page. They take as their theme the seasons or a recent event. The end of the letter refers to the relationship between reader and writer and looks to the future.

Some organizations routinely send contact letters to keep their names before clients and customers, particularly for items that are purchased infrequently. After the September 11, 2001, terrorist attacks, many organizations sent contact letters to customers and donors; the event seemed to cry out for comment. One of the best letters came from Amnesty International (see Figure 10.4).

Strategy in Brochures

Brochures can serve several purposes: they can build general support for an organization or candidate, give specific information ("How to Cope with Chemotherapy"), or even have a reply coupon that readers can return to buy a book, register for a conference, or donate to a cause.

Brochures can have many sizes. The simplest (and least expensive) brochures are an 8½-by-11-inch sheet of paper folded into three panels on each side for a total of six panels ("tri-fold"). The Heifer Project International brochure in Figure 10.5 uses a 6-by-12-inch page folded into four panels on each side. Brochures can also be quite large.

To create a brochure, determine your purpose(s) and your audience(s). Think about where and how your brochure will be distributed. A charity distributing brochures at a booth at the state fair needs to have information relevant to people all over the state, not just in the city where the fair is held. Determine whether gatekeepers such as doctors or travel agents will decide whether to distribute your brochures. Think about visual constraints and clutter that your brochure needs to overcome: other brochures, a holder that will block the bottom portion of the cover, and so forth. Plan photos and other visual elements.

Draft the text you want to include to get a sense of how much space you need. To keep a brochure size manageable, you may want to focus on just one of the programs or products you offer. For example, the Heifer Project brochure focuses on the Kids 2 Kids program and doesn't mention any of its other programs. Choose a central selling point or theme.

If you have too much text for the available space, tighten one more time. If the text still won't fit, consider using a larger page size, narrowing the purpose further, or creating a series of brochures. If you have extra space, add anecdotes, testimonials, maps, or more information.

See Chapter 6 for information on designing brochures and the BAC Web site for examples of brochures and templates to make simple brochures.

FIGURE 10.4 A Contact Letter

WILLIAM F. SCHULZ
EXECUTIVE DIRECTOR

September 21, 2001

Dear Amnesty Member,

Repetition of "Sometimes death comes . . . But not this time" creates powerful opener.

alliteration

Sometimes death comes in the dark, in the dead of night. But not this time. This time the day could not have been brighter or more beautiful.

Sometimes death comes when we are by ourselves. But not this time. This time it came to those who were surrounded by friends and colleagues.

Sometimes death comes on a battlefield or in a prison cell. But not this time. This time it came in commercial airplanes and pleasant office buildings. *Transition from the event to the organization sending the letter*

And sometimes death comes after a long struggle and much anticipation. But not this time. This time it came in an instant. And it appears to have swept in its wake family members of our staff and volunteers, friends of members of our Board and doubtless a good many Amnesty International members themselves.

In keeping with the organization's philosophy, the letter calls for a thoughtful, measured response.

Now that it has, you and I have work to do. Not the kind of work that sorts through rubble or loads up body bags, thank God. Those who do *that* work deserve a thousand tears of gratitude. Our work is of a different order but just as important nonetheless. The work of anger, to be sure, but an anger tempered by wisdom. The work of grieving, absolutely, but a grieving that pays homage to suffering. And the work of justice, no question about it, but a justice of which every one of us can be proud.

Rule of 3 with internal contrasts in each line.

alliteration

To get to grieving, we must go through anger. And to get to justice, we must go through grieving. Because, as the theologian Sam Keen so eloquently put it, "Every day we are not mourning is a day we will be taking vengeance" and vengeance is different from justice.

Those who died on September 11 represent the best that is in us as human beings, as citizens and people. The best that is in us knows that individuals are responsible for this crime – not *Repetition* anonymous masses of people. The best that is in us knows that the guilty deserve to be punished – not those who share their names or their language, their skin color or their religion. It knows that blind hatred corrupts the hater. It knows that the greatest power evil has is to entice the innocent to mimic its practices. It knows that every action has unintended consequences. It knows that the truly strong never forget that in the heart of every stranger lurks a reflection of our own.

Rule of 3 Those who died on September 11 represent the best that is in us, the calling of our highest selves. We owe them anger; we owe them grieving; we owe them justice. But everything that we do now must reflect the best, not the lowest, of our humanity. We pay those precious souls their rightful tribute only by leveling a wise justice, only by exhibiting a tender righteousness. We pay them tribute only by understanding what brought about their deaths and hewing to those principles that call us to a more abundant life.

AMNESTY INTERNATIONAL USA • 322 EIGHTH AVENUE • NEW YORK, NY 10001
(212) 807-8400 • www.amnestyusa.org

(continued)

FIGURE 10.4   A Contact Letter

Parallelism   Toward those ends, Amnesty International will mourn the victims; we will speak out against impunity for the perpetrators; we will demand that those innocent of crimes be protected and respected; and we will insist that justice is not justice if it fails to adhere to international human rights norms. Both the International Secretariat of Amnesty International and we in AIUSA have appointed Crisis Response Teams to work together in a coordinated, unified response to this tragedy and its aftermath. We will be determining as soon as possible how best our membership can help advance our common goals.

Short sentences ending in consonants bring a sense of closure.

For death has come in an instant. And now there is work to be done.

Repetition of sentence in ¶ 4

William F. Schulz
Executive Director

Writing Style

Direct mail is the one kind of business writing where elegance and beauty of language matter; in every other kind, elegance is welcome but efficiency is all that finally counts. Direct mail imitates the word choice and rhythm of conversation. The best sales, fund-raising, and promotional writing is closer to the language of poetry than to that of academia: it shimmers with images, it echoes with sound, it vibrates with energy.

Many of the things that make writing vivid and entertaining *add* words because they add specifics or evoke an emotional response. Individual sentences should flow smoothly. The passage as a whole may be fun to read precisely because of the details and images that "could have been left out."

1. Make Your Writing Interesting.

If the style is long-winded and boring, the reader will stop reading. Eliminating wordiness (⟵ p. 97) is crucial. You've already seen ways to tighten your writing in Chapter 4. Direct mail goes further, breaking some of the rules of grammar. In the following examples, note how sentence fragments and ellipses (spaced dots) are used in parallel structure to move the reader along:

FIGURE 10.5   A Brochure

Brochure Brings in $3.5 Million*

Inside Panels

"Foster Mother to the Human Race"

Quotation

In a world in which hunger seems to defy large-scale solutions, the answer may well lie with a much smaller one, the goat.

Startling statement

For most of the world's people, goat's milk is the only milk they have ever known. However, in many countries even goat's milk is in short supply. When children — at the most nutritionally vulnerable point in their lives — are deprived of milk, the consequences are disastrous. An absence of milk in their diet makes children easy targets for malnutrition and disease.

Goats offer an ideal solution to this grave situation. Goat's milk is as highly nutritious as that of any dairy animal. In fact, if children drink only one liter of goat's milk per day, they will be consuming all of the protein required for the first six years of life, and more than half of what they need to become teenagers and grow into adulthood. Even more impressive is the fact that this same single liter provides all the calcium required at almost every stage of life.

Just as important, goats require an extremely low investment and are very easy to keep. They will eat almost any kind of forage, need very little space, and are comfortable in a wide range of climates. They can also go longer without water than most other farm animals and reproduce quickly, allowing families to build their herds while producing extra milk to sell for income. Moreover, goat manure makes excellent fertilizer.

Details explain, "Why goats?"

Banners unify panels

Finally, goats and children appear to have a natural affinity for one another. Even young children are able to raise and take care of their family's goats. Such responsibility helps children gain the self-esteem that comes from playing a significant role in their family's economic life.

What money buys

At a cost of only $120 for a goat and the training in its care — or $10 for a share of a goat — Heifer Project's **Kids-2-Kids Campaign** makes it possible for us to send this four-footed economic miracle to needy children and their families all over the world. We invite you to take a glimpse into just some of the places where this miracle is taking place.

Logo banner separates stories

In Nepal

Most paragraphs should be 7 lines or less

Ten years ago, when she got the idea that would change her life, Gyandhari Basel could not even write her own name. Forced as a young girl to migrate from her native hill country to Nepal's southern plains, Gyandhari helped her family eke out a bare living as subsistence farmers. She was typical of many women in her situation, impoverished and soon married with four children of her own.

Gyandhari and several of her friends made the decision to band together to do what had previously been considered impossible. In a land

(continued)

So tiny, it fits virtually unnoticed in your pocket. So meticulously hand-assembled by unhurried craftsmen in Switzerland, that production may never exceed demand. So everyday useful, that you'll wonder how you ever got along without it.

Letter asking for inquiries about Dictaphone

Dear Member-elect:

If you still believe that there are only nine planets in our solar system . . . that wine doesn't breathe . . . and that you'd recognize a Neanderthal man on sight if one sat next to you on the bus . . . check your score. There aren't. It does. You wouldn't.

Subscription letter for *Natural History*

Indianapolis public TV/radio station WFYI needed new equipment. On-air fund-raising was already committed to operating costs. Hoping to raise $5 million in three years, the station started a capital improvements campaign.

The initial mailing used a cardboard brochure shaped like a greeting card. The cover had a silvery outline of a TV set and the words "In 1969, Indianapolis was the largest city in the nation without a public television station." Inside were an image of duct tape covering up the TV set on the cover and the words "It could be again."

A follow-up brochure provided a foldout time line of the station's history. Above the center line were printed, in black ink, the station's accomplishments. Below, in red, were the equipment failures. By the end, red ink covered the bottom of the page.

In nine months, the 500 mailers brought in $3.5 million.

*Based on Debra Ray, "'Poor-Mouth' Direct Mail Brochure Nets $3.5 Million in Contributions," *Direct Marketing*, February 1998, 38–39.

2. Use Sound Patterns to Emphasize Words

When you repeat sounds, you create patterns that catch the reader's attention, please the ear, and emphasize the words they occur in. **Alliteration** occurs when several syllables begin with the same sound. **Rhyme** is the repetition of the final vowel sounds and, if the words end with consonants, the final consonant sounds. **Rhythm** is the repetition of a pattern of accented and unaccented syllables. The **rule of three** explains that when you have a series of three items that are logically parallel, the last receives the most emphasis.

Political Direct Mail*

Political fund-raising letters entered national politics in 1952. Popular General Dwight Eisenhower had so little political identity that both the Democrats and Republicans asked him to run for them. The successful Republicans didn't know what campaign themes would be best. They chose to test themes by mailing out several letters, each with a different theme. To measure interest, the letter asked the reader to send in $1. The party received enough money to show that fund-raising letters could work.

Republicans are still ahead of Democrats in the fund-raising game and still using direct mail. In 1998, the Republican Party raised 51% of its receipts from responses to fund-raising letters. The Democratic Party received about 40% of its revenues from direct mail.

In addition to raising a significant amount of the money needed to mount a campaign, political direct mail also brings in the largest number of small contributors. And having lots of $100 to $200 donors—from as many states as possible in presidential primary elections— helps convince the big money donors that a candidate is electable and therefore worth supporting.

*Based on Jeanne Cummings, "Democrats Strike Gold Using Direct-Mail Drives Aimed at Small Donors amid Probe of Big Givers," *The Wall Street Journal*, August 20, 1998, A16; and Jeffrey H. Birnbaum, "The Money Chase," *Fortune*, September 7, 1998, 102.

FIGURE 10.5   A Brochure *(continued)*

where their husbands owned everything, they decided to seek a loan and raise goats.

The task seemed overwhelming for without collateral, no bank would help them. But when they applied to Heifer Project, they were answered with a miracle: 25 female goats, each with two kids! Each member of the group eagerly signed the agreement to pass on the first new kid to another woman in need.

As the kids were born and her income grew, Gyandhari — while organizing still more groups of women to accept and pass on the gift of a goat — finally had a chance to give her own children the kind of life she had always wanted for them. She bought them food, books, school uniforms and writing equipment, so they could begin their education. She rebuilt her crumbling house.

Today, with three of Gyandhari's children holding good jobs and the youngest in high school, she has turned her attention to the community — becoming the catalyst for a savings and loan program, a women's federation to advocate needed reforms with the government, a livestock management program, a cooperative investment program, and a literacy program taught by her husband.

This past year, the woman who once could not even write her own name had the privilege of addressing Nepal's most important dignitaries. At this important ceremony, Gyandhari was presented with Heifer Project's highest honor, the Golden Talent Award, in recognition of the lives she has changed for the better — all with the help of goats — made possible by people like you.

Four stories, from four continents, use details to build interest.

In Uganda

"Thank you for your kindness of helping the needy ones, especially me."

Many friends of Heifer Project know the story of Beatrice Biira, once so poor that as a 9-year-old she owned only one piece of clothing — a too-small red dress that had to be slit down the back in order for her to wear it.

Her life then was the stuff of poverty's worst nightmares: a four-mile walk along a dangerous road whenever her family needed water; hours at a time spent collecting firewood; a mile-long walk to the nearest classroom. However, Beatrice was so poor that when she walked to the classroom all she could do was look in and hope for the day her family might be able to afford for her to attend.

But Beatrice's life, like that of so many other children, changed forever on the day she received her HPI goat — through the generosity of people like you.

From that one beloved animal — which Beatrice's family named "Mugisa," meaning "luck" — came many blessings about which Beatrice once could only have dreamed.

Milk for nutrition. Healthy kids that grew,

Each story ends with acknowledgment of reader, encouraging new gifts.

(Inside panels, concluded)

Alliteration marks the opener-anecdote quoted earlier. The *s* and *z* sounds in the first sentence focus our attention on the snakes. The repetition of *st* in the second indented paragraph emphasizes those words. (Note that these paragraphs also use sentence fragments.)

> She hoisted herself up noiselessly so as not to disturb the rattlesnakes snoozing there in the sun.
>
> To her left, the high desert of New Mexico. Indian country. To her right, the rock carvings she had photographed the day before. Stick people. Primitive animals. Up ahead, three sandstone slabs stood stacked against the face of the cliff.

Subscription letter for *Science84*

Rhythm, rhyme, and the rule of three emphasize words in the following example:

> ① ② ③ ① ②
> Nightcalls, pratfalls, and jungle shrieks . . . a scattering of wings, a chattering of monkeys and big, yellow eyes in my headlights! ③

Headline, sales letter for Tom Timmins cigars

This letter goes on to tell the story of a search for tobacco in a tropical jungle—in a style that evokes the feeling of the Bogart-Hepburn movie *The African Queen*.

FIGURE 10.5 A Brochure *(continued)*

Outside Panels

were sold, and provided the money for the family's new home. And, most important to Beatrice, money for an <u>education</u>, first in the classroom she had always dreamed about, and later at one of the finest high schools in Uganda.

Today, Beatrice Biira speaks seven languages and dreams of becoming a veterinarian in Uganda, where she can care for the animals that mean so much to her people, and especially for the goats who changed her life forever, thanks to you.

In Honduras

Sometimes, all the hard work in the world doesn't seem to make any difference at all.

In Digna Campos' world, where families typically earn only $250 in an entire year, it didn't seem to matter how much she did.

Waking up at 3 a.m. to prepare the day's food, walking to a nearby coffee plantation to pick beans for two dollars a day and then working long hours after dinner, trying to get their small rented plot of land to yield just a bit more. None of it was enough. Her family's life never improved. And with no education, Digna appeared to have little hope of *making* anything better.

But then Digna received an HPI goat, and every definition of "hope" she had ever known changed.

With milk to drink, given by the goat they

Photos provide visual interest, show a variety of people and goats.

love and help care for, Digna's children have grown strong and healthy. And with money from the sale of extra milk, she was able to buy her own land. Fertilized with goat manure, the land produces enough food to eat *and* sell, and with her newfound income, Digna can afford clothes and medicine, a sturdy new home and, most importantly, school for her children.

"Before, we had no way to care for ourselves, no hope. Now that we have animals, we are much better off."

In Russia *Fourth story is about loneliness, not poverty.*

This is a story about healing, and it happened only because of the generosity of people like you, without whom Kids-2-Kids could not work.

The child who needed to be healed was a 6-year-old Armenian boy named Misha, whose father had been murdered shortly after travelling to Russia in search of work.

Crushed by depression, his mother retreated into her own world and left Misha with no one to help him heal. Four months after his father's death, Misha was barely communicating and never smiled.

(continued)

3. Use Psychological Description

Psychological description (p. 226) means describing your product or service in terms of reader benefits. In a sales letter, you can use psychological description to create a scenario so the reader can picture himself or herself using your product or service and enjoying its benefits. You can also use psychological description to describe the problem your product will solve.

A *Bon Appétit* subscription letter uses psychological description in its opener and in the P.S., creating a frame for the sales letter:

Dear Reader:

First, fill a pitcher with ice.

Now pour in a bottle of ordinary red wine, a quarter cup of brandy, and a small bottle of Club soda.

Sweeten to taste with a quarter to half cup of sugar, garnish with slices of apple, lemon, and orange. . . .

. . . then *move your chair to a warm, sunny spot.* You've just made yourself Sangria—one of the great glories of Spain, and the perfect thing to sit back with and sip while you consider this invitation. . . .

P.S. One more thing before you finish your Sangria. . . .

Ethics and Direct Mail, II

Direct mail letters are rarely written by the people who sign the letter. Al Gore and George W. Bush probably didn't actually draft the fund-raising letters you received. And their signatures were printed, not personally signed.

Sometimes, to create the effect of personal letters, direct mail includes a typo or two.

And one company specializes in producing handwritten letters: letters written by real people (but people whose only connection with the product or cause is that they're being paid as scribes).

Each of these practices is, strictly speaking, misleading. I would argue, however, that these tactics are acceptable. Savvy consumers know that actors and actresses in TV ads are being paid to enthuse about the product. Similarly, ghostwriters (and signers) in direct mail seem acceptable.

*Paragraph 3 based on Bethany McLean, "The Lost Art of Writing Meets the Black Art of Direct Mail," *Fortune*, February 5, 1996, 36.

FIGURE 10.5   A Brochure *(concluded)*

It's hard to imagine any reader really stopping to follow the recipe before finishing the letter, but the scenario is so vivid that one can imagine the sunshine even on a cold, gray day.

4. Make Your Letter Sound Like a Letter, Not an Ad.

Maintain the image of one person writing to one other person that is the foundation of all letters. Use an informal style with short words and sentences, and even slang.

You can also create **a persona**—the character who allegedly writes the letter—to make the letter interesting and keep us reading. Use the rhythms of speech, vivid images, and conversational words to create the effect that the author is a "character."

The following opening creates a persona who fits the product:

> Dear Friend:
>
> There's no use trying. I've tried and tried to tell people about my fish. But I wasn't rigged out to be a letter writer, and I can't do it. I can close-haul a sail with the best of them. I know how to pick out the best fish of the catch, I know just which fish will make the tastiest mouthfuls, but I'll never learn the knack of writing a letter that will tell people why my kind of fish—fresh-caught prime-grades, right off the fishing boats with the deep-sea tang still in it—is lots better than the ordinary store kind.

Sales letter, Frank Davis Fish Company

This letter, with its "Aw, shucks, I can't sell" persona, with language designed to make you see an unassuming fisherman ("rigged out," "close-haul"), was written by a professional advertiser.[10]

Parts of a Direct Mail Package

The letter is the most important part of a **direct mail package,** but several other parts help accomplish your purpose. The package includes the outer envelope and everything that goes in it: the main letter, brochures, samples, secondary letters, reply card, and the reply envelope.

The **envelope** can do more than simply protect the contents during mailing. One test found that an envelope marked "OPEN NOW" produced an 18% higher response rate than a plain envelope (the rest of the package parts were identical). Words on the envelope are called **teaser copy.** Like openers, teasers must get the reader's attention and have some logical link to the body of the letter.

Brochures give more information about the product or organization and, especially if they have color pictures, can involve the sense of sight and contribute to the package's emotional appeal. Magazines and products relating to food, decorating, scenery, gardening, sports, and history seem especially to lend themselves to good brochures, but you can use a brochure in almost any package.

Samples give the reader something to touch and may help sell your product. Swatches of cloth enable readers to check color and quality of the clothing you're selling; a small packet of seeds may motivate readers to order your book on gardening; a scratch-and-sniff card can help sell perfume or scented soap.

Many packages contain **secondary letters:** letters on small paper to readers who have decided not to accept the offer, letters from people who have benefited from the charity in the past, letters from recognized people corroborating the claims made in the main letter.

The **reply card** can be a separate card, a tear-off stub of the letter or brochure, or even the (large) inside flap of the reply envelope. Make the card easy to fill out. A good reply card not only has space for the reader to fill in mailing and ordering information but also repeats information from the letter such as the central selling point, basic product information, and price. Information from the letter is repeated because readers who plan to order or donate may throw away the letter and just keep the reply card.

If readers will be sending in checks, a separate **reply envelope** is necessary. In sales packages, the postage is normally paid. In fund-raising appeals, even if the postage is paid, the letter often invites the reader to affix a stamp, so that more of the organization's money can go to the cause. A postage-paid reply card, with no envelope, is possible if you are just asking for inquiries or if only credit sales are possible, but be careful—some readers prefer not to make their requests or their credit card numbers public.

Summary of Key Points

- Calling direct mail "junk mail" may cause us to respond to the symbol rather than to the reality.
- The first three steps in writing a sales or fund-raising letter are to (1) learn about the product or service, (2) choose and analyze the target audience, and (3) choose a central selling point. The **target audience** is the group of people one expects to be interested in the product, service, or cause. A **central selling point** is a reader benefit that by itself motivates your readers to act and covers all the other benefits.

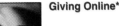

Giving Online*

According to the Mellman Group, more than 16 million Internet users say that they are willing to make a donation to charity online, while only about 12 million people currently respond to direct-mail solicitations from charities. The average age of direct-mail donors is 66, while the average age of online donors is 42. Finally, whereas an overwhelming majority of direct-mail donors describe themselves as liberal, potential online donors represent a wide range of ideologies.

Whatever their politics, potential Web donors are more skeptical and more demanding than traditional givers. They're more inclined to seek information about the charities they support and to insist on accountability regarding how their money is spent.

*Quoted from Tony Schwarz, "There Is a Disturbing Imbalance Today between Giving and Getting," *Fast Company*, August 2000, 228.

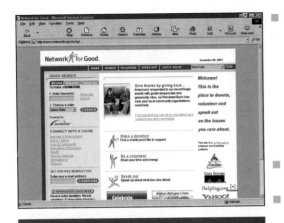

InSite

www.networkforgood.org

The Network for Good provides information about charities. Links let you donate online or find volunteer opportunities in your area.

- A good **star** (opener) makes readers want to read the letter and provides a reasonable transition to the body of the letter. Four modes for openers are questions, narration, startling statements, and quotations. A good **chain** (body) answers readers' questions, overcomes their objections, and involves them emotionally. A good **knot** (action close) tells readers what to do, makes the action sound easy, gives them a reason for acting promptly, and ends with a reader benefit or a picture of the reader's money helping to solve the problem.

- Specify price in the last fourth of a sales letter, after you've given your evidence and made the reader *want* the product.

- In a fund-raising letter, the basic strategy is vicarious participation. By donating money, readers participate vicariously in work they are not able to do personally.

- The primary purpose in a fund-raising letter is to get money. An important secondary purpose is to build support for the cause so that readers who are not persuaded to give will still have favorable attitudes toward the group and will be sympathetic when they hear about it again.

- The body of a fund-raising letter must prove that (1) the problem deserves the reader's attention, (2) the problem can be solved or at least alleviated, (3) your organization is helping to solve it, (4) private funds are needed, and (5) your organization will use the funds wisely.

- To increase the size of gifts, suggest amounts in descending order; ask for gifts slightly higher than the normal cut-off points; link the gift to what it will buy; offer a premium for giving; and ask for a monthly pledge.

- **Contact letters** keep in touch with customers or donors.

- Brochures can build general support for an organization or candidate, give specific information, or even have a reply coupon that readers can return.

- Good writing in direct mail is interesting. It uses sound patterns to emphasize words, uses psychological description, and is specific and conversational.

- A **direct mail package** includes the outer envelope and everything that goes in it: the main letter, brochures, samples, secondary letters, reply card, and the reply envelope.

CHAPTER 10   Exercises and Problems

Getting Started

10.1   Evaluating Envelope Teasers

In the following examples, the words in square brackets describe the appearance of the envelope or lettering. The name in parentheses is from the return address. If no name is listed, either the return address is a street address only or there is no return address. Unless otherwise noted, the teaser copy appeared on the front (address side) of the envelope.

Would you open the envelope? Why or why not? Do others in the class agree?

1. (National Glaucoma Research) [In blue handwriting above the address window]

    I didn't want to bother you over the phone.

    I hope I made the right decision.

2. (UNICEF) [Oversize 6-by-9-inch envelope. To the right of the address window, a child's color picture of three children. Below the address window, in blue type]

How good would it feel to know that a piece of your monthly phone bill can now go to children who need it most?

3. [Plain kraft envelope. In a window in the top right-hand corner, three real pennies show through.]

4. (Doctors without Borders. Médecins sans Frontieres) [In large red type to the right of the address window]

   The Enclosed Bracelet

   Is Not a Toy . . .

5. [Large 9-by-12-inch light gray envelope]

   The General figured he had nothing to lose.

When the brash young man who'd never held a pistol in his life boasted that he could cut training time IN HALF for the United States Army's pistol-shooting program, the General smiled.

When he vowed that he would raise its success rate at the same time, the General laughed.

But when the man insisted that he wouldn't take a penny in payment unless he was 100% successful, the General said, "You're on!"

Using the very same techniques that would make him a millionaire before his 29th birthday

[*continued inside*]

10.2   Evaluating P.S.'s

Evaluate the following P.S.'s. Will they motivate readers to read the whole letter if readers turn to them first? Do they create a strong ending for those who have already read the letter?

1. P.S. It only takes <u>one</u> night's stay in a hotel you read about here, <u>one</u> discounted flight, <u>one</u> budget-priced cruise, or <u>one</u> low-cost car rental to make mailing back your Subscription Certificate well worth it.

   P.P.S. About your free gift! Your risk-free subscription to CONSUMER REPORTS TRAVEL LETTER comes with a remarkable 314-page book as a FREE GIFT.

2. P.S. Help spread the tolerance message by using your personalized address labels on all your correspondence. And remember, you will receive a free *Teaching Tolerance* magazine right after your tax-deductible contribution arrives.

3. P.S. Every day brings more requests like that of Mr. Agyrey-Kwakey—for our "miracle seeds."

And it's urgent that we respond to the emergency in Malaysia and Indonesia by replanting those forests destroyed by fire. Please send <u>your gift today</u> and become a partner with us in these innovative projects around the world.

4. P.S. Your FREE GIFT, <u>Editor's Choice Video Clips</u>, is a CD-ROM collection of 250 high-quality AVI videos with sound. You can put these clips on your site with Emblaze VideoPro . . . or just have fun with them. You get action footage of people at work and at play . . . beautiful nature scenes . . . famous places around the world . . . and many other subjects. <u>Editor's Choice Video Clips</u> is worth $99, but it's yours to keep FREE—even if you decide to return Emblaze VideoPro.

5. P.S. Even as you read this letter, a donated load of food waits for the ticket that will move it to America's hungry. Please give today!

10.3   Evaluating Sales and Fund-Raising Letters

Collect the sales and fund-raising letters that come to you, your co-workers, landlord, neighbors, or family. Use the following questions to evaluate each package:

- What mode does the opener use? Is it related to the teaser, if any? Is it related to the rest of the letter? How good is the opener?

- What central selling point or common ground does the letter use?

- What kinds of proof does the letter use? Is the logic valid? What questions or objections are not answered?

- How does the letter create emotional appeal?

- Is the style effective? Where does the letter use sound to emphasize points?

- Does the close tell readers what to do, make action easy, give a reason for acting promptly, and end with a positive picture?

- Does the letter use a P.S.? How good is it?

- Is the letter visually attractive? Why or why not?

- What other items besides the letter are in the package?

As Your Instructor Directs,

a. Share your analysis of one or more letters with a small group of your classmates.

b. Analyze one letter in a presentation to the class. Make overhead transparencies or photocopies of the letter to use as a visual aid in your presentation.

c. Analyze one letter in a memo to your instructor. Provide a copy or photocopy of the letter along with your memo.

d. With several other students, write a group memo or report analyzing one part of the letter (e.g., openers) or one kind of letter (e.g., political letters, organizations fighting hunger, etc.). Use at least 10 letters for your analysis if you look at only one part; use at least 6 letters if you analyze one kind of letter. Provide copies or photocopies as an appendix to your report.

10.4   Brainstorming Openers for a Magazine Subscription Letter

a. Using at least **two** of the four different modes—question, narration, startling statement, and quotation—write **three** possible openers for a letter urging readers to subscribe to a magazine (you pick the magazine).

b. For each opener indicate (1) what mode it uses and (2) how you would make a transition to the body of the letter. (You may write out the transition or just describe it, whichever is easier.)

c. Rate the three openers in terms of their effectiveness, and briefly explain the reason for your ratings.

10.5   Evaluating Opener Drafts

The following are the results of a session brainstorming openers for a letter raising funds for a college that has suffered budget cuts. Suggest ways to improve each opener. Which seems the most promising? Why?

1. Do you realize that there are students who are getting a poorer education than you got from the same program you attended?

2. We are in danger of losing our accreditation.

3. Engineering students using dial calipers of only $\frac{1}{10}$ the accuracy needed . . . canceled library subscriptions . . . bigger classes . . . closed courses . . . obsolete equipment. . . . Budget cuts have made it harder for XYZ students to get a good education.

E-Mail Messages

10.6   Raising Money at the Office

A charity you support needs funds.

As Your Instructor Directs,

a. Write an e-mail message to your boss, to find out if it's OK to post fund-raising messages to the entire workforce.

b. Write a fund-raising e-mail message to everyone at your workplace. Be sure to tell where to send cash or checks.

Hints:

■ What's the office culture? Does it support volunteer work for and donations to charities?

■ How much are people at your workplace likely to know about the organization? What attitudes toward it are they likely to have?

■ Do people routinely post nonwork messages on the company e-mail system? If so, how will you differentiate your message from the clutter? In any case, how can you minimize negative feelings from people who don't like nonwork messages?

10.7   Selling Baked Goods at the Office

Your co-workers really appreciate the baked goods you occasionally bring in for office treats. (You may assume that you're the baker or that the baker is your partner, spouse, child, or parent.) Now the baker is planning to start a formal business, called Great Goodies. In addition to putting up posters on the bulletin board designated for nonwork announcements and telling the people you see, you want to announce the venture more widely. And you'd like to send messages to people who've enjoyed the goodies in the past, urging them to consider these goodies for upcoming events.

As Your Instructor Directs,

a. Write an e-mail message to your boss explaining what you're doing. Ask if it's OK to suggest that the organization buy from Great Goodies when it buys sweet rolls or other treats for meetings and receptions. If it is OK, whom do you write to? How could you find out whom to ask?

b. Think of a message that would be appropriate for each month (e.g., December could be Hanukkah, Christmas, Kwanzaa, or finals support). Write messages for three months, urging people to order appropriate treats from Great Goodies.

10.8   Answering an Ethics Question

You're a senior staffer in a charitable organization. Today, you get this message from your boss:

> Subject: Using "Handwritten" Messages
>
> I'd like your feedback on the suggestion from our direct mail consultant to use a mailing with handwritten notes. I understand the argument that this will increase response. But the idea of hiring people who don't have any relation to us to write notes—and implying that the notes are by loyal donors—seems unethical. And frankly, I worry about the image we'd create if our real donors learned that we'd done this.
>
> What do you think?

As Your Instructor Directs,

a.   Answer the question, using a charitable organization that you know something about.

b.   Answer the question, assuming that it comes from a congressional candidate.

c.   Answer the question, assuming that the strategy has been recommended for a sales rather than for a fund-raising letter.

d.   Write an e-mail message to your instructor, justifying your answer.

Web Pages

10.9   Creating a Web Page

The World Wide Web enables individuals and companies to sell products and services and organizations, causes, and candidates to raise funds. The cost can be much lower than other forms of marketing, and, because the consumer chooses to go to the page, Web pages may create a more positive response than other forms of marketing.

Create a Web page to sell a product or service or to raise funds for an organization or candidate. At the top of the page, catch the reader's attention, so that he or she is motivated to scroll down. Provide both a "snail mail" address to which funds can be sent and a form on which people can buy or contribute online by entering their credit card numbers. At the bottom of the page, put the creation/update date and your name and e-mail address.

As Your Instructor Directs,

a.   Turn in two laser copies of your page(s). On another page, give the URLs for any links.

b.   Turn in one laser copy of your page(s) and a disk with the HTML code and .gif files.

c.   Write a memo to your instructor (1) identifying the audience for which the page is designed and explaining (2) the search strategies you used to find material on this topic, (3) why you chose the information you've included, and (4) why you chose the layout and graphics you've used.

d.   Present your page orally to the class.

Hints:

- Pick a product, service, candidate, or organization you know something about.
- If you have a lot of information, divide it into several pages.
- Interest readers so that they stay with your page(s) as long as possible.
- Use links to pages sponsored by other organizations only if they support your purposes.
- Offer a reason for people to return to the page after their initial visit.

Letter and Brochure Assignments

10.10 Writing a Magazine Subscription Letter

Write a 2½- to 4-page letter persuading **new subscribers** to subscribe to a magazine of your choice. Assume that your letter would have a reply card and postage-paid envelope. You do NOT have to write these, but DO refer to them in your letter.

Choose a magazine you read or one that deals with a subject or sport you know something about. You may choose a narrower target audience for this letter than the magazine uses. For example, if the magazine is designed to appeal to women ages 18–35, for this assignment you could write to college women, ages 18–25. If you narrow the target audience, be sure to tell your instructor.

Hints:

■ Read several issues of the magazine, looking both at editorial content and at ads, to identify the magazine's target audience. Choose a central selling point that will appeal to that audience.

■ Pay special attention to language. To keep your letter moving quickly, consider occasionally using sentence fragments or ellipses. Try to choose vivid, evocative language; try your hand at alliteration or other repetitive patterns.

■ Everyone has had the experience of seeing interesting headlines on a magazine cover but then being disappointed by the stories inside. Be sure to prove your claims by giving examples and specifics. You may use material from previous issues of the magazine; you may need to edit or rewrite it for maximum effect. Choose details that will interest your reader.

■ Get current figures about subscription rates from the magazine itself. It's OK to offer a free issue, a premium, or a discount, but do not depend on the offer alone to motivate people. Your letter must be fully persuasive even without the special premium.

10.11 Writing a Contact Letter

Write a contact letter to go to customers, clients, or donors.

10.12 Creating a Brochure

Create a brochure for a campus group or a nonprofit organization. Turn in two copies of your brochure and a memo to your instructor explaining your choices for strategy, content, and design. Would this brochure be part of a series? What are the purposes of the brochure? Who are the audiences? Where will the brochure be phys-

ically available? Why did you choose your central selling point? Why did you choose to be more or less formal, more or less complete, and so forth? Explain your choices for strategy, content, wording, layout, visuals (if any), and color (if any).

10.13 Writing a Fund-Raising Letter

Write a 2½- to 4-page letter to raise money from **new donors** for an organization you support. You must use a real organization, but it does not actually have to be conducting a fund-raising drive now. Assume that your letter would have a reply card and postage-paid envelope. You do NOT have to write these, but DO refer to them in your letter.

Options for organizations include

■ Tax-deductible charitable organizations—churches; synagogues; hospitals; groups working to feed, clothe, and house poor people.

■ Lobbying groups—Mothers Against Drunk Driving, the National Abortion Rights Action League, the National Rifle Association, groups working against nuclear weapons, etc.

■ Groups raising money to fight a disease or fund research.

■ Colleges trying to raise money for endowments, buildings, scholarships, faculty salaries.

■ Athletic associations raising money for scholarships, equipment, buildings, facilities.

For this assignment, you may also use groups which do not regularly have fund-raising drives but which may have special needs. Perhaps a school needs new uniforms for its band or an automatic timing device for its swimming pool. Perhaps a sorority or fraternity house needs repairs, remodeling, or expansion.

10.14   Writing a Fund-Raising Letter for a Political Candidate

One of the problems in running for office is financing the campaign. Direct mail is a primary means of raising money. A letter can give far more information about a candidate's views than a TV or radio spot; unlike those media, it can target a specific group of voters. For presidential elections, direct mail is essential: candidates must demonstrate national support to qualify for federal matching funds.

Choose a real candidate and write a letter to raise funds for him or her. Use real information about the candidate's positions and the issues in the race. Let readers know ways to help the campaign instead of or in addition to giving money. Assume that your letter would have a reply card and postage-paid envelope. You do NOT have to write these, but DO refer to them in your letter.

Choose a target audience that would be likely to support this candidate. In a memo to your instructor, describe the audience and explain your decision to personalize or not to personalize the letter with the name and address of a specific voter.

Hints:

- Read newspapers and pick up the candidate's literature to find out where the candidate stands on the issues. The League of Women Voters can help you find each candidate's headquarters.
- Talk to some of the people who live in the district to see what their concerns are. Read material from other candidates so you'll know what you have to combat.

10.15   Attracting People to Your State, Province, or Country

Create a brochure or letter to attract people to your state, province, or country. Rather than trying to cover an entire state, province, or country, you may want to focus on one region, city, or tourist attraction. Possible audiences and purposes include the following:

a. Persuade people with high-tech skills to work in your state, province, or country.

b. Persuade growing businesses to move to your state, province, or country.

c. Persuade movie and TV producers to film in your state, province, or country.

d. Persuade retirees to move to your state, province, or country.

e. Persuade travelers to vacation in your state, province, or country.

Interpersonal Communication

11

Communicating across Cultures

Communicating across Cultures

Stefania Pinton
Director, International Training and Development, Bata

Stefania Pinton coordinates and supports the efforts of Bata companies worldwide in selecting, training, and relocating people for international assignments. Bata, a multinational company headquartered in Toronto, operates in 42 countries and is the world's largest manufacturer and marketer of footwear.

www.bata.com

Currently, 80% of our General Managers—the people responsible for running our operations around the world—are expatriates. These individuals have worked in an average of six different countries on different continents in 10–20 years. The same is true of many other senior employees. I became an expatriate myself in 1995 when I moved from Italy, my country of origin, to the Bata Limited international offices here in Canada. Communicating with managers from all over the world is a daily reality for me.

Our management development program, Elixir Vitae, identifies bright, highly motivated, well-educated individuals with an international mindset and education. We put them in a fast-track 12- to 14-month intensive training program and place them in a country of their choice. Our future expatriates visit and work in the host country two or three months before they and their families actually move there to get information about the country, the company environment, and the future job. They are our Bata international managers of the future.

In *The Seven Habits of Highly Effective People*, Stephen R. Covey argues that all our interactions are colored by the amount of *courage* we have to display our feelings and convictions and the amount of *consideration* we have for the feelings and convictions of others. Win/win situations/transactions/international business communication occur only when we adopt a paradigm of both high courage and high consideration. We want such people for international assignments: someone who knows how to demonstrate his/her culture's positive characteristics, but who also knows how to speak positively of the strengths of the other culture, who has the skills to bridge cultural gaps once he/she encounters them, and who knows how to understand and appreciate (or at least accept) differences.

Achieving cultural competence requires more than just memorizing a list of facts about a specific country or learning its language—important though these are. Cultural competence requires learning to expect differences and having a positive attitude toward challenges and change.

> "*Cultural competence requires learning to expect differences and having a positive attitude toward challenges and change.*"

Mission Statement*

Our values, priorities, and practices are shaped by the culture in which we grow up. Understanding other cultures is crucial if you want to sell your products in other countries, manage an international plant or office, or work in this country for a multinational company headquartered in another country.

As Brenda Arbeláez suggests, the successful international communicator is

- Aware that his or her preferred values and behaviors are influenced by culture and are not necessarily "right."
- Flexible and open to change.
- Sensitive to verbal and nonverbal behavior.
- Aware of the values, beliefs, and practices in other cultures.
- Sensitive to differences among individuals within a culture.[1]

The first step in understanding another culture is to realize that it may do things very differently, and that the difference is not bad or inferior. But people within a single culture differ. The kinds of differences summarized in this chapter can turn into stereotypes, which can be just as damaging as ignorance. Don't try to memorize the material here as a rigid set of rules. Instead, use the examples to get a sense for the kinds of things that differ from one culture to another. Test these generalizations against your experience. When in doubt, ask.

The Importance of Global Business

As we saw in Chapter 1, exports are essential both to the success of individual businesses and to a country's economy as a whole. Less technologically advanced countries may offer special opportunities for businesses in mature markets in the United States. Otis Elevator's largest market is in China.[2]

BusinessWeek reports that two-thirds of all industries either already operate globally or are in the process of doing so. An increasing share of profits comes from outside the headquarters country. Michelin earns 35% of its profits in the United States. McDonald's earns more than 62% of its income outside the United States, and almost 98% of Nokia's sales are outside its home country, Finland. In a global economy, good ideas don't have to come from headquarters. Chipmaker ST Microelectronics' Malaysian plant—not its headquarters in Europe—found a way to cut the assembly time for certain chips from five days to five hours. Now the company is transferring the technique to its Moroccan plant as well.[3]

For links to statistics on international business, see the BAC Web site.

The web of international business is not confined to exports and imports. Many companies—even service businesses—depend on vendors or operations in other countries. More software is written in Ireland than anywhere else in the world. General Electric Capital's customer service calls are answered by 1,000 English-speaking Indian employees in New Delhi 24 hours a day, seven days a week. Workers respond to customer service e-mails for Compaq and Palm Pilot from offices in Madras, India.[4]

For executives in global companies, international experience is often essential for career advancement. At Tupperware, each of the nine members of the executive committee speaks two to four languages and has worked outside his or her home country.[5] Robert Staley, Vice Chairman of Emerson Electric, says,

> If you want to be a senior manager in this company 20 years from now, you'd better get some experience in Asia.[6]

Diversity in the United States and Canada

Even if you stay in the United States and Canada, you'll work with people whose backgrounds differ from yours. Residents of small towns and rural areas have different notions of friendliness than do people from big cities. Californians may talk and dress differently than people in the Midwest. The cultural icons that resonate for baby boomers may mean little to members of Generation Ñ.

The last 15 years have seen a growing emphasis on diversity, with the "news" that more and more women and people of color are joining the US workforce.[7] But people outside the power structure have always worked. In the past, such people (including non-elite white males) may have been relegated to low-status and low-paying jobs, to agricultural or domestic work, or to staff rather than line work and management.

"Diversity" in the workplace comes from many sources:

- Gender.
- Race and ethnicity.
- Regional and national origin.
- Social class.
- Religion.
- Age.
- Sexual orientation.
- Physical ability.

Many young Americans are already multicultural. According to US census figures, a third of Americans aged 17 to 27 are African American, Latino, Asian, or Native American.[8] One study showed that 80% of teens have a close friend of another race.[9]

Bilingual Canada has long compared the diversity of its people to a mosaic. But now immigrants from Italy, Greece, and Hong Kong add their voices to the medley of French, English, and Inuit. Radio station CHIN in Toronto broadcasts in 32 languages.[10] In the 2000 US census, 2.4% of the population—about 6.8 million people—idenitified themselves as belonging to more than one race. US Census figures released in 2001 show that 17.6% of the population nationally and 39.5% in California speak a language other than English at home.[11] Employees at 3Com Corporation's modern factory in Chicago come from 65 countries and speak more than 20 languages.[12] Workers are religiously diverse as well, celebrating Muslim, Hindu, and Vietnamese holidays, to name only a few.[13]

Ways to Look at Culture

Each of us grows up in a **culture** that provides patterns of acceptable behavior and belief. We may not be aware of the most basic features of our own culture until we come into contact with people who do things differently. If we come from a culture where dogs are pets, that interpretation may seem "natural" until we learn that in other cultures, dogs, like chickens, are raised for food.

We can categorize cultures as high-context or low-context. In **high-context cultures,** most of the information is inferred from the context of a message; little is explicitly conveyed. Japanese, Arabic, and Latin American cultures are high-context. In **low-context cultures,** context is less important; most information is explicitly spelled out. German, Scandinavian, and North American cultures are low-context.

As David Victor points out, high- and low-context cultures value different kinds of communication and have different attitudes toward oral and written channels (◄ p. 63).[14] As Figure 11.1 shows, low-context cultures like those of the United States favor direct approaches and may see indirectness as dishonest or manipulative. The written word is seen as more important than oral statements, so contracts are binding but promises may be broken. Details matter. Business communication practices in the United States reflect these low-context preferences.

We Are Family*

Who is in your family? Middle-class baby boomers limit "family" to people joined by blood or marriage. Younger whites and people of color have a much more extended sense of family.

Generation Xers include step-parents, adopted and half-siblings, close friends, and live-in lovers.

For US African Americans, "family" may embrace "play kin," the children one played with regularly as a child, and their families. "Family" includes the people who raised one, who may be no blood relationship at all but simply friends who helped out when times were tough.

Similarly, in Hispanic cultures, "family" includes not only people related by blood or marriage but also godparents and the especially close relationship known as the *compadre.*

US businesses normally grant leaves for family emergencies. But the size and extent of the "family" will differ among different subcultures.

*Based on Karen Ritchie, "Marketing to Generation X," *American Demographics*, April 1995, 36; Deneen Shepherd, conversation with the author, July 29, 1993; and H. Ned Seelye and Alan Seelye-James, *Culture Clash* (Lincolnwood, IL: NTC Business Books, 1995), 108–9.

FIGURE 11.1   Views of Communication in High- and Low-Context Cultures

	High-context (Examples: Japan, United Arab Emirates)	Low-context (Examples: Germany, North America)
Preferred communication strategy	Indirectness, politeness, ambiguity	Directness, confrontation, clarity
Reliance on words to communicate	Low	High
Reliance on nonverbal signs to communicate	High	Low
Importance of written word	Low	High
Agreements made in writing	Not binding	Binding
Agreements made orally	Binding	Not binding
Attention to detail	Low	High

Source: Adapted from David A. Victor, *International Business Communication* (New York: HarperCollins, 1992), 148, 153, 160.

The discussion that follows focuses on national and regional cultures. But business communication is also influenced by the organizational culture and by personal culture, such as gender, race and ethnicity, social class, and so forth. As Figure 11.2 suggests, all of these intersect to determine what kind of communication is needed in a given situation. Sometimes one kind of culture may be more important than another. For example, in a study of aerospace engineers in Europe, Asia, and the United States, researchers John Webb and Michael Keene found that the similarities of the professional discourse community outweighed differences in national cultures.[15]

Values, Beliefs, and Practices

Values and beliefs, often unconscious, affect our response to people and situations. Most North Americans, for example, value "fairness." "You're not playing fair" is a sharp criticism calling for changed behavior. In some countries, however, people expect certain groups to receive preferential treatment. Most North Americans accept competition and believe that it produces better performance. The Japanese, however, believe that competition leads to disharmony. US business people believe that success is based on individual achievement and is open to anyone who excels. In England and in France, success is

FIGURE 11.2   National Culture, Organizational Culture, and Personal Culture Overlap

more obviously linked to social class. And in some countries, people of some castes or races are prohibited by law from full participation in society.

Many people in the United States value individualism. Other countries may value the group. In traditional classrooms, US students are expected to complete assignments alone; if they get much help from anyone else, they're "cheating." In Japan, in contrast, groups routinely work together to solve problems. In US white culture, quiet is a sign that people are working. In Japan people talk to get the work done.[16]

Values and beliefs are influenced by religion. Christianity coexists with a view of the individual as proactive. In some Muslim and Asian countries, however, it is seen as presumptuous to predict the future by promising action by a certain date. The Protestant work ethic legitimizes wealth by seeing it as a sign of divine favor. In other Christian cultures, a simpler lifestyle is considered to be closer to God.

Religion affects what foods may be eaten and on what days businesses are open. For example, Hindus do not eat beef; Muslims consider pork unclean; orthodox Jews eat only kosher meats. In many Muslim countries, Friday, a day of prayer, is an official holiday. During the ninth month of the Muslim lunar calendar, a devout Muslim may be on a pilgrimage to Mecca. An ordinary business day may be a holiday in the country you're visiting. A sampling of international holidays appears in Figure 11.3.

Even everyday practices differ from culture to culture. North Americans and Europeans put the family name last; Asians put it first. North American and European printing moves from top to bottom and from left to right; Arabic reads from right to left, but still from top to bottom. An American carpenter pushes a saw; a Japanese pulls it. Light switches and door knobs turn opposite ways in Japan and in the United States.[17]

Values are more pervasive than we sometimes realize. A US manager whose company was owned by the Japanese was asked to estimate the US sales potential for a piece of construction equipment that is widely used in Japan. The

Observing Ramadan*

[Some US companies are making] it easier for workers who observe the Islamic holy month, which requires Muslims to abstain from food, water, cigarettes and sex during daylight hours. Fort Bragg, N.C., excuses its 165 Muslim soldiers from physical training. Alaa Shoreibah, a financial analyst at American International Health Alliance, Washington, D.C., arrives at work an hour ahead of schedule so he can be home to break his fast at sundown.

With an estimated five million Muslims in the U.S. and their numbers growing, Ramadan is becoming a more common issue for employers. . . .

Houston Rockets basketball star Hakeem Olajuwon can't drink water even during day games. "The thing is to control your desire," he tells reporters.

*Quoted from Carl Quintanilla, "Work Week," *The Wall Street Journal,* February 4, 1997, A1.

Living and working in another country require being sensitive to religious beliefs and practices. Here, thousands of Muslims in India gather to attend a prayer service marking the last day of Islam's holy month of Ramadan.

FIGURE 11.3   A Sampling of International Holidays

Holiday	Date	Celebrated in	Commemorates
Chinese New Year (Spring Festival)	January or February (date varies)	Countries with Chinese residents	Beginning of lunar new year
Independence Day	March 6	Ghana	1957 independence from Great Britain
St. Patrick's Day	March 17	Ireland	Ireland's patron saint
Cinco de Mayo	May 5	Mexico	1867 victory over the French
St. Jean-Baptiste Day	June 24	Québec province of Canada	Québec's national holiday
Canada Day	July 1	Canada	1867 proclamation of Canada's status as dominion
Bastille Day	July 14	France	1789 fall of the Bastille prison during the French Revolution
Ramadan	Ninth month of lunar year	Countries with Muslim residents	Atonement; fasting from sunup to sundown
Respect for the Aged Day	September 15	Japan	Respect for elderly relatives and friends
Chun Ben	Last week of September	Cambodia, other Buddhist countries	The dead and actions for one's salvation
Diwali	October or November	Countries with Hindu residents	Festival of lights celebrating renewal of life
Guy Fawkes Day	November 5	England	Capture of Guy Fawkes, who plotted to blow up Parliament
Hanukkah	December (dates vary)	Countries with Jewish residents	Rededication of the temple in Jerusalem
Christmas	December 25	Countries with Christian residents	Birth of Jesus
Boxing Day	December 26	British Commonwealth	Tradition of presenting small boxed gifts to service workers

manager believed that the equipment was too small for US construction sites and knew that US builders were happy with the equipment they were using. But smallness is a virtue in crowded Japan, and technological innovation is more important. The manager felt that he had to defer to the values of the parent company in his report. He presented the potential problems of the equipment as mildly as possible and ended his report with a statement that if management decided to sell the equipment in the United States, he would do everything possible to market it. The statement was necessary, the man believed, so that his superiors in Japan would not see him as disloyal and attacking the company.[18]

The Web offers information about almost every country in the world. For links, see the BAC Web site.

Nonverbal Communication

Nonverbal communication—communication that doesn't use words—takes place all the time. Smiles, frowns, who sits where at a meeting, the size of an office, how long someone keeps a visitor waiting—all these communicate pleasure or anger, friendliness or distance, power and status. Most of the time we are no more conscious of interpreting nonverbal signals than we are conscious of breathing.

Yet nonverbal signals can be misinterpreted just as easily as can verbal symbols (words). And the misunderstandings can be harder to clear up because people may not be aware of the nonverbal cues that led them to assume that they aren't liked, respected, or approved. An Arab student assumed that his US roommate disliked him intensely because the US student sat around the room with his feet up on the furniture, soles toward the Arab roommate. Arab culture sees the foot in general and the sole in particular as unclean; showing the sole of the foot is an insult.[19]

Learning about nonverbal language can help us project the image we want to present and make us more aware of the signals we are interpreting. However, even within a single culture, a nonverbal symbol may have more than one meaning.

Body Language

The Japanese value the ability to sit quietly. They may see the US tendency to fidget and shift as an indication of lack of mental or spiritual balance. Even in North America, interviewers and audiences usually respond negatively to nervous gestures such as fidgeting with a tie or hair or jewelry, tapping a pencil, or swinging a foot.

People from different cultures learn to walk differently. Carmen Judith Nine-Curt observes that Caribbean people move the torso as though it was made up of separable parts, while North American Anglos and Northern Spaniards carry the torso as if it were one piece.[20] People from one culture often react negatively to another culture's walk. The French see the American walk as "uncivilized."[21] Anglo Americans sometimes see the way African American men walk as threatening and the way Latinos walk as sexual, although there is no evidence that these walks carry such meanings in the cultures where people have learned them.

Getting an International Assignment*

Eric Rosenkranz, executive VP at Grey Advertising International, has three suggestions for anyone trying to get his or her hands on an international assignment: "First, ask to go along with someone else on an overseas trip and use that chance to demonstrate your ability to perform. Become an expert in that country's language, markets, and political situation. Then go on a vacation to that country and use the time to write a detailed report, with recommendations, on a business opportunity." Doing your homework on, say, Asian customs and mores can also help you avoid breaches of etiquette when you do finally get to work there.

*Quoted from Anne Fisher, "Ask Annie: Overseas, U.S. Businesswomen May Have the Edge," *Fortune*, September 28, 1998, 304.

You've seen the laundry detergent cliché: the stern expert in the white coat rebukes the hapless housewife who has been washing her clothes in "ordinary laundry detergent." Now a Czech firm has started selling Ordinary Laundry Detergent, which comes in a box just like the one in the ads. "They talked about Ordinary Laundry Detergent so much on TV that someone had to manufacture it," says Frantisek Cerny, 26, whose tiny detergent manufacturer, Dedra, quickly sold out of the first run. "The mentality of Czechs," says Cerny, "is that when something is put down, they feel sorry for it and they like it. . . . We don't even have to spend any money on advertising. Our detergent is on TV every night."

Eye contact

North American whites see **eye contact** as a sign of honesty. But in many cultures, dropped eyes are a sign of appropriate deference to a superior. Puerto Rican children are taught not to meet the eyes of adults.[22] The Japanese are taught to look at the neck.[23] In Korea, prolonged eye contact is considered rude. The lower-ranking person is expected to look down first.[24]

Arab men in laboratory experiments looked at each other more than did two American men or two Englishmen.[25] Eye contact is so important that Arabs dislike talking to someone wearing dark glasses or while walking side by side. It is considered impolite not to face someone directly. In Muslim countries, women and men are not supposed to have eye contact.

These differences can lead to miscommunication in the multicultural workplace. Superiors may feel that subordinates are being disrespectful when the subordinate is being fully respectful—according to the norms of his or her culture.

Smiling

In the United States, smiling varies from region to region. Thirty years ago, Ray Birdwhistell found that "middle-class individuals" from Ohio, Indiana, and Illinois smiled more than did people from Massachusetts, New Hampshire, and Maine, who in turn smiled more than did western New Yorkers. People from cities in southern and border states—Atlanta, Louisville, Memphis, and Nashville—smiled most of all.[26] Some scholars speculate that northeasterners may distrust the sincerity of southerners who smile a lot (like former president Jimmy Carter). Students from other countries who come to US universities may be disconcerted by the American tendency to smile at strangers—until they realize that the smiles don't "mean" anything. In Germany, smiles are reserved for friends.[27] The Japanese smile not only when they are pleased or amused but also to say "That's none of your business" and to cover embarrassment, sadness, and even anger.[28]

The Japanese learn to control their emotions. In situations of strong emotion, it is considered acceptable to smile or laugh, but not to frown or cry. In some US businesses, it is considered acceptable to frown, swear, and yell, but not to cry. Yet both "anger" and "crying" may be expressions of the same emotion: frustration at not getting what we want.

Gestures

Americans sometimes assume that they can depend on gestures to communicate if language fails. But Birdwhistell reported that "although we have been searching for 15 years [1950–65], we have found no gesture or body motion which has the same meaning in all societies."[29] In Bulgaria, for example, people may nod their heads to signify *no* and shake their heads to signify *yes*.[30]

Gestures that mean approval in the United States may have very different meanings in other countries. The "thumbs up" sign, which means "good work" or "go ahead" in the United States and most of Western Europe, is a vulgar insult in Greece. The circle formed with the thumb and first finger that means *OK* in the United States is obscene in Southern Italy and can mean "you're worth nothing" in France and Belgium.[31]

In the question period after a lecture, a man asked the speaker, a Puerto Rican professor, if shaking the hands up and down in front of the chest, as though shaking off water, was "a sign of mental retardation." The professor was horrified: in her culture, the gesture meant "excitement, intense thrill."[32] Studies have found that Spanish-speaking doctors rate the mental abilities of Latino patients much higher than do English-speaking doctors. The language barrier is surely part of the misevaluation of English-speaking doctors. Cultural differences in gestures may contribute to the misevaluation. Similarly, Anglo supervisors in the workplace may underestimate the abilities of Hispanics because gestures differ in the two cultures.

Space

Personal space is the distance someone wants between himself or herself and other people in ordinary, nonintimate interchanges. Observation and limited experimentation show that most North Americans, North Europeans, and Asians want a bigger personal space than do Latin Americans, French, Italians, and Arabs. People who prefer lots of personal space are often forced to accept close contact on a crowded elevator or subway.

Even within a culture, some people like more personal space than do others. One US study found that men took more personal space than women did.[33] In many cultures, people who are of the same age and sex take less personal space than do mixed-age or mixed-sex groups. Latin Americans will stand closer to people of the same sex than North Americans would, but North Americans stand closer to people of the opposite sex.[34] Similarly, Laotians of the same sex sit very close together, almost "on top of each other" according to the space norms of the United States. But people of the opposite sex sit at a distance from each other.[35]

Touch

Repeated studies have shown that babies need to be touched to grow and thrive and that older people are healthier both mentally and physically if they are touched. But some people are more comfortable with touch than others. Each kind of person may misinterpret the other. A person who dislikes touch may seem unfriendly to someone who's used to touching. A toucher may seem overly familiar to someone who dislikes touch. Studies in the United States have shown that touch is interpreted as power: more powerful people touch less powerful people. When the toucher had higher status than the recipient, both men and women liked being touched.[36]

Most parts of North America allow opposite-sex couples to hold hands or walk arm-in-arm in public but frown on the same behavior in same-sex couples. People in Asia, the Middle East, South America, and parts of Africa have the opposite expectation: male friends or female friends can hold hands or walk arm-in-arm, but it is slightly shocking for an opposite-sex couple to touch in public.[37]

People who don't know each other well may feel more comfortable with each other if a piece of furniture separates them. For example, a group may work better sitting around a table than just sitting in a circle. In North America, a person sitting at the head of a table is generally assumed to be the group's leader. However, one experiment showed that when a woman sat at the head of a mixed-sex group, observers assumed that one of the men in the group was the leader.[38]

Lecterns and desks can be used as barricades to protect oneself from other people. One professor normally walked among his students as he lectured. But if anyone asked a question he was uncomfortable with, he retreated behind the lectern before answering it.

Spatial arrangements

In the United States, the size, placement, and privacy of one's office connotes status. Large corner offices have the highest status. An individual office with a

In Hong Kong, a Big Mac Is Bread*

[In Hong Kong,] hamburgers are referred to, in colloquial Cantonese, as *han bou bao*—*han* being a homophone for "ham " and *bou* the common term for stuffed buns or bread rolls. *Bao* are quintessential snacks, and however excellent or nutritious they might be, they do not constitute the basis of a satisfying (i.e., filling) meal. In South China that honor is reserved for culinary arrangements that rest, literally, on a bed of rice (*fan*). Foods that accompany rice are referred to as *sung*, probably best translated as "toppings" (including meat, fish, and vegetables). It is significant that hamburgers are rarely categorized as meat (*yuk*); Hong Kong consumers tend to perceive anything that is served between slices of bread (Big Macs, fish sandwiches, hot dogs) as bread. In American culture, the hamburger is categorized first and foremost as a meat item (with all the attendant worries about fat and cholesterol content), whereas in Hong Kong the same item is thought of primarily as bread.

*Quoted from James L. Watson, "McDonald's in Hong Kong: Consumerism, Dietary Change and the Rise of a Children's Culture," in *Golden Arches East: McDonald's in East Asia*, ed. James L. Watson (Stanford: Stanford University Press, 1997), 84–85.

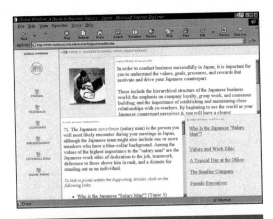

InSite

www.anderson.ucla.edu/research/japan/
mainfrm.htm

Extensive information about many countries is
available on the Web. This site was created by
Professor Archie Kleingartner of UCLA's Anderson
School of Management in collaboration with Meikai
and Asahi Universities in Japan. It has extensive
information about Japanese practices, laws, and
culture and has won several prestigious awards.

door that closes connotes more status than a desk in a common
area. Japanese firms, however, see private offices as "inappropriate and inefficient," reports Robert Christopher. Only the
very highest executives and directors have private offices in
the traditional Japanese company, and even they will also have
desks in the common areas.[39]

Time

Differences in time zones complicate international phone calls.
But even more important are different views of time and attitudes toward time.

Organizations in the United States—businesses, government, and schools—keep time by the calendar and the clock.
Being "on time" is seen as a sign of dependability. Other cultures may keep time by the seasons and the moon, the sun, internal "body clocks," or a personal feeling that "the time is
right."

North Americans who believe that "time is money" are often frustrated in negotiations with people who take a much
more leisurely approach. Part of the problem is that people in
many other cultures want to establish a personal relationship
before they decide whether to do business with each other.

The problem is made worse because various cultures men-
tally measure time differently. Many North Americans measure time in five-
minute blocks. Someone who's five minutes late to an appointment or a job interview feels compelled to apologize. If the executive or interviewer is running
half an hour late, the caller expects to be told about the likely delay upon arriving. Some people won't be able to wait that long and will need to resched-
ule their appointments. But in other cultures, 15 minutes or half an hour may
be the smallest block of time. To someone who mentally measures time in 15-
minute blocks, being 45 minutes late is no worse than being 15 minutes late is
to someone who is conscious of smaller units.

Edward T. Hall points out that different cultures have different lead times. In
some countries, you need to schedule important meetings at least two weeks in
advance. In other countries, not only are people not booked up so far in advance, but a date two weeks into the future may be forgotten. He advises scheduling appointments only three or four days in advance in Arab countries.[40]

Hall also distinguishes between **monochronic cultures,** which focus on
clock time, and **polychronic cultures,** which focus on relationships. When US
managers feel offended because a Latin American manager also sees other people during "their" appointments, the two kinds of time are in conflict.

According to some scholars, Europeans schedule fewer events in a comparable period of time than do North Americans. Perhaps as a result, Germans
and German Swiss see North Americans as too time-conscious.[41]

Other Nonverbal Symbols

Many other symbols can carry nonverbal meanings: clothing, colors, age, and
height, to name a few.

In North America, certain styles and colors of clothing are considered more
"professional" and more "credible." In Japan, clothing denotes not only status
but also occupational group. Students wear uniforms. Company badges indicate rank within the organization. Workers wear different clothes when they
are on strike than they do when they are working.[42]

Colors can also carry meanings in a culture. In the United States, mourners wear black to funerals, while brides wear white. In Japan, white is the color of death. Purple flowers are given to the dead in Mexico. In Korea, red ink is used to record deaths but never to write about living people.[43] In the United States, the first-place winner gets a blue ribbon. In the United Kingdom, the first-place ribbon is usually red.

In the United States, youth is valued. Some men as well as some women color their hair and even have face-lifts to look as youthful as possible. In Japan, younger people defer to older people. Americans attempting to negotiate in Japan are usually taken more seriously if at least one member of the team is noticeably gray-haired.

Height connotes status in many parts of the world. Executive offices are usually on the top floors; the underlings work below. Even being tall can help a person succeed. Studies have shown that employers are more willing to hire men over 6 feet tall than shorter men with the same credentials. Studies of real-world executives and graduates have shown that taller men make more money. In one study, every extra inch of height brought in an extra $1,300 a year.[44] But being too big can be a disadvantage. A tall, brawny football player complained that people found him intimidating off the field and assumed that he "had the brains of a Twinkie."

Oral Communication

Effective oral communication requires cultural understanding. As Figure 11.4 shows, the purpose of and information exchanged in business introductions differs across cultures.

For sites that help you learn foreign languages, see the BAC Web site. Learning at least a little of the language of the country where you hope to do business will help you in several ways. First, learning the language will give you at least a glimpse into the culture. In English, for example, we say that a clock "runs." The French say *"Il marche,"*—literally, "It is walking." Second, learning some of the language will help you manage the daily necessities of finding food and getting where you need to go while you're there. If you know enough, you'll even be able to sightsee and take advantage of the unique opportunities business travel can provide. Finally, in business negotiations, knowing a little of the language gives you more time to think. You'll catch part of the meaning when you hear your counterpart speak; you can begin thinking even before the translation begins.

Understanding the Host Nation*

Many US employees have learned, often through costly mistakes, that the key to successful international business relationships lies in a real understanding of the values, priorities, and practices of the counterparts in the host nation.

For example, to do business in Mexico, you need to develop a personal relationship. Tell me about you as a person. That's very important. Then I tell you about me, and we do this sometimes not just one time but several times. Then I will trust you and I will value your qualities. Then I will like to work with you. So that's the first step. In Mexican values, work is number 2, family is number 1. So if something happens, they take off to be there for their families.

Even within the United States, you can learn about other cultures. You can watch Spanish TV channels and listen to Spanish radio. You can buy tapes and cassettes, you have concerts, you have the Hispanic community growing in every single city. The language is incredible, and the culture is here for you to pick up.

*Quoted from Brenda Arbeláez, statement to Kitty Locker, December 12, 1996.

FIGURE 11.4   Cultural Contrasts in Business Introductions

	United States	**Japan**	**Arab countries**
Purpose of introduction	Establish status and job identity; network	Establish position in group, build harmony	Establish personal rapport
Image of individual	Independent	Member of group	Part of rich culture
Information	Related to business	Related to company	Personal
Use of language	Informal, friendly; use first name	Little talking	Formal; expression of admiration
Values	Openness, directness, action	Harmony, respect, listening	Religious harmony, hospitality, emotional support

Source: Adapted from Farid Elashmawi and Philip R. Harris, *Multicultural Management 2000: Essential Cultural Insights for Global Business Success* (Houston: Gulf, 1998), 113.

If at all possible, take your own translator when you travel abroad on business. Brief him or her with the technical terms you'll be using; explain as much of the context of your negotiations as possible. A good translator can also help you interpret nonverbal behavior and negotiating strategies.

Understatement and Exaggeration

To understand someone from another culture, you must understand the speaker's conversational style. The British have a reputation for understatement. Someone good enough to play at Wimbledon may say he or she "plays a little tennis." Many people in the United States exaggerate. An American businessman negotiating with a German said, "I know it's impossible, but can we do it?" The German saw the statement as nonsensical: by definition, something that is impossible cannot be done. The American saw "impossible" as merely a strong way of saying "difficult" and assumed that with enough resources and commitment, the job could in fact be done.[45]

Compliments

The kinds of statements that people interpret as compliments and the socially correct ways to respond to compliments also vary among cultures. The statement "You must be really tired" is a compliment in Japan since it recognizes the other person has worked hard. The correct response is "Thank you, but I'm OK." An American who is complimented on giving a good oral presentation will probably say "Thank you." A Japanese, in contrast, will apologize: "No, it wasn't very good."[46]

Statements that seem complimentary in one context may be inappropriate in another. For example, women in business are usually uncomfortable if male colleagues or superiors compliment them on their appearance: the comments suggest that the women are being treated as visual decoration rather than as contributing workers.

Silence

Silence also has different meanings in different cultures and subcultures. Muriel Saville-Troike reports that during a period of military tension, Greek traffic controllers responded with silence when Egyptian planes requested permission to land. The Greeks intended silence as a refusal; the Egyptians interpreted silence as consent. Several people were killed when the Greeks fired on the planes as they approached the runway.[47]

Voice Qualities

Tone of voice refers to the rising or falling inflection that tells you whether a group of words is a question or a statement, whether the speaker is uncertain or confident, whether a statement is sincere or sarcastic. Anyone who has written dialog with adverbs ("he said thoughtfully") has tried to indicate tone of voice.

When tone of voice and the meaning of words conflict, people "believe" the tone of voice. Jann Davis reports that one person responded to friends' "How are you?" with the words "Dying, and you?" Most of the friends responded "Fine." Because the tone of voice was cheerful, they didn't hear the content of the words.[48]

Pitch measures whether a voice uses sounds that are low (like the bass notes on a piano) or high. Low-pitched voices are usually perceived as being more authoritative, sexier, and more pleasant to listen to than are high-pitched voices. Most voices go up in pitch when the speaker is angry or excited; some people raise pitch when they increase volume. Women whose normal speaking voices are high may need to practice projecting their voices to avoid becoming shrill when they speak to large groups.

Stress is the emphasis given to one or more words in a sentence. As the following example shows, emphasizing different words can change the meaning.

I'll give you a raise.

[Implication, depending on pitch and speed: "Another supervisor wouldn't" or "I have the power to determine your salary."]

I'll **give** you a raise.

[Implication, depending on pitch and speed: "You haven't **earned** it" or "OK, all right, you win. I'm saying 'yes' to get rid of you, but I don't really agree," or "I've just this instant decided that you deserve a raise."]

I'll give **you** a raise.

[Implication: "But nobody else in this department is getting one."]

I'll give you **a** raise.

[Implication: "But just one."]

I'll give you a **raise.**

[Implication: "But you won't get the promotion or anything else you want."]

I'll give **you** a **raise.**

[Implication: "You deserve it."]

I'll give you a **raise!**

[Implication: "I've just this minute decided to act, and I'm excited about this idea. The raise will please both of us."]

Speakers who use many changes in tone, pitch, and stress as they speak usually seem more enthusiastic; often they also seem more energetic and more intelligent. Someone who speaks in a monotone may seem apathetic or unintelligent. Nonnative speakers whose first language does not use tone, pitch, and stress to convey meaning and attitude may need to practice varying these voice qualities when they give presentations in the United States.

Volume is a measure of loudness or softness. Very soft voices, especially if they are also breathy and high-pitched, give the impression of youth and inexperience. People who do a lot of speaking to large groups need to practice projecting their voices so they can increase their volume without shouting.

In some cultures, it is considered rude to shout; loud voices connote anger and imminent violence. In others, everyday conversations are loud.

Writing to International Audiences

Most cultures are more formal than the United States. When you write to international audiences, use titles, not first names; avoid contractions, slang, and sports metaphors. Do write in English unless you're extremely fluent in your reader's language.

Marcia Sweezey, a manager at Digital Equipment Corporation, offers the following advice for sending e-mail to Japanese recipients.

Silence, Please!*

In Japan, silence can mean "I don't like your idea," but it can also mean "I'm thinking." Knowing this is essential for international negotiators. One American businessman offered an apparatus to a Japanese customer for $100,000. The customer sat quietly. After 10 minutes, the American, who couldn't stand the silence any more, lowered his price $10,000.

Reading this through a US lens, you might think that the Japanese customer was happy and perhaps even used silence deliberately. Not so. In fact, he was deeply disappointed by the poor negotiation. Relationships are far more important than price in Japan. How could someone be so impatient?

*Based on J. M. Ulijn, "How Can a Multicultural Workforce of a Company Successfully Communicate in International Trade?" *Acta Universitatis Wratislaviensis*, No. 1774, 264–65.

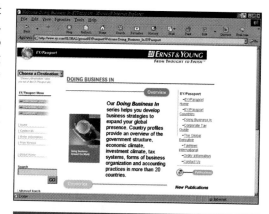

InSite

www.ey.com/GLOBAL/gcr.nsf/EYPassport/ Welcome-Doing_Business_In-EYPassport

Ernst & Young's *Doing Business In* series provides downloadable reports on more than 20 countries.

Translators Needed*

As the number of people speaking languages other than English has grown in Los Angeles, so has the need for translators.

Los Angeles businesses put up signs and flyers in Mandarin, Farsi, and Hebrew. Students and their parents in Cupertino elementary schools speak 52 different languages and 12 dialects. Hebrew, Russian, and Farsi are among the 10 most common. Cornish and Carey Real Estate handles about 40 tongues.

Translators have been called upon to translate courtroom testimony, Japanese operating manuals, and Arabic business contracts.

Translation, as always, works best when the translator knows connotations and context as well as the dictionary meaning of words. George Rimalower, president of Interpreting Services International in Van Nuys, California, reports that one church newsletter turned "our Lord in heaven" into "our guy in the sky."

*Based on Jan Lonsdale, "The Real L.A. Speak," *Los Angeles Times Magazine*, June 13, 1993, 8; and "New Companies Fuel Silicon Valley Boom," *The Wall Street Journal*, October 8, 1996, A12.

1. Be clear, but be adult. Don't write in second-grade English.
2. Use complete sentences.
3. Write "Dear Lastname-san" to begin your e-mail: Dear Abo-san. Use this form of address for both men and women. Also use this form to refer to your peers in a formal memo, such as a memo to that person's manager.
4. Tell your peers how to address you. Peers in Japan may write to you "Dear Smith-san" or "Dear Ellen-san." You may wish to invite them to call you by your first name. (The first time you correspond, let them know if you are a man or a woman so they know whether to use "Mr." or "Ms." when they address you formally.)
5. Be honest, friendly, and relaxed.[49]

The patterns of organization that work for North American audiences may need to be modified in international correspondence. For most cultures, buffer negative messages and make requests more indirect. As Figures 11.5 and 11.6 suggest, the style, structure, and strategies that would motivate a US audience may need to be changed for international readers. Make a special effort to avoid phrases that could seem cold and uncaring. Cultural mistakes made orally float away on the air; those made in writing are permanently recorded.

Business people from Europe and Japan who correspond frequently with North America are beginning to adopt US directness and patterns of organization. If you know that your reader understands North American behavior, you can write just as you would to someone in the United States or Canada. If you don't know your reader well, it may be safer to modify your message slightly.

If you're faxing the message, use at least 12-point type. If the transmission has static or if your message is re-faxed to another reader, the larger type will make it easier to read.

In international business correspondence, list the day before the month:

Not: April 8, 2000

But: 8 April 2000

Spell out the month to avoid confusion. A US professor wrote to the British library to reserve the books he would need for his visit on April 10th. However, he wrote "4/10" and the British assumed he wanted them on October 4th.

FIGURE 11.5   Cultural Contrasts in Written Persuasive Documents

	United States	Japan	Arab countries
Opening	Request action or get reader's attention	Offer thanks; apologize	Offer personal greetings
Way to persuade	Immediate gain or loss of opportunity	Waiting	Personal connections; future opportunity
Style	Short sentences	Modestly, minimize own standing	Elaborate expressions; many signatures
Closing	Specific request	Desire to maintain harmony	Future relationship, personal greeting
Values	Efficiency; directness; action	Politeness; indirectness; relationship	Status; continuation

Source: Adapted from Farid Elashmawi and Philip R. Harris, *Multicultural Management 2000: Essential Cultural Insights for Global Business Success* (Houston: Gulf, 1998), 139.

FIGURE 11.6 Cultural Contrasts in Motivation

	United States	Japan	Arab countries
Emotional appeal	Opportunity	Group participation; company success	Religion; nationalism; admiration
Recognition based on	Individual achievement	Group achievement	Individual status; status of class/society
Material rewards	Salary; bonus; profit sharing	Annual bonus; social services; fringe benefits	Gifts for self/family; salary
Threats	Loss of job	Loss of group membership	Demotion, loss of reputation
Values	Competition; risk taking; freedom	Group harmony; belonging	Reputation; family security; religion

Source: Adapted from Farid Elashmawi and Philip R. Harris, *Multicultural Management 2000: Essential Cultural Insights for Global Business Success* (Houston: Gulf, 1998), 169.

Learning More about International Business Communication

Learning to communicate with people from different backgrounds shouldn't be a matter of learning rules. Instead, use the examples in this chapter to get a sense for the kinds of factors that differ from one culture to another. Test these generalizations against your experience. And when in doubt, ask.

You can deepen your knowledge by reading. Figure 11.7 lists useful sources to check.

You can also learn by seeking out people from other backgrounds and talking with them. Many campuses have centers for international students. Some communities have groups of international business people who meet regularly to discuss their countries. By asking all these people what aspects of the dominant US culture seem strange to them, you'll learn much about what is "right" in their cultures.

FIGURE 11.7 Print Sources for More Information about International Business

Culturgrams, updated annually, offer 4-page overviews of every country in the world. Write or call:

Brigham Young University
The David M. Kennedy Center for International Studies
P.O. Box 24538
Provo, UT 84602-4538
1-800-528-6279

To learn more about a specific country or region, write the embassy for information or consult business magazines and reference books.

- American Society for Quality Control. Assistance in meeting manufacturing standards set by the International Organization for Standardization. 1-800-248-1946.
- Export Legal Assistance Network. Referrals to local attorneys with experience in international trade. 1-202-778-3000.
- Export Opportunity Hot Line. Free information provided by trade experts. Sponsored by the Small Business Foundation of America. 1-800-243-7332. In Washington, DC, call 1-202-223-1104.
- Service Corps of Retired Executives (SCORE). Matches small businesses with one of roughly 500 seasoned exporting counselors. 1-800-634-0245.
- US Commerce Department Hot Line. How to qualify for low tariffs under NAFTA. Free information. 1-800-USA-TRADE.
- US & Foreign Commercial Service. Offices in 68 US cities and in 129 cities in 67 other countries. Offers advice about exports, market research, and sales leads.

Overseas, US Businesswomen May Have the Edge*

[A] growing body of research suggest[s] that American businesswomen abroad may actually enjoy a significant edge over their male counterparts. A study conducted last year by international staffing consultants Cornelius Grove & Associates (www.grovewell.com) concluded that women are often more "nurturing" than men, tend to form close personal connections with colleagues and clients, and are highly respected for it. In China, for example, Cornelius Grove found that a quality called *ren*—which translates loosely as warm-heartedness, benevolence, and a readiness to look out for other people's welfare—is considered essential in business leaders. . . .

"In our interviews with Japanese executives, we find that many of them would much rather work with a woman than a man," [Professor John] Graham writes. Why? "Many American men's conversational style tends toward competitiveness, even aggressiveness, and can get in the way of a free-flowing exchange of information." By contrast, the negotiating style of their female counterparts, emphasizing interpersonal warmth and willingness to listen, [is] much less disconcerting.

*Quoted from Anne Fisher, "Ask Annie: Overseas, U.S. Businesswomen May Have the Edge," *Fortune,* September 28, 1998, 304.

Summary of Key Points

■ **Culture** provides patterns of acceptable behavior and beliefs.

■ The successful intercultural communicator is

   ■ Aware that his or her preferred values and behaviors are influenced by culture and are not necessarily "right."

   ■ Flexible and open to change.

   ■ Sensitive to verbal and nonverbal behavior.

   ■ Aware of the values, beliefs, and practices in other cultures.

   ■ Sensitive to differences among individuals within a culture.

■ In **high-context cultures,** most of the information is inferred from the context of a message; little is explicitly conveyed. In **low-context cultures,** context is less important; most information is explicitly spelled out.

■ **Nonverbal communication** is communication that doesn't use words. Nonverbal communication can include voice qualities, body language, space, time, and other miscellaneous matters such as clothing, colors, and age.

■ Nonverbal signals can be misinterpreted just as easily as can verbal symbols (words).

■ No gesture has a universal meaning across all cultures. Gestures that signify approval in North America may be insults in other countries, and vice versa.

■ **Personal space** is the distance someone wants between him or herself and other people in ordinary, nonintimate interchanges.

■ North Americans who believe that "time is money" are often frustrated in negotiations with people who want to establish a personal relationship before they decide whether to do business with each other or who measure time in 15- or 30-minute increments rather than the 5-minute intervals North Americans are used to.

■ In **monochronic** cultures, people focus on clock time. The United States is monochronic. In **polychronic** cultures, people focus on relationships.

■ The patterns of organization that work for North American audiences may need to be modified in international correspondence.

■ In international correspondence, spell out the month.

Exercises and Problems

Getting Started

11.1   Identifying Sources of Miscommunication

In each of the following situations, identify one or more ways that cultural differences may be leading to miscommunication.

1. Alan is a US sales representative in Mexico. He makes appointments and is careful to be on time. But the person he's calling on is frequently late. To save time, Alan tries to get right to business. But his hosts want to talk about sightseeing and his family. Even worse, his appointments are interrupted constantly, not only by business phone calls but also by long conversations with other people and even the customers' children who come into the office. Alan's first progress report is very negative. He hasn't yet made a sale. Perhaps Mexico just isn't the right place to sell his company's products.

2. To help her company establish a presence in Japan, Susan wants to hire a local interpreter who can advise her on business customs. Kana Tomari has superb qualifications on paper. But when Susan tries to probe about her experience, Kana just says, "I will do my best. I will try very hard." She never gives details about any of the previous positions she's held. Susan begins to wonder if the résumé is inflated.

3. Stan wants to negotiate a joint venture with a Chinese company. He asks Tung-Sen Lee if the Chinese people have enough discretionary income to afford his product. Mr. Lee is silent for a time, and then says, "Your product is good. People in the West must like it." Stan smiles, pleased that Mr. Lee recognizes the quality of his product, and he gives Mr. Lee a contract to sign. Weeks later, Stan still hasn't heard anything. If China is going to be so inefficient, he wonders if he really should try to do business there.

4. Elspeth is very proud of her participatory management style. On assignment in India, she is careful not to give orders but to ask for suggestions. But people rarely suggest anything. Even a formal suggestion system doesn't work. And to make matters worse, she doesn't sense the respect and camaraderie of the plant she managed in the United States. Perhaps, she decides gloomily, people in India just aren't ready for a woman boss.

E-Mail Messages

11.2   Sending a Draft to Japan

You've drafted instructions for a consumer product that will be sold in Japan. Before the text is translated, you want to find out if the pictures will be clear. So you send an e-mail to your Japanese counterpart, Takashi Haneda, asking for a response within a week.

Write an e-mail message; assume that you will send the pictures as an attachment.

11.3   Asking about Travel Arrangements

The CEO is planning a trip to visit colleagues in another country (you pick the country). As Executive Assistant to the CEO of your organization, it's your job to make travel plans. At this stage, you don't know anything except dates and flights. (The CEO will arrive in the country at 7 AM local time on the 28th of next month and stay for three days.) It's your job to find out what the plans are and communicate any of the CEO's requirements.

Write an e-mail message to your contact.

Hints:

■ Pick a business, nonprofit organization, or government agency you know something about, making assumptions about the kinds of things its executive would want to do during an international visit.

■ How much international traveling does your CEO do? Has he or she ever been to this country before? What questions will he or she want answered?

Communicating at Work

11.4   Studying International Communication at Your Workplace

Does your employer buy from suppliers or sell to customers outside the country? Get a sampling of international messages, or interview managers about the problems they've encountered.

As Your Instructor Directs,

a. Share your results orally with a small group of students.

b. Present your findings orally to the class.

c. Summarize your findings in a memo to your instructor.

d. Join with other students in your class to write a group report.

Web Pages

11.5   Creating a Web Page

Create a Web page for international managers who are planning assignments in other countries or who work in this country for a multinational company headquartered in another country.

Assume that this page can be accessed from another of the organization's pages. Offer at least seven links. (More is better.) You may offer information as well as links to other pages with information. At the top of the page, offer an overview of what the page covers. At the bottom of the page, put the creation/update date and your name and e-mail address.

As Your Instructor Directs,

a. Turn in two laser copies of your page(s). On another page, give the URLs for each link.

b. Turn in one laser copy of your page(s) and a disk with the HTML code and .gif files.

c. Write a memo to your instructor (1) identifying the audience for which the page is designed and explain-

ing (2) the search strategies you used to find material on this topic, (3) why you chose the pages and information you've included, and (4) why you chose the layout and graphics you've used.

d. Present your page orally to the class.

Hints:

■ Limit your page to just one country or one part of the world.

■ You can include some general information about working abroad and culture, but most of your links should be specific to the country or part of the world you focus on.

■ Try to cover as many topics as possible: history, politics, geography, culture, money, living accommodations, transport, weather, business practices, and so forth.

■ Chunk your links into small groups under headings.

11.6   Comparing Company Web Pages for Various Countries

Many multinationals have separate Web pages for their operations in various countries. For example, Coca-Cola's pages include

Coca-Cola Belgium (www.cocacola.be)

Coca-Cola France (www.coca-cola.fr)

Coca-Cola Japan (www.cocacola.co.jp)

Analyze three of the country pages of a company of your choice.

▪ Is a single template used for pages in different countries, or do the basic designs differ?

▪ Are different images used in different countries? What do the images suggest?

▪ If you can read the language, analyze the links. What information is emphasized?

▪ To what extent are the pages similar? To what extent do they reveal national and cultural differences?

As Your Instructor Directs,

a. Write a memo analyzing the similarities and differences you find. Attach printouts of the pages to your memo.

b. Post a message to the class analyzing the pages. Include the URLs as hotlinks.

c. Make an oral presentation to the class. Paste the Web pages into PowerPoint slides.

d. Join with a small group of students to create a group report comparing several companies' Web pages in three specific countries. Attach printouts of the pages.

e. Make a group oral presentation to the class.

Memo and Report Assignments

11.7   Planning an International Trip

Assume that you're going to the capital city of another country on business two months from now. (You pick the country.) Use a search engine or the links on the BAC Web site to find out

▪ What holidays will be celebrated in that month.

▪ What the climate will be.

▪ What current events are in the news.

▪ What key features of business etiquette you should know.

▪ What kinds of gifts you should bring to your hosts.

▪ What sight-seeing you should try to include.

As Your Instructor Directs,

a. Write a memo to your instructor reporting the information you found.

b. Post a message to the class analyzing the pages. Include the URLs as hotlinks.

c. Make an oral presentation to the class.

d. Join with a small group of students to create a group report on several countries in a region.

e. Make a group oral presentation to the class.

11.8   Recommending a Candidate for an Overseas Position

Your company sells customized computer systems to businesses large and small around the world. The Executive Committee needs to recommend someone to begin a three-year term as Manager of Eastern European Marketing.

As Your Instructor Directs,

a. Write a memo to each of the candidates, specifying the questions you would like each to answer in a final interview.

b. Assume that it is not possible to interview the candidates. Use the information here to write a memo to the CEO recommending a candidate.

c. Write a memo to the CEO recommending the best way to prepare the person chosen for his or her assignment.

d. Write a memo to the CEO recommending a better way to choose candidates for international assignments.

e. Write a memo to your instructor explaining the assumptions you made about the company and the candidates that influenced your recommendation(s).

Information about the Candidates:

All the candidates have applied for the position and say they are highly interested in it.

1. **Deborah Gere,** 39, white, single. Employed by the company for eight years in the Indianapolis and New York offices. Currently in the New York office as Assistant Marketing Manager, Eastern United States; successful. University of Indiana MBA. Speaks Russian fluently; has translated for business negotiations that led to the setting up of the Moscow office. Good technical knowledge, acceptable managerial skills, excellent communication skills, good interpersonal skills. Excellent health; excellent emotional stability. Swims. One child, age 12. Lived in the then–Soviet Union for one year as an exchange student in college; business and personal travel in Europe.

2. **Claude Chabot,** 36, French, single. Employed by the company for 11 years in the Paris and London offices. Currently in the Paris office as Assistant Sales Manager for the European Economic Community; successful. No MBA, but degrees from MIT in the United States and l'Ecole Supérieure de Commerce de Paris. Speaks native French; speaks English and Italian fluently; speaks some German. Good technical knowledge, excellent managerial skills, acceptable communication skills, excellent interpersonal skills. Excellent health, good emotional stability. Plays tennis. No children.

French citizen; lived in the United States for two years, in London for five years (one year in college, four years in the London office). Extensive business and personal travel in Europe.

3. **Linda Moss,** 35, African American, married. Employed by the company for 10 years in the Atlanta and Toronto offices. Currently Assistant Manager of Canadian Marketing; very successful. Howard University MBA. Speaks some French. Good technical knowledge, excellent managerial skills, excellent communication skills, excellent interpersonal skills. Excellent health; excellent emotional stability. Does Jazzercize classes. Husband is an executive at a US company in Detroit; he plans to stay in the States with their children, ages 11 and 9. The couple plans to commute every two to six weeks. Has lived in Toronto for five years; business travel in North America; personal travel in Europe and Latin America.

4. **Steven Hsu,** 42, of Asian American descent, married. Employed by the company for 18 years in the Los Angeles office. Currently Marketing Manager, Western United States; very successful. UCLA MBA. Speaks some Korean. Excellent technical knowledge, excellent managerial skills, good communication skills, excellent interpersonal skills. Good health, excellent emotional stability. Plays golf. Wife is an engineer who plans to do consulting work in eastern Europe. Children ages 8, 5, and 2. Has not lived outside the United States; personal travel in Europe and Asia.

Your committee has received this memo from the CEO.

To:	Executive Committee
From:	Ed Conzachi ERC
Subject:	Choosing a Manager for the New Eastern European Office

Please write me a memo recommending the best candidate for Manager of East European Marketing. In your memo, tell me whom you're choosing and why; also explain why you have rejected the unsuccessful candidates.

This person will be assuming a three-year appointment, with the possibility of reappointment. The company will pay moving and relocation expenses for the manager and his or her family.

The Eastern European division currently is the smallest of the company's international divisions. However, this area is poised for growth. The new manager will supervise the Moscow office and establish branch offices as needed.

The committee has invited comments from everyone in the company. You've received these memos.

To: Executive Committee

From: Robert Osborne, US Marketing Manager   RO

Subject: Recommendation for Steve Hsu

Steve Hsu would be a great choice to head up the new Moscow office. In the past seven years, Steve has increased sales in the Western Region by 15%—in spite of recessions, earthquakes, and fires. He has a low-key, participative style that brings out the best in subordinates. Moreover, Steve is a brilliant computer programmer. He probably understands our products better than any other marketing or salesperson in the company.

Steve is clearly destined for success in headquarters. This assignment will give him the international experience he needs to move up to the next level of executive success.

To: Executive Committee

From: Becky Exter, Affirmative Action Officer   RRE

Subject: Hiring the New Manager for East European Marketing

Please be sensitive to affirmative action concerns. The company has a very good record of appointing women and minorities to key positions in the United States and Canada; so far our record in our overseas divisions has been less effective.

In part, perhaps, that may stem from a perception that women and minorities will not be accepted in countries less open than our own. But the experience of several multinational firms has been that even exclusionary countries will accept people who have the full backing of their countries. Another concern may be that it will be harder for women to establish a social support system abroad. However, different individuals have different ways of establishing support. To assume that the best candidate for an international assignment is a male with a stay-at-home wife is discriminatory and may deprive our company of the skills of some of its best people.

We have several qualified women and minority candidates. I urge you to consider their credentials carefully.

To: Executive Committee   *WED*

From: William E. Dortch, Marketing Manager, European Economic Community

Subject: Recommendation for Debbie Gere

Debbie Gere would be my choice to head the new Moscow office. As you know, I recommended that Europe be divided and that we establish an Eastern European division. Of all the people from the States who have worked on the creation of the new division, Debbie is the best. The negotiations were often complex. Debbie's knowledge of the language and culture was invaluable. She's done a good job in the New York office and is ready for wider responsibilities. Eastern Europe is a challenging place, but Debbie can handle the pressure and help us gain the foothold we need.

To: Ed Conzachi, President

From: Pierre Garamond, Sales Representative,
          European Economic Community   *PG*

Subject: Recommendation for Claude Chabot

Claude Chabot would be the best choice for Manager of Eastern European Marketing. He is a superb supervisor, motivating us to the highest level of achievement. He understands the complex legal and cultural nuances of selling our products in Europe as only a native can. He also has the budgeting and managerial skills to oversee the entire marketing effort.

You are aware that the company's record of sending US citizens to head international divisions is not particularly good. European Marketing is an exception, but our records in the Middle East and Japan have been poor. The company would gain stability by appointing Europeans to head European offices, Asians to head Asian offices, and so forth. Such people would do a better job of managing and motivating staffs which will be comprised primarily of nationals in the country where the office is located. Ending the practice of reserving the top jobs for US citizens would also send a message to international employees that we are valued and that we have a future with this company.

To: Executive Committee

From: Elaine Crispell, Manager, Canadian Marketing *EC*

Subject: Recommendation for Linda Moss

Linda Moss has done well as Assistant Manager for the last two and a half years. She is a creative, flexible problem solver. Her productivity is the highest in the office. Though she could be called a "workaholic," she is a warm, caring human being.

As you know, the Canadian division includes French-Speaking Montreal and a large Native Canadian population; furthermore, Toronto is an international and intercultural city. Linda has gained intercultural competence both on a personal and professional level.

Linda has the potential to be our first woman CEO fifteen years down the road. She needs more international experience to be competitive at that level. This would be a good opportunity for her, and she would do well for the company.

12

Working and Writing in Groups

Working and Writing in Groups

Valeria Maltoni

Marketing Communications Specialist, Destiny WebSolutions

Valeria Maltoni drives company positioning and messaging through various media. Her collaborative projects include writing for the Web, brochures, advertising campaigns, client proposals, and presentations. A specialized consultancy to the financial industry, Destiny helps some of the world's top financial institutions solve real business problems through technology.

www.destiny.com

Companies looking for better practices have discovered the power of groups. Collaborative work capitalizes on the different perspectives, experiences, ideas, styles, and strengths each individual contributes. Whenever our marketing group needs to come up with a new name or concept for a campaign, we get together to brainstorm. Four people think more creatively and generate better ideas than one.

Successful group work requires thoughtful up-front planning. During the initial phase of a project, group members need to discuss and agree on their vision and objectives as well as expectations. Documenting the planning process goes a long way to realizing it.

Business pressures often dictate tight timelines, and that's where technology can help. By using project planning and virtual meeting software, along with instant messaging and e-mail, teams can record their progress and overcome the constraints of physical location. I'm often called to participate in cross-divisional/office teams where members from strategy work alongside experienced designers and business analysts from three different locations. Technology helps greatly in keeping the team on the same page, but it does not replace communication. It is even more challenging but ever rewarding to work across time zones and through cultural differences.

In group writing, individuals need to check their egos at the door. During the draft phase, don't get attached to any particular word, phrase, or expression. Rather, commit to finding the best flow for the project and discovering the gaps in the material for further research. I find that working with a strong editor while writing helps integrate group thinking into early drafts, thus shortening the review process. Regardless of individual styles, the final copy needs to read in one voice. Good team results need not come at anyone's expense. Collaboration goes hand in hand with respect and communication.

Not everyone enjoys all aspects of teamwork. My advice is—be honest. Spend more time listening than talking, and ask for help frequently. No one expects you to know everything, and everyone is happy to help. You just need to ask.

> *"Successful group work requires thoughtful up-front planning."*

Teamwork is crucial to success in an organization. Some teams produce products, provide services, or recommend solutions to problems. Other teams—perhaps in addition to providing a service or recommending a solution—also produce documents. For examples of award-winning work teams, see the BAC Web site. **Interpersonal communication** is communication between people. Interpersonal skills such as listening and dealing with conflict are used in one-to-one interchanges, in problem-solving groups, and in writing groups. These skills will make you more successful on the job, in social groups, and in community service and volunteer work. In writing groups, giving careful attention to both group process and writing process (◄ p. 112) improves both the final product and members' satisfaction with the group.

Listening

Listening is crucial to building trust. However, listening on the job may be more difficult than listening in classes. Many classroom lectures are well organized, with signposts and repetition of key points to help hearers follow. But conversations usually wander. A key point about when a report is due may be sandwiched in among statements about other due dates for other projects. Finally, in a classroom you're listening primarily for information. In interchanges with friends and co-workers, you need to listen for feelings, too. Feelings of being rejected or overworked need to be dealt with as they arise. But you can't deal with a feeling unless you are aware of it.

As Appendix C explains, to receive a message, the receiver must first perceive the message, then decode it (that is, translate the symbols into meaning), and then interpret it. In interpersonal communication, **hearing** denotes perceiving sounds. **Listening** means decoding and interpreting them correctly.

Some listening errors happen because the hearer wasn't paying enough attention to a key point. After a meeting with a client, a consultant waited for the client to send her more information, which she would use to draft a formal proposal to do a job for the client. It turned out the client thought the next move was up to the consultant. The consultant and the client had met together, but they hadn't remembered the same facts.

Take notes when you can. In addition,

■ As early as possible, make a mental or paper list of the questions you have. When is the project due? What resources do you have? What is the most important aspect of this project, from the other person's point of view? During a conversation, listen for answers to your questions.

■ At the end of the conversation, check your understanding with the other person. Especially check who does what next.

■ After the conversation, write down key points that affect deadlines or how work will be evaluated.

Many listening errors are errors in interpretation. In 1977 when two Boeing 747 jumbo jets ran into each other on the ground in Tenerife, the pilots seemed to have heard the control tower's instructions. The KLM pilot was told to taxi to the end of the runway, turn around, and wait for clearance. But the KLM pilot didn't interpret the order to wait as an order he needed to follow. The Pan Am pilot interpreted *his* order to turn off at the "third intersection" to mean the third *unblocked* intersection. He didn't count the first blocked ramp, so he was still on the main runway when the KLM pilot ran into his plane at 186 miles an hour. The planes exploded in flames; 576 people died.[1]

To reduce listening errors caused by misinterpretation,

- Don't ignore instructions you think are unnecessary. Before you do something else, check with the order giver to see if there is a reason for the instruction.

- Consider the other person's background and experiences. Why is this point important to the speaker? What might he or she mean by it?

- Paraphrase what the speaker has said, giving him or her a chance to correct your understanding.

Listening to people is an indication that you're taking them seriously. **Acknowledgment responses**—nods, *uh huhs,* smiles, frowns—help carry the message that you're listening. However, listening responses vary in different cultures. Research has found that US whites almost always respond nonverbally when they listen closely, but that African Americans respond with words rather than nonverbal cues (◀ p. 296). This difference in response patterns may explain the fact that some whites think that African Americans do not understand what they are saying. Studies in the mid-1970s showed that white counselors repeated themselves more often to black clients than to white clients.[2] Similarly, black supervisors may miss verbal feedback when they talk to white subordinates who only nod.

In **active listening,** receivers actively demonstrate that they've heard and understood a speaker by feeding back either the literal meaning or the emotional content or both. Five strategies create active responses:

- Paraphrase the content. Feed back the meaning in your own words.
- Mirror the speaker's feelings. Identify the feelings you think you hear.
- State your own feelings. This strategy works especially well when you are angry.
- Ask for information or clarification.
- Offer to help solve the problem.

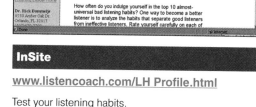

InSite

www.listencoach.com/LH Profile.html

Test your listening habits.

City Year, a Boston-based, nationwide nonprofit service organization, opens meetings with a show of hands. Smaller groups reach their hands in to form a circle. Larger groups raise their hands high. Conversations stop, all is quiet, and group members are physically engaged in a common action.

FIGURE 12.1   Blocking Responses versus Active Listening

Blocking response	Possible active response
Ordering, threatening	**Paraphrasing content**
"I don't care how you do it. Just get that report on my desk by Friday."	"You're saying that you don't have time to finish the report by Friday."
Preaching, criticizing	**Mirroring feelings**
"You should know better than to air the department's problems in a general meeting."	"It sounds like the department's problems really bother you."
Interrogating	**Stating one's own feelings**
"Why didn't you *tell* me that you didn't understand the instructions?"	"I'm frustrated that the job isn't completed yet, and I'm worried about getting it done on time."
Minimizing the problem	**Asking for information or clarification**
"You think *that's* bad. You should see what *I* have to do this week."	"What parts of the problem seem most difficult to solve?"
Advising	**Offering to help solve the problem together**
"Well, why don't you try listing everything you have to do and seeing which items are most important?"	"Is there anything I could do that would help?"

Source: The 5 responses that block communication are based on a list of 12 in Thomas Gordon and Judith Gordon Sands, *P.E.T. in Action* (New York: Wyden, 1976), 117–18.

Instead of simply mirroring what the other person says, many of us immediately respond in a way that analyzes or attempts to solve or dismiss the problem. People with problems need first of all to know that we hear that they're having a rough time. Figure 12.1 lists some of the responses that block communication. Ordering and interrogating both tell the other person that the speaker doesn't want to hear what he or she has to say. Preaching attacks the other person. Minimizing the problem suggests the other person's concern is misplaced. Even advising shuts off discussion. Giving a quick answer minimizes the pain the person feels and puts him or her down for not seeing (what is to us) the obvious answer. Even if it is a good answer from an objective point of view, the other person may not be ready to hear it. And sometimes, the off-the-top-of-the-head solution doesn't address the real problem.

Active listening takes time and energy. Even people who are skilled active listeners can't do it all the time. Furthermore, as Thomas Gordon and Judith Gordon Sands point out, active listening works only if you genuinely accept the other person's ideas and feelings. Active listening can reduce the conflict that results from miscommunication, but it alone cannot reduce the conflict that comes when two people want apparently inconsistent things or when one person wants to change someone else.[3]

Group Interactions

Groups can focus on three different dimensions. **Informational messages** focus on content: the problem, data, and possible solutions. **Procedural messages** focus on method and process. How will the group make decisions? Who will do what? When will assignments be due? **Interpersonal messages** focus on people, promoting friendliness, cooperation, and group loyalty. Different kinds of communication dominate during the four stages of the life of a task group: orientation, formation, coordination, and formalization.[4]

During **orientation,** when members meet and begin to define their task, groups need to develop some sort of social cohesiveness and to develop pro-

FIGURE 12.2   Possible Group Ground Rules

- Start on time; end on time.
- Come to the meeting prepared.
- Focus comments on the issues.
- Avoid personal attacks.
- Listen to and respect members' opinions.
- NOSTUESO (No One Speaks Twice Until Everybody Speaks Once)
- If you have a problem with another person, tell that person, not everyone else.
- Everyone must be 70% comfortable with the decision and 100% committed to implementing it.
- If you agree to do something, do it.
- Communicate immediately if you think you may not be able to fulfill an agreement.

Sources: Nancy Schullery and Beth Hoger, "Business Advocacy for Students in Small Groups," Association for Business Communication Annual Convention, San Antonio, November 9–11, 1998; "An Antidote to Chronic Cantankerousness," *Fast Company,* February/March 1998, 176; John Grossmann, "We've Got to Start Meeting Like This," *Inc.,* April 1998, 70; Gary Dessler, *Winning Commitment,* quoted in *Team Management Briefings,* preview issue (September 1998), 5; and 3M Meeting Network, "Groundrules and Agreements," www.3M.com/meetingnetwork/readingroom/meetingguide_grndrules.html (September 25, 2001).

cedures for meeting and acting. Interpersonal and procedural comments reduce the tension that always exists in a new group. Insistence on information in this first stage can hurt the group's long-term productivity.

Groups are often most effective when they explicitly adopt ground rules. Figure 12.2 lists some of the most common ground rules used by workplace teams.

During **formation,** conflicts almost always arise when the group chooses a leader and defines the problem. Successful leaders make the procedure clear so that each member knows what he or she is supposed to do. Interpersonal communication is needed to resolve the conflict that surfaces during this phase. Successful groups analyze the problem carefully before they begin to search for solutions.

Coordination is the longest phase and the phase during which most of the group's work is done. While procedural and interpersonal comments help maintain direction and friendliness, most of the comments need to deal with information. Good information is essential to a good decision. Conflict occurs as the group debates alternate solutions.

In **formalization,** the group seeks consensus. The success of this phase determines how well the group's decision will be implemented. In this stage, the group seeks to forget earlier conflicts.

Roles in Groups

Individual members can play several roles in groups. These roles can be positive or negative.

Positive roles and actions that help the group achieve its task goals include the following:[5]

- **Seeking information and opinions**—asking questions, identifying gaps in the group's knowledge.
- **Giving information and opinions**—answering questions, providing relevant information.

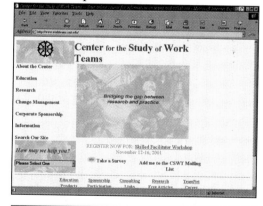

InSite

www.workteams.unt.edu

The Center for the Study of Work Teams offers abstracts of research reports, newsletter archives, and an extensive list of links.

The Power and Peril of Teams*

[Shaunna Sowell at Texas Instruments] was tapped for a product-quality steering committee that was loaded with bosses. She was intimidated at first but her confidence grew with her experience.

"I left one meeting thinking, . . . 'I've ruined my career,' " she recalls. "I'd just told a guy four levels above me he was wrong."

Actually, she impressed an executive on the team who was casting about for a vice president of corporate environmental safety. "You have to be a great individual contributor," she says, "that's how you get picked for the next team." . . .

In leading a team charged with redesigning Boston Gas's distribution operation, [Mary] Kinnear, a human-resources specialist, also knew she risked offending some influential executives whose turf was being threatened. Some had already voiced skepticism about her abilities to do effective work on the team. . . .

When the project ended, however, she was eventually named general manager of one of the eight regional operating divisions created by the project team. Absent the project team, she says she wouldn't have had the experience or the exposure to land her current job.

*Quoted from Hal Lancaster, "That Team Spirit Can Lead Your Career to New Victories," *The Wall Street Journal*, January 14, 1997, B1.

- **Summarizing**—restating major points, pulling ideas together, summarizing decisions.
- **Evaluating**—comparing group processes and products to standards and goals.
- **Coordinating**—planning work, giving directions, and fitting together contributions of group members.

Positive roles and actions that help the group build loyalty, resolve conflicts, and function smoothly include the following:

- **Encouraging participation**—demonstrating openness and acceptance, recognizing the contributions of members, calling on quieter group members.
- **Relieving tensions**—joking and suggesting breaks and fun activities.
- **Checking feelings**—asking members how they feel about group activities and sharing one's own feelings with others.
- **Solving interpersonal problems**—opening discussion of interpersonal problems in the group and suggesting ways to solve them.
- **Listening actively**—showing group members that they have been heard and that their ideas are being taken seriously.

Negative roles and actions that hurt the group's product and process include the following:

- **Blocking**—disagreeing with everything that is proposed.
- **Dominating**—trying to run the group by ordering, shutting out others, and insisting on one's own way.
- **Clowning**—making unproductive jokes and diverting the group from the task.
- **Withdrawing**—being silent in meetings, not contributing, not helping with the work, not attending meetings.

Some actions can be positive or negative depending on how they are used. Criticizing ideas is necessary if the group is to produce the best solution, but criticizing every idea raised without ever suggesting possible solutions blocks a group. Jokes in moderation can defuse tension and make the group more fun. Too many jokes or inappropriate jokes can make the group's work more difficult.

Leadership in Groups

You may have noted that "leader" was not one of the roles listed above. Being a leader does *not* mean doing all the work yourself. Indeed, someone who implies that he or she has the best ideas and can do the best work is likely playing the negative roles of blocking and dominating.

Effective groups balance three kinds of leadership, which parallel the three group dimensions:

- Informational leaders generate and evaluate ideas and text.
- Interpersonal leaders monitor the group's process, check people's feelings, and resolve conflicts.
- Procedural leaders set the agenda, make sure that everyone knows what's due for the next meeting, communicate with absent group members, and check to be sure that assignments are carried out.

While it's possible for one person to do all of these responsibilities, in many groups, the three kinds of leadership are taken on by three (or more) different people. Some groups formally or informally rotate or share these responsibilities, so that everyone—and no one—is a leader.

Several studies have shown people who talk a lot, listen effectively, and respond nonverbally to other members in the group are considered to be leaders.[6]

Decision-Making Strategies

Probably the least effective decision-making strategy is to let the person who talks first, last, loudest, or most determine the decision.

Voting is quick but may leave people in the minority unhappy with and uncommitted to the majority's plan.

Coming to consensus takes time but results in speedier implementation of ideas.

Two strategies that are often useful in organizational groups are the standard agenda and dot planning.

The **standard agenda** is a seven-step process for solving problems:

1. Understand what the group has to deliver, in what form, by what due date. Identify available resources.
2. Identify the problem. What exactly is wrong? What question(s) is the group trying to answer?
3. Gather information, share it with all group members, and examine it critically.
4. Establish criteria. What would the ideal solution include? Which elements of that solution would be part of a less-than-ideal but still acceptable solution? What legal, financial, moral, or other limitations might keep a solution from being implemented?
5. Generate alternate solutions. Brainstorm and record ideas for the next step.
6. Measure the alternatives against the criteria.
7. Choose the best solution.[7]

Dot planning offers a way for large groups to choose priorities quickly. First, the group brainstorms ideas, recording each on pages that are put on the wall. Then each individual gets two strips of three to five adhesive dots in different colors. One color represents high priority, the other lower priority. People then walk up to the pages and affix dots by the points they care most about. Some groups allow only one dot from one person on any one item; others allow someone who is really passionate about an idea to put all of his or her dots on it. As Figure 12.3 shows, the dots make it easy to see which items the group believes are most important.

Characteristics of Successful Student Groups

A case study of six student groups completing class projects found that students in successful groups were not necessarily more skilled or more experienced than students in less successful groups. Instead, successful and less successful groups communicated differently in three ways.[8]

First, in the successful groups, the leader set clear deadlines, scheduled frequent meetings, and dealt directly with conflict that emerged in the group. In less successful groups, members had to ask the leader what they were supposed to be doing. The less successful groups met less often, and they tried to pretend that conflicts didn't exist.

Second, the successful groups listened to criticism and made important decisions together. Perhaps as a result, everyone in the group could articulate the group's goals. In the less successful groups, a subgroup made decisions and told other members what had been decided.

Third, the successful groups had a higher proportion of members who worked actively on the project. The successful groups even found ways to use

Evaluating Teams*

[A]t Con-Way Transportation Services, . . . teams evaluate *themselves* through a process called the Team Improvement Review (TIR). . . .

The TIR process . . . separates feedback sessions from salary reviews. . . .

The TIR also guarantees that feedback takes place in a safe environment. . . . [M]anagers are usually not present. Instead, the groups often bring in a neutral facilitator who leads the discussions.

Last, the TIR has a formal process by which teams offer feedback. The reviews happen about every three months. A week before the TIR meeting, participants rate team performance on a 1-to-5 scale for 31 criteria. During the meeting, people discuss the team's performance as well as individual performance in the context of the team. . . . [T]o keep the discussions focused on performance rather than on personality [, . . . the team uses techniques such as] the Round Robin. Each person creates two columns on a sheet of paper, one labeled "Strengths" and the other "Something to Work On." Then each person lists all the strengths that he or she brings to the team as well as one thing to work on. The papers get passed around the room, and each team member comments on everyone else's forms.

*Quoted from "How Con-Way Reviews Teams," *Fast Company*, September 1998, 152.

FIGURE 12.3   Dot Planning Allows Groups to Set Priorities Quickly

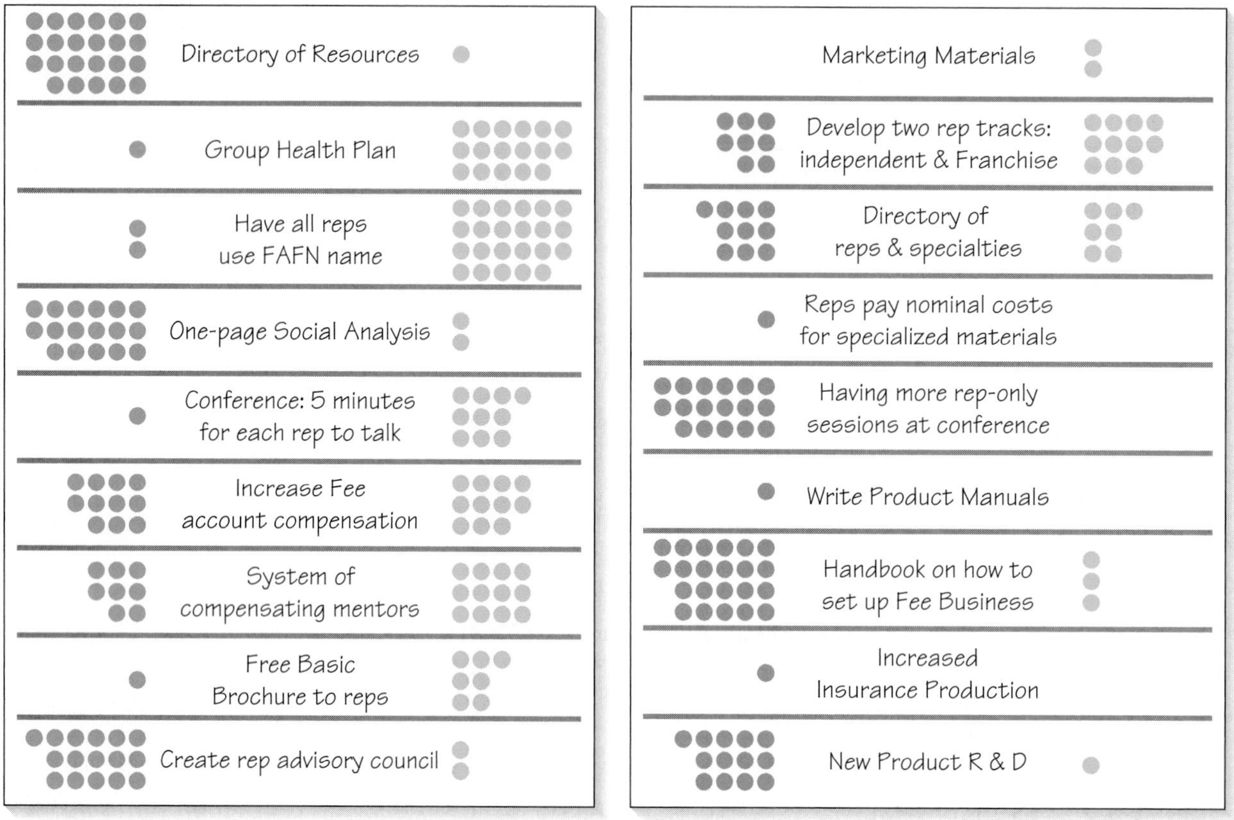

Directory of Resources	Marketing Materials
Group Health Plan	Develop two rep tracks: independent & Franchise
Have all reps use FAFN name	Directory of reps & specialties
One-page Social Analysis	Reps pay nominal costs for specialized materials
Conference: 5 minutes for each rep to talk	Having more rep-only sessions at conference
Increase Fee account compensation	Write Product Manuals
System of compensating mentors	Handbook on how to set up Fee Business
Free Basic Brochure to reps	Increased Insurance Production
Create rep advisory council	New Product R & D

Here, green dots mean "high priority" and orange dots mean "low priority." One can see at a glance which items have widespread support, which are controversial, and which are low priority.

Source: "The Color-Coded Priority Setter," *Inc.*, June 1995, 70–71.

members who didn't like working in groups. For example, one student who didn't want to be a "team player" functioned as a "freelancer" for her group, completing assignments by herself and giving them to the leader. The less successful groups had a much smaller percentage of active members and each had some members who did very little on the final project.

Rebecca Burnett has shown that student groups produce better documents when they disagree over substantive issues of content and document design. The disagreement does not need to be angry: a group member can simply say, "Yes, and here's another way we could do it." Deciding among two (or more) alternatives forces the proposer to explain the rationale for an idea. Even when the group adopts the original idea, considering alternatives rather than quickly accepting the first idea produces better writing.[9]

Kimberly Freeman found that the students who spent the most time meeting with their groups had the highest grades—on their individual as well as on group assignments.[10]

Peer Pressure and Groupthink

Groups that never express conflict may be experiencing groupthink. **Groupthink** is the tendency for groups to put such a high premium on agreement that they directly or indirectly punish dissent.

Many people feel so much reluctance to express open disagreement that they will say they agree even when objective circumstances would suggest the first speaker cannot be right. In a series of experiments in the 1950s, Solomon Asch showed the influence of peer pressure. People sitting around a table were shown a large card with a line and asked to match it to the line of the same length on another card. It's a simple test: people normally match the lines correctly almost 100% of the time. However, in the experiment, all but one of the people in the group had been instructed to give false answers for several of the trials. When the group gave an incorrect answer, the focal person accepted the group's judgment 36.8% of the time. When someone else also gave a different answer—even if it was another wrong answer—the focal person accepted the group's judgment only 9% of the time.[11]

The experimenters varied the differences in line lengths, hoping to create a situation in which even the most conforming subjects would trust their own senses. But some people continued to accept the group's judgment, even when one line was seven inches longer than the other.

Groups that "go along with the crowd" and suppress conflict ignore the full range of alternatives, seek only information that supports the positions they already favor, and fail to prepare contingency plans to cope with foreseeable setbacks. A business suffering from groupthink may launch a new product that senior executives support but for which there is no demand. Student groups suffering from groupthink turn in inferior documents.

The best correctives to groupthink are to consciously search for additional alternatives, to test one's assumptions against those of a range of other people, and to protect the right of people in a group to disagree.

Working in Diverse Groups

In any organization, you'll work with people whose backgrounds differ from yours. Residents of small towns and rural areas have different notions of friendliness than do people from big cities. Californians look, talk, and dress differently from people in the Midwest. Advertising executives and truck drivers have different lifestyles.

Even people who come from the same part of the country and who have the same jobs may differ in personality type. Savvy group members play to each other's strengths and devise strategies for dealing with differences.

In addition, differences arise from gender, class, race and ethnicity, religion, age, sexual orientation, and physical ability. A growing body of literature shows that ethnically diverse teams produce more and higher-quality ideas.[12]

See the BAC Web page for links to sites for various ethnic groups in the United States. One problem with our awareness of difference, however, is that when someone feels shut out, he or she can attribute the negative interaction to prejudice, when other factors may be responsible. Conversational style and nonverbal communication are two of the areas that may cause miscommunication.

Conversational Style

Deborah Tannen uses the term **conversational style** to denote our conversational patterns and the meaning we give to them: the way we show interest, politeness, appropriateness.[13] Your answers to the following questions reveal your own conversational style:

- How long a pause tells you that it's your turn to speak?
- Do you see interruption as rude? or do you say things while other people are still talking to show that you're interested and to encourage them to say more?
- Do you show interest by asking lots of questions? or do you see questions as intrusive and wait for people to volunteer whatever they have to say?

"Assertiveness" May Be a Matter of Conversational Style*

Rachel regularly led training groups with a male colleague. He always did all the talking, and she was always angry at him for dominating and not giving her a chance to say anything. . . . He would begin to answer questions from the group while she was still waiting for a slight pause to begin answering. And when she was in the middle of talking, he would jump in—but always when she had paused. So she tried pushing herself to begin answering questions a little sooner than felt polite, and not to leave long pauses when she was talking. The result was that she talked a lot more, and the man was as pleased as she was. Her supervisor complimented her on having become more assertive.

Whether or not Rachel actually became more assertive is debatable. . . . [S]he solved her problem with a simple and slight adjustment of her way of speaking, without soul-searching, self-analysis, external intervention, and—most important—without defining herself as having an emotional problem or a personality defect: unassertiveness.

*Quoted from Deborah Tannen, *That's Not What I Meant!* (New York: William Morrow, 1986), 177–78.

Are Interruptions Impolite?*

In the dominant US culture, interrupting can seem impolite, especially if a lower-status person interrupts a superior.

Simulated negotiations have measured the interruptions by business people in 10 countries. The following list is ordered by decreasing numbers of interruptions:

    Korea

    Germany

    France

    China

    Brazil

    Russia

    Taiwan

    Japan

    United Kingdom

    United States

This list does not mean that US business people are more polite, but rather that how people show politeness differs from culture to culture. Chinese and Italians (who also interrupt frequently) use interruptions to offer help, jointly construct a conversation, and show eagerness to do business—all of which are polite.

*Based on Jan M. Ulijn and Xiangling Li, "Is Interrupting Impolite? Some Temporal Aspects of Turn-Taking in Chinese-Western and Other Intercultural Encounters," *Text* 15, no. 4 (1995), 600, 621.

Tannen concludes that the following features characterize her own conversational style:

Fast rate of speech.

Fast rate of turn-taking.

Persistence—if a turn is not acknowledged, try again.

Preference for personal stories.

Tolerance of, preference for simultaneous speech.

Abrupt topic shifting.

Different conversational styles are not better or worse than each other, but people with different conversational styles may feel uncomfortable without knowing why. A subordinate who talks quickly may be frustrated by a boss who speaks slowly. People who talk more slowly may feel shut out of a conversation with people who talk more quickly. Someone who has learned to make requests directly ("Please pass the salt") may be annoyed by someone who uses indirect requests ("This casserole needs some salt").

In the workplace, conflicts may arise because of differences in conversational style. Generation Xers often use a rising inflection on statements as well as questions. Xers see this style as gentler and more polite. But baby boomer bosses may see this speech pattern as hesitant, as if the speaker wants advice—which they then proceed to deliver.[14] Thomas Kochman claims that blacks often use direct questions to criticize or accuse.[15] If Kochman is right, a black employee might see a question ("Will that report be ready Friday?") as a criticism of his or her progress. One supervisor might mean the question simply as a request for information. Another supervisor might use the question to mean "I want that report Friday."

Daniel N. Maltz and Ruth A. Borker believe that differences in conversational style (Figure 12.4) may be responsible for the miscommunication that often occurs in male–female conversations. Certainly conversational style is not the same for all men and for all women, but research has found several common patterns in the US cultures studied so far. For example, researchers have found that women are much more likely to nod and to say *yes* or *mm hmm* than men are. Maltz and Borker hypothesize that to women, these symbols mean simply "I'm listening; go on." Men, on the other hand, may decode these symbols as "I agree" or at least "I follow what you're saying so far." A man who receives nods and *mms* from a woman may feel that she is inconsistent and unpredictable if she then disagrees with him. A woman may feel that a man who doesn't provide any feedback isn't listening to her.[16]

Nonverbal Communication

Posture and body movements connote energy and openness. North American **open body positions** include leaning forward with uncrossed arms and legs, with the arms away from the body. **Closed** or **defensive body positions** include leaning back, sometimes with both hands behind the head, arms and legs crossed or close together, or hands in pockets. As the labels imply, open positions suggest that people are accepting and open to new ideas. Closed positions suggest that people are physically or psychologically uncomfortable, that they are defending themselves and shutting other people out.

People who cross their arms or legs often claim that they do so only because the position is more comfortable. But notice your own body the next time you're in a perfectly comfortable discussion with a good friend. You'll probably find that you naturally assume open body positions. The fact that so many

FIGURE 12.4 Different Conversational Styles

	Debating	Relating
Interpretation of questions	See questions as requests for information.	See questions as way to keep a conversation flowing.
Relation of new comment to what last speaker said	Do not require new comment to relate explicitly to last speaker's comment. Ignoring previous comment is one strategy for taking control.	Expect new comments to acknowledge the last speaker's comment and relate directly to it.
View of aggressiveness	See aggressiveness as one way to organize the flow of conversation.	See aggressiveness as directed at audience personally, as negative, and as disruptive to a conversation.
How topics are defined and changed	Tend to define topics narrowly and shift topics abruptly. Interpret statements about side issues as effort to change the topic.	Tend to define topics gradually, progressively. Interpret statements about side issues as effort to shape, expand, or limit the topic.
Response to someone who shares a problem	Offer advice, solutions.	Offer solidarity, reassurance. Share troubles to establish sense of community.

Sources: Based on Daniel N. Maltz and Ruth A. Borker, "A Cultural Approach to Male-Female Miscommunication," *Language and Social Identity,* ed. John J. Gumperz (Cambridge: Cambridge University Press, 1982), 213; and Deborah Tannen, *Talking from 9 to 5: Women and Men in the Workplace: Language, Sex and Power* (New York: William Morrow, 1995).

people in organizational settings adopt closed positions may indicate that many people feel at least slightly uncomfortable in school and on the job.

As Chapter 11 explains, even within a culture, a nonverbal sign may have more than one meaning. A young woman took a new idea into her boss, who sat there and glared at her, brows together in a frown, as she explained her proposal. The stare and lowered brows symbolized anger to her, and she assumed that he was rejecting her idea. Several months later, she learned that her boss always "frowned" when he was concentrating. The facial expression she had interpreted as anger had not been intended to convey anger at all.

Misunderstandings are even more common when people communicate with people from other cultures or other countries. A white teacher sends two African American students to the principal's office because they're "fighting." US whites consider fighting to have started when loud voices, insults, and posture indicate that violence is likely. But the US African American culture does not assume that those signs will lead to violence: they can be part of nonviolent disagreements.[17]

Knowing something about other cultures may help you realize that a subordinate who doesn't meet your eye may be showing respect rather than dishonesty. But it's impossible to memorize every meaning that every nonverbal sign has in every culture. And in a multicultural workforce, you can't know whether someone retains the meanings of his or her ancestors or has adopted the dominant US meanings. The best solution is to state an observation: "I see you're wearing black." The other person's response will let you know whether the color is a fashion statement or a sign of mourning.

Conflict Resolution

Conflicts are going to arise in any group of intelligent people who care about the task. Yet many of us feel so uncomfortable with conflict that we pretend it doesn't exist. However, unacknowledged conflicts rarely go away: they fester, making the next interchange more difficult.

To reduce the number of conflicts in a group,

- Make responsibilities and ground rules clear at the beginning.
- Discuss problems as they arise, rather than letting them fester till people explode.
- Realize that group members are not responsible for each others' happiness.

Once a conflict arises, groups may need to reopen discussions about responsibilities and confront a troublesome group member.[18]

Figure 12.5 suggests several possible solutions to conflicts that student groups often experience. Often the symptom arises from a feeling of not being respected or appreciated by the group. Therefore, many problems can be averted if people advocate for their ideas in a positive way. As Nancy Schullery and Beth Hoger point out, the best time to advocate for an idea is when the group has not yet identified all possible options, seems dominated by one view, or seems unable to choose among solutions. A tactful way to advocate for the position you favor is to recognize the contributions others have made, to summarize, and then to hypothesize: "What if . . . ?" "Let's look six months down the road." "Let's think about *x*."[19]

To see how comfortable you are with conflict, take the quizzes on the BAC Web site. You'll also find links on conflict resolution.

Steps in Conflict Resolution

Dealing successfully with conflict requires both attention to the issues and to people's feelings. This four-step procedure will help you resolve conflicts constructively.

1. Make sure the people involved really disagree.

Sometimes someone who's under a lot of pressure may explode. But the speaker may just be venting anger and frustration; he or she may not in fact be angry at the person who receives the explosion. One way to find out if a person is just venting is to ask, "Is there something you'd like me to do?"

2. Check to see that everyone's information is correct.

Sometimes different conversational styles, differing interpretations of symbols, or faulty inferences create apparent conflicts when no real disagreement exists. (See Appendix C ➡ for a discussion of symbols and inferences.) During a negotiation between a US businessman and a Balinese businessman, the Balinese man dropped his voice and lowered his eyes when he discussed price. The US man saw the low voice and breaking of eye contact as an indication of dishonesty. But the Balinese believe that it is rude to mention price specifically. He was embarrassed, but he wasn't lying.[20]

Similarly, misunderstanding can arise from faulty assumptions. A US student studying in Colombia quickly learned that only cold water was available for his evening shower. Since his host family washed dinner dishes in cold water, he assumed the family didn't have hot water. They did. Colombians turn off the water heater in the morning after everyone has bathed; washing later in the day is done with cold water. He could have hot water for his showers if he took them in the morning.[21]

3. Discover the needs each person is trying to meet.

Sometimes determining the real needs makes it possible to see a new solution. The **presenting problem** that surfaces as the subject of dissention may or may not be the real problem. For example, a worker who complains about the hours he's

FIGURE 12.5 Troubleshooting Group Problems

Symptom	Possible solutions
We can't find a time to meet that works for all of us.	a. Find out why people can't meet at certain times. Some reasons suggest their own solutions. For example, if someone has to stay home with small children, perhaps the group could meet at that person's home. b. Assign out-of-class work to "committees" to work on parts of the project. c. Use e-mail to share, discuss, and revise drafts.
One person isn't doing his or her fair share.	a. Find out what is going on. Is the person overcommitted? Does he or she feel unappreciated? Those are different problems you'd solve in different ways. b. Early on, do things to build group loyalty. Get to know each other as writers and as people. Sometimes, do something fun together. c. Encourage the person to contribute. "Mary, what do you think?" "Jim, which part of this would you like to draft?" Then find something to praise in the work. "Thanks for getting us started." d. If someone misses a meeting, assign someone else to bring the person up to speed. People who miss meetings for legitimate reasons (job interviews, illness) but don't find out what happened may become less committed to the group. e. Consider whether strict equality is the most important criterion. On a given project, some people may have more knowledge or time than others. Sometimes the best group product results from letting people do different amounts of "work." f. Even if you divide up the work, make all decisions as a group: what to write about, which evidence to include, what graphs to use, what revisions to make. People excluded from decisions become less committed to the group.
I seem to be the only one in the group who cares about quality.	a. Find out why other members "don't care." If they received low grades on early assignments, stress that good ideas and attention to detail can raise grades. Perhaps the group should meet with the instructor to discuss what kinds of work will pay the highest dividends. b. Volunteer to do extra work. Sometimes people settle for something that's just OK because they don't have the time or resources to do excellent work. They might be happy for the work to be done—if they didn't have to do it. c. Be sure that you're respecting what each person can contribute. Group members sometimes withdraw when one person dominates and suggests that he or she is "better" than other members.
People in the group don't seem willing to disagree. We end up going with the first idea suggested.	a. Appoint someone to be a devil's advocate. b. Brainstorm so you have several possibilities to consider. c. After an idea is suggested, have each person in the group suggest a way it could be improved. d. Have each person in the group write a draft. It's likely the drafts will be different, and you'll have several options to mix and match. e. Talk about good ways to offer criticism. Sometimes people don't disagree because they're afraid that other group members won't tolerate disagreement.
One person just criticizes everything.	a. Ask the person to follow up the criticism with a suggestion for improvement. b. Talk about ways to express criticism tactfully. "I think we need to think about x" is more tactful than "You're wrong." c. If the criticism is about ideas and writing (not about people), value it. Ideas and documents need criticism if we are to improve them.

Who Does What

Working successfully in a group depends on being open about preferences, constraints, and skills and then using creative problem-solving techniques.

A person who prefers to outline the whole project in advance may be in a group with someone who expects to do the project at the last minute. Someone who likes to talk out ideas before writing may be in a group with someone who wants to work on a draft in silence and revise it before showing it to anyone. By being honest about your preferences, you make it possible for the group to find a creative solution that builds on what each person can offer.

In one group, Rob wanted to wait to start the project because he was busy with other class work. David and Susan, however, wanted to go ahead now because their schedules would get busier later in the term. A creative solution would be for David and Susan to do most of the work on parts of the project that had to be completed first (such as collecting data and writing the proposal) and for Rob to do work that had to be done later (such as revising, editing, and proofreading).

putting in may in fact be complaining not about the hours themselves but about not feeling appreciated. A supervisor who complains that the other supervisors don't invite her to meetings may really feel that the other managers don't accept her as a peer. Sometimes people have trouble seeing beyond the presenting problem because they've been taught to suppress their anger, especially toward powerful people. One way to tell whether the presenting problem is the real problem is to ask, "If this were solved, would I be satisfied?" If the answer is *no*, then the problem that presents itself is not the real problem. Solving the presenting problem won't solve the conflict. Keep probing until you get to the real conflict.

4. Search for alternatives.

Sometimes people are locked into conflict because they see too few alternatives. At one data-entry company, productivity fell because women employees took time off to visit their children at day care. Men on the board wanted to solve the problem by docking pay. The one woman on the board proposed installing software to let mothers check on their children online. That solved the problem.[22]

5. Repair bad feelings.

Conflict can emerge without anger and without escalating the disagreement, as the next section shows. But if people's feelings have been hurt, the group needs to deal with those feelings to resolve the conflict constructively. Only when people feel respected and taken seriously can they take the next step of trusting others in the group.

Responding to Criticism

Conflict is particularly difficult to resolve when someone else criticizes or attacks us directly. When we are criticized, our natural reaction is to defend ourselves—perhaps by counterattacking. The counterattack prompts the critic to defend him- or herself. The conflict escalates; feelings are hurt; issues become muddied and more difficult to resolve.

Just as resolving conflict depends on identifying the needs each person is trying to meet, so dealing with criticism depends on understanding the real concern of the critic. Constructive ways to respond to criticism and get closer to the real concern include paraphrasing, checking for feelings, checking inferences, and buying time with limited agreement.

Paraphrasing

To **paraphrase,** repeat in your own words the verbal content of the critic's message. The purposes of paraphrasing are (1) to be sure that you have heard the critic accurately, (2) to let the critic know what his or her statement means to you, and (3) to communicate the feeling that you are taking the critic and his or her feelings seriously.

Criticism: You guys are stonewalling my requests for information.

Paraphrase: You think that we don't give you the information you need quickly enough.

Checking for feelings

When you check the critic's feelings, you identify the emotions that the critic seems to be expressing verbally or nonverbally. The purposes of checking feelings are to try to understand (1) the critic's emotions, (2) the importance of the criticism for the critic, and (3) the unspoken ideas and feelings that may actually be more important than the voiced criticism.

| Criticism: | You guys are stonewalling my requests for information. |
| Feeling check: | You sound pretty angry. |

Always *ask* the other person if you are right in your perception. Even the best reader of nonverbal cues is sometimes wrong.

Checking for inferences

When you check the inferences you draw from criticism, you identify the implied meaning of the verbal and nonverbal content of the criticism, taking the statement a step further than the words of the critic to try to understand *why* the critic is bothered by the action or attitude under discussion. The purposes of checking inferences are (1) to identify the real (as opposed to the presenting) problem and (2) to communicate the feeling that you care about resolving the conflict.

| Criticism: | You guys are stonewalling my requests for information. |
| Inference: | Are you saying that you need more information from our group? |

Inferences can be faulty. In the above interchange, the critic might respond, "I don't need *more* information. I just think you should give it to me without my having to file three forms in triplicate every time I want some data."

Buying time with limited agreement

Buying time is a useful strategy for dealing with criticisms that really sting. When you buy time with limited agreement, you avoid escalating the conflict (as an angry statement might do) but also avoid yielding to the critic's point of view. To buy time, restate the part of the criticism you agree to be true. (This is often a fact, rather than the interpretation or evaluation the critic has made of that fact.) *Then let the critic respond, before you say anything else.* The purposes of buying time are (1) to allow you time to think when a criticism really hits home and threatens you, so that you can respond to the criticism rather than simply reacting defensively, and (2) to suggest to the critic that you are trying to hear what he or she is saying.

| Criticism: | You guys are stonewalling my requests for information. |
| Limited agreement: | It's true that the cost projections you asked for last week still aren't ready. |

DO NOT go on to justify or explain. A "Yes, but . . ." statement is not a time-buyer.

You-attitude in conflict resolution

You-attitude means looking at things from the audience's point of view, respecting the audience, and protecting the audience's ego. The *you* statements that many people use when they're angry attack the audience; they do not illustrate you-attitude. Instead, substitute statements about your own feelings. In conflict, *I* statements show good you-attitude!

Lacks you-attitude:	You never do your share of the work.
You-attitude:	I feel that I'm doing more than my share of the work on this project.
Lacks you-attitude:	Even you should be able to run the report through a spelling checker.
You-attitude:	I'm not willing to have my name on a report with so many spelling errors. I did lots of the writing, and I don't think I should have to do the proofreading and spell checking, too.

Getting to the Root of the Problem*

Magazine advertising account representative Beverly Jameson received a phone call from an ad agency saying that a client wanted to cancel the space it had bought. Jameson saw the problem as an opportunity: "Instead of hearing 'cancel,' I heard, 'There's a problem here—let's get to the root of it and figure out how to make the client happy.'" Jameson met with the client, asked the right questions, and discovered that the client wanted more flexibility. She changed some of the markets, kept the business, and turned the client into a repeat customer.

*Based on "Listen Up and Sell," *Selling Power*, July/August 1999, 34.

Being Taken Seriously*

It's frustrating to speak in a meeting and have people ignore what you say. Here are some tips for being taken seriously:

- Link your comment to the comment of a powerful person, even if logic suffers a bit. For example, say, "John is saying that we should focus on excellence, AND I think we can become stronger by encouraging diversity."

- Show that you've done your homework. Laura Sloate, who is blind, establishes authority by making sure her first question is highly technical: "In footnote three of the 10K, you indicate . . ."

- Find an ally in the organization and agree ahead of time to acknowledge each other's contributions to the meeting, whether you agree or disagree with the point being made. Explicit disagreement signals that the comment is worth taking seriously: "Duane has pointed out . . . , but I think that . . . ."

- Use the style of language that powerful people in your organization use.

- Repeat your ideas. Put important ideas in a memo before the meeting.

*Based on Joan E. Rigdon, "Managing Your Career," *The Wall Street Journal*, December 1, 1993, B1; Cynthia Crossen, "Spotting Value Takes Smarts, Not Sight, Laura Sloate Shows," *The Wall Street Journal*, December 10, 1987, A1, A14; and Anne Fisher, "Ask Annie: Putting Your Money Where Your Mouth Is," *Fortune*, September 3, 2001, 238.

Effective Meetings

Meetings have always taken a large part of the average manager's week. Although e-mail has eliminated some meetings, the increased number of teams means that meetings are even more frequent.

Meetings can have any of at least six purposes:

- To share information.
- To brainstorm ideas.
- To evaluate ideas.
- To make decisions.
- To create a document.
- To motivate members.

When meetings combine two or more purposes, it's useful to make the purposes explicit. For example, in the meeting of a university senate or a company's board of directors, some items are presented for information. Discussion is possible, but the group will not be asked to make a decision. Other items are presented for action; the group will be asked to vote. A business meeting might specify that the first half hour will be time for brainstorming, with the second half hour devoted to evaluation.

Intel's agendas also specify *how* decisions will be made. The company recognizes four different decision-making processes:

- Authoritative (the leader makes the decision alone).
- Consultative (the leader hears group comments, but then makes the decision alone).
- Voting (the majority wins).
- Consensus (discussion continues until everyone can buy into the decision).[23]

Specifying how input will be used makes expectations clear and focuses the conversation.

Formal meetings are run under strict rules, like the rules of parliamentary procedure summarized in *Robert's Rules of Order.* Motions must be made formally before a topic can be debated. Each point is settled by a vote. **Minutes** record each motion and the vote on it. See the BAC Web site for links to minutes posted on the Web. Formal rules help the meeting run smoothly if the group is very large or if the agenda is very long. **Informal meetings,** which are much more common in the workplace, are run more loosely. Votes may not be taken if most people seem to agree. Minutes may not be kept. Informal meetings are better for team-building and problem solving.

See the BAC Web site for links to pages about meetings, parliamentary procedure, and writing meeting minutes.

Planning the agenda is the foundation of a good meeting. A good agenda indicates

- Whether each item is presented for information, for discussion, or for a decision.
- Who is sponsoring or introducing each item.
- How much time is allotted for each item.

Many groups put first routine items on which agreement will be easy. If there's a long list of routine items, save them till the end or dispense with them in an omnibus motion. An **omnibus motion** allows a group to approve many items together rather than voting on each separately. A single omnibus motion might cover multiple changes to operational guidelines, or a whole slate of candidates for various offices, or various budget recommendations. It's important to schedule controversial items early in the meeting, when people's energy level is high, and to allow enough time for full discussion. Giving a controversial item only half an hour at the end of the day or evening makes people suspect that the leaders are trying to manipulate them.

Pay attention to people and process as well as to the task at hand. At informal meetings, a good leader observes nonverbal feedback and invites everyone to participate. If conflict seems to be getting out of hand, a leader may want to focus attention on the group process and ways that it could deal with conflict, before getting back to the substantive issues.

If the group doesn't formally vote, the leader should summarize the group's consensus after each point. At the end of the meeting, the leader must summarize all decisions and remind the group who is responsible for implementing or following up on each item. If no other notes are taken, someone should record the decisions and assignments. Long minutes will be most helpful if assignments are set off visually from the narrative.

If you're planning a long meeting, for example, a training session or a conference, recognize that networking is part of the value of the meeting. Allow short breaks at least every two hours and generous breaks twice a day so participants can talk informally to each other. If participants will be strangers, include some social functions so they can get to know each other. If they will have different interests or different levels of knowledge, plan concurrent sessions on different topics or for people with different levels of expertise.

Collaborative Writing

Whatever your career, it is likely that some of the documents you produce will be written with a group. Lisa Ede and Andrea Lunsford found that 87% of the 700 professionals in seven fields who responded to their survey sometimes wrote as members of a team or a group.[24] Collaboration is often prompted by one of the following situations:

1. The task is too big or the time is too short for one person to do all the work.
2. No one person has all the knowledge required to do the task.
3. A group representing different perspectives must reach a consensus.
4. The stakes for the task are so high that the organization wants the best efforts of as many people as possible; no one person wants the sole responsibility for the success or failure of the document.

Collaborative writing can be done by two people or by a much larger group. The group can be democratic or run by a leader who makes decisions alone. The group may share or divide responsibility for each of the eight stages in the writing process.

Research in collaborative writing is beginning to tell us about the strategies that produce the best writing. Rebecca Burnett found that student groups that voiced disagreements as they analyzed, planned, and wrote a document produced significantly better documents than those that suppressed disagreement, going along with whatever was first proposed.[25] A case study of two collaborative writing teams in a state agency found that the successful group distributed power in an egalitarian way, worked to soothe hurt feelings, and was careful to involve all group members. In terms of writing process, the successful group understood the task as a response to a rhetorical situation, planned revisions as a group, saw supervisors' comments as legitimate, and had a positive attitude toward revision.[26] Ede and Lunsford's detailed case studies of collaborative teams in business, government, and science create an

Long-Distance Collaboration*

Every new commercial aircraft that we [at Boeing] create involves hundreds of design teams that are located in different cities throughout the United States. We've studied how teams work together, and we've come up with a few guidelines to help improve that process.

First, technology should never replace face-to-face contact. When Boeing begins building a new airplane, the first thing that it does is to bring the project's team leaders and other key people together. That initial face-to-face meeting helps people get to know one another, builds trust, and helps people to agree on goals.

Second, when people are teleconferencing, everyone involved must be very conscious of social behavior. . . . For instance, it's important to designate a meeting facilitator—someone who makes sure that everyone feels included and gets heard.

Third, one person should be responsible for setting up equipment. . . .

Finally, in real estate, it's location, location, location; in long-distance collaboration it's audio, audio, audio. I have observed 25 engineers try to have a conference call using a tiny speakerphone. My most important piece of teleconferencing advice: Use good speakerphones!

*Quoted from Steve Poltrock, "In Long-Distance Collaboration, It's Audio, Audio, Audio," *Fast Company*, June 2000, 142.

The Integrative Approach*

I have had the opportunity to write in groups . . . in my MBA program at the University of Chicago. The most effective writing process was a truly integrative approach. Our group wrote a paper on leadership that combined six hour-long interviews. The final paper was clear and well organized and read like a single document.

One of the worst ways I have approached group writing is the divide-and-conquer model. . . . On the day before the paper is due, everyone slams the parts together. When you read a paper like this, you realize the problems cut-and-paste writing causes. . . . Simply pasting sections together makes it painfully obvious that there is no continuous style in the document, and that detracts from the content. Had we done this with our leadership paper, it would have been simply six summations of interviews without any comparison of our leaders' styles and experiences.

As we worked, we shared drafts among the six group members by e-mail. This allowed us to revise and edit the document quickly and efficiently. You simply cannot do this with a faxed copy. One person, usually the strongest writer in the group, should complete the final edit of the document to standardize its look and feel.

*Quoted from George Fogel, statement to Kitty Locker, February 18, 1997.

"emerging profile of effective collaborative writers": "They are flexible; respectful of others; attentive and analytical listeners; able to speak and write clearly and articulately; dependable and able to meet deadlines; able to designate and share responsibility, to lead and to follow; open to criticism but confident in their own abilities; ready to engage in creative conflict."[27]

Planning the Work and the Document

Collaborative writing is most successful when the group articulates its understanding of the document's purposes and audiences and explicitly discusses the best way to achieve these rhetorical goals. Businesses schedule formal planning sessions for large projects to set up a time line specifying intermediate and final due dates, meeting dates, who will attend each meeting, and who will do what. Putting the plan in writing reduces misunderstandings during the project.

When you plan a collaborative writing project,

- Make your analysis of the problem, the audience, and your purposes explicit so you know where you agree and where you disagree.
- Plan the organization, format, and style of the document before anyone begins to write to make it easier to blend sections written by different authors.
- Consider your work styles and other commitments. A writer working alone can stay up all night to finish a single-authored document. But members of a group need to work together to accommodate each other's styles and to enable members to meet other commitments.
- Build some leeway into your deadlines. It's harder for a group to finish a document when one person's part is missing than it is for a single writer to finish the last section of a document on which he or she has done all the work.

Composing the Drafts

Most writers find that composing alone is faster than composing in a group. However, composing together may reduce revision time later, since the group examines every choice as it is made.

When you draft a collaborative writing project,

- Use word processing to make it easier to produce the many drafts necessary in a collaborative document.
- If the quality of writing is crucial, have the best writer(s) draft the document after everyone has gathered the necessary information.

Revising the Document

Revising a collaborative document requires attention to content, organization, and style. The following guidelines can make the revision process more effective:

- Evaluate the content and discuss possible revisions as a group. Brainstorm ways to improve each section so the person doing the revisions has some guidance.
- Recognize that different people favor different writing styles. If the style satisfies the demands of standard English and the conventions of business writing, accept it even if you wouldn't say it that way.
- When the group is satisfied with the content of the document, one person—probably the best writer—should make any changes necessary to make the writing style consistent throughout.

Meeting rooms equipped with laptops, pagers, and cell phones help Intel employees collaborate on group projects with colleagues around the world.

Editing and Proofreading the Document

Since writers' mastery of standard English varies, a group report needs careful editing and proofreading.

- Have at least one person check the whole document for correctness in grammar, mechanics, and spelling and for consistency in the way that format elements, names, and numbers are handled.
- Run the document through a spell checker if possible.
- Even if you use a computerized spell checker, at least one human being should proofread the document too.

Making the Group Process Work

All of the information in this chapter can help your collaborative writing group listen effectively, run meetings efficiently, and deal with conflict constructively. The following suggestions apply specifically to writing groups:

- Give yourselves plenty of time to discuss problems and find solutions. Purdue students who are writing group reports spend six to seven hours a week outside class in group meetings—not counting the time they spend gathering information and writing their drafts.[28]
- Take the time to get to know group members and to build group loyalty. Group members will work harder and the final document will be better if the group is important to members.
- Be a responsible group member. Attend all the meetings; carry out your responsibilities.
- Be aware that people have different ways of experiencing reality and of expressing themselves. Use the principles of semantics discussed in Appendix C ⟹ to reduce miscommunication.
- Because talking is "looser" than writing, people in a group can think they agree when they don't. Don't assume that because the discussion went smoothly, a draft written by one person will necessarily be acceptable.

The Importance of Planning, I*

Chris Higgins, . . . [BankAmerica's senior vice president responsible for national currency services] says, spend less time "doing" and more time "planning." Higgins warns that teams are often too quick to act and too slow to think. "If you spend enough time planning," he says, "execution time can be very short. If you work on the fly, you do things fast. But you may do the wrong things, and that slows down the project."

Recently, for example, Higgins led a 500-person team that had one year to develop a system for BankAmerica to accept deposits across state lines. Everyone was eager to "get to work." But Higgins insisted that the team devote six months to planning the system, evaluating business implications, and anticipating technical challenges—all before it wrote a single line of code. After writing the code, the team spent three months testing and refining it. "My approach is 50% planning, 25% doing, and 25% testing and training."

*Quoted from Gina Imperato, "He's Become BankAmerica's 'Mr. Project,' " *Fast Company*, January 1998, 42–44.

The Importance of Planning, II*

Higgins has a second piece of advice: Remember that different projects have lots in common. . . .

Higgins first learned this principle in the army, when he was in charge of supplying a Ranger battalion stationed at Fort Lewis, Washington. He led a unit of 120 people that supported 650 Rangers. Higgins and his team had to supply diverse missions in four different climates: mountain, tropical, desert, and arctic. The goal was to have the support group airborne, headed to meet the Rangers with the right equipment, 18 hours after receiving its orders. Under the previous leader, the . . . best time was 72 hours. Higgins's team eventually did the job in 12 hours.

How? "The previous team always waited until it knew where the mission was headed before assembling gear," Higgins says. "But a lot of what the Rangers need—food, medical supplies, ammunition—is the same no matter where they go." So Higgins and his unit figured out how to prepackage such supplies and how to pack them onto airplanes with maximum efficiency. "Focusing on what's common between projects [has] worked for us time and again."

*Quoted from Gina Imperato, "He's Become BankAmerica's 'Mr. Project,'" *Fast Company*, January 1998, 42–44.

Summary of Key Points

- **Interpersonal communication** is communication between people.
- In interpersonal communication, **hearing** denotes perceiving sounds. **Listening** means decoding and interpreting them correctly.
- To avoid listening errors caused by inattention,
  - Be conscious of the points you need to know and listen for them.
  - At the end of the conversation, check your understanding with the other person.
  - After the conversation, write down key points that affect deadlines or how work will be evaluated.
- To reduce listening errors caused by misinterpretation,
  - Don't ignore instructions you think are unnecessary.
  - Consider the other person's background and experiences. Why is this point important to the speaker?
  - Paraphrase what the speaker has said, giving him or her a chance to correct your understanding.
- In **active listening,** receivers actively demonstrate that they've heard and understood a speaker by feeding back either the literal meaning or the emotional content or both.
- Effective groups balance information leadership, interpersonal leadership, and procedural group management.
- The **standard agenda** is a seven-step process for solving problems. In **dot planning** the group brainstorms ideas. Then each individual affixes adhesive dots by the points or proposals he or she cares most about.
- A case study of six student groups completing class projects found that students in successful groups had leaders who set clear deadlines, scheduled frequent meetings, and dealt directly with conflict that emerged in the group; an inclusive decision-making style; and a higher proportion of members who worked actively on the project.
- Students who spent the most time meeting with their groups got the highest grades.
- **Groupthink** is the tendency for groups to put such a high premium on agreement that they directly or indirectly punish dissent. The best correctives to groupthink are to consciously search for additional alternatives, to test one's assumptions against those of a range of other people, and to protect the right of each person in the group to disagree.
- **Conversational style** denotes our conversational patterns and the meaning we give to them: the way we show interest, politeness, and appropriateness.
- To resolve conflicts, first make sure that the people involved really disagree. Next, check to see that everyone's information is correct. Discover the needs each person is trying to meet. The **presenting problem** that surfaces as the subject of dissention may or may not be the real problem. Search for alternatives.
- Constructive ways to respond to criticism include paraphrasing, checking for feelings, checking inferences, and buying time with limited agreement.
- Use statements about your own feelings to own the problem and avoid attacking the audience. In conflict, *I* statements are good you-attitude!
- To make meetings more effective,
  - State the purpose of the meeting at the beginning.
  - Distribute an agenda that indicates whether each item is for information, for discussion, for action, and how long each is expected to take.

- Allow enough time to discuss controversial issues.
- Pay attention to people and process as well as to the task at hand.
- If you don't take formal votes, summarize the group's consensus after each point. At the end of the meeting, summarize all decisions and remind the group who is responsible for implementing or following up on each item.
- **Collaborative writing** means working with other writers to produce a single document. Writers producing a joint document need to pay attention not only to the basic steps in the writing process but also to the processes of group formation and conflict resolution.

Using Informal Meetings to Advance Your Career

You'll see your supervisor several times a week. Some of these meetings will be accidental: you'll meet by the coffee pot or ride up the elevator together. Some of them will be deliberately initiated: your boss will stop by your work station, or you'll go to your boss's office to ask for something.

Take advantage of these meetings by planning for them. These informal meetings are often short. An elevator ride, for example, may last about three minutes. So plan 90-second scripts that you can use to give your boss a brief report on what you're doing, ask for something you need, or lay the groundwork for an important issue.

Planning scripts is especially important if your boss doesn't give you much feedback or mentoring. In this case, your boss probably doesn't see you as promotable. You need to take the initiative. Make statements that show the boss you're thinking about ways to work smarter. Show that you're interested in learning more so that you can be more valuable to the organization.

| CHAPTER 12 | Exercises and Problems |

Getting Started

12.1   Making Ethical Choices

Indicate whether you consider each of the following actions ethical, unethical, or a gray area. Which of the actions would you do? Which would you feel uncomfortable doing? Which would you refuse to do?

1. Taking home office supplies (e.g., pens, markers, calculators, etc.) for personal use.
2. Inflating your evaluation of a subordinate because you know that only people ranked *excellent* will get pay raises.
3. Making personal long-distance calls on the company phone.
4. Writing a feasibility report about a new product and de-emphasizing test results that show it could cause cancer.
5. Coming in to the office in the evening to use the company's word processor and computer for personal projects.
6. Designing an ad campaign for a cigarette brand.
7. Working as an accountant for a company that makes or advertises cigarettes.
8. Working as a manager in a company that exploits its nonunionized hourly workers.

9. Writing copy for a company's annual report hiding or minimizing the fact that the company pollutes the environment.

10. "Padding" your expense account by putting on it charges you did not pay for.

11. Writing a subscription letter for a sex magazine that glamorizes rape, violence, and sadism.

12. Doing the taxes of a client who publishes a sex magazine that glamorizes rape, violence, and sadism.

13. Telling a job candidate that the company "usually" grants cost-of-living raises every six months, even though you know that the company is losing money and plans to cancel cost-of-living raises for the next year.

14. Laughing at the racist or sexist jokes a client makes, even though you find them offensive.

15. Reading *The Wall Street Journal* on company time.

12.2   Identifying Responses That Show Active Listening

Which of the following responses show active listening? Which responses block communication?

1. Comment: Whenever I say something, the group just ignores me.

   Responses:

   a. That's because your ideas aren't very good. Do more planning before group meetings.
   b. Nobody listens to me, either.
   c. You're saying that nobody builds on your ideas.

2. Comment: I've done more than my share of work on this project. But the people who have been freeloading are going to get the same grade I've worked so hard to earn.

   Responses:

   a. Yes, we're all going to get the same grade.
   b. Are you afraid we won't do well on the assignment?
   c. It sounds like you feel resentful.

3. Comment: My parents are going to kill me if I don't have a job lined up when I graduate.

   Responses:

   a. You know they're exaggerating. They won't *really* kill you.
   b. Can you blame them? I mean, it's taken you six years to get a degree. Surely you've learned something to make you employable!
   c. If you act the way in interviews that you do in our class, I'm not surprised. Companies want people with good attitudes and good work ethics.

12.3   Practicing Active Listening

Go around the room for this exercise. In turn, let each student complain about something (large or small) that really bothers him or her. Then the next student(s) will

a. Offer a statement of limited agreement that would buy time.

b. Paraphrase the statement.
c. Check for feelings that might lie behind the statement.
d. Offer inferences that might motivate the statement.

12.4   Brainstorming Ways to Resolve Conflicts

Suggest one or more ways that each of the following groups could deal with the conflict(s) it faces.

1. Mike and Takashi both find writing hard. Elise has been getting better grades than either of them, so they offer to do all the research if she'll organize the document and write, revise, edit, and proofread it. Elise thinks that this method would leave her doing a disproportionate share of the work. Moreover, scheduling the work would be difficult, since she wouldn't know how good their research was until the last minute.

2. Because of their class and work schedules, Lars and Andrea want to hold group meetings from 8 to 10 PM, working later if need be. But Juan's wife works the evening shift, and he needs to be home with his children, two of whom have to be in bed before 8. He wants to meet from 8 to 10 AM, but the others don't want to meet that early.

3. Lynn wants to divide up the work exactly equally, with firm due dates. Marcia is trying to get into medical school. She says she'd rather do the lion's share of the work so that she knows it's good.

Jessie's father is terminally ill. This group isn't very important in terms of what's going on in her life, and she knows she may have to miss some group meetings.

4. Sherry is aware that she is the person in her group who always points out the logical flaws in arguments: she's the one who reminds the group that they haven't done all the parts of the assignment. She doesn't want her group to turn in a flawed product, but she wonders whether the other group members see her as too critical.

5. Jim's group missed several questions on their group quiz. Talking to Tae-Suk after class, Jim learns that Tae-Suk knew all the answers. "Why didn't you say anything?" Jim asks angrily. Tae-Suk responds quietly, "Todd said that he knew the answers. I did not want to argue with him. We have to work together, and I do not want anyone to lose face."

12.5 Taking Minutes

As Your Instructor Directs, have two or more people take minutes of each class or collaborative group meeting for a week. Compare the accounts of the same meeting.

- To what extent do they agree on what happened?
- Does one contain information missing in other accounts?
- Do any accounts disagree on a specific fact?
- How do you account for the differences you find?

12.6 Keeping a Journal about a Group

As you work in a collaborative writing group, keep a journal after each group meeting.
- What happened?
- What roles did you play in the meeting?
- What conflicts arose? How were they handled?
- What strategies could you use to make the next meeting go smoothly?
- Record one observation about each group member.

E-Mail Messages

In Problems 12.7 through 12.11, assume that your group has been asked to recommend a solution.

As Your Instructor Directs,
- Send e-mail messages to group members laying out your initial point of view on the issue and discussing the various options.
- As a group, answer the message.
- Write a memo to your instructor telling how satisfied you are with
  a. The decision your group reached.
  b. The process you used to reach it.

12.7 Recommending a Policy on Student Entrepreneurs

Assume that your small group comprises the officers in student government on your campus. You receive this e-mail from the Dean of Students:

As you know, campus policy says that no student may use campus resources to conduct business-related activities. Students can't conduct business out of dorm rooms or use university e-mail addresses for business. They can't post business Web pages on the university server.

On the other hand, a survey conducted by the Kauffman Center for Entrepreneurial Leadership showed that 7 out of 10 teens want to become entrepreneurs.

Should campus policy be changed to allow students to use dorm rooms and university e-mail addresses for business? (And then what happens when roommates complain and our network can't carry the increased e-mail traffic?) Please recommend what support (if any) should be given to student entrepreneurs.

Write a group report recommending what (if anything) your campus should do for student entrepreneurs and supporting your recommendation.

Hints:

■ Does your campus offer other support for entrepreneurs (courses, a business plan competition, a start-up incubator)? What should be added or expanded?

■ Is it realistic to ask alumni for money to fund student start-ups?

■ Are campus dorms, e-mail, phone, and delivery services funded by tax dollars? If your school is a public institution, do state or local laws limit business use?

12.8   Recommending a Fair Way to Assign Work around the Holidays

Assume that your small group comprises your organization's Labor-Management Committee. This e-mail arrives from the general manager:

> Subject: Allocating Holiday Hours
>
> As you know, lots of people want to take extra time off around holidays to turn three-day weekends into longer trips. But we do need to stay open. Right now, there are allegations that some supervisors give the time off to their friends. But even "fair" systems, such as giving more senior workers first choice at time off, or requiring that workers with crucial skills work, also create problems. And possibly we need a different system around Christmas, when many people want to take off a week or more, than around lesser holidays, when most people take only an extra day or two.
>
> Please recommend an equitable way to decide how to assign hours.

Write a group response recommending the best way to assign hours and supporting your recommendation.

Hint:

Agree on an office, factory, store, hospital, or other workplace to use for this problem.

12.9   Recommending a Dress Policy

Assume that your small group comprises your organization's Labor-Management Committee
    This e-mail arrives from the CEO:

> In the last 10 years, we became increasingly casual. But changed circumstances seem to call for more formality. Is it time to reinstate a dress policy? If so, what should it be?

Write a group response recommending the appropriate dress for employees and supporting your recommendation.

Hint:

Agree on an office, factory, store, or other workplace to use for this problem.

12.10   Responding to an Employee Grievance

Assume that your small group comprises the Labor-Management committee at the headquarters of a chain of grocery stores. This e-mail arrives from the vice president for human resources:

As you know, company policy requires that employees smile at customers and make eye contact with them. In the past 9 months, 12 employees have filed grievances over this rule. They say they are being harassed by customers who think they are flirting with them. A produce clerk claims customers have propositioned her and followed her to her car. Another says "Let *me* decide who I am going to say hello to with a big smile." The union wants us to change the policy to let workers *not* make eye contact with customers, and to allow workers to refuse to carry groceries to a customer's car at night. My own feeling is that we want to maintain our image as a friendly store that cares about customers, but that we also don't want to require behavior that leads to harassment. Let's find a creative solution.

Write a group response recommending whether to change the policy and supporting your recommendation.

12.11   Recommending Whether to Keep the Skybox

Assume that your small group comprises the executive committee of a large company that has a luxury football skybox. (Depending on the stadium, a skybox for a professional football team may cost as little as $100,000 a year or 10 times that much. A portion—perhaps up to 30%—of the cost may be deductible as a business expense.) The CEO says, "Times are tight. We need to reevaluate whether we should retain the skybox."

Write a group response recommending whether to keep the skybox and supporting your recommendation.

Hints:

- Agree on a company to use for this problem.
- Does having a skybox match the values in the company's mission statement? If you keep the skybox, who should have priority in using it?
- How is the company doing financially? Is it laying off workers?

Web Pages

As Your Instructor Directs,

in Problems 12.12 and 12.13,

a. Turn in two laser copies of your page(s). On another page, give the URL for each link.

b. Turn in one laser copy of your page(s) and a disk with the HTML code and .gif files.

c. Write a group memo to your instructor (1) identifying the audience for which the page is designed and explaining (2) the search strategies you used to find material on this topic, (3) why you chose the pages and information you've included, (4) why you chose the layout and graphics you've used, and (5) who did what on the project.

d. Present your page orally to the class.

12.12   Creating a Web Page for Multicultural Managers and Workers

1. Create a Web page for multicultural managers. What links would help managers better understand the multicultural workforce?

2. Create a Web page for members of a group that has not traditionally been part of the power structure of US business. (The group could be defined by class, gender, race and ethnicity, religion, physical ability, age, sexual orientation, or education.) What links would provide support to members of this group and help them attain their full potential in their work lives?

3. Create a Web page for a nonprofit, business, or government organization devoted to the advancement of a group that has not traditionally been part of the power structure of US business. (The group could be defined by class, gender, race and ethnicity, religion, physical ability, age, sexual orientation, or education.) You must choose an organization that does not already have a Web page.

12.13   Creating a Web Page on a Topic of Your Choice

Create a Web page on a topic of your choice. Possibilities include

- Information for students new to your campus.
- Study tips for students in your major.
- Links about speakers, bands, or events coming to your town.

- Links to advice about online résumés and to good (and poor) résumés on the Web.
- Information about how to construct a Web page.

Memo and Brochure Assignments

12.14   Answering an Ethics Question

Assume that your small group comprises your organization's Ethics Committee. You receive the following anonymous note:

> People are routinely using the company letterhead to write letters to members of Congress, senators, and even the president stating their positions on various issues. Making their opinions known is of course their right, but doing so on letterhead stationery implies that they are speaking for the company, which they are not.
>
> I think that the use of letterhead for anything other than official company business should be prohibited.

Determine the best solution to the problem. Then write a message to all employees stating your decision and building support for it.

12.15   Answering an Inquiry about Photos

You've just been named Vice President for Diversity, the first person in your organization to hold this position. Today, you receive this memo from Sheila Lathan, who edits the employee newsletter.

Subject: Photos in the Employee Newsletter

Please tell me what to do about photos in the monthly employee newsletter. I'm concerned that almost no single issue represents the diversity of employees we have here.

As you know, our layout allows two visuals each month. One of those is always the employee of the month (EM). In the last year, most of those have been male and all but two have been white. What makes it worse is that people want photos that make them look good. You may remember that Ron Olmos was the EM two months ago; in the photo he wanted me to use, you can't tell that he's in a wheelchair. Often the EM is the only photo; the other visual is often a graph of sales or something relating to quality.

Even if the second visual is another photo, it may not look balanced in terms of gender and race. After all, 62% of our employees are men, and 78% are white. Should the pictures try to represent those percentages? The leadership positions (both in management and in the union) are even more heavily male and white. Should we run pictures of people doing important things, and risk continuing the imbalance?

I guess I could use more visuals, but then there wouldn't be room for as many stories—and people really like to see their names in print. Plus, giving people information about company activities and sales is important to maintaining goodwill. A bigger newsletter would be one way to have more visuals and keep the content, but with the cost-cutting measures we're under, that doesn't look likely.

What should I do?

As Your Instructor Directs,

a. Work in a small group with other students to come up with a recommendation for Sheila.

b. Write a memo responding to her.

c. Write an article for the employee newsletter about the photo policy you recommend and how it relates to the company's concern for diversity.

12.16   Writing a Meeting Manual

Create a manual for students next term telling them how to have effective meetings as they work on collaborative projects.

Source: Adapted from Miles McCall, Beth Stewart, and Timothy Clipson, "Teaching Communication Skills for Meeting Management," *1998 Refereed Proceedings,* Association for Business Communication Southwestern United States, ed. Marsha L. Bayless (Nacogdoches, TX), 68.

12.17   Planning a Game

Many companies are using games and contests to solve problems in an enjoyable way. One company promised to give everyone $30 a month extra if they got the error rate below 0.5%. The rate improved immediately. After several successful months, the incentive went to $40 a month for getting it under 0.3% and finally to $50 a month for getting it under 0.2%. Another company offered workers two "well hours" if they got in by 7 AM every day for a month. An accounting and financial-services company divided its employees into two teams. The one that got the most referrals and new accounts received a meal prepared and served by the losing team (the firm paid for the food). Games are best when the people who will play them create them. Games need to make business sense and give rewards to many people, not just a few. Rewards should be small.

Think of a game or contest that could improve productivity or quality in your classroom, on campus, or in a workplace you know well.

As Your Instructor Directs,

a. Write a message to persuade your instructor, boss, or other decision maker to authorize the game or contest.

b. Write a message announcing the game and persuading people to participate in it.

Source: Based on John Case, *The Open-Book Experience: Lessons from Over 100 Companies Who Successfully Transformed Themselves* (Reading, MA: Addison-Wesley, 1998), 129–201.

12.18   Creating Brochures

In a collaborative group, create a series of brochures for an organization and present your design and copy to the class in a group oral presentation. Your brochures should work well as a series but also be capable of standing alone if a reader picks up just one. They should share a common visual design and be appropriate for your purposes and audience. You may use sketches rather than photos or finished drawings. Text, however, should be as it will appear in the final copy.

As you prepare your series, talk to a knowledgeable person in the organization. For this assignment, as long

as the person is knowledgeable, he or she does not have to have the power to approve the brochures.

In a manila folder, turn in

1. Two copies of each brochure.

2. A copy of your approved proposal (see Chapter 13).

3. A narrative explaining (a) how you responded to the wishes of the person in the organization who was your contact and (b) five of the choices you made in terms of content, visuals, and design and why you made these choices.

12.19   Interviewing Workers about Listening

Interview someone who works in an organization about his or her on-the-job listening. Possible questions to ask include the following:

- Whom do you listen to as part of your job? Your superior? Subordinates? (How many levels down?) Customers or clients? Who else?

- How much time a day do you spend listening?

- What people do you talk to as part of your job? Do you feel they hear what you say? How do you tell whether or not they're listening?

- Do you know of any problems that came up because someone didn't listen? What happened?

- What do you think prevents people from listening effectively? What advice would you have for someone on how to listen more accurately?

As Your Instructor Directs,

a. Share your information with a small group of students in your class.

b. Present your findings orally to the class.

c. Present your findings in a memo to your instructor.

d. Join with other students to present your findings in a group report.

12.20   Analyzing the Dynamics of a Group

Analyze the dynamics of a task group of which you are a member. Answer the following questions:

1. Who was the group's leader? How did the leader emerge? Were there any changes in or challenges to the original leader?

2. Describe the contribution each member made to the group and the roles each person played.

3. Did any members of the group officially or unofficially drop out? Did anyone join after the group had begun working? How did you deal with the loss or addition of a group member, both in terms of getting the work done and in terms of helping people work together?

4. What planning did your group do at the start of the project? Did you stick to the plan or revise it? How did the group decide that revision was necessary?

5. How did your group make decisions? Did you vote? reach decisions by consensus?

6. What problems or conflicts arose? Did the group deal with them openly? To what extent did they interfere with the group's task?

7. Evaluate your group both in terms of its task and in terms of the satisfaction members felt. How did this group compare with other task groups you've been part of? What made it better or worse?

As you answer the questions,

▪ Be honest. You won't lose points for reporting that your group had problems or did something "wrong."

▪ Show your knowledge of good group dynamics. That is, if your group did something wrong, show that you know what *should* have been done. Similarly, if your group worked well, show that you know *why* it worked well.

▪ Be specific. Give examples or anecdotes to support your claims.

As Your Instructor Directs,

a. Discuss these questions with the other group members.

b. Present your findings orally to the class.

c. Present your findings in an individual memo to your instructor.

d. Join with the other group members to write a collaborative memo to your instructor.

13

Planning, Proposing, and Researching Reports

Planning, Proposing, and Researching Reports

James B. Lane
Vice President, Cap Gemini Ernst & Young

A specialist in business change management, Jim Lane is the City Lead for Cap Gemini's high growth practice in the Columbus, Ohio, office. Cap Gemini is one of the largest management and IT consulting firms in the world.

www.cgey.com

A recent competitive bidding process for what I'll call ABC Motors illustrates three key points about sales proposals.

Be Prepared to Work Quickly.

Three days after the request for proposals came out, we met with ABC's CFO. That was a Wednesday. Before the weekend was out, we had established a proposal war room complete with white boards, LAN access, a PC projection system, and a globally accessible Lotus Notes database for sharing proposal work products across the planet. Three weeks after the initial meeting, we presented the winning proposal in a facsimile of ABC's office space complete with desks, computers, graphical posters, and a 3,000-step mural-size work plan outlining the changes we proposed.

Study Your Audience and the Problem.

In order to win consistently, you must listen to the client. Design your proposal to meet the client's spoken and unspoken needs.

We assembled a team of 15 subject-matter experts to work one-on-one with client personnel in a two-day information-gathering session. We used what we learned to propose redesigning the work to reduce costs and increase return on investment. This focus on value also enabled us to identify an opportunity related to but not part of the original RFP.

> *"In order to win consistently, you must listen to the client."*

Identify Win Themes.

The written proposal, your oral presentation, your attire, and the staff associated with the sale must all join in a harmonious whole. Focus on a few key messages. Our Win themes included our automotive industry experience, our technical depth in related areas, our program management capabilities, and our knowledge management and reuse processes.

We tailored our themes to competitive information we heard from the client. For example, the competitor who held the current contract for services had not interacted effectively with ABC's senior executives. To exploit this weakness, we included specific steps in the proposed work plan to help stakeholders in the company buy into the project.

Summary.

As a result of intense work, audience analysis, and insight, we won a seven-figure contract for the firm.

Proposals and reports depend on research. The research may be as simple as pulling up data with a computer program or as complicated as calling many different people, conducting focus groups and surveys, or even planning and conducting experiments. Care in planning, proposing, and researching reports is needed to produce reliable data.

In writing any report, there are five basic steps:

1. Define the problem.
2. Gather the necessary data and information.
3. Analyze the data and information.
4. Organize the information.
5. Write the report.

After reviewing the varieties of reports, this chapter focuses on the first two steps. Chapter 14 discusses the last three steps.

Varieties of Reports

Many kinds of documents are called *reports*. In some organizations, a report is a long document or a document that contains numerical data. In others, one- and two-page memos are called *reports*. In still others, *reports* consist of PowerPoint slides printed out and bound together. A short report to a client may use letter format. **Formal reports** contain formal elements such as a title page, a transmittal, a table of contents, and a list of illustrations. **Informal reports** may be letters and memos or even computer printouts of production or sales figures. But all reports, whatever their length or degree of formality, provide the information that people in organizations need to make plans and solve problems.

Reports can just provide information, both provide information and analyze it, or provide information and analysis to support a recommendation (see Figure 13.1). Reports can be called **information reports** if they collect data for the reader, **analytical reports** if they interpret data but do not recommend action, and **recommendation reports** if they recommend action or a solution.

The following reports can be information, analytical, or recommendation reports, depending on what they provide:

- *Accident reports* can simply list the nature and causes of accidents in a factory or office. These reports can also recommend ways to make conditions safer.
- *Credit reports* can simply summarize an applicant's income and other credit obligations. These reports can also evaluate the applicant's collateral and creditworthiness.
- *Progress* and *interim reports* can simply record the work done so far and the work remaining on a project. These reports can also recommend that a project be stopped, continued, or restructured.
- *Trip reports* can simply share what the author learned at a conference or during a visit to a customer or supplier. These reports can also recommend action based on that information.
- *Closure reports* can simply document the causes of a failure or of possible products that are not economically or technically feasible under current conditions. They can also recommend action to prevent such failures in the future.

A Timeline for Writing Reports

When you write a report, plan to spend half your time analyzing your data, writing and revising the draft, and preparing visuals and slides. Figure 5.1

FIGURE 13.1 Three Levels of Reports

Reports can provide

Information only

■ **Sales reports** (sales figures for the week or month).

■ **Quarterly reports** (figures showing a plant's productivity and profits for the quarter).

Information plus analysis

■ **Annual reports** (financial data and an organization's accomplishments during the past year).

■ **Audit reports** (interpretations of the facts revealed during an audit).

■ **Make-good or pay-back reports** (calculations of the point at which a new capital investment will pay for itself).

Information plus analysis plus a recommendation

■ **Feasibility reports** evaluate two or more alternatives and recommend which alternative the organization should choose.

■ **Justification reports** justify the need for a purchase, an investment, a new personnel line, or a change in procedure.

■ **Problem-solving reports** identify the causes of an organizational problem and recommend a solution.

The Questions behind the Question*

Barbara Waugh is Worldwide Personnel Manager at Hewlett Packard Labs. Five years ago, she was asked to investigate the following question: Why wasn't HP labs ranked as the best in the business?

To answer that question, she asked even more basic questions: What does it mean to be the "best" research lab? Having the most Nobel laureates? Filing the most patents? What would it take to become "the best"? Hire more people? Different people? Start different projects? Market current projects better?

A survey asking those questions yielded 800 single-spaced pages of data. She distilled the data into challenges in three areas. *Programs:* HP labs needed clearer priorities and fewer projects. *People:* HP needed to get rid of poor performers more quickly and give good workers more freedom. *Processes:* People needed to share information more effectively.

*Quoted from Katherine Mieszkowski, "I Grew Up Thinking That Change Was Cataclysmic. The Way We've Done It Here Is to Start Slow and Work Small," *Fast Company*, December 1998, 149–50.

(◄▥ p. 114) shows how a writer might divide the time for a report to be prepared in 30 days of full-time work. When you write a report for a class project, plan to complete at least one-fourth of your research before you write the proposal. Begin analyzing your data as you collect it; prepare your list of sources and drafts of visuals as you go along. Save at least one-fourth of your time at the end of the project to think and write after all your data are collected. For a collaborative report, you'll need even more time to write and revise.

Up-front planning helps you use your time efficiently. Start by thinking about the whole report process. Read the sample reports in Chapter 14 even before you write your proposal. Talk to your readers to understand how much detail and formality they want. In a company, look at earlier reports. List all the parts of the report you'll need to prepare. Then articulate—to yourself or your group members—the purposes, audiences, and generic constraints for each part. The fuller idea you have of the final product when you start, the fewer drafts you'll need to write and the better your final product will be.

Defining Report Problems

Good report problems grow out of real problems: disjunctions between reality and the ideal, choices that must be made. When you write a report as part of your job, the organization may define the topic. To think of problems for class reports, think about problems that face your college or university; housing units on campus; social, religious, and professional groups on campus and in your city; local businesses; and city, county, state, and federal governments and their agencies. Read your campus and local papers and newsmagazines; watch the news on TV, or listen to it on National Public Radio.

Definitions and Problem Solving*

Microscan asked its sales force to identify "customer defectors." At first, salespeople assumed that a "defector" was a former customer who no longer bought anything. By that definition, very few defectors existed.

But then the term was redefined as customers who had stopped buying *some* products and services. By this definition, quite a few defectors existed. And the fact that each of them had turned to a competitor for some of what they used to buy from Microscan showed that improvements—and improved profits—were possible.

*Based on Frederick F. Reichheld, "Learning from Customer Defects," *Harvard Business Review*, March–April 1996, 56–69.

A good report problem in business or administration meets the following criteria:

1. The problem is
   ■ Real.
   ■ Important enough to be worth solving.
   ■ Narrow but challenging.
2. The audience for the report is
   ■ Real.
   ■ Able to implement the recommended action.
3. The data, evidence, and facts are
   ■ Sufficient to document the severity of the problem.
   ■ Sufficient to prove that the recommendation will solve the problem.
   ■ Available to *you*.
   ■ Comprehensible to *you*.

Often problems need to be narrowed. For example, "improving the college experiences of international students studying in the United States" is far too broad. First, choose one college or university. Second, identify the specific problem. Do you want to increase the social interaction between US and international students? Help international students find housing? Increase the number of ethnic grocery stores and restaurants? Third, identify the specific audience that would have the power to implement your recommendations.

Alissa Kozuh analyzes the words customers type in on the search feature at www.nordstrom.com. She's found five patterns: customers key in particular items ("shoes"), trends ("leopard prints"), departments from the bricks-and-mortar stores ("Brass Plum," the juniors department), designer names, and special occasions ("prom"). The changes she suggested for the site based on her research increased Web sales 32%.

Depending on the specific topic, the audience might be the Office of International Studies, the residence hall counselors, a service organization on campus or in town, a store, or a group of investors.

Pick a problem you can solve in the time available. Six months of full-time (and overtime) work and a team of colleagues might allow you to look at all the ways to make a store more profitable. If you're doing a report in 6 to 12 weeks for a class that is only one of your responsibilities, limit the topic. Depending on your interests and knowledge, you could choose to examine the prices and styles of clothes a store carried, its inventory procedures, its overhead costs, its layout and decor, or its advertising budget.

How you define the problem shapes the solutions you find. For example, suppose that a manufacturer of frozen foods isn't making money. If the problem is defined as a marketing problem, the researcher may analyze the product's price, image, advertising, and position in the market. But perhaps the problem is really that overhead costs are too high due to poor inventory management, or that an inadequate distribution system doesn't get the product to its target market. Defining the problem accurately is essential to finding an effective solution.

Once you've defined your problem, you're ready to write a purpose statement. The purpose statement goes both in your proposal and in your final report. A good **purpose statement** makes three things clear:

- The organizational problem or conflict.
- The specific technical questions that must be answered to solve the problem.
- The rhetorical purpose (to explain, to recommend, to request, to propose) the report is designed to achieve.

The following purpose statements have all three elements:

> Current management methods keep the elk population within the carrying capacity of the habitat but require frequent human intervention. Both wildlife conservation specialists and the public would prefer methods that controlled the elk population naturally. This report will compare the current short-term management techniques (hunting, trapping and transporting, and winter feeding) with two long-term management techniques, habitat modification and the reintroduction of predators. The purpose of this report is to recommend which techniques or combination of techniques would best satisfy the needs of conservationists, hunters, and the public.

Report audience: The superintendent of Yellowstone National Park

> When banner ads on Web pages first appeared in 1994, the initial reponse, or "click-through" rate was about 10%. However, as ads have proliferated on Web pages, the click-through rate has dropped sharply. Rather than assuming that any banner ad will be successful, we need to ask, What characteristics do successful banner ads share? Are ads for certain kinds of products and services or for certain kinds of audiences more likely to be successful on the Web? The purpose of this report is to summarize the available research and anecdotal evidence and to recommend what Leo Burnett should tell its clients about whether and how to use banner ads.

Report audience: Leo Burnett Advertising Agency

To write a good purpose statement, you must understand the basic problem and have some idea of the questions that your report will answer. Note, however, that you can (and should) write the purpose statement before researching the specific alternatives the report will discuss.

FIGURE 13.2   Relationship among Situation, Proposal, and Final Report

Company's current situation	The proposal offers to	The final report will provide
We don't know whether we should change.	Assess whether change is a good idea.	Insight, recommending whether change is desirable.
We need to/want to change, but we don't know exactly what we need to do.	Develop a plan to achieve desired goal.	A plan for achieving the desired change.
We need to/want to change, and we know what to do, but we need help doing it.	Implement the plan, increase (or decrease) measurable outcomes.	A record of the implementation and evaluation process.

Source: Adapted from Richard C. Freed, Shervin Freed, and Joseph D. Romano, *Writing Winning Proposals: Your Guide to Landing the Client, Making the Sale, Persuading the Boss* (New York: McGraw-Hill, 1995), 21.

Writing Proposals

Proposals suggest a method for finding information or solving a problem.[1] Finding the information or solving the problem helps an organization decide whether to change, decide how to change, or implement a change that is agreed on. (See Figure 13.2.)

As Donna Kienzler points out, proposals have two goals: to get the project accepted and to get you accepted to do the job. Proposals must stress reader benefits and provide specific supporting details. Attention to details—including good visual impact and proofreading—helps establish your professional image and suggests that you'd give the same care to the project if your proposal is accepted.[2]

Proposals may be competitive or noncompetitive. *Competitive proposals* compete against each other for limited resources. When you collaborate on a group report, each student may propose a topic; only one can be accepted. Similarly, applications for research funding are often very competitive. The National Science Foundation, for example, funds only 12% of the proposals submitted.[3] Many companies will bid for corporate or government contracts, but only one will be accepted. *Noncompetitive proposals* have no real competition. For example, a company could accept all of the internal proposals it thought would save money or improve quality. Similarly, when students write proposals for reports or theses, the proposals compete not against each other but against standards for doing good research. Therefore, all of the proposals can be accepted. And often a company that is satisfied with a vendor asks for a noncompetitive proposal to renew the contract.

To write a good proposal, you need to have a clear view of the problem you hope to solve and the kind of research or other action needed to solve it. A proposal must answer the following questions convincingly:

■ **What problem are you going to solve?** Show that you understand the problem and the organization's needs. Define the problem as the audience sees it, even if you believe that the presenting problem is part of a larger problem that must first be solved.

■ **How are you going to solve it?** Prove that your methods are feasible. Show that a solution can be found in the time available. Specify the topics you'll investigate. Explain how you'll gather data.

■ **What exactly will you provide for us?** Specify the tangible products you'll produce; explain how you'll evaluate them.

▓ **Can you deliver what you promise?** Show that you have the knowledge, the staff, and the facilities to do what you say you will. Describe your previous work in this area, your other qualifications, and the qualifications of any people who will be helping you.

▓ **What benefits can you offer?** In a sales proposal, several vendors may be able to supply the equipment needed. Show why the company should hire you. Discuss the benefits—direct and indirect—that your firm can provide.

▓ **When will you complete the work?** Provide a detailed schedule showing when each phase of the work will be completed.

▓ **How much will you charge?** Provide a detailed budget that includes costs for materials, salaries, and overhead.

Government agencies and companies often issue **requests for proposals,** known as **RFPs.** Follow the RFP exactly when you respond to a proposal. Competitive proposals are often scored by giving points in each category. Evaluators look only under the heads specified in the RFP. If information isn't there, the proposal gets no points in that category.

Proposals for Class Research Projects

You may be asked to submit a proposal for a report that you will write for a class. Your instructor wants evidence that your problem is not too big and not too small, that you understand it, that your method will give you the information you need, and that you have the knowledge and resources to collect and analyze the data.

A proposal for a student report usually has the following sections:

1. In your first paragraph (no heading), summarize in a sentence or two the topic and purposes of your report.
2. **Problem.** What organizational problem exists? What is wrong? Why does it need to be solved? Is there a history or background that is relevant?
3. **Feasibility.** Are you sure that a solution can be found in the time available? How do you know?
4. **Audience.** Who in the organization would have the power to implement your recommendation? What secondary audiences might be asked to evaluate your report? What audiences would be affected by your recommendation? Will anyone in the organization serve as a gatekeeper, determining whether your report is sent to decision makers? What watchdog audiences might read the report?

    For each of these audiences and for your initial audience (your instructor), give the person's name, job title, and business address and answer the following questions:

    ▓ What is the audience's major concern or priority? What "hot buttons" must you address with care?

    ▓ What will the audience see as advantages of your proposal? What objections, if any, is the reader likely to have?

    ▓ How interested is the audience in the topic of your report?

    ▓ How much does the audience know about the topic of your report?

    List any terms, concepts, equations, or assumptions that one or more of your audiences may need to have explained. Briefly identify ways in which your audiences may affect the content, organization, or style of the report.

5. **Topics to investigate.** List the questions and subquestions you will answer in your report, the topics or concepts you will explain, the aspects of the

Planning a Proposal*

As an Associate Planner for Leo Burnett, I answer key marketing and communication questions to support strategic planning for our clients. . . .

Either the client or someone at the agency asks "Why?" Why do children flip over hamburgers at their favorite restaurants? Why have teens embraced the fashions of the 70s? The questions never end.

Once we identify what we need to know, we usually set up a brainstorming meeting among key agency team members. . . . Here we develop an action plan, which is presented to the client in a written proposal. The proposal outlines the project background (what led to the initiative), the objectives of the project (what we hope to learn), the recommended methods (how and by whom the study will be conducted), the timeline and cost, and any next steps that need to be taken.

*Quoted from Kendra Hatcher to Kitty Locker, March 26, 1997.

Choosing Topics to Investigate*

No report investigates all possible topics. Choose the ones that decision makers care most about and will find most useful.

Specific topics will relate to the specific topic of the report. General topics can include managerial, technical, and social criteria. Here are some examples:

Managerial Criteria

- Cost (e.g., acquisition, maintenance, disposal; taxes).
- Market demand.
- Staffing requirements.
- Organizational impact (distribution of resources; effect on personnel, other projects, and image).
- Consistency with organizational goals.

Technical Criteria

- Availability of technology, materials, parts.
- Compatibility with existing systems.
- Adaptability, flexibility, ability to be upgraded.
- Reliability, longevity, repair record.
- Compliance with legal codes (e.g., environment, Americans with Disabilities Act).

Social Criteria

- Human impact (jobs, morale, employment benefits).
- Environmental impact.
- Safety.
- Quality.
- Ethical issues (e.g., conflict of interest, use of resources, impact on stakeholders).

*Based on Mary M. Lay, Billie J. Wahlstrom, Carolyn Rude, Cindy Selfe, and Jack Selzer, *Technical Communication*, 2nd ed. (Burr Ridge, IL: Irwin/McGraw-Hill, 2000), 510.

problem you will discuss. Indicate how deeply you will examine each of the aspects you plan to treat. Explain your rationale for choosing to discuss some aspects of the problem and not others.

6. **Methods/procedure.** How will you get answers to your questions? Whom will you interview or survey? Provide a draft of your questions. What published sources will you use? Give the full bibliographic references.

   Your METHODS section should clearly indicate how you will get the information needed to answer the questions in the TOPICS TO INVESTIGATE section.

7. **Qualifications/facilities/resources.** Do you have the knowledge and skills needed to conduct this study? Do you have adequate access to the organization? Do you have access to any equipment you will need to conduct your research (computer, books, etc.)? Where will you turn for help if you hit an unexpected snag?

   You'll be more convincing if you have already scheduled an interview, checked out books, or printed out online sources.

8. **Work schedule.** List both the total time you plan to spend on and the date when you expect to finish each of the following activities:

   - Gathering information.
   - Analyzing information.
   - Preparing the progress report.
   - Organizing information.
   - Writing the draft.
   - Revising the draft.
   - Preparing the visuals.
   - Editing the draft.
   - Proofreading the report.

   Organize your work schedule either in a chart or in a calendar. A good schedule provides realistic estimates for each activity, allows time for unexpected snags, and shows that you can complete the work on time.

9. **Call to action.** In your final section, indicate that you'd welcome any suggestions your instructor may have for improving the research plan. Ask your instructor to approve your proposal so that you can begin work on your report.

   Figure 13.3 shows a student proposal for a long report.

   For examples of additional student proposals, see the BAC Web site.

Proposals for Action

You can write a proposal for action or change in your organization. Normally, proposals for action recommend new programs or ways to solve organizational problems. As a new hire in the finance department of International Paper, P. J. Smoot saw a need for career development programs for employees. She wrote a proposal to Human Resources, which accepted the idea and hired her to implement it. Patti Douglas, a customer service representative for Phelps County Bank in Rolla, Missouri, proposed that her bank create a marketing program for mature adults.[4]

Organize a proposal for action as a direct request (p. 216). Explain in detail how your idea could be implemented. Be sure to answer your readers' questions and to overcome objections.

FIGURE 13.3 Proposal for a Student Report Using Survey Research

July 19, 2001

To: Kitty O. Locker   ESR

In subject line ① indicate that this is a proposal ② specify the kind of report ③ specify the topic.

From: Elizabeth Ryan

Subject: Proposal to Write a Problem-Solving Report Recommending Ways to Increase Student Attendance Rates at Ohio State University Women's Basketball Games

Summarize topic and purposes of report.

Ohio State University's (OSU) men's basketball team is a crowd pleaser, selling out home games at the Schottenstein Center in good years. However, the women's basketball team suffers from low attendance figures, filling less than half the Schottenstein Center. The Ohio State University Athletic Department would like to find ways to increase attendance at the women's games. I will assume that this department has asked me to assess possible factors leading to low attendance and suggest marketing and education plans to increase attendance. I will survey students, interview numbers of the Athletic Department, and read online and print sources to find solutions to the problem.

Some reports will need a "Background" section so that the reader can understand what led to the problem statement.

Problem *If "Problem" section is detailed and well-written, you may be able to use it unchanged in your report.*

The Schottenstein Center holds 19,100 fans, but the average general attendance at one of this past year's 17 women's basketball games was 6,256 (Liz Cook, personal communication, June 26, 2001).

The 2001 attendance rate was the lowest of the past three years even though the team went 22-11, the best record of the three years, and won the Women's NIT championship. The highest attendance in the past three years was in the 1998-99 season, when 7,588 fans attended each home game. During that season, the team had a 17-12 record and made the first round of the NCAA finals. Such low attendance, though disappointing, is not unusual. Ironically, in all of the past three years, attendance at the OSU women's basketball team has ranked in the top 10 nationally among collegiate women's basketball games (Liz Cook, personal communication, June 26, 2001).

OSU would like to increase attendance, particularly student attendance, at women's basketball games. Student attendance builds school spirit and the morale of student athletes.

Feasibility *Convince your instructor that you have a backup plan if your original proposal proves unworkable.*

Since basketball is a popular sport, it seems likely that attendance can be increased. Certainly students respond to marketing appeals for sports and other products. If I am unable to demonstrate that possible strategies will increase attendance, I will show readers why the obvious solutions won't work and recommend that the university hire a professional sports marketing consulting firm.

Audience *Show how your audiences will affect how you'll present information in your report.*

All of my audiences are at least somewhat interested in creasing attendance. None of them are hostile, so I will be able to present information straightforwardly. The topic is not technical, so I don't expect to need a glossary. *List your major audiences. Identify their knowledge, interests, and concerns.*

(continued)

FIGURE 13.3   Proposal for a Student Report Using Survey Research *(continued)*

Proposal to Write a Recommendation Report on Attendance at OSU Women's Basketball Games
July 19, 2001
Page 2

My primary audience will be Andy Geiger, Director of the OSU Athletic Department. He has the power to accept or reject my recommendations. I don't know how interested he is in women's basketball, but I assume he is at least somewhat knowledgeable about sports marketing. He will look good if attendance increases.

Secondary audiences to this report include staffers in the Athletic Department who will be asked to implement the recommendations. Director of Marketing Dave Brown and the coaching staff of the basketball team may be asked to evaluate the report. Finally, players and students are part of the secondary audience. Players benefit from student support at games, and the sudents are the people being targeted for increased attendance. Only a few of these secondary audiences will be very interested in my report.

The Athletic Council will act as a watchdog audience. The Council, composed of university faculty, staff, and students, oversees the Athletic Department and encourages strong academics with athletes. The Council wants to promote the university's image. Any suggestions I make will be evaluated on the basis of upholding OSU's image and supporting academics.

You will be my initial audience. You've told me that you like men's basketball but have never been to a women's basketball game, even though several of your friends have season tickets.

Topics to Investigate

Indicate what you'll discuss briefly and what you'll discuss in more detail. This list should match your audience's concerns.

I plan to answer these questions in detail:

1. What factors affect student attendance?
    - Why do the students who attend women's basketball games do so?
    - Why do the students who don't attend stay away?
    - What promotions or publicity could make students more likely to attend?

All items in list must be grammatically parallel. Here, all are questions.

2. How can student awareness of the team be increased?
    - What short-term strategies exist?
    - What long-term strategies exist?
    - Does it make sense to market the team to female audiences?

3. Would a loyalty program help?
    - What programs are available, and what is involved?
    - What are some university examples of programs?

If it is well-written, "Topics to Investigate" section will become the "Scope" section of the report —with minor revisions.

I will briefly discuss how attendance and newspaper publicity correlate to the win/loss record.

If you'll administer a survey or conduct interviews, tell how many subjects you'll have, how you'll choose them, and what you'll ask them.

I will not discuss the cost or the return on investment of my recommendations. I will not discuss how changes in coaching or recruiting might affect attendance. *Indicate any topics relevant to your report that you choose not to discuss.*

Methods

I expect to get data from four sources: (1) surveys of 50 to 100 students, (2) interviews with members of the Athletic Department, (3) my observations of marketing tatics on campus and in Columbus, and (4) library and online sources about attendance at basketball games.

A draft of my questionnaire is attached. I will distribute the survey to a convenience sample at the Union.

(continued)

FIGURE 13.3 Proposal for a Student Report Using Survey Research *(continued)*

Proposal to Write a Recommendation Report on Attendance at OSU Women's Basketball Games
July 19, 2001
Page 3

The follwing articles and Web sites appear useful:

If you're using library or Web research, list sources you hope to use. Use full bibliographic citations.

Justarrive. (2000, November 10). Justarrive redefines college sports marketing rewarding both fans and teams alike. [Electronic version.] Business Wire, p. 145.

Kurdek, R. (2000, November 20). $5M just arrives for sporting start-up. Private Equity Week, p. 4.

This list uses APA format.

Lee, J. (2000, July 7). Stanford gets on the ball with online ticket alliance. San Francisco Business Times, p. 47.

Ohio State University. (2001). Ohio State Buckeyes. Retrieved July 3, 2001, from the World Wide Web: http://ohiostatebuckeyes.fansonly.com.

Raymond, J. (2001, April). Home field advantage. American Demographics, 34–36.

University of Nebraska. (2001). Husker Fever card. Retrieved June 20, 2001 from the World Wide Web: http://www.huskerfevercard.com.

Qualifications

Cite knowledge and skills from other classes, jobs, and activities that will enable you to conduct the research and interpret your data. If you've already done some of the work, say so.

I am a student majoring in English at the Ohio State University and a sports fan. I would like to see the student community offer more support to the Lady Buckeyes. I have already e-mailed a director at Justarrive, a loyalty program consulting firm focusing on collegiate sports, and received a response. I also know a former athletic director from OSU who is now at Bowling Green State University. He can give me information about the Athletic Department and the names of people I should talk to.

Work Schedule

The following schedule will enable me to finish this report by the end of the summer quarter.

Activity	Total Time	Completion Date
Gathering information	15 hours	July 6
Analyzing information	10 hours	July 19
Organizing information	7 hours	July 25
Preparing the progress report	3 hours	July 30
Writing the draft/creating visuals	15 hours	August 6
Revising the draft/visuals	12 hours	August 10
Editing the draft	5 hours	August 13
Proofreading the report	3 hours	August 20
Preparing Power Point slides	5 hours	August 20

Time needed will depend on the length and topic of the report, your knowledge of the topic, and your writing skills.

Allow plenty of time!

Good reports need good revision, editing, and proofreading as well as good research.

Call to Action

Could we schedule a conference to discuss my proposal and questionnaire? I would appreciate any suggestions you may have for strengthening my ideas and making the report better. Please approve my proposal so I may continue my research and begin the report.

It's tactful to indicate you'll accept suggestions. End on a positive note.

(continued)

FIGURE 13.3   Proposal for a Student Report Using Survey Research *(concluded)*

A catchy title can help.

In your introductory ¶,
①tell how to return the survey
②tell how the information will be used

Survey: Why Do Students Attend Athletic Events?

The purpose of this survey is to determine why students attend sports events, and what might increase attendance. All information is to be used solely for a student research paper. Please return completed surveys to Elizabeth or Vicki in the Union. Thank you for your assistance!

Start with easy–to–answer questions

1. Gender (Please circle one)   M   F

2. What is your rank? (Please circle)   1   2   3   4   Grad   Other

The words below each number anchor responses, while still allowing you to average the data numerically

3. How do you feel about women's sports? (Please circle)

1	2	3	4	5
I enjoy watching women's sports		I'll watch, but it doesn't really matter		Women's sports are boring/ I'd rather watch men's sports

Seeing a response in a survey can make respondents more willing to admit to feelings they may be embarrassed to admit.

4. Do you like to attend OSU men's basketball games or watch them on TV? (Please circle)
   Y   N

5. How often do you attend OSU women's basketball games? (Please circle)

1	2	3	4	5
All/most games	Few games a season	Once a season	Less than once a year	Never

6. If you do not attend all of the women's basketball games, why not? (Please check all that apply. If you attend all the games, skip to #7.)

__I've never thought to go.
__I don't like basketball.
__I don't like sporting events.
__The team isn't good enough.
__My friends are not interested in going.
__I want to go, I just haven't had the opportunity.
__The tickets cost too much ($3).
__Other (please specify) _____

Think about factors that affect the problem you're studying, and write survey questions to get information about them.

7. To what extent would each of the following make you more likely to attend an OSU women's basketball game? (please rank all)

1	2	3
Much more likely to attend	Possibley more likely	No effect

__Increased awareness on campus (fliers, chalking on the Oval, more articles in The Lantern)
__Marketing to students (give-aways, days for residence halls or fraternities/sororities)
__Student loyalty program (awarding points towards free tickets, clothing, food for attending games)
__Education (pocket guide explaining the rules of the game provided at the gate)
__Other (please specify) _____

Thank you!
Please return this survey to Elizabeth or Vicki.

Repeat where to turn in or mail completed surveys.

Writing a proposal for action requires considerable research. To get the information she needed for her proposal for a marketing program for mature adults, Patti Douglas

- Read articles in trade journals about mature-adult programs.
- Visited local competitors to find out what (if any) programs they offered for mature adults.
- Called the National Center of Health Statistics to find out how long people lived.
- Asked the switchboard operator to track inquiries about a program for mature adults.
- Found out how much free customer checks and other services for mature adults would cost.
- Assembled a group of current customers to find out what benefits would attract mature adults.[5]

Sales Proposals

To sell expensive goods or services, you may be asked to submit a proposal.

Be sure that you understand the buyer's priorities. A phone company lost a $36 million sale to a university because it assumed the university's priority would be cost. Instead, the university wanted a state-of-the-art system. The university accepted a higher bid.

Don't assume that the buyer will understand why your product or system is good. For everything you offer, show the reader benefits (◀ p. 70) of each feature. Be sure to present the benefits using you-attitude (◀ p. 34). Consider using psychological description (◀ p. 226) to make the benefits vivid.

Use language appropriate for your audience. Even if the buyers want a state-of-the-art system, they may not want the level of detail that your staff could provide; they may not understand or appreciate technical jargon (◀ p. 93).

Sales proposals, particularly for complicated systems costing millions of dollars, are often long. Provide a one-page cover letter to present your proposal succinctly. The best organization for this letter is a modified version of the sales pattern in Chapter 10:

1. Catch the reader's attention and summarize up to three major benefits you offer.
2. Discuss each of the major benefits in the order in which you mentioned them in the first paragraph.
3. Deal with any objections or concerns the reader may have.
4. Mention other benefits briefly.
5. Ask the reader to approve your proposal and provide a reason for acting promptly.

Proposals for Funding

Proposals for funding include both **business plans** (documents written to raise capital for new business ventures) and proposals submitted to a foundation, a corporation, a government agency, or a religious agency to seek money for public service projects. In a proposal for funding, stress the needs your project will meet and show how your project helps fulfill the goals of the organization you are asking for funds.

See the BAC Web site for advice about writing business plans.

Every funding source has certain priorities; some have detailed lists of the kind of projects they fund. *The Foundation Directory* indexes founda-

Customizing a Sales Proposal*

Our average contract value [was only] $100,000 . . . so when I found a contract worth $18 million, I jumped at the chance to win it. First I convinced the purchasing manager that my company could handle the business, then I spent weeks writing a custom proposal. I addressed every buyer expectation from the request for a quote and even included a quote from their senior vice president on the benefit of specialized training that matched our training program. My proposal earned me the chance to make a presentation, and although my competitors brought along their VPs and senior management, I brought only two project managers who had worked for the prospect company before and had connections I didn't. I explained to the buyer that we didn't need our senior management because we would be accountable for our performance if we got the job. The mammoth companies I competed against couldn't believe it, but I won the sale. They thought I cut our prices to "buy" the job, but the truth is I earned it by writing a proposal that gave them just what they wanted.

*Quoted from Greg Cecchi, "Whale of a Sale," *Selling Power*, July/August 1999, 141.

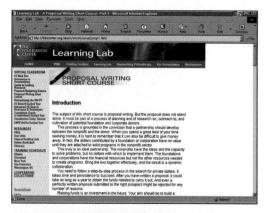

InSite

fdncenter.org/learn/shortcourse/prop1.html

The Foundation Center offers an online short course
on proposal writing and extensive information about
finding and applying for grants.

tions by state and city and by field of interest. *The Foundation
Grants Index Annual* lists grants of $5,000 or more made by the
425 biggest foundations. Check recent awards to discover
foundations that may be interested in your project. *Source Book
Profiles* describes 1,000 national and regional foundations.

Figuring the Budget and Costs

For a class research project, you may not be asked to prepare a
budget. However, many proposals do require budgets, and a
good budget is crucial to making the winning bid. Ask for
everything you need to do a quality job. Asking for too little
may backfire, leading the funder to think that you don't understand the scope of the project.

Do some research. Read the RFP to find out what is and isn't
fundable. Talk to the program officer and read successful past
proposals to find answers to the following questions:

- What size projects will the organization fund in theory?
- Does the funder prefer making a few big grants or many
  smaller grants?
- Does the funder expect you to provide in-kind or cost-sharing funds from
  other sources?

Think about exactly what you'll do and who will do it. What will it cost to
get that person? What supplies or materials will he or she need? Also think
about indirect costs for using office space, about retirement and health benefits
as well as salaries, about office supplies, administration, and infrastructure.

Make the basis of your estimates specific.

Weak:	75 hours of transcribing interviews	$1,500
Better:	25 hours of interviews; a skilled transcriber can complete 1 hour of interviews in 3 hours; 75 hours @ $20/hour	$1,500

Figure your numbers conservatively. For example, if the going rate for
skilled transcribers is $20 an hour, but you think you might be able to train
someone and pay only $12 an hour, use the higher figure. Then, even if your
grant is cut, you'll still be able to do the project well.

Writing Progress Reports

When you're assigned to a single project that will take a month or more, you'll
probably be asked to file one or more progress reports. A progress report reas-
sures the funding agency or employer that you're making progress and allows
you and the agency or employer to resolve problems as they arise. Different
readers may have different concerns. An instructor may want to know whether
you'll have your report in by the due date. A client may be more interested in
what you're learning about the problem. Adapt your progress report to the
needs of the audience.

Christine Barabas's study of the progress reports in a large research and development organization found that poor writers tended to focus on what they
had done and said very little about the value of their work. Good writers, in
contrast, spent less space writing about the details of what they'd done but
much more space explaining the value of their work for the organization.[6]

Subject lines for progress reports are straightforward. Specify the project on
which you are reporting your progress.

Subject: Progress on Developing a Marketing Plan for TCBY

Subject: Progress on Group Survey on Campus Parking

If you are submitting weekly or monthly progress reports on a long project, number your progress reports or include the time period in your subject line. Include dates for the work completed since the last report and work to be completed before the next report.

Make your progress report as positive as you honestly can. You'll build a better image of yourself if you show that you can take minor problems in stride and that you're confident of your own abilities.

Negative: I have not deviated markedly from my schedule, and I feel that I will have very little trouble completing this report by the due date.

Positive: I am back on schedule and expect to complete my report by the due date.

Progress reports can be organized in three ways: by chronology, by task, and to support a recommendation.

Chronological Progress Reports

The following pattern of organization focuses on what you have done and what work remains.

1. **Summarize your progress in terms of your goals and your original schedule.** Use measurable statements.

   Poor: My progress has been slow.

   Better: The research for my report is about one-third complete.

2. **Under the heading "Work Completed," describe what you have already done.** Be specific, both to support your claims in the first paragraph and to allow the reader to appreciate your hard work. Acknowledge the people who have helped you. Describe any serious obstacles you've encountered and tell how you've dealt with them.

   Poor: I have found many articles about Procter & Gamble on the Web. I have had a few problems finding how the company keeps employees safe from chemical fumes.

   Better: On the Web, I found Procter & Gamble's home page, its annual report, and mission statement. No one whom I interviewed could tell me about safety programs specifically at P&G. I have found seven articles about ways to protect workers against pollution in factories, but none mentions P&G.

3. **Under the heading "Work to Be Completed," describe the work that remains.** If you're more than three days late (for school projects) or two weeks late (for business projects) submit a new schedule, showing how you will be able to meet the original deadline. You may want to discuss "Observations" or "Preliminary Conclusions" if you want feedback before writing the final report or if your reader has asked for substantive interim reports.

4. **Either express your confidence in having the report ready by the due date or request a conference to discuss extending the due date or limiting the project.** If you are behind your original schedule, show why you think you can still finish the project on time.

The student progress report in Figure 13.4 uses this pattern of organization.

The Bullet-Proof Business Plan*

[D]escribe the business in an understandable fashion. . . .

[T]alk about your competitors in detail in your business plan: identify direct, indirect, and even potential competitors and describe their offerings, their percentage of the market, their funding, and their pricing, distribution, and promotion strategies. . . . [B]e crystal clear about how your own offering is different and why it gives customers a better value.

Some evidence that customers will buy your product—and buy it at the price you're charging—is essential. . . .

[I]nvestors expect to see a highly qualified management team in place. . . . At a minimum, you need an experienced and proven CEO. . . . [D]on't cut corners on the sales-and-marketing side. . . .

The path to profitability has to be both clear and short—a year to 18 months. . . . Savvy entrepreneurs will also want to include the slowing economy in their assumptions. . .
[I]nvestors still want to cash out in five to seven years. Investors like to see potential acquirers named in the business plan because it shows knowledge of the market.

*Quoted from Emily Barker, "The Bullet-Proof Business Plan," *Inc.*, October 2001, 102–4.

FIGURE 13.4   A Student Chronological Progress Report

November 10, 2003

To: Kitty O. Locker

From: David G. Bunnel   *DGB*

Subject: Progress on CAD/CAM Software Feasibility Study for the Architecture Firm, Patrick
               and Associates, Inc.

*¶ 1:
Summarize
results in
terms of
purpose,
schedule.*

I have obtained most of the information necessary to recommend whether CADAM or CATIA is
better for Patrick and Associates, Inc. (P&A). I am currently analyzing and organizing this information and am on schedule.

Work Completed   *Underline headings
or bold.*

*Be very
specific
about
what
you've
done.*

To learn how computer literate P&A employees are, I interviewed a judgment sample of five
employees. My interview with Bruce Ratekin, the director of P&A's Computer-Aided Design
(CAD) Department on November 3 enabled me to determine the architectural drafting needs of
the firm. Mr. Ratekin also gave me a basic drawing of a building showing both two- and three-
dimensional views so that I could replicate the drawing with both software packages.

*Show how
you've
overcome
minor
problems.*

I obtained tutorials for both packages to use as a reference while making the drawings. First I
drew the building using CADAM, the package designed primarily for two-dimensional architectural drawings. I encountered problems with the isometric drawing because there was a mistake
in the manual I was using; I fixed the problem by trying alternatives and finally getting help from
another CADAM user. Next, I used CATIA, the package whose strength is three-dimensional
drawings, to construct the drawing. I am in the process of comparing the two packages based
on these criteria: quality of drawing, ease of data entry (lines, points, surfaces, etc.) for computer experts and novices, and ease of making changes in the completed drawings. Based on
my experience with the packages, I have analyzed the training people with and without experience in CAD would need to learn to use each of these packages.

*Indicate changes in purpose, scope, or recommendations.
Progress report is a low-risk way to bring the readers on board.*

Work to Be Completed

Making the drawings has shown that neither of the packages can do everything that P&A
needs. Therefore, I want to investigate the feasibility of P&A's buying both packages.

*Specify
the work
that
remains.*

As soon as he comes back from an unexpected illness that has kept him out of the office, I will
meet with Tom Merrick, the CAD systems programmer for The Ohio State University, to learn
about software expansion flexibility for both packages as well as the costs for initial purchase,
installation, maintenance, and software updates. After this meeting, I will be ready to begin the
first draft of my report.

Whether I am able to meet my deadline will depend on when I am able to meet with Mr. Merrick. Right now, I am on schedule and plan to submit my report by the December 10th deadline.

End on a positive note.

Task Progress Reports

In a task progress report, organize information under the various tasks you have worked on during the period. For example, a task progress report for a group report project might use the following headings:

> Finding Background Information on the Web and in Print
> Analyzing Our Survey Data
> Working on the Introduction of the Report and the Appendices

Under each heading, the group could discuss the tasks it has completed and those that remain.

Recommendation Progress Reports

Recommendation progress reports recommend action: increasing the funding for a project, changing its direction, canceling a project that isn't working out. When the recommendation will be easy for the reader to accept, use the direct request pattern of organization from Chapter 9 (◀▥ p. 216). If the recommendation is likely to meet strong resistance, the problem-solving pattern (◀▥ p. 218) may be more effective.

Research Strategies for Reports

Research for a report may be as simple as getting a computer printout of sales for the last month; it may involve finding published material or surveying or interviewing people. **Secondary research** retrieves information that someone else gathered. Library research and online searches are the best known kinds of secondary research. **Primary research** gathers new information. Surveys, interviews, and observations are common methods for gathering new information for business reports.

Finding Information Online and in Print

You can save time and money by checking online and published sources of data before you gather new information. Many college and university libraries provide

- Workshops on research techniques.
- Handouts explaining how to use printed and computer-based sources.
- Free or inexpensive access to computer databases.
- Research librarians who can help you find and use sources.

Categories of sources that may be useful include

- Specialized encyclopedias for introductions to a topic (for example, *Kodansha Encyclopedia of Japan*).
- Indexes to find articles. Most permit searches by keyword, by author, and often by company name.
- Abstracts for brief descriptions or summaries of articles. Sometimes the abstract will be all you'll need; almost always, you can tell from the abstract whether an article is useful for your needs.
- Citation indexes to find materials that cite previous research. Citation indexes thus enable you to use an older reference to find newer articles on the topic. The *Social Sciences Citation Index* is the most useful for researching business topics.
- Newspapers for information about recent events.
- US Census reports, for a variety of business and demographic information.

The Political Uses of Progress Reports

Progress reports can do more than just report progress. You can use progress reports to

- Enhance your image. Details about the number of documents you've read, people you've surveyed, or experiments you've conducted create a picture of a hardworking person doing a thorough job.

- Float trial balloons. Explain, "I could continue to do X [what you approved]; I could do Y instead [what I'd like to do now]." The detail in the progress report can help back up your claim. Even if the idea is rejected, you don't lose face because you haven't made a separate issue of the alternative.

- Minimize potential problems. As you do the work, it may become clear that implementing your recommendations will be difficult. In your regular progress reports, you can alert your boss or the funding agency to the challenges that lie ahead, enabling them to prepare psychologically and physically to act on your recommendations.

Bermuda *Not* Onion

Searches on the Web can yield hundreds, sometimes thousands, of matches. The computer just matches words. If you enter "Bermuda" as your search term, you'll get articles and pages about Bermuda onions as well as about the cruise market in Bermuda. "Bermuda *and* Travel" limits the search to articles with both the words *Bermuda* and *travel*. But maybe that's too narrow. What if the article uses the word *cruise* or *vacation* instead of *travel?* To capture those variations, use "Bermuda *and* (Cruise* *or* Vacation* *or* Travel)." The parentheses group the "or" items together to flag any one of them with *Bermuda*. The asterisks are wild card endings allowing for plurals and other forms. Some databases use different symbols for wild cards. Specify articles printed in the last two to three years (maybe even more recently, if your topic has been changing quickly). Then read the articles and pages the search finds. When one is relevant, copy or download it so that you can use it in your research.

FIGURE 13.5   Example of a Boolean Search

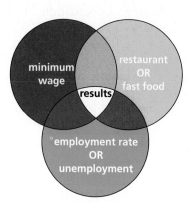

To use a computer database efficiently, identify the concepts you're interested in and choose keywords that will help you find relevant sources. **Keywords** or **descriptors** are the terms that the computer searches for. If you're not sure what terms to use, check the ABI/Inform Thesaurus for synonyms and the hierarchies in which information is arranged in various databases.

Specific commands allow you to narrow your search. For example, to study the effect of the minimum wage on employment in the restaurant industry, you might use a Boolean search (see Figure 13.5):

(minimum wage) *and* (restaurant *or* fast food) *and*
(employment rate *or* unemployment).

This descriptor would give you the titles of articles that treat all three of the topics in parentheses. Without *and,* you'd get articles that discuss the minimum wage in general, articles about every aspect of *restaurants,* and every article that refers to *unemployment,* even though many of these would not be relevant to your topic. The *or* descriptor calls up articles that use the term *fast food* but not the term *restaurant.* An article that used the phrase *food service industry* would be eliminated unless it also used the term *restaurant.* Alta Vista and some other Web search engines allow you to specify words that cannot appear in a source.

Many words can appear in related forms. To catch all of them, use the database's **wild card** or **truncated code** for shortened terms and root words.

Web search engines are particularly effective for words, people, or phrases that are unlikely to have separate pages devoted to them. For general topics or famous people, directories like E-Blast or Yahoo! are more useful, since they yield a smaller number of hits. Figures 13.6 and 13.7 list a few of the specialized sources available.

Evaluating Web Sources

Some of the material on the Web is excellent, but some of it is wholly unreliable. With print sources, the editor or publisher serves as a gatekeeper, so you can trust the material in good journals. To put up a Web page, all one needs is access to a server.

Use four criteria to decide whether a Web site is good enough to use for a research project:

1. **Authors.** What person or organization sponsors the site? What credentials do the authors have?
2. **Objectivity.** Does the site give evidence to support its claims? Does it give both sides of controversial issues? Is the tone professional?

FIGURE 13.6   Sources for Electronic Research

CD-ROM databases are available in many university libraries. Check your college or university library to find additional sources.

ABI/Inform (indexes and abstracts 800 journals in management and business)

Black Studies on Disc

ComIndex (indexes and abstracts journals in communication)

Congressional Masterfile

Dun's Million Dollar Disc

Ethnic Newswatch

Foreign Trade and Economic Abstracts

GPO on SilverPlatter (government publications)

Handbook of Latin American Studies

LEXIS/NEXIS Services

A Matter of Fact

Newspaper Abstracts

PAIS International—Public Affairs Information Service

Statistical Masterfile (statistics collected by the US government)

Wilson Business Abstracts

Women's Resources International

FIGURE 13.7   Sources for Web Research

Subject matter directories

AccountingNet

   www.accounting.smartpros.com/

Rutger's Accounting Web (RAW)

   www.accounting.rutgers.edu

Education index

   www.educationindex.com

Resources for economists on the Internet

   http://rfe.wustl.edu/Econ FAQ.htm

FINWeb

   www.finweb.com

Human resource management resources on the Internet

   www.nbs.ntu.ac.uk/depts/hrm/hrm_link.htm

Global Edge

   www.globaledge.msu.edu/ibrd/ibrd.asp

International Business Kiosk

   www.calintel.org/kiosk

Management and entrepreneurship

   www.lib.lsu.edu/bus/managemt.html

The WWW Virtual Library: Marketing

   www.knowthis.com

Internet marketing resources

   www.lib.lsu.edu/bus/marketin.html

Not Necessarily True*

Information on the Web is not necessarily true.

Press releases from "Independent Financial Reports" touted an Internet stock. "Independent Financial Reports" did not exist; the press releases were fakes, designed to boost the price of the stock. (The SEC has filed suit.)

The satirical newspaper *The Onion* (www.theonion.com) posted an "interview" in which *Harry Potter* author J. K. Rowling "admitted" that she worshipped Satan. The interview was a spoof.

A Minnesota Web page showed a sunny beach where "thanks to a freak of nature: the Farr/Sclare Fissure" hot springs warmed water year round. The spoof caused so many people to ask for information on lodging that the page finally posted a disclaimer and was eventually removed.

For nearly a year in 2000–01, a Web site chronicled Kaycee Nicole Swenson's losing battle with leukemia. Only after her "death" did mourners realize that no one had ever met her. In fact, Kaycee was a fiction.

For information on Web frauds and hoaxes, see www.snopes.2.com or www.scambusters.org.

*Based on "Beware the Press Release," *BusinessWeek,* April 24, 2000, 153; "You Said It," *Reader's Digest,* April 2001, 18; Laura Gurak, "'Is This the Party to Whom I Am Speaking?' Women, Credibility, and the Internet," *The Women's Review of Books* 18, no. 5 (February 2001): 5; and Katie Hafter, "Friends Mourn a Life That Never Was," *The Columbus Dispatch,* July 9, 2001, E6.

FIGURE 13.7   Sources for Web Research *(concluded)*

News sites

Business Week
   www.businessweek.com

CNN/CNNFN
   www.cnn.com (news)
   www.cnnfn.cnn.com (financial news)

National Public Radio
   www.npr.org

NewsLink (links to US, Canadian, and international newspapers, magazines, and resources online)
   http://newslink.org

New York Times
   www.nyt.com

The Wall Street Journal
   www.wsj.com

Washington Post
   www.WashingtonPost.com

US government information

EDGAR Online (SEC's online database)
   www.edgar-online.com
   www.sec.gov/edgar.shtml

FEDSTATS (links to 70 US government agencies)
   www.fedstats.gov

STAT-USA (fast-breaking statistics on US trade and economy)
   www.stat-usa.gov

US Census (including Data FERRET)
   www.census.gov

US government publications (search databases online)
   www.access.gpo.gov/su_docs

US Small Business Administration
   www.sbaonline.sba.gov

White House Briefing Room (economic issues)
   www.whitehouse.gov/fsbr/esbr.html

White House Briefing Room (social issues and statistics)
   www.whitehouse.gov/fsbr/ssbr.html

Reference collections

Hoover's Online (information on more than 13,000 public and private companies worldwide)
   www.hoovers.com

Industry Research Desk
   www.virtualpet.com/industry/rdindex2.htm

My Virtual Reference Desk
   www.refdesk.com

Tile.Net's Guide to Listservs
   http://tile.net/lists

3. **Information.** How complete is the information? What is it based on?

4. **Revision date.** When was the site last updated?

Answers to these questions may lead you to discard some of the relevant sites you find. For example, if you find five different Web pages about the cell phones and car accidents that all cite the same Toronto study, you have one source, not five. Choose the most complete for your project.

For more information on evaluating Web sites, see the BAC Web page.

Designing Questions for Surveys and Interviews

A **survey** questions a large group of people, called **respondents** or **subjects.** The easiest way to ask many questions is to create a **questionnaire,** a written list of questions that people fill out. An **interview** is a structured conversation with someone who will be able to give you useful information. Surveys and interviews can be useful only if the questions are well designed.

Good questions ask only one thing, are phrased neutrally, avoid making assumptions about the respondent, and mean the same thing to different people.

Phrase questions in a way that won't bias the response. In Gallup polls, 62% of respondents favored school vouchers for "tuition at the public, private or religious school of your choice." Support dropped to 48% when the tuition was just for "a private school." Support dropped even lower—to 39%—when the question specified that students would attend private schools "at public expense."[7]

Avoid questions that make assumptions about your subjects. The question "Does your wife have a job outside the home?" assumes that your respondent is a married man.

Use words that mean the same thing to you and to the respondents. If a question can be interpreted in more than one way, it will be. Words like *often* and *important* mean different things to different people. Whenever possible, use more objective measures:

Vague: Do you study in the library frequently?

Better: How many hours a week do you study in the library?

Even questions that call for objective information can be confusing. For example, consider the owner of a small business confronted with the question "How many employees do you have?" Does the number include the owner as well as subordinates? Does it include both full- and part-time employees? Does it include people who have been hired but who haven't yet started work, or someone who is leaving at the end of the month? A better wording would be

How many full-time employees were on your payroll the week of May 16?

As discussed in chapter 4, bypassing occurs when two people use the same symbol but interpret it differently. To reduce bypassing,

1. Train your observers. Decide on definitions in advance; do some practice coding to allow observers to apply the definitions.

2. Avoid terms that are likely to mean different things to different people.

3. Pretest your questions with several people who are like those who will fill out the survey to catch questions that

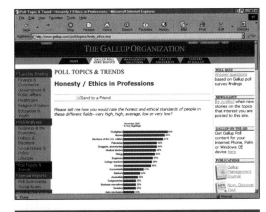

InSite

www.gallup.com/poll/indicators/
indhnsty_ethics.asp

The Gallup Organization Web page posts questions, responses, and brief analyses for many of its polls.

Market Research on the Web*

can be misunderstood. Even a small pretest with 10 people can help you refine your questions.

Questions can be categorized in several ways.

Closed questions have a limited number of possible responses. **Open questions** do not lock the subject into any sort of response. Figure 13.8 gives examples of closed and open questions. The second question in Figure 13.8 is an example of a Likert-type scale. Closed questions are faster for subjects to answer and easier for researchers to score. However, since all answers must fit into prechosen categories, they cannot probe the complexities of a subject. You can improve the quality of closed questions by conducting a pretest with open questions to find categories that matter to respondents.

Use an "Other, Please Specify" category when you want the convenience of a closed question but cannot foresee all the possible responses:

> What is the single most important reason that you ride the bus?
> _____ I don't have a car.
> _____ I don't want to fight rush-hour traffic.
> _____ Riding the bus is cheaper than driving my car.
> _____ Riding the bus conserves fuel and reduces pollution.
> _____ Other (Please specify) _____

When you use multiple-choice questions, make sure that any one answer fits only in one category. In the following example of overlapping categories, a

FIGURE 13.8   Closed and Open Questions

Closed questions

Are you satisfied with the city bus service? (yes/no)

How good is the city bus service?

   Excellent   5   4   3   2   1   Terrible

Indicate whether you agree or disagree with each of the following statements about city bus service:

   A   D   The schedule is convenient for me.

   A   D   The routes are convenient for me.

   A   D   The drivers are courteous.

   A   D   The buses are clean.

Rate each of the following improvements in the order of their importance to you (1 = most important, 6 = least important)

_____ Buy new buses.

_____ Increase non-rush-hour service on weekdays.

_____ Increase service on weekdays.

_____ Provide earlier and later service on weekdays.

_____ Buy more buses with wheelchair access.

_____ Provide unlimited free transfers.

Open questions

How do you feel about the city bus service?

Tell me about the city bus service.

Why do you ride the bus? (or, Why don't you ride the bus?)

What do you like and dislike about the city bus service?

How could the city bus service be improved?

person who worked for a company with exactly 25 employees could check either *a* or *b*. The resulting data would be unreliable.

Overlapping categories: Indicate the number of full-time employees in your company on May 16:

    ___ a. 0–25

    ___ b. 25–100

    ___ c. 100–500

    ___ d. over 500

Discrete categories: Indicate the number of full-time employees on your payroll on May 16:

    ___ a. 0–25

    ___ b. 26–100

    ___ c. 101–500

    ___ d. more than 500

Giving several options is more important the older your respondents are. Psychologist Cynthia Adams notes that older people are uncomfortable choosing between only two options. When asked "Are discounts important to you," more mature people want to answer, "It depends."[8] A good survey will specify the context or allow the respondent to do so.

Branching questions direct different respondents to different parts of the questionnaire based on their answers to earlier questions.

> 10. Have you talked to an academic adviser this year?   yes   no
> (If "no," skip to question 14.)

Use closed multiple-choice questions for potentially embarrassing topics. Seeing their own situation listed as one response can help respondents feel that it is acceptable. However, very sensitive issues are perhaps better asked in an interview, where the interviewer can build trust and reveal information about himself or herself to encourage the interviewee to answer.

Generally, put early in the questionnaire questions that will be easy to answer. Put questions that are harder to answer or that people may be less willing to answer (e.g., age and income) near the end of the questionnaire. Even if people choose not to answer such questions, you'll still have the rest of the survey filled out.

If subjects will fill out the questionnaire themselves, pay careful attention to the physical design of the document. Use indentations and white space effectively; make it easy to mark and score the answers. Include a brief statement of purpose if you (or someone else) will not be available to explain the questionnaire or answer questions. Pretest the questionnaire to make sure the directions are clear. One researcher mailed a two-page questionnaire without pretesting it. Twenty-five respondents didn't answer the questions on the back of the first page.[9]

For examples of survey questions, responses and brief analyses, see the BAC Web page.

Conducting Surveys and Interviews

Face-to-face surveys are convenient when you are surveying a fairly small number of people in a specific location. In a face-to-face survey, the interviewer's sex, race, and nonverbal cues can bias results. Most people prefer not to say things they think their audience will find unacceptable. For that reason, women will be more likely to agree that sexual harassment is a problem if the

If People Can Misunderstand the Question, They Will*

Q: Give previous experience with dates.
A: Moderately successful in the past, but I am now happily married!

Q: How many autopsies have you performed on dead people?
A: All my autopsies have been on dead people.

Q: James stood back and shot Tommy Lee?
A: Yes.
Q: And then Tommy Lee pulled out his gun and shot James in the fracas?
A: (After hesitation) No sir, just above it.

Q: What is the country's mortality rate?
A: 100%. Everybody dies.

Q: Give numbers of employees broken down by sex.
A: None. Our problem is booze.

Q: Sex?
A: I feel this is a very personal subject.

*Based on James Hartley, *Designing Instructional Text* (London: Kogan Page, 1978), 109; Richard Lederer, *Anguished English* (New York: Wyrick, 1988); and folklore.

Who Tallies That Survey?*

When we think about information and privacy, we usually think about how a company will use the information we've provided. But sometimes the person who tallies the survey puts the respondent at risk.

One woman filled out a questionnaire that promised she'd receive free product samples for her time and answers about products she used. What the instructions didn't say was that prison inmates were hired to enter the data.

The woman got a 12-page letter from a man imprisoned for rape; the letter referred to the magazines she liked, the fact that she was divorced, and her birthday. The letter spun sexual fantasies involving the products she used.

That company says it no longer uses inmates to tally surveys. But inmates in more than a dozen states routinely process data, answer 800 numbers, and even work as telemarketers. Optimistically, most states require convicts to sign a confidentiality agreement before handling sensitive data.

*Based on James P. Miller, "Privacy Issue Raised in Direct-Mail Case," *The Wall Street Journal*, May 6, 1996, B8; and James P. Miller, "Work Week," *The Wall Street Journal*, December 7, 1999, A1.

interviewer is also a woman. Members of a minority group are more likely to admit that they suffer discrimination if the interviewer is a member of the same minority.

Telephone surveys are popular because they can be closely supervised. Interviewers can read the questions from a computer screen and key in answers as the respondent gives them. The results can then be available just a few minutes after the last call is completed.

The major limitation of phone surveys is that they reach only people who have phones and thus underrepresent poor people. Other limitations can be avoided with good designs. Since a survey based on a phone book would exclude people with unlisted numbers, professional survey-takers use automatic random-digit dialing. Since women are more likely to answer the phone than men are,[10] decide in advance to whom you want to speak, and ask for that person rather than surveying whoever answers the phone.

To increase the response rate for a phone survey, call at a time respondents will find convenient. Avoid calling between 5 and 7 PM, a time when many families have dinner.

Mail surveys can reach anyone who has an address. Some people may be more willing to fill out an anonymous questionnaire than to give sensitive information to a stranger over the phone. However, mail surveys are not effective for respondents who don't read and write well. Further, it may be more difficult to get a response from someone who is reluctant to participate. Over the phone, the interviewer can try to persuade the subject and overcome his or her objections.

A major concern with any kind of survey is the **response rate,** the percentage of people who respond. People who refuse to answer may differ from those who respond quickly, and you need information from both groups to be able to generalize to the whole population. However, professional pollsters find that about 60% of Americans refuse to answer phone surveys. Mail surveys are better but still get refusal rates of 40%. A seven-month media blitz of TV, radio, print, outdoor, and Internet ads in 17 languages was needed to achieve a 67% response rate for Census 2000.[11] To get as high a response rate as possible, good researchers follow up, contacting nonrespondents at least once and preferably twice to try to persuade them to participate in the survey.

Selecting a sample for surveys and interviews

To keep research costs reasonable, only a sample of the total population is polled. How that sample is chosen and the attempts made to get responses from nonrespondents will determine whether you can infer that what is true of your sample is also true of the population as a whole. The **population** is the group you want to make statements about. Depending on the purpose of your research, your population might be all Fortune 1000 companies, all business students at your college, or all consumers.

A **convenience sample** is a group of subjects who are easy to get: students who walk through the union, people at a shopping mall, workers in your own unit. Convenience samples are useful for a rough pretest of a questionnaire and may be acceptable for some class research projects. However, you cannot generalize from a convenience sample to a larger group.

A **judgment sample** is a group of people whose views seem useful. Someone interested in surveying the kinds of writing done on campus might ask each department for the name of a faculty member who cared about writing, and then send surveys to those people.

In a **random sample,** each person in the population theoretically has an equal chance of being chosen. See the BAC Web page for various ways of taking random samples.

When people say they did something *randomly* they often mean *without conscious bias.* However, unconscious bias exists. Someone passing out surveys in front of the library will be more likely to approach people who seem friendly and less likely to ask people who seem intimidating, in a hurry, much older or younger, or of a different race, class, or sex. True random samples rely on random digit tables, published in statistics texts and books such as *A Million Random Digits.* Computers can also be programmed to generate random numbers. If you take a true random sample, you can generalize your findings to the whole population from which your sample comes. For example, a random phone survey that shows that 65% of the respondents approve of a presidential policy may be accurate $\pm$ 7%. That is, in the population as a whole, between 58% and 72% approve the policy. The accuracy range is based on the size of the sample and the expected variation within the population. Statistics texts tell you how to calculate these figures.

Conducting research interviews

Schedule interviews in advance; tell the interviewee about how long you expect the interview to take. A survey of technical writers (who get much of their information from interviews) found that the best times to interview subject-matter experts are Tuesdays, Wednesdays, and Thursday mornings.[12]

Interviews can be structured or unstructured. In a **structured interview,** the interviewer uses a detailed list of questions to guide the interview. Indeed, a structured interview may use a questionnaire just as a survey does. In an **unstructured interview,** the interviewer has three or four main questions. Other questions build on what the interviewee says. To prepare for an unstructured interview, learn as much as possible about the interviewee and the topic. Go into the interview with three or four main topics you want to cover.

Interviewers sometimes use closed questions to start the interview and set the interviewee at ease. The strength of an interview, however, is getting at a person's attitudes, feelings, and experiences. Situational questions let you probe what someone would do in a specific circumstance. Hypothetical questions that ask people to imagine what they would do generally yield less reliable answers than questions about **critical incidents** or key past events.

Hypothetical question:	What would you say if you had to tell an employee that his or her performance was unsatisfactory?
Critical incident question:	You've probably been in a situation where someone who was working with you wasn't carrying his or her share of the work. What did you do the last time that happened?

A **mirror question** paraphrases the content of the last answer: "So you confronted him directly?" "You think that this product costs too much?" Mirror questions are used both to check that the interviewer understands what the interviewee has said and to prompt the interviewee to continue talking. **Probes** follow up an original question to get at specific aspects of a topic:

Question:	What do you think about the fees for campus parking?
Probes:	Would you be willing to pay more for a reserved space? How much more? Should the fines for vehicles parked illegally be increased? Do you think fees should be based on income?

Probes are not used in any definite order. Instead, they are used to keep the interviewee talking, to get at aspects of a subject that the interviewee has not yet mentioned, and to probe more deeply into points that the interviewee brings up.

If you read questions to subjects in a structured interview, use fewer options than you might in a written questionnaire.

Research on a Shoestring*

Traditional market research can cost $20,000 to $50,000 or even more. What does a company do if its budget isn't that big?

Mark Bissel used diaries and observations to collect data about a European home-cleaning product he wanted to sell in the United States. In return for a $1,500 donation, his local Parent-Teacher Association let him make a presentation at a meeting. Twenty people agreed to try the product in their homes. Each kept a diary about experiences using the "Steam Gun," and Bissel's marketing director visited homes to watch people using the product.

The first lesson was that the product's name was a problem. Kids threatened to blow their siblings away with the "Steam Gun." And US consumers didn't believe that steam without soap or chemicals would get stuff clean. So the company changed the name to "Steam N' Clean."

People serious about cleaning liked the product best. The product was great for blasting dirt out of corners and crevices in the kitchen and bathroom. So the company developed infomercials touting the benefits of steam for cleaning. The product sold well both from the infomercials and in Kmart.

*Based on Alison Stein Wellner, "Research on a Shoestring," *American Demographics*, April 2001, 38–39.

Ethical Issues in Interviewing

If you're trying to get sensitive information, interviewees may give useful information when the interview is "over" and the tape recorder has been turned off. Is it ethical to use that information?

If you're interviewing a hostile or very reluctant interviewee, you may get more information if you agree with everything you can legitimately agree to, and keep silent on the rest. Is it ethical to imply acceptance even when you know you'll criticize the interviewee's ideas in your report?

Most people would say that whatever public figures say is fair game: they're supposed to know enough to defend themselves. Many people would say that different rules apply when you'll cite someone by name than when you'll use the information as background or use a pseudonym so that the interviewee cannot be identified.

As a practical matter, if someone feels you've misrepresented him or her, that person will be less willing to talk to you in the future. But quite apart from practical considerations, interview strategies raise ethical issues as well.

> I'm going to read a list of factors that someone might look for in choosing a restaurant. After I read each factor, please tell me whether that factor is Very Important to you, Somewhat Important to you, or Not Important to you.

If the interviewee hesitates, reread the scale.

Always tape the interview. Test your equipment ahead of time to make sure it works. If you think your interviewee may be reluctant to speak on tape, take along two tapes and two recorders; offer to give one tape to the interviewee.

Pulitzer Prize winner Nan Robertson offers the following advice to interviewers:[13]

- Do your homework. Learn about the subject and the person before the interview.

- To set a nervous interviewee at ease, start with nuts-and-bolts questions, even if you already know the answers.

- Save controversial questions for the end. You'll have everything else you need, and the trust built up in the interview makes an answer more likely.

- Go into an interview with three or four major questions. Listen to what the interviewee says and let the conversation flow naturally.

- At the end of the interview, ask for office and home telephone numbers in case you need to ask an additional question when you write up the interview.

Ethnographic research closely observes how people choose and use products. Videotapes showed that many customers bought only a few cuts of meat because they didn't know how to cook other cuts. As a result, many grocers are now rearranging meat products by cooking methods and offering simple, three-step instructions on packages.

Observing Customers and Users

Answers to surveys and interviews may differ from actual behavior—sometimes greatly. To get more accurate consumer information, many marketers observe users.

When she introduced Growing Healthy, a line of frozen baby foods, founder Julia Knight enlisted friends with kids to join her on research shopping trips. She quickly realized that the frozen food section wasn't a good location. Kids didn't like the cold, and parents sped through as quickly as possible. So she persuaded supermarket managers to place cutaway freezers in the baby food section, and her company succeeded. Her observations also showed Knight why survey and interview data can be so unreliable: "What mother, especially in front of other mothers, would really tell you that she spent more on cat food than on baby food?"[14]

Sometimes the insights from observation are obvious—once the retailer or marketer sees. When Judy George, founder and CEO of Domain furniture stores, watched six hours of videotape of customers in one of her stores, she realized for the first time that almost all shoppers came in couples, and many of the men looked uncomfortable. George knew that people were more likely to buy the longer they stayed in the store. So she's creating entertainment centers in each of her 23 stores with sports on cable TV.[15]

Observation can also be used for in-house research. A custom-machine-parts manufacturer in Danvers, Massachusetts, videotaped tool-setup processes at one milling work center. Management and work teams watched the tape, suggested changes in the processes, and were able to cut setup time 14 to 20% throughout the work center.[16]

Observation is often combined with other techniques to get the most information. *Think-aloud protocols* ask users to voice their thoughts as they use a document or product: "First I'll try. . . ." These protocols are tape-recorded and later analyzed to understand how users approach a document or product. *Interruption interviews* interrupt users to ask them what's happening. For example, a company testing a draft of computer instructions might interrupt a user to ask, "What are you trying to do now? Tell me why you did that." *Discourse-based interviews* ask questions based on documents that the interviewee has written: "You said that the process is too complicated. Tell me what you mean by that."

Consumers in the Mist*

The 60-ish woman caught on the grainy videotape is sitting on her hotel bed, addressing her husband after a long day spent on the road. "Good job!" she exults. "We beat the . . . out of the front desk and got a terrific room!" . . . [T]he couple was part of the latest effort by marketers to figure out what consumers really think about their products. . . .

Best Western International . . . paid 25 over-55 couples to tape themselves on cross-country journeys. . . . [T]he effort convinced the hotel chain that it didn't need to boost its standard 10% senior citizen discount. The tapes showed that seniors who talked the hotel clerk into a better deal . . . were after the thrill of the deal. Instead of attracting new customers, bigger discounts would simply allow the old customers to trade up to a fancier dinner down the street somewhere[,] doing absolutely nothing for Best Western.

*Quoted from Gerry Khermouch, "Consumers in the Mist," *BusinessWeek*, January 26, 2001, 92–94.

Using and Documenting Sources

In a good report, sources are cited and documented smoothly and unobtrusively. **Citation** means attributing an idea or fact to its source *in the body of the report:* "According to the 2000 Census . . ." "Jane Bryant Quinn argues that . . ." Citing sources demonstrates your honesty and enhances your credibility. **Documentation** means providing the bibliographic information readers would need to go back to the original source. The two usual means of documentation are notes and lists of references.

Note that citation and documentation are used in addition to quotation marks. If you use the source's exact words, you'll use the name of the person you're citing and quotation marks in the body of the report; you'll indicate the source in parentheses and a list of references or in a footnote or endnote. If you put the source's idea into your own words, or if you condense or synthesize information, you don't need quotation marks, but you still need to tell whose idea it is and where you found it.

Long quotations (four typed lines or more) are used sparingly in business reports. Since many readers skip quotes, always summarize the main point of

Market Research Creates an Ad Campaign*

[The tiny company that made Boker knives was considering dropping the brand. But before making the decision, executives and ad agency personnel talked to current and potential customers: people who hunt and fish.]

They knew they were onto something when they ran into a longtime Boker customer who told them what he liked about the knife. He said that whenever he wants to make French fries, he just opens his Boker, puts it in the glove box of his four-by-four pickup with a bunch of potatoes, and drives over a rocky road in second gear. He added, "Of course, for hash browns I use third gear."

As they began to collect stories like this, others poured in. The agency ran a print campaign featuring fanciful pictures of old-time Boker users. The title of the ad ran: IN EVERY LIE ABOUT THE BOKER THERE'S A LITTLE BIT OF TRUTH. The ads recounted the tall tales, which guaranteed high readership. Then the ads told the serious part of the Boker message. Within a year, both market share and profits had doubled.

*Quoted from Robert H. Waterman, *The Renewal Factor* (Toronto: Bantam, 1987), 163.

the quotation in a single sentence before the quotation itself. End the sentence with a colon, not a period, since it introduces the quote. Indent long quotations on the left and right to set them off from your text. Indented quotations do not need quotation marks; the indentation shows the reader that the passage is a quote.

You may want to interrupt a quotation to analyze, clarify, or question it.

To make a quotation fit the grammar of your report, you may need to change one or two words. Sometimes you may want to add a few words to explain something in the longer original. In both cases, use square brackets to indicate words that are your replacements or additions. Omit any words in the original source that are not essential for your purposes. Use ellipses (spaced dots) to indicate where your omissions are.

Document every fact and idea that you take from a source except facts that are common knowledge. Historical dates and facts are considered common knowledge. Generalizations are considered common knowledge ("More and more women are entering the workforce") even though specific statements about the same topic (such as the percentage of women in the workforce in 1975 and in 2000) would require documentation.

The three most widely used formats for footnotes, endnotes, and bibliographies in reports are those of the American Psychological Association (APA), the Modern Language Association (MLA), and the University of Chicago *Manual of Style* format, which this book uses. The APA format uses internal documentation with a list of references; it does not use footnotes or endnotes. **Internal documentation** provides the work and the page number where the reference was found in parentheses in the text. The work may be indicated by the author's last name (if that isn't already in the sentence), or by the last name plus the date of the work (if you're using two or more works by the same author, or if the dates of the works are important). The full bibliographical citation appears in a list of references or works cited at the end of the report. Figure 13.9 and 13.10 show a portion of a report in APA and MLA formats, respectively, with the list of references (APA) or works cited (MLA). Figure 13.11 shows the APA and MLA formats for the sources used most often in reports.

Frito-Lay used innovative and traditional research methods to develop products for the growing Hispanic market. Because Hispanics are less likely than non-Hispanics to shop at malls, site of traditional taste tests, the company turned giant RVs into traveling test kitchens. Focus groups showed that ads in Spanish would be most effective and that the "Happy Face" logo, an icon of Frito-Lay's sister company in Mexico, reminded Mexican Americans of snacks from home.

FIGURE 13.9 Report Paragraphs with APA Documentation

Heading, ¶ number help readers find material in Web site without page numbers.

APA Format

Modern office buildings contain a surprising number of pollutants. Printing and copying documents creates particles which can be harmful to health. Office carpets and furniture emit chemical pollutants (Environmental Protection Agency, "Management of pollutant sources" section, ¶s 4-5). Indeed, the dyes and sealants used in many office chairs are considered hazardous waste. "Most people are sitting on chairs that are an amalgam of hundreds of chemicals that have never been [tested]. . . . The [more deeply] we look, [the more] we find . . . cancer-causing chemicals," says William McDonough, an architectural consultant who specializes in air-quality concerns (Conlin, 2000, p. 128).

Ellipses (spaced dots) indicate some material has been omitted.

An extra dot serves as the period of the sentence.

Square brackets indicate a change from the original to make the quote fit into the structure of your sentence.

The problem is compounded by inadequate ventilation. The American Society of Heating, Refrigeration, and Air-Conditioning Engineers recommends that a building's heating, ventilation, and cooling system deliver 20 cubic feet per minute of outside air for each occupant (Areas, 2001, "Ventilation rates" section, ¶ 5). But, Conlin reports (2000), some buildings provide only 5 cubic feet of fresh air per person a minute. And that "fresh air" may not be pure. Some buildings have fresh air vents over loading docks and parking garages. Revolving doors pull in second-hand smoke "like a chimney" (p. 117) from smokers who stand by the door.

All material from citation to end of ¶ is from a single source.

Use page number for direct quote (no need to repeate source when named earlier in ¶).

In the 1990s, responses to "sick buildings" often focused on the cost of solving the problem—a cost sometimes undertaken only after a lawsuit was filed (Nai, 1995). But recently, several companies have found that improving air quality pays for itself. Pennsylvania Power and Light's remodeling paid for itself in just 69 days by cutting absenteeism 25%, increasing productivity 13%, and reducing energy costs 69% (Aerias, 2001, "Why indoor air quality should be improved," ¶ 4).

Place author, date in parentheses (use page numbers only for a direct quote).

References

List all works (but only those works) cited in text.

Don't abbreviate month.

Aerias. (2001). Overview of IAQ problems in offices. Retrieved September 24, 2001 from the World Wide Web: http://www.aerias.org/office_overview.htm

List sources alphabetically.

Use URL of home page.

List source only once, even when it's used more than once.

Conlin, M. (with Carey, J.). (2000, June 5). Is your office killing you? *BusinessWeek*, 114–128.

Copyright/update date

Repeat hundreds.

Environmental Protection Agency. (2001, July 19). An office building occupant's guide to indoor air quality. Retrieved September 19, 2001, from the World Wide Web: http://www.epa.gov/iaq/pubs/occupgd.html

No punctuation at the end of a URL

Nai, A. K. (1995, October 26). Squabbles delay cure of "sick" office building. *The Wall Street Journal*, pp. B1, B3.

If you have used many sources that you have not cited, you may want to list both works cited and works consulted. The term *bibliography* covers all sources on a topic.

If you use a printed source that is not readily available, consider including it as an appendix in your report. For example, you could copy an ad or include an organization's promotional brochure.

FIGURE 13.10   Report Paragraphs with MLA Documentation

MLA Format

An extra dot serves as the period of the sentence. Modern office buildings contain a surprising number of pollutants. Printing and copying documents creates particles which can be harmful to health. Office carpets and furniture emit chemical pollutants (Environmental Protection Agency, "Management of Pollutant Sources" section, pars. 4-5). Indeed, the dyes and sealants used in many office chairs are considered hazardous waste. "Most people are sitting on chairs that are an amalgam of hundreds of chemicals that have never been [tested] . . . The [more deeply] we look, [the more] we find . . . cancer-causing chemicals," says William McDonough, an architectural consultant who specializes in air-quality concerns (Conlin 128).

Square brackets indicate a change from the original to make the quote fit into the structure of your sentence.

No comma between author, page number; no "p." before page number.

The problem is compounded by inadequate ventilation. The American Society of Heating, Refrigeration, and Air-Conditioning Engineers recommends that a building's heating, ventilation, and cooling system deliver 20 cubic feet per minute of outside air for each occupant (Aerias, 2001, "Ventilation Rates" section, par. 5). But, Michelle Conlin reports, some buildings provide only 5 cubic feet of fresh air per person a minute. And that "fresh air" may not be pure. Some buildings have fresh air vents over loading docks and parking garages. Revolving doors pull in second-hand smoke "like a chimney" (117) from smokers who stand by the door.

Use only page number since author identified in sentence.

In the 1990s, responses to "sick buildings" often focused on the cost of solving the problem—a cost sometimes undertaken only after a lawsuit was filed (Nai B1). But recently, several companies have found that improving air quality pays for itself. Pennsylvania Power and Light's remodeling paid for itself in just 69 days by cutting absenteeism 25%, increasing productivity 13%, and reducing energy costs 69% (Aerias, 2001, "Why Indoor Air Quality Should Be Improved," par. 4).

Heading, paragraph number helps reader find material in Web sites without page numbers.

Give page number for facts, not just quotes.

Works Cited

Copyright/update date
Date you visited site
List all works cited in text.

Aerias. "Overview of IAQ Problems in Offices." 2001. 24 Sept. 2001 <http://www.aerias.org/office_overview.htm>.

List sources alphabetically.   *URL in angle brackets; period after angle bracket.*

Conlin, Michelle with John Carey. "Is Your Office Killing You?" *BusinessWeek* 5 June 2000: 114-28.

Don't repeat hundreds.

Environmental Protection Agency. "An Office Building Occupant's Guide to Indoor Air Quality." 19 July 2001. 19 Sept. 2001 <http://www.epa.gov/iaq/pubs/occupgd.html>.

Use date month year; abbreviate month.   *If URL is too long to fit on one line, break after a punctuation mark.*

Nai, Amal Kumar. "Squabbles Delay Cure of 'Sick' Office Building." *The Wall Street Journal* 26 October 1995: B1+.

"+" indicates article continues.

FIGURE 13.11 APA and MLA Formats for Sources Used Most Often in Reports

APA Format

APA internal documentation gives the author's last name and the date of the work in parentheses in the text. A comma separates the author's name from the date (Gilsdorf & Leonard, 2001). The page number is given only for direct quotations (Cross, 2001, p. 74). If the author's name is used in the sentence, only the date is given in parentheses. (See Figure 13.9.) A list of REFERENCES gives the full bibliographic citation, arranging the entries alphabetically by the first author's last name.

In titles of articles and books capitalize only ①first word, ②first word of subtitle, ③proper nouns.

Article in a Periodical *comma   last name first   No quotes around title of article*

Year (period outside parenthesis).

Gilsdorf, J., & Leonard, D. (2001). Big stuff, little stuff: A decennial measurement of executives' and academics' reactions to questionable usage elements. *The Journal of Business Communication, 38*, 439-475. *no "pp." when journal has a volume number   Capitalize all major words in title of journal, magazine, or newspaper.*

Italicize volume.

McCartney, S. (2000, December 27). Why a baseball superstar's megacontract can be less than it seems. *The Wall Street Journal*, p. B1, B3.

Separate discontinuous pages with comma and space.

Article in an Edited Book *Ampersands join names of co-authors, co-editors.* *Editors' names have last names last.*

Killingsworth, M. J., & Jacobsen, M. (1999). The rhetorical construction of environmental risk narratives in government and activist websites: A critique. In J. M. Perkins & N. Blyler (Eds.), *Narrative and professional communication* (pp. 167-177). Stamford, CT: Ablex.

Editors before book title   *Repeat "1" in 177.*   *Give state when city is not well known.*

Article from a Publication on the Web

Greengard, S. (2001, May). Scoring web wins. *Business Finance Magazine*. p. 37. Retrieved July 12, 2001, from http://www.businessfinancemag.com/archives/appfiles/Article.cfm?IssueID=348&ArticleID=13750 *← no punctuation after URL*

Initials only

Book *Italicize title of book.*

Cross, G. A. (2001). *Forming the collective mind: A contextual exploration of large-scale collaborative writing in industry*. Creskill, NJ: Hampton Press.

Put in square brackets information known to you but not printed in document.

Book or Pamphlet with a Corporate Author

Citibank. (1994). *Indonesia: An investment guide*. [Jakarta:] Author.

Indicates organization authoring document also published it.

E-Mail Message

[Identify e-mail messages in the text as personal communications. Give name of author and as specific a date as possible. Do not list in References.]

Government Document

No abbreviations

Senate Special Committee on Aging. (2001). *Long-term care: States grapple with increasing demands and costs*. Hearing before the Special Committee on Aging, Senate, One Hundred Seventh Congress, first session, hearing held in Washington, DC, July 11, 2001 (Doc ID: 75-038). Washington, DC: U.S. Government Printing Office.

Document number   *APA uses periods for "U.S."*

(continued)

FIGURE 13.11   APA and MLA Formats for Sources Used Most Often in Reports *(continued)*

copyright or update date

Government Document Available on the Web from the GPO Access Database

U.S. General Accounting Office. (2001, September 20.) Aviation security: Terrorist acts demonstrate urgent need to improve security at the nation's airports. Testimony before the Committee on Commerce, Science, and Transportation, U.S. Senate (GAO-01-1162T). Retrieved December 20, 2001, from General Accounting Office Reports Online via GPO Access: http://www.gao.gov/new.items/d011162t.pdf

date you visited site

keep "http://"

Interview Conducted by the Researcher

[Identify interviews in the test as personal communications. Give name of interviewee and as specific a date as possible. Do not list in References.]

Posting to a Listserv

[Identify messages on listservs to which one must subscribe in the text as personal communications. Give name of author and as specific a date as possible. Do not list in References.]

Web Site

American Express. (2001). Creating an effective business plan. Retrieved December 20, 2001, from the World Wide Web: http://home3.americanexpress.com/smallbusiness/tool/biz_plan/index.asp

comma

no punctuation

Break long web address at a slash or other punctuation mark.

MLA Format

MLA internal documentation gives the author's last name and page number in parentheses in the text for facts as well as for quotations (Gilsdorf and Leonard 470). Unlike APA, the year is not given, no comma separates the name and page number, and the abbreviation "p." is not used (Cross 74). If the author's name is used in the sentence, only the page number is given in parentheses. (See Figure 13.10.) A list of WORKS CITED gives the full bibliographic citation, arranging the entries alphabetically by the first author's last name.

first name first for second author

Put quotation marks around title of article.

Article in a Periodical

Gilsdorf, Jeanette and Don Leonard. "Big Stuff, Little Stuff: A Decennial Measurement of Executives' and Academics' Reactions to Questionable Usage Elements." *The Journal of Business Communication* 38 (2001): 448-75.

Capitalize all major words in titles of articles, books, journals magazines, and newspapers.

omit "4" in "475"

Italicize title of journal, magazine, or newspaper.

McCartney, Scott. "Why a Baseball Superstar's Megacontract Can Be Less Than It Seems." *The Wall Street Journal*, 27 Dec. 2000: B1+.

Indicates article continues past first page.

Article from an Edited Book

Killingsworth, M. Jimmie and Martin Jacobsen. "The Rhetorical Construction of Environmental Risk Narratives in Government and Activist Websites: A Critique." *Narrative and Professional Communication.* Ed. Jane M. Perkins and Nancy Blyler. Stamford, CT: Ablex. 167-77.

Give authors', editors' names as printed in the source.

Give state when city is not well known.

Spell out editors' names. Join with "and."

(continued)

FIGURE 13.11   APA and MLA Formats for Sources Used Most Often in Reports *(concluded)*

Article from a Publication on the Web

Greengard, Samuel. "Scoring Web Wins." *Business Finance Magazine*. May 2001. 12 July 2001. <http://www.businessfinancemag.com/archives/appfiles/Article.cfm? IssueID=348&ArticleID=13750>.

↖ Put Web address in angle brackets.
End entry with a period.

Don't add any extra hyphens when you break a long Web address.

Book

Cross, Geoffrey A. *Forming the Collective Mind: A Contextual Exploration of Large-Scale Collaborative Writing in Industry*. Creskill, NJ: Hampton Press, 2001.

Put in square brackets information known to you

Book or Pamphlet with a Corporate Author *but not printed in source.*

Citibank. *Indonesia: An Investment Guide*. [Jakarta:] Citibank, 1994.

Date after city and publisher

E-Mail Message

Abbreviate long months.

Locker, Kitty O. "Could We Get a New Photo?" E-mail to Rajani J. Kamuth. 17 Dec. 2001.

day month year

Government Document

United States. Sen. Special Committee on Aging. *Long-Term Care: States Grapple with Increasing Demands and Costs*. 107th Cong., 1st sess. Washington: GPO, 2001.

Abbreviate
Omit state when city is well known.   ↖   "Government

Government Document Available on the Web from the GPO Access Database *Printing Office."*

United States. General Accounting Office. *Aviation Security: Terrorist Acts Demonstrate Urgent Need to Improve Security at the Nation's Airports*. Testimony before the Committee on Commerce, Science, and Transportation, U.S. Senate (GAO-01-1162T). 20 Sept. 2001. 20 Dec. 2001 <http://www.gao.gov/new.items/d011162t.pdf>.

Interview Conducted by the Researcher

Drysdale, Andrew. Telephone interview. 12 Apr. 1999.

Date of posting.

Posting to a Listserv

Dietrich, Dan. "Re: Course on Report and Proposal Writing." Online posting. 14 Feb. 2000. BizCom Discussion Group. 23 Dec. 2001 <bizcom@ebbs.English.vt.edu>.

If discussion group has a Web archive, give the Web address.

Date you accessed posting

Web Site

If it doesn't have a Web page, give the

American Express. *Creating an Effective Business Plan*. 2001. 20 Dec. 2001. <http://home3.americanexpress.com/smallbusiness/tool/biz_plan/index.asp>

email address of the list.

**Does That
Method
Work?***

[Some research methods don't really capture what they hope to capture. Consider, for example, the Nielsen TV diaries.] Nielsen's diaries divide an hour's worth of viewing into four 15-minute time blocks, under the impression, apparently, that viewers tend to watch at least a quarter of an hour of any given show. That's a misplaced assumption. . . . On any given morning, in one 15-minute Nielsen time block, I've typically surfed through four major networks, plus CNBC. That averages out to 3 minutes per station. Pathetic but true. So how did I account for such channel-surfing in the diary? I pretended to watch a half-hour of morning TV instead of 15 minutes, and knocked out the two stations I watched least. . . .

I also didn't jot down everything. Does anyone care that at 5 a.m. one morning my eyes were glued to Suzanne Somers and Patrick Duffy explaining what muscles the Torso Track targets? It's not as if I was really watching: I was simply too low on caffeine to begin my remote-control-pressing exercises.

*Quoted from Seema Nayyar, "Confessions of a Nielsen Household," *American Demographics*, May 2001, 6.

Summary of Key Points

- **Information reports** collect data for the reader; **analytical reports** present and interpret data; **recommendation reports** recommend action or a solution.
- A good purpose statement must make three things clear:
    - The organizational problem or conflict.
    - The specific technical questions that must be answered to solve the problem.
    - The rhetorical purpose (to explain, to recommend, to request, to propose) that the report is designed to achieve.
- A proposal must answer the following questions:
    - What problem are you going to solve?
    - How are you going to solve it?
    - What exactly will you provide for us?
    - Can you deliver what you promise?
    - When will you complete the work?
    - How much will you charge?
- In a proposal for a class research project, prove that your problem is the right size, that you understand it, that your method will give you the information you need to solve the problem, and that you have the knowledge and resources.
- Use the following pattern of organization for the cover letter for a sales proposal:
    1. Catch the reader's attention and summarize up to three major benefits you offer.
    2. Discuss each of the major benefits in the order in which you mentioned them in the first paragraph.
    3. Deal with any objections or concerns the reader may have.
    4. Mention other benefits briefly.
    5. Ask the reader to approve your proposal and provide a reason for acting promptly.
- In a proposal for funding, stress the needs your project will meet. Show how your project will help fulfill the goals of the organization you are asking for funds.
- Progress reports may be organized chronologically, by task, or to support a recommendation.
- Use positive emphasis in progress reports to create an image of yourself as a capable, confident worker.
- Use indexes and directories to find information about a specific company or topic.
- To decide whether to use a Web site as a source in a research project, evaluate the site's authors, objectivity, information, and revision date.
- A **survey** questions a large group of people, called **respondents** or **subjects**. A **questionnaire** is a written list of questions that people fill out. An **interview** is a structured conversation with someone who will be able to give you useful information.
- Good questions ask just one thing, are phrased neutrally, avoid making assumptions about the respondent, and mean the same thing to different people.

- **Closed questions** have a limited number of possible responses. **Open questions** do not lock the subject into any sort of response. **Branching questions** direct different respondents to different parts of the questionnaire based on their answers to earlier questions. A **mirror question** paraphrases the content of the last answer. **Probes** follow up an original question to get at specific aspects of a topic.

- Good researchers attempt to reach nonrespondents at least once and preferably twice.

- A **convenience sample** is a group of subjects who are easy to get. A **judgment sample** is a group of people whose views seem useful. In a **random sample,** each person in the population theoretically has an equal chance of being chosen. A sample is random only if a formal, approved random sampling method is used. Otherwise, unconscious bias exists.

- **Citation** means attributing an idea or fact to its source in the body of the report. **Documentation** means providing the bibliographic information readers would need to go back to the original source.

CHAPTER 13 Exercises and Problems

Getting Started

13.1 Identifying the Weaknesses in Problem Statements

Identify the weaknesses in the following problem statements.

- Is the problem narrow enough?
- Can a solution be found in a semester or quarter?
- What organization could implement any recommendations to solve the problem?
- Could the topic be limited or refocused to yield an acceptable problem statement?

1. One possible report topic I would like to investigate would be the differences in women's intercollegiate sports in our athletic conference.

2. How to market products effectively to college students.

3. Should Web banners be part of a company's advertising?

4. How can US and Canadian students get jobs in Europe?

5. We want to explore ways our company can help raise funds for the Open Shelter. We will investigate whether collecting and recycling glass, aluminum, and paper products will raise enough money to help.

6. How can XYZ university better serve students from traditionally underrepresented groups?

7. What are the best investments for the next year?

13.2 Writing a Preliminary Purpose Statement

Answer the following questions about a topic on which you could write a formal report. (See Problems 14.4, 14.6, 14.7, 14.9, and 14.10.)

As Your Instructor Directs,

a. Be prepared to answer the questions orally in a conference.

b. Bring written answers to a conference.

c. Submit written answers in class.

d. Give your instructor a photocopy of your statement after it is approved.

1. What problem will you investigate or solve?

a. What is the name of the organization facing the problem?

b. What is the technical problem or difficulty?

c. Why is it important to the organization that this problem be solved?

d. What solution or action might you recommend to solve the problem?

e. List the name and title of the person in the organization who would have the power to accept or reject your recommendation.

2. Will this report use information from other classes or from work experiences? If so, give the name and topic of the class and/or briefly describe the job. If you will need additional information (that you have not already gotten from other classes or from a job), how do you expect to find it?

3. List the name, title, and business phone number of a professor who can testify to your ability to handle the expertise needed for this report.

4. List the name, title, and business phone number of someone in the organization who can testify that you have access to enough information about that organization to write this report.

13.3   Choosing Research Strategies

For each of the following reports, indicate the kinds of research that might be useful. If a survey is called for, indicate the most efficient kind of sample to use.

a. How can XYZ store increase sales?

b. What is it like to live and work in [name of country]?

c. Should our organization have a dress code?

d. Is it feasible to start a monthly newsletter for students in your major?

e. How can we best market to mature adults?

f. Can compensation programs increase productivity?

g. What skills are in demand in our area? Of these, which could the local community college offer courses in?

13.4   Identifying Keywords for Computer Searches

As Your Instructor Directs,
Identify the keyword combinations that you could use in researching one or more of the following topics:

a. Ways to evaluate whether recycling is working.

b. Safety of pension funds.

c. Ethical issues in accounting.

d. Effects of advertising on sales of automobiles.

e. What can be done to increase the privacy of personal data.

f. Accounting for intellectual capital.

g. Advantages and problems of Web advertising.

13.5   Comparing Web Search Engines

Using at least three different search engines, search for sources on a topic on which you could write a formal report. (See Problems 14.5, 14.6, 14.7, 14.9, and 14.10.) Compare the top 30 sources. Which sites turn up on all three search engines? Which search engine appears to be most useful for your project?

As Your Instructor Directs,

a. Share your results orally with a small group of students.

b. Present your results to the class.

c. Write a memo to your instructor summarizing your results.

d. With a small group of students, write a report recommending guidelines for using search engines.

13.6   Evaluating Web Sites

Evaluate 10 Web sites related to the topic of your report. For each, consider

■   Authors.

■   Objectivity.

■   Information.

■   Revision date.

Based on these criteria, which sites are best for your report? Which are unacceptable? Why?

As Your Instructor Directs,

a. Share your results with a small group of students.

b. Present your results in a memo to your instructor.

c. Present your results to the class in an oral presentation.

13.7   Choosing Samples for Surveys and Interviews

Indicate the best sample(s) to use in surveys and interviews for reports on the following topics.

a. Would XYZ organization raise more money if it sold items besides donuts every morning in [classroom building]?

b. Improving access to computers for students at XYZ College.

c. How can XYZ organization attract more student members?

d. How can XYZ restaurant reduce turnover?

e. Improving communication with international students at XYZ University.

f. Dealing with hate speech at XYZ College.

g. How teaching can be improved in [Department].

13.8   Evaluating Survey Questions

Evaluate each of the following questions. Are they acceptable as they stand? If not, how can they be improved?

a. Survey of clerical workers:
    Do you work for the government? ☐
    or the private sector? ☐

b. Questionnaire on grocery purchases:
    1. Do you *usually* shop at the same grocery store?
        a. Yes
        b. No
    2. Do you use credit cards to purchase items at your grocery store?
        a. Yes
        b. No
    3. How much is your average grocery bill?
        a. Under $25
        b. $25–50
        c. $50–100
        d. $100–150
        e. Over $150

c. Survey on technology:
    1. Would you generally welcome any technological advancement that allowed information to be sent and received more quickly and in greater quantities than ever before?
    2. Do you think that all people should have free access to all information, or do you think that information should somehow be regulated and monitored?

d. Survey on job skills:
    How important are the following skills for getting and keeping a professional-level job in US business and industry today?

	Low				High
Ability to communicate	1	2	3	4	5
Leadership ability	1	2	3	4	5
Public presentation skills	1	2	3	4	5
Selling ability	1	2	3	4	5
Teamwork capability	1	2	3	4	5
Writing ability	1	2	3	4	5

13.9   Designing Questions for an Interview or Survey

Submit either a one- to three-page questionnaire or questions for a 20- to 30-minute interview AND the information listed below for the method you choose.

Questionnaire
1. Purpose(s), goal(s).
2. Subjects (who, why, how many).
3. How and where to be distributed.
4. Any changes in type size, paper color, etc., from submitted copy.
5. Rationale for order of questions, kinds of questions, wording of questions.
6. References, if building on questionnaires by other authors.

Interview
1. Purpose(s), goal(s).
2. Subjects (who, and why).
3. Proposed site, length of interview.
4. Rationale for order of questions, kinds of questions, wording of questions, choice of branching or follow-up questions.
5. References, if building on questions devised by others.

As Your Instructor Directs,

a. Create questions for a survey on one of the following topics:

- Survey students on your campus about their knowledge of and interest in the programs and activities sponsored by a student organization.

- Survey workers at a company about what they like and dislike about their jobs.

- Survey people in your community about their willingness to pay more to buy products using recycled materials and to buy products that are packaged with a minimum of waste.

- Survey students and faculty on your campus about whether adequate parking exists.

- Survey two groups on a topic that interests you.

b. Create questions for an interview on one of the following topics:

- Interview an international student about the forms of greetings and farewells, topics of small talk, forms of politeness, festivals and holidays, meals at home, size of families, and roles of family members in his or her country.

- Interview a TV producer about what styles and colors work best for people appearing on TV.

- Interview a worker about an ethical dilemma he or she faced on the job, what the worker did and why, and how the company responded.

- Interview the owner of a small business about the problems the business has, what strategies the owner has already used to increase sales and profits and how successful these strategies were, and the owner's attitudes toward possible changes in product line, decor, marketing, hiring, advertising, and money management.

- Interview someone who has information you need for a report you're writing.

13.10   Choosing Subject Lines for Memo Reports

Identify the strengths and weaknesses of each subject line, and choose the best subject line(s) from each group.

1. A proposal to conduct research.
   a. Membership Survey
   b. Proposal to Survey Former Members to Learn Their Reasons for Not Rejoining
   c. Proposal to Investigate Former Members' Reasons for Not Rejoining

2. A survey to find out why former members did not renew their memberships.

   a. 2003 Delinquency Survey
   b. Results of 2003 Former Member Survey
   c. Why Members Did Not Renew Their Memberships in 2003

3. A progress report.
   a. Progress Report
   b. Work Completed, October 15–November 5
   c. Status of the Survey of Former Members

E-Mail Messages

13.11   Writing a Progress Report

As Your Instructor Directs,

send an e-mail message

a. To the other members of your group, describing your progress since the last group meeting.

b. To your instructor, describing your progress.

c. To your instructor, asking for help solving a problem you have encountered.

Communicating at Work

As Your Instructor Directs in Problems 13.12 through 13.14,

a. Create a document or presentation to achieve the goal.

b. Write a memo to your instructor describing the situation at your workplace and explaining your rhetorical choices (medium, strategy, tone, wording, graphics or document design, and so forth).

13.12   Proposing a Change

No organization is perfect. Propose a change that would improve your organization. The change can affect only your unit or the whole organization; it can relate to productivity and profits, to quality of life, or to any other aspect your organization can control. Direct your proposal to the person or committee with the power to authorize the change.

13.13   Proposing to Undertake a Research Project

Pick a project you would like to study whose results could be used by your organization. (See Problem 14.4.) Write a proposal to your supervisor requesting time away from other duties to do the research. Show how your research (whatever its outcome) will be useful to the organization.

13.14   Writing a Progress Report to Your Superior

Describe the progress you have made this week or this month on projects you have been assigned. You may describe progress you have made individually, or progress your unit has made as a team.

Memo and Letter Assignments

13.15   Writing a Report Based on a Survey

As Your Instructor Directs,

a. Survey 40 to 50 people on some subject of your choice.

b. Team up with your classmates to conduct a survey and write it up as a group. Survey 50 to 80 people if your group has two members, 75 to 120 people if it has three members, 100 to 150 people if it has four members, and 125 to 200 people if it has five members.

c. Keep a journal during your group meetings and submit it to your instructor.

d. Write a memo to your instructor describing and evaluating your group's process for designing, conducting, and writing up the survey. (See Chapter 12 on working and writing in groups.)

For this assignment, you do **not** have to take a random sample. Do, however, survey at least two different groups so that you can see if they differ in some way. Possible groups are men and women, business majors and English majors, Greeks and independents, first-year students and seniors, students and townspeople.

As you conduct your survey, make careful notes about what you do so that you can use this information when you write up your survey. If you work with a group, record who does what. Use complete memo format. Your subject line should be clear and reasonably complete. Omit unnecessary words such as "Survey of." Your first paragraph serves as an introduction, but it needs no heading. The rest of the body of your memo will be divided into four sections with the following headings: Purpose, Procedure, Results, and Discussion.

In your first paragraph, briefly summarize (not necessarily in this order) who conducted the experiment or survey, when it was conducted, where it was conducted, who the subjects were, what your purpose was, and what you found out. You will discuss all of these topics in more detail in the body of your memo.

In your **Purpose** section, explain why you conducted the survey. What were you trying to learn? What hypothesis were you testing? Why did this subject seem interesting or important?

In your **Procedure** section, describe in detail *exactly* what you did. "The first 50 people who came through the Union on Wed., Feb. 2" is not the same as "The first 50 people who came through the south entrance of the Union on Wed., Feb. 2, and agreed to answer my questions." Explain any steps you took to overcome possible sources of bias.

In your **Results** section, first tell whether your results supported your hypothesis. Use both visuals and words to explain what your numbers show. (See Chapter 15 on how to design visuals.) Process your raw data in a way that will be useful to your reader.

In your **Discussion** section, evaluate your survey and discuss the implications of your results. Consider these questions:

1. What are the limitations of your survey and your results?

2. Do you think a scientifically valid survey would have produced the same results? Why or why not?

3. Were there any sources of bias either in the way the questions were phrased or in the way the subjects were chosen? If you were running the survey again, what changes would you make to eliminate or reduce these sources of bias?

4. Do you think your subjects answered honestly and completely? What factors may have intruded? Is the fact that you did or didn't know them, were or weren't of the same sex relevant? If your results seem to contradict other evidence, how do you account for the discrepancy? Were your subjects shading the truth? Was your sample's unrepresentativeness the culprit? Or have things changed since earlier data were collected?

5. What causes the phenomenon your results reveal? If several causes together account for the phenomenon, or if it is impossible to be sure of the cause, admit this. Identify possible causes and assess the likelihood of each.

6. What action should be taken?

The discussion section gives you the opportunity to analyze the significance of your survey. Its insight and originality lift the otherwise well-written memo from the ranks of the merely satisfactory to the ranks of the above-average and the excellent.

The whole assignment will be more interesting if you choose a question that interests you. It does not need to be "significant" in terms of major political or philosophic problems; a quirk of human behavior that fascinates you will do nicely.

13.16   Writing a Proposal for a Student Report

Write a proposal to your instructor to do the research for a formal or informal report. (See Problems 14.4, 14.6, 14.7, 14.9, and 14.10.)

The headings and the questions in the section titled "Proposals for Class Research Projects" are your RFP; be sure to answer every question and to use the headings exactly as stated in the RFP. Exception: where alternate heads are listed, you may choose one, combine the two ("Qualifications and Facilities"), or treat them as separate headings in separate categories.

13.17   Writing a Proposal for Funding for a Nonprofit Group

Pick a nonprofit group you care about. Examples include professional organizations, a school sports team, a charitable group, a community organization, a religious group, or your own college or university.

As Your Instructor Directs,

a. Check the Web or a directory of foundations to find one that makes grants to groups like yours. Brainstorm a list of businesses that might be willing to give money for specific projects. Check to see whether state or national levels of your organization make grants to local chapters.

b. Write a proposal to obtain funds for a special project your group could undertake if it had the money. Address your proposal to a specific organization.

c. Write a proposal to obtain operating funds or money to buy something your group would like to have. Address your proposal to a specific organization.

13.18   Writing a Sales Proposal

Pick a project that you could do for a local company or government office. Examples include

■ Creating a brochure or Web page.

■ Revising form letters.

■ Conducting a training program.

■ Writing a newsletter or an annual report.

■ Developing a marketing plan.

■ Providing plant care, catering, or janitorial services.

Write a proposal specifying what you could do and providing a detailed budget and work schedule.

As Your Instructor Directs,

a. Phone someone in the organization to talk about its needs and what you could offer.

b. Write an individual proposal.

c. Join with other students in the class to create a group proposal.

d. Present your proposal orally.

13.19   Writing a Progress Report

Write a memo to your instructor summarizing your progress on your report.

In the introductory paragraph, summarize your progress in terms of your schedule and your goals. Under a heading titled *Work Completed,* list what you have already done. (This is a chance to toot your own horn: if you have solved problems creatively, say so! You can also describe obstacles you've encountered that you have not yet solved.) Under *Work to Be Completed,* list what you still have to do. If you are more than two days behind the schedule you submitted with your proposal, include a revised schedule, listing the completion dates for the activities that remain.

In your last paragraph, either indicate your confidence in completing the report by the due date or ask for a conference to resolve the problems you are encountering.

13.20   Writing a Progress Report for a Group Report

Write a memo to your instructor summarizing your group's progress.

In the introductory paragraph, summarize the group's progress in terms of its goals and its schedule, your own progress on the tasks for which you are responsible, and your feelings about the group's work thus far.

Under a heading titled *Work Completed,* list what has already been done. Be most specific about what you yourself have done. Describe briefly the chronology of group activities: number, time, and length of meetings; topics discussed and decisions made at meetings.

If you have solved problems creatively, say so! You can also describe obstacles you've encountered that you have not yet solved. In this section, you can also comment on problems that the group has faced and whether or not they've been solved. You can comment on things that have gone well and have contributed to the smooth functioning of the group.

Under *Work to Be Completed,* list what you personally and other group members still have to do. Indicate the schedule for completing the work.

In your last paragraph, either indicate your confidence in completing the report by the due date or ask for a conference to resolve the problems you are encountering.

Analyzing Information and Writing Reports

Analyzing Information and Writing Reports

At Custom Research, Inc. (CRI), our analysis and report writing process begins with the very first conversation we have with a client. We identify objectives up front.

Then, *before* any data are collected, we decide what kinds of analysis we will use and create a preliminary outline of the report. Identifying the data needed to answer the objectives ensures that the right data are collected.

While there is no one right style for a report, you need to develop *some* style, some viewpoint to give your writing consistency. When parts of a report are written at different times or by different people, make sure that the whole report uses the same style.

To make a report come alive, link the various pieces of information together to create a story or build a case. First *understand* the information, then *organize* it by checking and revising the outline that was created earlier, and then *write* the report. Headings can organize and synthesize information. Instead of just restating the data ("Product A is preferred over Product B by 70% of the people"), use headings that interpret the data ("Product A is a clear winner").

Report format allows varied audiences to find what they need. CRI reports begin with an Executive Summary written for the CEO or Marketing VP. This summary contains a short description of the research and objectives along with key conclusions and recommendations. Giving the basic support for the recommendations here allows executives to understand and approve the basic recommendations without getting bogged down in all the details. Next come the Detailed Findings, written for the marketing or market research manager. This section has detailed information and analysis that can be used to make more specific decisions.

Finally, edit and proofread! Your report should be concise. *And,* it should be error free. Just one wrong number will make the entire report suspect. A good report offers analysis in an interesting, concise, and error-free document.

Diane Kokal
Executive Vice President, Custom Research, Inc.

Diane Kokal has written reports for many of Custom Research, Inc.'s Fortune 500 clients, including McDonald's, General Mills, Quaker Oats, and Kraft Foods. Custom Research is a market research consulting firm and a recipient of the 1996 Malcolm Baldrige National Quality Award. Kokal was a key part of the team that wrote the application.

www.customresearch.com

> " *A good report offers analysis in an interesting, concise, and error-free document.* "

Reports at Toyota*

Most companies use meetings to hammer out the many decisions and compromises necessary to design a new vehicle. Toyota, in contrast, relies on written reports. When a cross-functional problem arises, the person who identified the problem writes a report identifying the problem, analyzing it, and recommending a solution. These reports focus on a single issue and are brief—often only a page or two long. They may be presented orally as well or supplemented with a phone call. Afterward, the recipient reads the report carefully, then responds in another report.

A couple of rounds of report and response solve most conflicts. If problems remain, the parties meet. At this point, everyone has thought about the issue; the precision that writing demands has focused thinking. So meetings are brief and productive.

*Based on Durward K. Sobek, II, Jeffrey K. Liker, and Allen C. Ward, "Another Look at How Toyota Integrates Product Development," *Harvard Business Review* 76, no. 4 (July/August 1998), 38–40.

Careful analysis, smooth writing, and effective document design work together to make effective reports, whether you're writing a 2½-page memo report or a 250-page formal report complete with all the report components. See the BAC Web site for links to reports on the Web.

Chapter 13 covered the first two steps in writing a report:

1. Define the problem.
2. Gather the necessary data and information.

This chapter covers the last three steps:

3. Analyze the data and information.
4. Organize the information.
5. Write the report.

Other chapters that are especially useful for reports are Chapters 9, 12, 15, and 16. Appendix C, on making and communicating meaning, and Appendix D, on Toulmin logic, are also helpful.

Using Your Time Efficiently

To use your time efficiently, think about the parts of the report before you begin writing. Much of the introduction comes from your proposal, with only minor revisions. You can write six sections even before you've finished your research: Purpose, Scope, Assumptions, Methods, Criteria, and Definitions.

The background reading for your proposal can form the first draft of your list of references.

Save a copy of your questionnaire or interview questions to use as an appendix. As you tally and analyze the data, prepare an appendix summarizing all the responses to your questionnaire, your figures and tables, and a complete list of references. You can print appendixes before the final report is ready if you number their pages separately. Appendix A pages would be A-1, A-2, and so forth; Appendix B pages would be B-1, B-2, and so forth.

You can write the title page and the transmittal as soon as you know what your recommendation will be.

After you've analyzed your data, write the executive summary, the body, and the conclusions and recommendations. Prepare a draft of the table of contents and the list of illustrations.

When you write a long report, list all the sections (headings) that your report will have. Mark those that are most important to your reader and your logic, and spend most of your time on them. Write the important sections early. That way, you won't spend all your time on Background or History of the Problem. Instead, you'll get to the meat of your report.

Analyzing Data and Information for Reports

Analyzing the data you have gathered is essential to produce the tight logic needed for a good report. Analyze your data with healthy skepticism. Professor Raymond Panko found that 30% of spreadsheets had errors, such as misplaced decimal points, transposed digits, and wrong signs, built into their rules.[1]

Identifying the Source of the Data

Check to be sure that your data come from a reliable source. Use the strategies outlined in Chapter 13 to evaluate Web sources (◀ p. 365). When the source has a vested interest (◀▦ p. 213) in the results, scrutinize them with special care. To analyze a company's financial prospects, use independent information as well as the company's annual report and press releases.

If your report is based upon secondary data from library and online research, look at the sample, the sample size, and the exact wording of questions to see what the data actually measure. Some studies bias results by limiting the alternatives. Ninety percent of students surveyed by Levi Strauss & Co. said Levi's 501 jeans would be the most popular clothes that year. But Levi's were the only brand of jeans on the list of choices. Some studies ask biased questions. A poll sponsored by the disposable diaper industry asked, "It is estimated that disposable diapers account for less than 2% of the trash in today's landfills. In contrast, beverage containers, third-class mail, and yard waste are estimated to account for about 21% of the trash in landfills. Given this, in your opinion, would it be fair to ban disposable diapers?" Not surprisingly, 84% of respondents said *no*.[2]

Identify exactly what the data measure. For example, using a Dun & Bradstreet database, many people claim that only 28% of small businesses survive for eight years. But that database counts a small business as "surviving" only if it remains under the same ownership. Researcher Bruce Kirchoff found that another 26% survive with ownership changes, for a total survival rate of 54%.[3]

Identify the assumptions used in analyzing the data. When studies contradict each other, the explanation sometimes lies in the assumptions. For example, a study that found disposable diapers were better for the environment than cloth diapers assumed that each diaper change used 1.9 or 1.79 diapers and that a cloth diaper lasted for 92.5 uses. A study that found that cloth diapers were better assumed that each diaper change used 1.72 diapers and that each cloth diaper lasted for 167 uses.[4]

Analyzing Numbers

Many reports analyze numbers—either numbers from databases and sources or numbers from a survey you have conducted.

If you've conducted a survey, your first step is to transfer the responses on the survey form into numbers. For some categories, you'll assign numbers arbitrarily. For example, you might record men as 1 and women as 2—or vice versa. Such assignments don't matter, as long as you're consistent throughout your project. In these cases, you can report the number and percentage of men and women who responded to your survey, but you can't do anything else with the numbers.

When you have numbers for salaries or other figures, start by figuring the average, or mean, the median, and the range. The **average** or **mean** is calculated by adding up all the figures and dividing by the number of samples. The **mode** is the number that occurs most often. The **median** is the number that is exactly in the middle. When you have an odd number of observations, the median will be the middle number. When you have an even number, the median will be the average of the two numbers in the center. The **range** is the difference between the high and low figures for that variable. Figure 14.1 shows the raw data that a student recorded in a report evaluating a hospital's emergency room procedures. To analyze the data, we could rearrange them, listing them from low to high (see Figure 14.2). The average waiting time is 26.6 minutes, but the median (the middle number) is only 22.

Finding the average takes a few more steps when you have different kinds of data. For example, it's common to ask respondents whether they find a feature "very important," "somewhat important," or "not important." You might

Analyzing Numbers, I*

Beth Baldwin, Director of Marketing Information at Terra Lycos, the giant dotcom portal, knew the numbers didn't add up. Last November, New York–based Web audience measurement service Media Matrix reported that Lycos Zone—the portal's site for kids—had seen a 5 percent decline from the previous month. Baldwin's own numbers, however, showed that in fact the amount of traffic to the site had increased during that period.

Baldwin believed that her numbers, generated by Terra Lycos's site-metrics software, were probably right, but she had to prove it because Wall Street was more inclined to treat Media Matrix as the final word. It took two months, but she finally found the answer in a study, conducted by market research firm Roper Starch Worldwide, that reported on Web usage in schools and listed popular K–12 sites. Baldwin realized that many of the visitors to Lycos Zone were kids logging on from school, and that Media Matrix doesn't count those users. Her numbers were indeed correct.

*Quoted from Brian Caulfield, "Why Your Site Traffic Numbers Are Out of Whack," *www.ecompany.com*, March 2001, 122.

Analyzing Numbers, II*

True story. One of the Big Three Detroit Automakers put together a customer relationship management (CRM) system that helped it decide which cars to manufacture based on what was going on in dealers' lots. It worked great.

Well, except for one catch. According to Eric Almquist, VP at Mercer Management Consulting, the company's marketing team had just created sales incentives to get rid of a lot of lime-green cars, which no one wanted. As consumers snapped up the special deals on the cars, the CRM software noticed the surge of sales in lime-green cars and instructed the factory to produce more. The automaker lost millions of dollars before it caught the error.

*Quoted from Brian Caulfield, "Facing Up to CRM," *www.ecompany.com*, August/September 2001, 149.

FIGURE 14.1   Raw Data from Observations for a Report

Amount of time (rounded off to the nearest minute) that patients wait in the emergency room before being examined in triage.

Patient	Wait	Patient	Wait	Patient	Wait
1	12	6	17	11	19
2	17	7	35	12	31
3	15	8	12	13	41
4	22	9	54	14	23
5	35	10	50	15	17

FIGURE 14.2   Rearranging Data to Find the Average (Mean), Mode, and Median

```
12, 12           Average: 26.6 minutes
15               Median: 22 minutes
17, 17, 17       Mode: 17 minutes
19               Range: 12 – 54 minutes
22
23
31
35, 35
41
50
54
```

code "very important" as "3," "somewhat important" as "2," and "not important" as "1." To find the average in this kind of data,

1. For each response, multiply the code by the number of people who gave that response.
2. Add up the figures.
3. Divide by the total number of people responding to the question.

For example, suppose you have the following data after surveying 50 people about the features they want in a proposed apartment complex:

	Very important (coded as "3")	Somewhat important (coded as "2")	Not important (coded as "1")
Party house	26	12	13
Extra parking for guests	26	23	1

Following step 1, to get the average for "party house," multiply $3 \times 26 = 78$; $2 \times 12 = 24$; and $1 \times 13 = 13$. Then add $78 + 24 + 13 = 115$. Divide by the number of people answering the question and you get the average for that factor: 115 divided by 50 = 2.3. Repeat the process for the next factor, "extra parking": $3 \times 26 = 78$; $2 \times 23 = 46$; $1 \times 1 = 1$. Adding $78 + 46 + 1 = 125$; dividing by 50 = 2.5.

The average then gives an easy way to compare various features. If the party house averages 2.3 while extra parking for guests is 2.5, you know that your re-

FIGURE 14.3   A Quadrant Analysis Shows Which Accounts Meet Two Desirable Criteria

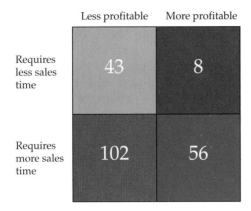

spondents would find extra parking more important than a party house. You can now arrange the factors in order of importance:

Table 4. "How Important Is Each Factor to You in Choosing an Apartment?"

n = 50; 3 = "Very Important"

Extra parking for guests	2.5
Party house	2.3
Pool	2.2
Convenient to bus line	2.0

Often it's useful to simplify numerical data: rounding it off, combining similar elements. Then you can see that one number is about 2½ times another. Charting it can also help you see patterns in your data. (See Chapter 15 for a full discussion of charts as a way of analyzing and presenting numerical data.) Look at the raw data as well as at percentages. For example, a 50% increase in shoplifting incidents sounds alarming—but an increase from two to three shoplifting incidents sounds well within normal variation.

Yet another way to analyze numerical data is use a **quadrant analysis.** A quadrant analyzes two factors of interest. For example, a company interested in knowing whether it was using its sales representatives effectively might analyze its accounts into more and less profitable and more and less time-consuming. (See Figure 14.3.) The dividing points are arbitrary. A small business might label accounts yielding profits of up to $25,000 a year "less profitable" and accounts yielding $25,000 or more "more profitable." A big company would have a much higher cut-off to divide "less" from "more" profitable.

The ideal situation, from the company's point of view, would be to have lots of highly profitable accounts that needed little time from sales representatives. The next best condition is to spend time on profitable accounts. Figure 14.3 shows how many accounts fall into each of the four possibilities. The highest number of accounts is in the quadrant of "less profit, but lots of time." The sales representatives would better use their time on more accounts that yield more profits.

Analyzing Words

If your data include words, try to find out what the words mean to the people who said them. Respondents to Whirlpool's survey of 180,000 households said they wanted "clean refrigerators." After asking more questions, Whirlpool found that what people really wanted were refrigerators that *looked* clean, so the company developed models with textured fronts and sides to hide fingerprints.[5] Also try to measure words against numbers. When he researched possible investments, Peter Lynch found that people in mature industries were pessimistic, seeing clouds. People in immature industries saw pie in the sky, even when the numbers weren't great.[6]

Look for patterns. If you have library sources, on which points do experts agree? Which disagreements can be explained by early theories or numbers that have now changed? Which disagreements are the result of different interpretations of the same data? Which are the result of having different values and criteria? In your interviews and surveys, what patterns do you see?

- Have things changed over time?
- Does geography account for differences?
- What similarities do you see?
- What differences do you see?
- What confirms your hunches?
- What surprises you?

Checking Your Logic

State accurately what your data show. For example, suppose that you've asked people who use computers if they could be as productive without them and the overwhelming majority say *no*. This finding shows that people *believe* that computers make them more productive, but it does not prove that they in fact *are* more productive.

Don't confuse causation with correlation. *Causation* means that one thing causes or produces another. *Correlation* means that two things happen at the same time. One might cause the other, but both might be caused by a third. For example, suppose you're considering whether to buy PCs for everyone in your company, and suppose your surveys show that the people who currently have computers are, in general, more productive than people who don't use computers. Does having a computer lead to higher productivity? Perhaps. But perhaps productive people are more likely to push to get computers from company funds, while less productive people are more passive. Perhaps productive people earn more and are more likely to be able to buy their own computers if the organization doesn't provide them. Perhaps some third factor—experience in the company, education, or social background—leads both to increased productivity and to acquiring computers.

Consciously search for at least three possible causes for each phenomenon you've observed and at least three possible solutions for each problem. The more possibilities you brainstorm, the more likely you are to find good options. In your report, mention all of the possibilities; discuss in detail only those that will occur to readers and that you think are the real reasons and the best solutions.

When you have identified patterns that seem to represent the causes of the problem or the best solutions, check these ideas against reality. Can you find support in the quotes or in the numbers? Can you answer counterclaims? If you can, you will be able to present evidence for your argument in a convincing way. See Appendix D for a discussion of Toulmin logic.

Make the nature of your evidence clear to your reader. Do you have observations that you yourself have made? Or do

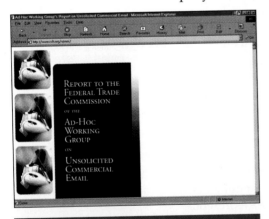

InSite

www.cdt.org/spam

The Ad-Hoc Working Group's report on unsolicited commercial e-mail is one of many government reports on the Web.

you have inferences based on observations or data collected by others? Check the principles of semantics in Appendix C. Old data and *either–or* classifications are not good guides to future action. A statement—even one from a computer printout—is never the whole story.

If you can't prove the claim you originally hoped to make, modify your conclusions to fit your data. Even when your market test is a failure or your experiment disproves your hypothesis, you can still write a useful report.

- Identify changes that might yield a different result. For example, selling the product at a lower price might enable the company to sell enough units.
- Divide the discussion to show what part of the test succeeded.
- Discuss circumstances that may have affected the results.
- Summarize your negative findings in progress reports to let readers down gradually and to give them a chance to modify the research design.
- Remember that negative results aren't always disappointing to the audience. For example, the people who commissioned a feasibility report may be relieved to have an impartial outsider confirm their suspicions that a project isn't feasible.[7]

Choosing Information for Reports

Don't put information in reports just because you have it or just because it took you a long time to find it. Instead, choose the information that your reader needs to make a decision.

If you know your readers well, you may know what their priorities are. If you don't know your readers, you may be able to get a sense for what is important by showing them a tentative table of contents (a list of your headings) and asking, "Have I included everything?" When you cannot contact an external audience, show your draft to superiors in your organization.

One report writer was asked to examine a building that had problems with heating, cooling, and air circulation. The client who owned the building wanted quick answers to three questions: Should we put in a new system or can we repair the old one? What will it cost? When will it pay for itself? The report could have been three pages with a seven-page appendix showing the payback figures.[8]

How much information you need to include depends on whether your audience is likely to be supportive, neutral, or skeptical. As Jeanne Halpern of McKinsey says,

> If the audience is very likely to go along with you, then you can give the message directly and explain how to do it. If you have a message that the people have no conviction about or don't feel happy about, then you have to show the reasons why and explain your thinking in a persuasive way.[9]

You must also decide whether to put information in the body of the report or in appendixes. Put material in the body of the report if it is crucial to your proof or if it is short. (Something less than half a page won't interrupt the reader.)

Anything that a careful reader will want but that is not crucial to your proof can go in an appendix. Appendixes can include

- A copy of a survey questionnaire or interview questions.
- A tally of responses to each question in a survey.
- A copy of responses to open-ended questions in a survey.
- A transcript of an interview.
- Computer printouts.
- Previous reports on the same subject.

What Does the Reader Want? I*

What criteria do experienced investors use to read strategic business plans? Researchers Evelyn Pierce, Richard Young, and Thomas Hajduk found that the return on investment and the management team were the most important criteria. Investors didn't really care what product or service the business would provide, and they skipped most of the material in business plans that didn't relate to their criteria.

*Based on Evelyn Pierce, Richard Young, and Thomas Hajduk, "Using Experienced Audience Insights That Reveal How Readers Respond to Business Documents," Southeast Association for Business Communication, Kiawah Island, South Carolina, March 7–9, 1996.

Tell Them a Story*

To persuade people, tell them a story or anecdote that proves your point.

Experiments with both high school teachers and quantitatively trained MBA students show that people are more likely to believe a point and more likely to be committed to it when points were made by examples, stories, and case studies. Stories alone were more effective than a combination of stories and statistics; the combination was more effective than statistics alone. In another experiment, attitude changes lasted longer when the audience had read stories than when they had only read numbers. Recent research suggests that stories are more persuasive because people remember them.

In many cases, you'll need to provide statistics or numbers to convince the careful reader that your anecdote is a representative example. But give the story first. It's more persuasive.

*Based on Daniel J. O'Keefe, *Persuasion* (Newbury Park, CA: Sage, 1990), 168; Joanne Martin and Melanie E. Powers, "Truth or Corporate Propaganda," *Organizational Symbolism*, eds. Louis R. Pondy, Thomas C. Dandridge, Gareth Morgan, and Peter J. Frost (Greenwich, CT: JAI Press 1983), 97–107; and Dean C. Kazoleas, "A Comparison of the Persuasive Effectiveness of Qualitative versus Quantitative Evidence: A Test of Explanatory Hypotheses," *Communication Quarterly* 41, no. 1 (Winter 1993), 40–50.

Organizing Information in Reports

Most sets of data can be organized in several logical ways. Choose the way that makes your information easiest for the reader to understand and use. If you were compiling a directory of all the employees at your plant, for example, alphabetizing by last name would be far more useful than listing people by height, social security number, or length of service with the company, although those organizing principles might make sense in other lists for other purposes.

In one company, a young employee comparing the economics of two proposed manufacturing processes gave his logic and his calculations in full before getting to his conclusion. But his superiors didn't want to wade through eight single-spaced pages; they wanted his recommendation up front.[10]

The following three guidelines will help you choose the arrangement that will be the most useful for your reader:

1. **Process your information before you present it to your reader.** The order in which you became aware of information usually is not the best order to present it to your reader.

2. **When you have lots of information, group it into three to seven categories.** The average person's short-term memory can hold only seven chunks, though the chunks can be of any size.[11] By grouping your information into seven categories (or fewer), you make your report easier to read.

3. **Work with the reader's expectations, not against them.** Introduce ideas in the overview in the order in which you will discuss them.

Basic Patterns for Organizing Information

Seven basic patterns for organizing information are useful in reports:

1. Comparison/contrast.
2. Problem-solution.
3. Elimination of alternatives.
4. General to particular or particular to general.
5. Geographic or spatial.
6. Functional.
7. Chronological.

Any of these patterns can be used for a whole report or for only part of it.

1. Comparison/contrast

Many reports use comparison/contrast sections within a larger report pattern. Comparison/contrast can also be the purpose of the whole report. Feasibility studies usually use this pattern. You can focus either on the alternatives you are evaluating or on the criteria you use. See Figure 14.4 for examples of these two patterns in a report.

Focus on the alternatives when

- One alternative is clearly superior.
- The criteria are hard to separate.
- The reader will intuitively grasp the alternative as a whole rather than as the sum of its parts.

Focus on the criteria when

- The superiority of one alternative to another depends on the relative weight assigned to various criteria. Perhaps Alternative A is best if we are

FIGURE 14.4 Two Ways to Organize a Comparison/Contrast Report

Focus on alternatives	
Alternative A	Opening a New Store on Campus
Criterion 1	Cost of Renting Space
Criterion 2	Proximity to Target Market
Criterion 3	Competition from Similar Stores
Alternative B	Opening a New Store in the Suburban Mall
Criterion 1	Cost of Renting Space
Criterion 2	Proximity to Target Market
Criterion 3	Competition from Similar Stores
Focus on criteria	
Criterion 1	Cost of Renting Space for the New Store
Alternative A	Cost of Campus Locations
Alternative B	Cost of Locations in the Suburban Mall
Criterion 2	Proximity to Target Market
Alternative A	Proximity on Campus
Alternative B	Proximity in the Suburban Mall
Criterion 3	Competition from Similar Stores
Alternative A	Competing Stores on Campus
Alternative B	Competing Stores in the Suburban Mall

most concerned about Criterion 1, cost, but worst if we are most concerned about Criterion 2, proximity to target market.

■ The criteria are easy to separate.

■ The reader wants to compare and contrast the options independently of your recommendation.

A variation of the divided pattern is the **pro-and-con pattern.** In this pattern, under each specific heading, give the arguments for and against that alternative. A report recommending new plantings for a university quadrangle uses the pro-and-con pattern:

> Advantages of Monocropping
>   High Productivity
>   Visual Symmetry
> Disadvantages of Monocropping
>   Danger of Pest Exploitation
>   Visual Monotony

Whatever information comes second will carry more psychological weight. This pattern is least effective when you want to deemphasize the disadvantages of a proposed solution, for it does not permit you to bury the disadvantages between neutral or positive material.

2. Problem-solution

Identify the problem; explain its background or history; discuss its extent and seriousness; identify its causes. Discuss the factors (criteria) that affect the decision. Analyze the advantages and disadvantages of possible solutions.

UPS bought more than $5 billion worth of Airbus A300 planes. To decide which plane to buy, UPS formed a cross-functional acquisition team with members from its accounting, meteorology, aircraft maintenance, network planning, flight control, and dispatch departments. The team used external reports from government agencies, airplane manufacturers, and consultants and generated five reports analyzing the various factors important in the decision.

Conclusions and recommendation can go either first or last, depending on the preferences of your reader. This pattern works well when the reader is neutral.

A report recommending ways to eliminate solidification of a granular bleach during production uses the problem-solution pattern:

> Recommended Reformulation for Vibe Bleach
> Problems in Maintaining Vibe's Granular Structure
>   Solidifying during Storage and Transportation
>   Customer Complaints about "Blocks" of Vibe in Boxes
> Why Vibe Bleach "Cakes"
>   Vibe's Formula
>   The Manufacturing Process
>   The Chemical Process of Solidification
> Modifications Needed to Keep Vibe Flowing Freely

3. Elimination of alternatives

After discussing the problem and its causes, discuss the *impractical* solutions first, showing why they will not work. End with the most practical solution. This pattern works well when the solutions the reader is likely to favor will not work, while the solution you recommend is likely to be perceived as expensive, intrusive, or radical.

A report on toy commercials eliminates alternatives:

> The Effect of TV Ads on Children
> Camera Techniques Used in TV Advertisements

Alternative Solutions to Problems in TV Toy Ads
   Leave Ads Unchanged
   Mandate School Units on Advertising
   Ask the Industry to Regulate Itself
   Give FCC Authority to Regulate TV Ads Directed at Children

4. General to particular or particular to general

General to particular starts with the problem as it affects the organization or as it manifests itself in general and then moves to a discussion of the parts of the problem and solutions to each of these parts. Particular to general starts with the problem as the audience defines it and moves to larger issues of which the problem is a part. Both are good patterns when you need to redefine the reader's perception of the problem to solve it effectively.

The directors of a student volunteer organization, VIP, have defined their problem as "not enough volunteers." After studying the subject, the writer is convinced that problems in training, supervision, and campus awareness are responsible both for a high dropout rate and a low recruitment rate. The general-to-particular pattern helps the audience see the problem in a new way:

Why VIP Needs More Volunteers
Why Some VIP Volunteers Drop Out
   Inadequate Training
   Inadequate Supervision
   Feeling That VIP Requires Too Much Time
   Feeling That the Work Is Too Emotionally Demanding
Why Some Students Do Not Volunteer
   Feeling That VIP Requires Too Much Time
   Feeling That the Work Is Too Emotionally Demanding
   Preference for Volunteering with Another Organization
   Lack of Knowledge about VIP Opportunities
How VIP Volunteers Are Currently Trained and Supervised
Time Demands on VIP Volunteers
Emotional Demands on VIP Volunteers
Ways to Increase Volunteer Commitment and Motivation
   Improving Training and Supervision
   Improving the Flexibility of Volunteers' Hours
   Providing Emotional Support to Volunteers
   Providing More Information about Community Needs and VIP Services

5. Geographic or spatial

In a geographic or spatial pattern, you discuss problems and solutions by units by their physical arrangement. Move from office to office, building to building, factory to factory, state to state, region to region, etc.

A sales report uses a geographic pattern of organization:

Sales Have Risen in the European Community
Sales Are Flat in Eastern Europe
Sales Have Fallen Sharply in the Middle East
Sales Are Off to a Strong Start in Africa
Sales Have Risen Slightly in Asia
Sales Have Fallen Slightly in South America
Sales Are Steady in North America

Failure Isn't Final*

Researchers write closure reports when the company decides that the project they're working on isn't feasible. However, a few years later, new technologies, new conditions, or new ideas may make a "failed" idea feasible.

Post-It® notes use a "failed" adhesive because one 3M employee saw the weak adhesive as a solution to a problem:

> I was singing in the choir in my church. . . . I would mark the pages with little pieces of paper normally. And sometimes they would fall out. . . . I thought what I really need is . . . a bookmark that's going to stick to those pages . . . and still not damage the book when I pull them off. . . . I knew that Spence Silver back in our laboratory had just developed an adhesive that would do that. And I made . . . rough samples of the bookmarks. . . . I had also made up some larger sizes and found, hey, these are really handy for notes.

An adhesive that failed in its original application was a spectacular success in a new and highly profitable product.

*Based on John Nathan, *In Search of Excellence* (Waltham, MA: Nathan/Tyler Productions, 1985), 9.

6. Functional

In functional patterns, discuss the problems and solutions of each functional unit. For example, a report on a new plant might divide data into sections on the costs of land and building, on the availability of personnel, on the convenience of raw materials, and so on. A government report might divide data into the different functions an office performed, taking each in turn.

A strategy report for a political party uses a functional pattern of organization:

Current Makeup of the House and Senate
Congressional Seats Open in 2006
   Seats Held by a Democratic Incumbent
     Races in Which the Incumbent Has a Commanding Lead
     Races in Which the Incumbent Is Vulnerable
   Seats Held by a Republican Incumbent
     Races in Which the Incumbent Has a Commanding Lead
     Races in Which the Incumbent Is Vulnerable
   Seats Where No Incumbent Is Running
  Senate Seats Open in 2006
   Seats Held by a Democratic Incumbent
     Races in Which the Incumbent Has a Commanding Lead
     Races in Which the Incumbent Is Vulnerable
   Seats Held by a Republican Incumbent
     Races in Which the Incumbent Has a Commanding Lead
     Races in Which the Incumbent Is Vulnerable
   Seats Where No Incumbent Is Running

7. Chronological

A chronological report records events in the order in which they happened or are planned to happen. Many progress reports are organized chronologically:

Work Completed in October
Work Planned for November

How to Organize Specific Varieties of Reports

Informative, feasibility, and justification reports will be more successful when you work with the readers' expectations for that kind of report.

Informative and closure reports

Informative and **closure reports** summarize completed work or research that does not result in action or recommendation.

Informative reports often include the following elements:

- Introductory paragraph summarizing the problems or successes of the project.
- Purpose and scope section(s) giving the purpose of the report and indicating what aspects of the topic it covers.
- Chronological account of how the problem was discovered, what was done, and what the results were.
- Concluding paragraph with suggestions for later action. In a recommendation report, the recommendations would be based on proof. In contrast, the suggestions in a closure or recommendation report are not proved in detail.

Figure 14.5 presents this kind of informative closure report.

FIGURE 14.5 An Informative Memo Report Describing How a Company Solved a Problem

March 14, 2003

To: Kitty O. Locker

From: Sara A. Ratterman *SAR*

Informal short reports use letter or memo format.

Subject: Recycling at Bike Nashbar

First paragraph summarizes main points.

Two months ago, Bike Nashbar began recycling its corrugated cardboard boxes. The program was easy to implement and actually saves the company a little money compared to our previous garbage pickup.

Purpose and scope of report.

In this report, I will explain how, why, and by whom Bike Nashbar's program was initiated; how the program works and what it costs; and why other businesses should consider similar programs.

Bold or underline headings.

The Problem of Too Many Boxes and Not Enough Space in Bike Nashbar

Cause of problem.

Every week, Bike Nashbar receives about 40 large cardboard boxes containing bicycles and other merchandise. As many boxes as possible would be stuffed into the trash bin behind the building, which also had to accommodate all the other solid waste the shop produces. Boxes that didn't fit in the trash bin ended up lying around the shop, blocking doorways, and taking up space needed for customers' bikes. The trash bin was only emptied once a week, and by that time, even more boxes would have arrived.

Triple space before heading.

The Importance of Recycling Cardboard Rather than Throwing It Away

Arranging for more trash bins or more frequent pickups would have solved the immediate problem at Bike Nashbar but would have done nothing to solve the problem created by throwing away so much trash in the first place.

Double space between paragraphs within heading.

Further seriousness of problem.

According to David Crogen, sales representative for Waste Management, Inc., 75% of all solid waste in Columbus goes to landfills. The amount of trash the city collects has increased 150% in the last five years. Columbus's landfill is almost full. In an effort to encourage people and businesses to recycle, the cost of dumping trash in the landfill is doubling from $4.90 a cubic yard to $9.90 a cubic yard next week. Next January, the price will increase again, to $12.95 a cubic yard. Crogen believes that the amount of trash can be reduced by cooperation between the landfill and the power plant and by recycling.

How Bike Nashbar Started Recycling Cardboard

Capitalize first letter of major words in heading.

Solution.

Waste Management, Inc., is the country's largest waste processor. After reading an article about how committed Waste Management, Inc., is to waste reduction and recycling, I decided to see whether Waste Management could recycle our boxes. Corrugated cardboard (which is what Bike Nashbar's boxes are made of) is almost 100% recyclable, so we seemed to be a good candidate for recycling.

(continued)

FIGURE 14.5   An Informative Memo Report Describing How a Company Solved a Problem *(continued)*

Kitty O. Locker
March 14, 2003
Page 2

Reader's name, date, page number.

To get the service started,

1.   I looked up Waste Management's phone number and called the company.

2.   I met with a friendly sales rep, David Crogen, that same afternoon to discuss the service.

Waste Management, Inc., took care of all the details. Two days later, Bike Nashbar was recycling its cardboard.

How the Service Works and What It Costs

Talking heads tell reader what to expect in each section.

Details of solution.   Waste Management took away our existing 8-cubic-yard garbage bin and replaced it with two 4-yard bins. One of these bins is white and has "cardboard only" printed on the outside; the other is brown and is for all other solid waste. The bins are emptied once a week, with the cardboard being taken to the recycling plant and the solid waste going to the landfill or power plant.

Double space between paragraphs.   Since Bike Nashbar was already paying more than $60 a week for garbage pickup, our basic cost stayed the same. (Waste Management can absorb the extra overhead only if the current charge is at least $60 a week.) The cost is divided 80/20 between the two bins: 80% of the cost pays for the bin that goes to the landfill and power plant; 20% covers the cardboard pickup. Bike Nashbar actually receives $5.00 for each ton of cardboard it recycles.

Each employee at Bike Nashbar is responsible for putting all the boxes he or she opens in the recycling bin. Employees must follow these rules:

- The cardboard must have the word "corrugated" printed on it, along with the universal recycling symbol.

Indented lists provide visual variety.

- The boxes must be broken down to their flattest form. If they aren't, they won't all fit in the bin and Waste Management would be picking up air when it could pick up solid cardboard. The more boxes that are picked up, the more money and space that will be made.

- No other waste except corrugated cardboard can be put in the recycling bin. Other materials could break the recycling machinery or contaminate the new cardboard.

- The recycling bin is to be kept locked with a padlock provided by Waste Management so that vagrants don't steal the cardboard and lose money for Waste Management and Bike Nashbar.

(continued)

FIGURE 14.5 An Informative Memo Report Describing How a Company Solved a Problem *(concluded)*

Kitty O. Locker
March 14, 2003
Page 3

Dis-advantages of solution. **Minor Problems with Running the Recycling Program**

The only problems we've encountered have been minor ones of violating the rules. Sometimes employees at the shop forget to flatten boxes, and air instead of cardboard gets picked up. Sometimes people forget to lock the recycling bin. When the bin is left unlocked, people do steal the cardboard, and plastic cups and other solid waste get dumped in the cardboard bin. I've posted signs where the key to the bin hangs, reminding employees to empty and fold boxes and relock the bin after putting cardboard in it. I hope this will turn things around and these problems will be solved.

Advantages of the Recycling Program

Advantages of solution. The program is a great success. Now when boxes arrive, they are unloaded, broken down, and disposed of quickly. It is a great relief to get the boxes out of our way, and knowing that we are making a contribution to saving our environment builds pride in ourselves and Bike Nashbar.

Our company depends on a clean, safe environment for people to ride their bikes in. Now we have become part of the solution. By choosing to recycle and reduce the amount of solid waste our company generates, we can save money while gaining a reputation as a socially responsible business.

Why Other Companies Should Adopt Similar Programs

Argues that her company's experience is relevant to other companies. Businesses and institutions in Franklin County currently recycle less than 4% of the solid waste they produce. David Crogen tells me he has over 8,000 clients in Columbus alone, and he acquires new ones every day. Many of these businesses can recycle a large portion of their solid waste at no additional cost. Depending on what they recycle, they may even get a little money back.

The environmental and economic benefits of recycling as part of a comprehensive waste reduction program are numerous. Recycling helps preserve our environment. We can use the same materials over and over again, saving natural resources such as trees, fuel, and metals and decreasing the amount of solid waste in landfills. By conserving natural resources, recycling helps the U.S. become less dependent on imported raw materials. Crogen predicts that Columbus will be on a 100% recycling system by the year 2020. I strongly hope that his prediction will come true and the future may start to look a little brighter.

Two hospitals in Columbus, Ohio, had helicopter services that were each losing money. They commissioned a feasibility study to see whether the two services could merge. The report found that a merger was feasible. The resulting service, MedFlight, is profitable. Here, a MedFlight helicopter team transports the survivor of an automobile accident.

Closure reports also allow a firm to document the alternatives it has considered before choosing a final design and to prove its right to copyrights and patents. Dwight W. Stevenson has shown that firms challenged in product liability suits need to be able to document in detail the evaluation process that led to the product design.[12] In another kind of case, the Wells Fargo bank fought off a $480 million suit charging that it had misappropriated someone else's idea for a credit card operation. The bank used materials from its archives going back 20 years to prove that it had developed the idea itself.[13]

Feasibility reports

Feasibility reports evaluate two or more alternatives and recommend one of them. (Doing nothing or delaying action can be one of the alternatives.)

Feasibility reports normally open by explaining the decision to be made, listing the alternatives, and explaining the criteria. In the body of the report, each alternative will be evaluated according to the criteria using one of the two comparison/contrast patterns. Discussing each alternative separately is better when one alternative is clearly superior, when the criteria interact, and when each alternative is indivisible. If the choice depends on the weight given to each criterion, you may want to discuss each alternative under each criterion.

Whether your recommendation should come at the beginning or the end of the report depends on your reader and the culture of your organization. Most readers want the "bottom line" up front. However, if the reader will find your recommendation hard to accept, you may want to delay your recommendation until the end of the report when you have given all your evidence.

Justification reports

Justification reports recommend or justify a purchase, investment, hiring, or change in policy. If your organization has a standard format for justification reports, follow that format. If you can choose your headings and organization, use this pattern when your recommendation will be easy for your reader to suggest:

1. **Indicate what you're asking for and why it's needed.** Since the reader has not asked for the report, you must link your request to the organization's goals.
2. **Briefly give the background of the problem or need.**

3. **Explain each of the possible solutions.** For each, give the cost and the advantages and disadvantages.
4. **Summarize the action needed to implement your recommendation.** If several people will be involved, indicate who will do what and how long each step will take.
5. **Ask for the action you want.**

If the reader will be reluctant to grant your request, use this variation of the problem-solving pattern described in Chapter 9:

1. **Describe the organizational problem (which your request will solve).** Use specific examples to prove the seriousness of the problem.
2. **Show why easier or less expensive solutions will not solve the problem.**
3. **Present your solution impersonally.**
4. **Show that the disadvantages of your solution are outweighed by the advantages.**
5. **Summarize the action needed to implement your recommendation.** If several people will be involved, indicate who will do what and how long each step will take.
6. **Ask for the action you want.**

How much detail you need to give in a justification report depends on the corporate culture and on your reader's knowledge of and attitude toward your recommendation. Many organizations expect justification reports to be short—only one or two pages. Other organizations may expect longer reports with much more detailed budgets and a full discussion of the problem and each possible solution.

Presenting Information Effectively in Reports

The advice about style in Chapter 4 also applies to reports, with three exceptions:

1. **Use a fairly formal style, without contractions or slang.**
2. **Avoid the word *you*.** In a document with multiple audiences, it will not be clear who *you* is. Instead, use the company name.
3. **Include in the report all the definitions and documents needed to understand the recommendations.** The multiple audiences for reports include readers who may consult the document months or years from now; they will not share your special knowledge. Explain acronyms and abbreviations the first time they appear. Explain the history or background of the problem. Add as appendixes previous documents on which you are building.

The following points apply to any kind of writing, but they are particularly important in reports:

1. Say what you mean.
2. Tighten your writing.
3. Introduce sources and visuals gracefully.
4. Use blueprints, transitions, topic sentences, and headings to make your organization clear to your reader.

Let's look at each of these principles as they apply to reports.

1. Say What You Mean.

Not-quite-right word choices are particularly damaging in reports, which may be skimmed by readers who know very little about the subject. Occasionally you can simply substitute a word.

Incorrect:	With these recommendations, we can overcome the solutions to our problem.
Correct:	With these recommendations, we can overcome our problem.
Also correct:	With these recommendations, we can solve our problem.

Putting the meaning of your sentence in the verbs will help you say what you mean.

Vague:	My report revolves around the checkout lines and the methods used to get price checks when they arise.
Better:	My report shows how price checks slow checkout lines and recommends ways to reduce the number of price checks needed.

Sometimes you'll need to completely recast the sentence.

Incorrect:	The first problem with the incentive program is that middle managers do not use good interpersonal skills in implementing it. For example, the hotel chef openly ridicules the program. As a result, the kitchen staff fear being mocked if they participate in the program.
Better:	The first problem with the incentive program is that some middle managers undercut it. For example, the hotel chef openly ridicules the program. As a result, the kitchen staff fear being mocked if they participate in the program.

2. Tighten Your Writing.

Eliminate unnecessary words, use gerunds and infinitives, combine sentences, and reword sentences to cut the number of words.

Wordy:	Campus Jewelers' main objective is to increase sales. Specifically, the objective is to double sales in the next five years by becoming a more successful business.
Better:	Campus Jewelers' objective is to double sales in the next five years.

Wordiness in reports may arise from two sources that are less likely to affect shorter messages: writers may deliberately put in extra words to create a longer document, and repetition may occur in different sections that are written at different times.

No reader wants length for the sake of length. Even in a class report, the page requirement is an indication of the complexity of analysis that the instructor expects. If you've chosen an appropriate topic, collected enough data, and analyzed the data thoroughly, you should reach any minimum page requirement easily. (If you suspect that you don't have enough data to yield an adequate report, talk to your instructor well before the due date to revise your topic.)

Some repetition in reports is legitimate. The conclusion restates points made in the body of the report; the recommendations appear in the transmittal, the abstract or executive summary, and in the recommendations sections of the report. However, repetitive references to earlier material ("As we have already seen") may indicate that the document needs to be reorganized. Read the document through at a single sitting to make sure that any repetition serves a useful purpose. If the repetition is boring, eliminate it.

3. Introduce Sources and Visuals Gracefully.

The first time you cite an author's work, use his or her full name: "Rosabeth Moss Kanter points out. . . ." In subsequent citations, use only the last name: "Kanter shows. . . ." Use active rather than passive verbs.

The verb you use indicates your attitude toward the source. *Says* and *writes* are neutral. *Points out, shows, suggests, discovers,* and *notes* suggest that you agree with the source. Words such as *claims, argues, contends that, believes,* and *alleges* distance you from the source. At a minimum, they suggest that you know that not everyone agrees with the source; they are also appropriate to report the views of someone with whom you disagree.

Use active verbs to refer to visuals, too:

As Table 1 shows, . . .
See Figure 4.

4. Use Blueprints, Transitions, Topic Sentences, and Headings.

Blueprints are overviews or forecasts that tell the reader what you will discuss in a section or in the entire report. Make your blueprint easy to read by telling the reader how many points there are and using bullets or numbers (either words or figures). In the following example, the first sentence in the revised paragraph tells the reader to look for four points; the numbers separate the four points clearly. This overview paragraph also makes a contract with readers, who now expect to read about tax benefits first and employee benefits last.

Paragraph without numbers:	Employee stock ownership programs (ESOPs) have several advantages. They provide tax benefits for the company. ESOPs also create tax benefits for employees and for lenders. They provide a defense against takeovers. In some organizations, productivity increases because workers now have a financial stake in the company's profits. ESOPs are an attractive employee benefit and help the company hire and retain good employees.
Revised paragraph with numbers:	Employee stock ownership programs (ESOPs) provide four benefits. First, ESOPs provide tax benefits for the company, its employees, and lenders to the plan. Second, ESOPs help create a defense against takeovers. Third, ESOPs may increase productivity by giving workers a financial stake in the company's profits. Fourth, as an attractive employee benefit, ESOPs help the company hire and retain good employees.

Transitions are words, phrases, or sentences that tell the reader whether the discussion is continuing on the same point or shifting points.

There are economic advantages, too.
(Tells the reader that we are still discussing advantages but that we have now moved to economic advantages.)
An alternative to this plan is . . .
(Tells reader that a second option follows.)
The second factor . . .
(Tells reader that the discussion of the first factor is finished.)
These advantages, however, are found only in A, not in B or C.
(Prepares reader for a shift from A to B and C.)

A topic sentence (see Chapter 4) introduces or summarizes the main idea of a sentence. Readers who skim reports can follow your ideas more easily if each paragraph begins with a topic sentence.

Legal Liability and Report Drafts*

During civil litigation (such as a tort case charging that a product has injured a user), rough drafts may be important to establish the state of mind and intent of a document's drafters.

To protect the company, one lawyer recommends labeling all but the final draft "Preliminary Draft: Subject to Change." That way, if there's ever a lawsuit, the company will be able to argue that only the final report, not the drafts, should be used as evidence.

*Based on Elizabeth McCord, "'But What You Really Meant Was . . .': Multiple Drafts and Legal Liability," paper presented at the Association for Business Communication Midwest Regional Conference, Akron, OH, April 3–5, 1991.

Hard to read (no topic sentence):	Another main use of ice is to keep the fish fresh. Each of the seven kinds of fish served at the restaurant requires one gallon twice a day, for a total of 14 gallons. An additional 6 gallons a day are required for the salad bar.
Better (begins with topic sentence):	Twenty gallons of ice a day are needed to keep food fresh. Of this, the biggest portion (14 gallons) is used to keep the fish fresh. Each of the seven kinds of fish served at the restaurant requires one gallon twice a day (7 × 2 = 14). An additional 6 gallons a day are required for the salad bar.

Headings (see Chapter 6) are single words, short phrases, or complete sentences that indicate the topic in each section. A heading must cover all of the material under it until the next heading. For example, *Cost of Tuition* cannot include the cost of books or of room and board. You can have just one paragraph under a heading or several pages. If you do have several pages between headings you may want to consider using subheadings. Use subheadings only when you have two or more divisions within a main heading.

Topic headings focus on the structure of the report. As you can see from the following example, topic headings give very little information.

Topic headings are vague.

Recommendation

Problem

    Situation 1

    Situation 2

Causes of the Problem

    Background

    Cause 1

    Cause 2

Recommended Solution

Talking heads, in contrast, tell the reader what to expect. Talking heads, like those in the examples in this chapter, provide an overview of each section and of the entire report.

Talking heads are specific.

Recommended Reformulation for Vibe Bleach

Problems in Maintaining Vibe's Granular Structure

    Solidifying during Storage and Transportation

    Customer Complaints about "Blocks" of Vibe in Boxes

Why Vibe Bleach "Cakes"

    Vibe's Formula

    The Manufacturing Process

    The Chemical Process of Solidification

Modifications Needed to Keep Vibe Flowing Freely

Headings must be parallel (p. 101); that is, they must use the same grammatical structure. Subheads must be parallel to each other but do not necessarily have to be parallel to subheads under other headings.

Not parallel: Are Students Aware of VIP?

Current Awareness among Undergraduate Students

Graduate Students

Ways to Increase Volunteer Commitment and Motivation

We Must Improve Training and Supervision

Can We Make Volunteers' Hours More Flexible?

Providing Emotional Support to Volunteers

Provide More Information about Community Needs and VIP Services

Parallel: Campus Awareness of VIP

Current Awareness among Undergraduate Students

Current Awareness among Graduate Students

Ways to Increase Volunteer Commitment and Motivation

Improving Training and Supervision

Improving the Flexibility of Volunteers' Hours

Providing Emotional Support to Volunteers

Providing More Information about Community Needs and VIP Services

In a very complicated report, you may need up to three levels of headings. Figure 14.6 illustrates one way to set up headings. Although the figure shows only one example of each level of headings, in an actual report you would not use a subheading unless you had at least two subsections under the next higher heading.

Whatever the format for headings, avoid having a subhead come immediately after a heading. Instead, some text should follow the main heading before the subheading. (If you have nothing else to say, give an overview of the division.) Avoid having a heading or subheading all by itself at the bottom of the page. Instead, have at least one line (preferably two) of type. If there isn't room for a line of type under it, put the heading on the next page. Don't use a heading as the antecedent for a pronoun. Instead, repeat the noun.

Writing Formal Reports

Formal reports are distinguished from informal letter and memo reports by their length and by their components. A full formal report may contain the following components (see Figures 14.7 and 14.8):

Cover

Title Page

Letter or Memo of Transmittal

Table of Contents

List of Illustrations

Executive Summary

Report Body

   Introduction (Orients the reader to the report. Usually has subheadings for Purpose and Scope; depending on the situation, may also have Limitations, Assumptions, Methods, Criteria, and Definitions.)

   Background or History of the Problem (Orients the reader to the topic of the report. Serves as a record for later readers of the report.)

   Body (Presents and interprets data in words and visuals. Analyzes causes of the problem and evaluates possible solutions. Specific headings will depend on the topic of the report.)

Quality Packaging*

Quality packaging means that the final report is clear, concise and well organized. . . .

The most critical piece of the final report is the Executive Summary. Why? Because most time-pressed executives never read beyond this section. Therefore the writer should make certain that the key findings, conclusions and recommendation(s) are laid out clearly here. The rest of the report, in all its detail, is attached so the reader may decide whether she or he would like more information on a particular topic.

How much detail should you include? As much as you believe the audience reading the report will want. . . . Put yourself in the reader's shoes. Would you rather read about the problem and solution in 5 pages or in 50 pages? In each of the supporting sections, state the question you answer, your analytic method, findings, and conclusions. Put the raw data in appendices.

The final piece of the process is editing and revising. . . . This step is necessary to "polish" your report and refine your thinking. How well you perform this step is often the difference between a good report and a great report.

*Quoted from Dayton J. D. Semerjian, statement to Kitty Locker, February 3, 1997.

FIGURE 14.6   Setting Up Headings in a Single-Spaced Document

Center the title
use bold and
a bigger font.   **Typing Titles and Headings for Reports**   *14-point type.*

For the title of a report, use a bold font two point sizes bigger than the largest size in the body of the report. You may want to use an even bigger size or a different font to create an attractive title page. Capitalize the first word and all major words of the title.

Heading for main   ↕ *Two empty spaces (triple space)*
divisions

Typing Headings for Reports   *12-point type.*
↕ *One empty space (double space)*

11-point   Center main headings, capitalize the first and all major words, and use bold. In single-spaced text, leave
type   two empty spaces before main headings and one after. Also leave an extra space between paragraphs. You
for body   may also want to use main headings that are one point size bigger than the body text.
text

This example provides just one example of each level of heading. However, in a real document, use headings only when you have at least two of them in the document. In a report, you'll have several.

↕ *Two empty spaces (triple space)*

Typing Subheadings *Bold; left margin*
↕ *One empty space*

Most reports use subheadings under some main headings. Use subheadings only if you have at least two of them under a given heading. It is OK to use subheadings in some sections and not in others. Normally you'll have several paragraphs under a subheading, but it's OK to have just one paragraph under some subheadings.

11-point   Subheadings in a report use the same format as headings in letters and memos. Bold subheadings and set
type   them at the left margin. Capitalize the first word and major words. Leave two empty spaces before the
subheading and one empty space after it, before the first paragraph under the subheading. Use the same
size font as the body paragraphs.

Period   ↕ *One empty space (normal paragraph spacing)*
after   **Typing Further Subdivisions.** For a very long report, you may need further subdivisions under a
heading   subheading. Bold the further subdivision, capitalizing the first word and major words, and end the phrase
with a period. Begin the text on the same line. Use normal spacing between paragraphs. Further subdivide a
subheading only if you have at least two such subdivisions under a given subheading. It is OK to use
divisions under some subheadings and not under others.

Conclusions (Summarizes main points of report.)

Recommendations (Recommends actions to solve the problem. May be combined with Conclusions; may be put at beginning of body rather than at the end.)

Notes, References, or Works Cited (Document sources cited in the report.)

Appendixes (Provide additional materials that the careful reader may want: transcript of an interview, copies of questionnaires, tallies of all the questions, computer printouts, previous reports.)

As Figure 14.7 shows, not every formal report necessarily has all these components. In addition, some organizations call for additional components or arrange these components in a different order. As you read each section below, you may want to turn to the corresponding pages of the long report in Figure 14.8 to see how the component is set up and how it relates to the total report.

FIGURE 14.7 The Components in a Report Can Vary

More formal ←	→ Less formal

More formal		Less formal
Cover	Title Page	Introduction
Title Page	Table of Contents	Body
Transmittal	Executive Summary	Conclusions
Table of Contents	Body	Recommendations
List of Illustrations	Introduction	
Executive Summary	Body	
Body	Conclusions	
Introduction	Recommendations	
Body		
Conclusions		
Recommendations		
References/Works Cited		
Appendixes		
Questionnaires		
Interviews		
Computer Printouts		
Related Documents		

Title Page

The title page of a report usually contains four items: the title of the report, whom the report is prepared for, whom it is prepared by, and the release date. Sometimes reports also contain a brief summary or abstract of the contents of the report; some title pages contain decorative artwork.

The title of the report should be as informative as possible. Like subject lines, report titles are straightforward.

Poor title: New Plant Site

Better title: Why Eugene, Oregon, Is the Best Site for the New Kemco Plant

Poor title: Planting for the Quadrangle

Better title: Why Honey Locusts Are the Best Trees for the New Quadrangle

Large organizations that issue many reports may use two-part titles to make it easier to search for reports electronically. For example, US government reports titles first give the agency sponsoring the report, then the title of that particular report.

Small Business Administration: Management Practices Have Improved for the Women's Business Center Program

Small Business Administration: Steps Taken to Better Manage Its Human Capital, but More Needs to Be Done

Small Business: SBA Could Better Focus Its 8(a) Program to Help Firms Obtain Contracts

In many cases, the title will state the recommendation in the report: "Why the United Nations Should Establish a Seed Bank." However, the title should omit recommendations when

- The reader will find the recommendations hard to accept.
- Putting all the recommendations in the title would make it too long.
- The report does not offer recommendations.

If the title does not contain the recommendation, it normally indicates what problem the report tries to solve.

Eliminate any unnecessary words:

Wordy: Report of a Study on Ways to Market Life Insurance to Urban Professional People Who Are in Their Mid-40s

Better: Ways to Market Life Insurance to the Mid-40s Urban Professional

The statement of whom the report is prepared for normally includes the name of the person who will make a decision based on the report, his or her job title, the organization's name, and its location (city, state, and zip code). Government reports often omit the person's name and simply give the organization that authorized the report.

If the report is prepared primarily by one person, the *Prepared by* section will have that person's name, his or her title, the organization, and its location (city, state, and zip code). In internal reports, the organization and location are usually omitted if the report writer works at the headquarters office.

If several people write the report, government reports normally list all their names, using a separate sheet of paper if the group working on the report is large. Practices in business differ. In some organizations, all the names are listed; in others, the division to which they belong is listed; in still others, the name of the chair of the group appears.

The **release date,** the date the report will be released to the public, is usually the date the report is scheduled for discussion by the decision makers. The report is due four to six weeks before the release date so that the decision makers can review the report before the meeting.

If you have the facilities and the time, try using different sizes and styles of type, color, and artwork to create a visually attractive and impressive title page. However, a plain typed page is acceptable. The format in Figure 14.8 will enable you to create an acceptable title page by typing it only once.

Letter or Memo of Transmittal

Use a letter of transmittal if you are not a regular employee of the organization for which you prepare the report; use a memo if you are a regular employee. See Appendix A for letter and memo formats.

The transmittal has several purposes: to transmit the report, to orient the reader to the report, and to build a good image of the report and of the writer. An informal writing style is appropriate for a transmittal even when the style in the report is more formal. A professional transmittal helps you create a good image of yourself and enhances your credibility. Personal statements are appropriate in the transmittal, even though they would not be acceptable in the report itself.

Organize the transmittal in this way:

1. **Transmit the report.** Tell when and by whom it was authorized and the purpose it was to fulfill.

2. **Summarize your conclusions and recommendations.** If the recommendations will be easy for the reader to accept, put them early in the transmittal. If they will be difficult, summarize the findings and conclusions before the recommendations.

3. **Mention any points of special interest in the report. Indicate minor problems you encountered in your investigation and show how you surmounted them. Thank people who helped you.** These optional items can build goodwill and enhance your credibility.

4. **Point out additional research that is necessary, if any.** Sometimes your recommendation cannot be implemented until further work is done. If you'd be interested in doing that research, or if you'd like to implement the recommendations, say so.

5. **Thank the reader for the opportunity to do the work and offer to answer questions.** Even if the report has not been fun to do, expressing satisfaction in doing the project is expected. Saying that you'll answer questions about the report is a way of saying that you won't charge the reader your normal hourly fee to answer questions (one more reason to make the report clear!).

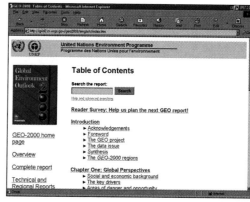

InSite

http://grid2.cr.usgs.gov/geo2000/english/index.htm

Tables of Contents for Web reports can have search boxes and clickable links for chapter titles and headings, as does this United Nations report on the state of the global environment.

The letter of transmittal on page i of Figure 14.8 uses this pattern of organization.

Table of Contents

In the table of contents, list the headings exactly as they appear in the body of the report. If the report is less than 25 pages, you'll probably list all the levels of headings. In a very long report, pick a level and put all the headings at that level and above in the table of contents.

Page ii of Figure 14.8 shows the table of contents.

List of Illustrations

A list of illustrations enables readers to refer to your visuals.

Report visuals comprise both tables and figures. *Tables* are words or numbers arranged in rows and columns. *Figures* are everything else: bar graphs, pie charts, flow charts, maps, drawings, photographs, computer printouts, and so on. Tables and figures may be numbered independently, so you may have both a Table 1 and a Figure 1. In a report with maps and graphs but no other visuals, the visuals are sometimes called Map 1 and Graph 1. Whatever you call the illustrations, list them in the order in which they appear in the report; give the name of each visual as well as its number.

See Chapter 15 for information about how to design and label visuals.

Executive Summary

An **executive summary** or **abstract** tells the reader what the document is about. It summarizes the recommendation of the report and the reasons for the recommendation or describes the topics the report discusses and indicates the depth of the discussion.

A good abstract is easy to read, concise, and clear. Edit your abstract carefully to tighten your writing and eliminate any unnecessary words.

What Does the Reader Want? II*

In the US Army, a general wanted a one-page Executive Summary. If—and only if—he disagreed with the summary, he read the relevant sections of the report to get more information.

*Based on James Dubinski, personal communication, December 27, 2000.

Wordy: The author describes two types of business jargon, *businessese* and *reverse gobbledygook.* He gives many examples of each of these and points out how their use can be harmful.

Tight: The author describes and gives examples of two harmful types of business jargon, *businessese* and *reverse gobbledygook.*

It's OK to use exactly the same words in the abstract and the report. Abstracts generally use a more formal style than other forms of business writing. Avoid contractions. Use second-person *you* only if the article uses the second person; even then, use *you* sparingly.

It is not necessary to follow the organization, wording, or proportions of the original report or article. The abstract usually uses a logical pattern of organization, putting the thesis first, even though the report may use another pattern (a psychological problem-solving pattern, for instance).

Summary abstracts present the logical skeleton of the article: the thesis or recommendation and its proof. Use a summary abstract to give the most useful information in the shortest space.

> To market life insurance to mid-40s urban professionals, Interstate Fidelity Insurance should advertise in upscale publications and use direct mail.
>
> Network TV and radio are not cost-efficient for reaching this market. This group comprises a small percentage of the prime-time network TV audience and a minority of most radio station listeners. They tend to discard newspapers and general-interest magazines quickly, but many of them keep upscale periodicals for months or years. Magazines with high percentages of readers in this group include *Architectural Digest, Bon Appetit, Business Week, Forbes, Golf Digest, Metropolitan Home, Southern Living,* and *Smithsonian.* Most urban professionals in their mid-40s are already used to shopping by mail and respond positively to well-conceived and well-executed direct mail appeals.
>
> Any advertising campaign needs to overcome this group's feeling that they already have the insurance they need. One way to do this would be to encourage them to check the coverage their employers provide and to calculate the cost of their children's expenses through college graduation. Insurance plans that provide savings and tax benefits as well as death benefits might also be appealing.

To write abstracts of business and government reports, conference papers, and published articles, write a sentence outline. A **sentence outline** not only uses complete sentences rather than words or phrases but also contains the thesis sentence or recommendation and the points that prove that point. Combine the sentences into paragraphs, adding transitions if necessary, and you'll have your abstract.

Descriptive abstracts indicate what topics the article covers and how deeply it goes into each topic, but they do not summarize what the article says about each topic. Phrases that describe the paper ("this paper reports," "it includes," "it summarizes," "it concludes") are marks of a descriptive abstract. An additional mark of a descriptive abstract is that the reader can't tell what the article says about the topics it covers.

> This report recommends ways Interstate Fidelity Insurance could market insurance to mid-40s urban professionals. It examines demographic and psychographic profiles of the target market. Survey results are used to show attitudes toward insurance. The report suggests some appeals that might be successful with this market.

A **mixed abstract** is a hybrid: part summary, part description. Mixed abstracts enable you both to comment about the kind of information and present the thesis and its proof.

Introduction

The **Introduction** of the report always contains a statement of purpose and scope and may include all the parts in the following list.

- **Purpose.** The purpose statement (◄▥ p. 351) identifies the organizational problem the report addresses, the technical investigations it summarizes, and the rhetorical purpose (to explain, to recommend).

- **Scope.** The scope statement identifies how broad an area the report surveys. For example, Company XYZ is losing money on its line of radios. Does the report investigate the quality of the radios? The advertising campaign? The cost of manufacturing? The demand for radios? A scope statement allows the reader to evaluate the report on appropriate grounds. If the person who approved the proposal accepted a focus on advertising, then one cannot fault a report that considers only that factor.

- **Limitations.** Limitations make your recommendations less valid or valid only under certain conditions. Limitations usually arise because time or money constraints haven't permitted full research. For example, a campus pizza restaurant considering expanding its menu may ask for a report but not have enough money to take a random sample of students and townspeople. Without a random sample, the writer cannot generalize from the sample to the larger population.

  Many recommendations are valid only for a limited time. For instance, a campus store wants to know what kinds of clothing will appeal to college men. The recommendations will remain in force only for a short time: Three years from now, styles and tastes may have changed, and the clothes that would sell best now may no longer be in demand.

- **Assumptions.** Assumptions in a report are like assumptions in geometry: statements whose truth you assume, and which you use to prove your final point. If they are wrong, the conclusion will be wrong too.

  For example, to plan cars that will be built five years from now, an automobile manufacturer commissions a report on young adults' attitudes toward cars. The recommendations would be based on assumptions both about gas prices and about the economy. If gas prices radically rose or fell, the kinds of cars young adults wanted would change. If there were a major recession, people wouldn't be able to buy new cars.

  Almost all reports require assumptions. A good report spells out its assumptions so that readers can make decisions more confidently.

- **Methods.** If you conducted surveys, focus groups, or interviews, you need to tell how you chose your subjects, and how, when, and where they were interviewed. Reports based on scientific experiments usually put the methods section in the body of the report, not in the Introduction.

  If your report is based solely on library or online research, omit the methods section; simply cite your sources in the text and document them in notes or references. See Chapter 13 on how to cite and document sources.

- **Criteria.** The criteria section outlines the factors or standards that you are considering and the relative importance of each. If a company is choosing a city for a new office, is the cost of office space more or less important than the availability of skilled workers? Check with your audience before you write the draft to make sure that your criteria match those of your readers.

FIGURE 14.8 A Formal Report

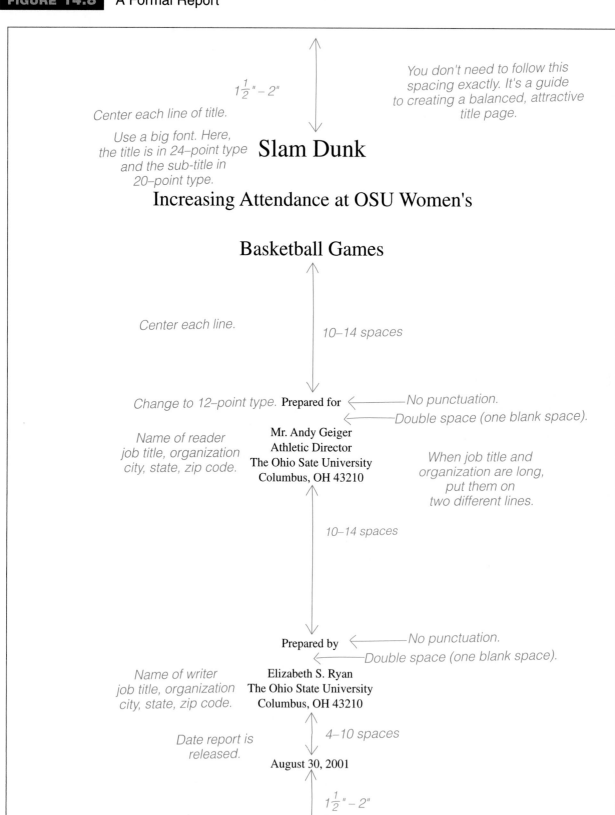

(continued)

FIGURE 14.8 A Formal Report *(continued)*

*You may also design
a letterhead for yourself,
especially if you're assuming
that you are doing the report
as a consultant.*

*This letter uses modified
block format (see Figure A.5).
Block format is also acceptable.*

7571 Saunderlane Road
Columbus, OH 43235
August 19, 2001

Mr. Andy Geiger, Director
The Ohio State University Athletic Department
St. John's Arena
410 Woody Hayes Drive
Columbus, OH 43210

*In paragraph 1, release the report.
Note when and by whom the report
was authorized. Note report's purpose.*

Dear Mr. Geiger:

Here is the report you authorized in July identifying why attendance at women's OSU basketball games is low and recommending ways to increase student attendance at the games.

As you know, even though the team has been doing well, attendance at women's home games has fallen over the last three years. When I surveyed a convenience sample of students, I found no season ticket holders and only two people who said they attended "a few" games each season. Fully 34% had never been to an OSU women's basketball game.

Because most students do like basketball (62% follow the men's team), it's reasonable to think that some students could be persuaded to attend women's games as well. The two biggest reasons for not attending, according to my survey, were "I never thought to go" and "my friends aren't interested in going." I therefore recommend strategies that would remind students that the women's team exists and is playing and encourage groups of people to go to the games together.

*Give
recommendations
or thesis.*

Short-term solutions that could be implemented this year include having team members visit the Oval to drum up support and posting an abundance of signs about upcoming games around campus. Longer-term strategies include creating a calendar of special days for specific groups, offering giveaways, cultivating sports writers, and considering a loyalty program. Because further research is needed, you might want to put a staff member in charge of marketing the women's basketball team and hire a student intern to do the legwork for this research.

*Thank
people
who
helped
you.*

The information in this report came from print and online sources, a survey of OSU students, and interviews with several members of the Athletic Department. Liz Cook of the OSU Women's Basketball office and the Athletic Department's Sports Information office were particularly helpful.

Thank the reader for the opportunity to do the research.

Thank you for the opportunity to conduct this research. I've enjoyed learning more about the basketball team, the workings of the Athletic Department, and sports marketing strategies. If you have any questions about the material in this report, please call me.

*Offer to answer questions about the report.
Answers would be included in your fee—no extra charge!*

Sincerely,

Elizabeth Ryan

Elizabeth Ryan

*Center page number at the bottom
of the page.
Use a lower-case Roman numeral.*

i

(continued)

FIGURE 14.8 A Formal Report *(continued)*

Headings or subheadings must be parallel within a section. Here, headings are nouns and non (gerund) phases. Questions and complete sentences can also be used.

Table of Contents

Use lowercase Roman numerals for front matter.

Table of Contents does not list itself.

Intro begins on page 1.

Capitalize first letter of each major word in headings.

Indentations show level or heading at a glance.

Some reports have separate sections for "Conclusions" and "Recommendations."

Line up right margin (justify).

Add a "List of Illustrations" at the bottom of the Table of Contents or on a separate page if the report has graphs and other visuals. Omit "List of Illustrations" if you have only tables.

List of Illustrations

Figures and Tables are numbered independently, so you can have both a "Figure 1" and a "Table 1".

ii

418

(continued)

FIGURE 14.8 A Formal Report *(continued)*

Report title. **Slam Dunk**
Increasing Attendance at OSU Women's Basketball Games

Many readers read only the Executive Summary, not the report. Include enough information to give the reader the key points you make.

Executive Summary

Start with recommendations or thesis.

To increase student attendance at OSU women's basketball games, the Ohio State Athletic Department should implement short- and long-term marketing strategies and consider implementing a loyalty program.

Even though the team has been doing well, attendance at women's home games has fallen over the last three years. Student attendance at games is especially important because there are a lot of students; attending games is fun, promotes bonding with other students, and creates school spirit; and athletes do better when other students cheer them on.

Provide brief support for recommendations.

Because most students do like basketball (62% follow the men's team), it's reasonable to think that some students could be persuaded to attend women's games as well. The two biggest reasons for not attending, according to my survey, were "I never thought to go" and "My friends aren't interested in going." Students might be interested in going to the OSU women's games if it occurred to them to go or if their friends went, too.

To increase attendance, the Athletic Department should

1. **Implement short-term marketing this fall**. Capitalize on the Lady Buckeyes' winning streak last year to attract a higher attendance this year. Since basketball season is only a quarter away, it might be smart to focus on increased awareness for the upcoming season.
   - Chalk the Oval before each home game.
   - Ask the women basketball players to host impromptu meet-and-greets or pickup games on the Oval.
   - Provide information about the rules for women's basketball.

2. **Use OSU students to develop a long-term marketing program and a formal publicity campaign.** Changing perceptions takes time and many messages.
   - Designate days for specific groups.
   - Offer deals and freebies. Ask sponsors to donate freebies or items to be raffled or auctioned.
   - Create an advertising campaign focusing on women students in sororities, women's floors in residence halls, and Women's Studies classes.
   - Buy more advertising space in *The Lantern* and *The Columbus Dispatch*.
   - Try to persuade more reporters to write more stories in more prominent locations about the women's team.

3. **Consider adopting a loyalty program**. A loyalty program allows the Athletic Department to reward students for behaviors it wants to encourage by giving it useful marketing information. Further research is needed to study the financial implications of implementing such a program.

Language in Executive Summary can come from report. Make sure any repeated language is well written!

iii

The abstract or executive summary contains the logical skeleton of the report: the recommendation(s) and evidence supporting them.

(continued)

FIGURE 14.8 A Formal Report *(continued)*

A running header is optional.

Also OK to omit "Page."

Here, the running heads and page numbers are one point size smaller than body.

Start with "Introduction."   *Center main headings. This head uses bold (one point larger than body).*

Spell out term the first time you use it; put abbreviation in parentheses.

Introduction

Ohio State University's (OSU) men's basketball team is a crowd pleaser, selling out home games at the Schottenstein Center in good years. However, the women's basketball team suffers from low attendance figures, filling less than half the Schottenstein Center.

"Purpose" and "Scope" can also be separate sections if either is long.

Purpose and Scope   *rhetorical purpose*

The purpose of this report is to <u>recommend</u> ways to increase student attendance at OSU women's basketball games.

Tell what you discuss and how thoroughly you discuss each topic.

In this report, I will focus on the three topics: the factors that affect student attendance, ways that student awareness of the women's team can be increased, and loyalty programs as a way of increasing attendance. I will briefly discuss how attendance and newspaper publicity correlate to the win/loss record.

Give topics in the order in which you'll discuss them.

"Scope" section should match report. You may need to revise "Topics to Investigate" from the proposal.

I will not discuss the cost of or the return on investment of my recommendations. I will not discuss how changes in coaching or recruiting might affect attendance.

List any relevant topics you don't discuss.

Assumption   *Assumptions cannot be proved. But if they are wrong, the report's recommendation may no longer be valid.*

My recommendations are based on the assumption that reasons for Ohio State student attendance at games are similar to those of students at other universities, so that loyalty programs at other schools are good models for Ohio State.

If you collected original data (surveys, interviews, or observations), tell how you chose whom to study, what kind of a sample you used, and on what date(s) you collected the information.

If you use only library and online services you do not need a "Methods" section. Instead, briefly describe your services in a short paragraph under "Purpose."

Methods

My information for this report comes from library and online sources, interviews with Athletic Department staff, and a survey of 50 Ohio State students, using a convenience sample. I surveyed students during the lunch hour in the Ohio Union dining area on July 27, 2001. I walked around the room and asked everyone if he or she would be willing to answer the survey, until I had 50 people.

Summarize the demographic information about your respondents.

The students filling out my survey represent all academic ranks at OSU from undergraduate students (including incoming first-year students) to graduate students. Sixty percent of the respondents are male, and forty percent are female. Sixty-eight percent of the people surveyed have never attended a women's basketball game, although 62% watch men's games. (See Appendix A for the raw data.)

Refer to your Appendixes in the text of your report.

If your report has limitations, state them.

Limitations

Giving the number makes it easier for the reader to read the paragraph.

My research has <u>four</u> limitations. First, because I used a convenience survey, I cannot generalize from the people I surveyed to all Ohio State students. Second, the timing of the survey was a problem. In the summer, many of the people in the Union are international students and incoming

(continued)

FIGURE 14.8 A Formal Report *(continued)*

10–point type Slam Dunk: Increasing Attendance at OSU Women's Basketball Games Page 2

11–point type first-year students (or their parents) participating in orientation. However, incoming students will be here for at least four years, so they are the most interested in a long-term marketing program, such as a loyalty program. Third, 11 of my respondents circled "other." I cannot tell whether they are incoming first-year students, faculty, or visitors who are not students. Fourth, some interviewer error may have occurred. I was able to clarify questions for some students, but not all. I tried to be available to all students and answer all questions, but my words were not always consistent. I also found that the wording on my last question was not clear enough and caused some confusion.

Use Talking Heads. Note how much more specific this head is than "Background" would be.

12–point type **Attendance at OSU Women's Basketball Home Games**

Try for a mix of paragraph lengths.
The Schottenstein Center holds 19,100 fans, but the average general attendance at one of this past year's 17 women's home basketball games was only 6,256 (Liz Cook, personal communication, June 26, 2001). This low attendance exists even though student tickets to the women's games ($3) are only half as expensive as student tickets to the men's games ($6).

Begin most paragraphs with topic sentences.

Most paragraphs should be seven lines or less.
The 2001 attendance rate was the lowest of the past three years even though the team went 22-11, the best record of the three years, and won the Women's NIT championship. The highest attendance in the past three years was in the 1998–99 season, when 7,588 fans attended each home game. During that season, coach Beth Burns joined the team, which had a 17–12 record and made the first round of the NCAA Finals. The 1999–2000 season attracted 7,277 fans per game with a 13–15 record (Liz Cook, personal communication, June 26, 2001). As Figure 1 shows, attendance has been falling even though the percentage of games won has increased.

APA format puts "Figure #" above the title of the Figure.

Figure 1

OSU Women Win More Games . . .

But Attract Fewer Fans

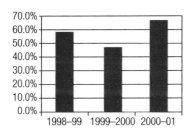

Percentage of Games Won

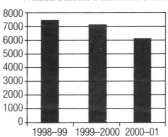

Average Attendance at Each Women's Home Basketball Game

Such low attendance, though disappointing, is not unusual. Ironically, in all of the past three years, attendance at the OSU women's basketball team has ranked in the top 10 nationally among collegiate women's basketball games (Liz Cook, personal communication, June 26, 2001).

Triple space before heading (two blank spaces).
The Importance of Increasing Student Attendance
Double space (one blank space) after.
To increase attendance, it would be possible to look to faculty or townspeople rather than to students. But students provide a promising audience for three reasons. First, there are a lot of them: 55,000. Second, attending games is fun and creates school spirit. Student attendance at sporting events (as well as theatrical performances and club meetings) brings students together and helps them

In APA use "personal communication" for interviews, e–mails, and other information to which the reader has no access.

FIGURE 14.8   A Formal Report *(continued)*

realize common interests. Athletic events provide a break for students and allow for bonding, whether with a residence hall floor, fraternities and sororities, or with friends. Attending games is one way to make a large campus feel smaller. Third, student attendance helps the athletes. Students provide moral support for one another. Attending games is a win-win situation for all. Student performance is better on the court when more people are cheering the team on. Athletes know their performance is enjoyed and like being watched.

In indented quote, period goes at end of quote. No punctuation after parenthesis.

Increased attendance can also benefit the team in more tangible ways. When the Lady Bucks competed for a qualifying spot in the NIT last season, Coach Beth Burns hoped for higher attendance rates so the women could play at home:

Indent quotes of 40 words or more. The quote is itself a quote. No extra quotation marks are necessary.

"The attendance that we have Sunday could ensure that we could host a championship game if we're fortunate enough to get there," Burns said. "The NIT is totally attendance-driven. They want to put [the championship game] on where the most interest is." ("Burns," 2000, p. 2E)

Use first word of title in quotation marks for an article with no author.

Ohio State played two of its three NIT games at home, drawing 1,846 and 1,918 fans, respectively. Games in New Mexico and Hawaii had bigger crowds, averaging 6,000 and 3,400 fans, respectively, for their home NIT games. The championship game was held at New Mexico, site of the biggest crowds ("Burns," 2000). Higher attendance at Ohio State might have moved the championship game here and allowed the OSU Lady Buckeyes to win the championship (which they did) before students, faculty, staff, and the Columbus community.

Factors Leading to Low Attendance at OSU Women's Basketball Games

At Ohio State, basketball is less popular than football. Women's basketball attracts fewer fans than does men's basketball. Few people I surveyed on the OSU campus could say they had been to a women's basketball game last year. Out of 50 surveys, 34 respondents—68%—say they have never been to an OSU women's basketball game. As Figure 2 shows, the two biggest reasons that students give for not attending the games is that they "have never thought to go" and their "friends are not interested" in attending the games.

Give both numbers and percentages.

Refer to Figure in text before you give it. Tell what point it makes.

Quote to give the exact wording of survey question.

Figure 2

Most Students Who Don't Attend Games "Never Thought" About Going

Use bars rather than columns when labels are long. Reorder bars in order of length— don't simply repeat the order from the survey. OK to shorten labels from survey questions.

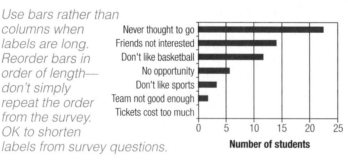

Label both axes. See Chapter 15 for more information on creating graphs and other visuals.

FIGURE 14.8 A Formal Report *(continued)*

10-point type

Slam Dunk: Increasing Attendance at OSU Women's Basketball Games   Page 4

11-point type

It's true that almost one-fourth of the respondents don't like basketball. But most do, and indeed, 62% watch men's games. Two people felt that the team wasn't "good enough." However, this past year, the team won the women's NIT championship. It seems that perception, not reality, is likely the issue for these students. No one in my sample felt that the tickets cost too much. It is obvious that the three-dollar ticket price is not an issue for students. Men's tickets cost double, yet more are sold.

Summarize the point of a quote before you give the quote.

12-point type

Increasing Attendance Through Marketing

Heading must cover everything under that heading until the next head or subhead at that level.

Marketing sports events can increase attendance, as Clay Daughtrey and Andy Gillentine of the University of Mississippi found in their research about marketing swim meets:

> Marketing techniques such as advertising, posters, word of mouth, and expanded ticket distribution were all identified as effective in increasing attendance. Making the meet more enjoyable for fans was also seen as imperative to increase fan attendance. This [goal] was achieved through music, giveaways, promotions, and fan participation exercises. Results could be useful to other Olympic or youth sport organizations that are attempting to market, increase public interest and generate funds for their sport (2000, p. A-118).

Use square brackets around words you add.

Don't need authors' names in parentheses when they're in the sentence introducing the quote.

The three most promising options for OSU are short-term marketing to educate and increase awareness of games, long-term marketing programs, and loyalty programs. All of these methods should be used, but, as Table 1 shows, long-term marketing and a loyalty program are likely to have the greatest effect.

Tables and Figures are numbered independently, so you can have both a "Figure 1" and "Table 1."

Table 1

A Loyalty Program May Make Loyal Fans

Give question from survey.

"To what extent would each of the following make you more likely to attend an OSU women's basketball game?"

Tell what numbers in a Likert-type scale mean.

Average; N=50

Reorder from high to low.

(3 = Much more likely, 2 = Possibly more likely, 1 = No effect)

Rank	Option	
1	Loyalty Program	1.88
2	Long-Term Marketing	1.76
3	Increased Awareness	1.56
4	Education	1.28

"N" is the total number of people responding to the question. Use "n" to give the number of people giving a particular response.

Short-Term Marketing: Education and Increasing Awareness

Just walking across the Ohio State campus each day is a learning experience. Daily, groups pass out fliers, chalk the sidewalks, and set up booths with messages about credit cards, club meetings, textbook and class notes deals, Web sites, clothing sales, and parties. Most of this "publicity" takes place on the Oval, the center of campus. Students run for the university government, professors hold classes, and the ROTC, student organizations, and religious groups try to recruit students on the Oval.

Not every idea needs a source.

Use your knowledge of people and of business.

Short-term marketing can be as simple as chalking messages on the sidewalk or tacking posters on the information poles near the library and administration buildings about upcoming games and when and where they will be held. If the team is not playing at home, the messages can remind students to watch a televised game, the nightly sports wrap-up on the local news or ESPN, or to look for a report on the game's outcome the next morning in the university newspaper, *The Lantern*, or the

Italicize newspaper titles.

(continued)

FIGURE 14.8 A Formal Report *(continued)*

Slam Dunk: Increasing Attendance at OSU Women's Basketball Games   Page 5

Limit claims you cannot prove with certainty.

local *Columbus Dispatch*. Many of the students surveyed say they've never thought to go to a game; maybe a friendly reminder in rather busy schedules would work.   *Italicize newspaper titles.*
Begin most paragraphs with topic sentences.

A visit from the female basketball players on the Oval is another way to attract fans. The Lady Bucks could set up a booth to sell tickets in advance for a game, erect a temporary basketball hoop and play a pickup game, or host a shooting contest against interested students walking across the Oval. Some respondents said they do not attend games because they do not know any players.

A lesson in the rules of the game may be in order. When the National Hockey League (NHL) Columbus Blue Jackets arrived in Columbus, one of the sponsoring companies, BankOne, provided pocket-size pamphlets that unfolded into a cheat sheet with facts about the playing surface and players and explanations of the rules of the game, playing times, scoring, referee signals, and penalties. This pocket "rules of the game" was helpful to many Columbus fans who were new to hockey. A pocket guide for women's basketball may be helpful to students who are new to women's college basketball (which has different rules than men's), or in fact new to the game of basketball. The 2001 NCAA rules book for men's and women's basketball (2000) lists differences in the ball circumference and weight ($\pm$ 2 inches smaller and $\pm$ 2 ounces lighter for women), shot clock times (35 seconds for men, 30 seconds for women), number of players allowed in a free throw (6 for men, 5 for women), and explains personal control fouls.

Long-Term Marketing   *Divide a heading only when you have two or more subheads.*

People like to do things in groups. The fact that OSU football games are "events" means that students want to go to the games whether they like football or not. The Athletic Department needs to work to increase interest in women's basketball in general. As Figure 2 showed, the second most-common reason that students do not attend games is that their friends aren't interested. *APA does not capitalize words after a colon*

Limit claims that you cannot prove with certainty.

The Athletic Department could designate days for specific groups: fraternities and sororities, *when the words* residential halls, and student organizations. Invite these groups to a game, seat them together in a *are not a* certain spot in the arena, recognize them, and offer them a price break on food or merchandise for the *complete* game. The groups come for a break from studying and the bonding experience, and it is inevitable *sentence.* that some of the students will invite friends from outside of the group to join in the fun. People who come just to be with their friends may enjoy the experience and return for other games.

In the past, the Athletic Department has offered deals to residence halls, giving students the opportunity to purchase so many tickets to hockey or baseball for a flat fee, and in turn, students receive T-shirts at the first game. The T-shirts are white and use just one color of printing, but nobody is going to turn down a free T-shirt. Students still wear the "Jim Rat #6" shirts that were given out at a men's basketball game during Jim O'Brien's first year as head coach.

Offering freebies to the first so many fans attending a game will attract students. Besides shirts, other giveaways could include hats (which have been given away at a Major League Soccer Columbus Crew game), ear coverings for the winter, drink and food coupons, promotional music CDs, signed posters of the team, or key chains. Fans also like raffles. The Scarlet and Gray pep rally at the beginning of the year attracts students because everyone hopes his or her ticket will be pulled for the quarter of free tuition. The campus bookstores could give away a gift certificate to be used towards textbooks, as most students know what a chunk of money books require each quarter. Campus travel agents could donate a plane ticket to fly home or to be used for Spring Break travel.

Ohio State already has a multimillion-dollar contract with Coca-Cola. The Department could

(continued)

FIGURE 14.8 A Formal Report *(continued)*

Slam Dunk: Increasing Attendance at OSU Women's Basketball Games   Page 6

approach the company for more sponsorship at the games, whether it be to provide basketball shirts with the Coca-Cola logo on the back or contribute to a student's tuition. The clothing chain Aeropostale holds quarterly campus warehouse sales with great clothing buys. Aeropostale provided the T-shirts for last year's hockey and baseball promotions and might be willing to do the same thing for women's basketball.

Limit claims that you cannot prove with certainty.

Men's basketball attracts many students, and men will always identify with the men's sport first. Therefore, it might make sense for the Athletic Department to launch a campaign appealing to women students. The Department could work with sororities, the advisors on women's residence hall floors, and Women's Studies classes to find out what the students would like to see at games. The Department can create an advertising campaign for women, posting information on the floor bulletin boards, holding informational sessions throughout the year in the dorms with basketball players as speakers, and holding "Women's Nights" at the games. Once women students are recognized and catered to at games, they are going to attend more often and bring their male friends, classmates, and boyfriends to games. Increasing women students' attendance will increase men's attendance.

APA calls for a capital letter after a colon when the words after the colon form a complete sentence.

Last, the Department could launch a formal publicity campaign: Buy more advertising space in *The Lantern* and *The Columbus Dispatch*, and push for more articles to be written. In a search on Academic Universe for articles over the past year about the women's basketball team in *The Columbus Dispatch,* I found approximately fifty articles. With an average of 537 words an article, a majority of the articles rehash the statistics of games or discuss injuries that plagued the team last season. Only 26% of the articles appeared on the front or inside front page of the Sports section. After the NIT win last season several Columbus residents wrote to the Sports editor to complain about the coverage of the team, or lack thereof:

Use ellipses (3 spaces dots) when you omit part of a quote.

> I understand that women's basketball usually doesn't produce the same crowds and therefore the same revenue that men's basketball produces. But one would think that they would deserve the same respect and praise that comes along with winning a championship. However, all that was awarded them was a passing mention on the TV news, and a small mention on the bottom of the front page of this newspaper and one article in the sports section compared with the multiple mentions that the men's team receives. . . . One of my co-workers didn't even know that the women's team was in a tournament, let alone that they won it. (Cofer, 2001, p. 3D)

Use author's name in parentheses when it isn't in the sentence introducing quote.

Although the men's team did not win a tournament this past season, it had more and longer articles (averaging 603 words). Most of the articles built interest in the team, rather than simply rehashing the game. Almost twice as many articles about the men's team (49%) appeared on the front or inside front page of the Sports section. Several reporters wrote articles about the men's team, while one reporter wrote almost all the articles about women. Inviting more reporters for more interviews with the women's team and encouraging more reports on the front page would boost awareness of the team.

When quote is part of your sentence, period goes after the parenthesis.

The more the public sees of the team, the more likely people will be to attend games. And reporters will write more stories if they know the team better. Daughtrey found "the most effective method used to generate media attention was to create a personal relationship with members of the media. Sponsorship was increased most when signage, hospitality, recognition through plaques/announcements, newspaper articles, and personal thank you notes were offered" (2000, p. A-118).

Hire a business student on an hourly salary to do the legwork for a long-term marketing program, contacting other university marketing programs, evaluating the financial expectations, and presenting a business plan to the Athletic Department. In return, the student gains real-world experience that serves him or her well when interviewing for jobs later on.

(continued)

FIGURE 14.8 A Formal Report *(continued)*

Slam Dunk: Increasing Attendance at OSU Women's Basketball Games   Page 7

Loyalty Program

Most Americans today have at least one "club card" for the local grocery store hanging from their key chains. Many have three or four cards ranging from the supermarket to the drugstore and the video store that award points and give discounts on certain items each time the cards are swiped (as an ATM card is) and a purchase is made.

When author's name is in the sentence, it isn't repeated in the parentheses.

Short quotes (less than 40 words) go in your sentence.

In recent years, professional and collegiate athletic teams have joined the phenomenon. Joan Raymond explains, "Each time fans use their card, they rack up attendance points redeemable for promotional coupons or items such as food, drinks, and souvenirs. The more points they compile, the more 'rewards' they receive" (2001, p. 35). When fans sign up for the club cards, they provide basic information that the teams can use to tailor their offerings to the target audience. Customer relationship marketing (CRM) uses databases to track fan attendance and identify those most likely to buy season tickets.

When the original has a word in quotation marks, use single quotes (and double quotation marks for the whole quote).

OSU can use the information that students give to create e-mail updates about the basketball team, give advance notice for tickets and giveaways, and attract more season ticket holders. The information can also clue the Schottenstein in on what kind of concessions students want and what kind of merchandise penny-pinching college students are going to spend their money on.

Further subdivisions within a sub-heading use bold. Capitalize all main words. End with a period, and continue ¶ on the same line.

Justarrive's Loyalty Programs. Justarrive is a company that creates technologically savvy loyalty programs for collegiate teams. Students just swipe their college Ids at the gate and are billed later for the games that they actually attend (Justarrive, 2001). The swipe terminals at the gate recognize students' names and attendance patterns and print out paper tickets/coupons. "The paper coupon also provides teams and corporate sponsors with a marketing opportunity, since personalized messages and discounts for products and services can be printed on the reverse side of the 'ticket'" (Raymond, 2001, p. 36).

Use author's name in parentheses when it isn't in the sentence.

Justarrive began its program in time for the 1999 Stanford basketball season. Thanks to the program, Raymond notes, Stanford fans "received e-mails with updated point totals, and the fans with the most points were guaranteed entrance to the major Stanford games, and entered multiple times in the lottery for NCAA tournament tickets" (Raymond, 2001, p. 36). The program replaced the old first-come, first-serve admission policy, rewarding "die-hard" fans with the most points and guaranteeing that they could get in.

Student season-ticket holders who cannot attend a game may lend their student ID or Justarrive card to a friend who can attend the game (Justarrive, 2001). Students still receive points, and the university keeps attendance rates high:

Summarize the point of an indented quote before you give it.

"Typically, students with season tickets don't go to every game, and even when stadiums are sold out, anywhere from 20% to 30% of the seats are empty on game day," said Ana Witherow, Justarrive's chief operating officer. "It's not fair to fans who   [are turned away] because they couldn't get tickets, and it's hard psychologically on players, to look up at the stands and see empty seats." (Kurdek, 2000, p. 4) *APA uses "p." before the page number.*

After Stanford's success, Justarrive has signed on Georgia Tech and UCLA.

Husker Fever Card. Rather than contracting with a marketing company, Ohio State could consult the University of Nebraska for ways to improve upon the Go Bucks! Card. The Go Bucks! Card costs $25 plus a $5 service fee and provides free general admission to baseball, gymnastics, lacrosse, soccer, volleyball, women's ice hockey, and wrestling events (Ohio State University, 2001).

OK to have subheadings under some heads and not under others.

Students get their money's worth if they attend at least 10 games or matches during the year.

(continued)

FIGURE 14.8 A Formal Report *(continued)*

However, women's basketball is not one of the sports included on the card, and many of the students that the Department hopes to attract to the women's basketball games don't attend many sports events. The card would not be a good investment for students who attend a few games a year or are interested only in a specific sport.

URLs will be easiest to read if you put them in angle brackets.
Underlining cuts off descenders and makes words harder to read.

The University of Nebraska introduced its Husker Fever Card last year. Fans sign up for the free card on the Web: <www.huskerfevercard.com>. The card can be used for admission to all 24 sports, and each swipe awards Husker Fever points that can be used for merchandise and in online auctions. Using the card also enters fans to win vacations and tickets to sporting and entertainment events (University of Nebraska, 2001). Every time a member logs on the Web site, he or she earns more points or bucks for the auctions. Cardholders earn points when using the card at sponsoring businesses like Pizza Hut, 66 Gas, Pepsi, Omaha Favorites.com, convenience stores, and grocery stores throughout Nebraska. In grocery stores, the card entitles the student to discounts on certain name-brand products each week.

The Husker Fever Card seems to be a rather large program and might be something for OSU to consider working up to in the future.

Conclusions repeat points made in the report.   *Some companies ask for Conclusions and*
Recommendations are actions the readers should take. *Recommendations at the beginning of reports.*

Conclusions and Recommendations

A majority of students like basketball and might be interested in going to the OSU women's games if it occurred to them to go or if their friends went, too. To increase attendance, the Athletic Department should

Numbering points makes it easy for readers to discuss them. The list also provides visual variety.

1. **Implement short-term marketing this fall.** Capitalize on the Lady Buckeyes' winning streak last year to attract a higher attendance this year. Since basketball season is only a quarter away, it might be smart to focus on increased awareness for the upcoming season.
   - Chalk the Oval before each home game.
   - Ask the women basketball players to host impromptu meet-and-greets or pickup games on the Oval.
   - Provide information about the rules for women's basketball.

2. **Use OSU students to develop a long-term marketing program and a formal publicity campaign.** Changing perceptions takes time and many messages.
   - Designate days for specific groups.
   - Offer deals and freebies. Ask sponsors to donate freebies or items to be raffled or auctioned.
   - Create an advertising campaign focusing on women students in sororities, women's floors in residence halls, and Women's Studies classes.
   - Buy more advertising space in *The Lantern* and *The Columbus Dispatch*.
   - Try to persuade more reporters to write more stories in more prominent locations about the women's team.

Make sure items in a list are parallel.

3. **Consider adopting a loyalty program.** A loyalty program allows the Athletic Department to reward students for behaviors it wants to encourage by giving it useful marketing information. Further research is needed to study the financial implications of implementing such a program.

Because many readers turn to the "Recommendations" first, provide enough information so that the reason is clear all by itself. The ideas in this section must be logical extensions of the points made and supported in the body of the report.

(continued)

FIGURE 14.8 A Formal Report *(continued)*

References *APA Format*

Cofer, E. (2001, April 8). OSU women deserved more attention from the media. *The Columbus Dispatch*, p. 3D.

Start with the title of the article when no author is given.

Use "p." when you don't have volume number.

Burns looks for OSU victory, big crowd. (2001, March 24). *The Columbus Dispatch*, p. 2E.

Month follows year. Period outside parentheses.

Daughtrey, C., & Gillentine, A. (2000, March). The marketing of swim meets [Electronic Version]. *Research Quarterly for Exercise and Sport, 71*, A-118. *No "p." when you give volume number.*

Italicize volume number

Justarrive. (1999–2001). *Case study*. Retrieved June 19, 2001, from the World Wide Web: http://www.justarrive.com *No punctuation after Web address*

Kurdek, R. (2000, November 20). $5M Just arrives for sporting start-up [Electronic Version]. *Private Equity Week*, p. 4.

NCAA. (2000). *Playing rules: Men's and women's basketball rules and interpretations.* Retrieved August 30, 2001, from the World Wide Web: http://www.ncaa.org/library/rules.html

Ohio State University. (2001). *Ohio State Buckeyes*. Retrieved July 3, 2001, from the World Wide Web: http://www.hangonsloopy.com

Raymond, J. (2001, April). Home field advantage. *American Demographics*, 34–36.

Copyright/update date   *Date you visited site*

University of Nebraska. (2001). Husker Fever card. Retrieved June 20, 2001 from the World Wide Web: http://www.huskerfevercard.com

List all the printed and online sources cited in your report. Do not list sources you used for background but did not cite. Do not list interviews, phone calls, or other information to which the reader has no access.

(continued)

FIGURE 14.8 A Formal Report *(concluded)*

Include a copy of your survey with the raw data. It's OK to change the format a bit to make room for the data.

Appendix A: Raw Survey Data

N = 50.   *Tell how many people responded.*

1. Gender   M   30 (60%)
                   F   20 (40%)

2. Rank   First-Year   4 (8%)   *Give numbers*
            Sophomore   9 (18%)   *and percentages.*
            Junior   13 (26%)
            Senior   5 (10%)
            Graduate student   7 (14%)
            Other   12 (24%)

3. How do you feel about women's sports?
   9 (18%)   1   I enjoy watching women's sports.
   10 (20%)   2
   20 (40%)   3   I'll watch, but it doesn't really matter.
   7 (14%)   4
   5 (10%)   5   Women's sports are boring/I'd rather watch men's sports.

4. Do you like to attend OSU men's basketball games or watch them on TV?
   31 (62%) Y   19 (38%) N

5. How often do you attend OSU women's basketball games?
   0 (0%)   All/most games
   2 (4%)   Few games a season
   6 (12%)   Once a season
   8 (16%)   Less than once a year
   34 (68%)   Never

6. If you do not attend all of the women's basketball games, why not?
   22 (44%)   I've never thought to go.
   12 (24%)   I don't like basketball.
   3 (6%)   I don't like sporting events.
   2 (4%)   The team isn't good enough.
   14 (25%)   My friends are not interested in going.
   6 (12%)   I want to go, I just haven't had the opportunity.
   0 (0%)   The tickets cost too much ($3).

7. To what extent would each of the following make you more likely to attend an OSU women's basketball game?   (3 = Much more likely, 2 = Possibly more likely, 1 = No effect)
   Increased awareness   1.56
   Long-term marketing   1.76
   Student loyalty program   1.88
   Education   1.28

Definitions. When you know that some members of your primary, secondary, or immediate audience will not understand technical terms, define them. If you have only a few definitions, you can put them in the Introduction. If you have many terms to define, use a **glossary** either early in the report or at the end. If the glossary is at the end, refer to it in the Introduction so that readers know that you've provided it.

Background or History

Formal reports usually have a section that gives the background of the situation or the history of the problem. Even though the current audience for the report probably knows the situation, reports are filed and consulted years later. These later audiences will probably not know the background, although it may be crucial for understanding the options that are possible.

In some cases, the history section may cover many years. For example, a report recommending that a US hotel chain open hotels in Romania will probably give the history of that country for at least the last hundred years. In other cases, the history section is much briefer, covering only a few years or even just the immediate situation.

Conclusions and Recommendations

Conclusions summarize points you have made in the body of the report; **Recommendations** are action items that would solve or ameliorate the problem. These sections are often combined if they are short: *Conclusions and Recommendations.*

The Conclusions section is the most widely read part of the report.[14] No new information should be included in the Conclusions. Conclusions are usually presented in paragraphs, but you could also use a numbered or bulleted list.

Many readers turn to the recommendations section first; some organizations ask that recommendations be presented early in the report. Number the recommendations to make it easy for people to discuss them. If the recommendations will seem difficult or controversial, give a brief paragraph of rationale after each recommendation. If they'll be easy for the audience to accept, you can simply list them without comments or reasons. The recommendations will also be in the executive summary and perhaps in the title and the transmittal.

Summary of Key Points

- *Causation* means that one thing causes or produces another. *Correlation* means that two things happen at the same time. One might cause the other, but both might be caused by a third.

- In **comparison/contrast,** you can focus on alternatives or on criteria. The **pro-and-con pattern** divides the alternatives and discusses the arguments for and against that alternative. A **problem-solving report** identifies the problem, explains its causes, and analyzes the advantages and disadvantages of possible solutions. **Elimination** identifies the problem, explains its causes, and discusses the least practical solutions first, ending with the one the writer favors. **General to particular** begins with the problem as it affects the organization or as it manifests itself in general, then moves to a discussion of the parts of the problem and solutions to each of these parts. **Particular to general** starts with specific aspects of the problem, then moves to a discussion of the larger implications of the problem for the organization. **Geographical or spatial** patterns discuss the problems and solutions by units. **Functional** patterns discuss the problems and solutions of each functional unit.

- Reports use the same style as other business documents, with three exceptions:
  1. Reports use a more formal style than do many letters and memos.
  2. Reports rarely use the word *you*.
  3. Reports should be self-explanatory.

- To create good report style,
  1. Say what you mean.
  2. Tighten your writing.
  3. Introduce sources and visuals gracefully.
  4. Use blueprints, transitions, topic sentences, and headings.

- **Headings** are single words, short phrases, or complete sentences that cover all of the material under it until the next heading. **Talking heads** tell the reader what to expect in each section.

- Headings must use the same grammatical structure. Subheads under a heading must be parallel to each other but do not necessarily have to be parallel to subheads under other headings.

- The title page of a report usually contains four items: the title of the report, whom the report is prepared for, whom it is prepared by, and the date.

- The title of a report should contain the recommendations unless
  - The reader will find the recommendations hard to accept.
  - Putting all the recommendations in the title would make it too long.
  - The report does not offer recommendations.

- If the title does not contain the recommendations, it normally indicates what problem the report tries to solve.

- If the report is 25 pages or less, list all the headings in the table of contents. In a long report, pick a level and put all the headings at that level and above in the contents.

- Organize the transmittal in this way:
  1. Release the report.
  2. Summarize your conclusions and recommendations.
  3. Mention any points of special interest in the report. Indicate minor problems you encountered in your investigation and show how you surmounted them. Thank people who helped you.
  4. Point out additional research that is necessary, if any.
  5. Thank the reader for the opportunity to do the work and offer to answer questions.

- **Summary abstracts** present the logical skeleton of the article: the thesis or recommendation and its proof. **Descriptive abstracts** indicate what topics the article covers and how deeply it goes into each topic, but do not summarize what the article says about each topic. **Mixed abstracts** have some characteristics of both summary and descriptive abstracts. They may list all of the topics covered in an article and summarize some of the points about some of the topics.

- A summary abstract is based on a sentence outline. A descriptive abstract is based on a topic outline.

Report Your Way to a Better Job*

Joan was hired by a computer company to find references to the computer industry in current publications. To expand her job description, Joan wrote reports summarizing the data instead of just sending files of clippings. The receivers were delighted because she was saving them time.

Her second step was to meet with the people who got her reports to ask them what sorts of information they needed. Now she was able to target her reports to her readers' needs. People in each unit began to invite her to meetings discussing the projects she was researching.

As a member of the various groups within the company, Joan now had the information she needed to take a third step: drafting the report for decision makers. For example, if the sales department wanted information for a proposal to a client, she presented her information in a sales proposal. If the president wanted material for a speech, she arranged her information in a speech outline.

When the director of business communications resigned, Joan was the obvious choice for the job.

*Based on Janice LaRouche, "I'm Stuck in a Dead-End Job," *Family Circle*, March 24, 1987, 121.

- A good abstract or executive summary is easy to read, concise, and clear. A good abstract can be understood by itself, without the original article or reference books.

- The **Introduction** of the report always contains a statement of purpose and scope. The **Purpose** statement identifies the organizational problem the report addresses, the technical investigations it summarizes, and the rhetorical purpose (to explain, to recommend). The **Scope** statement identifies how broad an area the report surveys. The introduction may also include **Limitations,** problems or factors that limit the validity of your recommendations; **Assumptions,** statements whose truth you assume, and which you use to prove your final point; **Methods,** an explanation of how you gathered your data; **Criteria** used to weigh the factors in the decision; and **Definitions** of terms readers may not know.

- A **Background** or **History** section is included because reports are filed and may be consulted years later.

- **Conclusions** summarize points made in the body of the report; **Recommendations** are action items that would solve or ameliorate the problem. These sections are often combined if they are short.

CHAPTER 14   Exercises and Problems

Getting Started

14.1   Identifying Assumptions and Limitations

Indicate whether each of the following would be an Assumption or a Limitation in a formal report.

a. Report on Ways to Encourage More Students to Join XYZ Organization

   1. I surveyed a judgment sample rather than a random sample.

   2. These recommendations are based on the attitudes of current students. Presumably, students in the next several years will have the same attitudes and interests.

b. Report on the Feasibility of Building Hilton Hotels in Vietnam

   1. This report is based on the expectation that the country will be politically stable.

   2. All of my information is based on library research. The most recent articles were published two months ago; much of the information was published a year ago or more. Therefore some of my information may be out of date.

c. Report on Car-Buying Preferences of Young Adults

   1. These recommendations may change if the cost of gasoline increases dramatically or if there is another deep recession.

   2. This report is based on a survey of adults ages 20 to 24 in California, Texas, Illinois, Ontario, and Massachusetts.

   3. These preferences are based on the cars now available. If a major technical or styling innovation occurs, preferences may change.

14.2   Revising an Executive Summary

The following Executive Summary is poorly organized and too long. Rearrange information to make it more effective. Cut information that does not belong in the summary. You may use different words as you revise.

> In this report I will discuss the communication problems which exist at Rolling Meadows Golf Club. The problems discussed will deal with channels of communication. The areas which are causing problems are internal. Radios would solve these internal problems.
>
> Taking a 15-minute drive on a golf cart in order to find the superintendent is a common occurrence. Starters and rangers need to keep in touch with the clubhouse to maintain a smooth flow of players around the course. The rangers have expressed an interest in being able to call the clubhouse for advice and support.
>
> Purchasing two-channel FM radios with private channels would provide three advantages. First, radios would make the golf course safer by providing a means of notifying someone in the event of an emergency. Second, radios would make the staff more efficient by providing a faster channel of communication. Third, radios would enable clubhouse personnel to keep in touch with the superintendent, the rangers, and the starters.
>
> During the week, radios can be carried by the superintendent, the golf pro, and another course worker. On weekends and during tournaments, one radio will be used by the golf professional. The other two will be used by one starter and one ranger. Three radios is the minimum needed to meet basic communication needs. A fourth radio would provide more flexibility for busy weekends and during tournaments.
>
> Tekk T-20 radios can be purchased from Page-Com for $129 each. These radios have the range and options needed for use on the golf course. Radios are durable and easy to service. It is possible that another brand might be even less expensive.
>
> Rolling Meadows Golf Club should purchase four radios. They will cost under $600 and can be paid for from the current equipment budget.

Communicating at Work

As Your Instructor Directs, In Problems 14.3 and 14.4,

a. Create a document or presentation to achieve the goal.

b. Write a memo to your instructor describing the situation at your workplace and explaining your rhetorical choices (medium, strategy, tone, wording, graphics or document design, and so forth).

14.3   Explaining "Best Practices"

Write a report explaining the "best practices" of your unit that could also be adopted by other units in your organization.

14.4   Recommending Action

Write a report recommending an action that your unit or organization should take. Possibilities include

- Buying more equipment for your department.
- Hiring an additional worker for your department.
- Making your organization more family-friendly.

- Making a change that will make the organization more efficient.
- Making changes to improve accessibility for customers or employees with disabilities.

Address your report to the person who would have the power to approve your recommendation.

14.5   Evaluating a Report from Your Workplace

Consider the following aspects of a report from your workplace:

- How much information is included? How is it presented?
- Visuals and layout. Are visuals used effectively? Are they accurate and free from chartjunk? What image do the pictures and visuals create? Are color and white space used effectively? (See Chapter 15 on visuals.)
- Emphasis. What points are emphasized? What points are deemphasized? What verbal and visual techniques are used to highlight or minimize information?

As Your Instructor Directs,

a.   Write a memo to your instructor analyzing the report.

b.   Join with a small group of students to compare and contrast several reports. Present your evaluation in an informal group report.

c.   Present your evaluation orally to the class.

Report Assignments

14.6   Writing a Feasibility Study

Write a report evaluating the feasibility of two or more alternatives. Possible topics include the following:

1.   Is it feasible for a local restaurant to open another branch? Where should it be?

2.   Is it feasible to create a program to mentor women and minorities in your organization?

3.   Is it feasible to produce a video yearbook in addition to or instead of a paper yearbook at your college, community college, or university?

4.   Is it feasible to create or enlarge a day care center for the children of students?

5.   Could your college host a regional meeting of the Association for Business Communication on campus or in town?

6.   Is it feasible to start a monthly newsletter for students in your major?

7.   Is it feasible for local grocery stores to stock (or increase their stock of) carambolas, mamey, longans, lychees, atemoyas, sugar apples, jackfruit, and other exotic Asian and Latin American fruits and vegetables? If so, where should the additional space come from: Less space for traditional fruits and vegetables? Less space for another department? (If so, which one?) Store expansion?

Pick a limited number of alternatives, explain your criteria clearly, evaluate each alternative, and recommend the best course of action.

14.7 Writing an Informative or Closure Report

Write an informative report on one of the following topics.

1. What should a US or Canadian manager know about dealing with workers from _____ [you fill in the country or culture]? What factors do and do not motivate people in this group? How do they show respect and deference? Are they used to a strong hierarchy or to an egalitarian setting? Do they normally do one thing at once or many things? How important is clock time and being on time? What factors lead them to respect someone? Age? Experience? Education? Technical knowledge? Wealth? Or what? What conflicts or miscommunications may arise between workers from this culture and other workers due to cultural differences? Are people from this culture similar in these beliefs and behaviors, or is there lots of variation?

2. What benefits do companies offer? To get information, check the Web pages of three companies in the same industry. Information about benefits is usually on the page about working for the company. For example, Eddie Bauer's Associate Benefits page is www.eddiebauer.com/about/company_info/careers_benefits.asp.

3. Describe an ethical dilemma encountered by workers in a specific organization. What is the background of the situation? What competing loyalties exist? In the past, how have workers responded? How has the organization responded? Have "whistle-blowers" been rewarded or punished? What could the organization do to foster ethical behavior?

4. Describe a problem or challenge encountered by an organization where you've worked. Describe the problem, show why it needed to be solved, tell who did what to try to solve it, and tell how successful the efforts were. Possibilities include

   - How the organization is implementing work teams, downsizing, or a change in organizational culture.
   - How the organization uses e-mail or voice mail, statistical process control, or telecommuting.
   - How managers deal with stress, make ethical choices, or evaluate subordinates.
   - How the organization is responding to changing US demographics, the Americans with Disabilities Act, or international competition and opportunities.

14.8 Writing a Consultant's Report—Restaurant Tipping

Your consulting company has been asked to conduct a report for Diamond Enterprises, which runs three national chains: FishStix, The Bar-B-Q Pit, and Morrie's. All are medium-priced, family-friendly restaurants. The CEO is thinking of replacing optional tips with a 15% service fee automatically added to bills.

You read articles in trade journals, surveyed a random sample of 200 workers in each of the chains, and conducted an e-mail survey of the 136 restaurant managers. Here are your findings:

1. Trade journals point out that the Internal Revenue Service (IRS) audits restaurants if it thinks that servers underreport tips. Dealing with an audit is time-consuming and often results in the restaurant's having to pay penalties and interest.

2. Only one Morrie's restaurant has actually been audited by the IRS. Management was able to convince the IRS that servers were reporting tips accurately. No penalty was assessed. Management spent $1,000 on CPA and legal fees and spent over 80 hours of management time gathering data and participating in the audit.

3. Restaurants in Europe already add a service fee (usually 15%) to the bill. Patrons can add more if they choose. Local custom determines whether tips are expected and how much they should be. In Germany, for example, it is more usual to round up the bill (from 27 € to 30 €, for example), than to figure a percentage.

4. If the restaurant collected a service fee, it could use the income to raise wages for cooks and hosts and pay for other benefits, such as health insurance, rather than giving all the money to servers and bussers.

5. Morrie's servers tend to be under 25 years of age. FishStix employs more servers over 25, who are doing this for a living. The Bar-B-Q Pit servers are students in college towns.

6. In all three chains, servers oppose the idea. Employees other than servers generally support it.

	Retain tips	Change to service fee added to bill	Don't care
FishStix servers (n = 115)	90%	7%	3%
Bar-B-Q servers (n = 73)	95%	0%	5%
Morrie's servers (n = 93)	85%	15%	0%
Morrie's nonservers (n = 65)	25%	70%	5%
FishStix nonservers (n = 46)	32%	32%	37%
Bar-B-Q nonservers (n = 43)	56%	20%	25%

(Numbers do not add up to 100% due to rounding.)

7. Servers said that it was important to go home with money in their pockets (92%), that their expertise increased food sales and should be rewarded (67%), and that if a service fee replaced tips they would be likely to look for another job (45%). Some (17%) thought that if the manager distributed service-fee income, favoritism rather than the quality of work would govern how much tip income they got. Most (72%) thought that customers would not add anything beyond the 15% service fee, and many (66%) thought that total tip income would decrease and their own portion of that income would decrease (90%).

8. Managers generally support the change.

	Retain tips	Change to service fee added to bill	Don't care
FishStix managers (n = 44)	20%	80%	0%
Bar-B-Q managers (n = 13)	33%	67%	0%
Morrie's managers (n = 58)	55%	45%	0%

9. Comments from managers include: "It isn't fair for a cook with eight years of experience to make only $12 an hour while a server can make $25 an hour in just a couple of months," and "I could have my pick of employees if I offered health insurance."

10. Morale at Bar-B-Q seems low. This is seen in part in the low response rate to the survey.

11. In a tight employment market, some restaurants might lose good servers if they made the change. However, hiring cooks and other nonservers would be easier.

12. The current computer systems in place can handle figuring and recording the service fee. Since bills are printed by computer, an additional line could be added. Allocating the service-fee income could take extra managerial time, especially at first.

14.9   Writing a Library Research Report

Write a library research report.

As Your Instructor Directs,

Turn in the following documents:

a. The approved proposal.

b. Two copies of the report, including

Cover.

Title Page.

Letter or Memo of Transmittal.

Table of Contents.

List of Illustrations.

Executive Summary or Abstract.

Body (Introduction, all information, recommendations). Your instructor may specify a minimum length, a minimum number or kind of sources, and a minimum number of visuals.

References or Works Cited.

c. Your notes and rough drafts.

Choose one of the following topics.

1. **Making Money from Football.** Your boss, the athletic director at your college, community college, or university, is interested in increasing revenue. "NFL teams make money in lots of ways—and some of the teams that are successful financially don't have good teams. Look at what they're doing, and recommend whether we could copy any of their strategies. Also recommend ways to ensure that students aren't priced out of attending the games." Start with Sam Walker, "Pro Football: Scoring in a Slow Economy," *The Wall Street Journal,* September 7, 2001, W1, W4.

2. **Recommending a Dress Policy.** Your boss asks you to look into "business casual" dress. "Is it time to retire it? And what *is* 'business casual'? Recommend how our employees should dress, and why. Include some photos of what is and isn't appropriate." To start, read Anne Field, "What Is

Business Casual?" *BusinessWeek,* October 30, 2000, 180–90.

> *Hint:* Choose a business, nonprofit, or government agency you know well and recommend a dress policy for it.

3. **Accounting for Intellectual Capital.** You work for the Securities Exchange Commission (SEC). Your boss hands you a copy of Thomas A. Stewart, "Accounting Gets Radical," *Fortune,* April 1, 2001, 184–94. "Many experts believe that traditional, generally accepted accounting principles don't work well now that knowledge and intellectual property can be a firm's most important assets. Write a report summarizing proposals for alternate accounting schemes and explain the advantages and disadvantages of each."

4. **Evaluating Online Voting.** As an aide to one of your state's members of Congress, you frequently research topics for legislation. You have been told, "Look into online voting. It's going to be recommended, and I want to know what the problems are and whether it's feasible for the next election." Start with Stephen H. Wildstrom, "Click and Be Counted," *BusinessWeek,* April 24, 2000, 22; and Thomas E. Weber, " 'Scalable' Ballot Fraud: Why One Tech Maven Fears Computer Voting," *The Wall Street Journal,* March 19, 2001, B1.

5. **Evaluating the Ethics of "Weblining."** You're an aide to one of your state's senators. You've been told, "I'm concerned that information on the Web allows companies to 'rank' customers and then charge rates and provide customer service based on how 'good' a customer is. Poor people and small businesses will be hurt. Find out how widespread the practice is. Especially consider the ethical implications. Should the federal government outlaw the practice?" Start with Marcia Stepanek, "Weblining," *BusinessWeek e.biz,* April 3, 2000, EB26–E34.

6. **Understanding Demographic Changes.** You work for a major political party. Your boss says, "As you know, the number of so-called minorities is growing. Moreover, they're increasingly middle class. I want you to analyze one ethnic group in our state. What issues are they interested in? Which party do they favor? What appeals might persuade them to vote for a candidate of the other party?" Depending on the group you pick, you may want to read Jonathan J. Higuera, "No Political Pigeonhole," *Hispanic Business,* December 2001, 33; Robert H. Brischetto, "The Hispanic Middle Class Comes of Age," *Hispanic Business,* December 2001, 21–36; or Deborah Kong, "Number Crunch," *aMagazine,* December 2001/January 2002, 38–39, 78.

7. **Improving Laptop Security.** Your boss hands you a copy of Charles C. Mann, "Where the Hell Is My Laptop?" *www.ecompany.com,* March 2001, 84–90. She says, "This article is frightening. Laptop theft is rising. My concern is not just the cost of the computers stolen, but the danger of data theft as well. Thieves can even re-create what's on a laptop screen in another room. Put together a report on how we can protect our data and our computers."

8. **Raising Military Pay.** Your boss is a member of the House Committee on Armed Services. He says, "We need to look at military pay. Civilian pay for highly skilled people is much higher than military pay. As a result, reenlistment is falling—at a time when the military needs more technological sophistication than ever. Study the issue of compensation. How can we continue to pay for education and training without losing people as soon as they have new skills?" Start with Gary S. Becker, "Yes, Raise Military Pay. Just Do It Cleverly," *BusinessWeek,* February 12, 2001, 24.

9. **Evaluating Welfare Reform.** You work for a local foodbank. The director says, "We're serving more people than ever. I think part of the problem is that lifetime limits for families receiving welfare are going into effect. Yet rising unemployment means that many former welfare recipients are out of work again. And even people who still have jobs may lack health insurance and have trouble making ends meet. I'd like you to look into the situation. Is the state doing enough in terms of job counseling? Do people need child care or transportation? Should we try to persuade Washington to change welfare reform?" Start with Alexandra Starr, "Welfare Reform's Toughest Test," *BusinessWeek,* December 10, 2001, 52–53.

10. With your instructor's permission, investigate a topic of your choice.

14.10   Writing a Recommendation Report

Write an individual or a group report.

As Your Instructor Directs,

Turn in the following documents:

1. The approved proposal.
2. Two copies of the report, including
    Cover.
    Title Page.
    Letter or Memo of Transmittal.
    Table of Contents.
    List of Illustrations.
    Executive Summary or Abstract.
    Body (Introduction, all information, recommendations). Your instructor may specify a minimum length, a minimum number or kind of sources, and a minimum number of visuals.
    Appendixes if useful or relevant.
3. Your notes and rough drafts.

    Pick one of the following topics.

1. **Improving Customer Service.** Many customers find that service is getting poorer and workers are getting ruder. Evaluate the service in a local store, restaurant, or other organization. Are customers made to feel comfortable? Is workers' communication helpful, friendly, and respectful? Are workers knowledgeable about products and services? Do they sell them effectively? Write a report analyzing the quality of service and recommending what the organization should do to improve.
2. **Recommending Courses for the Local Community College.** Businesses want to be able to send workers to local community colleges to upgrade their skills; community colleges want to prepare students to enter the local workforce. What skills are in demand in your community? What courses at what levels should the local community college offer?
3. **Improving Sales and Profits.** Recommend ways a small business in your community can increase sales and profits. Focus on one or more of the following: the products or services it offers, its advertising, its decor, its location, its accounting methods, its cash management, or any other aspect that may be keeping the company from achieving its potential. Address your report to the owner of the business.
4. **Increasing Student Involvement.** How could an organization on campus persuade more of the students who are eligible to join or to become active in its programs? Do students know that it exists? Is it offering programs that interest students? Is it retaining current members? What changes should the organization make? Address your report to the officers of the organization.
5. **Evaluating a Potential Employer.** What training is available to new employees? How soon is the average entry-level person promoted? How much travel and weekend work are expected? Is there a "busy season," or is the workload consistent year-round? What fringe benefits are offered? What is the corporate culture? Is the climate nonracist and nonsexist? How strong is the company economically? How is it likely to be affected by current economic, demographic, and political trends? Address your report to the Placement Office on campus; recommend whether it should encourage students to work at this company.
6. With your instructor's permission, choose your own topic.

15

Using Graphs and Other Visuals

Using Graphs and Other Visuals

Cindy Huffman
Development Tester, SAS Institute

Cindy Huffman tests the functionality of visuals such as bar, pie, and scatter charts and Java applets displaying maps, various graphs, and contour plots. SAS Institute develops, markets, and supports the world's foremost data warehousing and decision support software.

www.sas.com

Just as a picture is worth a thousand words, a good visual *replaces* a thousand words (of documentation). It is important for users to produce high-end graphics that are intuitive and easy to understand. It's even more useful when the user can place these graphics within a Web page, presentation, paper, or even an application.

Data mining—analyzing data for relationships or patterns—plays an important role in producing visualizations. With piles and piles of data available, data mining allows users to find trends and stories in their data.

For example, a market analysis can find patterns in data identifying which products are commonly purchased together in a grocery store. These items can be easily identified graphically (by the height in a bar chart, or the size of a slice in a pie chart). With this information, the grocery store can place commonly purchased items together for greater success.

Computers give users the ability to generate powerful visuals, but it is up to the user to understand the data and figure out what type of graph represents the data accurately. As one of my Computer Science professors said throughout three semesters of classes, "Computers are dumb machines. They only do what you tell them to do."

It is important for graphs to be accurate, because they can be used in very important business decisions (opening a business in an area that matches the demographics portrayed in a graph). It's unethical to use graphics to mislead people with a visual that uses made-up or skewed data to support an agenda (for example, implying that sales are up, when they're not). However, verifying the accuracy can be as difficult as hand–calculating numbers and figures to support what is displayed. One way to validate graphs is to try several different types and determine if the visualizations are similar.

> "*Data mining allows users to find trends and stories in their data.*"

Showing Trends and Changes*

Jerry Atkinson gives his clients not only financial statements but also graphs of key trends. Atkinson is managing director of Atkinson and Company, a 62-employee CPA firm in Albuquerque, New Mexico.

Current-month or -year information isn't enough, he says. Clients need to see trends and changes. And graphs offer an easy way to show that.

Atkinson personalizes the graphs by using the colors of the company being profiled.

*Based on John von Brachel, "Interpreting Financial Statements: How One Firm Uses the Language of Graphics," *Journal of Accountancy* 180, no. 2 (August 1995), 42–43.

Visuals help make numbers meaningful and thus help communicate your points in telecasts, oral presentations, memos, letters, reports, and meetings. This chapter shows you how to turn data into graphs and other visuals. See Chapter 6 for a discussion of designing slides for oral presentations and Chapter 16 for a discussion of other aspects of good oral presentations.

Visuals can present numbers dramatically. The Consumer Federation of America crystallized discontent with high interest rates on consumer loans by issuing a simple three-page study with a graph showing that while the prime rate was going down, interest on consumer loans was going up. Dan Rather showed the graph and discussed the report on the evening news; the publicity helped persuade Congress to pass laws requiring fuller disclosure and some caps on interest rates.[1]

Numbers are no more "objective" than words are: both require interpretation and context to have meaning. On November 1, 1990, both *The Wall Street Journal* and *The Columbus Dispatch* carried stories about General Motors' third-quarter loss, which had been announced the day before. *The Dispatch*'s headline was negative: "GM's $2 Billion Quarterly Loss Biggest Ever." *The Wall Street Journal,* in contrast, saw the loss as a positive strategic move: "Smaller Giant: Huge GM Write-Off Positions Automaker to Show New Growth."[2] The two headlines come from and suggest very different ways to view the loss and GM's potential.

The same numbers can be presented in different ways to create very different impressions. In 1999, a pharmaceutical company announced that, in a year-long clinical test, people taking its anti-obesity drug lost 50% more weight than people receiving a placebo. That statement is true but isn't a reason to rush to a doctor to get a prescription. People in the group getting only the placebo lost an average of 13 pounds. People taking the drug lost an extra 6½ pounds—in a year.[3]

When to Use Visuals

The ease of creating visuals by computer may make people use them uncritically. Use a visual only to achieve a specific purpose. Never put in numbers or visuals just because you have them; instead, use them to convey information the audience needs or wants.

In your rough draft, use visuals

- **To see that ideas are presented completely.** A table, for example, can show you whether you've included all the items in a comparison.
- **To find relationships.** For example, charting sales on a map may show that the sales representatives who made quota all have territories on the East or the West Coast. Is the central United States suffering a recession? Is the product one that appeals to coastal lifestyles? Is advertising reaching the coasts but not the central states? Even if you don't use the visual in your final document, creating the map may lead you to questions you wouldn't otherwise ask.

In the final presentation or document, use visuals

- **To make points vivid.** Readers skim memos and reports; a visual catches the eye. The brain processes visuals immediately. Understanding words—written or oral—takes more time.
- **To emphasize material** that might be skipped if it were buried in a paragraph. The beginning and end are places of emphasis. However, something has to go in the middle, especially in a long document. Visuals allow you to emphasize important material, wherever it logically falls.

■ **To present material more compactly and with less repetition** than words alone would require. Words can call attention to the main points of the visual, without repeating all of the visual's information.

The number of visuals you will need depends on your purposes, the kind of information, and the audience. You'll use more visuals when you want to show relationships and to persuade, when the information is complex or contains extensive numerical data, and when the audience values visuals. Some audiences and discourse communities (◄▦ p. 59) expect oral presentations and reports to use lots of visuals. Other audiences may see visuals as frivolous and time spent making visuals as time wasted. For these audiences, you'd sharply limit the number of visuals you use—but you'd still use them when your own purposes and the information called for them.

Designing Visuals

Use these six steps to create good visuals:

1. Check the source of the data.
2. Determine the story you want to tell.
3. Choose the right visual for the story.
4. Follow the conventions for designing typical visuals.
5. Use color and decoration with restraint.
6. Be sure the visual is accurate and ethical.

Let's discuss each of these briefly.

1. Check the Source of the Data.

Your chart is only as good as the underlying data. Check to be sure that your data come from a reliable source. See "Identifying the source of the Data" in Chapter 14 ◄▦.

You may be able to use data based on assumptions and definitions in careful titles or notes: "Under the Fast-Growth Scenario, Sales Will Triple." "Over One-Fourth of Small Businesses Last Eight Years under Original Owners." If the data themselves are unreliable, you're better off not using visuals. The visual picture will be more powerful than verbal disclaimers, and the audience will be misled.

2. Determine the Story You Want to Tell.

Every visual should tell a story. Stories can be expressed in complete sentences that describe something that happens or changes. The sentence also serves as the title of the visual.

Not a story:	US Sales, 1996–2000
Possible stories:	Forty Percent of Our Sales Were to New Customers.
	Growth Was Highest in the South.
	Sales Increased from 1996 to 2000.
	Most Sales Representatives Have 2–5 Years' Experience.
	Sales Were Highest in the Areas with More Sales Representatives.

Stories that tell us what we already know are rarely interesting. Instead, good stories may

■ Support a hunch you have.

■ Surprise you or challenge so-called common knowledge.

Why the Numbers Don't Add Up*

How many people work at home? We don't know. Even different US government agencies get different numbers, because their calculations are based on different data.

In 1997, the US Bureau of Labor Statistics counted 4.1 million people working at home who were not incorporated.

The same year, the Small Business Administration estimated that there were 9.2 million home-based businesses. Those figures included businesses whether they were incorporated or not—but counted them only if they had at least $500 in receipts.

Business tax returns don't yield a good count, because someone who has three businesses fills out three separate returns.

*Based on *Inc. State of Small Business 2001*, 39.

Interpreting Statistics*

In 1982, Stephen Jay Gould, author of *The Panda's Thumb* and other essays on evolution, learned that he had a rare, incurable form of cancer. Patients lived a median of eight months after the disease was discovered.

Gould knew that "lived a median of eight months" meant half the people lived longer. Some of them lived a lot longer.

Furthermore, he knew that the statistics referred to cases treated by conventional means. Gould entered an experimental protocol. He thus had the opportunity to be in a new group with a new median and a new distribution curve.

Gould was young; his disease had been caught early; he had excellent medical care; he wanted to live; and he knew enough about statistics to read the data correctly and avoid despair.

As this book goes to press 20 years after the initial diagnosis, Gould is alive and doing well. And he's still writing essays helping us understand science and statistics.

*Based on Stephen Jay Gould, "The Median Isn't the Message," *Discover*, June 1985, 40–42.

■ Show trends or changes you didn't know existed.

■ Have commercial or social significance.

■ Provide information needed for action.

■ Be personally relevant to you and the audience.

To find stories,

1. Focus on a topic (purchases of cars, who likes jazz, etc.).
2. Simplify the data on that topic and convert the numbers to simple, easy-to-understand units.
3. Look for relationships and changes. For example, compare two or more groups: do men and women have the same attitudes? Look for changes over time. Look for items that can be seen as part of the same group. For example, to find stories about entertainers' incomes, you might compare the number of writers, actors, and musicians in three rankings.
4. Process the data to find more stories. Find the average and the median (◄■ p. 391). Calculate the percentage change from one year to the next.

When you think you have a story, test it against all the data to be sure it's accurate.

Some stories are simple straight lines: "Sales Increased." But other stories are more complex, with exceptions or outlying cases. Such stories will need more nuanced titles to do justice to the story. And sometimes the best story arises from the juxtaposition of two or more stories. In Figure 15.1, *Business-Week* uses three **paired graphs** to tell a complex story.

Gene Zelazny points out that the audience should be able to *see* what the message *says:*

> [D]oes the chart support the title; and does the title reinforce the chart? So if I *say* in my title that "sales have increased significantly" I want to *see* a trend moving up at a sharp angle. If not, if the trend parallels the baseline, it's an instant clue that the chart needs more thinking.[4]

Almost every data set allows you to tell several stories. You must choose the story you want to tell. Dumps of uninterpreted data confuse and frustrate your audience; they undercut the credibility and goodwill you want to create.

Sometimes several stories will be important. When that's the case, you'll need a separate visual for each.

3. Choose the Right Visual for the Story.

Visuals are not interchangeable. Good writers choose the visual that best matches the purpose of presenting the data.

■ Use a **table** when the reader needs to be able to identify exact values. (See Figure 15.2a.)

■ Use a chart or graph when you want the reader to focus on relationships.[5]

   ■ To compare a part to the whole, use a **pie chart.** (See Figure 15.2b.)

   ■ To compare one item to another item, use a **map** or a **bar chart.** (See Figure 15.2c.)

   ■ To compare items over time, use a **bar chart** or a **line graph.** (See Figure 15.2d.)

   ■ To show frequency or distribution, use a **line graph** or **bar chart.** (See Figure 15.2e.)

   ■ To show correlations, use a **bar chart,** a **line graph,** or a **dot chart.** (See Figure 15.2f.)

FIGURE 15.1   A Complex Story Using Paired Graphs

The Big Headache

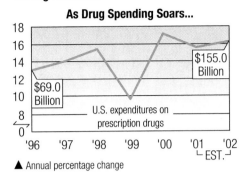

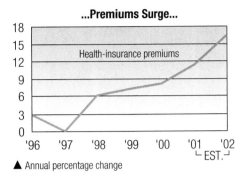

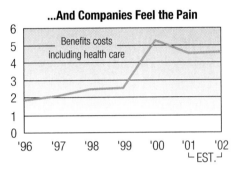

▲ Annual percentage change, year ended June 30

Data: Bureau of Labor Statistics, economy.com, Health Care Financing Administration, Kaiser Family Foundation, William M. Mercer Inc.

Source: BusinessWeek, September 17, 2001, 46–47.

- ▪ Use photographs to create a sense of authenticity or show the item in use. If the item is especially big or small, include something in the photograph that can serve as a reference point: a dime, a person.
- ▪ Use drawings to show dimensions or emphasize detail.
- ▪ Use sketches to show processes in an interesting way.
- ▪ Use maps to emphasize location.
- ▪ Use **Gantt charts** to show timelines for proposals or projects.

4. Follow the Conventions for Designing Typical Visuals.

Every visual should contain six components:

1. A title that tells the story that the visual shows.
2. A clear indication of what the data are. For example, what people *say* they did is not necessarily what they really did. An estimate of what a number will be in the future differs from numbers in the past that have already been measured.
3. Clearly labeled units.
4. Labels or legends identifying axes, colors, symbols, and so forth.
5. The source of the data, if you created the visual from data someone else gathered and compiled.
6. The source of the visual, if you reproduce a visual someone else created.

FIGURE 15.2   Choose the Visual to Fit the Story

US sales reach $44.5 million.

	Millions of dollars		
	1998	2000	2002
Northeast	10.2	10.8	11.3
South	7.6	8.5	10.4
Midwest	8.3	6.8	9.3
West	11.3	12.1	13.5
Totals	37.4	38.2	44.5

a. Tables show exact values.

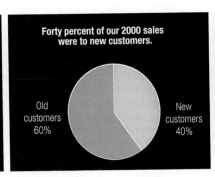

b. Pie charts compare a component to the whole.

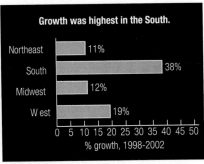

c. Bar charts compare items or show distribution or correlation.

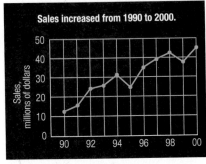

d. Line charts compare items over time or show distribution or correlation.

e. Bar charts can show frequency.

f. Dot charts show correlation.

Formal visuals are divided into tables and figures. **Tables** are numbers or words arrayed in rows and columns; **figures** are everything else. In a document, formal visuals have both numbers and titles, e.g., "Figure 1. The Falling Cost of Computer Memory, 1990–2000." In an oral presentation, the title is usually used without the number: "The Falling Cost of Computer Memory, 1990–2000." The title should tell the story so that the audience knows what to look for in the visual and why it is important. **Spot visuals** are informal visuals that are inserted directly into the text; they do not have numbers or titles.

Tables

Use tables only when you want the audience to focus on specific numbers. Graphs convey less specific information but are always more memorable. Figure 15.3 illustrates the basic structure of tables. The **boxhead** is the variable whose label is at the top; the **stub** is the variable listed on the side.

- Use common, understandable units. Round off to simplify the data (e.g., 35% rather than 35.27%; 44.5 million rather than 44,503,276).
- Provide column and row totals or averages when they're relevant.
- Put the items you want readers to compare in columns rather than in rows to facilitate mental subtraction and division.
- When you have many rows, screen alternate entries or double-space after every five entries to help readers line up items accurately.

FIGURE 15.3 Tables Show Exact Values

Table Number – Title

	Boxhead		
Stub			

Rank		Company(Country)	Market Value
2001	2000		Billions of U.S. Dollars
1	1	General Electric (US)	486.67
2	4	Microsoft (US)	369.10
3	5	Exxon Mobil (US)	306.67
4	20	Pfizer (US)	270.80
5	11	Citigroup (US)	260.80
6	7	Wal-Mart Stores (US)	231.15
7	29	AOL Time Warner (US)	230.48
8	10	Royal Dutch/Shell Group (Neth./Britain)	216.50
9	12	BP (Britain)	199.79
10	14	International Business Machines (US)	196.86

Source: "US Companies Dominate the Business Week Global 1000," *Business Week*, July 9, 2001, p. 75.

Pie charts

Pie charts force the audience to measure area. Research shows that people can judge position or length (which a bar chart uses) much more accurately than they judge area. The data in any pie chart can be put in a bar chart.[6] Therefore, use a pie chart only when you are comparing one segment to the whole. When you are comparing one segment to another segment, use a bar chart, a line graph, or a map—even though the data may be expressed in percentages.

- Start at 12 o'clock with the largest percentage or the percentage you want to focus on. Go clockwise to each smaller percentage or to each percentage in some other logical order.
- Make the chart a perfect circle. Perspective circles distort the data.
- Limit the number of segments to no more than seven. If your data have more divisions, combine the smallest or the least important into a single "miscellaneous" or "other" category.
- Label the segments outside the circle. Internal labels are hard to read.

Bar charts

Bar charts are easy to interpret because they ask people to compare distance along a common scale, which most people judge accurately. Bar charts are useful in a variety of situations: to compare one item to another, to compare items over time, and to show correlations. Use horizontal bars when your labels are long; when the labels are short, either horizontal or vertical bars will work.

- ▪ Order the bars in a logical or chronological order.
- ▪ Put the bars close enough together to make comparison easy.
- ▪ Label both horizontal and vertical axes.
- ▪ Put all labels inside the bars or outside them. When some labels are inside and some are outside, the labels carry the visual weight of longer bars, distorting the data.
- ▪ Make all the bars the same width.
- ▪ Use different colors for different bars only when their meanings are different: estimates as opposed to known numbers, negative as opposed to positive numbers.
- ▪ Avoid using perspective. Perspective makes the values harder to read and can make comparison difficult.

Several varieties of bar charts exist. See Figure 15.4 for examples.

- ▪ **Grouped bar charts** allow you to compare either several aspects of each item or several items over time. Group together the items you want to compare. Figure 15.4a shows that sales were highest in the west each year. If we wanted to show how sales had changed in each region, the bars should be grouped by region, not by year.
- ▪ **Segmented, subdivided,** or **stacked bars** sum the components of an item. It's hard to identify the values in specific segments; grouped bar charts are almost always easier to use.

FIGURE 15.4   Varieties of Bar Charts

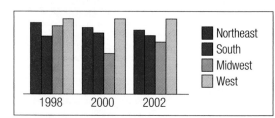

a. Grouped bar charts compare several aspects of each item, or several items over time.

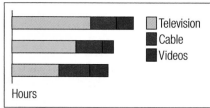

b. Segmented, subdivided, or **stacked bars** sum the components of an item.

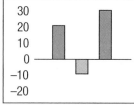

c. Deviation bar charts identify positive and negative values.

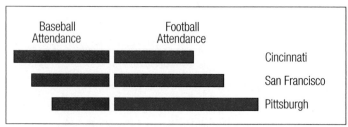

d. Paired bar charts show the correlation between two items.

e. Histograms or **pictograms** use images to create the bars.

- **Deviation bar charts** identify positive and negative values, or winners and losers.
- **Paired bar charts** show the correlation between two items.
- **Histograms** or **pictograms** use images to create the bars.

Line graphs

Line graphs are also easy to interpret. Use line graphs to compare items over time, to show frequency or distribution, and to show correlations.

- Label both horizontal and vertical axes.
- When time is a variable, put it on the horizontal axis.
- Avoid using more than three different lines on one graph. Even three lines may be too many if they cross each other.
- Avoid using perspective. Perspective makes the values harder to read and can make comparison difficult.

Line graphs with the area below the line filled in are sometimes called **landscape graphs.**

Dot charts

Dot charts show correlations or other large data sets.

- Label both horizontal and vertical axes.
- Keep the dots fairly small. If they get too big, they no longer mark data "points"; some of the detail is lost.

Photographs

Photographs convey a sense of authenticity. The photo of a prototype helps convince investors that a product can be manufactured; the photo of a devastated area can suggest the need for government grants or private donations.

You may need to **crop,** or trim, a photo for best results. If someone else is doing the production, mark the places for cropping in the margins of the photo or attach nonsticky paper. Never write or mark on the photo or the negative.

A growing problem with photos is that they may be edited or staged, purporting to show something as reality even though it never occurred.

Drawings

The richness of detail in photos makes them less effective than drawings for focusing on details. With a drawing, the artist can provide as much or as little detail as is needed to make the point; different parts of the drawing can show different layers or levels of detail. Drawings are also better for showing structures underground, undersea, or in the atmosphere.

Sketches

Unlike drawings, sketches omit details. In the sketch in Figure 15.5, no attempt is made to draw a specific person; instead, a generic male is shown. Sketches are good to help readers visualize processes. Here, the sketch shows how workers in Mexico get paid in a virtual system that eliminates paychecks and the need to have a bank account.

Putting Business on the Map*

Geographic information systems (GIS) software lets you map information on your own PC.

Archadeck in Richmond, Virginia, builds decks. Using a GIS "prospect-finder" called GeoWizard, Archadeck's marketing director identifies homeowners living near new projects. Before construction starts, likely prospects get a soft-sell notice asking them to call Archadeck if there's too much noise. Once construction starts, a second postcard invites people to stop by to take a look. GeoWizard has cut direct mail costs and, by providing better lists, tripled the response rate.

Another company learned that its high-end garden implement stores were saturating some affluent areas—and competing against themselves—while neglecting others. GIS software showed the right population mix for new stores.

*Based on Kazumi Tanaka, "Putting Your Business on the Map," *Inc. Technology* (1996), 94–99.

FIGURE 15.5   Sketches Can Show Processes

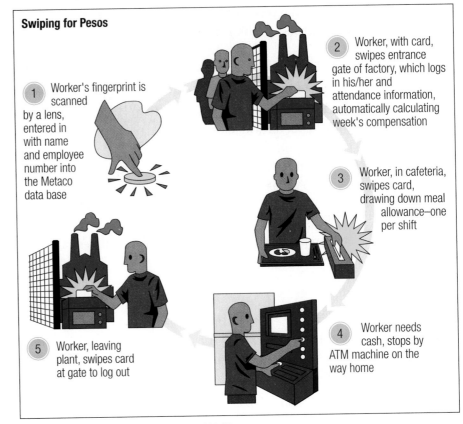

Source: The Wall Street Journal, November 23, 1998, B1.

Maps

Use maps to emphasize location or to compare items in different locations. Several computer software packages now allow users to generate local, state, national, or global maps, adding color or shadings, and labels. (See Figure 15.6.)

- Label states, provinces, or countries if it's important that people be able to identify levels in areas other than their own.
- Avoid using perspective. Perspective makes the values harder to read and can make comparison difficult.

Gantt charts

Gantt charts are bar charts used to show schedules. They're most commonly used in proposals. (See Figure 15.7.)

- Color-code bars to indicate work planned and work completed.
- Use a red outline to indicate **critical activities,** which must be completed on time if the project is to be completed by the due date.
- Use diamonds to indicate progress reports, major achievements, or other accomplishments.

5. Use Color and Decoration with Restraint.

Color makes visuals more dramatic, but it creates at least two problems. First, readers try to interpret color, an interpretation that may not be appropriate.

FIGURE 15.6   Maps Show Where High-Tech Jobs Are

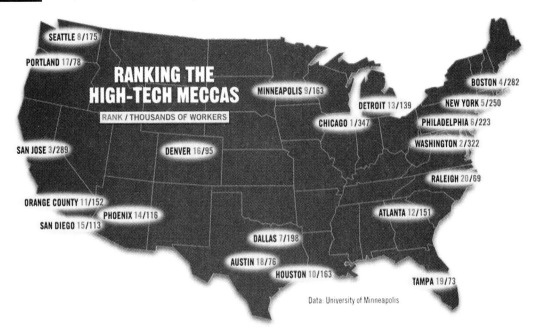

Source: Stan Cook "Rust Belts Try Tech Belts," *BusinessWeek,* August 13, 2001, p. 55.

FIGURE 15.7   Gantt Charts Show the Schedule for Completing a Project

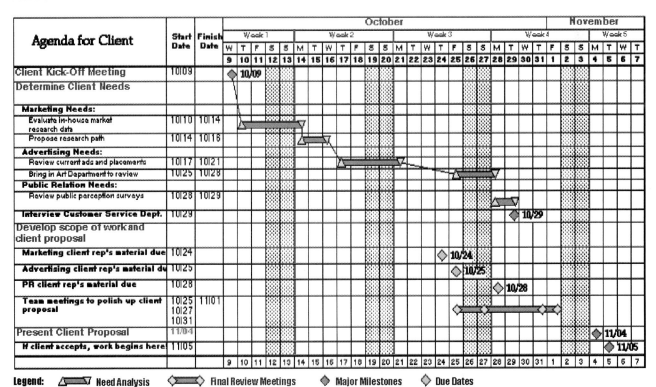

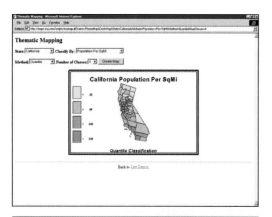

InSite

www.esri.com

To see how mapping works, visit the Web site developed by Environmental Systems Research Institute. Scroll down to "Demography: Map Census Data for Any State in the United States" and click. Use the boxes to find your state and the variable you want to map: population, rent, and so forth.

Perhaps the best use of color occurs in the weather maps printed daily in many newspapers. Blue seems to fit cold; red seems to fit hot temperatures. Second, meanings assigned to colors differ depending on the audience's national background and profession.

As we have seen in Chapter 11, connotations for color vary from culture to culture. Blue suggests masculinity in the United States, criminality in France, strength or fertility in Egypt, and villainy in Japan. Red is sometimes used to suggest danger or *stop* in the United States; it means *go* in China and is associated with festivities. Red suggests masculinity or aristocracy in France, death in Korea, blasphemy in some African countries, and luxury in many parts of the world. Yellow suggests caution or cowardice in the United States, prosperity in Egypt, grace in Japan, and femininity in many parts of the world.[7]

These general cultural associations may be superseded by corporate, national, or professional associations. Some people associate blue with IBM or Hewlett-Packard and red with Coca-Cola, communism, or Japan. People in specific professions learn other meanings for colors. Blue suggests *reliability* to financial managers, *water* or *coldness* to engineers, and *death* to health care professionals. Red means *losing money* to financial managers, *danger* to engineers, but *healthy* to health care professionals. Green usually means *safe* to engineers, but *infected* to health care professionals.[8]

These various associations suggest that color is safest with a homogenous audience that you know well. In an increasingly multicultural workforce, color may send signals you do not intend.

When you do use color in visuals, L. G. Thorell and W. J. Smith suggest these guidelines:[9]

- Use no more than five colors when colors have meanings.
- Use glossy paper to make colors more vivid.
- Be aware that colors on a computer screen always look brighter than the same colors on paper because the screen sends out light.

In any visual, use as little shading and as few lines as are necessary for clarity. Don't clutter up the visual with extra marks. When you design black-and-white graphs, use shades of gray rather than stripes, wavy lines, and checks to indicate different segments or items.

Resist the temptation to make your visual "artistic" or "relevant" by turning it into a picture or adding clip art. **Clip art** consists of predrawn images that you can import into your newsletter, sign, or graph. A small drawing of a car in the corner of a line graph showing the number of miles driven is acceptable in an oral presentation but out of place in a written report. Turning a line graph into a highway to show miles driven makes it harder to read: it's hard to separate the data line from lines that are merely decorative. Edward Tufte uses the term **chartjunk** for decorations that at best are irrelevant to the visual and at worst mislead the reader.[10] If you use clip art, be sure that the images of people show a good mix of both sexes, various races and ages, and various physical conditions.

6. Be Sure the Visual Is Accurate and Ethical.

Always double-check your visuals to be sure the information is accurate. Also, many visuals have accurate labels but misleading visual shapes. Visuals communicate quickly; audiences remember the shape, not the labels. If the reader has to study the labels to get the right picture, the visual is unethical even if the labels are accurate.

Figure 15.8 is distorted by chartjunk and dimensionality. In an effort to make the visual interesting, the artist used a picture of a young man (presumably an engineer) rather than simple bars. By using a photograph rather than a bar, the chart implies that all engineers are young, nerdy-looking white men. Women, people of color, and men with other appearances are excluded. The photograph also makes it difficult to compare the numbers. The number represented by the tallest figure is not quite 5 times as great as the number represented by the shortest figure, yet the tallest figure takes up 12 times as much space and appears even bigger than that. Two-dimensional figures distort data by multiplying the apparent value by the width as well as by the height—four times for every doubling in value. Perspective graphs are especially hard for readers to interpret and should be avoided.[11]

Even simple bar and line graphs may be misleading if part of the scale is missing, or truncated. **Truncated graphs** are most acceptable when the audience knows the basic data set well. For example, graphs of the stock market almost never start at zero; they are routinely truncated. This omission is acceptable for audiences who follow the market closely.

Since part of the scale is missing in truncated graphs, small changes seem like major ones. The graph in Figure 15.9, from Philadelphia Suburban's 1994 annual report, seems to show a healthy growth. But a close look at the numbers shows a different story. It turns out that the bottom of the glass is 230,000 customers, not zero. The real growth was 6.4%, not the 300% that the visual shows.[12] Another annual report disguised losses by using a negative base.[13] Because readers expect zero to be the base, they're almost certain to misread the visual. Labels may make the visual literally "accurate," but a visual is unethical if someone who looks at it quickly is likely to misinterpret it.

Data can also be distorted when the context is omitted. As Tufte suggests, a drop may be part of a regular cycle, a correction after an atypical increase, or a permanent drop to a new, lower plateau.

FIGURE 15.8 Chartjunk and Dimensions Distort Data

Source: "Valley Horror Show: The Incredible Shrinking Engineer," Adam Lashinsky, *Fortune*, December 10, 2001, p. 40.

FIGURE 15.9   Truncated Scales Distort Data

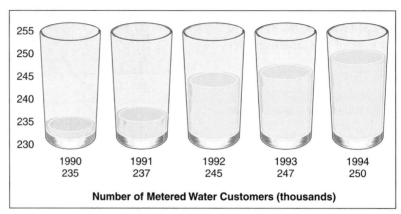

Source: *The Wall Street Journal*, May 25, 1995, B1.

To make your visuals more accurate,

- Differentiate between actual and estimated or projected values.
- When you must truncate a scale, do so clearly with a break in the bars or in the background.
- Avoid perspective and three-dimensional graphs.
- Avoid combining graphs with different scales.
- Use images of people carefully in histographs to avoid sexist, racist, or other exclusionary visual statements.

Integrating Visuals in Your Text

Refer to every visual in your text. Normally one gives the table or figure number in the text but not the title. Put the visual as soon after your reference as space and page design permit. If the visual must go on another page, tell the reader where to find it:

As Figure 3 shows (page 10), . . .

(See Table 2 on page 14.)

Summarize the main point of a visual *before* you present the visual itself. Then when readers get to it, they'll see it as confirmation of your point.

Weak: Listed below are the results.

Better: As Figure 4 shows, sales doubled in the last decade.

The weak statement mirrors the thought processes that occur as the writer processes data: one first categorizes the data in a very general way ("results"); one next looks at the data; and one finally decides what the data mean. But when this mental process becomes the writer's organizing pattern, the reader is forced to duplicate the whole process by which the writer reached a conclusion. Most readers, understandably, are unwilling to do work which the writer is supposed to do, so they will skim or skip the data presented in this unsatisfactory fashion. When the writer finally comes to the point, readers may be unconvinced because they haven't recognized the significance of the evidence in the table. Remember that you are writing not to reveal how your own mind works but to explain something to your readers and to convince them that your analysis is correct.

How much discussion a visual needs depends on the audience, the complexity of the visual, and the importance of the point it makes. If the material is new to the audience, you'll need a fuller explanation than if similar material is presented to this audience every week or month. If the visual is complex, you may want to help the reader find key data points in it. If the point is important, you'll want to discuss its implications in some detail. In contrast, one sentence about a visual may be enough when the audience is already familiar with the topic and the data, when the visual is simple and well designed, and when the information in the visual is a minor part of your proof.

When you discuss visuals, spell out numbers that fall at the beginning of a sentence. If spelling out the number or year is cumbersome, revise the sentence so that it does not begin with a number.

Forty-five percent of the cost goes to pay wages and salaries.

In 2002, euronotes and coins became legal tender.

Put numbers in parentheses at the end of the clause or sentence to make the sentence easier to read:

Hard to read: As Table 4 shows, teachers participate (54%) in more community service groups than do members of the other occupations surveyed; dentists (20.8%) participate in more service groups than do members of five of the other occupations.

Better: As Table 4 shows, teachers participate in more community service groups than do members of the other occupations surveyed (54%); dentists participate in more service groups than do five of the other occupations (20.8%).

Using Visuals in Your Presentation

Visuals for presentations need to be simpler than visuals the audience reads on paper. The table in Figure 15.3, for example, is too complex for a slide. Depending on the point you needed to make, you might be able to cut out one of the columns, round off the data even more, or present the material in a chart rather than a table.

Visuals for presentations should have titles but don't need figure numbers. Do know where each visual is so that you can return to one if someone asks about it during the question period. Decorative clip art, even though technically chartjunk, is acceptable in oral presentations as long as it does not obscure the story you're telling with the visual.

Rather than reading the visual to the audience, summarize the story and then elaborate on what it means for the audience. If you have copies of all the visuals for your audience, hand them out at the beginning of the talk.

Summary of Key Points

- Numbers are not "objective." Like words, they require interpretation and context to make sense.

- In the rough draft, use visuals to see that ideas are presented completely and to see what relationships exist. In the final report, use visuals to make points vivid, to emphasize material that the reader might skip, and to present material more compactly and with less repetition than words alone would require.

- You'll use more visuals when you want to show relationships and to persuade, when the information is complex or contains extensive numerical data, and when the audience values visuals.

Japanese Children and Statistics*

Japanese children outscore US children on math tests. The difference is not just the result of a longer school year, but of a different national attitude toward numbers.

In Japan, statistics are the subject of a holiday, local and national conventions, award ceremonies and nationwide statistical collections and graph-drawing contests. "This year," said Yoshiharu Takahashi, a Government statistician, "we had almost 30,000 entries. Actually, we had 29,836."

Entries in the [children's] statistical graph contest were screened three times by judges, who gave first prize this year to the work of five 7-year-olds. Their graph creation, titled, "Mom, play with us more often," was the result of a survey of 32 classmates on the frequency that mothers play with their offspring and the reasons given for not doing so. . . . Other children's work examined the frequency of family phone usage and correlated the day's temperature with cicada singing.

*Paragraphs 2 and 3 quoted from Andrew H. Malcolm, "Data-Loving Japanese Rejoice on Statistics Day," *New York Times*, October 28, 1977, A1.

- Pick data to tell a story, to make a point.
- To find stories,
    1. Focus on a topic.
    2. Simplify the data.
    3. Look for relationships and changes.
- **Paired graphs** juxtapose two or more simple stories to create a more powerful story.
- Visuals are not interchangeable. The best visual depends on the kind of data and the point you want to make with the data.
- Tables are numbers or words arrayed in rows and columns; figures are everything else. Formal visuals have both numbers and titles that indicate what to look for in the visual or why the visual is included and is worth examining.
- Visuals must present data accurately, both literally and by implication. **Chartjunk** denotes decorations that at best are irrelevant to the visual and at worst mislead the reader. **Truncated graphs** omit part of the scale and visually mislead readers. Perspective graphs and graphs with negative bases mislead readers.
- Summarize the main point of a visual before it appears in the text.
- Visuals for presentations need to be simpler than visuals on paper.
- How much discussion a visual needs depends on the audience, the complexity of the visual, and the importance of the point it makes.

CHAPTER 15   Exercises and Problems

Getting Started

15.1   Identifying Stories

Of the following, which are stories?
1. Results
2. Computer Use
3. Computer Prices Fall
4. More Single Parents Buy Computers than Do Any Other Group
5. Where Your Tax Dollars Go
6. Sixty Percent of Tax Dollars Pay Entitlements, Interest
7. Percent of Tax Dollars Spent on Entitlements

15.2   Choosing Titles for Stories and Visuals

Which is the best title in each group? Why? Would the other titles ever be acceptable? Why or why not?

1. a. Single Women Are Buying More Computers than Are Single Men.
   b. More Women than Men Will Live Alone with Computers.
   c. What Do Single Women Want? Computers!
2. a. Lawyers in Private Practice Make More than Those in Public Practice.
   b. Lawyers Should Be Private in Choosing Their Salaries.
   c. Private Practice Pays.
3. a. The Poor Give More.
   b. People Making under $11,000 a Year Gave a Larger Percentage of Their Incomes to Churches than Did People Making over $100,000 a Year.
   c. People Making Least Give the Highest Percentage to Church.

15.3   Matching Visuals with Stories

What visual(s) would make it easiest to see each of the following stories?

1. Canada buys 20% of US exports.
2. Undergraduate enrollment rises, but graduate enrollment declines.
3. Population growth will be greatest in the West and South.
4. Open communication ranks Number 1 in reasons to take a job.

5. Companies with fewer than 200 employees created a larger percentage of new jobs than did companies with more than 5,000 employees.
6. Men are more likely than women to see their chances for advancement as good.
7. The NFL teams with the best records aren't necessarily the most profitable.

15.4   Evaluating Visuals

Evaluate each of the following visuals.

▪ Is visual's message clear?
▪ Is it the right visual for the story?
▪ Is the visual designed appropriately? Is color, if any, used appropriately?

▪ Is the visual free from chartjunk?
▪ Does the visual distort data or mislead the reader in any way?

1.

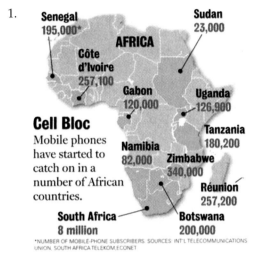

Source: Newsweek, August 27, 2001.

2.

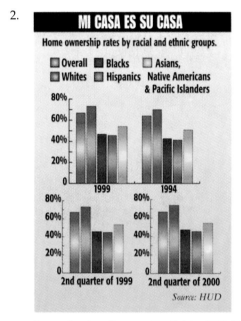

Source: American Demographics, October 2000, 24.

3.

How My Time Will Be Used

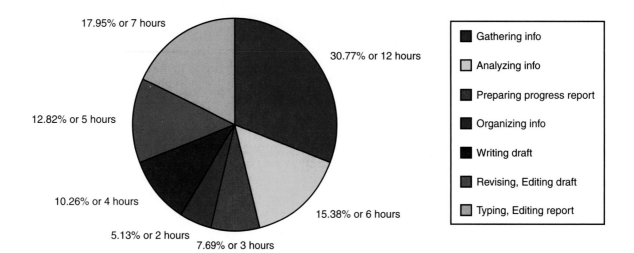

17.95% or 7 hours

30.77% or 12 hours

12.82% or 5 hours

10.26% or 4 hours

15.38% or 6 hours

5.13% or 2 hours

7.69% or 3 hours

■ Gathering info

□ Analyzing info

■ Preparing progress report

■ Organizing info

■ Writing draft

■ Revising, Editing draft

□ Typing, Editing report

4.

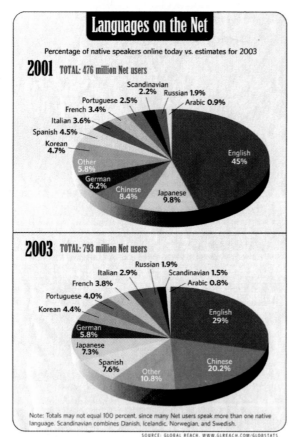

Languages on the Net

Percentage of native speakers online today vs. estimates for 2003

2001 TOTAL: 476 million Net users

Scandinavian 2.2%   Russian 1.9%
Portuguese 2.5%   Arabic 0.9%
French 3.4%
Italian 3.6%
Spanish 4.5%
Korean 4.7%
Other 5.8%
German 6.2%
Chinese 8.4%
Japanese 9.8%
English 45%

2003 TOTAL: 793 million Net users

Russian 1.9%
Italian 2.9%   Scandinavian 1.5%
French 3.8%   Arabic 0.8%
Portuguese 4.0%
Korean 4.4%
German 5.8%
Japanese 7.3%
Spanish 7.6%
Other 10.8%
English 29%
Chinese 20.2%

Note: Totals may not equal 100 percent, since many Net users speak more than one native language. Scandinavian combines Danish, Icelandic, Norwegian, and Swedish.

SOURCE: GLOBAL REACH, WWW.GLREACH.COM/GLOBSTATS

Source: Business 2.0, November 2001, 121.

5.

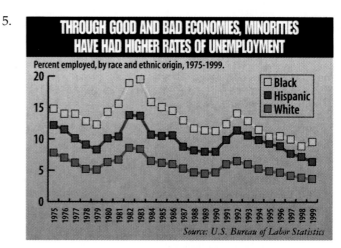

THROUGH GOOD AND BAD ECONOMIES, MINORITIES HAVE HAD HIGHER RATES OF UNEMPLOYMENT

Percent employed, by race and ethnic origin, 1975-1999.

□ Black
■ Hispanic
■ White

Source: U.S. Bureau of Labor Statistics

Source: American Demographics, June 2000, 22.

6. **Half Full...**

Both at home and at work, more and more consumers enjoy broadband access to the Web, which makes online entertainment a better experience (projections, in millions)

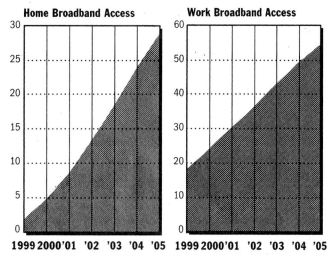

Source: Media Metrix

Source: The Wall Street Journal, March 26, 2001, R6.

7.

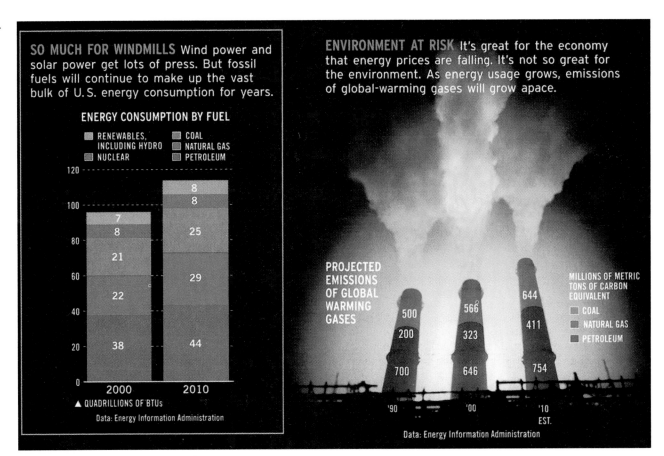

Source: BusinessWeek, August 27, 2001, 97.

8.

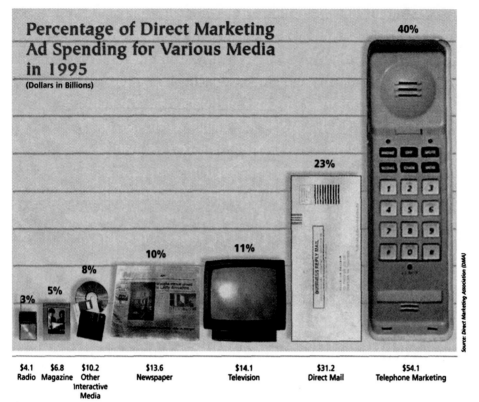

Percentage of Direct Marketing Ad Spending for Various Media in 1995

(Dollars in Billions)

| 3% | 5% | 8% | 10% | 11% | 23% | 40% |

| $4.1 Radio | $6.8 Magazine | $10.2 Other Interactive Media | $13.6 Newspaper | $14.1 Television | $31.2 Direct Mail | $54.1 Telephone Marketing |

Source: Direct Marketing Association (DMA)

Source: Direct Marketing, Special Advertising Section, np.

Web Page

15.5   Creating a Web Guide to Graphs

Create a Web page explaining how to create good visuals. Offer general principles and at least seven links to examples of good and poor visuals. (More is better.) At the top of the page, offer an overview of what the page covers. At the bottom of the page, put the creation/update date and your name and e-mail address.

As Your Instructor Directs,

a. Turn in two laser copies of your page(s). On another page, give the URLs for each link.

b. Turn in one laser copy of your page(s) and a disk with the HTML code and .gif files.

c. Write a memo to your instructor (1) identifying the audience for which the page is designed and explaining (2) the search strategies you used to find material on this topic, (3) why you chose the pages and information you've included, and (4) why you chose the layout and graphics you've used.

d. Present your page orally to the class.

Hints:

■ Searching for words (*graphs, maps, Gantt charts, data*) will turn up only pages with those words. Also check pages on topics that may use graphs to explain their data: finance, companies' performance, sports, cost of living, exports, and so forth.

■ In addition to finding good and bad visuals on the Web, you can also scan in examples you find in newspapers, magazines, and textbooks.

■ If you have more than nine links, chunk them in small groups under headings.

Visuals, Memos, and Report Assignments

15.6 Creating Visuals

As Your Instructor Directs,

a. Identify visuals that you might use to help analyze each of the following data sets.

b. Identify and create a visual for one or more of the stories in each set.

c. Identify additional information that would be needed for other stories related to these data sets.

1. Online sales

	1997 sales	2001 estimated sales
Financial services	$1.2 billion	$5 billion
Apparel and footware	$92 million	$514 million
PC hardware and software	$863 million	$3.8 billion
Entertainment	$298 million	$2.7 billion
Travel	$654 million	$7.4 billion
Books and music	$156 million	$1.1 billion
Ticket event sales	$79 million	$2 billion
Business-to-business sales	$8 billion	$183 billion

Source: "Online Sales Are Soaring," *BusinessWeek*, June 22, 1998, 124–25.

2. Women of color in corporate management

Catalyst surveyed 1,700 women (African American: 54%; Asian American: 21%; Hispanic: 24%)

Satisfied with content of job: 57% (African American: 55.2%; Asian American: 53.4%; Hispanic: 65.8%)

Believe affirmative action helped them get hired and/or promoted (African American: 54.4%; Asian American: 29.5%; Hispanic: 42%)

Believe opportunities for advancement have improved: (African American: 47.9%; Asian American: 41.8; Hispanic: 50%)

Plan to leave current employer: 21.6% (African American: 24.5%; Asian American: 19.3%; Hispanic: 16.7%)

Source: "Hispanic Professional Women Say Opportunities Looking Good," *Hispanic Business*, May 1998, 70.

3. Responses to TV commercials

Exhibit III: Percent of Adults Who Report They Often Respond to Television Commercials in Selected Ways

	TOTAL	FEMALE	MALE
Watch commercials	22%	19%	24%
Turn down the sound	14	13	14
Change channels	27	31	24
Leave television	45	44	47
Get annoyed	51	51	50
Talk to others, ignoring commercials	35	36	34
Talk to others about commercials	14	13	16
Get amused by funny commercials	26	24	29
Pay attention to information on new products and services	10	8	11
Fast forward through commercials when watching a taped program	35	38	32
Learn about products and services of interest	17	14	19

Source: The Roper Organization, 1993

Source: "Special Report," Internet Advertising Bureau, supplement to *Advertising Age*, Spring 1998, 68A.

15.7 Interpreting Data

As Your Instructor Directs,

a. Identify at least seven stories in one or more of the following data sets.

b. Create visuals for three of the stories.

c. Write a memo to your instructor explaining why you chose these stories and why you chose these visuals to display them.

d. Write a memo to some group that might be interested in your findings, presenting your visuals as part of a short report. Possible groups include career counselors, radio stations, advertising agencies, and Mothers Against Drunk Driving.

e. Brainstorm additional stories you could tell with additional data. Specify the kind of data you would need.

1. Data on Tipping

Tipping Made Easy

The vast majority (74 percent) of Americans tip their waiter or waitress a percentage of the final bill, about 17 percent on average. But 22 percent tip a flat amount instead, $4.67 on average.

	PEOPLE WHO TIP A PERCENTAGE OF THE BILL		PEOPLE WHO TIP A FLAT AMOUNT		PEOPLE WHO DON'T TIP
		AVG. PERCENT		AVG. AMOUNT	
Waiter or waitress	74%	17%	22%	$4.67	2%
Bartender	20%	16%	48%	$1.85*	18%
Barber, hair stylist, or cosmetician	26%	17%	52%	$4.21	18%
Cab or limousine driver	31%	14%	43%	$5.55	16%
Food delivery person	31%	15%	50%	$2.88	12%
Hotel maid	14%	14%	53%	$8.08**	26%
Skycap or bellhop	N/A	N/A	71%	$3.68***	10%
Masseuse	26%	16%	28%	$7.50	25%
Usher at theatre, sporting events, etc.	5%	13%	17%	$5.26	70%

*for one drink; ** for a two-night stay; *** for two bags
Note: "No Answer/Refused" not shown

Source: Taylor Nelson Sofres Intersearch

Beauty Gets Bucks

While only 11 percent of all Americans say they give a bigger tip to service providers they find attractive, single people are twice as likely to make a habit of it (16 percent) than their married counterparts (8 percent).

PERCENTAGE OF AMERICANS WHO SAY THEY TIP MORE WHEN THEIR SERVICE PROVIDER IS:

	OVERALL	MEN	WOMEN	MARRIED	UNMARRIED	WHITE	BLACK
Older than others who usually do the job	20%	17%	22%	16%	24%	18%	30%
A student	25%	24%	27%	25%	26%	24%	36%
A parent	17%	14%	19%	17%	16%	16%	27%
Attractive	11%	17%	5%	8%	16%	11%	14%
Someone I know	38%	38%	38%	34%	42%	39%	29%
A female	6%	9%	3%	4%	9%	6%	8%
A male	3%	3%	3%	3%	4%	3%	6%
Disabled	33%	34%	32%	33%	34%	32%	47%
A racial minority	3%	3%	3%	2%	4%	2%	9%
Flirtatious	11%	17%	5%	7%	15%	11%	9%

Source: Taylor Nelson Sofres Intersearch

Source: American Demographics, May 2001, 11.

2. Projected drinking patterns, 1997–2007

HAPPY HOUR IN AMERICA

(projected thousands of adults who drank any alcoholic beverage in the past six months, by sex and age, 1997, 2000, and 2007, and percent change, 1997–2000, and 1997–2007)

	1997	2000	2007	percent change 1997–2000	percent change 1997–2007
MEN					
Total	54,481	54,472	54,419	0.0%	−0.1%
21 to 24 ..	4,579	4,596	4,685	0.4	2.3
25 to 34 ..	13,446	12,273	11,268	−8.7	−16.2
35 to 44 ..	14,182	14,140	12,287	−0.3	−13.4
45 to 54 ..	10,304	11,201	12,558	8.7	21.9
55 to 64 ..	5,465	5,798	7,088	6.1	29.7
65 and older	6,506	6,465	6,534	−0.6	0.4
WOMEN					
Total	47,637	46,890	44,948	−1.6%	−5.6%
21 to 24 ..	3,649	3,573	3,375	−2.1	−7.5
25 to 34 ..	11,315	10,156	8,864	−10.2	−21.7
35 to 44 ..	12,691	12,531	10,746	−1.3	−15.3
45 to 54 ..	8,838	9,466	10,197	7.1	15.4
55 to 64 ..	5,062	5,348	6,486	5.7	28.1
65 and older	6,083	5,815	5,279	−4.4	−13.2

Source: Mediamark Research, Inc., Census Bureau, and American Demographics

SIPPING IN THE 21ST CENTURY

(projected thousands of men and women who drank alcohol in the past six months, by type of alcohol, 1997 and 2007, and percent change 1997–2007)

	1997	2007	percent change 1997–2007
MEN			
Any	54,481	54,419	−0.1%
Wine	24,972	21,751	−12.9
Beer	46,549	46,547	0.0
White goods .	18,530	16,829	−9.2
Brown goods	22,603	18,745	−17.1
WOMEN			
Any	47,637	44,948	−5.6%
Wine	32,045	29,061	−9.3
Beer	28,071	25,761	−8.2
White goods .	18,410	17,064	−7.3
Brown goods	16,326	10,541	−35.4

Note: White goods are distilled spirits, such as vodka and gin; brown goods include whiskey and cognac.

Source: Mediamark Research Inc, Census Bureau, and American Demographics

Source: American Demographics, January 1997, 4, 6.

3. Top Celebrities, 2001

Forbes magazine's Web site provides the full list of 100 top celebrities, explains the methodology, and re-ranks the list on any column. For example, you can click on "money rank" and get a list ordered by earnings. You can also find lists for other years. New lists generally come out each March.

Power Rank	Name	Money Rank	Earnings ($mil)	Web Hits	Press Clips	Magazine Covers	TV/Radio Hits
1	Tom Cruise	13	43.2	139,000	11,715	11	136
2	Tiger Woods	7	53.0	363,000	47,149	5	235
3	Beatles	3	70.0	1,430,000	26,142	1	166
4	Britney Spears	16	38.5	981,000	19,607	5	18
5	Bruce Willis	4	70.0	125,000	8,841	2	74
6	Michael Jordan	17	37.0	261,000	28,350	1	228
7	Backstreet Boys	20	35.5	619,000	11,666	3	80
8	'N Sync	14	42.0	391,000	12,506	5	9
9	Oprah Winfrey	2	150.0	104,000	9,495	0	108
10	Mel Gibson	24	31.8	262,000	9,591	4	84
11	Mike Tyson	10	48.0	125,000	15,770	0	48
12	George Lucas	1	250.0	146,000	4,002	0	27
13	Stephen King	12	44.0	144,000	6,747	1	46
14	Steven Spielberg	8	51.0	152,000	10,950	1	8
15	Michael Schumacher	6	59.0	97,900	8,595	0	20
16	Julia Roberts	51	18.9	136,000	10,422	7	100
17	Shaquille O'Neal	42	24.0	326,000	21,380	2	58
18	Metallica	32	28.0	731,000	5,077	0	87
19	Eddie Murphy	15	39.5	71,700	4,689	0	50
20	J.K. Rowling	19	36.0	336,000	3,109	0	26
21	Dr. Dre	25	31.5	112,000	7,157	1	32
22	Regis Philbin	21	35.0	23,700	10,133	0	139
23	David Copperfield	5	60.0	46,400	2,010	0	21
24	David Letterman	49	20.0	103,000	12,576	2	209
25	Kobe Bryant	48	20.0	140,000	15,554	2	33

Source of data: www.forbes.com/lists.

15.8   Graphing Data from the Web

Find data on the Web about a topic that interests you. Sites with data include the following:

American Demographics Archives
  www.marketingtools.com/search.htm
Catalyst
  www.catalystwomen.org/research
FEDSTATS (links to 70 US government agencies)
  www.fedstats.gov
Statistical Universe (US government statistics back to the 1970s)
  www.cispubs.com
White House Briefing Room (economic issues)
  www.whitehouse.gov/fsbr/esbr.html

As Your Instructor Directs,
a. Identify at least seven stories in the data.
b. Create visuals for three of the stories.
c. Write a memo to your instructor explaining why you chose these stories and why you chose these visuals to display them.
d. Write a memo to some group which might be interested in your findings, presenting your visuals as part of a short report.
e. Print out the data and include it with a copy of your memo or report.

16

Making Oral Presentations

Making Oral Presentations

Guy Kawasaki
CEO, Garage Technology Ventures

A noted speaker and the founder of various personal computer companies, Guy Kawasaki is the CEO of Garage Technology Ventures, a venture capital investment bank that provides funding for high-tech startups. Formerly, he was an Apple Fellow at Apple Computer, Inc.

www.garage.com

At the start of a speech, you have the attention of the audience. The key to keeping their attention is to start fast—for example, don't go into a 10-minute recap of your personal history as fascinating as (only) you think it might be. Get to the meat of the talk. Skip the build-up.

Even an informative presentation has to entertain. Only an interesting, entertaining speaker will get rapt attention. I want intellectual involvement, and it's my job as a speaker to make that happen.

Presentations don't have to use visuals. Indeed, visuals can be crutches for weak speakers. Visuals can emphasize key points, make the talk more interesting, and keep my company's logo on the screen in front of the audience. For a one-hour presentation, I use about 15 PowerPoint slides with short phrases or sentences like "Jump to the next curve."

I talk only about topics that I truly understand. I believe that someone who has nothing relevant to say to an audience shouldn't speak to them. Further, if the audience is relevant, but you have nothing to say (because nothing new has happened), then you should also decline the invitation.

> *"Even an informative presentation has to entertain"*

I used to be very afraid of speaking in public. I've found that there are no magical fixes for this fear—you just have to speak. I speak about 60 times a year as a keynote speaker or moderator. It takes this volume to truly be comfortable, and, I hope, good.

The next-to-last message in a talk should be something positive, uplifting, and optimistic. The last message should be gratefulness. Don't worry about trying to end on a "strong note." You can't pull a bad presentation out of a hole with a clever sentence. The key is for the whole speech to be good, so you can end on an "even note" and be just fine.

Make Your Message Memorable*

At a beverage conference in Spain, Nick Rosa, then president of The NutraSweet Company, began, "Every time I practice soccer with my sons, aged seven and eight, I am reminded of the generation game. When I consider my area of expertise, my boys represent this new generation perfectly. First, they're young. Second, they're thirsty. Third, they have grown up with diet drinks in the fridge." Then Nick launched into his speech. Six months later he met a conference delegate who greeted him by saying, "How's it going? I haven't seen you since that great speech where you talked about your kids."

By adding a personal touch, Nick helped make his speech memorable.

*Quoted from Elizabeth Urech, *Speaking Globally: Effective Presentations across International and Cultural Barriers* (Dover, NH: Kogan Page, 1998), 31.

The power to persuade people to care about something you believe in is crucial to business success. Making a good oral presentation is more than just good delivery: it also involves developing a strategy that fits your audience and purpose, having good content, and organizing material effectively. The choices you make in each of these areas are affected by your purposes, the audience, and the situation.

Purposes in Oral Presentations

Oral presentations have the same three basic purposes that written documents have: to inform, to persuade, and to build goodwill. Like written messages, most oral presentations have more than one purpose.

Informative presentations inform or teach the audience. Training sessions in an organization are primarily informative. Secondary purposes may be to persuade new employees to follow organizational procedures, rather than doing something their own way, and to help them appreciate the organizational culture (◀ p. 59).

Persuasive presentations motivate the audience to act or to believe. Giving information and evidence is an important means of persuasion. Stories, visuals, and self-disclosure are also effective. In addition, the speaker must build goodwill by appearing to be credible and sympathetic to the audience's needs. The goal in many presentations is a favorable vote or decision. For example, speakers making business presentations may try to persuade the audience to approve their proposals, to adopt their ideas, or to buy their products. Sometimes the goal is to change behavior or attitudes or to reinforce existing attitudes. For example, a speaker at a meeting of factory workers may stress the importance of following safety procedures. A speaker at a church meeting may talk about the problem of homelessness in the community and try to build support for community shelters for the homeless.

Goodwill presentations entertain and validate the audience. In an after-dinner speech, the audience wants to be entertained. Presentations at sales meetings may be designed to stroke the audience's egos and to validate their commitment to organizational goals.

Make your purpose as specific as possible.

Weak: The purpose of my presentation is to discuss saving for retirement.

Better: The purpose of my presentation is to persuade my audience to put their 401k funds in stocks and bonds, not in money market accounts and CDs.

or: The purpose of my presentation is to explain how to calculate how much money someone needs to save in order to maintain a specific lifestyle after retirement.

Note that the purpose *is not* the introduction of your talk; it is the principle that guides your choice of strategy and content.

Comparing Written and Oral Messages

Giving a presentation is in many ways very similar to writing a message. All of the chapters up to this point—on using you-attitude and positive emphasis, developing reader benefits, analyzing your audience, designing slides, overcoming objections, doing research, and analyzing data—remain relevant as you plan an oral presentation.

A written message makes it easier to

- Present extensive or complex financial data.
- Present many specific details of a law, policy, or procedure.
- Minimize undesirable emotions.

Oral messages make it easier to

- Use emotion to help persuade the audience.
- Focus the audience's attention on specific points.
- Answer questions, resolve conflicts, and build consensus.
- Modify a proposal that may not be acceptable in its original form.
- Get immediate action or response.

Oral and written messages have many similarities. In both, you should

- Adapt the message to the specific audience.
- Show the audience how they would benefit from the idea, policy, service, or product.
- Overcome any objections the audience may have.
- Use you-attitude and positive emphasis.
- Use visuals to clarify or emphasize material.
- Specify exactly what the audience should do.

Planning a Strategy for Your Presentation

A **strategy** is your plan for reaching your specific goals with a specific audience.

In all oral presentations, simplify what you want to say. Identify the one idea you want the audience to take home. Simplify your supporting detail so it's easy to follow. Simplify visuals so they can be taken in at a glance. Simplify your words and sentences so they're easy to understand.

| Too complicated: | Information Storage Devices provides voice solutions using the company's unique, patented multilevel storage technique. |
| Simple: | We make voice chips. They're extremely easy to use. They have unlimited applications. And they last forever.[1] |

An oral presentation needs to be simpler than a written message to the same audience. If readers forget a point, they can turn back to it and reread the paragraph. Headings, paragraph indentation, and punctuation provide visual cues to help readers understand the message. Listeners, in contrast, must remember what the speaker says. Whatever they don't remember is lost. Even asking questions requires the audience to remember which points they don't understand.

Analyze your audience for an oral presentation just as you do for a written message. If you'll be speaking to co-workers, talk to them about your topic or proposal to find out what questions or objections they have. For audiences inside the organization, the biggest questions are often practical ones: Will it work? How much will it cost? How long will it take?

Think about the physical conditions in which you'll be speaking. Will the audience be tired at the end of a long day of listening? Sleepy after a big meal? Will the group be large or small? The more you know about your audience, the better you can adapt your message to them.

Choosing the Kind of Presentation

Choose one of three basic kinds of presentations: monologue, guided discussion, or interactive.

In a **monologue presentation,** the speaker speaks without interruption; questions are held until the end of the presentation, where the speaker functions as an expert. The speaker plans the presentation in advance and delivers it without deviation. This kind of presentation is the most common in class

What CEOs Learn about Presentations*

Executives preparing to take their companies public make scores of presentations in dozens of towns over a few short weeks. The purpose of this "road show" is to introduce the company to investment professionals—persuading them to buy, or at least to chart, the stock.

To prepare for these crucial presentations, many CEOs take lessons. Four days of intensive training from one expert costs $20,000. Here are some of the lessons three CEOs learned:

- Trip Hawkins, CEO of The 3DO Co. *"I had to suppress my 'ums' and 'ahs'—people don't know how many times they use those in conversation. And I have a tendency to look around too much—my eyes were zigging and zagging around the room."*

- Scott Cook, Chairman of Intuit *"If I got negative questions, I'd get defensive and put a chill on things. . . . He taught me that when somebody asks a negative question, restate it positively, answer it positively."*

- Timothy Koogle, CEO of Yahoo! *"He had me . . . loosen up. Get rid of the podium death grip. . . . Connect with the audience physically, with my eyes. Encourage them to drink in a really important slide by having a big pause in my speech."*

*Quotations quoted from Quentin Hardy, "Meet Jerry Weisman, Acting Coach to CEOs," *The Wall Street Journal,* April 21, 1998, B1.

Interactive Multimedia Presentations*

Black Gold sells furnaces that burn waste engine oil cleanly. Its customers include service stations, car washes, airports, and Department of Transportation garages. Using Authorware from Macromedia, consulting from Duthie Associates created an interactive multimedia presentation for Black Gold.

If a prospect asks about current customers, the salesperson can bring up a map of the United States with dots indicating current installations. Clicking on one of those dots brings up a short video testimonial from the customer. When the prospect asks about cost, the salesperson can say, "If you're spending money on heat now, Black Gold won't cost you anything. It will save you money." A series of 10 short questions leads to a chart comparing the customer's current system to the Black Gold system, showing the breakeven point when the prospect's company will start making money with the Black Gold furnace.

Sales went up 25% when Black Gold started using the new presentation.

*Based on "Presentations," *Selling Power*, May 2001, 118.

situations, but it's often boring for the audience. Good delivery skills are crucial, since the audience is comparatively uninvolved.

Linda Driskill suggests that **guided discussions** offer a better way to present material and help an audience find a solution it can "buy into." In a guided discussion, the speaker presents the questions or issues that both speaker and audience have agreed on in advance. Rather than functioning as an expert with all the answers, the speaker serves as a facilitator to help the audience tap its own knowledge. This kind of presentation is excellent for presenting the results of consulting projects, when the speaker has specialized knowledge, but the audience must implement the solution if it is to succeed. Guided discussions need more time than monologue presentations, but produce more audience response, more responses involving analysis, and more commitment to the result.[2]

An **interactive presentation** is a conversation, even if the speaker stands up in front of a group and uses charts and overheads. Most sales presentations are interactive presentations. The sales representative uses questions to determine the buyer's needs, probe objections, and gain provisional and then final commitment to the purchase. Even in a memorized sales presentation, the buyer will talk at least 30% of the time. In a problem-solving sales presentation, top salespeople let the buyer do 70% of the talking up until the action close (p. 261).[3]

Adapting Your Ideas to the Audience

Measure the message you'd like to send against where your audience is now. If your audience is indifferent, skeptical, or hostile, focus on the part of your message the audience will find most interesting and easiest to accept.

Don't seek a major opinion change in a single oral presentation. If the audience has already decided to hire an advertising agency, then a good presentation can convince them that your agency is the one to hire. But if you're talking to a small business that has always done its own ads, limit your purpose. You may be able to prove that an agency can earn its fees by doing things the owner can't do and by freeing the owner's time for other activities. A second presentation may be needed to prove that an ad agency can do a *better* job than the small business could do on its own. Only after the audience is receptive should you try to persuade the audience to hire your agency rather than a competitor.

Make your ideas relevant to your audience by linking what you have to say to their experiences and interests. Showing your audience that the topic affects them directly is the most effective strategy. When you can't do that, at least link the topic to some everyday experience.

> When was the last time you were hungry? Maybe you remember being hungry while you were on a diet, or maybe you had to work late at a lab and didn't get back to the dorm in time for dinner.

Speech about world hunger to an audience of college students

Planning a Strong Opening and Close

The beginning and the end of a presentation, like the beginning and the end of a written document, are positions of emphasis. Use those key positions to interest the audience and emphasize your key point. You'll sound more natural and more effective if you talk from notes but write out your opener and close in advance and memorize them. (They'll be short: just a sentence or two.)

Consider using one of the four modes for openers that appeared in Chapter 10: startling statement, narration or anecdote, question, or quotation. The more you can do to personalize your opener for your audience, the better. Recent events are better than things that happened long ago; local events are better than events at a distance; people they know are better than people who are only names.

Startling statement

> Twelve of our customers have canceled orders in the past month.

This presentation to a company's executive committee went on to show that the company's distribution system was inadequate and to recommend a third warehouse located in the Southwest.

Narration or anecdote

> A mother was having difficulty getting her son up for school. He pulled the covers over his head.
> "I'm not going to school," he said. "I'm not ever going again."
> "Are you sick?" his mother asked.
> "No," he answered. "I'm sick of school. They hate me. They call me names. They make fun of me. Why should I go?"
> "I can give you two good reasons," the mother replied. "The first is that you're 42 years old. And the second is *you're the school principal.*"[4]

This speech to a seminar for educators went on to discuss "the three knottiest problems in education today." Educators had to face those problems; they couldn't hide under the covers.

Even better than canned stories are anecdotes that happened to you. The best anecdotes are parables that contain the point of your talk.

Question

> Are you going to have enough money to do the things you want to when you retire?

This presentation to a group of potential clients discusses the value of using the services of a professional financial planner to achieve one's goals for retirement.

Quotation

> According to Towers Perrin, the profits of Fortune 100 companies would be 25% lower—they'd go down $17 billion—if their earnings statements listed the future costs companies are obligated to pay for retirees' health care.

This presentation on options for health care for retired employees urges executives to start now to investigate options to cut the future costs.

Your opener should interest the audience and establish a rapport with them. Some speakers use humor to achieve those goals. However, an inappropriate joke can turn the audience against the speaker. Never use humor that's directed against the audience. In contrast, speakers who can make fun of themselves almost always succeed:

> It's both a privilege and a pressure to be here.[5]

Strategy for a Corporate Speech*

Security directors of the 50 most prominent international banks meet periodically to discuss common problems. BankAmerica's Bob Beck wanted to talk to the group about chemical dependency and BankAmerica's approach to the problem.

Audience's initial position: Resistant. Most favored testing, not treatment.

One point to leave with audience: Treatment is a practical alternative that works.

Adapting message to audience: Used terms from sports, banking, and security to make it easy for audience to identify with message. Backed up points with details and statistics. Explained problems of drug testing. Did not ask for action.

Opener: Hard-hitting statistics on how much chemical dependency costs US businesses—$26 billion a year.

Outline: (1) Chemical dependency as a disease; the size of the problem; testing as the usual response. (2) BankAmerica's treatment approach: policy, program design, and education in the workplace. (3) The business advantages of treatment: protects investment in trained people; confines business losses caused by chemical dependency.

*Based on Robin Welling, *No Frills, No Nonsense, No Secrets* (San Francisco: International Association of Business Communicators, 1988), 290–93.

Cultural Styles of Presentations*

When you make an international presentation, be sensitive to your host country's cultural preferences for presentations.

In Japan, speak in a modest, personal, conversational style. Look at the whole group; remember that the oldest person is probably the most important. Plan carefully so that your presentation fits in the available time—and remember that interpretation cuts your actual speaking time in half.

In Sweden, don't save points for a question-and-answer session. Swedes consider it rude to ask questions at the end of a presentation: to do so suggests the speaker has not been clear. Instead, include all your material in the body of the presentation. The best close is a well-crafted question that applies the material from the presentation, leaving the audience something to think about.

*Based on Bronwen Jones, *Doing Business in Japan: An ABC for Better Communications* ([Tokyo:] JETRO, 1991), 16; and H. Ned Seelye and Alan Seelye-James, *Culture Clash* (Lincolnwood, IL: NTC Business Books, 1995), 30–31.

Humor isn't the only way to set an audience at ease. Smile at your audience before you begin; let them see that you're a real person and a nice one.

The end of your presentation should be as strong as the opener. For your close, you could do one or more of the following:

- Restate your main point.
- Refer to your opener to create a frame for your presentation.
- End with a vivid, positive picture.
- Tell the audience exactly what to do to solve the problem you've discussed.

The following close from a fund-raising speech combines a restatement of the main point with a call for action, telling the audience what to do.

> Plain and simple, we need money to run the foundation, just like you need money to develop new products. We need money to make this work. We need money from you. Pick up that pledge card. Fill it out. Turn it in at the door as you leave. Make it a statement about your commitment . . . make it a big statement.[6]

When you write out your opener and close, be sure to use oral rather than written style. As you can see in the example close above, oral style uses shorter sentences and shorter, simpler words than writing does. Oral style can even sound a bit choppy when it is read by eye. Oral style uses more personal pronouns, a less varied vocabulary, and more repetition.

Planning Visuals and Other Devices to Involve the Audience

Visuals can give your presentation a professional image. A 1986 study showed that presenters using overhead transparencies were perceived as "better prepared, more professional, more persuasive, more credible, and more interesting" than speakers who did not use visuals. They were also more likely to persuade a group to adopt their recommendations.[7] In 2000, a study found that in an informative presentation, multimedia (PowerPoint slides with graphics and animation) produced 5% more learning than overheads made from the slides and 16% more learning than text alone. In sales presentations by two different banks, one bank's use of multimedia (PowerPoint slides with graphics, animation, and video) motivated 58% more students to choose that bank over the bank that used overheads only. When the second bank used text alone, 50% more students chose the bank that used multimedia. Although the two banks offered identical fees and services, students said that the bank represented by

PowerPoint slides aren't the only or necessarily the best way to involve the audience. Dan Leeber persuaded UPS to switch to Valeo clutches by completely disassembling the competitor's clutch and showing part by part why Valeo's product was better.

FIGURE 16.1 PowerPoint Slides for an Informative Presentation

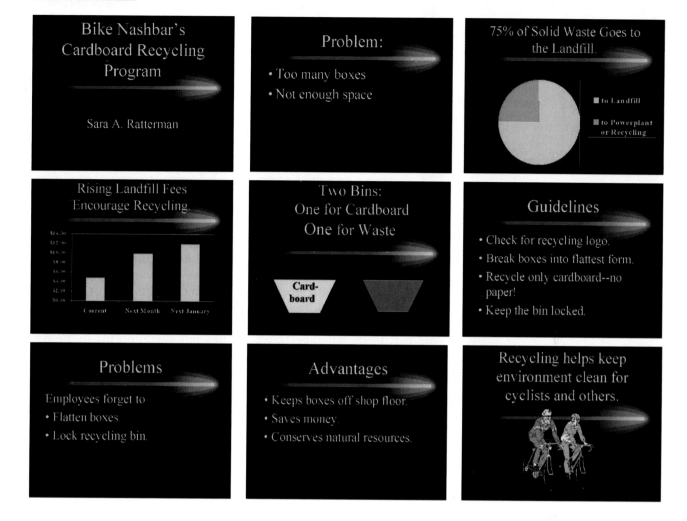

the multimedia presentation "was more credible, was more professional and offered better services and fees."[8]

Use at least 18-point type for visuals you prepare with a word processor. When you prepare slides with PowerPoint, Corel, or another presentation program, use at least 24-point type for the smallest words. You should be able to read the smallest words easily when you print a handout version of your slides.

Well-designed visuals can serve as an outline for your talk (see Figure 16.1), eliminating the need for additional notes. Visuals should highlight your main points, not give every detail.

Use these guidelines to create and show visuals for presentations:

- Make only one point with each visual. Break a complicated point down into several visuals.
- Give each visual a title that makes a point.
- Limit the amount of information on a visual. Use 35 words or less on seven lines or less; use simple graphs, not complex ones.
- Don't put your visual up till you're ready to talk about it. Leave it up until your next point; don't turn the projector or overhead off.

See Chapter 6 for information on designing slides and Chapter 15 for information on how to present numerical data through visuals.

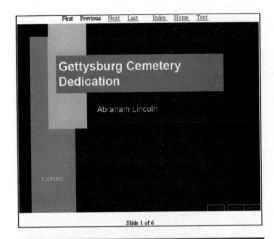

First Previous Next Last Index Home Text

Gettysburg Cemetery
Dedication

Abraham Lincoln

11/19/1863

Slide 1 of 6

InSite

www.norvig.com/Gettysburg

Not every speech needs visuals. As Peter Norvig shows, Lincoln's Gettysburg Address is hurt, not helped, by adding bland PowerPoint slides.

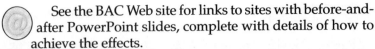

See the BAC Web site for links to sites with before-and-after PowerPoint slides, complete with details of how to achieve the effects.

Visuals work only if the technology they depend on works. When you give presentations in your own office, check the equipment in advance. When you make a presentation in another location or for another organization, arrive early so that you'll have time not only to check the equipment but also to track down a service worker if the equipment isn't working. Be prepared with a backup plan to use if you're unable to show your slides or videotape.

You can also involve the audience in other ways. A student giving a presentation on English-French business communication demonstrated the differences in US and French handshakes by asking a fellow class member to come up to shake hands with her. Another student discussing the need for low-salt products brought in a container of salt, a measuring cup, a measuring spoon, and two plates. As he discussed the body's need for salt, he measured out three teaspoons onto one plate: the amount the body needs in a month. As he discussed the amount of salt the average US diet provides, he continued to measure out salt onto the other plate, stopping only when he had 1¼ pounds of salt—the amount in the average US diet. The demonstration made the discrepancy clear in a way words or even a chart could not have done.[9] To make sure that his employees understood where money went, the CEO of a specialty printing shop in Algoma, Wisconsin, printed up $2 million in play money and handed out big cards to employees marked *Labor, Depreciation, Interest,* and so forth. Then he asked each "category" to come up and take its share of the revenues. The action was more dramatic than a color pie chart could ever have been.[10] Another speaker who was trying to raise funds used the simple act of asking people to stand to involve them, to create emotional appeal, and to make a statistic vivid:

> [A speaker] was talking to a luncheon club about contributing to the relief of an area that had been hit by a tornado. The news report said that 70% of the people had been killed or disabled. The room was set up [with] ten people at each round table. He asked three persons at each table to stand. Then he said, ". . . You people sitting are dead or disabled. You three standing have to take care of the mess. You'd need help, wouldn't you?"[11]

Choosing Information to Include in a Presentation

Choose the information that is most interesting to your audience and that answers the questions your audience will have. Limit your talk to three main points. In a long presentation (20 minutes or more) each main point can have subpoints. Your content will be easier to understand if you clearly show the relationship between each of the main points. Turning your information into a story also helps. For example, a controller might turn charts of financial data into the following story:

> The increase in sales income is offset by an increase in manufacturing costs. Why? Because the cost of material is out of line. Material costs for product #503 tripled last month. An analysis of the three shifts shows that the cost of materials jumped 800% on the second shift. Now, the problem is to find out why the second shift uses so much more material than the other shifts making the same product.[12]

Back up each point with solid support. Statistics and numbers can be convincing if you present them in ways that are easy to hear. Simplify numbers by reducing them to two significant digits.

Hard to hear:	If the national debt were in pennies, it would take 17,006,802,720 people, each carrying 100 pounds of pennies, to carry all of our debt.
Easier to hear:	If the national debt were in pennies, it would take 17 billion people, each carrying 100 pounds of pennies, to carry all of our debt.[13]

In an informative presentation, link the points you make to the knowledge your audience has. Show the audience members that your information answers their questions, solves their problems, or helps them do their jobs. When you explain the effect of a new law or the techniques for using a new machine, use specific examples that apply to the decisions they make and the work they do. If your content is detailed or complicated, give people a written outline or handouts. The written material both helps the audience keep track of your points during the presentation and serves as a reference after the talk is over.

Quotations work well as long as you cite authorities whom your audience genuinely respects. Often you'll need to paraphrase a quote to put it into simple language that's easy to understand. Be sure to tell whom you're citing: "According to Al Gore," "An article in *BusinessWeek* points out that," and so forth.

Demonstrations can prove your points dramatically and quickly. During the investigation of the space shuttle *Challenger* disaster, the late physicist Richard Feynman asked for a glass of water. When it came, he put a piece of the space shuttle's O-ring into the cold water. After less than a minute, he took it out and pinched it with a small clamp. The material kept the pinched shape when the clamp came off. The material couldn't return to its original shape.[14] A technical explanation could have made the same point: the O-ring couldn't function in the cold. But the demonstration was fast and easy to understand. It didn't require that the audience follow complex chemical or mathematical formulas. In an oral presentation, seeing is believing.

To be convincing, you must answer the audience's questions and objections.

> Some people think that working women are less reliable than men. But the facts show that women take fewer sick days than men do.

However, don't bring up negatives or inconsistencies unless you're sure that the audience will think of them. If you aren't sure, save your evidence for the question phase. If someone does ask, you'll have the answer.

Organizing Your Information

Most presentations use a direct pattern of organization, even when the goal is to persuade a reluctant audience. In a business setting, the audience is in a hurry and knows that you want to persuade them. Be honest about your goal, and then prove that your goal meets the audience's needs too.

In a persuasive presentation, start with your strongest point, your best reason. If time permits, give other reasons as well and respond to possible objections. Put your weakest point in the middle so that you can end on a strong note.

Often one of five standard patterns of organization will work:

- **Chronological.** Start with the past, move to the present, and end by looking ahead.
- **Problem–causes–solution.** Explain the symptoms of the problem, identify its causes, and suggest a solution. This pattern works best when the audience will find your solution easy to accept.

An Alternative to PowerPoint*

[Once Barbara Waugh had analyzed her survey data—p. 349—she had to plan a presentation.] But how could she capture and communicate what she'd learned? How could she share this powerful critique with senior management? The last thing she wanted to do was preach through PowerPoint. So instead of creating bullet-point slides, she drew on her experience with street theatre and created a "play" about HP Labs. She worked passages from the surveys into dialogue and then recruited executives to act as staff members, and junior people to act as executives. The troupe performed for 30 senior managers. "At the end of the play, the managers were very quiet," Waugh remembers. "Then they started clapping. It was exciting. They really got it. They finally understood."

*Quoted from Katherine Mieszkowski, "I Grew Up Thinking That Change Was Cataclysmic. The Way We've Done It Here Is to Start Slow and Work Small." *Fast Company*, December 1998, p. 152.

Advice from the Pros*

Creation

1. Think of your last summary slide first—then make sure each of those key bullet points are clearly explained in the body of your presentation.

2. Use simple, clear graphics and pictures of familiar people to capture attention and build audience identification.

3. Get someone else to check spellings and the logical flow of your slide show. Another pair of eyes will often pick up an error that you have missed.

Presentation

1. Practice, Practice, Practice. Rehearse several times— aloud and standing up, with the same equipment you will use for your presentation.

2. Make eye contact with more than one audience member during the course of your presentation.

3. Always carry backup disks of your presentation program, your slide show, and any special fonts that were used in its creation.

*Quoted from Shonan Noronha and John Rhodes, "Power Presentations," *Presentations,* special advertising section, n.p.

- **Excluding alternatives.** Explain the symptoms of the problem. Explain the obvious solutions first and show why they won't solve the problem. End by discussing a solution that will work. This pattern may be necessary when the audience will find the solution hard to accept.

- **Pro–con.** Give all the reasons in favor of something, then those against it. This pattern works well when you want the audience to see the weaknesses in its position.

- **1–2–3.** Discuss three aspects of a topic. This pattern works well to organize short informative briefings. "Today I'll review our sales, production, and profits for the last quarter."

Make your organization clear to your audience. Written documents can be reread; they can use headings, paragraphs, lists, and indentations to signal levels of detail. In a presentation, you have to provide explicit clues to the structure of your discourse.

Early in your talk—perhaps immediately after your opener—provide an overview of the main points you will make.

> First, I'd like to talk about who the homeless in Columbus are. Second, I'll talk about the services The Open Shelter provides. Finally, I'll talk about what you—either individually or as a group—can do to help.

An overview provides a mental peg that hearers can hang each point on. It also can prevent someone from missing what you are saying because he or she wonders why you aren't covering a major point that you've saved for later.[15]

Offer a clear signpost as you come to each new point. A **signpost** is an explicit statement of the point you have reached. Choose wording that fits your style. The following statements are four different ways that a speaker could use to introduce the last of three points:

> Now we come to the third point: what you can do as a group or as individuals to help homeless people in Columbus.

> So much for what we're doing. Now let's talk about what you can do to help.

> You may be wondering, what can I do to help?

> As you can see, the Shelter is trying to do many things. We could do more things with your help.

Delivering an Effective Presentation

Audiences want the sense that you're talking directly to them and that you care that they understand and are interested. They'll forgive you if you get tangled up in a sentence and end it ungrammatically. They won't forgive you if you seem to have a "canned" talk that you're going to deliver no matter who the audience is or how they respond. You can convey a sense of caring to your audience by making direct eye contact with them and by using a conversational style.

Dealing with Fear

Feeling nervous is normal. But you can harness that nervous energy to help you do your best work. As one student said, you don't need to get rid of your butterflies. All you need to do is make them fly in formation.

To calm your nerves before you give an oral presentation,

■ Be prepared. Analyze your audience, organize your thoughts, prepare visual aids, practice your opener and close, check out the arrangements.

■ Use only the amount of caffeine you normally use. More or less may make you jumpy.

■ Avoid alcoholic beverages.

■ Relabel your nerves. Instead of saying, "I'm scared," try saying, "My adrenaline is up." Adrenaline sharpens our reflexes and helps us do our best.

Just before your presentation,

■ Consciously contract and then relax your muscles, starting with your feet and calves and going up to your shoulders, arms, and hands.

■ Take several deep breaths from your diaphragm.

During your presentation,

■ Pause and look at the audience before you begin speaking.

■ Concentrate on communicating well.

■ Use body energy in strong gestures and movement.

Using Eye Contact

Look directly at the people you're talking to. In one study, speakers who looked more at the audience during a seven-minute informative speech were judged to be better informed, more experienced, more honest, and friendlier than speakers who delivered the same information with less eye contact.[16] An earlier study found that speakers judged sincere looked at the audience 63% of the time, while those judged insincere looked at the audience only 21% of the time.[17]

The point in making eye contact is to establish one-on-one contact with the individual members of your audience. People want to feel that you're talking to them. Looking directly at individuals also enables you to be more conscious of feedback from the audience, so that you can modify your approach if necessary.

Developing a Good Speaking Voice

People will enjoy your presentation more if your voice is easy to listen to. To find out what your voice sounds like, tape-record it. Also tape the voices of people on TV or on campus whose voices you like and imitate them. In a few weeks, tape yourself again.

To find your best speaking voice, close your ears with your fingers and hum up and down the scale until you find the pitch where the hum sounds loudest or most vibrant to you. This pitch will be near your optimum pitch.[18]

When you speak to a group, talk loudly enough so that people can hear you easily. If you're using a microphone, adjust your volume so you aren't shouting. When you speak in an unfamiliar location, try to get to the room early so you can check the size of the room and the power of the amplification equipment. If you can't do that, ask early in your talk, "Can you hear me in the back of the room?"

The bigger the group is, the more carefully you need to **enunciate,** that is, voice all the sounds of each word. Words starting or ending with *f, t, k, v,* and *d* are especially hard to hear. "Our informed and competent image" can sound like "Our informed, incompetent image."

Being Interviewed by the Press*

Business people and community leaders are often interviewed by the press. To appear your best on camera, on tape, or in a story,

■ Try to find out in advance why you're being interviewed and what information the reporter wants.

■ Practice answering possible questions in a single sentence. A long answer is likely to be cut for TV or radio news.

■ Talk slowly. You'll have time to think, the audience will have more time to understand what you're saying, and a reporter taking notes will record your words more accurately.

■ To reduce the possibility of being misquoted, bring along a cassette recorder to tape the interview. Better still, bring two—and offer to give one tape to the interviewer.

*Based on James L. Graham, "What to Do When a Reporter Calls," *IABC Communication World*, April 1985, 15; and Robert A. Papper, conversation with Kitty Locker, March 17, 1991.

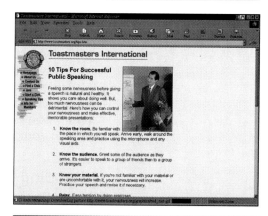

InSite

www.toastmasters.org/tips.html

Toastmasters International suggests ways to deal with nervousness. The clubs provide forums where members can practice their speaking skills.

To enunciate, use your tongue and lips. Researchers have identified 38 different sounds. Of these, you make 31 with your tongue and 7 with your lips. None are made with the jaw, so how wide you open your mouth really doesn't matter. If the tongue isn't active enough, muscles in the throat try to compensate, producing sore throats and strained voices.[19]

Tongue twisters can help you exercise your tongue and enunciate more clearly. Stephen Lucas suggests the following:

- Sid said to tell him that Benny hid the penny many years ago.
- Fetch me the finest French-fried freshest fish that Finney fries.
- Three gray geese in the green grass grazed.
- Shy Sarah saw six Swiss wristwatches.
- One year we had a Christmas brunch with Merry Christmas mush to munch. But I don't think you'd care for such. We didn't like to munch mush much.[20]

You can also reduce pressure on your throat by fitting phrases to your ideas. If you cut your sentences into bits, you'll emphasize words beginning with vowels, making the vocal cords hit each other. Instead, run past words beginning with vowels to emphasize later syllables or later words:[21]

Choppiness hurts vocal cords:

We must take more responsibility not
Only for
Ourselves
And
Our families but for
Our communities
And
Our country.

Smooth phrasing protects throat:

We must take more
Responsibility
Not only for our
Selves and our
Families but for our
Communities and our
Country.

You can reduce the number of *uhs* you use by practicing your talk several times. Filler sounds aren't signs of nervousness. Instead, say psychologists at Columbia University, they occur when speakers pause searching for the next word. Searching takes longer when people have big vocabularies or talk about topics where a variety of word choices are possible. Practicing your talk makes your word choices automatic, and you'll use fewer *uhs*.[22]

Vary your volume, pitch, and speed. Speakers who speak quickly and who vary their volume during the talk are more likely to be perceived as competent.[23] Sound energetic and enthusiastic. If your ideas don't excite you, why should your audience find them exciting?

Standing and Gesturing

Stand with your feet far enough apart for good balance, with your knees flexed. Unless the presentation is very formal or you're on camera, you can walk if you want to. Some speakers like to come in front of the lectern to remove that barrier between themselves and the audience.

If you use slides or transparencies, stand beside the screen so that you don't block it.

Build on your natural style for gestures. Gestures usually work best when they're big and confident.

Using Notes and Visuals

Put your notes on cards or on sturdy pieces of paper and number them. Most speakers like to use 4-by-6-inch or 5-by-7-inch cards because they hold more information than 3-by-5 inch cards. Your notes need to be complete enough to help you if you go blank, so use long phrases or complete sentences. Under each main point, jot down the evidence or illustration you'll use. Indicate where you'll refer to visuals.

Look at your notes infrequently. Most of your gaze time should be directed to members of the audience. Hold your notes high enough so that your head doesn't bob up and down like a yo-yo as you look from the audience to your notes and back again.

If you have lots of visuals and know your topic well, you won't need notes. Face the audience, not the screen. With transparencies, you can use colored marking pens to call attention to your points as you talk. Show the entire visual at once: don't cover up part of it. If you don't want the audience to read ahead, prepare several visuals that build up. In your overview, for example, the first visual could list your first point, the second the first and second, and the third all three points.

Keep the room lights on if possible; turning them off makes it easier for people to fall asleep and harder for them to concentrate on you.

Handling Questions

Prepare for questions by listing every fact or opinion you can think of that challenges your position. Treat each objection seriously and try to think of a way to deal with it. If you're talking about a controversial issue, you may want to save one point for the question period, rather than making it during the presentation. Speakers who have visuals to answer questions seem especially well prepared.

During your presentation, tell the audience how you'll handle questions. If you have a choice, save questions for the end. In your talk, answer the questions or objections that you expect your audience to have. Don't exaggerate your claims so that you won't have to back down in response to questions later.

During the question period, don't nod your head to indicate that you understand a question as it is asked. Audiences will interpret nods as signs that you agree with the questioner. Instead, look directly at the questioner. As you answer the question, expand your focus to take in the entire group. Don't say, "That's a good question." That response implies that the other questions have been poor ones.

If the audience may not have heard the question or if you want more time to think, repeat the question before you answer it. Link your answers to the points you made in your presentation. Keep the purpose of your presentation in mind, and select information that advances your goals.

If a question is hostile or biased, rephrase it before you answer it: "You're asking whether. . . ." Or suggest an alternative question: "I think there are problems with both the positions you describe. It seems to me that a third solution which is better than either of them is. . . ."

Occasionally someone will ask a question that is really designed to state the speaker's own position. Respond to the question if you want to. Another option is to say, "I'm not sure what you're asking," or even, "That's a clear statement of your position. Let's move to the next question now." If someone asks about something that you already explained in your presentation, simply answer the question without embarrassing the questioner. No audience will understand and remember 100% of what you say.

Responding to Hostile Questions*

In environmental public meetings, people who represent organizations must often respond to hostile questions. One study testing five kinds of responses showed that the most effective responses fell into two categories:

- Things have changed; that problem no longer exists; that charge is no longer true.

- The problem is outweighed by positive results.

Least effective was "passing the buck":

- We aren't responsible for that; someone else is.

*Based on Kim Sydow Campbell, Saroya I. Follender, and Guy Shane, "Preferred Strategies for Responding to Hostile Questions in Environmental Meetings," *Management Communication Quarterly* 11 (1998): 401–21.

Twice as Prepared*

Ralph Oliva made sales presentations for Texas Instruments. Each presentation to senior executives could, if successful, win a multimillion-dollar account for his company.

Oliva learned to prepare not one, but two presentations. In the first presentation, time didn't matter. He included every piece of support and tried to anticipate and respond to every possible objection. The second presentation hits just the main points in 10 to 15 minutes.

The second presentation is the one he actually gives. But because his preparation is so thorough, he isn't nervous. He can answer questions that may arise. The thorough preparation "makes me certain that the audience won't find me lacking in preparation. I can even say, 'I don't know' with confidence because I know I haven't done a sloppy job."

*Based on and quoted from "No Sweat: How to Deliver Winning Presentations for Million-Dollar Accounts," *Selling Power*, January/February 2000, 116.

If you don't know the answer to a question, say so. If your purpose is to inform, write down the question so that you can look up the answer before the next session. If it's a question to which you think there is no answer, ask if anyone in the room knows. When no one does, your "ignorance" is vindicated. If an expert is in the room, you may want to refer questions of fact to him or her. Answer questions of interpretation yourself.

At the end of the question period, take two minutes to summarize your main point once more. (This can be a restatement of your close.) Questions may or may not focus on the key point of your talk. Take advantage of having the floor to repeat your message briefly and forcefully.

Making Group Presentations

Plan carefully to involve as many members of the group as possible in speaking roles.

The easiest way to make a group presentation is to outline the presentation and then divide the topics, giving one to each group member. Another member can be responsible for the opener and the close. During the question period, each member answers questions that relate to his or her topic.

In this kind of divided presentation, be sure to

- Plan transitions.
- Enforce time limits strictly.
- Coordinate your visuals so that the presentation seems a coherent whole.
- Practice the presentation as a group at least once; more is better.

The best group presentations are even more fully integrated: the group writes a very detailed outline, chooses points and examples, and creates visuals together. Then, within each point, voices trade off. This presentation is most effective because each voice speaks only a minute or two before a new voice comes in. However, it works only when all group members know the subject well and when the group plans carefully and practices extensively.

Whatever form of group presentation you use, be sure to introduce each member of the team to the audience and to pay close attention to each other. If other members of the team seem uninterested in the speaker, the audience gets the sense that that speaker isn't worth listening to.

Summary of Key Points

- **Informative presentations** inform or teach the audience. **Persuasive presentations** motivate the audience to act or to believe. **Goodwill presentations** entertain and validate the audience. Most oral presentations have more than one purpose.
- A written message makes it easier to present extensive or complex information and to minimize undesirable emotions. Oral messages make it easier to use emotion, to focus the audience's attention, to answer questions and resolve conflicts quickly, to modify a proposal that may not be acceptable in its original form, and to get immediate action or response.
- In both oral and written messages, you should
  - Adapt the message to the specific audience.
  - Show the audience how they benefit from the idea, policy, service, or product.
  - Overcome any objections the audience may have.
  - Use you-attitude and positive emphasis.

- Use visuals to clarify or emphasize material.
- Specify exactly what the audience should do.

■ An oral presentation needs to be simpler than a written message to the same audience.

■ In a **monologue presentation,** the speaker plans the presentation in advance and delivers it without deviation. In a **guided discussion,** the speaker presents the questions or issues that both speaker and audience have agreed on in advance. Rather than functioning as an expert with all the answers, the speaker serves as a facilitator to help the audience tap its own knowledge. An **interactive presentation** is a conversation using questions to determine the buyer's needs, probe objections, and gain provisional and then final commitment to the purchase.

■ Adapt your message to your audience's beliefs, experiences, and interests.

■ Use the beginning and end of the presentation to interest the audience and emphasize your key point.

■ Use visuals to seem more prepared, more interesting, and more persuasive.

■ Use a direct pattern of organization. Put your strongest reason first.

■ Limit your talk to three main points. Early in your talk—perhaps immediately after your opener—provide an **overview of the main points** you will make. Offer a clear signpost as you come to each new point. A **signpost** is an explicit statement of the point you have reached.

■ To calm your nerves as you prepare to give an oral presentation,
  - Be prepared. Analyze your audience, organize your thoughts, prepare visual aids, practice your opener and close, check out the arrangements.
  - Use only the amount of caffeine you normally use.
  - Avoid alcoholic beverages.
  - Relabel your nerves. Instead of saying, "I'm scared," try saying, "My adrenaline is up." Adrenaline sharpens our reflexes and helps us do our best.

  Just before your presentation,
  - Consciously contract and then relax your muscles, starting with your feet and calves and going up to your shoulders, arms, and hands.
  - Take several deep breaths from your diaphragm.

  During your presentation,
  - Pause and look at the audience before you begin speaking.
  - Concentrate on communicating well.
  - Use body energy in strong gestures and movement.

■ Convey a sense of caring to your audience by making direct eye contact with them and by using a conversational style.

■ Treat questions as opportunities to give more detailed information than you had time to give in your presentation. Link your answers to the points you made in your presentation.

■ Repeat the question before you answer it if the audience may not have heard it or if you want more time to think. Rephrase hostile or biased questions before you answer them.

■ The best group presentations result when the group writes a very detailed outline, chooses points and examples, and creates visuals together. Then, within each point, voices trade off.

@ See the BAC Web site for links on planning and delivering effective presentation.

Cut to the Chase*

When a student took a job at Intel, her first assignment was to present a strategic plan to CEO Andy Grove two weeks later.

Five minutes into her presentation, he interrupted her: "Please flip to page 22. That's what I need to know."

*Based on Evelyn Pierce, Thomas Hadjuk, and Richard Young, "Using Verbal Protocol Research to Determine What Business Audiences Want in Documents," Association for Business Communication Conference, Chicago, IL, November 6–9, 1996.

Getting Started

16.1   Analyzing Openers and Closes

The following openers and closes came from class presentations on information interviews.

- Does each opener make you interested in hearing the rest of the presentation?
- Does each opener provide a transition to the overview?
- Does the close end the presentation in a satisfying way?

a.   Opener: I interviewed Mark Perry at AT&T.

Close: Well, that's my report.

b.   Opener: How many of you know what you want to do when you graduate?

Close: So, if you like numbers and want to travel, think about being a CPA. Ernst & Young can take you all over the world.

c.   Opener: You don't have to know anything about computer programming to get a job as a technical writer at CompuServe.

Close: After talking to Raj, I decided technical writing isn't for me. But it is a good career if you work well under pressure and like learning new things all the time.

d.   Opener: My report is about what it's like to work in an advertising agency.

Middle: They keep really tight security; I had to wear a badge and be escorted to Susan's desk.

Close: Susan gave me samples of the agency's ads and even a sample of a new soft drink she's developing a campaign for. But she didn't let me keep the badge.

16.2   Developing Stories

Think of personal anecdotes that you could use to open or illustrate presentations on the following topics:

1. Why people need to plan.
2. Dealing with change.
3. The importance of lifelong learning.
4. The value of good customer service.
5. The culture of an organization you know well.

As Your Instructor Directs,

a.   Share your stories with a small group of students.

b.   Turn in your stories in a memo to your instructor.

c.   Make an oral presentation using one of the stories.

Presentation Assignments

16.3   Making a Short Oral Presentation

As Your Instructor Directs,

Make a short (three- to five-minute) presentation with PowerPoint slides on one of the following topics:

a.   Explain how what you've learned in classes, in campus activities, or at work will be useful to the employer who hires you after graduation.

b.   Profile someone who is successful in the field you hope to enter and explain what makes him or her successful.

c.   Describe a specific situation in an organization in which communication was handled well or badly.

d.   Make a short presentation based on another problem in this book.

1.5	Introduce yourself to the class.
3.11	Analyze your boss.
3.12	Analyze your co-workers.
7.5	Explain a "best practice" in your organization.
7.12	Explain what a new hire in your unit needs to know to be successful.
8.10	Tell your boss about a problem in your unit.
10.13	Make a presentation to raise funds for an organization.
12.18	Describe your choices in creating a brochure.
17.2	Tell the class in detail about one of your accomplishments.
18.4	Explain one of the challenges (e.g., technology, ethics, international competition) that the field you hope to enter is facing.

18.5 Profile a company you would like to work for and explain why you think it would be a good employer.

18.6 Share the results of an information interview.

19.2 Share the advice of students currently on the job market.

19.3 Share what you learn when you interview an interviewer.

19.4 Explain your interview strategy.

16.4 Making a Longer Oral Presentation

As Your Instructor Directs,

Make a 5- to 12-minute presentation on one of the following. Use visuals to make your talk effective.

a. Show why your unit is important to the organization and either should be exempt from downsizing or should receive additional resources.

b. Persuade your supervisor to make a change that will benefit the organization.

c. Persuade your organization to make a change that will improve the organization's image in the community.

d. Persuade classmates to donate time or money to a charitable organization. (Read Chapter 10.)

e. Persuade an employer that you are the best person for the job.

f. Use another problem in this book as the basis for your presentation.

3.14 Analyze an organization's culture.

3.15 Analyze a discourse community.

5.1 Describe the composing process(es) of a writer you've interviewed.

6.7 Evaluate the page design of one or more documents.

6.8 Evaluate the design of a Web page.

7.8 Present a Web page you have designed.

8.16 Analyze rejection letters students on your campus have received.

9.17 Persuade your campus to make a change.

10.3 Analyze one or more sales or fund-raising letters.

11.4 Analyze international messages that your workplace has created or received.

13.15 Summarize the results of a survey you have conducted.

14.10 Summarize the results of your research.

16.5 Making a Group Oral Presentation

As Your Instructor Directs,

Make a 5- to 12-minute presentation on one of the following. Use visuals to make your talk effective.

1.4 Explain the role of communication in one or more organizations.

11.7 Report on another country.

12.18 Present brochures you have designed to the class.

12.19 Describe the listening strategies of workers you have interviewed.

16.6 Evaluating Oral Presentations

Evaluate an oral presentation given by a classmate or given by a speaker on your campus. Use the following categories:

Strategy

1. Choosing an effective kind of presentation for the situation.
2. Adapting ideas to audience's beliefs, experiences, and interests.
3. Using a strong opening and close.
4. Using visual aids or other devices to involve audience.

Content

5. Using specific, vivid supporting material and language.
6. Providing rebuttals to counterclaims or objections.

Organization

7. Providing an overview of main points.
8. Signposting main points in body of talk.
9. Providing adequate transitions between points and speakers.

Visuals

10. Using an appropriate design or template.
11. Using standard edited English.
12. Being creative.

Delivery

13. Making direct eye contact with audience.
14. Using voice and gestures effectively.
15. Handling questions effectively.
16. Stance, position (not blocking screen)

As Your Instructor Directs,

a. Fill out a form indicating your evaluation in each of the areas.
b. Share your evaluation orally with the speaker.
c. Write a memo to the speaker evaluating the presentation. Send a copy of your memo to your instructor.

16.7   Evaluating Team Presentations

Evaluate team presentations using the following questions:

1. How thoroughly were all group members involved?
2. Did members of the team introduce themselves or each other?
3. Did team members seem interested in what their teammates said?
4. How well was the material organized?
5. How well did the material hold your interest?
6. How clear did the material seem to you?
7. How effective were the visuals?
8. How well did the team handle questions?
9. What could be done to improve the presentation?
10. What were the strong points of the presentation?

As Your Instructor Directs,

a. Fill out a form indicating your evaluation in each of the areas.
b. Share your evaluation orally with the speaker.
c. Write a memo to the speaker evaluating the presentation. Send a copy of your memo to your instructor.

16.8   Evaluating the Way a Speaker Handles Questions

Listen to a speaker talking about a controversial subject. (Go to a talk on campus or in town, or watch a speaker on a TV show like *Face the Nation* or *60 Minutes*.) Observe the way he or she handles questions.

■ About how many questions does the speaker answer?
■ What is the format for asking and answering questions?
■ Are the answers clear? responsive to the question? something that could be quoted without embarrassing the speaker and the organization he or she represents?
■ How does the speaker handle hostile questions? Does the speaker avoid getting angry? Does the speaker retain control of the meeting? How?

■ If some questions were not answered well, what (if anything) could the speaker have done to leave a better impression?
■ Did the answers leave the audience with a more or less positive impression of the speaker? Why?

As Your Instructor Directs,

a. Share your evaluation with a small group of students.
b. Present your evaluation formally to the class.
c. Summarize your evaluation in a memo to your instructor.

Job Hunting

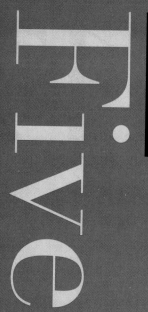

Résumés

Résumés

Kevin Slakey

University Relations Representative, Cisco Systems

Kevin Slakey builds relationships among Cisco, universities, and students. His many job responsibilities include reviewing résumés and conducting interviews. Cisco Systems, Inc. is the worldwide leader in networking for the Internet.

www.cisco.com

On average, a recruiter will spend 30 to 60 seconds looking at your résumé. Recruiters look as much for things to disqualify you (like typos, misspellings, and poor grammar) as for things to capture their interest and get them to linger longer over your qualifications. Here's how to capture more "eyeball time" and increase the odds of having your résumé placed in the "interview" stack:

- Highlight any relevant internships or co-ops. Provide details about the projects you worked, tools you used, accomplishments you achieved. Spent the summer flipping burgers? Then downplay your work experience and expand upon projects you completed during coursework.

- Provide a short list of the major courses you took, especially if they were the most difficult courses offered at your school in your major.

- Use industry buzzwords and acronyms. Recruiters and hiring managers zero in on them. Remember—anything you put in your résumé is fair game for interview questions. If you state that you have "in-depth" experience with something, you better have it.

> *"A good résumé actually helps your interviewer ask questions that showcase your strengths."*

- Create different versions of your résumé, including one that can be scanned into a résumé database and one in ASCII to e-mail to appropriate company contacts.

A résumé is only one tool in your career search arsenal. Just as important is developing a good network of contacts in the industry you are targeting. Get as much relevant work experience as you can during summers and the school year. It isn't enough these days to have a sought-after major or high GPA. What increasingly sets candidates apart is work experience gained while in pursuit of their degrees.

A good résumé actually helps your interviewer ask questions that showcase your strengths. Good luck!

Jump-Starting Your Job Search*

While you're in college,

- Join the student organization in your specialty.

- Get summer internships before you're a senior.

- Use alumni connections. Mary E. Schilling, director of career services at the College of William and Mary, says, "It isn't that these folks can give you a job, but they can give you some advice and pass along your résumé."

- "Treat e-mail as official correspondence, not as informal conversation," says Tom Wunderlich of Old Dominion University's career center. Avoid goofy or suggestive e-mail addresses or phone messages. "No song of the day or joke of the week on your voicemail," Wunderlich advises.

*Based on "Get an Edge on Competition before School Lets Out," *Chicago Tribune Internet Edition*, December 19, 2001.

A **résumé** is a persuasive summary of your qualifications for employment. If you're on the job market, having a résumé makes you look well organized and prepared. When you're employed, having an up-to-date résumé makes it easier to take advantage of opportunities that may come up for an even better job. If you're several years away from job hunting, preparing a résumé now will help you become more conscious of what to do in the next two or three years to make yourself an attractive candidate. Writing a résumé is also an ego-building experience: The person who looks so good on paper is **you!**

This chapter covers paper, Web, and scannable résumés. Job application letters (sometimes called cover letters) are discussed in Chapter 18. Chapter 19 discusses interviews and the communication after the interview. All three chapters focus on job hunting in the United States. Conventions, expectations, and criteria differ from culture to culture: different norms apply in different countries.

All job communications must be tailored to your unique qualifications. Adopt the wording or layout of an example if it's relevant to your own situation, but don't be locked into the forms in this book. You've got different strengths; your résumé will be different, too.

A Time Line for Job Hunting

Informal preparation for job hunting should start soon after you arrive on campus. Join extracurricular organizations on campus and in the community to increase your knowledge and provide a network for learning about jobs. Find a job that gives you experience. Note which courses you like—and why you like them. If you like thinking and learning about a subject, you're more likely to enjoy a job in that field.

Formal preparation for job hunting should begin a full year *before you begin interviewing.* Visit the campus placement office to see what services it provides. Ask friends who are on the job market about their experiences in interviews; find out what kinds of job offers they get. Check into the possibility of getting an internship or a co-op job that will give you relevant experience before you interview.

The year you interview, register with your Placement Office early. If you plan to graduate in the spring, prepare your résumé and plan your interview strategy early in the fall. Initial campus interviews occur from October to February for May or June graduation. In January or February, write to any organization you'd like to work for that hasn't interviewed on campus. From February to April, you're likely to visit one or more offices for a second interview.

Try to have a job offer lined up *before* you get the degree. People who don't need jobs immediately are more confident in interviews and usually get better job offers. If you have to job-hunt after graduation, plan to spend at least 30 hours a week on your job search. The time will pay off in a better job that you find more quickly.

Evaluating Your Strengths and Interests

A self-assessment is the first step in producing a good résumé. Each person could do several jobs happily. Personality and aptitude tests can tell you what your strengths are, but they won't say, "You should be a _____." You'll still need to answer questions like these:

- What achievements have given you the most satisfaction? *Why* did you enjoy them?

- Would you rather have firm deadlines or a flexible schedule? Do you prefer working alone or with other people? Do you prefer specific instructions and standards for evaluation or freedom and uncertainty? How comfortable are you with pressure? Are you willing to pay your dues for several years before you are promoted? How much challenge do you want?

- Are you willing to take work home? To travel? How important is money to you? Prestige? Time to spend with family and friends?

- Where do you want to live? What features in terms of weather, geography, cultural and social life do you see as ideal?

- Is it important to you that your work achieve certain purposes or values, or do you see work as just a way to make a living? Are the organization's culture and ethical standards important to you?

Once you know what is most important to you, analyze the job market to see where you could find what you want. For example, Peter's greatest interest is athletics, but he isn't good enough for the pros. Studying the job market might suggest several alternatives. He could teach sports and physical fitness as a high school coach or a corporate fitness director. He could cover sports for a newspaper, a magazine, or a TV station. He could go into management or sales for a professional sports team, a health club, or a company that sells sports equipment.

Using the Internet in Your Job Search

Every candidate should check the Internet as part of a job search. Some Web pages are merely advertisements for for-fee services, but several comprehensive sites give detailed information about writing résumés and application letters, researching companies, and preparing for interviews. Figure 17.1 lists some of the best sites.

FIGURE 17.1   Comprehensive Web Job Sites Covering the Entire Job Search Process

Archeus WorkSearch
 www.garywill.com/worksearch

CareerBuilder
 www.careerbuilder.com

College Grad Job Hunter
 www.collegegrad.com

The Five O'Clock Club
 www.fiveoclockclub.com

JobHuntersBible.com (Dick Bolles)
 www.jobhuntersbible.com/intro/intromez.shtml

JobOptions
 www.joboptions.com/jo_main/index.jsp

JobStar Central
 http://jobstar.org

Monster.com
 www.monster.com

MonsterTrak
 www.monstertrak.com

Quintessential Careers
 www.quintcareers.com/index.html

The Riley Guide
 www.rileyguide.com

The Rockport Institute
 www.rockportinstitute.com/main.html

What Employers Want*

Good communication skills are what employers want most when hiring new people, according to a survey conducted by the National Association of Colleges and Employers.

Honesty/integrity ranked second.

The ability to work in a team came next, followed by interpersonal skills and a strong work ethic.

*Based on "The Perfect Candidate," Job Outlook 2002, www.jobweb.com.

How Employers Use Résumés

Understanding how employers use résumés will help you create a résumé that works for you.

1. **Employers use résumés to decide whom to interview.** (The major exceptions are on-campus interviews, where the campus placement office has policies that determine who meets with the interviewer.) Since résumés are used to screen out applicants, omit anything that may create a negative impression.

2. **Résumés are scanned or skimmed.** At many companies, résumés are scanned into an electronic job applicant tracking system. Only résumés that match keywords are skimmed by a human being. A human may give a résumé 3 to 30 seconds before deciding to keep or toss it. You must design your résumé to pass both the "scan test" and the "skim test."

3. **Employers assume that your letter and résumé represent your best work.** Neatness, accuracy, and freedom from typographical errors are essential.

4. **Interviewers usually reread your résumé before the interview to refresh their memories.** Be ready to offer fuller details about everything on your résumé.

5. **After the search committee has chosen an applicant, it submits the applicant's résumé to people in the organization who must approve the appointment.** These people may have different backgrounds and areas of expertise. Spell out acronyms. Explain Greek-letter honor societies, unusual job titles, or organizations that may be unfamiliar to the reader.

Guidelines for Résumés

Writing a résumé is not an exact science. If your skills are in great demand, you can violate every guideline here and still get a good job. But when you must compete against many applicants, these guidelines will help you look as good on paper as you are in person.

Length

A one-page résumé is sufficient, but do fill the page. Less than a full page suggests that you do not have very much to say for yourself.

The average résumé is now two pages, according to career-planning consultant Marilyn Moats Kennedy. An experiment that mailed one- or two-page résumés to recruiters at Big Five accounting firms showed that even readers who said they preferred short résumés were more likely to want to interview the candidate with the longer résumé.[1]

If you do use more than one page, the second page should have at least 10 to 12 lines. Use a second sheet and staple it to the first so that readers who skim see the staple and know that there's more. Leave less important information for the second page. Put your name and "Page 2" or "Cont." on the page. If the pages are separated, you want the reader to know who the qualifications belong to and that the second page is not your whole résumé.

Emphasis

Emphasize the things you've done that (a) are most relevant to the position for which you're applying, (b) show your superiority to other applicants, and (c) are recent.

Show that you're qualified by giving details on relevant course projects, activities, and jobs where you've done similar work. Marketing recruiters responded more positively to résumés giving details about course projects, especially when candidates had little relevant work experience.[2] Be brief about low-level jobs that simply show dependability. To prove that you're the best candidate for the job, emphasize items that set you apart from other applicants: promotions, honors and achievements, experience with computers or other relevant equipment, foreign languages, and so on.

If you're getting a two-year or a four-year degree, omit high school jobs, activities, and honors unless you need them to fill the page. When you're 25 or older, include information about high school only if you need it to show geographical flexibility. Focus on achievements in the last three to five years. Whatever your age at the time you write a résumé, you want to suggest that you are now the best you've ever been.

Include full-time work after high school before you returned to college and work during college to support yourself or to earn expenses. If the jobs you held then were low-level ones, present them briefly or combine them:

> 2000–04   Part-time and full-time jobs to support family

You can emphasize material by putting it at the top or the bottom of a page, by giving it more space, and by setting it off with white space. The beginning and end—of a document, a page, a list—are positions of emphasis. When you have a choice (e.g., in a list of job duties), put less important material in the middle, not at the end, to avoid the impression of "fading out."

Weak order: Coordinated weekly schedules, assigned projects to five staff members, evaluated their performance, and submitted weekly time sheets.

Emphatic order: Coordinated weekly schedules and submitted weekly time sheets. Assigned projects to five staff members and evaluated their performance.

You can also emphasize material by presenting it in a vertical list, by using a phrase in a heading, and by providing details. For example, rather than presenting your internship work in long paragraphs, use bulleted lists to make your accomplishments stand out.

Details

Details provide evidence to support your claims, convince the reader, and separate you from other applicants. Tell how many people you trained or supervised, how much money you budgeted or raised. Describe the aspects of the job you did.

Too vague: Sales Manager, *The Daily Collegian*, University Park, PA, 2000–03. Supervised staff; promoted ad sales.

Good details: Sales Manager, *The Daily Collegian*, University Park, PA, 2002–03. Supervised 22-member sales staff; helped recruit, interview, and select staff; assigned duties and scheduled work; recommended best performers for promotion. Motivated staff to increase paid ad inches 10% over previous year's sales.

Omit details that add nothing to a title, that are less impressive than the title alone, or that suggest a faulty sense of priorities (e.g., listing minor offices in an organization that tries to give everyone something to do). Either use strong details or just give the office or job title without any details.

Writing Style

Without sacrificing content, be as concise as possible.

A Flexible Marketing Document*

A good résumé is a flexible marketing document that can be customized for different situations. . . . [E]mployers like to see facts on achievements—such as sales figures or quotas that have been attained—in the resume as long as they're concise. Beyond that, common sense rules. Be brief and clear and tailor the document to each employer['s] needs.

*Quoted from Hal Lancaster, "The Standard Résumé Still Has a Role in Job Searches," *The Wall Street Journal*, February 3, 1998, B1.

Templates: Use Caution

Many Web sites have templates for paper and online résumés. If you choose to use one of them, print out a copy before you submit your résumé. Less sophisticated programs use fixed spacing before headings. If you skip the objective, or have less experience than the template allows, you may get blank space—hardly a way to build a good impression.

Almost certainly, you can create a better résumé by adapting a basic style you like to your own unique qualifications.

Wordy:	Member, Meat Judging Team, 2000–01
	Member, Meat Judging Team, 2001–02
	Member, Meat Judging Team, 2002–03
	Captain, Meat Judging Team, 2003–04
Tight:	Meat Judging Team, 2000–04; Captain 2003–04

Wordy:	Performed foundation load calculations
Tight:	Calculated foundation loads

Résumés normally use phrases and sentence fragments. Complete sentences are acceptable if they are the briefest way to present information. To save space and to avoid sounding arrogant, never use *I* in a résumé. *Me* and *my* are acceptable if they are unavoidable or if using them reduces wordiness.

Verbs or gerunds (the *-ing* form of verbs) create a more dynamic image of you than do nouns, so use them on résumés that will be read by people. (Rules for scannable résumés to be read by computers come later in this chapter.) In the following revisions, nouns, verbs, and gerunds are in bold type:

Nouns:	Chair, Income Tax Assistance Committee, Winnipeg, MB, 2003–04. Responsibilities: **recruitment** of volunteers; flyer **design, writing,** and **distribution** for **promotion** of program; **speeches** to various community groups and nursing homes to advertise the service.
Verbs:	Chair, Income Tax Assistance Committee, Winnipeg, MB, 2003–04. **Recruited** volunteers for the program. **Designed, wrote,** and **distributed** a flyer to promote the program; **spoke** to various community groups and nursing homes to advertise the service.
Gerunds:	Chair, Income Tax Assistance Committee, Winnipeg, MB, 2003–04. Responsibilities included **recruiting** volunteers for the program; **designing, writing,** and **distributing** a flyer to promote the program; and **speaking** to various community groups and nursing homes to advertise the service.

Note that the items in the list must be in parallel structure (◄▥ p. 101).

Layout, Printing, and Paper

Experiment with layout, fonts, and spacing to get an attractive résumé. Consider creating a letterhead that you use for both your résumé and your application letter.

Use enough white space to make your résumé easy to read, but not so much that you look as if you're padding. Even if you pay someone else to produce your résumé, *you* must specify the exact layout: you cannot expect a paid typist to care as much about your résumé as you do.

Print your résumé on a laser printer. Take advantage of different sizes of type and perhaps of rules (thin lines) to make your résumé look professional.

Print your résumé on standard 8½-by-11-inch paper (never legal size). White paper is standard; a very pale color is also acceptable. If you have a two-page résumé, consider having it printed on the front and left-inside page of a folded 11-by-17-inch page, with your application letter on the right-inside page.

Kinds of Résumés

There are two kinds of résumés: chronological and skills. A **chronological résumé** summarizes what you did in a time line (starting with the most recent events, and going backward in **reverse chronology**). It emphasizes degrees, job titles, and dates. It is the traditional résumé format. Figures 17.2 and 17.5 show chronological résumés.

FIGURE 17.2 Chronological Résumé

Vary font sizes. The name is in 18–point, the main headings in 12–point, and the text in 11–point type.

Jerry A. Jackson

Campus Address
1636½ Highland Street
Columbus, OH 43201
(614) 555-5718
jackson.2495@osu.edu
www.fisher.osu/students/jackson.2495/home.htm

Permanent Address
45 East Mulberry
Huntington, NY 11746
516) 555-7793

If you have a professional Web page, include its URL.

List 3–7 qualifications. Use keywords. Quantify when possible.

Summary of Qualifications

- High energy. Played sports during four years of college. Started two businesses.
- Sales experience. Sold both clothing and investments successfully.
- Presentation skills. In individual and group presentations, spoke to groups ranging from 2 to 75 people. Gave informative, persuasive, and inspirational talks.
- Knowledgeable about stocks and bonds, especially energy and telecommunication companies.
- Computer experience. Microsoft Word, Excel, SPSS, PowerPoint, and Dreamweaver. Experience creating Web pages. *Specify computer programs you know well.*

Education

B.S. in Family Financial Management, June 2004, The Ohio State University, Columbus, OH
"B" Average   *Give your grade average if it's good.*

Sports Experience

BAAD (Buckeye Athletes Against Drugs)
Intramural Hockey Team (Division Champions, Winter 2003)
Three-year Varsity Letterman, Ohio State University, Columbus, OH
Men's NCAA Division I Lacrosse   *(The Lacrosse team did poorly, so he omits its ranking.)*

Experience

Financial Sales Representative, Primerica Company, Columbus, OH, February 2003-present.
- Work with clients to plan investment strategies to meet family and retirement goals.
- Research and recommend specific investments.

Ways to handle self-employment

Entrepreneur, Huntington, NY, and Columbus, OH, September 2002-January 2003.
- Created a saleable product, secured financial backing, found a manufacturer, supervised production, and sold product–12 dozen T-shirts at a $5.25 profit each–to help pay for college expenses.

Landscape Maintenance Supervisor, Huntington, NY, Summers 1994-2002.
- Formed a company to cut lawns, put up fences, fertilize, garden, and paint houses.
- Hired, fired, trained, motivated, and paid friends to complete jobs.

Specify large sums of money

Collector and Repair Worker, ACN Inc., Huntington, NY, Summers 1994-2000.
- Collected and counted up to $10,000 a day in New York metro area.
- Worked with technicians troubleshooting and repairing electronic and coin mechanisms of video and pinball games, cigarette machines, and jukeboxes.

Honesty in the Résumé

Never lie in a résumé.

It's OK to omit negative information (like a low grade point average). If you were an officer in an organization, it's OK to list the title even if you didn't do much. It's OK to provide details when you did more than the job title indicates, or to give the job title alone if you had an inflated official title (e.g., Assistant Manager) but didn't really do much.

But it isn't OK to lie.

Interviewers will ask you about items in the résumé. If you have to back down, you destroy your credibility. And if lies are discovered after you are hired, you will be fired.

Use a chronological résumé when

- Your education and experience are a logical preparation for the position for which you're applying.
- You have impressive job titles, offices, or honors.

A **skills résumé** emphasizes the skills you've used, rather than the job in which or the date when you used them. Figures 17.6 and 17.7 (pp. 501 and 508) show skills résumés. Use a skills résumé when

- Your education and experience are not the usual route to the position for which you're applying.
- You're changing fields.
- You want to combine experience from paid jobs, activities or volunteer work, and courses to show the extent of your experience in administration, finance, speaking, and so on.

The two kinds differ in what information is included and how that information is organized. You may assume that the advice in this chapter applies to both kinds of résumés unless there is an explicit statement that the two kinds of résumés would handle a category differently.

What to Include in a Résumé

Although the résumé is a factual document, its purpose is to persuade. In a job application form or an application for graduate or professional school, you answer every question even if the answer is not to your credit. In a résumé, you cannot lie, but you can omit anything that does not work in your favor.

Résumés commonly contain the following information. The categories marked with an asterisk are essential.

> *Name, Address, and Phone Number
> Career Objective
> Summary of Qualifications
> *Education
> *Experience
> Honors
> Activities
> References

You may choose other titles for these categories and add categories that are relevant for your qualifications: COMPUTER SKILLS, FOREIGN LANGUAGES.

EDUCATION and EXPERIENCE always stand as separate categories, even if you have only one item under each head. Combine other headings so that you have at least two long or three short items under each heading. For example, if you're in one honor society, two social clubs, and on one athletic team, combine them all under ACTIVITIES AND HONORS.

If you have more than seven items under a heading, consider using subheadings. For example, a student who had a great many activities might divide them into STUDENT GOVERNMENT, OTHER CAMPUS ACTIVITIES, and COMMUNITY SERVICE.

Put your strongest categories near the top and at the bottom of the first page. If you have impressive work experience, you might want to put that category first after your name, put EDUCATION in the middle of the page, and put your address at the bottom.

Name, Address, and Phone Number

Use your full name, even if everyone calls you by a nickname. You may use an initial rather than spelling out your first or middle name. Put your name in big type.

If you use only one address, consider centering it under your name. If you use two addresses (office and home, campus and permanent, until _____/ after _____) set them up side by side to balance the page visually. Use a comma after the city before the state. It is OK to use either post office (two-letter, full caps, no period) abbreviations for the state or to spell out the state name. Be consistent throughout the résumé.

Urbana, IL 61801

Wheaton, Illinois 60187

If you have an e-mail address, give it too.

Give a complete phone number, including the area code. Either put the area code in parentheses, space, then put the number OR separate the area code by a hyphen.

(217) 555-1212 or 217-555-1212

If you don't have a phone, try to make arrangements with someone to take messages for you—employers usually call to schedule interviews and make job offers.

Omit your age, marital status, race, sex, and health. Questions about these topics are illegal.

Career Objective

CAREER OBJECTIVE statements should sound like the job descriptions an employer might use in a job listing. Keep your statement brief—two or three lines at most. Tell what you want to do, what level of responsibility you want to hold.

Ineffective career objective:	To offer a company my excellent academic foundation in hospital technology and my outstanding skills in oral and written communication
Better career objective:	Hospital and medical sales requiring experience with state-of-the-art equipment

Good CAREER OBJECTIVES are hard to write. If you talk about entry-level work, you won't sound ambitious; if you talk about where you hope to be in 5 or 10 years, you won't sound as though you're willing to do entry-level work. When you're applying for a job that is a natural outgrowth of your education and experience, omit this category and specify the job you want in your cover letter.

Often you can avoid writing a CAREER OBJECTIVE statement by putting the job title or field under your name:

Joan Larson Ooyen	Terence Edward Garvey	David R. Lunde
Marketing	Technical Writer	Corporate Fitness Director

Note that you can use the field you're in even if you're a new college graduate. To use a job title, you should have some relevant work experience.

If you use a separate heading for CAREER OBJECTIVE, put it immediately after your address, before the first major heading.

Objectional Objectives*

The following quotations show how bad a poor objective can be.

Objective: Easy work, pleasant surroundings, large expense account, high wages, and close to home.

Objective: To work with real people again.

Objective: To have something to do.

Objective: To get out of a rut.

Objective: Cash for talent.

Objective: A management position in which I can make order out of chaos and evil.

Objective: To have fun and live large.

*Quoted from "Robert Half's Resumania," in Taunee Besson, *The Wall Street Journal National Employment Business Weekly: Resumes*, 3rd ed. (New York: Wiley, 1999), 69; and Web sites that will remain unidentified.

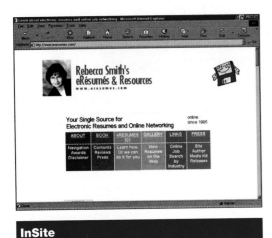

InSite

www.eresumes.com

Rebecca Smith's eRésumés & Resources provides extensive examples of keywords and Web résumés.

Summary of Qualifications

A section summarizing the candidate's qualifications seems to have first appeared in scannable résumés, where its keywords helped to increase the number of matches a résumé produced. But the section proved useful for human readers as well and now is a standard part of most résumés. The best summaries show your knowledge of the specialized terminology of your field and offer specific, quantifiable achievements.

Weak: Reliable

Better: Achieved zero sick days in four years with UPS.

Weak: Staff accountant

Better: Experience with accounts payable, accounts receivable, audits, and month-end closings. Prepared monthly financial reports.

Weak: Presentation skills

Better: Gave 20 individual and 7 team presentations to groups ranging from 5 to 100 people.

Your real accomplishments should go in the SUMMARY section. Include as many keywords as you legitimately can. Terms suggested by Rebecca Smith appear in Figure 17.3; see her Web site for even more.

Education

EDUCATION can be your first major category if you've just earned (or are about to earn) a degree, if you have a degree that is essential or desirable for the position you're seeking, or if you can present the information briefly. Put EDUCATION later if you need all of page 1 for another category or if you lack a degree that other applicants may have (see Figure 17.5).

Under EDUCATION, include information about your undergraduate and graduate degrees. You may set up the information in one of three ways. In all of them, use commas to separate elements:

FIGURE 17.3   Keywords for Sample Jobs

Accountant	Hotel manager	Human resources generalist	Marketing director
Accounts payable	Hospitality management	EEO regulations	Strategic planning skills
Accounts receivable	Banquet sales	ADA	Market research
Audits	Marketing	Applicant screening	New product transition
G/L	Guest relations	Applicant tracking	Trade show management
Microsoft Excel	Employee training	401(K)	Competitive market analysis
Financial reports	Front office management	Merit pay program	Team skills
SEC filings	Occupancy rate	Training and development	Multiple priorities
Budget analysis	Guest services	Compensation	Direct marketing campaigns
Gross margin analysis	Convention management	Recruitment	Business models
Month-end closings	Reservations	Diversity	Marketing business plans

Source: Rebecca Smith, *Electronic Résumés & Online Networking: How to Use the Internet to Do a Better Job Search, Including a Complete, Up-to-Date Resource Guide* (Franklin Lakes, NJ: Career Press, 1999), 192–94.

Bachelor of Science in Business Administration, May 2005, University of Illinois at
   Urbana–Champaign
Options: University of Illinois, Urbana, IL
               University of Illinois (Urbana, Illinois)

Use the same form for city, state of all schools. If you continue information about education on the same line, put a period after the state. Otherwise, use no punctuation.

B.S. in Education, June 2005, The Ohio State University, Columbus, OH.
   Undeclared minor in business.

But . . .

B.S. in Education, June 2005, The Ohio State University, Columbus, OH

When you're getting a four-year degree, include junior college if it gave you an area of expertise different from the area of your major. Include summer school if you took courses to fit in extra electives or to graduate early but not if you were making up a course you flunked during the year. Include study abroad, even if you didn't earn college credits. If you got a certificate for international study, give the name and explain the significance of the certificate.

To punctuate your degrees, do not space between letters and periods:

A.S. in Office Administration

B.S. in Accountancy

Ed.D. in Business Education

Current usage also permits you to omit the periods:

MBA

PhD in Finance

Highlight proficiency in foreign or computer languages by using a separate category.

Professional certifications can be listed under EDUCATION or in a separate category.

If your GPA is good, include it. Because grade point systems vary, specify what your GPA is based on: "3.4/4.0" means 3.4 on a 4.0 scale. If your GPA is under 3.0 on a 4.0 scale, use words rather than numbers: "B− average." If your GPA isn't impressive, calculate your average in your major and your average for your last 60 hours. If these are higher than your overall GPA, consider using them.

There are two basic options for presenting your educational information. Option I just gives degrees, dates, school, and city; option II also tells about your course work.

Option I: List in reverse chronological order (most recent first) each degree earned, field of study, date, school, city, state of any graduate work, short courses and professional certification courses, college, junior college, or school from which you transferred.

Master of Accounting Science, May 2005, Arizona State University, Tempe, AZ
Bachelor of Arts in Finance, May 2003, New Mexico State University, Las Cruces, NM

Plan to sit for the CPA exam November 2005

Résumé Goofs*

Flunked my CPA exam with high grades.

Typing speed: 756 wpm.

Statistics mayor.

My GPA at night is 3.0.

Cities of preference: Mexico City. Languages Spoken: French.

Exposure to German for two years, but many words are not appropriate for business.

Married girls 16 and 18 years.

Delivered papers at age 12 like many other great Americans. The only difference is that they became great.

I am not smart, but I am not stupid.

I am considered charming. References available.

*Quoted from Robert Half, "Resume goofs," *Managing Your Career,* Spring 1989, 37, 39; Selwyn Feinstein, "Labor Letter," *The Wall Street Journal,* April 5, 1989, A1; Geoff Martz, *How to Survive without Your Parents' Money: Making It from College to the Real World* (New York, Villard Books, 1993), 112; and Web sites that will remain unidentified.

BS in Personnel Management, June 2006, Georgia State University, Milledgeville, GA

AS in Office Management, June 2003, Georgia Community College, Atlanta, GA

Option II: After giving the basic information (degree, field of study, date, school, city, state) about your degree, list courses, using short descriptive titles rather than course numbers. Use a subhead like "Courses Related to Major" or "Courses Related to Financial Management" that will allow you to list all the courses (including psychology, speech, and business communication) that will help you in the job for which you're applying. Don't say "Relevant Courses," as that implies your other courses were irrelevant.

Bachelor of Science in Management, May 2004, Illinois State University, Normal, IL

GPA: 3.8/4.0

Courses Related to Management:

Personnel Administration	Business Decision Making
Finance	International Business
Management I and II	Marketing
Accounting I and II	Legal Environment of Business
Business Report Writing	Business Speaking

Salutatorian, Niles Township East High School, June 1999, Niles, IL

Listing courses is an unobtrusive way to fill a page. You may also want to list courses or the number of hours in various subjects if you've taken an unusual combination of courses that uniquely qualify you for the position for which you're applying.

BS in Marketing, May 2005, California State University at Northridge

30 hours in marketing

15 hours in Spanish

9 hours in Chicano studies

Honors and Awards

It's nice to have the word HONORS in a heading where it will be obvious even when the reader skims the résumé. If you have fewer than three and therefore cannot justify a separate heading, consider a heading ACTIVITIES AND HONORS to get that important word in a position of emphasis.

Include the following kinds of entries in this category:

- Listings in recognition books (e.g., *Who's Who in the Southwest*).
- Academic honor societies. Specify the nature of Greek-letter honor societies so the reader doesn't think they're just social clubs.
- Fellowships and scholarships, including honorary scholarships for which you received no money and fellowships you could not hold because you received another fellowship at the same time.
- Awards given by professional societies.
- Major awards given by civic groups.
- Varsity letters; selection to all-state or all-America teams; finishes in state, national, or Olympic meets. (These could also go under ACTIVITIES but may look more impressive under HONORS. Put them under one category or the other—not both.)

Omit honors like "Miss Congeniality" that work against the professional image you want your résumé to create.

As a new college graduate, try to put HONORS on page 1. In a skills résumé, put HONORS on page 1 if they're major (e.g., Phi Beta Kappa, Phi Kappa Phi). Otherwise, save them till page 2—EXPERIENCE will probably take the whole first page.

Experience

You may use other headings if they work better: WORK EXPE-RIENCE, SUMMER AND PART-TIME JOBS, MILITARY EX-PERIENCE, MARKETING EXPERIENCE, ACHIEVEMENTS RELATED TO CAREER OBJECTIVE.

What to include

Under this section, include the following information for each job you list: position or job title, organization, city and state (no zip code), dates of employment, and other details, such as full- or part-time status, job duties, special responsibilities, or the fact that you started at an entry-level position and were promoted. Use the verbs in Figure 17.4 to brainstorm what you've done. Include unpaid jobs and self-employment if they provided relevant skills (e.g., supervising people, budgeting, planning, persuading).

Normally, go back as far as the summer after high school. Include earlier jobs if you started working someplace before graduating from high school but continued working there after graduation. However, give minimal detail about high school jobs. If you worked full-time after high school, make that clear. Give details of relevant skills, such as those listed in Figure 17.4.

If as an undergraduate you've earned a substantial portion of your college expenses, say so in a separate sentence either under EXPERIENCE or in the section on personal data. (Graduate students are expected to support themselves.)

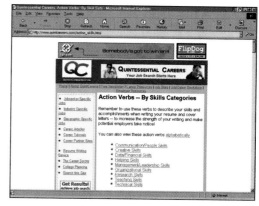

InSite

www.quintcareers.com/action_skills.html

Quintessential Careers offers long lists of action verbs, arranged both alphabetically and by skill.

FIGURE 17.4   Action Verbs for Résumés

analyzed	directed	led	reviewed
budgeted	earned	managed	revised
built	edited	motivated	saved
chaired	established	negotiated	scheduled
coached	examined	observed	simplified
collected	evaluated	organized	sold
conducted	helped	persuaded	solved
coordinated	hired	planned	spoke
counseled	improved	presented	started
created	increased	produced	supervised
demonstrated	interviewed	recruited	trained
designed	introduced	reported	translated
developed	investigated	researched	wrote

Part Five Job Hunting

But I Haven't Done Anything!*

Some students have trouble coming up with details. "I've never really done anything." That's too negative. *Everybody* has done *something*. How have you spent the last five years?

One woman's only job was as a part-time salesclerk in the lighting department of a department store. Her official duties weren't important. But when she focused on what she'd actually done, she had evidence of skills employers want.

She had done research. To answer customers' questions, she read about lighting, vision, and energy consumption. She visited competitors and noticed their products and displays.

She had demonstrated creativity. In August, she rigged up a mannequin to look like a student—slouched in a chair, holding textbook and pop bottle, surrounded by clothes, a football, and a guitar. On the table was a lamp positioned to provide good study light with a sign, "At least he won't ruin his eyes."

Her display worked. The store sold four times as many lamps that August as it ever had, including the month before Christmas.

A résumé entry could give these details to support claims for experience in research and persuading. And she had increased sales in her unit 400%.

*Based on John L. Munschauer, *Jobs for English Majors and Other Smart People* (Princeton, NJ: Peterson's Guides, 1986), 36–37.

> These jobs paid 40% of my college expenses.

> Paid for 65% of expenses with jobs, scholarships, and loans.

Note that a complete sentence is acceptable if it does not use *I.*

Formats for setting up EXPERIENCE

There are two basic ways to set up the EXPERIENCE section of your résumé. In **indented format,** items that are logically equivalent begin at the same space, with carryover lines indented four spaces or three-tenths of an inch. Indented format emphasizes job titles. Figure 17.5 uses indented format. Use commas to separate items. Put a period after the date, before other details about the job (responsibilities, etc.):

Job title, name of organization, city, state, dates. Other information.

EXPERIENCE

Engineering Assistant, Sohio Chemical Company, Lima, Ohio, Summer 2004. Originally hired as a laboratory technician, Summer 2003; promoted following year. As laboratory technician, tested wastewater effluents for compliance with Federal EPA standards. As engineering assistant, helped chemists design a test to analyze groundwater quality and seepage around landfills. Presented weekly oral and written progress reports to Director of Research and Development.
Animal Caretaker, Animalcare, Worthington, Ohio, June 1999–September 2002. Full-time during summers; part-time during senior year of high school.

Two-margin or **block format** emphasizes *when* you worked, so it is appropriate if you've only held low-level jobs. Don't use two-margin format if your work history has gaps or if you've worked as an intern or held another job directly relevant to the position you're applying for.

EXPERIENCE	
Summers, 2002–04	Repair worker, Bryant Heating and Cooling, Providence, RI.
2002–03	Library Clerk, Boston University Library, Boston, MA. Part-time during school year.
2000–02	Food Service Worker, Boston University, Boston, MA. Part-time during school year.
Summer, 2001	Delivery person, Domino's Pizza, Providence, RI.

Use a hyphen to join inclusive dates:

March-August, 2004 (or write out March to August, 2004)

1999-2003

2004-05

If you use numbers for dates, do not space before or after the slash:

10/03–5/04

Choosing headings for skills résumés

In a skills résumé the subheadings under EXPERIENCE will be the *skills* used in or the *aspects* of the job you are applying for, rather than the title or the dates of the jobs you've held (as in a chronological résumé). For entries under each skill, combine experience from paid jobs, unpaid work, classes, activities, and community service.

FIGURE 17.5 A Community College Student's Chronological Résumé

Steven W. Zajano

921 South Seventh Street
Cambridge, Ohio 43725
(740) 555-4715

Summary of Qualifications
- Dependable, detail-minded, results-oriented
- Strong background in environmental practices and concepts
- Hands-on experience in aquaculture, landscaping, and land restoration

Work Experience

Use present tense when you're doing the job now.

Groundskeeper, Muskingum College, New Concord, Ohio, 2002–present.
- Maintain campus grounds, athletic fields, and equipment
- Perform electrical, plumbing, and carpentry work as needed

How to present a job where you've been promoted.

Crew Leader, Seneca National Fish Hatchery, Senecaville, Ohio, 1999–2001.
Started as Young Adult Conservation Corps (YACC) member; promoted to crew leader after five months. As crew leader,

Use past tense for a job that's over.

Be specific about the number of people you've supervised.

- Maintained hatchery facilities
- Planned work activities and schedules for 12 YACC workers

Put this duty second so extra white space below it emphasizes it.

Landscaper, R.G.'s Landscaping Service, Canton, Ohio, Summer 1999.
- Maintained existing lawns; landscaped and established new lawns

Use parallel structure for all duties.

Farm Worker, Hanover Stud Horse Farm, Canal Fulton, Ohio, 1995–99.
- Maintained tractors and mended fences
- Baled hay and straw
- Cared for thoroughbred racing horses

Put most interesting duty last where it stands out.

Activities and Interests
Boy Scout Troop, Cambridge, Ohio (Leader)
Bus Ministry, Cambridge United Christian Church
Hunting, fishing, camping, swimming, hiking

Some readers may respond negatively. But this ministry is an important part of Steve's life, and he wants to suggest that he isn't just interested in outdoor recreational pursuits.

Education
Associate of Applied Sciences, June 2004, Hocking Technical College, Nelsonville, Ohio
Specialization: Natural Resources Management

References

Give phone number and e-mail address of each reference.

James Heidler, Grounds Supervisor, Muskingum College, Cambridge, Ohio 43725
(740) 555-5024 <heidlermc@yahoo.com>
Richard Jordet, YACC Program Director, Seneca National Fish Hatchery, Byesville, Ohio
43723 (740) 555-5541 <rjourdet@snfh.gov>
Gerald Sagan, Professor of Natural Resources Management, Hocking Technical College,
Nelsonville, Ohio 43765 (740) 555-3492 <sagan.12@hocking.edu>

Put e-mail addresses in brackets unless the address is on a line by itself. Avoid underlines: they make the address hard to read.

I Do Good Work*

Use headings that reflect the jargon of the job for which you're applying: *logistics* rather than *planning* for a technical job; *procurement* rather than *purchasing* for a job with the military. Figure 17.6 shows a skills résumé for someone who is changing fields.

A job description can give you ideas for headings. Possible headings and subheadings for skills résumés include

Administration	Communication
Alternates or Subheadings:	Alternates or Subheadings:
Budgeting	Conducting Meetings
Coordinating	Editing
Evaluating	Fund-Raising
Implementing	Interviewing
Negotiating	Oral Skills
Planning	Negotiating
Keeping Records	Persuading
Scheduling	Proposal Writing
Solving Problems	Report Writing
Supervising	

Many jobs require a mix of skills. Try to include the skills that you know will be needed in the job you want. For example, one study identified the six top communication skills for jobs in finance and in management.[3] Applicants who had experience in some of these areas could list them as well as subject-related skills and knowledge.

Finance	Management
Listening	Listening
Advising	Motivating
Building Relationships	Advising
Exchanging Routine Information	Building Relationships
Giving Feedback	Persuading
Persuading	Instructing

You need at least three subheadings in a skills résumé; six or seven is not uncommon. Give enough detail under each subheading so the reader will know what you did. Put the most important category from the reader's point of view first.

In a skills résumé, list your paid jobs under WORK HISTORY or EMPLOYMENT RECORD near the end of the résumé (see Figure 17.6). List only job title, employer, city, state, and dates. Omit details that you have already used under EXPERIENCE.

Activities

Employers are very interested in your activities if you're a new college graduate. If you've worked for several years after college or have an advanced degree (MBA, JD), you can omit ACTIVITIES and include PROFESSIONAL ACTIVITIES AND AFFILIATIONS or COMMUNITY AND PUBLIC SERVICE. If you went straight from college to graduate school but have an unusually strong record under ACTIVITIES, include this category even if all the entries are from your undergraduate days.

FIGURE 17.6 A Skills Résumé for Someone Changing Fields

On the first page of a skills résumé, put skills directly related to the job for which you're applying.

Marcella G. Cope

370 Monahan Lane
Dublin, OH 43016
614-555-1997
mcope@postbox.acs.ohio-state.edu

Objective

Put company's name in objective.

To help create high quality CD-ROM products in Metatec's New Media Solutions Division

Editing and Proofreading Experience

An extra half space creates good visual impact.

- **Edited** a textbook published by Simon and Schuster, revising with attention to format, consistency, coherence, document integrity, and document design.

- **Proofed** training and instructor's manuals, policy statements, student essays and research papers, internal documents, and promotional materials.

- **Worked with authors** in a variety of fields including English, communication, business, marketing, economics, education, history, sociology, biology, agriculture, computer science, law, and medicine to revise their prose and improve their writing skills by giving them oral and written feedback.

Writing Experience

- **Wrote** training and instructor's manuals, professional papers, and letters, memos, and reports.

- **Co-authored** the foreword to a forthcoming textbook (Fall 2003) from NCTE press.

- **Contributed** to a textbook forthcoming (Fall 2003) from Bedford Books/St. Martin's press.

Computer Experience

- **Designed** a Web page using Dreamweaver (www.cohums.ohio-state.edu/english/People/Bracken.1/Sedgwick/)

- **Learned and used** a variety of programs on both Macintosh and PC platforms:
Word Processing and Spreadsheets	Dreamweaver
Microsoft Project	PageMaker
E-Mail	PowerPoint
Aspects (a form for online synchronous discussion)	
Storyspace (a hypertext writing environment)	

Computer experience is crucial for almost every job. Specify the hardware and software you've worked with.

Other Business and Management Experience

- **Developed** policies, procedures, and vision statements.

- **Supervised** new staff members in a mentoring program.

- **Coordinated** program and individual schedules, planned work and estimated costs, set goals, and evaluated progress and results.

- **Member of team that directed** the nation's largest first-year writing program.

FIGURE 17.6 A Skills Résumé for Someone Changing Fields *(concluded)*

Marcella G. Cope

Page 2

*If you use two pages
be sure to put your name
and "Page 2" on the second page.
The reader may remove a staple.*

Employment History

*Most
recent
job
first.*

Graduate Teaching Associate, Department of English, The Ohio State University, September 1999-Present. Taught Intermediate and First-Year Composition.

Writing Consultant, University Writing Center, The Ohio State University, January-April 2002

Program Administrator, First-Year Writing Program, The Ohio State University, September 2000-January 2002

Honors

*Explain honor societies that the
reader may not know.*

Phi Kappa Phi Honor Society, inducted 2000. Membership based upon performance in top ten percent of graduate students nationwide.

Letters of Commendation, 1999-2002. Issued by the Director of Graduate Studies in recognition of outstanding achievement.

Dean's List, Northwestern University, Evanston, IL

Education

Master of Arts, June 2001, The Ohio State University, Columbus, OH. Cumulative GPA: 4.0/4.0

Bachelor of Arts, June 1999, Northwestern University, Evanston, IL. Graduated with Honors.

References

Kitty O. Locker
Associate Professor, Business and Administrative Communication
The Ohio State University
421 Denney Hall, 164 W. 17th Ave.
Columbus, OH 43210
614-555-6556
locker.1@osu.edu

Marilyn Duffey
Director, Ohio University Writing Program
Ohio University
140 Chubb Hall
Athens, OH 45701
614-555-9443
duffeymc@ohiou.edu

*Choose references who
can speak about your skills
for the job for which you're
applying.*

James Bracken
Associate Professor, English and Library Science
The Ohio State University
224 Main Library, 1858 Neil Avenue Mall
Columbus, OH 43210
614-555-2786
bracken@osu.edu

Include the following kinds of items under ACTIVITIES:

- Volunteer work. Include important committees and leadership roles.
- Membership in organized student activities. Include important subcommittees, leadership roles. Include minor offices only if they're directly related to the job for which you're applying or if they show growing responsibility (you held a minor office one year, a bigger office the following year). Include so-called major offices (e.g., vice president) even if you did very little. Provide descriptive details if (but only if) they help the reader realize how much you did and the importance of your work.
- Membership in professional associations. To find out about the association(s) in your field, ask your professors or check scholarly journals.
- Participation in organized activities that require talent or responsibility (e.g., choir, new student orientation).
- Participation in varsity, intramural, or independent athletics. However, don't list so many sports that you appear not to have had any time to study.
- Social clubs, if you held a major leadership role or if social skills are important for the job for which you're applying.
- Religious organizations if you held a major leadership role or if you're applying for a church-related job.

Major leadership roles may look more impressive if they're listed under EXPERIENCE instead of under ACTIVITIES.

Finding Your Flaws Online*

Ever file a workers' compensation claim? Wrecked a company car? Received a speeding ticket?

Prospective employers can find out if you did. And now, thanks to the Internet, they can do it almost instantly.

Informus Corp. makes a living giving curious employers information such as the names and phone numbers of your neighbors. Besides access to workers' compensation claims, Informus connects employers to credit bureaus and state agencies that store financial and criminal information.

*Quoted from Tawn Nhan, "On-line Service Checks Out Job Applicants," *The Columbus Dispatch*, May 19, 1996.

References

Including references anticipates the employer's needs and removes a potential barrier to your getting the job. To make your résumé fit on one page, you can omit this category. However, include REFERENCES if you're having trouble filling the page. Don't say "References Available on Request" since no job applicant is going to refuse to supply references. If you don't want your current employer to know you're job-hunting, omit the category in the résumé and say in the letter, "If I become a finalist for the job, I will supply the names of current references."

When you list references, include at least three, usually no more than five, never more than six. As a college student or a new graduate, include at least one professor and at least one employer or adviser—someone who can comment on your work habits and leadership skills. Don't use relatives or roommates, even if you've worked for them. Omit personal or character references who can say nothing about your work. If you're changing jobs, include your current superior.

Always ask the person's permission to list him or her as a reference. Don't say, "May I list you as a reference?" Instead, say, "Can you speak specifically about my work?" Jog the person's memory by taking along copies of work you did for him or her and a copy of your current résumé. Tell the person what points you'd like him or her to stress in a letter. Keep your list of references up to date. If it's been a year or more since you asked someone, ask again—and tell the person about your recent achievements.

For each reference, list name, title or position, organization, city and state, and phone number. You could also give the full mailing address if you think people are more likely to write than to call. Use courtesy titles (*Dr., Mr., Ms.*) for all or for none. By convention, all faculty with the rank of assistant professor or above may be called *Professor*. If you want to list teaching assistants, omit titles for all references.

References whom the reader knows are by far the most impressive. In a skills résumé, choose references who can testify to your abilities in the most important skills areas.

Include the name and address of your placement office if you have written recommendations on file there.

Ways to set up REFERENCES

To save space, present references in indented line format (see Figure 17.5). If you have slightly more room, double-space between the names of references. In indented line format, use a comma to separate lines. Do not put any punctuation after the zip code.

> REFERENCES
> Thomas Elgee, Professor of Community Health, University of Northern Colorado, Greeley, CO 80639 (302) 351-1111
> Elizabeth Tormei, Professor of Women's Studies, University of Northern Colorado, Greeley, CO 80639 (302) 351-2222
> Amy Wilson, Director, Rape Crisis Center, Denver, CO 80203 (303) 555-3333
> Matthew J. Kohl, Director, Brethren Community Services, Eugene, CO 80689 (302) 726-4444

When you list references vertically, omit punctuation at the end of a line, just as you would in the lines of an address on an envelope. Two-margin format takes up more space and can help you fill a page.

> REFERENCES
>
> Thomas Elgee   Elizabeth Tormei
> Professor of Community Health   Professor of Women's Studies
> University of Northern Colorado   University of Northern Colorado
> 321 Blevins Building   100 Humanities Building
> Greeley, CO 80639   Greeley, CO 80639
> (302) 351-1111   (302) 351-2222
>
> Amy Wilson   Matthew J. Kohl
> Director   Director
> Rape Crisis Center   Brethren Community Services
> 100 Main Street   4835 Goodale Blvd.
> Denver, CO 80203   Eugene, CO 80689
> (303) 351-3333   (302) 726-4444

Dealing with Difficulties

Some job hunters face special problems. This section gives advice for five common problems.

"All My Experience Is in My Family's Business."

In your résumé, simply list the company you worked for. For a reference, instead of a family member, list a supervisor, client, or vendor who can talk about your work. Since the reader may wonder whether "Jim Clarke" is any relation to the owner of "Clarke Construction Company," be ready to answer interview questions about why you're looking at other companies. Prepare an answer that stresses the broader opportunities you seek but doesn't criticize your family or the family business.

"I've Been Out of the Job Market for a While."

You need to prove to a potential employer that you're up-to-date and motivated. Carl Quintanilla suggests the following ways to do that:

- Be active in professional organizations. Attend meetings; read trade journals.
- Learn the computer programs that professionals in your field use.
- Find out your prospective employer's immediate priorities. If you can show you'll contribute from day one, you'll have a much easier sell. But to do that, you need to know what skills the employer is looking for, what needs the employer has.
- Show how your at-home experience relates to the workplace. Dealing with unpredictable situations, building consensus, listening, raising money, and making presentations are transferable skills.
- Create a portfolio of your work—even if it's for imaginary clients—to demonstrate your expertise.[4]

"I Want to Change Fields."

Have a good reason for choosing the field in which you're looking for work. "I want a change" or "I need to get out of a bad situation" does not convince an employer that you know what you're doing.

Think about how your experience relates to the job you want. Jack is an older-than-average student who wants to be a pharmaceutical sales representative. He has sold woodstoves, served subpoenas, and worked on an oil rig. A chronological résumé makes his work history look directionless. But a skills résumé could focus on persuasive ability (selling stoves), initiative and persistence (serving subpoenas), and technical knowledge (courses in biology and chemistry).[5]

Learn about the skills needed in the job you want: learn the buzzwords of the industry. (Chapter 18 has suggestions for ways to find these things out.) Figure 17.6 shows a skills résumé of someone changing fields.

"I Was Fired."

First, deal with the emotional baggage. You need to reduce negative feelings to a manageable level before you're ready to job-hunt.

Second, try to learn from the experience. You'll be a much more attractive job candidate if you can show that you've learned from the experience—whether your lesson is improved work habits or that you need to choose a job where you can do work you can point to with pride.

Third, suggests Phil Elder, an interviewer for an insurance company, call the person who fired you and say something like this: "Look, I know you weren't pleased with the job I did at _____. I'm applying for a job at _____ now and the personnel director may call you to ask about me. Would you be willing to give me the chance to get this job so that I can try to do things right this time?" All but the hardest of heart, says Elder, will give you one more chance. You won't get a glowing reference, but neither will the statement be so damning that no one is willing to hire you.[6]

"I Don't Have Any Experience."

If you have a year or more before you job hunt, you can get experience in several ways:

- Take a fast-food job—and keep it. If you do well, you'll be promoted to a supervisor within a year. Use every opportunity to learn about the management and financial aspects of the business.

Wacky Résumés*

In search of a position as a marketing manager, Olivia Scott created a CD titled "Who Is Olivia Scott?" She burned seven songs, including "She Works Hard for the Money" and "Southern Girl." The "liner notes" contained her résumé. She got an interview from one of the five companies to which she sent the CD.

To find a public relations job, Peter Shankman had his résumé printed on two 4-foot-by-3-foot poster boards and wore them, sandwich style, over his suit and overcoat. He stood on a Manhattan street corner on a cold January day from 6 AM to 7:15 PM and handed out 1,000 résumés. He got 200 phone calls, 45 interviews, and 20 job offers. He attributes his success to the fact that people saw him.

Aaron Rabinowitz e-mailed a photo of himself relaxing on an Israeli kibbutz with his dog. He got the public relations job he applied for.

But job candidates who have sent ransom notes, five dollar bills, and garden spades (from a job candidate named Forrest—"plant this Forrest and watch your company grow") got no nibbles.

*Based on Kemba J. Dunham, "Wacky Résumés Get Attention—But a Job, Too?" *The Wall Street Journal*, December 19, 2000, B1, B16.

- Join a volunteer organization that interests you. If you work hard, you'll quickly get an opportunity to do more: manage a budget, write fund-raising materials, and supervise other volunteers.
- Freelance. Design brochures, create Web pages, do tax returns for small businesses. Use your skills—for free, if you have to at first.
- Write. Create a portfolio of ads, instructions, or whatever documents are relevant for the field you want to enter. Ask a professional—an instructor, a local business person, someone from a professional organization—to critique them. Volunteer your services to local fund-raising organizations and small businesses.

Getting experience is particularly important for students with good grades. Pick something where you interact with other people, so that you can show that you can work well in an organization.

If you're on the job market now, think carefully about what you've really done. Complete sentences using the action verbs in Figure 17.4. Think about what you've done in courses, in volunteer work, in unpaid activities. Especially focus on skills in problem solving, critical thinking, teamwork, and communication. Solving a problem for a hypothetical firm in an accounting class, thinking critically about a report problem in business communication, working with a group in a marketing class, and communicating with people at the senior center where you volunteer are experience, even if no one paid you.

If you're not actually looking for a job but just need to create a résumé for this course, ask your instructor whether you may assume that you're a senior and add the things you hope to do between now and your senior year.

How an Average Student Created an Excellent Résumé

Allyson was convinced that she had nothing to put on her résumé. In a conference, her instructor asked Allyson to describe exactly what she'd done. Allyson's "baby-sitting" was actually house management and child care. But a summer job at Harvard had consisted of changing beds and cleaning rooms for conference guests.

Her five summers of work at a law firm sounded more promising. She went to the library, formulated medical and legal questions, and searched for answers. The information she found helped the firm win a $7 million out-of-court settlement. Not bad for a sophomore in college. But Allyson was in advertising and wanted to go into copywriting, not market research. The experience was certainly worth putting on her résumé, but the kind of thinking she'd done as a law clerk wasn't the kind of thinking she needed to demonstrate to an ad agency.

Some of the items under ACHIEVEMENTS were interesting. The Locker Room was a restaurant in town where Allyson had had dinner. Its menu said the restaurant "had a long history." In fact, the restaurant was new; it was the *building* that was old. Allyson went up to the owner, told him several of the things that were wrong with the menu, and offered to rewrite it. The owner told her he'd pay her for doing that and also invited her to submit ideas for ads.

The instructor was impressed. The whole anecdote might work in a job application letter, while the résumé could highlight the fact that Allyson had written menu and advertising copy for a real business (not just a class). "What you need," the instructor said, "is a skills résumé."

"Are skills résumés very common?"

"Not as common as chronological résumés. And they're a little harder to write. You can write a chronological résumé just by going through the list and remembering what you've done under EDUCATION, under EXPERIENCE, and so on. You can almost fill in the blanks: the job title, the organization, the city and state, the dates. With a skills résumé, you think about the skills you'd need in the job you want to have, the skills the employer is looking for, and show how you've used those skills in what you've already done. A skills résumé lets you take things from classes, from paid jobs, from volunteer work and put them all together.

"How do employers feel about skills résumés?"

"There isn't any good research. One survey asked employers which they'd rather get, and more people said 'the traditional résumé.' But that's just because they know where to look for things on the traditional résumé. Nobody's ever done research taking the same qualifications, presenting them in two different ways, and seeing which way got more interviews or more job offers. I know people who've gotten jobs using skills résumés.

"You want a résumé that immediately says 'WOW' to the employer. People always get more résumés than they want to deal with. To survive the cut, a résumé has to stand out. You want the résumé to have the same punch that you have in person."

The next step was to answer two questions: "What do you want to do? What do you think the employer is looking for?" Allyson replied, "I want to get a job as a copywriter in Cleveland. It's the 10th biggest market, and I'd rather work as a copywriter in a smaller market than have to start as a secretary at a New York agency. I think the agencies want someone who shows creativity, who has a strong personality, who isn't afraid to take risks."

"Then your résumé needs to do that. And it can. You're coming across as a self-starter, a problem solver. When you actually write your résumé, use the language of your field. *Problem solver* is a positive term in most fields, but it may or may not be right for advertising. Given what you've done, you could have headings for WRITING EXPERIENCE, CREATING ADS, PLANNING PROMOTIONAL CAMPAIGNS, RESEARCH, and SPEAKING, with a list of items under each one.

"Your résumé is going to make you look qualified. Highly qualified. Other students are going to read it and say, 'But she has done so much. *I* haven't done anything.' They're going to feel just the way you felt when you said you hadn't done much in the last four years. But you *have* done a lot. You'll look great in your résumé. Anyone can, who understands the options and who puts in the time and energy."

Allyson still had to tinker with headings, decide what details to use, and experiment with layout and spacing. The final product (Figure 17.7) is worth the work.

Online Résumés

Most large companies scan résumés into an electronic job-applicant tracking system.[7] Creating a Web résumé is optional, but prepare a scannable version of your résumé to send any company that asks for it.

Sending Your Résumé by E-mail

Hiring managers and recruiters now use e-mail for most of their correspondence. According to a survey by the Society for Human Resource Management, more than one-third of human resource professionals reported a preference for e-mailed résumés.[8] Here are some basic guidelines of e-mail job-hunting etiquette:

- Don't use your current employer's e-mail system for your job search. You'll leave potential employers with the impression that you spend company time on writing résumés and other nonwork-related activities.

Online "Salvaging"*

You post a résumé online and wait for the offers to come in. Then you get an e-mail—from the boss. Seems a sharp-eyed guy in personnel saw your résumé on Getajob.com. If you're lucky and the company has decided that you're worth "salvaging," you'll get a raise and a warning. If not, you'll be shown the door. . . .

Usually based on the human resources department, "salvagers" monitor online job-listing sites, which range from general ones like Monster.com to such specialty sites as Layover.com for truckers and Taxsearchinc.com for tax preparers. . . . [S]alvaging operations can range from a full-time staff of salvagers to "find and tell" policies that require any employee who finds a colleague's résumé online to inform a supervisor immediately. . . .

A quality control officer at a midsize telecom company posted his résumé in the "confidential" section of a highly specialized job site, which withheld his name and his employer's and blocked anyone logging in from his employer's domain name from seeing his résumé. The employee got several offers— including one from his employer. The personnel officer who smoked him out used a free Yahoo! account to avoid the job site's filters. . . . After a few sleepless nights, he came clean. The company gave him a small raise and warned that he would lose certain assignments if his résumé was found again within a year.

*Quoted from Richard Miniter, "Watch Out, or You Might Get 'Salvaged,'" *The Wall Street Journal*, November 1, 1999, A54.

FIGURE 17.7 A Skills Résumé for a Graduate Entering the Job Market

A border creates visual variety.

Allyson Karnes

195 W. Ninth
Columbus, OH 43210
(614) 555-3498
karnes.173@osu.edu

6782 Fenwick Drive
Solon, OH 44121
(216) 555-6182

She varies the usual "Summary of Qualifications" to make it specific to the job. This really is Allyson's philosophy— and it's one an agency will appreciate.

Qualifications for Writing Creative Ads That Make People Remember the Product

➤ Created headlines and print ads for a variety of audiences.
➤ Persuaded team members, business owners, and lawyers to accept my ideas.
➤ Self-starter who sees a project through from start to finish.

Skills résumé allows her to combine experience from classes and life.

Education

B.A. in Advertising, June 2004, The Ohio State University, Columbus, OH
    Core courses: Copywriting, promotional strategies, magazine writing, graphics, media planning
    Harvard University Writing Program, Summer 2001, Boston, MA

Experience Creating Ads

Led the team that developed the winning promotional strategy for Max & Erma's Restaurants.
    ➤ Developed idea for theme for a year's campaign of ads.
    ➤ Wrote copy for radio spots, magazine ads, and billboards. One billboard ad had the headline "Multiple Choice" and boxes for burgers, chicken, and salads--with all the boxes checked.
    ➤ Presented creative strategy to Max & Erma's CEO and the Head of Advertising.
    ➤ Strategy won first place from among 17 proposals.

Details, wording demonstrate her ability.

Wrote more than 15 ads for Copywriting class, including
    ➤ Ad for cordless phone: "Isn't It Time to Cut the Cord?"
    ➤ Slogan for Ohio University's Springfest Jamboree: "In Short, It Jams"
    ➤ Billboard for Columbus Boys' School: "Who Said It's Lonely at the Top?"

Created ads and revised menu for The Locker Room (restaurant).

Allyson chooses unusual bullets rather than the standard dots or squares. In a résumé for an ad agency, the bullets work.

Other Writing Experience

Wrote "Commuter Flights" (humor).
Created more than 30 magazine articles as part of courses at Harvard University and Ohio State.
Researched and wrote legal briefs as part of course at Harvard.
Summarized research on $7 million medical malpractice case for Garson and Associates.

Employment History

2001-04   Child care and house management, Worthington, OH. Part-time daily during school year.

Summer   Maid, Harvard Student Agency, Boston, MA. Part-time while attending Harvard
2001   University Writing Program.

Summers   Law Clerk, Garson and Associates, Cleveland, OH. Did independent case research
1997-2000   used by the firm to win $7 million malpractice out-of-court settlement for the client.

Reverse chronology.

Portfolio Available on Request   *A position of emphasis.*

- Set up a free, Internet-based e-mail account using services such as Hotmail or Yahoo! to manage correspondence related to your job hunt.

- Avoid using silly or cryptic e-mail addresses. Instead of bubbles@aol.com, opt for something businesslike: yourname@yahoo.com.

- Understand that e-mail isn't confidential. Don't put address or phone number on your e-résumé. Instead write "Confidential Résumé" and list a personal e-mail address where you can be reached.

- Send individual, targeted messages rather than mass mailings. You don't want a coveted employer to see that you're also sending your résumé to 20 other companies.

- Write a simple subject line that makes a good first impression: Résumé—Kate Sanchez. A good subject line will improve the chances that your résumé is actually read, since e-mail from unknown senders is often deleted without being opened.

Prepare a résumé that looks good on a computer screen. Computer systems vary widely and have differently installed fonts, printer drivers, and word processing software, so your beautifully designed Microsoft Word résumé could turn into an eyesore on the hiring manager's computer. If you design the résumé in a font that the recipient lacks, your résumé will appear in a default font and you'll lose control of how it looks.

Use a plain text résumé. Save your fully formatted résumé in your word processing program as "text" or "rich-text format" (rtf)—a document type that's compatible with all systems. It's important to heed the specific directions of employers that you are e-mailing. Some may want a Microsoft Word attachment of your résumé, while others may specify that you paste the e-mail directly into the body of your e-mail message. Paste the plain text résumé into the body of your e-mail message and, unless instructed otherwise, include it as an attachment as well. Also include a brief cover letter in your message. In it, mention the types of files you've included. (See Figure 18.9.) Before sending your résumé into cyberspace, test to see how it will look when it comes out on the other end. E-mail it to yourself and a friend, then critique and fix it.

Creating a Web Résumé

With the popularity of the Web, you may want to post your résumé online. If you don't know hypertext markup language (HTML), the behind-the-scenes programming that displays Web pages in your browser, you can save your résumé as HTML in Word or WordPerfect. However, be aware that the HTML editors in word-processing programs create messy codes that computer programmers deplore. If you're claiming the ability to code Web pages as one of your skills and abilities, use real HTML, not the code created by Word or Word-Perfect.

In your Web résumé,

- Include an e-mail link at the top of the résumé under your name.

- Omit your street addresses and phone numbers. (A post office box is OK.) Employers who find your résumé on the Web will have the technology to e-mail you.

- Consider having links under your name and e-mail address to the various parts of your résumé. Use phrases that give the viewer some idea of what you offer: e.g., *Marketing Experience.*

- Link to other pages that provide more information about you (a list of courses, a document you've written), but not to organizations (your university, an employer) that shift emphasis away from your credentials.

- Don't be cute. Do be professional. Link to other pages you've created only if they convey the same professional image as your résumé.
- Put your strongest qualification immediately after your name and e-mail address. If the first screen doesn't interest readers, they won't scroll through the rest of the résumé.
- Specify the job you want. Recruiters respond negatively to scrolling through an entire résumé only to find that the candidate is in another field.[9]
- Specify city and state for educational institutions and employers.
- Use lists, indentations, and white space to create visual variety.
- Most commercial and many university sites offer lists of applicants, with a short phrase after each name. Craft this phrase to convince the recruiter to click on your résumé.
- Proofread the résumé carefully.

Be prepared during the job interview to create HTML or Java text or provide an in-office writing sample. Firms know that candidates can get help with Web pages and online portfolios and may want confirmation that the skills they represent indeed belong to the candidate.[10]

Creating a Scannable Résumé

Increasingly, large companies such as Bank of America, Ford Motor Company, Walt Disney, and the Clorox Company use electronic job-applicant-tracking systems like Resumix and Res-Track. After paper résumés are scanned in, the systems can search them by keyword to match job descriptions. Advanced systems take care of the paperwork throughout the hiring process, notifying each applicant when the résumé has been scanned in, saving interview notes and results of pre-employment testing, automatically generating an "offer" letter, and updating the candidate's file to "hired" and the job requisition to "filled" after the candidate accepts.

Figure 17.8 is an example of a scannable résumé.
To increase the chances that the résumé is scanned correctly,

- Use a standard typeface. Beverly Nelson, William Gallé, and Donna Luse recommend Helvetica, Futura, Optima, Times Roman, New Century Schoolbook, Courier, Univers, and Bookman.[11]
- Use 12- or 14-point type.
- Use a ragged right margin rather than full justification. Scanners can't always handle the extra spaces between words and letters that full justification creates.
- Don't italicize or underline words—even titles of books or newspapers that grammatically require such treatment.
- Check text in full caps or bold to make sure letters don't touch each other.
- Don't use lines, boxes, script, leader dots, or borders.
- Don't use two-column formats.
- Print the résumé using portrait (standard page) rather than landscape orientation.
- Put each phone number on a separate line.
- Use plenty of white space.
- Don't fold or staple the pages.
- Don't write anything by hand on your résumé.
- Send a laser copy or a high-quality photocopy. Stray marks defeat scanners.

FIGURE 17.8 A Scannable Résumé

Use 12– or 14–point type in a standard typeface. Here, Times Roman is used.

Jerry A. Jackson

Keywords: family financial management; investment sales; computer modeling; competitive; self-starter; hard worker; responsible; collegiate athletics; sales experience; willing to travel

In keywords, use labels and terms that employers might use in a job listing.

Campus Address
$1636\frac{1}{2}$ Highland Street
Columbus, OH 43201
(614) 555-5718
E-mail address: Jackson.2495@osu.edu
Created a Web page on saving for life goals, such as a home, children's education, and retirement: http://www.fisher.osu/students/Jackson.2495/home.htm

Permanent Address
45 East Mulberry
Huntington, NY 11746
(516) 555-7793

Don't use columns. Scanners can't handle them.

Summary of Qualifications
High energy. Played sports during four years of college. Started two businesses.
Sales experience. Sold both clothing and investments successfully.
Presentation skills. In individual and group presentations, spoke to groups ranging from 2 to 75 people. Gave informative, persuasive, and inspirational talks.
Knowledgeable about stocks and bonds, especially energy and telecommunication companies.
Computer experience. Microsoft Word, Excel, SPSS, PowerPoint, and Dreamweaver. Experience creating Web pages.

Education
B.S. in Family Financial Management, June 2004, The Ohio State University, Columbus, OH
"B" Grade Point Average
Comprehensive courses related to major provide not only the basics of family financial management but also skills in communication, writing, speaking, small groups, and computer modeling
Accounting I and II
Business and Professional Writing
Computer Programming
Finance
Economics I and II
Family Resource Management
Family and Human Development Statistics
Public Speaking
Interpersonal Communication

Give as much information as you like. The computer doesn't care how long the document is.

(continued)

FIGURE 17.8   A Scannable Résumé *(concluded)*

Sports Experience
BAAD (Buckeye Athletes Against Drugs)
Intramural Hockey Team (Division Champions, Winter 1997)
Three-year Varsity Letterman, Ohio State University, Columbus, OH
Men's NCAA Division I Lacrosse

Don't just justify margins. Doing so creates extra spaces which confuse scanners.

Omit bold and italics. Some scanners can handle bullets, but they aren't needed in a scannable résumé.

Experience
Financial Sales Representative, Primerica Company, Columbus, OH, February 2003-present.
Work with clients to plan investment strategies.
Research and recommend specific investments, including stocks, bonds, mutual funds, and annuities.

Entrepreneur, Huntington, NY and Columbus, OH, September 2002-January 2003.
Created a saleable product, secured financial backing, found a manufacturer, supervised production, and sold product–12 dozen T-shirts at a $5.25 profit each–to help pay for college expenses.

Landscape Maintenance Supervisor, Huntington, NY, Summers 1994-2002.
Formed a company to cut lawns, put up fences, fertilize, garden, and paint houses.
Hired, fired, trained, motivated, and paid friends to complete jobs.

Collector and Repair Worker, ACN Inc., Huntington, NY, Summers 1994-2000.
Collected and counted up to $10,000 a day.
Worked with technicians troubleshooting and repairing electronic and coin mechanisms of video and pinball games, cigarette machines, and jukeboxes.

Willing to relocate
U.S. citizen

To increase the number of matches, or hits,

- Prepare a traditional chronological résumé. Don't be "creative." It doesn't matter where information is; the system can find it anywhere.
- Use a *Keywords* summary under your name, address, and phone. In it, put not only degrees, job field or title, and accomplishments but also personality traits and attitude: *dependable, skill in time management, leadership, sense of responsibility.*[12]
- Use industry buzzwords and jargon, even if you're redundant. For example, "Web page design and HTML coding" will "match" either "Web" or "HTML" as a keyword.
- Use conventional terms, even if they're a bit wordy.
- Use specific, concrete nouns. Some systems don't handle verbs well, and tracking systems "key in" primarily on nouns.
- Use common headings such as *Summary of Qualifications, Strengths, Certifications,* and so forth as well as *Education, Experience,* and so on.

- Use as many pages as necessary.
- Mention specific software programs (e.g., *Dreamweaver*) you've used.
- Be specific and quantifiable. "Managed $2 million building materials account" will generate more hits than "manager" or "managerial experience."

Weak: Microsoft Front Page

Better: Used Microsoft Front Page to design an interactive Web page for a national fashion retailer, with links to information about style trends, current store promotions, employment opportunities, and an online video fashion show.

- Join honor societies, professional and trade organizations, since they're often used as keywords.[13] Spell out Greek letter societies (the scanner will mangle Greek characters, even if your computer has them): "Pi Sigma Alpha Honor Society." For English words, spell out the organization name; follow it with the abbreviation in parentheses: "College Newspaper Business and Advertising Managers Association (CNBAM)." That way, the résumé will be tagged whether the recruiter searches for the full name or the acronym.
- Put everything in the résumé rather than "saving" some material for the cover letter. While some applicant-tracking systems can search for keywords in cover letters and other application materials, most extract information only from the résumé, even though they store the other papers. The length of the résumé doesn't matter.

Send only one résumé, even if the firm has more than one position for which you qualify. Most recruiters have negative reactions to multiple résumés, and the tracking system allows the applicant to be coded "NH" (never hire), a coding that persists even if the original recruiter leaves the company. Do, however, bring a separate résumé (designed to be read by humans) to the interview.

Experts differ on whether candidates should phone to follow up. Taunee Besson advises phoning the administrator or verifier of the tracking system just once to be sure that your résumé arrived.[14]

Using Online Job Boards

The Internet has made it much easier for job seekers to connect directly with prospective employers through online job boards such as Monster.com and Hotjobs.com. Job Web sites allow you to post your résumé in online databases. Employers may then search for job candidates by entering key criteria of the positions they would like to fill.

One of the drawbacks of job Web sites is they do not post your résumé as is. It is usually necessary for you to enter the information directly online by answering a series of questions. The job board Web site then imports your data into a preformatted template for easy, uniform viewing by employers.

Answering questions directly online makes proofing more challenging, but not impossible. The best approach is to cut and paste as much of your information as possible from your final, proofed résumé. The job board may also ask you questions that are not in your résumé. For these questions compose, edit, and proof your response in a word processing program. You can then cut and paste your answers from the word processing document into the online template. This may require you to return to the job board more than once to complete your résumé, but most sites allow you to add your personal information incrementally.

Spell Check Doesn't Know Best*

My husband, an auto mechanic, was looking for higher-paying work and asked me to write his résumé on the computer. As I typed, I used spell check to make sure everything was perfect. I soon found another benefit to this function—it doubled as a career adviser. Every time it stopped on the word *Mazda*, it suggested I change it to *Mercedes*.

*Quoted from Wendy O'Lary in "Virtual Hilarity," *Reader's Digest*, October 1999, 49.

Summary of Key Points

- Informal preparation for job hunting should start soon after you arrive on campus. Formal preparation for job hunting should begin a full year before you begin interviewing. The year you interview, register with your placement office early.

- Employers skim résumés to decide whom to interview. Employers assume that the letter and résumé represent your best work. Interviewers normally reread the résumé before the interview. After the search committee has chosen an applicant, it submits the résumé to people in the organization who must approve the appointment.

- A résumé must fill at least one page. Use two pages if you have extensive activities and experience.

- Emphasize information that is relevant to the job you want, is recent (last three years), and shows your superiority to other applicants.

- To emphasize key points, put them in headings, list them vertically, and provide details.

- Résumés use sentence fragments punctuated like complete sentences. Items in the résumé must be concise and parallel. Verbs and gerunds create a dynamic image of you.

- A **chronological résumé** summarizes what you did in a time line (starting with the most recent events, and going backward in **reverse chronology**). It emphasizes degrees, job titles, and dates. Use a chronological résumé when
  - Your education and experience are a logical preparation for the position for which you're applying.
  - You have impressive job titles, offices, or honors.

- A **skills résumé** emphasizes the skills you've used, rather than the job in which or the date when you used them. Use a skills résumé when
  - Your education and experience are not the usual route to the position for which you're applying.
  - You're changing fields.
  - You want to combine experience from paid jobs, activities or volunteer work, and courses to show the extent of your experience in administration, finance, speaking, etc.
  - Your recent work history may create the wrong impression (e.g., it has gaps, shows a demotion, shows job-hopping, etc.).

- Résumés commonly contain the applicant's name, address, phone number, education, and experience. Activities, honors, references, and a summary of qualifications should be included if possible.

- To fill the page, list courses or list references vertically.

- Using a laser printer, print your résumé on quality paper.

- To e-mail your résumé, save it in plain text format.

- To create a scannable résumé, create a "plain vanilla" text using industry jargon, buzzwords, and acronyms.

- To post your résumé on an online job board, compose, edit, and proof your answers in word processing software before posting them online.

CHAPTER 17   Exercises and Problems

Getting Started

17.1   Analyzing Your Accomplishments

List the 10 accomplishments that give you the most personal satisfaction. These could be things that other people wouldn't notice. They can be things you've done recently or things you did years ago.

Answer the following question for each accomplishment:

1. What skills or knowledge did you use?
2. What personal traits did you exhibit?
3. What about this accomplishment makes it personally satisfying to you?

As Your Instructor Directs,

a. Share your answers with a small group of other students.
b. Summarize your answers in a memo to your instructor.
c. Present your answers orally to the class.

17.2   Remembering What You've Done

Use the following list to jog your memory about what you've done. For each, give three or four details as well as a general statement.

Describe a time when you

1. Used facts and figures to gain agreement on an important point.
2. Identified a problem that a group or organization faced and developed a plan for solving the problem.
3. Made a presentation or a speech to a group.
4. Won the goodwill of people whose continued support was necessary for the success of some long-term project or activity.
5. Interested other people in something that was important to you and persuaded them to take the actions you wanted.

6. Helped a group deal constructively with conflict.
7. Demonstrated creativity.
8. Took a project from start to finish.
9. Created an opportunity for yourself in a job or volunteer position.
10. Used good judgment and logic in solving a problem.

As Your Instructor Directs,

a. Identify which job(s) each detail is relevant for.
b. Identify which details would work well on a résumé.
c. Identify which details, further developed, would work well in a job letter.

17.3   Developing Action Statements

Use 10 of the verbs from Figure 17.4 to write action statements describing what you've done in paid or volunteer work, in classes, in extracurricular activities, or in community service.

17.4   Changing Verbs to Nouns

Revise the action statements you created for Problem 17.3, changing the verbs to nouns so that you could use the same information in a scannable résumé.

17.5   Evaluating Career Objective Statements

None of the following career objective statements is effective. What is wrong with each statement as it stands? Which statements could be revised to be satisfactory? Which should be dropped?

1. To use my acquired knowledge of accounting to eventually own my own business.

2. A progressively responsible position as a MARKETING MANAGER where education and ability would have valuable application and lead to advancement.

3. To work with people responsibly and creatively, helping them develop personal and professional skills.

4. A position in international marketing which makes use of my specialization in marketing and my knowledge of foreign markets.

5. To bring Faith, Hope, and Charity to the American workplace.

6. To succeed in sales.

7. To design and maintain Web pages.

17.6   Deciding How Much Detail to Use

In each of the following situations, how detailed should the applicant be? Why?

1. Ron Oliver has been steadily employed for the last six years while getting his college degree, but the jobs have been low-level ones, whose prime benefit was that they paid well and fit around his class schedule.

2. Adrienne Barcus was an assistant department manager at a clothing boutique. As assistant manager, she was authorized to approve checks in the absence of the manager. Her other duties were ringing up sales, cleaning the area, and helping mark items for sales.

3. Lois Heilman has been a clerk-typist in the Alumni Office. As part of her job, she developed a schedule for mailings to alumni, set up a merge system, and wrote two of the letters that go out to alumni. The merge system she set up has cut in half the time needed to produce letters.

4. As a co-op student, Stanley Greene spends every other term in a paid job. He now has six semesters of job experience in television broadcasting. During his last co-op he was the assistant producer for a daily "morning magazine" show.

17.7   Evaluating Web Résumés

Evaluate 10 résumés you find on the Web. Many schools of business have places where students can post résumés online. You may find other résumés on job boards (see the list in Figure 17.1).

As Your Instructor Directs,

a. Share your results with a small group of students.

b. Write an e-mail message analyzing what works and what doesn't. If your e-mail program supports hyperlinks, provide links to the pages you discuss.

c. Write a memo analyzing what works and what doesn't. Attach printouts of each page you discuss.

d. Join with a small group of students to analyze the pages.

e. Make a short oral presentation to the class discussing the best (or worst) page you found.

Résumé Assignments

For problems 17.8 through 17.10, write the kind of résumé (chronological, skills, a combination, or a new creation) that best represents your qualifications.

17.8   Writing a Web Résumé

Create a set of Web pages to present your qualifications to an employer. Provide links to course projects and other documents that support your claims.

17.9   Writing a Paper Résumé

Write a résumé on paper that you could mail to an employer or hand to an interviewer at an interview.

As Your Instructor Directs,

a.   Write a résumé for the field in which you hope to find a job.

b.   Write two different résumés for two different job paths you are interested in pursuing.

c.   Adapt your résumé to a specific company you hope to work for.

17.10   Writing a Scannable Résumé

Take the résumé you like best from problem 17.9, and create a scannable version of it.

18

Job Application Letters

Job Application Letters

Teresa Moburg
Midwest Area Assurance Recruiting Manager KPMG Peat Marwick LLP

Teresa Moburg recruits for all lines of business for KPMG Peat Marwick in 11 states. As one of the Big Five professional services firms, KPMG Peat Marwick LLP specializes in consulting, assurance and tax services, and process management in five lines of business

www.us.kpmg.com

You can find information about organizations and career opportunities on Web sites, in career libraries at colleges and universities, and sometimes directly from the organization, especially from the human resources office at the main location. Web sites are a wonderful source of quick and timely information. KPMG's Web site includes information about the firm, job postings, training opportunities, benefits, and key clients just to name a few.

To create a good application letter, apply for a specific position. Include where you learned of the position (Internet, advertisement, a current employee of the firm). For each of the position qualifications, show how your experience and skills meet the employer's needs. **Include specific but concise examples of your experience and skills that qualify you for the position.** In this era of team building, a good personality fit is important. Learn about the culture of the organization (the Web site can help) and adapt your writing style and content to the organization's style. Do not try to fit where you're not comfortable, though. It is always best to err on the conservative side if you are uncertain.

Send the letter to a specific person—and know the person's name and the correct title and spelling! Proofread your letter carefully, especially if you use a computer to adapt a basic letter to several different companies. I've received letters addressed to me with the content of the letter still bearing a competitor's name.

Remember, recruiters are very busy and see hundreds of applications a week. The easier you make it for them to identify you as a qualified candidate, the greater your chances of being contacted. By adapting the letter to the company, you're showing your knowledge of the business and how you could contribute to its continued success.

This first impression is critical in determining if you make it to the next step. Good luck!

"For each of the position qualifications, show how your experience and skills meet the employer's needs."

The purpose of a job application letter is to get an interview. If you get a job through interviews arranged by your campus placement office or through contacts, you may not need to write a letter. However, if you want to work for an organization that isn't interviewing on campus, or later when you change jobs, you will. Writing a letter is also a good preparation for a job interview, since the letter is your first step in showing a specific company what you can do for it.

How Job Letters Differ from Résumés

The job application letter accompanies your résumé. Although the two documents overlap slightly, they differ in several ways:

- A résumé is adapted to a position. As Teresa Moburg notes, the letter is adapted to the needs of a particular organization.
- The résumé summarizes all your qualifications. The letter shows how your qualifications can help the organization meet its needs, how you differ from other applicants, and that you have some knowledge of the organization.
- The résumé uses short, parallel phrases (← p. 101) and sentence fragments. The letter uses complete sentences in well-written paragraphs.

How to Find Out about Employers and Jobs

To adapt your letter to a specific organization, you need information both about the employer and about the job itself. You'll need to know

- **The name and address of the person who should receive the letter.** To get this information, check the ad, call the organization, check its Web site, or consult the directories listed in Figure 18.1. An advantage of calling is that you can find out what courtesy title (← p. 45) a woman prefers and get current information. A directory that went to press months ago will not include recent promotions.
- **What the organization does, and at least four or five facts about it.** Knowing the organization's larger goals enables you to show how your specific work will help the company meet its goals. Useful facts can include market

---

FIGURE 18.1   Print Sources for Addresses and Facts about Companies

General directories	Specialized directories and resource books
Directory of Corporate Affiliations	Accounting Firms and Practitioners
Dun's Million Dollar Directory	California Manufacturers Register
Standard & Poor's Register of Corporations, Directors, and Executives	Directory of American Firms Operating in Foreign Countries
Thomas Register of American Manufacturers	Directory of Hotel and Motel Systems
	Directory of Management Consultants
	Directory of New England Manufacturers
	Franchise Annual: Handbook and Directory
	O'Dwyer's Directory of Public Relations Firms
	The Rand McNally Banker's Directory
	Thomas Grocery Register
	Standard Directory of Advertisers ("Red Book")
	Who's Who in Direct Marketing Creative Services
	Television Factbook

share, new products or promotions, the kind of computer or manufacturing equipment it uses, plans for growth or downsizing, competitive position, challenges the organization faces, the corporate culture (◀▥ p. 59), and so forth.

The directories listed in Figure 18.1 provide information ranging from net worth, market share, and principal products to the names of officers and directors. To get specific financial data (and to see how the organization presents itself to the public), get the company's annual report from your library, the Web, or the company itself. (Note: Only companies whose stock is publicly traded are required to issue annual reports. In this day of mergers and buyouts, many companies are owned by other companies. The parent company may be the only one to issue an annual report.) Recruiting notebooks at your campus placement office may provide information about training programs and career paths for new hires. To learn about new products, plans for growth, or solutions to industry challenges, read business newspapers such as *The Wall Street Journal* or *The Financial Post*, business magazines such as *Fortune, BusinessWeek, Forbes*, and trade journals. Each of these has indexes listing which companies are discussed in a specific issue. A few of the trade journals available are listed in Figure 18.2.

■ **What the job itself involves.** Campus placement offices and Web listings often have fuller job descriptions than appear in ads. Talk to friends who have graduated recently to learn what their jobs involve. Conduct information interviews to learn more about opportunities that interest you.

Using the Internet

As Figure 18.3 shows, many job listings are on the Web. Even better, the Web can be a fast way to learn about the company you hope to join. Check professional listservs and electronic bulletin boards. Employers sometimes post specialized jobs on them, and they're always a good way to get information about the industry you hope to enter.

Information Interviews

In an **information interview** you talk to someone who works in the area you hope to enter to find out what the day-to-day work involves and how you can best prepare to enter that field. An information interview can let you know whether or not you'd like the job, give you specific information that you can use to present yourself effectively in your résumé and application letter, and

So Many Job Sites, So Little Time*

To use the Internet as the ultimate job-seeking tool, understand the kinds of employment sites it offers.

■ Help wanted sites are developed and maintained by employers and act as electronic versions of postings in store windows. They are informative and provide detailed job descriptions.

■ Classified sites are online versions of local newspapers' want ads.

■ Résumé sites showcase applicants' skills and experience rather than employer profiles.

■ Industry sites locate jobs in a specific industry. Most feature searchable lists as well as profiles of major industry employers and employment statistics.

■ Career sites are operated by independent companies and can advertise hundreds of thousands of job listings in their searchable databases.

*Based on Carolyn Gosselin, "Targeting a New Job: Where to Go in the Sea of Job Sites," *Chicago Tribune*, June 1, 2000.

FIGURE 18.2 Examples of Trade Journals

Advertising Age	*Direct Marketing*	*The Practical Accountant*
American Banker	*Discount Store News*	*Sales and Marketing Management*
Automotive News	*Electric Power Monthly*	*Software Canada*
Aviation Week	*Financial Analysts Journal*	*Television/Radio Age*
Beverage Industry	*Graphic Arts Monthly*	*Today's Realtor*
Benefits Canada	*HR Focus*	*Training & Development*
Cable Communication Magazine	*Internal Auditor*	*Travel Agent*
CA Magazine	*International Advertiser*	*Women's Wear Daily*
Canadian Business	*Logging and Sawmilling Journal*	*Variety*
CPA Practitioner	*Nation's Restaurant News*	

FIGURE 18.3   Job Listings on the Web

Job listings	
America's Job Bank www.ajb.dni.us/index.html	**Federal Jobs Central** www.fedjobs.com
Career Path Online www.careerpath.com Job listings from the *Boston Globe, Chicago Tribune, Los Angeles Times, New York Times, San Jose Mercury News, Washington Post,* and more	**Job Search Sites on the WWW** www.ups.purdue.edu/Student/jobsites.htm
	Monster.com www.monster.com
Careermag.com http://vertical.worklife.com/onlines/careermag	**Monster Trak.com** www.jobtrak.com
	Nonprofit Jobnet www.philanthropy-journal.org/jobnet/jobs.htm
Careers.org www.careers.org	
CareerWEB www.careerweb.com	**World Wide Web Employment Office** www.harbornet.com/biz/office/annex.html

create a good image of you in the mind of the interviewer. If you present yourself positively, the interviewer may remember you when openings arise.

In an information interview, you might ask the following questions:

- Tell me about the papers on your desk. What are you working on right now?
- How do you spend your typical day?
- Have your duties changed a lot since you first started working here?
- What do you like best about your job? What do you like least?
- What do you think the future holds for this kind of work?
- How did you get this job?
- What courses, activities, or jobs would you recommend to someone who wanted to do this kind of work?

To set up an information interview, you can phone or write a letter like the one in Figure 18.4. If you do write, phone the following week to set up a specific time.

Tapping into the Hidden Job Market

Many jobs are never advertised—and the number rises the higher on the job ladder you go. Over 60% of all new jobs come not from responding to an ad but from networking with personal contacts.[1] Some of these jobs are created especially for a specific person. These unadvertised jobs are called the **hidden job market.** Referral interviews, an organized method of networking, offer the most systematic way to tap into these jobs. **Referral interviews** are interviews you schedule to learn about current job opportunities in your field. Sometimes an interview that starts out as an information interview turns into a referral interview.

A referral interview should give you information about the opportunities currently available in the town in the area you're interested in, refer you to other people who can tell you about job opportunities, and enable the interviewer to see that you could make a contribution to his or her organization. Therefore, the goal of a referral interview is to put you face-to-face with someone who has the power to hire you: the president of a small company, the division vice president or branch manager of a big company, the director of the local office of a state or federal agency.

FIGURE 18.4 Letter Requesting an Information Interview

72 E. 13th Avenue
Columbus, OH 43210
November 4, 2003

Use the courtesy title the reader prefers.

Mrs. Kam Yuricich
Clary Communications
1372 Grandview Avenue
Suite 230
Columbus, OH 43212

Dear Mrs. Yuricich:

If starting with the request seems too abrupt, work up to it more gradually.

Could I schedule an information interview with you to learn more about how public relations consultants interact with their clients?

Refer to any previous contact with reader.

I was very interested in your talk to OSU's PRSSA Chapter last month about the differences between working for a PR firm and being a PR staff person within an organization. Last summer I had the chance to work as an intern at Management Horizons. While many of my assignments were "go-fer" jobs, my supervisor gave me the chance to work on several brochures and to draft two speeches for managers. I enjoyed this variety and would like to learn more about the possibility of working in a PR firm.

Ask about ways to enter the field.

Perhaps we could also talk about courses that would best prepare me for PR work. I have a year and a half left before I graduate, and I have room for several free electives in my schedule. I'd like to use them as productively as possible.

I'll call you early next week to set up an appointment. I look forward to your advice as I attempt to find my niche in the workforce.

Mentioning your qualifications and including a sample of your work may help persuade the reader to take time to see you.

Sincerely,

Lee Tan

Lee Tan
555-5932

Even though you shouldn't depend on the reader to call you, it's polite to give your phone number under your name.

Encl.: Marketing Brochure for Riverside Hospitals

Start by scheduling interviews with people you know who may know something about that field—professors, co-workers, neighbors, friends. Call your alumni office to get the names and phone numbers of alumni who now work where you would like to work. Your purpose in talking to them is (ostensibly) to get advice about improving your résumé and about general job-hunting strategy and (really) to get referrals to other people. In fact, go into the interview with the names of people you'd like to talk to. If the interviewee doesn't suggest anyone, say, "Do you think it would be a good idea for me to talk to _____?"

Then, armed with a referral from someone you know, you call Mr. or Ms. Big and say, "So-and-so suggested I talk with you about job-hunting strategy." If the person says, "We aren't hiring," you say, "Oh, I'm not asking *you* for a job. I'd just like some advice from a knowledgeable person about the opportunities in banking [or desktop publishing, or whatever] in this city." If this person

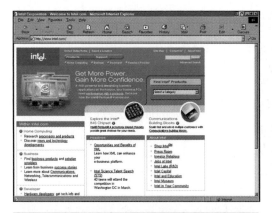

doesn't have the power to create a position, you seek more referrals at the end of *this* interview. (You can also polish your résumé, if you get good suggestions.)

Even when you talk to the person who could create a job for
you, you *do not ask for a job.* But to give you advice about your
résumé, the person has to look at it. When a powerful person
focuses on your skills, he or she will naturally think about the
problems and needs in that organization. When there's a
match between what you can do and what the organization
needs, that person has the power to create a position for you.

Some business people are cynical about information and referral interviewing. Prepare as carefully for these interviews as
you would for an interview when you know the organization
is hiring. Think in advance of good questions; know something
about the general field or industry; try to learn at least a little
bit about the specific company.

Always follow up information and referral interviews with
personal thank-you letters. Use specifics to show that you paid
attention during the interview, and enclose a copy of your revised résumé.

Content and Organization for Job Application Letters

In your letter, focus on

- Major requirements of the job for which you're applying.
- Points that separate you from other applicants.
- Points that show your knowledge of the organization.
- Qualities that every employer is likely to value: the ability to write and speak effectively, to solve problems, to get along with people.

Two different hiring situations call for two different kinds of application letters. Write a **solicited letter** when you know that the company is hiring: you've
seen an ad, you've been advised to apply by a professor or friend, you've read
in a trade publication that the company is expanding. This situation is similar
to a direct request in persuasion (p. 216): you can indicate immediately that
you are applying for the position. Sometimes, however, the advertised positions may not be what you want, or you may want to work for an organization
that has not announced openings in your area. Then you write a **prospecting
letter.** (The metaphor is drawn from prospecting for gold.) The prospecting letter is like a problem-solving persuasive message (p. 218).

Prospecting letters help you tap into the hidden job market. In some cases,
your prospecting letter may arrive at a company that has decided to hire but
has not yet announced the job. In other cases, companies create positions to get
a good person who is on the market. Even in a hiring freeze, jobs are sometimes
created for specific individuals.

In both solicited and prospecting letters you should

- Address the letter to a specific person.
- Indicate the specific position for which you're applying.
- Be specific about your qualifications.
- Show what separates you from other applicants.
- Show a knowledge of the company and the position.
- Refer to your résumé (which you would enclose with the letter).
- Ask for an interview.

FIGURE 18.5   How to Organize a Solicited Job Application Letter

1. State that you're applying for the job (phrase the job title as your source phrased it). Tell where you learned about the job (ad, referral, etc.). Include any reference number mentioned in the ad. Briefly show that you have the major qualifications required by the ad: a college degree, professional certification, job experience, etc. Summarize your other qualifications briefly in the same order in which you plan to discuss them in the letter.

2. Develop your major qualifications in detail. Be specific about what you've done; relate your achievements to the work you'd be doing in this new job. Remember that readers know only what you tell them. This is not the place for modesty!

3. Develop your other qualifications, even if the ad doesn't ask for them. (If the ad asks for a lot of qualifications, pick the most important three or four.) Show what separates you from the other applicants who will also answer the ad. Demonstrate your knowledge of the organization.

4. Ask for an interview; tell when you'll be available to be interviewed and to begin work. End on a positive, forward-looking note.

Be a Successful Job Hunter!*

A study by the Administrative Management Society revealed that successful job hunters were more likely to

- Make lots of contacts; schedule lots of interviews. Increasing the number of contacts and interviews increases the number of job offers.

- Adapt the approach to the individual employer. Many students use the same approach for all potential employers. Adapting the strategy to the employer sets you apart from other applicants and increases the chances of a job offer.

- Take control of the process. Employers prefer motivated, active, aggressive candidates.

- Polish communication and interpersonal skills. These skills are needed both to present your qualifications effectively and to make you competitive for the many jobs that require communicating and working with people in addition to specific technical skills.

- Investigate the hidden job market. Don't rely just on advertised openings. Use the techniques in this chapter to tap into the hidden job market.

*Based on Steven R. Dzubow, "Entering the Job Market," *Journal of College Placement* 45, no. 3 (Spring 1985), 49–50.

The following discussion follows the job letter from beginning to end. The two kinds of letters are discussed separately where they differ and together where they are the same. Letters for internships follow the same patterns: use a solicited letter to apply for an internship that has been advertised and a prospecting letter to create an internship with a company that has not announced one.

How to Organize Solicited Letters

When you know the company is hiring, use the pattern of organization in Figure 18.5. A sample solicited letter is shown in Figure 18.6.

How to Organize Prospecting Letters

When you don't have any evidence that the company is hiring, you cannot use the pattern for solicited letters. Instead, use the pattern of organization in Figure 18.7. A sample prospecting letter is shown in Figure 18.8.

First Paragraphs of Solicited Letters

When you know that the firm is hiring, announcing that you are applying for a specific position enables the firm to route your letter to the appropriate person, thus speeding consideration of your application. Identify where you learned about the job: "the position of junior accountant announced in Sunday's *Dispatch*," "William Paquette, our placement director, told me that you are looking for . . ."

Note how the following paragraph picks up several of the characteristics of the ad:

Ad: Business Education Instructor at Shelby Adult Education. Candidate must possess a Bachelor's degree in Business Education. Will be responsible for providing in-house training to business and government leaders. . . . Candidate should have at least six months' office experience. Prior teaching experience not required.

Letter: I am interested in your position in Business Education. I will receive a Bachelor of Science degree from North Carolina A & T University in December. I have two years' experience teaching word processing and computer accounting courses to adults and have developed leadership skills in the North Carolina National Guard.

FIGURE 18.6   A Solicited Letter from a Graduating Senior

Tracey has had only course work and one part-time job. But by being specific about what she's done in class and on the job, she creates a positive impression.

1072 Adams Street, Apt. 23
Waltham, MA 02254
April 17, 2003

Modified block format is good for letters of application.

Mr. Robert H. Catanga, Senior Accountant
IBM Corporation
1717 Central
New York, NY 10021

Tell where you learned about the job. If the job has a number, provide it.

Dear Mr. Catanga:

I am applying for the Accounting position announced on IBM's Web site (jof17747). I will receive a Bachelor of Science degree in accountancy from Bentley this August and plan to take the CPA exam in December.

In paragraph 1, show you have the qualifications the ad lists.

My courses in the accountancy curriculum at Bentley have given me not only the necessary theoretical background but also extensive practical experience in General Ledgers, Accounts Payable, and Travel Expenses. I have worked many cases and problems using computer data, including preparing simulated accounting records for hypothetical firms.

Many courses provide practice with simulated cases—you may be able to use Tracey's strategy, too.

These terms come from the job listing.

These true-to-life cases gave me the opportunity to interpret all sorts of data in order to prepare accurate financial statements. For instance, I've learned the best measures for fixed assets and property controls, how to figure inter/intra-company and travel expenses, and the best methods of matching revenues with expenditures. These I could then analyze and compare to past statements to identify trends and recommend ways that costs could be reduced so that the business could be run even more efficiently.

Referring to her Web page suggests her technological savvy.

Courses in speech communication and business writing have taught me how to communicate with various business audiences. This means that I would be able to provide reports, financial statements, and visuals to show how accounting information is related to management needs. I can use Excel and create computer graphics to provide the reliable accounting data that IBM needs to continue growing each year. Visit my Web page (www.bentley/business/students/mckenna/report.htm) to see the report I wrote on choosing the best method to accelerate depreciation.

Relates what she has done to what she could do for the company.

The ad asked for experience with spreadsheets and computer graphics.

My three years of experience working for Allstate Insurance Company have also given me the opportunity to take leadership and show responsibility. Although I was hired merely as a part-time typist, my supervisor frequently asked for my recommendations of ways to get work done more efficiently. In fact, I developed a procedure for making out arbitration reports which saved so much time that I was asked to teach it to the other employees in my department.

Phrase from the CEO's letter in the annual report, which Tracey read on the Web.

She gets a lot of mileage out of her part-time job by being specific.

One way to refer to résumé.

The enclosed résumé summarizes my qualifications. I can come to New York for an interview any Tuesday or Thursday afternoon. I can begin work in September and look forward to discussing with you ways in which I can help IBM continue its tradition of excellence.

Nice allusion to inclusion of IBM in In Search of Excellence.

Sincerely,

Tracey McKenna

Tracey McKenna

Encl.: Résumé

You don't have to note the enclosure, but doing so is a nice touch if you have room at the bottom of the page.

FIGURE 18.7 How to Organize a Prospecting Letter

1. Catch the reader's interest.
2. Create a bridge between the attention-getter and your qualifications. Focus on what you know and can do. Since the employer is not planning to hire, he or she won't be impressed with the fact that you're graduating. Summarize your qualifications briefly in the same order in which you plan to discuss them in the letter. This summary sentence or paragraph then covers everything you will talk about and serves as an organizing device for your letter.
3. Develop your strong points in detail. Be specific. Relate what you've done in the past to what you could do for this company. Show that you know something about the company. Identify the specific niche you want to fill.
4. Ask for an interview and tell when you'll be available for interviews. (Don't tell when you can begin work.) End on a positive, forward-looking note.

Libraries Are Excellent Resources*

Your public library is an excellent resource for finding a new job or career.

"There's a lot of stuff out there on the Internet, and libraries can serve an important function in pointing people to the most quality career resources," says Frances Roehm, a librarian and co-chairwoman of the Public Library Association's Job and Career Information Services Committee. "There is some fraud out there and some things that aren't current anymore."

Elisa Topper, assistant dean of the graduate library school at Dominican University's Graduate School of Library and Information Science, said she has seen more demands on public libraries for career information.

"The trend has shifted to career collections and using the Internet. I think people still feel safe in going to a library, and that people want the nurturing and the support that other people can give them."

*Quoted from Elizabeth Neff, "Libraries Lend Hand in Job Hunt," *Chicago Tribune,* July 13, 2000.

Your **summary sentence** or **paragraph** covers everything you will talk about and serves as an organizing device for your letter.

> I have a good background in standard accounting principles and procedures and a working knowledge of some of the special accounting practices of the oil industry. This working knowledge is based on practical experience in the oil fields: I've pumped, tailed rods, and worked as a roustabout.

> My business experience, experience using DeVilbiss equipment, and communication skills qualify me to be an effective part of the sales staff at DeVilbiss.

> Let me put my creative eye, artistic ability, and experience to work for McLean Design.

Good word choices can help set your letter apart from the scores or even hundreds of letters the company is likely to get in response to an ad. The following first paragraph of a letter in response to an ad by Allstate Insurance Company shows a knowledge of the firm's advertising slogan and sets itself apart from the dozens of letters that start with "I would like to apply for. . . ."

> The Allstate Insurance Company is famous across the nation for its "Good Hands Policy." I would like to lend a helping hand to many Americans as a financial analyst for Allstate, as advertised in the *Chicago Tribune.* I have a Bachelor of Science degree in Accounting from Iowa State University and I have worked with figures, computers, and people.

Note that the last sentence forecasts the organization of the letter, preparing for paragraphs about the student's academic background and (in this order) experience with "figures, computers, and people."

First Paragraphs of Prospecting Letters

In a prospecting letter, asking for a job in the first paragraph is dangerous: unless the company plans to hire but has not yet announced openings, the reader is likely to throw the letter away. Instead, catch the reader's interest. Then in the second paragraph you can shift the focus to your skills and experience, showing how they can be useful to the employer.

FIGURE 18.8   A Prospecting Letter from a Career Changer

Marcella G. Cope
370 Monahan Lane
Dublin, OH 43016
614-555-1997
mcope@postbox.acs.ohio-state.edu

Marcella creates a "letterhead" that harmonizes with her résumé (see Figure 17.6).

August 23, 2002

Mr. John Harrobin
New Media Solutions
Metatec Corporation
7001 Metatec Boulevard
Dublin, OH 43017

Block format with justified margins lets Marcella get this letter on one page.

Dear Mr. Harrobin:

In a prospecting letter, open with a sentence which (1) will seem interesting and true to the reader and (2) provides a natural bridge to talking about yourself.

One way to refer to the enclosed résumé.

Putting a textbook on a CD-ROM saves paper but does nothing to take advantage of the many possibilities the CD-ROM environment provides. Yet it can be a real challenge to find people who write well, proof carefully, and understand multimedia design. You will see from my enclosed résumé that I have this useful combination of skills.

Shows knowledge of the company.

Rita Haralabidis tells me that Metatec needs people to design and develop high-quality CD-ROM products to meet business and consumer deadlines. Most of the writing and editing that I do is subject to strict standards and even stricter deadlines, and I know information is useful only if it is available when clients need it.

Shows she can meet company needs.

When I toured Metatec this spring, members of the New Media Solutions Group shared some of their work from a series of interactive CD-ROM textbooks they were developing in tandem with Harcourt Brace. This project sparked my interest in Metatec because of my own experience with evaluating, contributing to, and editing college-level textbooks.

Relates what she's done to what she could do for this company.

As a program administrator at The Ohio State University, I examined dozens of textbooks from publishers interested in having their books adopted by the nation's largest First-Year Writing Program. This experience taught me which elements of a textbook--both content and design--were successful, and which failed to generate interest. Often, I worked closely with sales representatives to suggest changes for future editions. My own contributions to two nationally distributed textbooks further familiarized me with production processes and the needs of multiple audiences. My close contact with students convinces me of the need to produce educational materials that excite students, keep their attention, and allow them to learn through words, pictures, and sounds.

All of these terms fit Metatec's production of multimedia educational materials.

My communication and technology skills would enable me to adapt quickly to work with both individual clients and major corporations like CompuServe and The American Medical Association. I am a flexible thinker, a careful editor, a fluent writer, and, most important, a quick study. I will call you next week to find a mutually convenient time when we can discuss putting my talents to work for Metatec.

Names specific clients, showing more knowledge of the company.

Sincerely,

Marcella G. Cope

Marcella G. Cope

When you're changing fields, learning quickly is a real plus.

Enclosed: Résumé

Here are some effective first paragraphs and the second paragraphs that provide a transition to the writer's discussion of his or her qualifications:

■ First two paragraphs of a letter to the Director of Publications of Standard Oil:

> Americans are so concerned about the preservation of oil reserves that some are even beginning to walk instead of riding. If scarcity of resources makes us use them more carefully, perhaps it would be a good idea to announce that words are in short supply. If people used them more carefully, internal communications specialists like you would have fewer headaches because communications jobs would be done right the first time.
>
> I have worked for the last six years improving my communications skills, learning to use words more carefully and effectively. I have taught business communication at a major university, worked for two newspapers, completed a Master's degree in English, and would like to contribute my skills to your internal communications staff.

Relating What You've Done to the Job*

The letter continued . . .

As I looked into publishing, it occurred to me that of all the things I have done, the one I could most closely relate to the field was, strangely enough, an experience I had as a baby-sitter.

Immediately, he had the editor's full attention. How could baby-sitting fit in with publishing? During the summer of his junior year in college he had taken a job as a sailing instructor, tutor, and companion for the children of a wealthy family. . . . While the parents were on a cruise, the governess suffered a stroke, sending the cook into a tizzy, the maid into tears, and the chauffeur and gardener into the local bar. Only the student could cope, and he took charge and managed the estate for the rest of the summer.

In his letter of application he described the crisis, and subsequent problems he had faced, and told how he had met them. Then he related those experiences to the problems that he had learned editors, advertisers, printers, and others encounter in the publishing industry.

*Quoted from John L. Munschauer, *Jobs for English Majors and Other Smart People* (Princeton, NJ: Peterson's Guides, 1986), 75–76.

Avoid Fields. Jump Fences.

Help wanted.
Bruce Mau Design is looking for thinking designers to work in our intense, upbeat, fast-paced, intellectually demanding studio.

We're looking for people who:

· understand design culture as research – trials and errors, experiments, speculations

· read books (sorry, we must insist)

· work at the intersection of form and content

· don't see a clear distinction between work and play

· possess broad cultural experience and are excited by working in an international context.

You could win a job, and not just any job!

The BMDquiz is "scientifically" developed to test the depth of your cultural awareness. A score of more than 35 may qualify you for an interview, so go ahead, tell us a little bit about yourself. (By the way, research is allowed.)

Effective letters of application respond directly to the job description. This ad from Bruce Mau Design Inc. in Toronto asked applicants to answer 41 questions ("research allowed"). A good response would include not only the quiz answers but also digital files of design projects and paragraphs showing an understanding of design culture as research, documenting a broad cultural experience, and reporting any international experience or interests.

- First two paragraphs of a letter applying to be a computer programmer for an insurance company:

> Computers alone aren't the answer to demands for higher productivity in the competitive insurance business. Merging a poorly written letter with a database of customers just sends out bad letters more quickly. But you know how hard it is to find people who can both program computers and write well.
>
> My education and training have given me this useful combination. I'd like to put my associate's degree in computer technology and my business experience writing to customers to work in State Farm's service approach to insurance.

- Questions work well only if the answers aren't obvious. One student used the following paragraph in his first draft:

> Do you think that training competent and motivated operating personnel is a serious concern in the nuclear power industry?

If the reader says *yes*, the question will seem dumb. If the reader says *no*, the student has destroyed his common ground. In the next draft, the student revised the first paragraph to read:

> Competent and motivated operating personnel are just as important to the safe and efficient operation of a nuclear power plant as is high-quality equipment.

This paragraph gave him an easy transition into talking about himself as a competent, motivated person.

Showing a Knowledge of the Position and the Company

If you could substitute another inside address and salutation and send out the letter without any further changes, it isn't specific enough. A job application letter is basically a claim that you could do a job. Use your knowledge of the position and the company to choose relevant evidence from what you've done to support your claims that you could help the company. (See Figures 18.6 and 18.8.)

The following paragraphs also use the writer's knowledge of the company.

- A letter to Bendix Home Appliances uses information that the student got from information in the campus placement office about the job duties and market share.

> Coursework in business communication has taught me how to write reports that meet the needs of readers. I can use this knowledge to summarize the trends that show up in the Saturday Night Reports that your dealers submit. . . .
>
> A minor in personnel management plus public-relations study has taught me that trends are manifestations of human motives and human feelings, and not just cold numbers. My attention to this fact will enable me to interpret retailers' reports concretely—to keep that thirty cents of every washing machine dollar clinking into Bendix tills.

- A letter to PricewaterhouseCoopers's Minneapolis office uses information the student learned in a referral interview with a partner in an accounting firm. Because the reader will know that Herr Wollner is a partner in the Berlin office, the student does not need to identify him.

While I was studying in Berlin last spring, I had the opportunity to discuss accounting methods for multinational clients of PricewaterhouseCoopers with Herr Fritz Wollner. We also talked about communication among PricewaterhouseCoopers's international offices.

Herr Wollner mentioned that the increasing flow of accounting information between the European offices—especially those located in Germany, Switzerland, and Austria—and the US offices of PricewaterhouseCoopers makes accurate translations essential. My fluency in German enables me to translate accurately; and my study of communication problems in Speech Communication, Business and Professional Speaking, and Business and Technical Writing will help me see where messages might be misunderstood and choose words which are more likely to communicate clearly.

▨ A letter to KMPG uses information the student learned in a summer job.

As an assistant accountant for Pacific Bell during this past summer, I worked with its computerized billing and record-keeping system, BARK. I had the opportunity to help the controller revise portions of the system, particularly the procedures for handling delinquent accounts. When the KMPG audit team reviewed Pacific Bell's transactions completed for July, I had the opportunity to observe your System 2170. Several courses in computer science allow me to appreciate the simplicity of your system and its objective of reducing audit work, time, and costs.

The best job applications give an employer a sample of what you can do. Born with cerebral palsey, Miami Dolphins kicking coach Doug Blevins has never himself kicked a football. He won his first NFL job by faxing then–New York Jets general manager Dick Steinberg analyses of the flaw of the Jets' placekicker at the time. As an NFL coach, Blevins has helped Leo Araguz, Adam Vinatieri, and Olindo Mare become some of the league's best.

One or two specific details about the company usually are enough to demonstrate your knowledge. Be sure to use the knowledge, not just repeat it. Never present the information as though it will be news to the reader. After all, the reader works for the company and presumably knows much more about it than you do.

Showing What Separates You from Other Applicants

Your knowledge of the company separates you from other applicants. You can also use coursework, an understanding of the field, and experience in jobs and extracurricular events to show that you're unique. As Teresa Moburg points out, be specific but concise. Usually three to five sentences will enable you to give enough specific supporting details.

- This student uses both coursework and summer jobs to set herself apart from other applicants:

> My college courses have taught me the essential accounting skills required to contribute to the growth of Monsanto. Since you recently adopted new accounting methods for fluctuations in foreign currencies, you will need people knowledgeable in foreign currency translation to convert currency exchange rates. In two courses in international accounting, I compiled simulated accounting statements of hypothetical multinational firms in countries experiencing different rates of currency devaluation. Through these classes, I acquired the skills needed to work with the daily fluctuations of exchange rates and at the same time formulate an accurate and favorable representation of Monsanto.
>
> A company as diverse as Monsanto requires extensive record-keeping as well as numerous internal and external communications. Both my summer jobs and my coursework prepare me to do this. As Office Manager for the steamboat *Julia Belle Swain,* I was in charge of most of the bookkeeping and letter writing for the company. I kept accurate records for each workday, and I often entered over 100 transactions in a single day. In business and technical writing I learned how to write persuasive letters and memos and how to present extensive data in reports in a simplified style that is clear and easy to understand.

- This student uses her sorority experience and knowledge of the company to set herself apart from other applicants in a letter applying to be Assistant Personnel Manager of a multinational firm:

> As a counselor for sorority rush, I was also able to work behind the scenes as well as with the prospective rushees. I was able to use my leadership and communication skills for group activities for 70 young women by planning numerous activities to make my group a cohesive unit. Helping the women deal with rejection was also part of my job. Not all of the rushees made final cuts, and it was the rush counselor who helped put the rejection into perspective.
>
> This skill could be helpful in speaking to prospective employees wishing to travel to Saudi Arabia. Not all will pass the medical exams or make the visa application deadlines in time, and the Assistant Manager tells these people the news. An even more delicate subject to handle is conveying news of a death of a relative or employee to those concerned. My experience with helping people deal with small losses gives me a foundation to help others deal with more severe losses and deeper grief.

In your résumé, you may list activities, offices, and courses. In your letter, give more detail about what you did and show how that experience will help you contribute to the employer's organization more quickly.

When you discuss your strengths, don't exaggerate. No employer will believe that a new graduate has a "comprehensive" knowledge of a field. Indeed, most employers believe that six months to a year of on-the-job training is necessary before most new hires are really earning their pay. Specifics about what you've done will make your claims about what you can do more believable and ground them in reality.

The Last Paragraph

In the last paragraph, indicate when you'd be available for an interview. If you're free anytime, you can say so. But it's likely that you have responsibilities in class and work. If you'd have to go out of town, there may be only certain days of the week or certain weeks that you could leave town for several days. Use a sentence that fits your situation.

> I could come to Albany for an interview any Wednesday or Friday.

> I'll be attending the Oregon Forestry Association's November meeting and will be available for interviews there.

> I could come to Memphis for an interview March 17–21.

Should you wait for the employer to call you, or should you call the employer to request an interview? In a solicited letter, it's safe to wait to be contacted: you know the employer wants to hire someone, and if your letter and résumé show that you're one of the top applicants, you'll get an interview. In a prospecting letter, call the employer. Because the employer is not planning to hire, you'll get a higher percentage of interviews if you're aggressive.

If you're writing a prospecting letter to a firm that's more than a few hours away by car, say that you'll be in the area the week of such-and-such and could stop by for an interview. Companies pay for follow-up visits, but not for first interviews. A company may be reluctant to ask you to make an expensive trip when it isn't yet sure it wants to hire you.

End the letter on a positive note that suggests you look forward to the interview and that you see yourself as a person who has something to contribute, not as someone who just needs a job.

> I look forward to discussing with you ways in which I could contribute to The Limited's continued growth.

E-Mail Application Letters

Some Web ads give you a street address to submit applications but say "e-mail preferred." Other ads just give an e-mail address.

No research exists on whether e-mail application letters should be shorter than paper ones. Until we know which works better, you have two choices: paste a traditional letter into your e-mail screen, or edit your letter to create a shorter, one-screen letter (see Figure 18.9).

Getting a Job with an *Inc.* 500 Company*

Paul Moran decided he wanted to work for a small company. So he got the *Inc.* 500 list (the list of the 500 fastest-growing small companies, published each year by *Inc.* magazine). He sent letters to all 17 companies in the Los Angeles area, offering to work for free. "I am confident that any financial rewards will come later."

He included a reply coupon, asking employers to fill in a "preliminary job description" and check one of two boxes:

☐ Yes, we are interested in interviewing you for an UNPAID POSITION.

☐ Sorry, we are not interested in having you work for us WITHOUT PAY.

The coupon noted that Moran would call three finalists to set up interviews.

Paul Moran got a job with Collectech Systems. He's now regional president, and the firm is still on the *Inc.* 500 list.

*Based on George Gendron, "FYI," *Inc.*, October 1995, 13.

Follow the Hot Markets to Find a Job*

Bill Connors was worried sick when he lost his job in late September. Where would a 54-year-old career telecom executive find a job in an economy that was souring? Connors turned to online job board Monster.com. He found a new job with better pay. Now he manages quality control at Boston's Solectria Corporation, which makes parts for electric vehicles. "In this job market, you have to be flexible. Look outside your field if you're going to find work," he says.

Even in a tough economy, certain industries continue to produce new jobs. For example, in bioscience workers continue to flit among jobs. "I've been impressed with the number of positions available in the pharmaceutical industry," says Dr. Vanaja V. Ragavan, who just jumped from Aventis to Novartis to head up women's health research.

People who don't make the cut in one industry may find their luck better—and faster—in others.

*Based on Charles Haddad, "Hot Spots in Job Market," *BusinessWeek Online*, December 10, 2001.

FIGURE 18.9 An E-Mail Application Letter

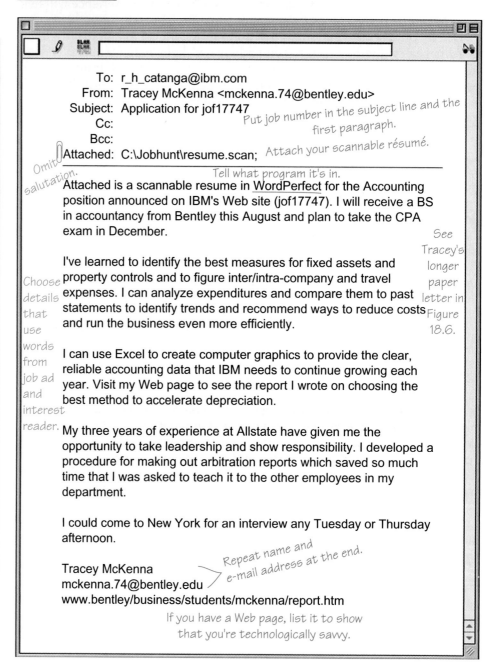

When you submit an e-mail letter with an attached résumé,

- Tell what word-processing program your scannable résumé is saved in.
- Put the job number or title for which you're applying in your subject line and in the first paragraph.
- Prepare your letter in a word-processing program with a spell checker to make it easier to edit and proof the document.
- Don't send anything in all capital letters.
- Don't use smiley faces or other emoticons.

- Put your name and e-mail address at the end of the message. Most e-mail programs send along the "sender" information at the top of the screen, but a few don't, and you want the employer to know whose letter this is!

Creating a Professional Image

Every employer wants businesslike employees who understand professionalism. To make your application letter professional,

- Create your letter in a word processing program so you can use features such as spell check. Use a standard font (Times Roman, Palatino, or Helvetica) in 11- or 12-point type.
- Address your letter to a specific person. If the reader is a woman, call the office to find out what courtesy title she prefers.
- Don't mention relatives' names. It's OK to use names of other people if the reader knows those people and thinks well of them, if they think well of you and will say good things about you, and if you have permission to use their names.
- Omit personal information not related to the job.
- Unless you're applying for a creative job in advertising, use a conservative style: few contractions, no sentence fragments, clichés, or slang.
- Edit the letter carefully and proof it several times to make sure it's perfect. Errors suggest that you're careless or inept.

Writing Style

Use a smooth, tight writing style (◀▥ p. 97). Use the technical jargon of the field, but avoid businessese and stuffy words like *utilize, commence,* and *transpire* (for *happen*).

Use a lively, energetic style that makes you sound like a real person.

Avoid words that can be interpreted sexually. A model letter distributed by the placement office at a midwestern university included the following sentence:

> I have been active in campus activities and have enjoyed good relations with my classmates and professors.

One young woman incorporated this sentence in a letter she mailed. The recipient circled the sentence and then passed the letter around the office (and did not invite the woman for an interview). That's not the kind of attention you want your letter to get!

Positive Emphasis

Be positive. Don't plead ("Please give me a chance") or apologize ("I cannot promise that I am substantially different from the lot"). Most negatives should be omitted in the letter.

Avoid word choices with negative connotations (◀▥ p. 92). Note how the following revisions make the writer sound more confident.

Negative: I have learned an excessive amount about writing through courses in journalism and advertising.

Positive: Courses in journalism and advertising have taught me to recognize and to write good copy. My profile of a professor was published in the campus newspaper; I earned an "A+" on my direct mail campaign for the American Dental Association to persuade young adults to see their dentist more often.

Getting a Job Overseas*

The Council on International Educational Exchange in New York City can provide information about work permits in Europe. Call 212-822-2600. Useful books include

- *Directory of Jobs and Careers Abroad* (Peterson's Guides).
- *How to Get a Job in Europe* (Surrey Books).
- *How to Get a Job in the Pacific Rim* (Surrey Books).

*Based on "Ask Annie," *Fortune,* December 9, 1996, 221.

Application Bloopers*

The following sentences came from separate application letters.

- Thank you for accepting me recent phone call.
- My position has been recently has been eliminated.
- I am seeking a position on the Eat Coast.
- Attached is a one-page summery.
- Please disregard my attached resume as it is woefully out of date.
- My talent is at an inordinately high level and my ability to maintain accurate figures and meet deadlines is unspeakable.
- In closing, let me outline the previous bookkeeping experience I've been able to endure.
- Thank you for your consideration. Hope to hear from you shorty.
- P.S. If you hire me away from this nightmare, you'll also save me thousands in therapy.

*Sentences quoted from Tom Burke, "How Do You Spell Quality?" *The Wall Street Journal*, April 8, 1996, A18; and Robert Half's *Resumania*, quoted in Taunee Besson, *Cover Letters: Proven Techniques for Writing Letters That Will Help You Get the Job You Want* (New York: John Wiley and Sons, 1995), 96–97, and in Rochelle Sharp, "Labor Letter," *The Wall Street Journal*, March 22, 1994, A1, and "Work Week," *The Wall Street Journal*, February 27, 1996, A1.

Excessive suggests that you think the courses covered too much—hardly an opinion likely to endear you to an employer.

Negative:　You can check with my references to verify what I've said.

Positive:　Professor Hill can give you more information about the program in Industrial Distribution Management.

Verify suggests that you expect the employer to distrust what you've said.

Negative:　I am anxious to talk with you about the opportunities for employment with Ernst & Young.

Positive:　I look forward to talking with you about opportunities at Ernst & Young.

Anxious suggests that you're worried about the interview.

You-Attitude

Unsupported claims may sound overconfident, selfish, or arrogant. Create you-attitude (◄ p. 34) by describing exactly what you have done and by showing how that relates to what you could do for this employer.

Lacks you-attitude:　An inventive and improvising individual like me is a necessity in your business.

You-attitude:　Building a summer house-painting business gave me the opportunity to find creative solutions to challenges. At the end of the first summer, for example, I had nearly 10 gallons of exterior latex left, but no more jobs. I contacted the home economics teacher at my high school. She agreed to give course credit to students who were willing to give up two Saturdays to paint a house being renovated by Habitat for Humanity. I donated the paint and supervised the students. I got a charitable deduction for the paint and hired the three best students to work for me the following summer. I could put these skills in problem solving and supervising to work as a personnel manager for Burroughs.

Lacks you-attitude:　A company of your standing could offer the challenging and demanding kind of position in which my abilities could flourish.

You-attitude:　Omit.

Lacks you-attitude:　I want a job with your company.

You-attitude:　I would like to apply for Procter & Gamble's management trainee program.

Remember that the word *you* refers to your reader. Using *you* when you really mean yourself or "all people" can insult your reader by implying that he or she still has a lot to learn about business:

Lacks you-attitude:　Running my own business taught me that you need to learn to manage your time.

You-attitude:　Running my own business taught me to manage my time.

Since you're talking about yourself, you'll use *I* in your letter. Reduce the number of *I*'s by revising some sentences to use *me* or *my*.

Under my presidency, the Agronomy Club . . .

Courses in media and advertising management gave me a chance to . . .

My responsibilities as a summer intern included . . .

In particular, avoid beginning every paragraph with *I*. Begin sentences with prepositional phrases or introductory clauses:

As my résumé shows, I . . .

In my coursework in media and advertising management, I . . .

As a summer intern, I . . .

Paragraph Length and Unity

Keep your first and last paragraphs fairly short—preferably no more than four or five typed lines. Vary paragraph length within the letter; it's OK to have one long paragraph, but don't use a series of eight-line paragraphs.

When you have a long paragraph, check to be sure that it covers only one subject. If it covers two or more subjects, divide it into two or more paragraphs. If a short paragraph covers several subjects, consider adding a topic sentence (◀▦ p. 103) to provide paragraph unity.

Length

Always use at least a full page. A short letter throws away an opportunity to be persuasive; it may also suggest that you have little to say for yourself or that you aren't very interested in the job.

Without eliminating content, tighten each sentence (◀▦ p. 97) to be sure that you're using space as efficiently as possible. If your letter is still a bit over a page, use slightly smaller margins, a type size that's one point smaller, or justified proportional type to get more on the page.

However, if you need more than a page, use it—as long as you have at least 6–12 lines of body text on the second page. The extra space gives you room to be more specific about what you've done and to add details about your experience that will separate you from other applicants. Employers don't *want* longer letters, but they will read them *if* the letter is well written and *if* the applicant establishes early in the letter that he or she has the credentials the company needs.

Summary of Key Points

- ▦ Résumés differ from letters of application in the following ways:
  - ▦ A résumé is adapted to a position. The letter is adapted to the needs of a particular organization.
  - ▦ The résumé summarizes all your qualifications. The letter shows how your qualifications can help the organization meet its needs, how you differ from other applicants, and that you have some knowledge of the organization.
  - ▦ The résumé uses short, parallel phrases and sentence fragments. The letter uses complete sentences in well-written paragraphs.
- ▦ Use directories, annual reports, recruiting literature, business periodicals, trade journals, and the Web to get information about employers and jobs to use in your letter.
- ▦ Information and referral interviews can help you tap into the **hidden job market**—jobs that are not advertised. In an **information interview** you find out what the day-to-day work involves and how you can best prepare to enter that field. **Referral interviews** are interviews you schedule to learn about current job opportunities in your field.

Separating Yourself from Other Applicants*

The following will help set you apart from other applicants:

- ■ Computer literacy. Be able to use word processing programs, spreadsheets, and databases. Graphics and page layout programs are a plus.

- ■ Foreign languages and international experience. Be able to speak at least one language other than English fluently. If funds permit, travel or study abroad. Cultivate the international students on your campus to gain experience interacting with people from other cultures.

- ■ Experience. Put your knowledge and skills to work in internships, volunteer work, and campus or community activities. Take a part-time or full-time job that's related to your field—both to earn money for college and to get experience to land a job after graduation.

- ■ The ability to sell yourself. Know about the product (you) and the customer (the employer).

*Based on Joan E. Rigdon, "Glut of Graduates Lets Recruiters Pick Only the Best," *The Wall Street Journal*, May 20, 1993, B1.

- When you know that a company is hiring, send a **solicited job letter.** When you want a job with a company that has not announced openings, send a **prospecting job letter.** In both letters, you should
  - Address the letter to a specific person.
  - Indicate the specific position for which you're applying.
  - Be specific about your qualifications.
  - Show what separates you from other applicants.
  - Show a knowledge of the company and the position.
  - Refer to your résumé (which you would enclose with the letter).
  - Ask for an interview.

- Organize a solicited letter in this way:
  1. State that you're applying for the job and tell where you learned about the job (ad, referral, etc.). Briefly show that you have the major qualifications required by the ad. Summarize your qualifications in the order in which you plan to discuss them in the letter.
  2. Develop your major qualifications in detail.
  3. Develop your other qualifications. Show what separates you from the other applicants who will also answer the ad. Demonstrate your knowledge of the organization.
  4. Ask for an interview; tell when you'll be available to be interviewed and to begin work. End on a positive, forward-looking note.

- Organize a prospecting letter in this way:
  1. Catch the reader's interest.
  2. Create a bridge between the attention-getter and your qualifications. Summarize your qualifications in the order in which you plan to discuss them in the letter.
  3. Develop your strong points in detail. Relate what you've done in the past to what you could do for this company. Show that you know something about the company. Identify the specific niche you want to fill.
  4. Ask for an interview and tell when you'll be available for interviews. End on a positive, forward-looking note.

- Use your knowledge of the company, your coursework, your understanding of the field, and your experience in jobs and extracurricular activities to show that you're unique.

- Don't repeat information that the reader already knows; don't seem to be lecturing the reader on his or her business.

- Never use relatives' names in a job letter. Using names of other people is OK if the reader knows those people and thinks well of them, if they think well of you and will say good things about you, and if you have permission to use their names.

- Use positive emphasis to sound confident. Use you-attitude by supporting general claims with specific examples and by relating what you've done to what the employer needs.

- Use at least a full page. It's desirable to limit your letter to one page, but use up to two pages if you need them to showcase all your credentials.

| CHAPTER 18 | Exercises and Problems |

Getting Started

18.1 Analyzing First Paragraphs of Prospecting Letters

All of the following are first paragraphs in prospecting letters written by new college graduates. Evaluate the paragraphs on these criteria:

■ Is the paragraph likely to interest the reader and motivate him or her to read the rest of the letter?

■ Does the paragraph have some content that the student can use to create a transition to talking about his or her qualifications?

■ Does the paragraph avoid asking for a job?

1. For the past two and one-half years I have been studying turf management. On August 1, I will graduate from _____ University with a BA in Ornamental Horticulture. The type of job I will seek will deal with golf course maintenance as an assistant superintendent.

2. Ann Gibbs suggested that I contact you.

3. Each year, the Christmas shopping rush makes more work for everyone at Nordstrom's, especially for the Credit Department. While working for Nordstrom's Credit Department for three Christmas and summer vacations, the Christmas sales increase is just one of the credit situations I became aware of.

4. Whether to plate a two-inch eyebolt with cadmium for a tough, brilliant shine or with zinc for a rust-resistant, less expensive finish is a tough question. But similar questions must be answered daily by your salespeople. With my experience in the electroplating industry, I can contribute greatly to your constant need of getting customers.

5. What a set of tractors! The new 9430 and 9630 diesels are just what is needed by today's farmer with his ever-increasing acreage. John Deere has truly done it again.

6. Prudential Insurance Company did much to help my college career as the sponsor of my National Merit Scholarship. Now I think I can give something back to Prudential. I'd like to put my education, including a B.S. degree in finance from _____ University, to work in your investment department.

7. Since the beginning of Delta Electric Construction Co. in 1993, the size and profits have grown steadily. My father, being a stockholder and vice president, often discusses company dealings with me. Although the company has prospered, I understand there have been a few problems of mismanagement. I feel with my present and future qualifications, I could help ease these problems.

18.2 Improving You-Attitude and Positive Emphasis in Job Letters

Revise each of these sentences to improve you-attitude and positive emphasis. You may need to add information.

1. I understand that your company has had problems due to the mistranslation of documents during international ad campaigns.

2. Included in my résumé are the courses in Finance that earned me a fairly attractive grade average.

3. I am looking for a position that gives me a chance to advance quickly.

4. Although short on experience, I am long on effort and enthusiasm.

5. I have been with the company from its beginning to its present unfortunate state of bankruptcy.

18.3 Evaluating Rough Drafts

Evaluate the following drafts. What parts should be omitted? What needs to be changed or added? What parts would benefit from specific supporting details?

1.

Dear _____:

There is more to a buyer's job than buying the merchandise. And a clothing buyer in particular has much to consider.

Even though something may be in style, customers may not want to buy it. Buyers should therefore be aware of what customers want and how much they are willing to pay.

In the buying field, request letters, thank-you letters, and persuasive letters are frequently written.

My interest in the retail field inspired me to read The Gap's annual report. I saw that a new store is being built. An interview would give us a chance to discuss how I could contribute to this new store. Please call me to schedule an interview.

Sincerely,

2.

Dear Sir or Madam:

I am taking the direct approach of a personnel letter. I believe you will under stand my true value in the areas of practical knowledge and promotional capabilities.

I am interested in a staff position with Darden in relation to trying to improve the operations and moral of the Olive Garden Restaurants, which I think that I am capable of doing. Please take a minute not to read my résumé (enclosed) and call to schedule an interview.

Sincerely,

3.

Dear _____:

I would like to apply for the opening you announced for an Assistant Golf Course Superintendent. I have the qualifications you are asking for.

Every year the Superintendent must go before the greens committee to defend its budget requests. To prepare myself to do this, I took courses in accounting, business and administrative writing, and speech.

I have done the operations necessary to maintain the greens properly.

I look forward to talking with you about this position.

Sincerely,

18.4 Gathering Information about an Industry

Use six recent issues of a trade journal to report on three to five trends, developments, or issues that are important in an industry.

As Your Instructor Directs,

a. Share your findings with a small group of other students.

b. Summarize your findings in a memo to your instructor.

c. Present your findings to the class.

d. Join with a small group of other students to write a report summarizing the results of this research.

18.5 Gathering Information about a Specific Organization

Gather information about a specific organization, using several of the following methods:

■ Check the organization's Web site.

■ Read the company's annual report.

■ Pick up relevant information at the Chamber of Commerce.

■ Read articles in trade publications and *The Wall Street Journal* or *The Financial Post* that mention the organization (check the indexes).

■ Get the names and addresses of its officers from a directory or the Web.

■ Read recruiting literature provided by the company.

As Your Instructor Directs,

a. Share your findings with a small group of other students.

b. Summarize your findings in a memo to your instructor.

c. Present your findings orally to the class.

d. Write a paragraph for a job letter using (directly or indirectly) the information you found.

18.6 Conducting an Information Interview

Interview someone working in a field you're interested in. Use the questions listed on page 522 or the shorter list here:

■ How did you get started in this field?

■ What do you like about your job?

■ What do you dislike about your job?

■ Can you give me names of three other people who could also give me information about this job?

As Your Instructor Directs,

a. Share the results of your interview with a small group of other students.

b. Write up your interview in a memo to your instructor.

c. Present the results of your interview orally to the class.

d. Write to the interviewee thanking him or her for taking the time to talk to you.

E-Mail Messages

18.7 Networking

Write to a friend who is already in the workforce, asking about one or more of the following topics:

■ Are any jobs in your field available in your friend's organization? If so, what?

■ If a job is available, can your friend provide information beyond the job listing that will help you write a more detailed, persuasive letter? (Specify the kind of information you'd like to have.)

■ Can your friend suggest people in other organizations who might be useful to you in your job search? (Specify any organizations in which you're especially interested.)

18.8 Applying Electronically

Write a one-screen application letter to accompany a résumé that you submit electronically.

Communicating at Work

As Your Instructor Directs in problems 18.9 and 18.10,

a. Create a document or presentation to achieve the goal.

b. Write a memo to your instructor describing the situation at your workplace and explaining your rhetorical choices (medium, strategy, tone, wording, graphics or document design, and so forth).

18.9   Applying for an Open Position

Many companies post open positions. Apply for one that interests you.

18.10   Creating a Position for Yourself

Identify a need that your employer has, and propose that you be hired (or promoted) to a full-time position working in this area.

Letter Assignments

18.11   Writing a Solicited Letter

Write a letter of application in response to an announced opening for a full-time job (not an internship) which a new college graduate could hold.

   Turn in a copy of the listing. If you use option (a), (b), or (d) below, your listing will be a copy. If you choose option (c), you will write the listing and can design your ideal job.

a. Respond to an ad in a newspaper, a professional journal, in the placement office, or on the Web. Use an ad that specifies the company, not a blind ad. Be sure that you are fully qualified for the job.

b. Take a job description and assume that it represents a current opening. Use a directory to get the name of the person to whom the letter should be addressed.

c. If you have already worked somewhere, you may assume that your employer is asking you to apply for full-time work after graduation. Be sure to write a fully persuasive letter.

d. Respond to one of the listings below. Use a directory to get the name and address of the person to whom you should write.

   1. Enterprise Rent-A-Car has an immediate opening for an entry-level **staff accountant.** Responsibilities will include but are not limited to A/P, A/R, Bank Recs and journal entries. To qualify you must possess a four-year accounting degree, strong written and oral skills, and a strong desire to succeed.

   2. A member of Congress in your state wants an **office manager** for a local office in your state and a **staff member** for the Washington, DC, office. The office manager will answer constituent questions, write press releases, assist with travel appearances, record contributions, and recruit and supervise volunteer staff. Good oral and interpersonal skills a must; political and financial skills helpful. The staff member in Washington will answer mail, help with political research, and draft bills and reports. Good writing and research skills a must; interpersonal skills and political savvy helpful.

   3. KPMG seeks **international human resources trainees** to interact with corporate human resources, payroll, relocation and accounting functions, and the expatriate. Bachelor's degree in an international field a plus. Personal expatriate experience preferred but not required. Must have computer skills. Please refer to job number MMGE-3W7LAY in your correspondence.

   4. Roxy Systems (Roxy.com) seeks **Internet Marketing Coordinators** to analyze online campaigns and put together detailed reports, covering ad impressions and click-through rates. Must have basic understanding of marketing; be organized, creative, and detail-oriented; know Microsoft Excel; have excellent communication skills; and be familiar with the Internet. Send letter and resume to mike@roxy.com.

   5. Bose Corporation seeks **public relations/communications administrative associate** (Job Code 117BD). Write, edit, and produce the in-house newsletter using desktop publishing software. Represent the company to external contacts (including the press). Provide

administrative support to the manager of PR by scheduling meetings, preparing presentations, tabulating and analyzing surveys, and processing financial requests. Excellent organizational, interpersonal, and communication skills (both written and oral) required. Must be proficient in MS Office and Filemaker Pro.

6. The Limited is hiring **executive development program trainees.** After completing 10-week training programs, trainees will become assistant buyers. Prefer people with strong interest and experience in retailing. Apply directly to the store for which you want to work.

7. Winterland, a leading supplier of screen-printed apparel, seeks an **Assistant Account Manager** (HR/AAM) to oversee day-to-day execution and service of client needs. The successful candidate will possess an extremely high degree of attention to detail and problem-solving abilities. Superior communication and interpersonal skills required. Proficiency with both MS Word and Excel an absolute must. Prior experience in the textile or apparel

industry highly desirable. Send correspondence to personnel@winterland.com (no attachments please).

8. A local nonprofit organization seeks a **Coordinator of Volunteer Services.** Responsibilities for this full-time position include coordinating volunteers' schedules, recruiting and training new volunteers, and evaluating existing programs. Excellent listening and communication skills required.

9. Your state wants **assistant international trade managers** for offices in London, Paris, Tokyo, Hong Kong, and Buenos Aires. Duties include promoting state exports, promoting the state as a site for foreign business investment and branch plants, and representing the state to government officials. Candidate should know language and culture of target country.

10. Ogilvie & Mather is hiring **assistant account executives.** You will be assigned to a major client account, and will help develop strategies for marketing and advertising, with specific assignments in one of the following: creative, media, research, or production.

18.12 Writing a Prospecting Letter

Pick a company you'd like to work for and apply for a specific position. The position can be one that already exists or one that you would create if you could to match your unique blend of talents. Give your instructor a copy of the job description with your letter.

Address your letter to the president of a small company, or the area vice president or branch manager of a large company. Use directories to get the name and address of the person with the power to create a job for you.

Job Interviews, Follow-Up Letters and Calls, and Job Offers

Job Interviews, Follow-Up Letters and Calls, and Job Offers

Tim R. Moore
Director of Human Resources,
The Northridge Group, Inc.

A recruiter since 1991, Tim Moore interviews hundreds of people each year and has helped thousands in their career searches. He currently serves as Director of Human Resources for Northridge Group, a network of professionals providing consulting, outsourcing, and interim staffing solutions to progressive enterprises worldwide.

www.northridgegroup.com

An interview is your opportunity to demonstrate that you're bright and energetic—the kind of person the company wants to hire. Doing a little pre-interview research and paying close attention to details is critical.

I can't tell you how many people I've interviewed over the years who came to my office without a clue about the company or the job they were interviewing for. I often ask, "What was it about our ad that caught your attention or interested you in our company?" The response "Umm, I don't really remember your ad. Could you tell me what it said?" is not the right one.

Before an interview, research the organization. When was it founded? What is the main line of business? Does it have subsidiaries? What is the annual revenue? Who owns the company? Formulate questions to ask the interviewer about the important issues the company faces.

> *"Good interviewing is a series of details that work together."*

Be prompt. Make sure that you know exactly where you are going and plan ahead so you'll have plenty of time to get there. Ideally, arrive 15–20 minutes early. Take a couple of paper copies of your résumé, even if you already sent one by fax or e-mail.

Wear a suit. An interview is not the time or place to make a trendy fashion statement. Even if the company is casual, I strongly recommend that you break out your best dark suit for the interview.

Be honest. Answer questions directly and without excessive "spin." Present yourself in the best light possible, but don't set false or unrealistic expectations.

Follow up. After an interview, send a brief note to the people with whom you met thanking them for their time and reaffirming your interest in the company.

Good interviewing is a series of details that work together to demonstrate that you are a thoughtful, bright, courteous person that the company should talk to more.

Distance Recruiting*

Recruiting by video conferencing has become even more common after the terrorist attacks in September 2001 made many people reluctant to fly.

Two kinds of video interviews exist. In the first, the company sends a list of questions, asking the applicant to tape the responses. The second kind is a live interview using videoconferencing equipment.

If you're asked to prepare a videotape,

- Practice your answers.
- Tape the interview as many times as necessary to get a tape that presents you at your best.
- Be specific. Since the employer can't ask follow-up questions, you need to be detailed about how your credentials could help the employer.

If you have an interview by videoconference.

- Tape yourself for practice so you can make any adjustments in pronunciation, voice qualities, posture, and clothing.
- Keep your answers short. Then say, "Would you like more information?" People are more reluctant to interrupt a speaker in another location, and body language is limited.

*Based on Steve Ralston, "Advances in Employment Interviewing Technology," and Jan Harding, Comments, both in Mini-Conference on Emerging Technologies: Focus on the World Wide Web and Its Uses in Business Communication, Columbus, OH, July 28–29, 1995; and "Distance Recruiting," *The Wall Street Journal*, September 25, 2001, B8.

Job interviews are scary, even when you've prepared thoroughly. But when you are prepared, you can harness the adrenaline to work for you, so that you put your best foot forward and get the job you want. See the BAC Web page for links to advice about job interviews.

Interviewing in the 21st Century

Interviews are changing as interviewers respond to interviewees who are prepared to answer the standard questions. Today, many employers expect you to

- Be more aggressive. One employer says he deliberately tells the company receptionist to brush off callers who ask about advertised openings. He interviews only those who keep calling and offer the receptionist reasons why they should be interviewed.

- Follow instructions to the letter. The owner of a delivery company tells candidates to phone at a precise hour. Failing to do so means that the person couldn't be trusted to deliver packages on time.[1]

- Participate in many interviews. Candidates for jobs with Electronic Arts, a maker of computer games, first answer questions online. Then they have up to five phone interviews—some asking candidates to solve problems or program functions. Candidates who get that far undergo "the gauntlet": three days of onsite interviewing.[2]

- Have one or more interviews by phone, computer, or video.

- Take one or more tests, including drug tests, psychological tests, aptitude tests, computer simulations, and essay exams where you're asked to explain what you'd do in a specific situation.

- Be approved by the team you'll be joining. In companies with self-managed work teams, the team has a say in who is hired.

- Provide—at the interview or right after it—a sample of the work you're applying to do. You may be asked to write a memo or a proposal, calculate a budget on a spreadsheet, or make a presentation.

All the phoning required in 21st-century interviews places a special emphasis on phone skills.

If you speak to a secretary, be nice to him or her. Find out the person's name on your first call and use it on subsequent calls. "Thank you for being so patient. Can you tell me when a better time might be to try to get Mr. or Ms. X? I'll try again on [date]." Sometimes, if you call after 5 PM, executives answer their own phones since clerical staff have gone home.

If you get someone's voice mail, leave a concise message—complete with your name and phone number. Even if you've called 10 times, keep your voice pleasant.

If you get voice mail repeatedly, call the main company number to speak with a receptionist. Ask whether the person you're trying to reach is in the building. If he or she is on the road, ask when the person is due in.

Developing an Interview Strategy

Develop an overall strategy based on your answers to these three questions:

1. **What about yourself do you want the interviewer to know?** Pick two to five points that represent your strengths for that particular job. These facts may be achievements, character traits (such as enthusiasm), experiences that qualify you for the job and separate you from other applicants, the fact that you really want to work for this company, and so on. For each strength, think of a specific action or accomplishment to support it. For ex-

Mirage Resorts sifted 75,000 applications to hire 9,600 workers in 24 weeks for its Bellagio resort. Here, a staffer asks an applicant for permission to do a background check. Mirage checked for criminal records and looked at job, school, and credit histories; finalists also took drug tests. Showing applicants courtesy and consideration helped keep the best candidates interested. Because background checks took time, job offers came a few months after interviews. But only 3% of the people Mirage liked dropped out during the process.

ample, be ready to give an example to prove that you're hardworking. Be ready to show how you helped an organization save money or serve customers better.

Then at the interview, listen to every question to see if you could make one of your key points as part of your answer. If the questions don't allow you to make your points, bring them up at the end of the interview.

2. **What disadvantages or weaknesses do you need to minimize?** Expect that you may be asked to explain weaknesses or apparent weaknesses in your record: age, sex, physical disabilities, lack of experience, so-so grades, and gaps in your record.

Plan how to deal with these issues if they arise. See the suggestions later in this chapter under "Kinds of Interviews" and "Traditional Questions."

3. **What do you need to know about the job and the organization to decide whether or not you want to accept this job if it is offered to you?** Plan *in advance* the criteria on which you will base your decision (you can always change the criteria). Use "Deciding Which Offer to Accept" below to plan questions to elicit the information you'll need to rank each offer.

Taking Care of the Details

Wearing inappropriate clothing or being late can cost you a job. Put enough time into planning details so that you can move on to substantive planning.

What to Wear

If you're interviewing for a management or office job, wear a business suit. What kind of suit? If you've got good taste and a good eye for color, follow your instincts. If fashion isn't your strong point, read John Molloy's *Dress for Success*

Using Your Portfolio in an Interview*

Take a portfolio with examples of your work to a job interview. The best items for a portfolio are documents that could be used in a business (not just school papers). Proof everything to make sure it's perfect.

Add labels that give the purpose and audience for each document. If you have evidence of the document's success, include that.

Let the interviewer turn the pages. When he or she stops to look at a document, give more information about your strategy.

Be sure to take the portfolio home with you. In both New York City and Minneapolis, one-third of the portfolios left at the client site are "lost." Ask interviewers to make copies of documents they want to read carefully, rather than leaving the whole portfolio at the site.

*Based on Pat O'Donnell, "What Recruiters Look for in Marcom Writers," *Impact!* 5, no. 3 (Spring 1999), 4.

(men's clothes) and *The New Woman's Dress for Success Book*. Perhaps the best suggestion in Molloy's books is the advice to visit expensive stores, noting details—the exact shade of blue in a suit, the number of buttons on the sleeve, the placement of pockets, the width of lapels—and then go to stores in your price range and buy a suit that has the details found on more expensive clothing.

For onsite interviews, show that you understand the corporate culture. Paul Capelli, former public relations executive at Amazon.com and now vice president of public relations at CNBC, suggests that applicants find out what employees wear "and notch it up one step":

> If the dress is jeans and a T-shirt, wear slacks and an open collar shirt. . . . If it's slacks and an open collar shirt, throw on a sport coat. If it's a sport coat, throw on a suit. At least match it and go one step up, but don't go three steps down.[3]

Choose comfortable shoes. You may do a fair amount of walking during an onsite interview.

Take care of all the details. Check your heels to make sure they aren't run down; make sure your shoes are shined. Have your hair cut or styled conservatively. Jewelry and makeup should be understated. Personal hygiene must be impeccable. Avoid cologne and perfumed aftershave lotions.

What to Bring to the Interview

Bring extra copies of your résumé. If your campus placement office has already given the interviewer a data sheet, present the résumé at the beginning of the interview: "I thought you might like a little more information about me."

Bring something to write on and something to write with. It's OK to bring in a small notepad with the questions you want to ask on it.

Bring copies of your work or a portfolio: an engineering design, a copy of a memo you wrote on a job or in a business writing class, an article you wrote for the campus paper. You don't need to present these unless the interview calls for them, but they can be very effective: "Yes, I have done a media plan. Here's a copy of a plan I put together in my advertising seminar last year. We had a fixed budget and used real figures for cost and rating points, just as I'd do if I joined Foote, Cone & Belding."

Bring the names, addresses, and phone numbers of references if you didn't put them on your résumé. Bring complete details about your work history and education, including dates and street addresses, in case you're asked to fill out an application form.

If you can afford it, buy a briefcase to carry these items. At this point in your life, an inexpensive vinyl briefcase is acceptable.

Note-Taking

During or immediately after the interview, write down

- The name of the interviewer (or all the people you talked to, if it's a group interview or an onsite visit).
- What the interviewer seemed to like best about you.
- Any negative points or weaknesses that came up that you need to counter in your follow-up letter or phone calls.
- Answers to your questions about the company.
- When you'll hear from the company.

The easiest way to get the interviewer's name is to ask for his or her card. You may be able to make all the notes you need on the back of the card.

Some interviewers say that they respond negatively to applicants who take notes during the interview. However, if you have several interviews back-to-back or if you know your memory is terrible, do take brief notes during the interview. That's better than forgetting which company said you'd be on the road every other week and which interviewer asked that *you* get in touch with him or her.

Practicing for the Interview

Rehearse everything you can: Put on the clothes you'll wear and practice entering a room, shaking hands, sitting down, and answering questions. Ask a friend to interview you. Saying answers out loud is surprisingly harder than saying them in your head.

Some campuses have videotaping facilities so that you can watch your own sample interview. Videotaping is more valuable if you can do it at least twice, so you can modify behavior the second time and check the tape to see whether the modification works.

During the Interview

Your interviewing skills will improve with practice. If possible, schedule a few interviews with other companies before your interview with the company that is your first choice. However, even if you're just interviewing for practice, you must still do all the research on that company. If interviewers sense that you aren't interested, they won't take you seriously and you won't learn much from the process.

How to Act

Should you be yourself? There's no point in assuming a radically different persona. If you do, you run the risk of getting into a job that you'll hate (though the persona you assumed might have loved it). Furthermore, as interviewers point out, you have to be a pretty good actor to come across convincingly if you try to be someone other than yourself. Yet keep in mind that all of us have several selves: we can be lazy, insensitive, bored, slow-witted, and tongue-tied, but we can also be energetic, perceptive, interested, intelligent, and articulate. Be your best self at the interview.

Interviews can make you feel vulnerable and defensive; to counter this, review your accomplishments—the things you're especially proud of having done. You'll make a better impression if you have a firm sense of your own self-worth.

Every interviewer repeats the advice that your mother probably gave you: sit up straight, don't mumble, look at people when you talk. It's good advice for interviews. Be aware that many people respond negatively to smoking.

Office visits that involve meals and semisocial occasions call for sensible choices. When you order, choose something that's easy and unmessy to eat. Watch your table manners. Eat a light lunch, with no alcohol, so that you'll be alert during the afternoon. At dinner or an evening party, decline alcohol if you don't drink. If you do drink, accept just one drink—you're still being evaluated, and you can't afford to have your guard down. Be aware that some people respond negatively to applicants who drink hard liquor.

Parts of the Interview

Every interview has an opening, a body, and a close.

In the **opening** (two to five minutes), good interviewers will try to set you at ease. Some interviewers will open with easy questions about your major or interests. Others open by telling you about the job or the company. If this happens, listen so you can answer questions later to show that you can do the job or contribute to the company that's being described.

The Stealth Job Interview*

I flew to Bangor, ME, for an interview for the director of photography position with a well-known studio. . . . I was told that Mr. Olive, the company president, had been detained. . . .

A few minutes later, a well-dressed family of five walked in. Surprised, the receptionist said, "Why Mr. Smith, we had you down for an appointment to be photographed next Saturday. We don't have a photographer on duty today.". . . The embarrassed receptionist turned to me: "Mr. Williams, would you be able to help us out and photograph these people?"

I agreed. . . . Everything went well, although about three-fourths of the way through I noticed someone lurking in a small closet nearby. When I finished, I bid the Smiths goodbye and turned on the room lights. A distinguished-looking little man stepped out of the closet and said, "I like the way you handle yourself, kid. You've got the job!"

It was Mr. Olive. Later I learned that the "Smith family" was really Mr. Olive's daughter, son-in-law, and grandchildren. The entire session had been an elaborate test.

*Quoted from Fred Williams, "Get the Picture?" *Selling Power*, March 2001, 20.

Stress Interviews for Salespeople at Dataflex*

Rick Rose, CEO of Dataflex, is "deliberately adversarial" at a first interview. After about five minutes, he tells interviewees they aren't very good—even if they are. He wants applicants who believe in themselves and will try to persuade him that he's wrong.

He challenges canned answers. If an applicant says he or she wants to be in sales "to help people," Rose responds, "You want to help people? Go be a nurse."

Rick tells candidates to call him after the interview. Those who do call back get second interviews with all the current salespeople.

And when all of that goes positively, the interviewee is invited to participate in a week's worth of sales meetings, which start at 7 AM four times a week. The people who do participate—not merely attend—are the people who get hired.

*Based on Richard C. Rose and Echo Montgomery Garrett, "Guerrilla Interviewing," *Inc.*, December 1992, 145–47.

The **body** of the interview (10 to 25 minutes) is an all-too-brief time for you to highlight your qualifications and find out what you need to know to decide if you want to accept a plant trip. Expect questions that give you an opportunity to showcase your strong points and questions that probe any weaknesses evident from your résumé. (You were neither in school nor working last fall. What were you doing?) Normally the interviewer will also try to sell you on the company and give you an opportunity to raise questions.

You need to be aware of time so that you can make sure to get in your key points and questions: "We haven't covered it yet, but I want you to know that I . . ." "I'm aware that it's almost 10:30. I do have some more questions that I'd like to ask about the company."

In the **close** of the interview (two to five minutes), the interviewer will usually tell you what happens next: "We'll be bringing our top candidates to the office in February. You should hear from us in three weeks." One interviewer reports that he gives applicants his card and tells them to call him. "It's a test to see if they are committed, how long it takes for them to call, and whether they even call at all."[4]

Close with an assertive statement. Depending on the circumstances, you could say: "I've certainly enjoyed learning more about General Electric." "I hope I get a chance to visit your Phoenix office. I'd really like to see the new computer system you talked about." "This job seems to be a good match between what you're looking for and what I'd like to do."

Stress Interviews

A **stress interview** deliberately puts the applicant under stress. If the stress is physical (for example, you're given a chair where the light is in your eyes), be assertive: move to another chair or tell the interviewer that the behavior bothers you.

Usually the stress is psychological. A group of interviewers fire rapid questions. A single interviewer probes every weak spot in your record and asks questions that elicit negatives. If you get questions that put you on the defensive, **rephrase** them in less inflammatory terms, if necessary, and then **treat them as requests for information.**

Q: Why did you major in physical education? That sounds like a pretty Mickey Mouse major.

A: You're asking whether I have the academic preparation for this job. I started out in physical education because I've always loved sports. I learned that I couldn't graduate in four years if I officially switched my major to business administration because the requirements were different in the two programs. But I do have 21 hours in business administration and 9 hours in accounting. And my sports experience gives me practical training in teamwork, motivating people, and management.

Respond assertively. The candidates who survive are those who stand up for themselves and who explain why indeed they *are* worth hiring.

Silence can also create stress. One woman walked into her scheduled interview to find a male interviewer with his feet up on the desk. He said, "It's been a long day. I'm tired and I want to go home. You have five minutes to sell yourself." Since she had planned the points she wanted to be sure interviewers knew, she was able to do this. "Your recruiting brochure said that you're looking for someone with a major in accounting and a minor in finance. As you may remember from my résumé, I'm majoring in accountancy and have had 12 hours in finance. I've also served as treasurer of a local campaign committee and have worked as a volunteer tax preparer through the Accounting Club." When she finished, the interviewer told her it was a test: "I wanted to see how you'd handle it."

Increasingly common is the variety of stress interview that asks you to do—on the spot—the kind of thing the job would require. An interviewer for a sales job handed applicants a ball-point pen and said, "Sell me this pen." (It's OK to ask who the target market is and whether this is a repeat or a new customer.) AT&T asks some applicants to deliver presentations or lead meetings. Massachusetts Mutual Life asked the finalists for a vice presidency to process memos and reports in a two-hour in-basket exercise and participate in several role plays.[5]

Sexist interviews are a special variety of stress interviews. Although questions about marriage and children are illegal, they occasionally are asked. An interview can also be categorized as sexist if the interviewer implies that an applicant can't do the job because she's female: "You're a woman and you're short. You'd be working with tall men in this job. How would you handle them?"

Although you're within your rights to say "I don't think that question is legal," a low-key response is more likely to lead to a job offer. Respond as you would to a stress question: **Rephrase the question and treat it as a legitimate request for information.**

Q: Aren't you just looking for a husband?

A: You may be asking whether I'll stay with you long enough to justify the expense of training me as a staff accountant. Well, I'm not promising to work for you the rest of my life, just as you're not promising to employ me for the rest of my life. How long I stay will depend upon whether my assignments continue to be interesting and challenging and whether I can advance.

Sometimes interviewers who do not ask sexist questions still have reservations about offering jobs to women. You may want to set at rest the interviewer's fears by bringing up the subject yourself: "You may have noticed that I'm married. My husband is a dentist and could relocate if the company wanted to transfer me."

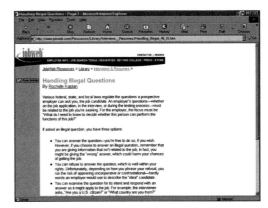

InSite

www.jobweb.com/Resources/Library/
Interviews_Resumes/
Handling_Illegal_46_02.htm

If you're asked an illegal interview question, Rochelle Kaplan advises that you figure out what job-related concern it may mask, and allay that concern.

Answering Traditional Interview Questions

First interviews seek to screen out less qualified candidates rather than to find someone to hire. Negative information will hurt you less if it comes out in the middle of the interview and is preceded and followed by positive information. If you blow a question near the end of the interview, don't leave until you've said something positive—perhaps restating one of the points you want the interviewer to know about you.

As Figure 19.1 shows, successful applicants use different communication behaviors than do unsuccessful applicants. Successful applicants are more likely to use the company name during the interview, support their claims with specific details, and ask specific questions about the company and the industry. In addition to practicing the content of questions, try to incorporate these tactics.

The following questions frequently come up at interviews. Do some unpressured thinking before the interview so that you'll be able to come up with answers that are responsive, honest, and paint a good picture of you. Choose answers that fit your qualifications and your interview strategy.

@   See the BAC Web page for additional questions asked at traditional interviews.

1.   Tell me about yourself.
     Don't launch into an autobiography. Instead, state the things about yourself that you want the interviewer to know. Give specifics to prove each of your strengths.

FIGURE 19.1   The Communication Behaviors of Successful Interviewees

Behavior	Unsuccessful interviewees	Successful interviewees
Statements about the position	Had only vague ideas of what they wanted to do; changed "ideal job" up to six times during the interview.	Specific and consistent about the position they wanted; were able to tell why they wanted the position.
Use of company name	Rarely used the company name.	Referred to the company by name four times as often as unsuccessful interviewees.
Knowledge about company and position	Made it clear that they were using the interview to learn about the company and what it offered.	Made it clear that they had researched the company; referred to specific brochures, journals, or people who had given them information.
Level of interest, enthusiasm	Responded neutrally to interviewer's statements: "OK," "I see." Indicated reservations about company or location.	Expressed approval of information provided by the interviewer nonverbally and verbally; "That's great!" Explicitly indicated desire to work for this particular company.
Nonverbal behavior	Made little eye contact; smiled infrequently.	Made eye contact often; smiled.
Picking up on interviewer's cues	Gave vague or negative answers even when a positive answer was clearly desired ("How are your math skills?").	Answered positively and confidently—and backed up the claim with a specific example of "problem solving" or "toughness."
Response to topic shift by interviewer	Resisted topic shift.	Accepted topic shift.
Use of industry terms and technical jargon	Used almost no technical jargon.	Used technical jargon: "point of purchase display," "NCR charge," "two-column approach," "direct mail."
Use of specifics in answers	Gave short answers—10 words or less, sometimes only one word; did not elaborate. Gave general responses: "fairly well."	Supported claims with specific personal experiences, comparisons, statistics, statements of teachers and employers.
Questions asked by interviewee	Asked a small number of general questions.	Asked specific questions based on knowledge of the industry and the company. Personalized questions: "What would my duties be?"
Control of time and topics	Interviewee talked 37% of the interview time, initiated 36% of the comments.	Interviewee talked 55% of the total time, initiated subjects 56% of the time.

Source: Based on research reported by Lois J. Einhorn, "An Inner View of the Job Interview: An Investigation of Successful Communicative Behaviors," *Communication Education* 30 (July 1981), 217–28; and Robert W. Elder and Michael M. Harris, eds., *The Employment Interview Handbook* (Thousand Oaks, CA: Sage, 1999), 300, 303, 327–28.

2.   What makes you think you're qualified to work for this company? Or, I'm interviewing 120 people for two jobs. Why should I hire you?

This question may feel like an attack. Use it as an opportunity to state your strong points: your qualifications for the job, the things that separate you from other applicants.

3. What two or three accomplishments have given you the greatest satisfaction?

   Pick accomplishments that you're proud of, that create the image you want to project, and that enable you to share one of the things you want the interviewer to know about you. Focus not just on the end result, but on the problem-solving and thinking skills that made the achievement possible.

4. Why do you want to work for us? What is your ideal job?

   Even if you're interviewing just for practice, make sure you have a good answer—preferably two or three reasons you'd like to work for that company. If you don't seem to be taking the interview seriously, the interviewer won't take you seriously, and you won't even get good practice.

   If your ideal job is very different from the ones the company has available, the interviewer may simply say there isn't a good match and end the interview. If you're interested in this company, do some research so that what you ask for is in the general ballpark of the kind of work the company offers.

5. What college subjects did you like best and least? Why?

   This question may be an icebreaker; it may be designed to discover the kind of applicant they're looking for. If your favorite class was something outside your major, prepare an answer that shows that you have qualities that can help you in the job you're applying for: "My favorite class was a seminar in the American novel. We got a chance to think on our own, rather than just regurgitate facts; we made presentations to the class every week. I found I really like sharing my ideas with other people and presenting reasons for my conclusions about something."

6. What is your class rank? Your grade point? Why are your grades so low?

   If your grades aren't great, be ready with a nondefensive explanation. If possible, show that the cause of low grades now has been solved or isn't relevant to the job you're applying for: "My father almost died last year, and my schoolwork really suffered." "When I started, I didn't have any firm goals. Once I discovered the field that was right for me, my grades have all been B's or better." "I'm not good at multiple-choice tests. But you need someone who can work with people, not someone who can take tests."

7. What have you read recently? What movies have you seen recently?

   These questions may be icebreakers; they may be designed to probe your intellectual depth. The term you're interviewing, read at least one book or magazine (regularly) and see at least one movie that you could discuss at an interview.

8. Show me some samples of your writing.

   Many jobs require the ability to write well. Employers no longer take mastery of basic English for granted, even if the applicant has a degree from a prestigious university.

   The year you're interviewing, go through your old papers and select the best ones, retyping them if necessary, so that you'll have samples if you're asked for them. If you don't have samples at the interview, mail them to the interviewer immediately after the interview.

9. Where do you see yourself in five years?

   Employers ask this question to find out if you are a self-starter or if you passively respond to what happens. You may want to have several scenarios for five years from now to use in different kinds of interviews. Or

Rescuing the Interview*

A smart question made Deborah Brown realize she had flubbed an interview for a diversity consultant's spot at Organizational Resources Counselors, a New York human-resources consulting firm. She felt her interview with two ORC officials "was going really well." So, near the end, she asked whether they had any objections to her candidacy.

"They said, 'This is a job that requires getting top-level commitment to launch a diversity initiative. You seem very nice and low-key.' " . . .

Translation: She wasn't aggressive enough to sway captains of industry. . . .

Ms. Brown tried to recover with a rapidly dispatched missive that strongly refuted the officials' misperception. The letter detailed how she had spearheaded a high-level initiative at her then-employer, New York's Port Authority.

Equally importantly, Ms. Brown dressed and acted differently during her next interview with the same ORC staffers. . . .

She substituted a strikingly bright maroon suit for the conservative blue one worn the first time. She sat forward, projected her voice, spoke more animatedly and used additional gestures to dramatize her numerous ideas.

She got the coveted job.

*Quoted from Joann S. Lublin, "You Blew the Interview, but You Can Correct Some of the Blunders," *The Wall Street Journal*, December 5, 2000, B1.

Tattoos and Interviews*

College students considering exactly where to place a tattoo or piercing would do well to heed the results of the 1999 Business Attire Survey. . . . When asked their attitudes toward a candidate's appearance during interviews, 90 campus recruiters preferred men and women without visible body art—including "multiple earrings.". . . As might be expected, the recruiters are being a little conservative—and perhaps a little unimaginative. Wouldn't they be intrigued if a candidate walked in sporting a tattoo of a Web site?

*Quoted from Robert P. Libbon, "Datadog," *American Demographics*, September 2000, 26.

you may want to say, "Well, my goals may change as opportunities arise. But right now, I want to. . . ."

10.   What are your interests outside work? What campus or community activities have you been involved in?

While it's desirable to be well-rounded, naming 10 interests is a mistake: the interviewer may wonder when you'll have time to work.

If you mention your fiancé, spouse, or children in response to this question ("Well, my fiancé and I like to go sailing"), it is perfectly legal for the interviewer to ask follow-up questions ("What would you do if your spouse got a job offer in another town?"), even though the same question would be illegal if the interviewer brought up the subject first.

11.   What have you done to learn about this company?

An employer may ask this to see what you already know about the company (if you've read the recruiting literature, the interviewer doesn't need to repeat it). This question may also be used to see how active a role you're taking in the job search process and how interested you are in this job.

12.   What adjectives would you use to describe yourself?

Use only positive ones. Be ready to illustrate each with a specific example of something you've done.

13.   What is your greatest strength?

Employers ask this question to give you a chance to sell yourself and to learn something about your values. Pick a strength related to work, school, or activities: "I'm good at working with people." "I really can sell things." "I'm good at solving problems." "I learn quickly." "I'm reliable. When I say I'll do something, I do it." Be ready to illustrate each with a specific example of something you've done.

14.   What is your greatest weakness?

Use a work-related negative, even if something in your personal life really is your greatest weakness. Interviewers won't let you get away with a "weakness" like being a workaholic or just not having any experience yet. Instead, use one of the following three strategies:

Amy's Ice Cream stores sell entertainment. To find creative, zany employees, Amy Miller gives applicants a white paper bag and a week to do something with it. People who produce something unusual are hired.

a. Discuss a weakness that is not related to the job you're being considered for and will not be needed even when you're promoted. (Even if you won't work with people or give speeches in your first job, you'll need those skills later in your career, so don't use them for this question.) End your answer with a positive that *is* related to the job:

> [For a creative job in advertising:] I don't like accounting. I know it's important, but I don't like it. I even hire someone to do my taxes. I'm much more interested in being creative and working with people, which is why I find this position interesting.

> [For a job in administration:] I don't like selling products. I hated selling cookies when I was a Girl Scout. I'd much rather work with ideas—and I really like selling the ideas that I believe in.

> [For a job in architecture:] I hate fund-raising. It always seemed to me if people wanted to give, they would anyway. I'd much rather have something to offer people which will help them solve their own problems and meet their own needs.

b. Discuss a weakness that you are working to improve:

> In the past, I wasn't a good writer. But last term I took a course in business writing that taught me how to organize my ideas and how to revise. I may never win a Pulitzer Prize, but now I'm a lot more confident that I can write effective reports and memos.

c. Discuss a work-related weakness:

> I procrastinate. Fortunately, I work well under pressure, but a couple of times I've really put myself in a bind.

15. Why are you looking for another job?

Stress what you're looking for in a new job, not why you want to get away from your old one.

If you were fired, say so. There are three acceptable ways to explain why you were fired:

a. It wasn't a good match. Add what you now know you need in a job, and ask what the employer can offer in this area.

b. You and your supervisor had a personality *conflict*. Make sure you show that this was an isolated incident, and that you normally get along well with people.

c. You made mistakes, but you've learned from them and are now ready to work well. Be ready to offer a specific anecdote proving that you have indeed changed.

16. What questions do you have?

This question gives you a chance to cover things the interviewer hasn't brought up; it also gives the interviewer a sense of your priorities and values. Don't focus on salary or fringe benefits. Better questions are

- What would I be doing on a day-to-day basis?
- What kind of training program do you have? If, as I'm rotating among departments, I find that I prefer one area, can I specialize in it when the training program is over?

Is There Life after Work?*

Questions about work-life balance—which in the past were saved for the final round of interviews or never asked at all—are surfacing in job candidates' first-round talks with employers.

A sampling of questions asked by undergraduate recruits . . . :

1. Do people who work for you have a life off the job?
2. Do your employees get to see their families?
3. What support can you offer my significant other?
4. Do you offer flextime?
5. If my job requires too much travel, can I change without doing serious damage to my career? . . .

[S]everal [recruiters] say many of the candidates who asked these questions in the past ended up being top performers in their jobs. "The thing I found is that these folks can set their priorities within time limits," says Faye Ambrefe Omasta, who recruits management trainees for GTE. Gordon Welton, placement manager for Principal Financial Group, adds, . . . "They know what's important to them. They're passionate not just about their work, but about themselves."

*Quoted from Sue Shellenbarger, "New Job Hunters Ask Recruiters, 'Is There Life After Work?' " *The Wall Street Journal*, January 29, 1996, B1.

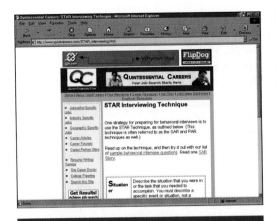

www.quintcareers.com/
STAR_interviewing.html

The STAR technique can help you answer behavioral
interview questions. The site also offers examples of
excellent answers to these and to traditional interview
questions.

- How do you evaluate employees? How often do you review them? Where would you expect a new trainee (banker, staff accountant) to be three years from now?
- What happened to the last person who had this job?
- How are interest rates (a new product from competitors, imports, demographic trends, government regulations, etc.) affecting your company?
- How would you describe the company's culture?
- This sounds like a great job. What are the drawbacks?

You won't be able to anticipate every question you may get. (One interviewer asked students, "What vegetable would you like to be?" Another asked, "If you were a cookie, what kind of cookie would you be?"[6]) Check with other people at your college or university who have interviewed recently to find out what questions are being asked in your field.

Behavioral and Situational Interviews

Many companies, dissatisfied with hires based on responses to traditional questions, are now using behavioral or situational interviews. **Behavioral interviews** ask the applicant to describe actual behaviors, rather than plans or general principles. Thus instead of asking "How would you motivate people?" the interviewer might ask, "Tell me what happened the last time you wanted to get other people to do something." Follow-up questions might include, "What exactly did you do to handle the situation? How did you feel about the results? How did the other people feel? How did your superior feel about the results?"

Additional behavioral questions may ask you to describe a situation in which you

1. Created an opportunity for yourself in a job or volunteer position.
2. Used writing to achieve your goal.
3. Went beyond the call of duty to get a job done.
4. Communicated successfully with someone you disliked.
5. Had to make a decision quickly.
6. Took a project from start to finish.
7. Used good judgment and logic in solving a problem.
8. Worked under a tight deadline.
9. Worked with a tough boss.
10. Worked with someone who wasn't doing his or her share of the work.

In your answer, describe the situation, tell what you did, and what happened. Think about the implications of what you did and be ready to talk about whether you'd do the same thing next time or if the situation were slightly different. For example, if you did the extra work yourself when a team member didn't do his or her share, does that fact suggest that you prefer to work alone? If the organization you're interviewing with values teams, you may want to go on to show why doing the extra work was appropriate in that situation but that you can respond differently in other situations.

Situational interviews put you in a situation that allows the interviewer to see whether you have the qualities the company is seeking. For example, Southwest Airlines found that 95% of the complaints it received were provoked by only 5% of its personnel. When managers explored further, they found that these 5% of employees were self-centered. To weed out self-centered applicants, Southwest now puts several candidates into a room and asks each to give a five-minute speech on "Why I Want to Work with Southwest Airlines." But the interviewers watch the *audience* to hire the people who are pulling for other speakers to do well, as opposed to those who are only thinking about their own performance.[7]

Situational interviews may also be conducted using traditional questions but evaluating behaviors other than the answers. Greyhound hired applicants for its customer-assistance center who made eye contact with the interviewer and smiled at least five times during a 15-minute interview.[8]

Figure 19.2 shows the poor responses to behavioral interview questions that cost candidates jobs at W. L. Gore & Associates. Figure 19.3 shows good responses to questions asked in Motley Fool interviews.

After the Interview

What you do after the interview can determine whether you get the job. One woman wanted to switch from banking, where she was working in corporate relations, to advertising. The ad agency interviewer expressed doubts about her qualifications. Immediately after leaving the agency, she tracked down a particular book the interviewer had mentioned he was looking for but had been unable to find. She presented it to him—and was hired.[9]

Xerox expects applicants for sales and repair positions to follow up within 10 days. If they don't, the company assumes that they wouldn't follow up with clients.[10]

FIGURE 19.2 Poor Responses to Behavioral Interview Questions

GORE-TEXT

Carolyn Murray (cmurray@wlgore.com), 37, a savvy recruiter at W.L. Gore & Associates, developers of Gore-Tex, pays little attention to a candidate's carefully scripted responses to her admittedly softball questions. Instead, she listens for a throwaway line that reveals the reality behind an otherwise benign reply. Herewith, Murray delivers a post-game analysis of how three job candidates whiffed during their interviews.

the PITCH	the SWING	the MISS
"Give me an example of a time when you had a conflict with a team member."	" 'Our leader asked me to handle all of the FedExing for our team. I did it, but I thought that FedExing was a waste of my time.' "	"At Gore, we work from a team concept. Her answer shows that she won't exactly jump when one of her teammates needs help."
"Tell me how you solved a problem that was impeding your project."	" 'One of the engineers on my team wasn't pulling his weight, and we were closing in on a deadline. So I took on some of his work. ' "	"The candidate may have resolved the issue for this particular deadline, but he did nothing to prevent the problem from happening again."
"What's the one thing that you would change about your current position?"	" 'My job as a salesman has become mundane. Now I want the responsibility of managing people.' "	"He's not maximizing his current position. Selling is never mundane if you go about it in the right way."

Source: Fast Company, January 1999, 156.

FIGURE 19.3   Good Responses to Interview Questions

FOOL'S TOOL

As CEO of Motley Fool, a wildly popular investment Web site, **Erik Rydholm** (erikr@fool.com), 31, has little time for fooling around with undesirable job candidates. To streamline the interview process, he's come up with three questions that quickly separate the fools from the Fools.

FOOLISH question	WISE answer	FOOL'S take-away
" 'What does Foolishness mean to you?' That's a great first question, one that separates those who get it from those who are clueless."	"One guy emphasized that we give people the power to gather investing information from many sources by visiting a single Web site."	"He understood that we're trying to revolutionize the way people lead their financial lives—by putting a lot of power at their disposal."
" 'Should the Motley Fool consider putting its name on mutual funds and selling a line of financial services?' "	"He encouraged us to consider whether branding a fund would undercut our integrity and whether it even related to our core competencies."	"He understood that there's integrity to the Motley Fool brand, and he recognized the risk of undercutting that integrity."
" 'How does the Motley Fool succeed?' That gets to the heart of how we can continue to capitalize on our current market share."	"One candidate argued that the Motley Fool is not a source—it's a service: We guide people through their investment decisions."	"He understood the difference between a 'source' and a 'service'—which made me confident that he could think distinctively for us."

Source: Fast Company, January 1999, 157.

If the employer sends you an e-mail query, answer it promptly. You're being judged not only on what you say but on how quickly you respond.

Follow-Up Phone Calls and Letters

After a first interview, make follow-up phone calls to reinforce positives from the first interview, to overcome any negatives, and to get information you can use to persuade the interviewer to hire you. Career coach Kate Wendleton suggests asking the following questions:

- "Is there more information I can give you?"
- "I've been giving a lot of thought to your project and have some new ideas. Can we meet to go over them?"
- "Where do I stand? How does my work compare with the work others presented?"[11]

A letter after an onsite visit is essential to thank your hosts for their hospitality as well as to send in receipts for your expenses. The letter should

- Remind the interviewer of what he or she liked in you.
- Counter any negative impressions that may have come up at the interview.
- Use the jargon of the company and refer to specific things you learned during your interview or saw during your visit.
- Be enthusiastic.
- Refer to the next move, whether you'll wait to hear from the employer or whether you want to call to learn about the status of your application.

Be sure the letter is well written and error-free. One employer reports,

> I often interviewed people whom I liked, . . . but their follow-up letters were filled with misspelled words and names and other inaccuracies. They blew their chance with the follow-up letter.[12]

Figure 19.4 is an example of a follow-up letter after an office visit.

Negotiating for Salary and Benefits

The best time to negotiate for salary and benefits is after you have the job offer. Try to delay discussing salary early in the interview process, when you're still competing against other applicants.

Prepare for salary negotiations by finding out what the going rate is for the kind of work you hope to do. Cultivate friends who are now in the workforce to find out what they're making. Ask the campus placement office for figures on what last year's graduates got. Check trade journals, such as, *Advertising Age, Direct Marketing and Telemarketing Guide,* or the *Robert Half and Accountemps Salary Guide.* Check the Web. See the BAC Web site for links that provide salary information.

This research is crucial. As recently as 2000, male students expected salaries in their first jobs that were 14% higher than the salaries female students expected. More than twice as many men as women expected to receive signing bonuses. Men were 16% more likely to expect annual bonuses, and the bonuses men expected were 16% higher than the bonuses women expected.[13] Knowing what a job is worth will give you the confidence to negotiate more effectively.

If the interviewer asks you about your salary requirements before a job offer has been made, try this response: "I'm sure your firm can pay me what I'm worth." Then either ask about pay ranges or go back to your qualifications for the job. If the interviewer demands a response, give a range using odd increments: "I'd expect to make between $32,300 and $36,900." As you say this, *watch the interviewer.* If he or she has that blank look we use to hide dismay, you may have asked for much more than the company was planning to offer. Quickly continue, ". . . depending, of course, on fringe benefits and how quickly I could be promoted. However, salary isn't the most important criterion for me in choosing a job, and I won't necessarily accept the highest offer I get. I'm interested in going somewhere where I can get good experience and use my talents to make a real contribution."

The best way to get more money is to convince the employer that you're worth it. During the interview process, show what you can do that the competition can't. Work to redefine the position in the employer's eyes from a low-level, anybody-could-do-it job to a complex combination of duties that only someone with your particular mix of talents could do.

After you have the offer, you can begin negotiating salary and benefits. You're in the strongest position when (1) you've done your homework and know what the usual salary and benefits are and (2) you can walk away from this offer if it doesn't meet your needs. Again, avoid naming a specific salary. Don't say you can't accept less. Instead, Kate Wendleton suggests, say you "would find it difficult to accept the offer" under the terms first offered.[14]

Remember that you're negotiating a package, not just a starting salary. A company that truly can't pay any more money now might be able to review you for promotion sooner than usual, or pay your moving costs, or give you a better job title. Some companies offer fringe benefits that may compensate for lower taxable income: use of a company car, reimbursements for education, child care or elder care subsidies, or help in finding a job for your spouse or

Interview Goofs*

We recently asked our site visitors for their responses to the following question: What's the funniest or most bizarre thing you've heard of a job candidate doing or saying in an interview? Here are some of the responses:

- "Showing up for an interview in a wrinkled shirt—for a position in a dry cleaning company."

- "While working for a staffing agency I interviewed a woman who wanted to work 'in computers.' When I asked what software packages she was familiar with and got a blank stare, I said, 'Such as WordPerfect, Lotus 1-2-3, etc.' Her response? 'Oh, yeah I know Lotus 1, Lotus 2 *and* Lotus 3!'"

- "When I told a candidate that our company had an attendance policy, he asked me if jail time counted as an acceptable absence from work."

- "A friend of mine was interviewing potential candidates for an administrative assistant job. One candidate came rushing in apologizing for being late . . . and said she hadn't had her lunch yet. She then pulled out a fast-food fish sandwich and consumed it during her (very short!) interview."

*Quoted from Robert Half International, *Resumania,* (www.resumania.com/respons1.shtml), April 5, 2001. Visited site December 26, 2001.

FIGURE 19.4   Follow-Up Letter after an Office Visit

405 West College, Apt. 201   *Single-space your address, date*
Thibodaux, LA 70301   *when you don't use letterhead.*
April 2, 2003

Mr. Robert Land, Account Manager
Sive Associates
378 Norman Boulevard
Cincinnati, OH 48528

Dear Mr. Land:

After visiting Sive Associates last week, I'm even more sure that writing direct mail is the career for me.

Refers to things she saw and learned during the interview.

I've always been able to brainstorm ideas, but sometimes, when I had to focus on one idea for a class project, I wasn't sure which idea was best. It was fascinating to see how you make direct mail scientific as well as creative by testing each new creative package against the control. I can understand how pleased Linda Hayes was when she learned that her new package for *Smithsonian* beat the control.

Reminds interviewer of her strong points.

Seeing Kelly, Luke, and Gene collaborating on the Sesame Street package gave me some sense of the tight deadlines you're under. As you know, I've learned to meet deadlines, not only for my class assignments, but also in working on Nicholls' newspaper. The award I won for my feature on the primary election suggests that my quality holds up even when the deadline is tight!

Thank you for your hospitality while I was in Cincinnati. You and your wife made my stay very pleasant. I especially appreciate the time the two of you took to help me find information about apartments that are accessible to wheelchairs. Cincinnati seems like a very livable city.

Be positive, not pushy. She doesn't assume she has the job.

I'm excited about a career in direct mail and about the (possibility) of joining Sive Associates. I look forward to hearing from you soon!

Refers to what will happen next.

Sincerely,

Gina Focasio

Gina Focasio
(504) 555-2948

Writer's phone number.

Puts request for reimbursement in P.S. to de-emphasize it, focuses on the job, not the cost of the trip.

P.S. My expenses totaled $454. Enclosed are receipts for my plane fare from New Orleans to Cincinnati ($367), the taxi to the airport in Cincinnati ($30), and the bus from Thibodaux to New Orleans ($57).

Encl.: Receipts for Expenses

partner. And think about your career, not just the initial salary. Sometimes a low-paying job at a company that will provide superb experience will do more for your career (and your long-term earning prospects) than a high salary now with no room to grow.

Work toward a win–win solution. You want the employer to be happy that you're coming on board and to feel that you've behaved maturely and professionally.

Deciding Which Offer to Accept

The problem with choosing among job offers is that you're comparing apples and oranges. The job with the most interesting work pays peanuts. The job that pays best is in a city where you really don't want to live. It's your life. The secret of professional happiness is taking a job where the positives are things you want and the negatives are things that don't matter much to you.

To choose among job offers, you need to know what is truly important to *you*. Start by answering questions like the following:

- Are you willing to take work home? To travel? How important is money to you? Prestige? Time to spend with family and friends?

- Would you rather have firm deadlines or a flexible schedule? Do you prefer working alone or with other people? Do you prefer specific instructions and standards for evaluation or freedom and uncertainty? How comfortable are you with pressure? How much challenge do you want?

- Where do you want to live? What features in terms of weather, geography, cultural and social life do you see as ideal?

- Is it important to you that your work achieve certain purposes or values, or do you see work as "just a way to make a living"? Are the organization's culture and ethical standards ones you find comfortable?

- Can you picture yourself doing this job 40 hours a week?

- Will you be able to do work you can point to with pride?

After you've done this brainstorming, make a list of *everything you'd like in your ideal job.* Then, to see which points are really important to you, do a forced choice. In a **forced choice,** you compare each item against every other one. Number the items in the order in which they happened to occur to you. Then, using the table of fractions in Figure 19.5, rank each pair. For "½" compare item 1 and item 2. If you could only have one of the two, which would you prefer? Circle that number. For "⅓," compare item 1 with item 3. Again, circle the item that's more important. Repeat until you've made a choice between each of the possible pairs. Then count the number of times you've chosen each item. The things you've chosen most often are the ones that matter: they're the ones you should look for in your job.

Figure 19.6 is the list that one man produced. The items are numbered in the order in which they occurred to him. To find out what's truly important and what's nice but not necessary, Jim can do a forced choice. If he had to choose between a high income and having time for his family, which would he prefer? Counting up the number of times he chooses each factor will tell him what he really wants.

Some employers offer jobs at the end of the office visit. In other cases, you may wait for weeks or even months to hear. Employers almost always offer jobs orally. You must say something in response immediately, so it's good to plan some strategies in advance.

If your first offer is not from your first choice, express your pleasure at being offered the job, but do not accept it on the phone. "That's great! I assume I

Finding Rewarding Work*

In the last nine years, a group of 22 business school graduates have averaged 4.3 jobs per person, with a few in their seventh job. Eight have had "involuntary departures." Their careers would have been more efficient and less painful if they had known more about themselves and about the world they were entering.

They didn't understand the changing nature of work.

They didn't expect business cycles and politics to affect them.

They didn't know people were irrational, driven by fear, greed, and jealously.

They hadn't thought about the nonfinancial sources of satisfaction they needed.

They hadn't realized that they had moral values.

The lesson their experience teaches is that the more you know about yourself, about the economy, and about the company you're considering joining, the more likely it is that your job will give you a sense of reward that goes beyond a paycheck.

*Based on Jan Harding, "Closing the Circle: Collaboration with Recent Graduates," Mini-Conference on Accounting and Business Communication, Columbus, OH, July 26–27, 1996.

FIGURE 19.5 Forced Choice Chart

When you're not sure which job to accept, use this table of fractions. See instructions on page 561.

1/2	1/3	1/4	1/5	1/6	1/7	1/8	1/9	1/10	1/11	1/12	1/13	1/14	1/15	1/16	1/17	1/18	1/19	1/20
2/3	2/4	2/5	2/6	2/7	2/8	2/9	2/10	2/11	2/12	2/13	2/14	2/15	2/16	2/17	2/18	2/19	2/20	
3/4	3/5	3/6	3/7	3/8	3/9	3/10	3/11	3/12	3/13	3/14	3/15	3/16	3/17	3/18	3/19	3/20		
4/5	4/6	4/7	4/8	4/9	4/10	4/11	4/12	4/13	4/14	4/15	4/16	4/17	4/18	4/19	4/20			
5/6	5/7	5/8	5/9	5/10	5/11	5/12	5/13	5/14	5/15	5/16	5/17	5/18	5/19	5/20				
6/7	6/8	6/9	6/10	6/11	6/12	6/13	6/14	6/15	6/16	6/17	6/18	6/19	6/20					
7/8	7/9	7/10	7/11	7/12	7/13	7/14	7/15	7/16	7/17	7/18	7/19	7/20						
8/9	8/10	8/11	8/12	8/13	8/14	8/15	8/16	8/17	8/18	8/19	8/20							
9/10	9/11	9/12	9/13	9/14	9/15	9/16	9/17	9/18	9/19	9/20								
10/11	10/12	10/13	10/14	10/15	10/16	10/17	10/18	10/19	10/20									
11/12	11/13	11/14	11/15	11/16	11/17	11/18	11/19	11/20										
12/13	12/14	12/15	12/16	12/17	12/18	12/19	12/20											
13/14	13/15	13/16	13/17	13/18	13/19	13/20												
14/15	14/16	14/17	14/18	14/19	14/20													
15/16	15/17	15/18	15/19	15/20														
16/17	16/18	16/19	16/20															
17/18	17/19	17/20																
18/19	18/20																	
19/20																		

Number of times I've chosen

1 _____	5 _____	9 _____	13 _____	17 _____
2 _____	6 _____	10 _____	14 _____	18 _____
3 _____	7 _____	11 _____	15 _____	19 _____
4 _____	8 _____	12 _____	16 _____	20 _____

have two weeks to let you know?" Then *call* the other companies you're interested in. Explain, "I've just got a job offer, but I'd rather work for you. Can you tell me what the status of my application is?" Nobody will put that information in writing, but almost everyone will tell you over the phone. With this information, you're in a better position to decide whether to accept the original offer.

Companies routinely give applicants two weeks to accept or reject offers. Some students have been successful in getting those two weeks extended to several weeks or even months. Certainly if you cannot decide by the deadline, it is worth asking for more time: the worst the company can do is say *no.* If you do try to keep a company hanging for a long time, be prepared for weekly phone calls asking you if you've decided yet.

Make your acceptance contingent upon a written job offer confirming the terms. That letter should spell out not only salary but also fringe benefits and any special provisions you have negotiated. If something is missing, call the interviewer for clarification: "You said that I'd be reviewed for a promotion and higher salary in six months, but that isn't in the letter." You have more power to resolve misunderstandings now than you will after six months or a year on the job.

When you've accepted one job, let the other places you visited know that you're no longer interested. Then they can go to their second choices. If you're

FIGURE 19.6   Jim's List for a Forced Choice

You can list more items or fewer, in any order. Then use the Forced Choice Chart to see which really matter to you.

1. High income
2. Time to spend with my family
3. Near mountains
4. Job opportunities for Linda
5. Opportunity for advancement
6. Nonracist environment
7. Company with other African Americans in leadership roles
8. Socially responsible company
9. Lots of open land near by
10. Challenging work
11. Minimal travel as part of job
12. Good college or pro sports teams in town
13. Cost of living not too high
14. Good schools
15. Town with large African American community
16. Town with parks, civic services
17. Lots of interaction with other people
18. Company that will encourage me to get a master's degree and even pay for it
19. Company with good fringe benefits
20. Not have to work weekends

Testing the Intangibles*

A growing number of companies, including General Motors and American Express, are no longer satisfied with traditional job interviews.

They are making applicants for many white-collar jobs run a gauntlet of paper-and-pencil tests, role-playing exercises, decision-making simulations, and brain teasers. Others put candidates through a long series of interviews by psychologists or trained interviewers. . . .

[E]mployers want to grade upper-echelon job candidates on intangible qualities. Is she creative and entrepreneurial? Can she lead and coach? Can he work in teams? Is he flexible and capable of learning? Does she have passion and a sense of urgency? How will he function under pressure?

Most important, will the potential recruit fit the corporate culture?

These tests . . . can take from an hour to two days.

*Quoted from Judith H. Dobrzynski, "Applicants Find It Takes More Than a Resume to Land a Job in the '90s," *The Columbus Dispatch*, September 8, 1996, 8I.

second on someone else's list, you'll appreciate other candidates' removing themselves so the way is clear for you.

Summary of Key Points

- Develop an overall strategy based on your answers to these three questions:
  1. What two to five facts about yourself do you want the interviewer to know?
  2. What disadvantages or weaknesses do you need to overcome or minimize?
  3. What do you need to know about the job and the organization to decide whether or not you want to accept this job if it is offered to you?

- Wear a conservative business suit to the interview.

- Bring an extra copy of your résumé, something to write on and write with, and copies of your work to the interview.

- Record the name of the interviewer, what the interviewer liked about you, any negative points that came up, answers to your questions about the company, and when you'll hear from the company.

- Rehearse everything you can. Ask a friend to interview you. If your campus has videotaping facilities, watch yourself on tape so that you can evaluate and modify your interview behavior.

- Be your best self at the interview.

- In a **stress interview,** the interviewer deliberately creates physical or psychological stress. Change the conditions that create physical stress. Meet psychological stress by rephrasing questions in less inflammatory terms and treating them as requests for information.

- Successful applicants know what they want to do, use the company name in the interview, have researched the company in advance, back up claims with specifics, use technical jargon, ask specific questions, and talk more of the time.

- As you practice answers to questions you may be asked, choose answers that fit your qualifications and your interview strategy.

- **Behavioral interviews** ask the applicant to describe actual behaviors, rather than plans or general principles. **Situational interviews** put you in a situation that allows the interviewer to see whether you have the qualities the company is seeking.

- To answer a behavioral question, describe the situation, tell what you did, and what happened. Think about the implications of what you did and be ready to talk about whether you'd do the same thing next time or if the situation were slightly different.

- Use follow-up phone calls to reinforce positives from the first interview, to overcome any negatives, and to get information you can use to persuade the interviewer to hire you.

- A follow-up letter should
    - Remind the interviewer of what he or she liked in you.
    - Allay any negative impressions that may have come up at the interview.
    - Use the jargon of the company and refer to specific things you learned during your interview or saw during your visit.
    - Be enthusiastic.
    - Refer to the next move you'll make.

- In a **forced choice,** you compare each item against every other one to learn which points are most important to you.

- If your first offer isn't from your first choice, call the other companies you're interested in to ask the status of your application.

CHAPTER 19   Exercises and Problems

Getting Started

19.1   Making a Forced Choice

On another sheet of paper, list the criteria you'd like in a job. Number each item. Then compare each pair of items.

If you have 20 items or fewer, you can use the Forced Choice Chart in Figure 19.5 to record your preferences. If you have more than 20 items, make a new chart so that each number will be compared with every other number.

On the chart, mark the number in each pair that corresponds with the item you'd choose if you could have only one of them. Then count how many times you've marked "1," how many times you've marked "2," etc. The items that you mark most often are the features you should try to find in a job.

As Your Instructor Directs,
a. Share your answers with a small group of other students.
b. Summarize your answers in a memo to your instructor.
c. Present your answers orally to the class.

19.2   Interviewing Job Hunters

Talk to students at your school who are interviewing for jobs this term. Possible questions to ask them include

- What field are you in? How good is the job market in that field this year?
- How long is the first interview with a company, usually?
- What questions have you been asked at job interviews? Were you asked any stress or sexist questions? Any really oddball questions?
- What answers seemed to go over well? What answers bombed?
- At an office visit or plant trip, how many people did you talk to? What were their job titles?
- Were you asked to take any tests (skills, physical, drugs)?

- How long did you have to wait after a first interview to learn whether you were being invited for an office visit? How long after an office visit did it take to learn whether you were being offered a job? How much time did the company give you to decide?
- What advice would you have for someone who will be interviewing next term or next year?

As Your Instructor Directs,

a. Summarize your findings in a memo to your instructor.
b. Report your findings orally to the class.
c. Join with a small group of students to write a group report describing the results of your survey.

19.3   Interviewing an Interviewer

Talk to someone who regularly interviews candidates for entry-level jobs. Possible questions to ask include the following:

- How long have you been interviewing for your organization? Does everyone on the management ladder at your company do some interviewing, or do people specialize in it?
- Do you follow a set structure for interviews? What are some of the standard questions you ask?
- What are you looking for? How important are (1) good grades, (2) leadership roles in extracurricular groups, or (3) relevant work experience? What advice would you give to someone who lacks one or more of these?
- What are the things you see students do that create a poor impression? Think about the worst candidate you've interviewed. What did he or she do (or not do) to create such a negative impression?

- What are the things that make a good impression? Recall the best student you've ever interviewed. Why did he or she impress you so much?
- How does your employer evaluate and reward your success as an interviewer?
- What advice would you have for someone who still has a year or so before the job hunt begins?

As Your Instructor Directs,

a. Summarize your findings in a memo to your instructor.
b. Report your findings orally to the class.
c. Join with a small group of students to write a group report describing the results of your survey.
d. Write to the interviewer thanking him or her for taking the time to talk to you.

19.4   Preparing an Interview Strategy

Based on your analysis in problems 17.1, 17.2, and 19.1, prepare an interview strategy.

1. List two to five things about yourself that you want the interviewer to know before you leave the interview.
2. Identify any weaknesses or apparent weaknesses in your record and plan ways to explain them or minimize them.
3. List the points you need to learn about an employer to decide whether to accept an office visit or plant trip.

As Your Instructor Directs,

a. Share your strategy with a small group of other students.
b. Describe your strategy in a memo to your instructor.
c. Present your strategy orally to the class.

19.5   Preparing Questions to Ask Employers

Prepare a list of questions to ask at job interviews.

1.   Prepare a list of three to five general questions that apply to most employers in your field.
2.   Prepare two to five specific questions for the three companies you are most interested in.

As Your Instructor Directs,

a.   Share the questions with a small group of other students.
b.   List the questions in a memo to your instructor.
c.   Present your questions orally to the class.

19.6   Preparing Answers to Questions You May Be Asked

Prepare answers to each of the interview questions listed in this chapter and to any other questions that you know are likely to be asked of job hunters in your field or on your campus.

As Your Instructor Directs,

a.   Write down the answers to your questions and turn them in.
b.   Conduct mini-interviews in a small group of students. In the group, let student A be the interviewer and ask five questions from the list. Student B will play the job candidate and answer the questions, using real information about student B's field and qualifications. Student C will evaluate the content of the answer. Student D will observe the nonverbal behavior of the interviewer (A); student E will observe the nonverbal behavior of the interviewee (B).

After the mini-interview, let students C, D, and E share their observations and recommend ways that B could be even more effective. Then switch roles. Let another student be the interviewer and ask five questions of another interviewee, while new observers note content and nonverbal behavior. Continue the process until everyone in the group has had a chance to be "interviewed."

c.   Assume that you are an independent behavioral psychologist hired to conduct screening interviews and interview yourself (silently, if you like). Then write a report to the organization considering the applicant, identifying each strength, weakness, and other characteristics. Support each claim with one or more behavioral examples. Write about yourself in the third person.

(Option c based on a problem written by William J. Allen, University of La Verne and University of Phoenix.)

E-Mail and Letter Assignments

19.7   Writing a Follow-Up Letter after an Onsite Visit

Write a follow-up e-mail message or letter after an office visit or plant trip. Thank your hosts for their hospitality; relate your strong points to things you learned about the company during the visit; allay any negatives that may remain; be enthusiastic about the company; and submit receipts for your expenses so you can be reimbursed.

19.8   Clarifying the Terms of a Job Offer

Last week, you got a job offer from your first choice company, and you accepted it over the phone. Today, the written confirmation arrived. The letter specifies the starting salary and fringe benefits you had negotiated. However, during the office visit, you were promised a 5% raise in six months. The job offer says nothing about the raise. You do want the job, but you want it on the terms you thought you had negotiated.

Write to your contact at the company, Damon Winters.

Formats for Letters, Memos, and E-Mail Messages

Formats for Letters

Alternate Format for Letters That Are Not Individually Typed

Formatting Envelopes

Format for Memos

Formats for E-Mail Messages

State and Province Abbreviations

Letters normally go to people outside your organization; **memos** go to other people in your organization. In very large organizations, corporate culture determines whether people in different divisions or different locations feel close enough to each other to write memos. Letters and memos do not necessarily differ in length, formality, writing style, or pattern of organization. However, letters and memos do differ in format. The format for e-mail messages is evolving. **Format** means the parts of a document and the way they are arranged on the page.

Formats for Letters

If your organization has a standard format for letters, use it.

Many organizations and writers choose one of three letter formats: **block format** (see Figure A.2), **modified block format** (see Figure A.3), or the **Administrative Management Society (AMS) Simplified format** (see Figure A.4). Your organization may make minor changes from the diagrams in margins or spacing.

Figure A.1 shows how the three formats differ.

Use the same level of formality in the **salutation,** or greeting, as you would in talking to someone on the phone: *Dear Glenn* if you're on a first-name basis, *Dear Mr. Helms* if you don't know the reader well enough to use the first name.

Some writers feel that the AMS Simplified format is better since the reader is not *Dear.* Omitting the salutation is particularly good when you do not know the reader's name or do not know which courtesy title (◄ p. 45) to use. (For a full discussion on nonsexist salutations and salutations when you don't know the reader's name, see Chapter 2.) However, readers like to see their names.

FIGURE A.1   Comparing and Contrasting Letter Formats

	Block	Modified block	AMS Simplified
Date and signature block	Lined up at left margin	Lined up ½ or ⅔ of the way over to the right	Lined up at left margin
Paragraph indentation	None	Optional	None
Salutation and complimentary close	Yes	Yes	None
Subject line	Optional	Rare	Yes
Lists, if any	Indented	Indented	At left margin
Writer's signature	Yes	Yes	None
Writer's typed name	Upper- and lower-case	Upper- and lower-case	Full capital letters
Paragraph spacing	Single-spaced, double-space between	Single-spaced, double-space between	Single-spaced, double-space between

Since the AMS Simplified omits the reader's name in the salutation, writers who use this format but who also want to be friendly often try to use the reader's name early in the body of the letter.

The Simplified letter format is good in business-to-business mail, or in letters where you are writing to anyone who holds a job (admissions officer, customer service representative) rather than to a specific person. It is too cold and distancing for cultures that place a premium on relationships.

Sincerely and *Yours truly* are standard **complimentary closes.** When you are writing to people in special groups or to someone who is a friend as well as a business acquaintance, you may want to use a less formal close. Depending on the circumstances, the following informal closes might be acceptable: *Yours for a better environment, Cordially, Thank you!,* or even *Ciao.*

In **mixed punctuation,** a colon follows the salutation and a comma follows the close. In a sales or fund-raising letter, it is acceptable to use a comma after the salutation to make the letter look like a personal letter rather than like a business letter. In **open punctuation,** omit all punctuation after the salutation and the close. Mixed punctuation is traditional. Open punctuation is faster to type.

A **subject line** tells what the letter is about. Subject lines are required in memos; they are optional in letters. Good subject lines are specific, concise, and appropriate for your purposes and the response you expect from your reader.

- When you have good news, put it in the subject line.
- When your information is neutral, summarize it concisely in the subject line.
- When your information is negative, use a negative subject line if the reader may not read the message or needs the information to act, or if the negative is your error.
- When you have a request that will be easy for the reader to grant, put either the subject of the request or a direct question in the subject line.
- When you must persuade a reluctant reader, use a common ground, a reader benefit, or a directed subject line that makes your stance on the issue clear.

For examples of subject lines in each of these situations, see Chapters 7, 8, and 9.

A **reference line** refers the reader to the number used on the previous correspondence this letter replies to, or the order or invoice number this letter is about. Very large organizations, like the IRS, use numbers on every piece of correspondence they send out so that it is possible to find quickly the earlier document to which an incoming letter refers.

Northwest Hardware Warehouse

100 Freeway Exchange   Provo, UT 84610   (801) 555-4683   www.northwesthardware.com

Line up everything at left margin

↕ 1–6 spaces depending on length of letter

June 20, 2003

Mr. James E. Murphy, Accounts Payable   *Title could be on a separate line*
Salt Lake Equipment Rentals
5600 Wasatch Boulevard
Salt Lake City, Utah 84121

1"–1½"

Use first name in salutation if you'd use it on the phone

Dear Jim: *Colon in mixed punctuation*

The following items totaling $393.09 are still open on your account. *¶ 1 never has a heading*

Invoice #01R-784391 *Bold or underline heading*

After the bill for this invoice arrived on May 14, you wrote saying that the material had not been delivered to you. On May 29, our Claims Department sent you a copy of the delivery receipt signed by an employee of Salt Lake Equipment. You have had proof of delivery for over three weeks, but your payment has not yet arrived.

⅝"–1"

Please send a check for $78.42.

Single-space paragraphs
Double-space between paragraphs (one blank space)

Triple-space before new heading (2 blank spaces)

Voucher #59351

Do not indent paragraphs

The reference line on your voucher #59351, dated June 16, indicates that it is the gross payment for invoice #01G-002345. However, the voucher was only for $1171.25, while the invoice amount was $1246.37. Please send a check for $75.12 to clear this item.

Voucher #55032

Voucher #55032, dated June 16, subtracts a credit for $239.55 from the amount due. Our records do not show that any credit is due on this voucher. Please send either an explanation or a check to cover the $239.55 immediately.

Total Amount Due   *Headings are optional in letters*

Please send a check for $393.09 to cover these three items and to bring your account up to date.

Sincerely,

↕ 1–2 spaces

2–4 spaces

Neil Hutchinson
Credit Representative

cc: Joan Stottlemyer, Credit Manager

Leave bottom margin of 3–6 spaces—more if letter is short

Bay City Information Systems

151 Bayview Road • San Francisco, CA 81153 • (650) 405-7849 • www.baycity.com

2–6 spaces

September 15, 2003
Line up date with signature block
$\frac{1}{2}$ or $\frac{2}{3}$ of the way over to the right

1–4 spaces

Ms. Mary E. Arcas
Personnel Director
Cyclops Communication Technologies
1050 South Sierra Bonita Avenue
Los Angeles, CA 90019 *Zip code on same line*

$1"–1\frac{1}{2}"$

Dear Ms. Arcas: *Colon in mixed punctuation*

$\frac{5}{8}"–1"$

Indenting ¶ is optional in modified block

Let me respond to your request for an evaluation of Colleen Kangas. Colleen was hired as a clerk-typist by Bay City Information Systems on April 4, 2001, and was promoted to Administrative Assistant on August 1, 2002. At her review in June, I recommended that she be promoted again. She is an intelligent young woman with good work habits and a good knowledge of computer software.

Single-space paragraphs

As an Adminstrative Assistant, Colleen not only handles routine duties such as processing time cards, ordering supplies, and entering data, but also screens calls for two marketing specialists, answers basic questions about Bay City Information Systems, compiles the statistics I need for my monthly reports, and investigates special assignments for me. In the past eight months, she has investigated freight charges, inventoried department hardware, and transferred files to CD-Roms. I need only to give her general directions: she has a knack for tracking down information quickly and summarizing it accurately.

Double-space between paragraphs (one blank line)

Although the department's workload has increased during the year, Colleen manages her time so that everything gets done on schedule. She is consistently poised and friendly under pressure. Her willingness to work overtime on occasion is particularly remarkable considering that she has been going to college part-time ever since she joined our firm.

At Bay City Information Systems, Colleen uses Microsoft Word and Access software. She tells me that she has also used WordPerfect and PowerPoint in her college classes.

If Colleen were staying in San Francisco, we would want to keep her. She has the potential either to become an Executive Secretary or to move into line or staff work, especially once she completes her degree. I recommend her highly.

1–2 spaces

Comma in mixed punctuation

Sincerely,

Headings are optional in letters

2–4 spaces

Jeanne Cederlind

Jeanne Cederlind
Vice President, Marketing
jeanne_c@baycity.com

Line up signature block with date

1–4 spaces

Encl.: Evaluation Form for Colleen Kangas

Leave at least 3–6 spaces at bottom of page—more if letter is short

McFarlane Memorial

1500 Main Street   Iowa City, IA 52232   (319) 555-3113

2–4 spaces

Line up everything at left margin

August 24, 2004

1–4 spaces

1"–1½"

Melinda Hamilton
Medical Services Division
Health Management Services, Inc.
4333 Edgewood Road, NE
Cedar Rapids, IA 52401

Triple space (2 blank spaces)   *Subject line in full capital letters*

REQUEST FOR INFORMATION ABOUT COMPUTER SYSTEMS

← No salutation

We're interested in upgrading our computer system and would like to talk to one of your marketing representatives to see what would best meet our needs. We will use the following criteria to choose a system:

1. Ability to use our current software and data files.   *Double-space (one blank space)*

2. Price, prorated on a three-year expected life.   *between items in list if any items are more than one line long*

3. Ability to provide auxiliary services, e.g., controlling inventory of drugs and supplies, monitoring patients' vital signs, and faster processing of insurance forms.

4. Freedom from downtime.

Triple-space (two blank spaces) between list, next paragraph

Do not indent paragraphs

McFarlane Memorial Hospital has 50 beds for acute care and 75 beds for long-term care. In the next five years, we expect the number of beds to remain the same while outpatient care and emergency room care increase.

Could we meet the first or the third week in September? We are eager to have the new system installed by Christmas if possible.

Please call me to schedule an appointment.   *Headings are optional in letters*

No close. No signature.

HUGH PORTERFIELD   *Writer's name in full capital letters*
Controller

1–4 spaces

Encl.:   Specifications of Current System
         Databases Currently in Use

cc: Rene Seaburg

Leave 3–6 spaces at bottom of page—more if letter is short

All three formats can use headings, lists, and indented sections for emphasis.

Each of the three formats has advantages. Both block and AMS Simplified can be typed quickly since everything is lined up at the left margin. Block format is the format most frequently used for business letters; readers expect it. Modified block format creates a visually attractive page by moving the date and signature block over into what would otherwise be empty white space. Modified block is a traditional format; readers are comfortable with it.

The examples of the three formats in Figures A.2–A.4 show one-page letters on company letterhead. **Letterhead** is preprinted stationery with the organization's name, logo, address, and phone number. Figure A.5 shows how to set up modified block format when you do not have letterhead. (It is also acceptable to use block format without letterhead.)

When your letter runs two or more pages, use a heading on the second page to identify it. Using the reader's name helps the writer, who may be printing out many letters at a time, to make sure the right second page gets in the envelope. The two most common formats are shown in Figures A.6, A.7, A.8, and below. Note even when the signature block is on the second page, it is still lined up with the date.

| Reader's Name |
| Date |
| Page Number |

or

| Reader's Name | Page Number | Date |

When a letter runs two or more pages, use letterhead only for page 1. (See Figures A.6, A.7, and A.8.) For the remaining pages, use plain paper that matches the letterhead in weight, texture, and color.

Set side margins of 1 inch to 1½ inches on the left and ⅝ inch to 1 inch on the right. If your letterhead extends all the way across the top of the page, set your margins even with the ends of the letterhead for the most visually pleasing page. The top margin should be three to six lines under the letterhead, or 2 inches down from the top of the page if you aren't using letterhead. If your letter is very short, you may want to use bigger side and top margins so that the letter is centered on the page.

To eliminate typing the reader's name and address on an envelope, some organizations use envelopes with cut-outs or windows so that the **inside address** (the reader's name and address) on the letter shows through and can be used for delivery. If your organization does this, adjust your margins, if necessary, so that the whole inside address is visible.

Many letters are accompanied by other documents. Whatever these documents may be—a multipage report or a two-line note—they are called **enclosures,** since they are enclosed in the envelope. The writer should refer to the enclosures in the body of the letter: "As you can see from my résumé, . . ." The enclosure line reminds the person who seals the letter to include the enclosures.

Sometimes you write to one person but send copies of your letter to other people. If you want the reader to know that other people are getting copies, list their names on the last page. The abbreviation *cc* originally meant *carbon copy* but now means *computer copy.* Other acceptable abbreviations include *pc* for *photocopy* or simply *c* for *copy.* You can also send copies to other people without telling the reader. Such copies are called **blind copies.** Blind copies are not mentioned on the original; they are listed on the copy saved for the file with the abbreviation *bc* preceding the names of people getting these copies.

6–12 spaces

Single space 11408 Brussels Ave. NE
Albuquerque, NM 87111
November 5, 2003

$1"–1\frac{1}{2}"$

1–6 spaces

Mr. Tom Miller, President
Miller Office Supplies Corporation
P.O. Box 2900
Lincolnshire, IL 60197-2900

Subject: Invoice No. 664907, 10/29/03   *Subject line is optional in block & modified block*

Indenting paragraphs is optional in modified block   Dear Mr. Miller *No punctuation in open punctuation*

My wife, Caroline Lehman, ordered and received the briefcase listed on page 71 of your catalog (881-CD-L-9Q-4). The catalog said that the Leatherizer, 881-P-4, was free. On the order blank she indicated that she did want the Leatherizer and marked "Free" in the space for price. Nevertheless, the bill charged us for the Leatherizer.

$\frac{5"}{8}–1"$

Please remove the $3.19 charge for the Leatherizer from our bill. The total bill was for $107.53, and with the $3.19 deducted, I assume the correct amount for the bill should be $104.34. I have enclosed a check for $104.34.

Please confirm that the charge has been removed and that our account for this order is now paid in full.

Sincerely *No punctuation in open punctuation*

2–4 spaces

William T. Mozing

1–4 spaces

Encl.: Check for $104.34 *Line up signature block with date*

State
University

4300 Gateway Boulevard
Midland, TX

August 11, 2003

1"–1½ "

Ms. Stephanie Voght
Stephen F. Austin High School
1200 Southwest Blvd.
San Antonio, TX 78214

↕ 1 – 2 spaces

Dear Ms. Voght: *Colon in mixed punctuation.*

⅝"–1"

Enclosed are 100 brochures about State University to distribute to your students. The brochures describe the academic programs and financial aid available. When you need additional brochures, just let me know.

Videotape about State University

You may also want to show your students the videotape "Life at State University." This

---

Plain paper for page 2.

↕ ½"–1"

Center

Stephanie Voght ← *Reader's name*   2   August 11, 2003

Also OK to line up page number date at left under reader's name.

campus life, including football and basketball games, fraternities and sororities, clubs and organizations, and opportunities for volunteer work. The tape stresses the diversity of the student body and the very different lifestyles that are available at State.

Triple space before each new heading (two blank spaces).

Scheduling the Videotape   *Bold or underline headings.*

Same margins as p 1.   To schedule your free showing, just fill out the enclosed card with your first, second, and third choices for dates, and return it in the stamped, self-addressed envelope. Dates are reserved in the order that requests arrive. Send in your request early to increase the chances of getting the date you want.

"Life at State University" will be on its way to give your high school students a preview of the college experience.

1–2 spaces ↕

Sincerely,   *Comma in mixed punctuation.*

2–4 spaces ↕   *Michael J. Mahler*

Michael L. Mahler
Director of Admissions

Headings are optional in letters.

↕ 1–4 spaces

Encl.: Brochures, Reservation Form

cc: R. J. Holland, School Superintendent
    Jose Lavilla, President, PTS Association

Glenarvon Carpets

1500 Summit Avenue   (612) 555-1002
Minneapolis, MN   Fax (612) 555-4032
                     www.glenarvon.biz

↕ 1–4 spaces

November 5, 2004

Line up date with signature block.

Mr. Roger B. Castino
Castino Floors and Carpets
418 E. North Street
Brockton, MA 02410

Indenting paragraphs is optional in modified block.

Dear Mr. Castino:

Welcome to the team of Glenarvon Carpet dealers!

Your first shipment of Glenarvon samples should reach you within ten days. The samples include

---

Plain paper for page 2

↕ ½"–1"

Mr. Roger B. Castino *← Reader's name*

Center

2

November 5, 2004

territory . In addition, as a dealer you receive

- Sales kit highlighting product features
- Samples to distribute to customers
- Advertising copy to run in local newspapers
- Display units to place in your store.

Indent or center list to emphasize it.

Use same margins as p 1.

The Annual Sales Meeting each January keeps you up-to-date on new products while you get to know other dealers and Glenarvon executives and relax at a resort hotel.

Make your reservations now for Monterey January 10-13 for your first Glenarvon Sales Meeting!

2–4 spaces ↕

Cordially, *Comma in mixed punctuation*

Barbara S. Charbonneau

Barbara S. Charbonneau
Vice President, Marketing

Line up signature block with date in heading and on p1.

↕ 1–4 spaces

Encl.: Organization Chart
       Product List
       National Advertising Campaigns in 2005
       1–4 spaces
cc: Nancy Magill, Northeast Sales Manager
    Edward Spaulding, Sales Representative
       ↕ 3–6 spaces – more if second page isn't a full page.

**ptions
for Living**

↕ 1–4 spaces

January 20, 2004

↕ 1–2 spaces

Gary Sammons, Editor
Southeastern Home Magazine
253 North Lake Street
Newport News, VA 23612

Triple space (two blank spaces)   *Subject line in full caps*

MATERIAL FOR YOUR STORY ON HOMES FOR PEOPLE WITH DISABILITIES

No salutation

Apartments and houses can easily be designed to accommodate people with disabilities. From the outside, the building is indistinguishable from conventional housing. But the modifications inside permit people who use wheelchairs or whose sight or hearing is impaired to do everyday things like shower, cook, and do laundry.

↕ $\frac{1}{2}''$–1''   *Plain paper for page 2*

Gary Sammons   *← Reader's
name*
January 20, 2004
Page 2

*Everything
lined up
at left
margin*

in hallways and showers and adjustable cabinets that can be raised or lowered. Cardinal says that the adaptations can run from a few dollars to $5000, depending on what the customer selects.

The Builders Association of South Florida will install many features at no extra cost: 36-inch doorways—eight inches wider than standard—to accommodate wheelchairs and extra wiring for electronic items for people whose sight or hearing is impaired.

*Same
margins
as page 1*

If you'd like pictures to accompany your story, just let me know.

MARILYN TILLOTSON   *No close, no signature*
Executive Director   *Writer's name in full caps*

Encl.: Blueprints for Housing for People with Disabilities

cc: Douglas Stringfellow, President, BASF
    Thomas R. Galliher, President, Cardinal Industries

↕ at least 3–6 spaces—more if page 2 is not a full page

You do not need to indicate that you have shown a letter to your superior or that you are saving a copy of the letter for your own files. These are standard practices.

Alternate Format for Letters That Are Not Individually Typed

Merge functions in word processing programs allow you to put in a reader's name and address even in a form letter. *If you use a specific name in the salutation,* also use the reader's name and address in the inside address.

If you cannot afford to type each reader's name and address individually on the page, you have two options. The first option is to omit the inside address and use a generic salutation: "Dear Voter." The second option is to omit the salutation and use the space where it and the inside address normally go for a benefit or attention-getter. Figure A.9 illustrates this option.

Formatting Envelopes

Business envelopes need to put the reader's name and address in the area that is picked up by the Post Office's Optical Character Readers (OCRs). Use side margins of at least 1 inch. Your bottom margin must be at least ⅝ inch but no bigger than 2¼ inches.

Most businesses use envelopes that already have the return address printed in the upper left-hand corner. When you don't have printed envelopes, type your name (optional), your street address, and your city, state, and zip code in the upper left-hand corner. Since the OCR doesn't need this information to route your letter, exact margins don't matter. Use whatever is convenient and looks good to you.

Format for Memos

Memos omit both the salutation and the close entirely. Memos never use indented paragraphs. Subject lines are required; headings are optional. Each heading must cover all the information until the next heading. Never use a separate heading for the first paragraph.

Figure A.10 illustrates the standard memo format typed on a plain sheet of paper. Note that the first letters of the reader's name, the writer's name, and the subject phrase are lined up vertically. Note also that memos are usually initialed by the To/From block. Initialing tells the reader that you have proofread the memo and prevents someone sending out your name on a memo you did not in fact write.

Some organizations have special letterhead for memos. When *Date/To/From/Subject* are already printed on the form, the date, writer's and reader's names, and subject are set at the main margin to save typing time. (See Figure A.11.)

Some organizations alter the order of items in the Date/To/From/Subject block. Some organizations ask employees to sign memos rather than simply initialing them. The signature goes below the last line of the memo, starting halfway over on the page, and prevents anyone's adding unauthorized information.

If the memo runs two pages or more, set up the second and subsequent pages in one of the following ways (see Figure A.12):

Brief Subject Line
Date
Page Number

COMPUTER SUPPORT
CORPORATION

2215 Midway Road • Carrollton, Texas 75006
(214) 661-8960 • Telex: 284831 CSCTX UR • Fax: (214) 661-1096

*"Johnson Box" used for emphasis
visual variety*

```
* * * * * * * * * * *
* Five FREE Libraries *
* Worth Up to $615!   *
* * * * * * * * * * *
```

*Attention–getter
visually
substitutes
for inside
address,
salutation*

*Date omitted so letter can be sent
out unchanged
Johnson Box visually substitutes
for date*

No Other Business
Graphics Software Can
Match the Versatility &
Flexibility of Diagraph!

Let us prove to you that Diagraph is a breakthrough in business
graphics software.

Use Diagraph to turn your ideas, concepts, plans, and data into
organization charts, signs, flow charts, diagrams, forms, and maps.
Diagraph comes with a money-back guarantee. Use it for 30 days and
we're certain that you will have discovered so many uses for
Diagraph that you won't want to part with it.

And now you have two choices: Diagraph/500 for only $99 or
Diagraph/2000 for $395.

Diagraph/500 files are fully compatible with Diagraph/2000 so you
can upgrade to Diagraph/2000 at any time. What's more, the cost of
Diagraph/500 is credited towards your purchase of Diagraph/2000.

See the enclosed data sheet for additional information or call us
today to see how the power of Diagraph can enhance everything you
write!

Sincerely,

4 sp. *[signature: Gail McCannon]*

Gail McCannon
Director, Customer Services

*Signature block lined up with
Johnson Box*

Initials of writer

GM:ec *← Initials of typist*

Encl.

P.S. As an added incentive, if you purchase Diagraph/2000 before
November 30, you can select five Diagraph libraries, worth up to
$615, absolutely free. Call for more details.

*Reader benefit saved for a P.S.
People's eyes go to P.S., which they may
read before returning to rest of letter*

Everything lined up at left

Plain paper

1–4 spaces

October 7, 2003

Line up

Double space (one blank space)

To: Annette T. Califero

From: Kyle B. Abrams *KBA* *Writer's initials added in ink*

1"–1½"

Subject: A Low-Cost Way to Reduce Energy Use *Capitalize first letter of each major word in subject line*

No heading for ¶ 1

As you requested, I've investigated low-cost ways to reduce our energy use. Reducing the building temperature on weekends is a change that we could make immediately, that would cost nothing, and that would cut our energy use by about 6%.

⅝"–1"

Triple space before each new heading (two blank spaces)

The Energy Savings from a Lower Weekend Temperature *Bold or underline headings*

Single-space paragraphs; double-space between paragraphs (one blank space)

Lowering the temperature from 68° to 60° from 8 p.m. Friday evening to 4 a.m. Monday morning could cut our total consumption by 6%. It is not feasible to lower the temperature on weeknights because a great many staff members work late; the cleaning crew also is on duty from 6 p.m. to midnight. Turning the temperature down for only four hours would not result in a significant heat saving.

Turning the heat back up at 4 a.m. will allow the building temperature to be back to 68° by 9 a.m. Our furnace already has computerized controls which can be set to automatically lower and raise the temperature.

Triple sp (two blank spaces)

How a Lower Temperature Would Affect Employees *Capitalize first letter of each major word of heading*

Do not indent paragraphs

A survey of employees shows that only 7 people use the building every weekend or almost every weekend. Eighteen percent of our staff have worked at least one weekend day in the last two months; 52% say they "occasionally" come in on weekends.

People who come in for an hour or less on weekends could cope with the lower temperature just by wearing warm clothes. However, most people would find 60° too cool for extended work. Employees who work regularly on weekends might want to install space heaters.

Action Needed to Implement the Change

Would you also like me to check into the cost of buying a dozen portable space heaters? Providing them would allow us to choose units that our wiring can handle and would be a nice gesture towards employees who give up their weekends to work. I could have a report to you in two weeks.

We can begin saving energy immediately. Just authorize the lower temperature, and I'll see that the controls are reset for this weekend.

Memos are initialed by To/From/Subject block — no signature

Headings are optional in memos

FIGURE A.11   Memo Format (on memo letterhead)

Kimball, Walls, and Morganstern

Date: March 15, 2004   *Line up horizontally with printed Date/To/From/Subject*

To: Annette T. Califero

From: Kyle B. Abrams *KBA* *Writer's initials added in ink*

Subject: The Effectiveness of Reducing Building Temperatures on Weekends

Capitalize first letter of each major word in subject line

Triple space(two blank spaces)

Margin lined up with items in To/From/Subject block to save typing time

Reducing the building temperature to 60° on weekends has cut energy use by 4% compared to last year's use from December to February and has saved our firm $22,000.

This savings is particularly remarkable when you consider that this winter has been colder than last year's, so that more heat would be needed to maintain the same temperature.

$\frac{5}{8}$"–1"

Fewer people have worked weekends during the past three months than during the preceding three months, but snow and bad driving conditions may have had more to do with keeping people home than the fear of being cold. Five of the 12 space heaters we bought have been checked out on an average weekend. On one weekend, all 12 were in use and some people shared their offices so that everyone could be in a room with a space heater.

Fully 92% of our employees support the lower temperature. I recommend that we continue turning down the heat on weekends through the remainder of the heating season and that we resume the practice when the heat is turned on next fall.

Headings are optional in memos

or

Brief Subject Line	Page Number	Date

Formats for E-Mail Messages

Most e-mail programs prompt you to supply the various parts of the format. For example, a blank Eudora screen prompts you to supply the name of the recipient(s) and the subject line. See Chapters 7, 8, and 9 for information about designing e-mail subject lines. "Cc:" denotes computer copies; the recipient will see that these people are getting the message. "Bcc:" denotes blind computer copies; the recipient does not see the names of these people. Most e-mail programs also allow you to attach documents from other programs. Thus you can send someone a document with formatting, drafts of PowerPoint slides, or

1"–1½"

February 18, 2003

To: Dorothy N. Blasingham

Double-space
(one blank space)

From: Roger L. Trout **R.L.T.** *Writer's initials added in ink*

Subject: Request for Third-Quarter Computer Training Sessions

Capitalize first letter of all major words in subject line

Triple space (two blank spaces)

¶ I never has a heading

⅝"–1"

Could you please run advanced training sessions on using Excel and WordPerfect in April and May and basic training sessions for new hires in June?

Triple-space before a heading (two blank spaces)

Advanced Sessions on Excel
Bold or underline headings

Double-space between paragraphs (one blank space)

Once the tax season is over, Jose Cisneros wants to have his first- and second-year people take your advanced course on Excel. Plan on about 45-50 people in three sessions. The people in the course already use Excel for basic spreadsheets but need to learn the fine points of macros and charting.

If possible, it would be most convenient to have the sessions run for four afternoons rather

---

Plain paper for page 2

½"–1"

Dorothy N. Blasingham   *Brief subject line or reader's name*   2 *Page number*   February 18, 2003

Also OK to line up page number, date at left under reader's name

Same margins as p 1.

before the summer vacation season begins.

Orientation for New Hires   *Capitalize first letter of all major words in heading*

With a total of 16 full-time and 34 part-time people being hired either for summer or permanent work, we'll need at least two and perhaps three orientation sessions. We'd like to hold these the first, second, and third weeks in June. By May 1, we should know how many people will be in each training session.

Would you be free to conduct training sessions on how to use our computers on June 9, June 16, and June 23? If we need only two dates, we'll use June 9 and June 16, but please block off the 23rd too in case we need a third session.

Triple-space before a heading (two blank spaces)

Request for Confirmation

Let me know whether you're free on these dates in June, and which dates you'd prefer for the sessions on Excel and WordPerfect. If you'll let me know by February 25, we can get information out to participants in plenty of time for the sessions.

Thanks!

Headings are optional in memos

Memos are initialed by To/From/Subject block

the design for a brochure cover. The computer program supplies the date and time automatically.

Some aspects of e-mail format are still evolving. In particular, some writers treat e-mail messages as if they were informal letters; some treat them as memos. Even though the e-mail screen has a "To" line (as do memos), some writers still use an informal salutation, as in Figure A.13. The writer in Figure A.13 ends the message with a signature block. You can store a signature block in the e-mail program and set the program to insert the signature block automatically. In contrast, the writer in Figure A.14 omits both the salutation and his name. When you send a message to an individual or a group you have set up, the "From:" line will have your name and e-mail address. If you post a message to a listserv, be sure to give at least your name and e-mail address at the end of your message, as some listservs strip out identifying information when they process messages.

When you hit "reply," the e-mail program automatically uses "Re:" (Latin for *about*) and the previous subject. The original message is set off with carats (see Figure A.15). You may want to change the subject line to make it more appropriate for your message.

Use short line lengths in your e-mail message. If the line lengths are too long, they'll produce awkward line breaks, as in Figure A.15.

State and Province Abbreviations

States with names of more than five letters are frequently abbreviated in letters and memos. The Post Office abbreviations use two capital letters with no punctuation. See Figure A.16.

FIGURE A.13 A Basic E-Mail Message in Eudora (direct request)

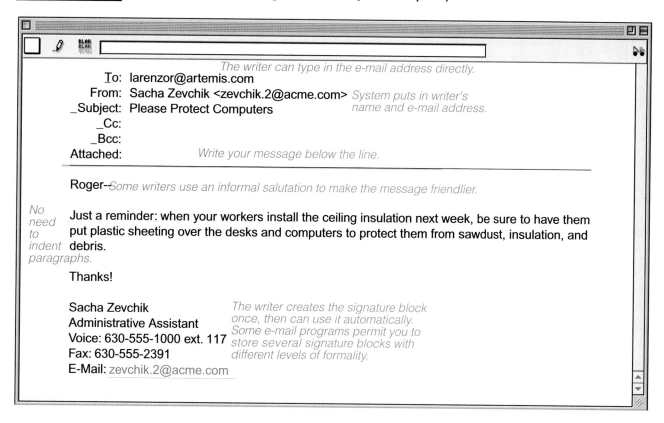

The writer can type in the e-mail address directly.

To: larenzor@artemis.com
From: Sacha Zevchik <zevchik.2@acme.com> *System puts in writer's name and e-mail address.*
Subject: Please Protect Computers
Cc:
Bcc:
Attached: *Write your message below the line.*

Roger-- *Some writers use an informal salutation to make the message friendlier.*

No need to indent paragraphs. Just a reminder: when your workers install the ceiling insulation next week, be sure to have them put plastic sheeting over the desks and computers to protect them from sawdust, insulation, and debris.

Thanks!

Sacha Zevchik
Administrative Assistant
Voice: 630-555-1000 ext. 117
Fax: 630-555-2391
E-Mail: zevchik.2@acme.com

The writer creates the signature block once, then can use it automatically. Some e-mail programs permit you to store several signature blocks with different levels of formality.

FIGURE A.14 An E-Mail Message with an Attachment (direct request)

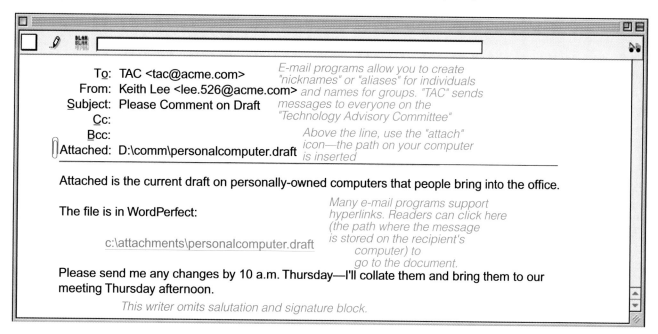

To: TAC <tac@acme.com> *E-mail programs allow you to create "nicknames" or "aliases" for individuals and names for groups. "TAC" sends messages to everyone on the "Technology Advisory Committee"*
From: Keith Lee <lee.526@acme.com>
Subject: Please Comment on Draft
Cc:
Bcc:
Attached: D:\comm\personalcomputer.draft *Above the line, use the "attach" icon—the path on your computer is inserted*

Attached is the current draft on personally-owned computers that people bring into the office.

The file is in WordPerfect:

c:\attachments\personalcomputer.draft

Many e-mail programs support hyperlinks. Readers can click here (the path where the message is stored on the recipient's computer) to go to the document.

Please send me any changes by 10 a.m. Thursday—I'll collate them and bring them to our meeting Thursday afternoon.

This writer omits salutation and signature block.

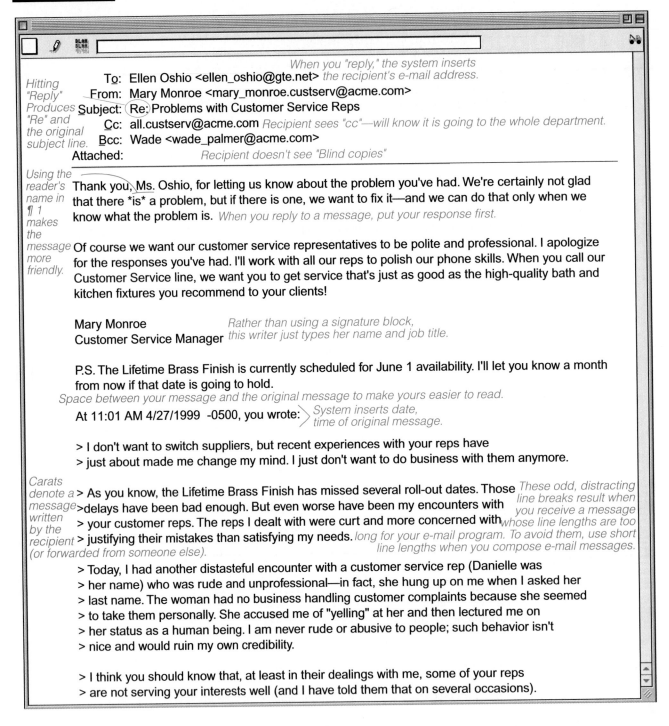

Hitting "Reply" Produces "Re" and the original subject line.

When you "reply," the system inserts the recipient's e-mail address.

To: Ellen Oshio <ellen_oshio@gte.net>
From: Mary Monroe <mary_monroe.custserv@acme.com>
Subject: Re: Problems with Customer Service Reps
Cc: all.custserv@acme.com *Recipient sees "cc"—will know it is going to the whole department.*
Bcc: Wade <wade_palmer@acme.com>
Attached: *Recipient doesn't see "Blind copies"*

Using the reader's name in ¶ 1 makes the message more friendly.

Thank you, Ms. Oshio, for letting us know about the problem you've had. We're certainly not glad that there *is* a problem, but if there is one, we want to fix it—and we can do that only when we know what the problem is. *When you reply to a message, put your response first.*

Of course we want our customer service representatives to be polite and professional. I apologize for the responses you've had. I'll work with all our reps to polish our phone skills. When you call our Customer Service line, we want you to get service that's just as good as the high-quality bath and kitchen fixtures you recommend to your clients!

Mary Monroe
Customer Service Manager *Rather than using a signature block, this writer just types her name and job title.*

P.S. The Lifetime Brass Finish is currently scheduled for June 1 availability. I'll let you know a month from now if that date is going to hold.
Space between your message and the original message to make yours easier to read.

At 11:01 AM 4/27/1999 -0500, you wrote: *System inserts date, time of original message.*

> I don't want to switch suppliers, but recent experiences with your reps have
> just about made me change my mind. I just don't want to do business with them anymore.

Carats denote a message written by the recipient (or forwarded from someone else).

> As you know, the Lifetime Brass Finish has missed several roll-out dates. Those
>delays have been bad enough. But even worse have been my encounters with
> your customer reps. The reps I dealt with were curt and more concerned with
> justifying their mistakes than satisfying my needs.

These odd, distracting line breaks result when you receive a message whose line lengths are too long for your e-mail program. To avoid them, use short line lengths when you compose e-mail messages.

> Today, I had another distasteful encounter with a customer service rep (Danielle was
> her name) who was rude and unprofessional—in fact, she hung up on me when I asked her
> last name. The woman had no business handling customer complaints because she seemed
> to take them personally. She accused me of "yelling" at her and then lectured me on
> her status as a human being. I am never rude or abusive to people; such behavior isn't
> nice and would ruin my own credibility.

> I think you should know that, at least in their dealings with me, some of your reps
> are not serving your interests well (and I have told them that on several occasions).

FIGURE A.16   Post Office Abbreviations for States, Territories, and Provinces

State name	Post Office abbreviation	State name	Post Office abbreviation
Alabama	AL	Missouri	MO
Alaska	AK	Montana	MT
Arizona	AZ	Nebraska	NE
Arkansas	AR	Nevada	NV
California	CA	New Hampshire	NH
Colorado	CO	New Jersey	NJ
Connecticut	CT	New Mexico	NM
Delaware	DE	New York	NY
District of Columbia	DC	North Carolina	NC
Florida	FL	North Dakota	ND
Georgia	GA	Ohio	OH
Hawaii	HI	Oklahoma	OK
Idaho	ID	Oregon	OR
Illinois	IL	Pennsylvania	PA
Indiana	IN	Rhode Island	RI
Iowa	IA	South Carolina	SC
Kansas	KS	South Dakota	SD
Kentucky	KY	Tennessee	TN
Louisiana	LA	Texas	TX
Maine	ME	Utah	UT
Maryland	MD	Vermont	VT
Massachusetts	MA	Virginia	VA
Michigan	MI	Washington	WA
Minnesota	MN	West Virginia	WV
Mississippi	MS	Wisconsin	WI
		Wyoming	WY

Territory	Post Office abbreviation	Province name	Post Office abbreviation
Guam	GU	Alberta	AB
Puerto Rico	PR	British Columbia	BC
Virgin Islands	VI	Labrador	LB
		Manitoba	MB
		New Brunswick	NB
		Newfoundland	NF
		Northwest Territories	NT
		Nova Scotia	NS
		Ontario	ON
		Prince Edward Island	PE
		Quebec	PQ
		Saskatchewan	SK
		Yukon Territory	YT

B

Writing Correctly

Too much concern for correctness at the wrong stage of the writing process can backfire: writers who worry about grammar and punctuation when they're writing a first or second draft are more likely to get writer's block. Wait till you have your ideas on paper to check your draft for correct grammar, punctuation, typing of numbers and dates, and word use. Use the proofreading symbols at the end of this appendix to indicate changes needed in a typed copy.

Most writers make a small number of grammatical errors repeatedly. Most readers care deeply about only a few grammatical points. Keep track of the feedback you get (from your instructors now, from your supervisor later) and put your energy into correcting the errors that bother the people who read what you write. A command of standard grammar will help you build the credible, professional image you want to create with everything you write.

Using Grammar

With the possible exception of spelling, grammar is the aspect of writing that writers seem to find most troublesome. Faulty grammar is often what executives are objecting to when they complain that college graduates or MBAs "can't write." See the BAC Web site for links that explain grammar.

Agreement

Subjects and verbs agree when they are both singular or both plural.

Incorrect: The accountants who conducted the audit was recommended highly.

Correct: The accountants who conducted the audit were recommended highly.

Subject–verb agreement errors often occur when other words come between the subject and the verb. Edit your draft by finding the subject and the verb of each sentence.

American usage treats company names and the words *company* and *government* as singular nouns. British usage treats them as plural:

Correct (US):   State Farm Insurance trains its agents well.

Correct (Great Britain):   Lloyds of London train their agents well.

Use a plural verb when two or more singular subjects are joined by *and*.

Correct: Larry McGreevy and I are planning to visit the client.

Use a singular verb when two or more singular subjects are joined by *or, nor,* or *but*.

Correct: Either the shipping clerk or the superintendent has to sign the order.

When the sentence begins with *Here* or *There,* make the verb agree with the subject that follows the verb.

Correct: Here is the booklet you asked for.

Correct: There are the blueprints I wanted.

Note that some words that end in *s* are considered to be singular and require singular verbs.

Correct: A series of meetings is planned.

When a situation doesn't seem to fit the rules, or when following a rule produces an awkward sentence, revise the sentence to avoid the problem.

Problematic: The Plant Manager in addition to the sales representative (was, were?) pleased with the new system.

Better: The Plant Manager and the sales representative were pleased with the new system.

Problematic: None of us (is, are?) perfect.

Better: All of us have faults.

Errors in **noun–pronoun agreement** occur if a pronoun is of a different number or person than the word it refers to.

Why Errors Matter*

Errors in a document can make it harder to figure out what the writer meant. On rare occasions, errors can even change the meaning.

Errors also create a negative image of the writer. Professor Larry Beason found that business people judged the authors of errors to be not only poor writers but also poor business people. Negative judgments included the following:

- Careless and hasty.
- Uncaring (about reader or message).
- Problems with thinking and logic.
- Not a detail person—what will you do with numbers?
- Poor oral communicator.
- Uneducated.

*Based on Larry Beason, "Language Errors in Business Documents: A Study of Business People's Reactions to Error," Southwest Federation of Administrative Disciplines Convention, Dallas, TX, March 4–7, 1998.

The Errors That Bother People in Organizations*

Professor Maxine Hairston constructed a questionnaire with 65 sentences, each with one grammatical error. The administrators, executives, and business people who responded were most bothered by the following:

- Wrong verb forms ("he brung his secretary with him")
- Double negatives
- Objective pronoun used for subject of sentence ("Him and Richards were the last ones hired.")
- Sentence fragments
- Run-on sentences
- Failure to capitalize proper names
- "Would of" for "would have"
- Lack of subject–verb agreement
- Comma between verb and complement ("Cox cannot predict, that street crime will diminish.")
- Lack of parallelism
- Adverb errors ("He treats his men bad.")
- "Set" for "sit"

They also disliked

- Errors in word meaning
- Dangling modifiers
- "I" as objective pronoun ("The army moved my husband and I")
- Not setting off interrupters (e.g., "However") with commas
- Tense switching
- Plural modifiers with singular nouns.

*Based on Maxine Hairston, "Not All Errors Are Created Equal: Nonacademic Readers in the Professions Respond to Lapses in Usage," *College English* 43, no. 8 (December 1981), 794–806.

Incorrect: All drivers of leased automobiles are billed $100 if damages to his automobile are caused by a collision.

Correct: All drivers of leased automobiles are billed $100 if damages to their automobiles are caused by collisions.

Incorrect: A manager has only yourself to blame if things go wrong.

Correct: As a manager, you have only yourself to blame if things go wrong.

The following words require a singular pronoun:

everybody	neither
each	nobody
either	a person
everyone	

Correct: Everyone should bring his or her copy of the manual to the next session on changes in the law.

If the pronoun pairs necessary to avoid sexism seem cumbersome, avoid the terms in this list. Instead, use words that take plural pronouns or use second-person *you.*

Each pronoun must refer to a specific word. If a pronoun does not refer to a specific term, add a word to correct the error.

Incorrect: We will open three new stores in the suburbs. This will bring us closer to our customers.

Correct: We will open three new stores in the suburbs. This strategy will bring us closer to our customers.

Hint: Make sure *this* and *it* refer to a specific noun in the previous sentence. If either refers to an idea, add a noun ("this strategy") to make the sentence grammatically correct.

Use *who* and *whom* to refer to people and *which* to refer to objects. *That* can refer to anything: people, animals, organizations, and objects.

Correct: The new Executive Director, who moved here from Boston, is already making friends.

Correct: The information which she wants will be available tomorrow.

Correct: This confirms the price that I quoted you this morning.

Case

Case refers to the grammatical role a noun or pronoun plays in a sentence. Figure B.1 identifies the case of each personal pronoun.

Use **nominative case** pronouns for the subject of a clause.

Correct: Shannon Weaver and I talked to the customer, who was interested in learning more about integrated software.

Use **possessive case** pronouns to show who or what something belongs to.

Correct: Microsoft Office will exactly meet her needs.

Use **objective case** pronouns as objects of verbs or prepositions.

Correct: When you send in the quote, thank her for the courtesy she showed Shannon and me.

Hint: Use *whom* when *him* would fit grammatically in the same place in your sentence.

| FIGURE B.1 | The Case of the Personal Pronoun |

	Nominative (subject of clause)	Possessive	Objective	Reflexive/intensive
Singular				
1st person	I	my, mine	me	myself
2nd person	you	your, yours	you	yourself
3rd person	he/she/it	his/her(s)/its	him/her/it	himself/herself/itself
	one/who	one's/whose	one/whom	oneself/(no form)
Plural				
1st person	we	our, ours	us	ourselves
2nd person	you	your, yours	you	yourselves
3rd person	they	their, theirs	them	themselves

I am writing this letter to (who/whom?) it may concern.
I am writing this letter to him.
Whom is correct.

Have we decided (who, whom?) will take notes?
Have we decided he will take notes?
Who is correct.

Use **reflexive** and **intensive case** pronouns to refer to or emphasize a noun or pronoun that has already appeared in the sentence.

Correct: I myself think the call was a very productive one.

Do not use reflexive pronouns as subjects of clauses or as objects of verbs or propositions.

Incorrect: Elaine and myself will follow up on this order.
Correct: Elaine and I will follow up on this order.

Incorrect: He gave the order to Dan and myself.
Correct: He gave the order to Dan and me.

Note that the first-person pronoun comes after names or pronouns that refer to other people.

Dangling Modifier

A **modifier** is a word or phrase that gives more information about the subject, verb, or object in a clause. A **dangling modifier** refers to a word that is not actually in the sentence. The solution is to reword the modifier so that it is grammatically correct.

Incorrect: Confirming our conversation, the truck will leave Monday. [The speaker is doing the confirming. But the speaker isn't in the sentence.]

Incorrect: At the age of eight, I began teaching my children about American business.
[This sentence says that the author was eight when he or she had children who could understand business.]

Anguished English*

Richard Lederer recorded the following howlers:

- CEMETERY ALLOWS PEOPLE TO BE BURIED BY THEIR PETS.
- KICKING BABY CONSIDERED TO BE HEALTHY
- DIRECTOR OF TRUMAN LIBRARY KNOWS NEWSMAN'S PROBLEMS—HE WAS ONE.
- MAN FOUND BEATEN, ROBBED BY POLICE

*Quoted from Richard Lederer, *More Anguished English* (New York: Delacorte Press, 1993), 166–67.

Correct a dangling modifier in one of these ways:

- Recast the modifier as a subordinate clause.

  Correct: As I told you, the truck will leave Monday.

  Correct: When they were eight, I began teaching my children about American business.

- Revise the main clause so its subject or object can be modified by the now-dangling phrase.

  Correct: Confirming our conversation, I have scheduled the truck to leave Monday.

  Correct: At the age of eight, my children began learning about American business.

Hint: Whenever you use a verb or adjective that ends in *-ing*, make sure it modifies the grammatical subject of your sentence. If it doesn't, reword the sentence.

Misplaced Modifier

A **misplaced modifier** appears to modify another element of the sentence than the writer intended.

  Incorrect: Customers who complain often alert us to changes we need to make. [Does the sentence mean that customers must complain frequently to teach us something? Or is the meaning that frequently we learn from complaints?]

Correct a misplaced modifier by moving it closer to the word it modifies or by adding punctuation to clarify your meaning. If a modifier modifies the whole sentence, use it as an introductory phrase or clause; follow it with a comma.

  Correct: Often, customers who complain alert us to changes we need to make.

Parallel Structure

Items in a series or list must have the same grammatical structure.

  Not parallel: In the second month of your internship, you will
  1. Learn how to resolve customers' complaints.
  2. Supervision of desk staff.
  3. Interns will help plan store displays.

  Parallel: In the second month of your internship, you will
  1. Learn how to resolve customers' complaints.
  2. Supervise desk staff.
  3. Plan store displays.

  Also parallel: Duties in the second month of your internship include resolving customers' complaints, supervising desk staff, and planning store displays.

Hint: When you have two or three items in a list (whether the list is horizontal or vertical) make sure the items are in the same grammatical form. Put lists vertically to make them easier to see.

Predication Errors

The predicate of a sentence must fit grammatically and logically with the subject.

In sentences using *is* and other linking verbs, the complement must be a noun, an adjective, or a noun clause.

FIGURE B.2   What Punctuation Tells the Reader

Mark	Tells the reader
Period	We're stopping.
Semicolon	What comes next is closely related to what I just said.
Colon	What comes next is an example of what I just said.
Dash	What comes next is a dramatic example of or a shift from what I just said.
Comma	What comes next is a slight turn, but we're going in the same basic direction.

What Bothers Your Boss?

Most bosses care deeply about only a few points of grammar. Find out which errors are your supervisor's pet peeves, and avoid them.

Any living language changes. New usages appear first in speaking. Here are four issues on which experts currently disagree:

1. Plural pronouns to refer to *everybody, everyone,* and *each.* Standard grammar says these words require singular pronouns.

2. Split infinitives. An infinitive is the form of a verb that contains *to: to understand.* An infinitive is **split** when another word separates the *to* from the rest of an infinitive: *to easily understand.*

3. *Hopefully* to mean *I hope that. Hopefully* means "in a hopeful manner." However, a speaker who says "Hopefully, the rain will stop" is talking about the speaker's hope, not the rain's.

4. *Verbal* to mean *oral. Verbal* means "using words." Both writing and speaking are verbal communication. Nonverbal communication (for example, body language) does not use words.

Ask your instructor and your boss whether they are willing to accept the less formal usage. When you write to someone you don't know, use standard grammar and usage.

Incorrect: The reason for this change is because the SEC now requires fuller disclosure.

Correct: The reason for this change is that the SEC now requires fuller disclosure.

Make sure that the verb describes the action done by or done to the subject.

Incorrect: Our goals should begin immediately.

Correct: Implementing our goals should begin immediately.

Understanding Punctuation

Punctuation marks are road signs to help readers predict what comes next. (See Figure B.2.)

When you move from the subject to the verb, you're going in a straight line; no comma is needed. When you end an introductory phrase or clause, the comma tells readers the introduction is over and you're turning to the main clause. When words interrupt the main clause, like this, commas tell the reader when to turn off the main clause for a short side route and when to return.

Some people have been told to put commas where they'd take breaths. That's bad advice. How often you'd take a breath depends on how big your lung capacity is, how fast and how loud you're speaking, and the emphasis you want. Commas aren't breaths. Instead, like other punctuation, they're road signs.

Punctuating Sentences

A sentence contains at least one main clause. A **main** or **independent clause** is a complete statement. A **subordinate** or **dependent clause** contains both a subject and verb but is not a complete statement and cannot stand by itself. A phrase is a group of words that does not contain both a subject and a verb.

Main clauses
    Your order will arrive Thursday.
    He dreaded talking to his supplier.
    I plan to enroll for summer school classes.
Subordinate clauses
    if you place your order by Monday
    because he was afraid the product would be out of stock
    since I want to graduate next spring
Phrases
    With our current schedule
    As a result
    After talking to my advisor

The Most Common Errors in First-Year Composition Papers*

A survey of hundreds of student papers found that the following errors were most common:

1. No comma after introductory element
2. Vague pronoun reference
3. No comma in compound sentence
4. Wrong word
5. No comma in nonrestrictive clause
6. Wrong/missing inflected endings
7. Wrong or missing preposition
8. Comma splice
9. Possessive apostrophe error
10. Tense shift
11. Unnecessary shift in person
12. Sentence fragment
13. Wrong tense or verb form
14. Subject–verb agreement error
15. Lack of comma in series
16. Pronoun agreement error
17. Unnecessary comma with restrictive clause
18. Run-on or fused sentence
19. Dangling or misplaced modifier
20. Its/it's error

*Based on Robert J. Connors and Andrea A. Lunsford, "Frequency of Formal Errors in Current College Writing, or Ma and Pa Kettle Do Research," *College Composition and Communication* 39, no. 4 (December 1988), 403.

A clause with one of the following words will be subordinate:

after
although, though
because, since
before, until
if
when, whenever
while, as

Using the correct punctuation will enable you to avoid three major sentence errors: comma splices, run-on sentences, and sentence fragments.

Comma Splices

A **comma splice** or **comma fault** occurs when two main clauses are joined only by a comma (instead of by a comma and a coordinating conjunction).

Incorrect: The contest will start in June, the date has not been set.

Correct a comma splice in one of the following ways:

- If the ideas are closely related, use a semicolon rather than a comma. If they aren't closely related, start a new sentence.

    Correct: The contest will start in June; the exact date has not been set.

- Add a coordinating conjunction.

    Correct: The contest will start in June, but the exact date has not been set.

- Subordinate one of the clauses.

    Correct: Although the contest will start in June, the exact date has not been set.

Remember that you cannot use just a comma with the following transitions:

however
therefore
nevertheless
moreover

Instead, either use a semicolon to separate the clauses or start a new sentence.

Incorrect: Computerized grammar checkers do not catch every error, however, they may be useful as a first check before an editor reads the material.

Correct: Computerized grammar checkers do not catch every error. However, they may be useful as a first check before an editor reads the material.

Run-on Sentences

A **run-on sentence** strings together several main clauses using *and, but, or, so,* and *for.* Run-on sentences and comma splices are "mirror faults." A comma splice uses *only* the comma and omits the coordinating conjunction, while a run-on sentence uses *only* the conjunction and omits the comma. Correct a short run-on sentence by adding a comma. Separate a long run-on sentence into two or more sentences. Consider subordinating one or more of the clauses.

Incorrect: We will end up with a much smaller markup but they use a lot of this material so the volume would be high so try to sell them on fast delivery and tell them our quality is very high.

Correct: Although we will end up with a much smaller markup, volume would be high since they use a lot of this material. Try to sell them on fast delivery and high quality.

Fused Sentences

A **fused sentence** results when two sentences or more are *fused*, or joined with neither punctuation nor conjunctions. To fix the error, add the punctuation, add a conjunction, or subordinate one of the clauses.

Incorrect: The advantages of Intranets are clear the challenge is persuading employees to share information.

Correct: The advantages of Intranets are clear; the challenge is persuading employees to share information.

Also correct: Although the advantages of Intranets are clear, the challenge is persuading employees to share information.

Sentence Fragments

In a **sentence fragment,** a group of words that is not a complete sentence is punctuated as if it were a complete sentence.

Incorrect: Observing these people, I have learned two things about the program. The time it takes. The rewards it brings.

To fix a sentence fragment, either add whatever parts of the sentence are missing or incorporate the fragment into the sentence before it or after it.

Correct: Observing these people, I have learned that the program is time-consuming but rewarding.

Remember that clauses with the following words are not complete sentences. Join them to a main clause.

after
although, though
because, since
before, until
if
when, whenever
while, as

Incorrect: We need to buy a new computer system. Because our current system is obsolete.

Correct: We need to buy a new computer system because our current system is obsolete.

Punctuation within Sentences

The good business and administrative writer knows how to use the following punctuation marks: apostrophes, colons, commas, dashes, hyphens, parentheses, periods, and semicolons.

Apostrophe

1. Use an apostrophe in a contraction to indicate that a letter has been omitted.

    We're trying to renegotiate the contract.

    The '90s were years of restructuring for our company.

The Fumblerules of Grammar*

1.   Avoid run-on sentences they are hard to read.
2.   A writer must not shift your point of view.
3.   Verbs has to agree with their subjects.
4.   No sentence fragments.
5.   Reserve the apostrophe for it's proper use and omit it when its not needed.
6.   Proofread carefully to see if you any words out.
7.   Avoid commas, that are unnecessary.
8.   Steer clear of incorrect forms of verbs that have snuck in the language.
9.   In statements involving two word phrases make an all out effort to use hyphens.
10. Last but not least, avoid clichés like the plague; seek viable alternatives.

*Quoted from William Safire, "On Language: The Fumblerules of Grammar," *New York Times Magazine*, November 11, 1979, 16, and "On Language: Fumblerule Follow-up," *New York Times Magazine*, November 25, 1979, 14.

The History of Punctuation*

WHENWRITINGBEGANTHERE
WERENOBREAKSBETWEEN
WORDS

In inscriptions on monuments in ancient Greece, breaks were chosen to create balance and proportion.

WHENWRITI
NGBEGANTH
EREWERENO
BREAKSBET
WEENWORDS

In the third century BC, Aristophanes added a dot high in the line (like this ˙), after a complete thought, or *periodos*. For part of a complete thought, or *colon*, he used a dot on the line (like this ●). For a comma, or subdivision of a colon, he used a dot halfway up (like this ●).

The monks in the Middle Ages substituted a strong slash for the midway dot. As time went on, the strong slash was shortened and acquired a curl—becoming our comma today.

*Based on Lionel Casson, "howandwhy punctuationevercametobeinvented," *Smithsonian* 19, no. 7 (October 1988), 216.

2.   To indicate possession, add an apostrophe and an *s* to the word.

The corporation's home office is in Houston, Texas.

Apostrophes to indicate possession are especially essential when one noun in a comparison is omitted.

This year's sales will be higher than last year's.

When a word already ends in an *s,* add only an apostrophe to make it possessive.

The meeting will be held at New Orleans' convention center.

With many terms, the placement of the apostrophe indicates whether the noun is singular or plural.

Incorrect: The program should increase the participant's knowledge. [Implies that only one participant is in the program.]

Correct: The program should increase the participants' knowledge. [Many participants are in the program.]

Hint: Use "of" in the sentence to see where the apostrophe goes.

The figures of last year = last year's figures

The needs of our customers = our customers' needs

Note that possessive pronouns (e.g., *his, ours*) usually do not have apostrophes. The only exception is *one's.*

The company needs the goodwill of its stockholders.

His promotion was announced yesterday.

One's greatest asset is the willingness to work hard.

3.   Use an apostrophe to make plurals that could be confused for other words.

I earned A's in all my business courses.

However, other plurals do not use apostrophes.

Colon

1.   Use a colon to separate a main clause and a list that explains the last element in the clause. The items in the list are specific examples of the word that appears immediately before the colon.

Please order the following supplies:

Printer cartridges

Computer paper (20-lb. white bond)

Bond paper (25-lb., white, 25% cotton)

Company letterhead

Company envelopes

When the list is presented vertically, capitalize the first letter of each item in the list. When the list is run in with the sentence, you don't need to capitalize the first letter after the colon.

Please order the following supplies: printer cartridges, computer paper (20-lb. white bond), bond paper (25-lb., white, 25% cotton), company letterhead, and company envelopes.

Do not use a colon when the list is grammatically part of the main clause.

Incorrect:	The rooms will have coordinated decors in natural colors such as: eggplant, moss, and mushroom.
Correct:	The rooms will have coordinated decors in natural colors such as eggplant, moss, and mushroom.
Also Correct:	The rooms will have coordinated decors in a variety of natural colors: eggplant, moss, and mushroom.

If the list is presented vertically, some authorities suggest introducing the list with a colon even though the words preceding the colon are not a complete sentence.

2. Use a colon to join two independent clauses when the second clause explains or restates the first clause.

Selling is simple: give people the service they need, and they'll come back with more orders.

Comma

1. Use commas to separate the main clause from an introductory clause, the reader's name, or words that interrupt the main clause. Note that commas both precede and follow the interrupting information.

R. J. Garcia, the new Sales Manager, comes to us from the Des Moines office.

A **nonessential clause** gives extra information that is not needed to identify the noun it modifies. Because nonessential clauses give extra information, they need extra commas.

Sue Decker, who wants to advance in the organization, has signed up for the company training program in sales techniques.

Do not use commas to set off information that restricts the meaning of a noun or pronoun. **Essential clauses** give essential, not extra, information.

Anyone ☐ who wants to advance in the organization ☐ should take advantage of on-the-job training.

Do not use commas to separate the subject from the verb, even if you would take a breath after a long subject.

Incorrect:	Laws requiring anyone collecting $5,000 or more on behalf of another person, apply to schools and private individuals as well to charitable groups and professional fund-raisers.
Correct:	Laws requiring anyone collecting $5,000 or more on behalf of another person ☐ apply to schools and private individuals as well to charitable groups and professional fund-raisers.

2. Use a comma after the first clause in a compound sentence if the clauses are long or if they have different subjects.

This policy eliminates all sick-leave credit of the employee at the time of retirement, and payment will be made only once to any individual.

Do not use commas to join independent clauses without a conjunction. Doing so produces comma splices.

3. Use commas to separate items in a series. Using a comma before the *and* or *or* is not required by some authorities, but using a comma always adds

---

Dashed Hopes*

To make up after a fight with his wife, a man ordered flowers for her and asked the florist to enclose a card saying "I'm sorry—I love you." However, he failed to dictate the punctuation, and the gesture went awry. The flowers arrived with a card reading "I'm sorry I love you."

*Based on Mark S. Maurer, "Life in These United States," *Reader's Digest,* January 1998, 86.

Spell Checkers' Errors*

The *Dallas Morning News* raised hackles in the computer industry . . . when an editor accidentally accepted all of a spell-checker's alternate spellings in a technology article that appeared in print— changing chip maker Intel into "Until" and Microsoft into "Microvolts."

*Quoted from Joan E. Rigdon, "Microsoft Word's Spell-Checker Gets Failing Grade in Computerese," *The Wall Street Journal*, November 15, 1995, B1.

clarity. The comma is essential if any of the items in the series themselves contain the word *and.*

The company pays the full cost of hospitalization insurance for eligible employees, spouses, and unmarried dependent children under age 23.

Dash

Use dashes to emphasize a break in thought.

Ryertex comes in 30 grades—each with a special use.

To type a dash, use two hyphens with no space before or after.

Hyphen

1. Use a hyphen to indicate that a word has been divided between two lines.

   Attach the original receipts for lodging, meals, tips, transportation, and registration fees.

   Divide words at syllable breaks. If you aren't sure where the syllables divide, look up the word in a dictionary. When a word has several syllables, divide it after a vowel or between two consonants. Don't divide words of one syllable (e.g., *used*); don't divide a two-syllable word if one of the syllables is only one letter long (e.g., *acre*).

2. Use hyphens to join two or more words used as a single adjective.

   Order five 10- or 12-foot lengths.

   The computer-prepared Income and Expense statements will be ready next Friday.

   The hyphen prevents misreading. In the first example, five lengths are needed, not lengths of 5, 10, or 12 feet. In the second example, without the hyphen, the reader might think that *computer* was the subject and *prepared* was the verb.

Parentheses

1. Use parentheses to set off words, phrases, or sentences used to explain or comment on the main idea.

   For the thinnest Ryertex (.015″) only a single layer of the base material may be used, while the thickest (10″) may contain over 600 greatly compressed layers of fabric or paper. By varying the fabric used (cotton, asbestos, glass, or nylon) or the type of paper, and by changing the kind of resin (phenolic, melamine, silicone, or epoxy), we can produce 30 different grades.

   Any additional punctuation goes outside the second parenthesis when the punctuation applies to the whole sentence. It goes inside when it applies only to the words in the parentheses.

   Please check the invoice to see if credit should be issued. (A copy of the invoice is attached.)

2. Use parentheses for the second of two numbers presented both in words and in figures.

   Construction must be completed within two (2) years of the date of the contract.

Period

1. Use a period at the end of a sentence. Leave two spaces before the next sentence.

2. Use a period after some abbreviations. When a period replaces a person's name, leave one space after the period before the next word. In other abbreviations, no space is necessary.

R. J. Tebeaux has been named Vice President for Marketing.

The U.S. division plans to hire 300 new M.B.A.s in the next year.

The tendency is to reduce the use of punctuation. It would also be correct to write

The US division plans to hire 300 new MBAs in the next year.

Semicolon

1. Use semicolons to join two independent clauses when they are closely related.

We'll do our best to fill your order promptly; however, we cannot guarantee a delivery date.

Using a semicolon suggests that the two ideas are very closely connected. Using a period and a new sentence is also correct but implies nothing about how closely related the two sentences are.

2. Use semicolons to separate items in a series when the items themselves contain commas.

The final choices for the new plant are El Paso, Texas; Albuquerque, New Mexico; Salt Lake City, Utah; Eureka, California; and Eugene, Oregon.

Hospital benefits are also provided for certain specialized care services such as diagnostic admissions directed toward a definite disease or injury; normal maternity delivery, Caesarean section delivery, or complications of pregnancy; and in-patient admissions for dental procedures necessary to safeguard the patient's life or health.

Hint: A semicolon could be replaced by a period and a capital letter. It has a sentence on both sides.

Special Punctuation Marks

Quotation marks, square brackets, ellipses, and underlining are necessary when you use quoted material.

Quotation Marks

1. Use quotation marks around the names of brochures, pamphlets, and magazine articles.

Enclosed are 30 copies of our pamphlet "Saving Energy."

You'll find articles like "How to Improve Your Golf Game" and "Can You Keep Your Eye on the Ball?" in every issue.

In US punctuation, periods and commas go inside quotation marks. Colons and semicolons go outside. Question marks go inside if they are part of the material being quoted.

2. Use quotation marks around words to indicate that you think the term is misleading.

These "pro-business" policies actually increase corporate taxes.

3. Use quotation marks around words that you are discussing as words.

International Punctuation*

Preferences in punctuation differ among cultures. US writers use exclamation points rarely and only one at a time: *Attention!* German writers use exclamation points more often and use them in multiples: *Attention!!!!!!!* US writers tend to use more commas than do writers in French, Spanish, Italian, and Portuguese.

Even when use is the same, the form of punctuation marks can differ. US quotation marks are like raised commas ("material quoted"). In contrast, French and Danish use double angle brackets, though of different kinds. The French use brackets that point away from the quote («material quoted»), while the Danish use brackets that point toward the quote (»material quoted«).

Translating material from one language to another requires translating the punctuation as well as the words.

*Based on Kirk R. St. Amant, "Problematic Punctuation," *Intercom,* November 1998, 40–41.

Forty percent of the respondents answered "yes" to the first question.

Use "Ms." as a courtesy title for a woman unless you know she prefers another title.

It is also acceptable to italicize words instead of using quotation marks.

4. Use quotation marks around words or sentences that you quote from someone else.

"The Fog Index," says its inventor, Robert Gunning, is "an effective warning system against drifting into needless complexity."

Square Brackets

Use square brackets to add your own additions to or changes in quoted material.

Senator Smith's statement:	"These measures will create a deficit."
Your use of Smith's statement:	According to Senator Smith, "These measures [in the new tax bill] will create a deficit."

The square brackets show that Smith did not say these words; you add them to make the quote make sense in your document.

Ellipses

Ellipses are spaced dots. In typing, use three spaced periods for an ellipsis. When an ellipsis comes at the end of a sentence, use a dot immediately after the last letter of the sentence for a period. Then add three spaced dots, with another space after the last dot.

1. Use ellipses to indicate that one or more words have been omitted in the middle of quoted material. You do not need ellipses at the beginning or end of a quote.

The Wall Street Journal notes that Japanese magazines and newspapers include advertisements for a "$2.1 million home in New York's posh Riverdale section . . . 185 acres of farmland [and] . . . luxury condos on Manhattan's Upper East Side."

2. In advertising and direct mail, use ellipses to imply the pace of spoken comments.

If you've ever wanted to live on a tropical island . . . cruise to the Bahamas . . . or live in a castle in Spain . . .

. . . you can make your dreams come true with Vacations Extraordinaire.

Underlining and Italics

1. Underline or italicize the names of newspapers, magazines, and books.

The Wall Street Journal	The Wall Street Journal
Fortune	Fortune
The Wealth of Nations	The Wealth of Nations

Titles of brochures and pamphlets are put in quotation marks.

2. Underline or italicize words to emphasize them.

Here's a bulletin that gives you, in handy chart form, workable data on over 50 different types of tubing and pipe.

You may also use bold to emphasize words. Bold type is better than either underlining or italics because it is easier to read. (See Chapter 6.)

Writing Numbers and Dates

Spell out **numbers** from one to nine. Use figures for numbers 10 and over in most cases. Always use figures for amounts of money.

Spell out any number that appears at the beginning of a sentence. If spelling it out is impractical, revise the sentence so that it does not begin with a number.

Fifty students filled out the survey.

In 2002, euro notes and coins entered circulation.

When two numbers follow each other, spell out the smaller number and use figures for the larger number.

In **dates,** use figures for the day and year. The month is normally spelled out. Be sure to spell out the month in international business communication. American usage puts the month first, so that *1/10/03* means *January 10, 2003.* European usage puts the day first, so that *1/10/03* means *October 1, 2003.* Modern punctuation uses a comma before the year only when you give both the month and the day of the month:

May 1, 2006

but

Summers 2001–04

August 2004

Fall 2005

No punctuation is needed in military or European usage, which puts the day of the month first: 13 July 2003. Do not space before or after the slash used to separate parts of the date: 10/03-5/04.

Use a hyphen to join inclusive dates.

March-August 2005 (or write out: March to August 2005)

'03-'04

1999-2001

Note that you do not need to repeat the century in the date that follows the hyphen: 2003-04.

Words That Are Often Confused

Here's a list of words that are frequently confused. Master them, and you'll be well on the way to using words correctly.

1. accede/exceed
    accede: to yield
    exceed: to go beyond, surpass
       I accede to your demand that we not exceed the budget.
2. accept/except
    accept: to receive
    except: to leave out or exclude; but
       I accept your proposal except for point 3.
3. access/excess
    access: the right to use; admission to
    excess: surplus
       As supply clerk, he had access to any excess materials.

More Anguished English*

- Family Physician. Hours: 10:30-12:20; 3:30-4:45 Monday-Friday. 10:30-11:45 Saturday. Limited Amount of Patience.

- Aunt and Roach Killer— 1.29.

- He is recovering from a near-fatal accident that sent him into a comma.

- The board voted by telephone pole.

- I found a liter of pups.

*Quoted from Richard Lederer, *More Anguished English* (New York: Delacorte Press, 1993), 166–67.

4. adept/adopt

    adept: skilled

    adopt: to take as one's own

    > She was adept at getting people to adopt her ideas.

5. advice/advise

    advice: (noun) counsel

    advise: (verb) to give counsel or advice to someone

    > I asked him to advise me, but I didn't like the advice I got.

6. affect/effect

    affect: (verb) to influence or modify

    effect: (verb) to produce or cause; (noun) result

    > He hoped that his argument would affect his boss's decision, but so far as he could see, it had no effect.

    > The tax relief effected some improvement for the citizens whose incomes had been affected by inflation.

7. affluent/effluent

    affluent: (adjective) rich, possessing in abundance

    effluent: (noun) something that flows out

    > Affluent companies can afford the cost of removing pollutants from the effluents their factories produce.

8. a lot/allot

    a lot: many (informal)

    allot: divide or give to

    > A lot of players signed up for this year's draft. We allotted one first-round draft choice to each team.

9. amount/number

    amount: (use with concepts that cannot be counted individually but can only be measured)

    number: (use when items can be counted individually)

    > It's a mistake to try to gauge the amount of interest he has by the number of questions he asks.

10. are/our

    are: (plural linking verb)

    our: belonging to us

    > Are we ready to go ahead with our proposal?

11. attributed/contributed

    attributed: was said to be caused by

    contributed: gave something to

    > The rain probably contributed to the accident, but the police officer attributed the accident to driver error.

12. between/among

    between: (use with only two choices)

    among: (use with more than two choices)

    > This year the differences between the two candidates for president are unusually clear.

    > I don't see any major differences among the candidates for city council.

13. cite/sight/site

    cite: (verb) to quote

    sight: (noun) vision, something to be seen

    site: (noun) location, place where a building is or will be built

    > She cited the old story of the building inspector who was depressed by the very sight of the site for the new factory.

14. complement/compliment

    complement: (verb) to complete, finish; (noun) something that completes

    compliment: (verb) to praise; (noun) praise

    > The compliment she gave me complemented my happiness.

15. compose/comprise

    compose: make up, create

    comprise: consist of, be made up of, be composed of

    > The city council is composed of 12 members. Each district comprises an area 50 blocks square.

16. confuse/complicate/exacerbate

    confuse: to bewilder

    complicate: to make more complex or detailed

    exacerbate: to make worse

    > Because I missed the first 20 minutes of the movie, I didn't understand what was going on. The complicated plot exacerbated my confusion.

17. dependant/dependent

    dependant: (noun) someone for whom one is financially responsible

    dependent: (adjective) relying on someone else

    > IRS regulations don't let us count our 25-year-old son as a dependant, but he is still financially dependent on us.

18. describe/prescribe

    describe: list the features of something, tell what something looks like

    prescribe: specify the features something must contain

    > The law prescribes the priorities for making repairs. This report describes our plans to comply with the law.

19. discreet/discrete

    discreet: tactful, careful not to reveal secrets

    discrete: separate, distinct

    > I have known him to be discreet on two discrete occasions.

20. do/due

    do: (verb) act or make

    due: (adjective) scheduled, caused by

    The banker said she would do her best to change the due date.

    > Due to the computer system, the payroll can be produced in only two days for all 453 employees.

21. elicit/illicit

    elicit: (verb) to draw out

    illicit: (adjective) not permitted, unlawful

    > The reporter could elicit no information from the senator about his illicit love affair.

The Knead for Approve Reed Her with a Spell Chequer*

Who wood have guest
The Spell Chequer would super seed
The assent of the editor
Who was once a mane figure? . . .
Once, awl sought his council;
Now nun prophet from him.
How suite the job was;
It was all sew fine. . . .
Never once was he board
As he edited each claws,
Going strait to his deer work
Where he'd in cyst on clarity.
Now he's holy unacceptable,
Useless and knot kneaded. . . .
This is know miner issue,
Fore he cannot urn a wage.
Two this he takes a fence,
Butt nose naught watt too due.
He's wade each option
Of jobs he mite dew,
But nothing peaks his interest
Like making pros clear.
Sum will see him silly
For being sew upset,
But doesn't good righting
Go beyond the write spelling?

*Quoted from Jeff Lovill, "On the Uselessness of an Editor in the Presents of a Spell Chequer," *Technical Communication* 35, no. 4 (1988), 267; and Edward M. Chilton, "Various Comments on 4Q88," *Technical Communication* 36, no. 2 (1989), 173.

22. eminent/immanent/imminent

    eminent: distinguished

    immanent: dwelling within tangible objects

    imminent: about to happen

    > The eminent doctor believed that death was imminent. The eminent minister believed that God was immanent.

23. fewer/less

    fewer: (use for objects that can be counted individually)

    less: (use for objects that can be measured but not counted individually)

    > There is less sand in this bucket; there are probably fewer grains of sand, too.

24. forward/foreword

    forward: ahead

    foreword: preface, introduction

    > The author looked forward to writing the foreword to the book.

25. good/well

    good: (adjective, used to modify nouns; as a noun, means something that is good)

    well: (adverb, used to modify verbs, adjectives, and other adverbs)

    > Her words "Good work!" told him that he was doing well.

    > He spent a great deal of time doing volunteer work because he believed that doing good was just as important as doing well.

26. i.e./e.g.

    i.e.: (*id est*—that is) introduces a restatement or explanation of the preceding word or phrase

    e.g.: (*exempli gratia*—for the sake of an example; for example) introduces one or more examples

    > Although he had never studied Latin, he rarely made a mistake in using Latin abbreviations, e.g., i.e., and etc. because he associated each with a mnemonic device (i.e., a word or image used to help one remember something). He remembered *i.e.* as *in effect*, pretended that *e.g.* meant *example given*, and used *etc.* only when *examples to continue* would fit.

27. imply/infer

    imply: suggest, put an idea into someone's head

    infer: deduce, get an idea out from something

    > She implied that an announcement would be made soon. I inferred from her smile that it would be an announcement of her promotion.

28. it's/its

    it's: it is, it has

    its: belonging to it

    > It's clear that a company must satisfy its customers to stay in business.

29. lectern/podium

    lectern: raised stand with a slanted top that holds a manuscript for a reader or notes for a speaker

    podium: platform for a speaker or conductor to stand on

    > I left my notes on the lectern when I left the podium at the end of my talk.

30. lie/lay

    lie: to recline; to tell a falsehood (never takes an object)

    lay: to put an object on something (always takes an object)

    > He was laying the papers on the desk when I came in, but they aren't lying there now.

31. loose/lose

    loose: not tight

    lose: to have something disappear

    > If I lose weight, this suit will be loose.

32. moral/morale

    moral: (adjective) virtuous, good; (noun: morals) ethics, sense of right and wrong

    morale: (noun) spirit, attitude, mental outlook

    > Studies have shown that coed dormitories improve student morale without harming student morals.

33. objective/rationale

    objective: goal

    rationale: reason, justification

    > The objective of the meeting was to explain the rationale behind the decision.

34. personal/personnel

    personal: individual, to be used by one person

    personnel: staff, employees

    > All personnel will get personal computers by the end of the year.

35. possible/possibly

    possible: (adjective) something that can be done

    possibly: (adverb) perhaps

    > It is possible that we will be able to hire this spring. We can choose from possibly the best graduating class in the past five years.

36. precede/proceed

    precede: (verb) to go before

    proceed: (verb) to continue; (noun: proceeds) money

    > Raising the money must precede spending it. Only after we obtain the funds can we proceed to spend the proceeds.

37. principal/principle

    principal: (adjective) main; (noun) person in charge; money lent out at interest

    principle: (noun) basic truth or rule, code of conduct

    > *The Prince*, Machiavelli's principal work, describes his principles for ruling a state.

38. quiet/quite

    quiet: not noisy

    quite: very

    > It was quite difficult to find a quiet spot anywhere near the floor of the stock exchange.

The Limits of Spell Checkers*

Treat a spell checker's recommendations with skepticism. Spell checkers can spot obvious errors such as reversed or omitted letters, but their ability to spot other problems is fairly primitive; many still don't recognize plural forms of words. . . . No spell checker can detect the difference between *their* and *there*, *which* and *witch*, or *watches* (several time pieces) and *watch's* (the possessive form).

They also miss the following:

- incorrect word usage, such as *anaesthetic* (numbing) for *unaesthetic* (unpleasing)

- homonymns and other sound-alikes (e.g., *o'er*, *or*, and *ore*), including phonetic misspellings

- added letters that create legitimate but incorrect words (e.g., when *the* becomes *then*)

- letter swaps that produce correctly spelled words that don't fit the context (e.g., replacing *type* with *typo*).

*Quoted from Geoffrey J. S. Hart, "Spelling and Grammar Checkers," *Intercom*, April 2001, 40.

Spelling Demons*

The words listed below (in order of increasing difficulty) are among the most frequently misspelled words in English. How many of them do you spell correctly?

1. Grammar
2. Argument
3. Surprise
4. Achieve
5. Definitely
6. Separate
7. Desirable
8. Development
9. Existence
10. Occasion
11. Assistant
12. Repetition
13. Privilege
14. Dependent
15. Consensus
16. Accommodate
17. Occurrence
18. Commitment
19. Allotted
20. Liaison
21. Proceed
22. Harass
23. Dissention
24. Prerogative
25. Inadvertent

*Based on Bruce O. Boston, ed., *Stet!* (Alexandria, VA: Editorial Experts, 1986), 267–68.

39. regulate/relegate

regulate: control

relegate: put (usually in an inferior position)

> If the federal government regulates the size of lettering on country road signs, we may as well relegate the current signs to the garbage bin.

40. residence/residents

residence: home

residents: people who live in a building

> The residents had different reactions when they learned that a shopping mall would be built next to their residence.

41. respectfully/respectively

respectfully: with respect

respectively: to each in the order listed

> When I was introduced to the queen, the prime minister, and the court jester, I bowed respectfully, shook hands politely, and winked, respectively.

42. role/roll

role: part in a play or script, function (in a group)

roll: (noun) list of students, voters, or other members; round piece of bread; (verb) move by turning over and over

> While the teacher called the roll, George—in his role as class clown—threw a roll he had saved from lunch.

43. simple/simplistic

simple: not complicated

simplistic: watered down, oversimplified

> She was able to explain the proposal in simple terms without making the explanation sound simplistic.

44. stationary/stationery

stationary: not moving, fixed

stationery: paper

> During the earthquake, even the stationery was not stationary.

45. their/there/they're

their: belonging to them

there: in that place

they're: they are

> There are plans, designed to their specifications, for the house they're building.

46. to/too/two

to: (preposition) function word indicating proximity, purpose, time, etc.

too: (adverb) also, very, excessively

two: (adjective) the number 2

> The formula is too secret to entrust to two people.

47. unique/unusual

unique: sole, only, alone

unusual: not common

> I believed that I was unique in my ability to memorize long strings of numbers until I consulted *Guinness World Records* and found that I was merely unusual: someone else had equaled my feat in 1993.

48. verbal/oral

    verbal: using words

    oral: spoken, not written

    > His verbal skills were uneven: his oral communication was excellent, but he didn't write well. His sensitivity to nonverbal cues was acute: he could tell what kind of day I had just by looking at my face.

    Hint: Oral comes from the Latin word for mouth, *os*. Think of Oral-B Toothbrushes: for the mouth. Verbal comes from the Latin word for word, *verba*. Nonverbal language is language that does not use words (e.g., body language, gestures).

49. whether/weather

    whether: (conjunction) used to introduce possible alternatives

    weather: (noun) state of the atmosphere: wet or dry, hot or cold, calm or storm

    > We will have to see what the weather is before we decide whether to hold the picnic indoors or out.

50. your/you're

    your: belonging to you

    you're: you are

    > You're the top candidate for promotion in your division.

Proofreading Symbols

Use the proofreading symbols in Figure B.3 to make corrections when you no longer have access to a computer. Figure B.4 shows how the symbols can be used to correct a typed text.

FIGURE B.3 Proofreading Symbols

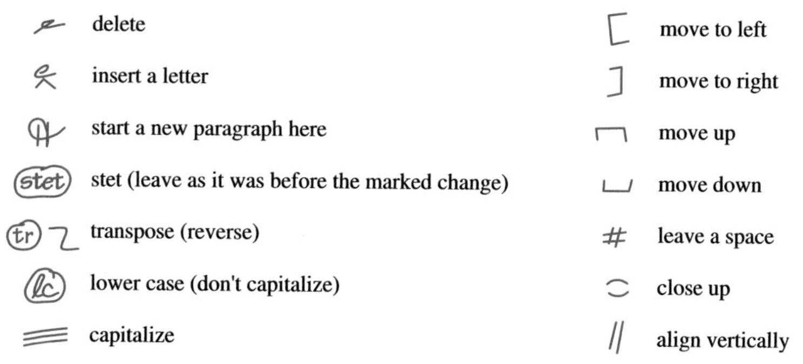

Symbol	Meaning		Symbol	Meaning
✄	delete		⌐	move to left
⤬	insert a letter		⌐	move to right
¶	start a new paragraph here		⌐	move up
(stet)	stet (leave as it was before the marked change)		⌐	move down
(tr)	transpose (reverse)		#	leave a space
(lc)	lower case (don't capitalize)		◠	close up
≡	capitalize		//	align vertically

FIGURE B.4   Marked Text

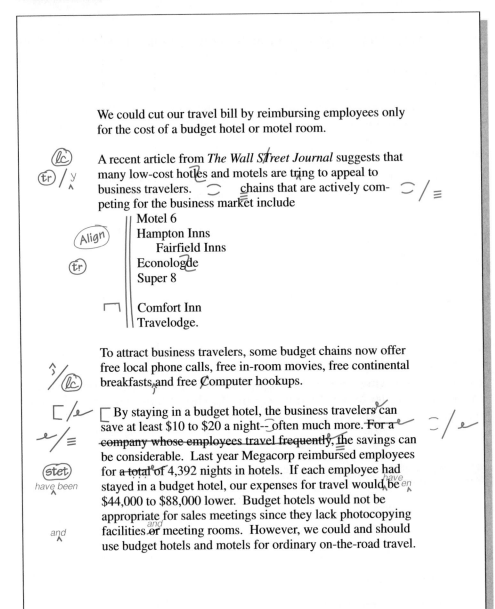

We could cut our travel bill by reimbursing employees only for the cost of a budget hotel or motel room.

A recent article from *The Wall Street Journal* suggests that many low-cost hotles and motels are tring to appeal to business travelers. chains that are actively competing for the business market include

Motel 6
Hampton Inns
Fairfield Inns
Econologde
Super 8

Comfort Inn
Travelodge.

To attract business travelers, some budget chains now offer free local phone calls, free in-room movies, free continental breakfasts, and free Computer hookups.

By staying in a budget hotel, the business travelers can save at least $10 to $20 a night--often much more. For a company whose employees travel frequently, the savings can be considerable. Last year Megacorp reimbursed employees for a total of 4,392 nights in hotels. If each employee had stayed in a budget hotel, our expenses for travel would be $44,000 to $88,000 lower. Budget hotels would not be appropriate for sales meetings since they lack photocopying facilities or meeting rooms. However, we could and should use budget hotels and motels for ordinary on-the-road travel.

APPENDIX B   Exercises and Problems

B.1   Diagnostic Test on Punctuation and Grammar

Identify and correct the errors in the following passages.

a.   Company's are finding it to their advantage to cultivate their suppliers. Partnerships between a company and it's suppliers can yield hefty payoffs for both company and supplier. One example is Bailey Controls, an Ohio headquartered company. Bailey make control systems for big factories. They treat suppliers almost like departments of their own company. When a Bailey employee passes a laser scanner over a bins bar code the supplier is instantly alerted to send more parts.

b.   Entrepreneur Trip Hawkins appears in Japanese ads for the video game system his company designed. "It plugs into the future! he says in one ad, in a cameo spliced into shots of U.S kids playing the games. Hawkins is one of several US celebrieties and business people whom plug products on Japanese TV. Jodie Foster, harrison ford, and Charlie Sheen adverstises canned coffee beer and cigarettes respectively.

c.   Mid size firms employing between 100 and 1000 peopole represent only 4% of companies in the U.S.; but create 33% of all new jobs. One observe attributes their success to their being small enough to take advantage of economic opportunity's agilely, but big enough to have access to credit and to operate on a national or even international scale. The biggest hiring area for midsize company's is wholesale and retail sales (38% of jobs), construction (20% of jobs, manufacturing (19% of jobs), and services (18 of jobs).

B.2   Providing Punctuation

Provide the necessary punctuation in the following sentences. Note that not every box requires punctuation.

1.   The system ☐ s ☐ user ☐ friendly design ☐ provides screen displays of work codes ☐ rates ☐ and client information.

2.   Many other factors also shape the organization ☐ s ☐ image ☐ advertising ☐ brochures ☐ proposals ☐ stationery ☐ calling cards ☐ etc.

3.   Charlotte Ford ☐ author of ☐ Charlotte Ford ☐ s ☐ Book of Modern Manners ☐☐ says ☐☐ Try to mention specifics of the conversation to fix the interview permanently in the interviewer ☐ s ☐ mind and be sure to mail the letter the same day ☐ before the hiring decision is made ☐☐

4.   What are your room rates and charges for food service ☐

5.   We will need accommodations for 150 people ☐ five meeting rooms ☐ one large room and four small ones ☐ ☐ coffee served during morning and afternoon breaks ☐ and lunches and dinners.

6.   The Operational Readiness Inspection ☐ which occurs once every three years ☐ is a realistic exercise ☐ which evaluates the National Guard ☐ s ☐ ability to mobilize ☐ deploy ☐ and fight.

7.   Most computer packages will calculate three different sets of percentages ☐ row percentages ☐ column percentages ☐ and table percentages ☐

8.   In today ☐ s ☐ economy ☐ it ☐ s almost impossible for a firm to extend credit beyond it ☐ s regular terms.

9.   The Department of Transportation does not have statutory authority to grant easements ☐ however ☐ we do have authority to lease unused areas of highway right ☐ of ☐ way.

10.   The program has two goals ☐ to identify employees with promise ☐ and to see that they get the training they need to advance.

B.3   Providing Punctuation

Provide the necessary punctuation in the following sentences. Note that not every box requires punctuation.

1. Office work ☐☐ especially at your desk ☐☐ can create back ☐ shoulder ☐ neck ☐ or wrist strain.
2. I searched for ☐ vacation ☐ and ☐ vacation planning ☐ on Google and Alta Vista.
3. I suggest putting a bulletin board in the rear hallway ☐ and posting all the interviewer ☐ s ☐ photos on it.
4. Analyzing audiences is the same for marketing and writing ☐ you have to identify who the audiences are ☐ understand how to motivate them ☐ and choose the best channel to reach them.
5. The more you know about your audience ☐☐ who they are ☐ what they buy ☐ where they shop ☐☐ the more relevant and effective you can make your ad.
6. The city already has five ☐ two ☐ hundred ☐ bed hospitals.
7. Students run the whole organization ☐ and are advised by a board of directors from the community.
8. The company is working on three team ☐ related issues ☐ interaction ☐ leadership ☐ and team size.
9. I would be interesting in working on the committee ☐ however ☐ I have decided to do less community work so that I have more time to spend with my family.
10. ☐ You can create you own future ☐☐ says Frank Montaño ☐☐ You have to think about it ☐ crystallize it in writing ☐ and be willing to work at it ☐ We teach a lot of goal ☐ setting and planning in our training sessions ☐☐

B.4   Creating Agreement

Revise the following sentences to correct errors in noun–pronoun and subject–verb agreement.

1. If there's any tickets left, they'll be $17 at the door.
2. A team of people from marketing, finance, and production are preparing the proposal.
3. Image type and resolution varies among clip art packages.
4. Your health and the health of your family is very important to us.
5. If a group member doesn't complete their assigned work, it slows the whole project down.
6. Baker & Baker was offended by the ad agency's sloppy proposal, and they withdrew their account from the firm.
7. The first step toward getting out of debt is not to add any more to it. This means cutting up your old credit card.
8. Contests are fun for employees and creates sales incentives.
9. The higher the position a person has, the more professional their image should be.
10. A new employee should try to read verbal and nonverbal signals to see which aspects of your job are most important.

B.5   Correcting Case Errors

Revise the following sentences to correct errors in pronoun case.

1. I didn't appreciate him assuming that he would be the group's leader.
2. Myself and Jim made the presentation.
3. Employees which lack experience in dealing with people from other cultures could benefit from seminars in international business communication.
4. Chandra drew the graphs after her and I discussed the ideas for them.
5. Please give your revisions to Cindy, Tyrone, or myself by noon Friday.

B.6   Improving Modifiers

Revise the following sentences to correct dangling and misplaced modifiers.

1. Originally a group of four, one member dropped out after the first meeting due to a death in the family.
2. Examining the data, it is apparent that most of our sales are to people on the northwest side of the city.
3. As a busy professional, we know that you will want to take advantage of this special offer.
4. Often documents end up in files that aren't especially good.
5. By making an early reservation, it will give us more time to coordinate our trucks to better serve you.

B.7   Creating Parallel Structure

Revise the following sentences to create parallel structure.

1. To narrow a Web search,
   - Put quotation marks around a phrase when you want an exact term.
   - Many search engines have wild cards (usually an asterisk) to find plurals and other forms of a word.
   - Reading the instructions on the search engine itself can teach you advanced search techniques.
2. Men drink more alcoholic beverages than women.
3. Each issue of *Hospice Care* has articles from four different perspectives: legislative, health care, hospice administrators, and inspirational authors.
4. The university is one of the largest employers in the community, brings in substantial business, and the cultural impact is also big.
5. These three tools can help competitive people be better negotiators:
   1. Think win–win
   2. It's important to ask enough questions to find out the other person's priorities, rather than jumping on the first advantage you find.
   3. Protect the other person's self-esteem.

   These three questions can help cooperative people be better negotiators:
   1. Can you developing a specific alternative to use if negotiation fails?
   2. Don't focus on the bottom line. Spend time thinking about what you want and why you need it.
   3. Saying "You'll have to do better than that because . . ." can help you resist the temptation to say "yes" too quickly.

B.8   Correcting Sentence Errors

Revise the following sentences to correct comma splices, run-on-sentences, fused sentences, and sentence fragments.

1. Members of the group are all experienced presenters, most have had little or no experience using PowerPoint.
2. Proofread the letter carefully and check for proper business format because errors undercut your ability to sell yourself so take advantage of your opportunity to make a good first impression.
3. Some documents need just one pass others need multiple revisions.
4. Videoconferencing can be frustrating. Simply because little time is available for casual conversation.
5. Entrepreneurs face two main obstacles. Limited cash. Lack of business experience.
6. The margin on pet supplies is very thin and the company can't make money selling just dog food and the real profit is in extras like neon-colored leashes, so you put the dog food in the back so people have to walk by everything else to get to it.
7. The company's profits jumped 15%. Although its revenues fell 3%.
8. The new budget will hurt small businesses it imposes extra fees it raises the interest rates small businesses must pay.
9. Our phones are constantly being used. Not just for business calls but also for personal calls.
10. Businesses are trying to cut travel costs, executives are taking fewer trips and flying out of alternate airports to save money.

B.9   Editing for Grammar and Usage

Revise the following sentences to eliminate errors in grammar and usage.

1. The number of students surveyed that worked more than 20 hours a week was 60%.
2. Not everyone is promoted after six months some people might remain in the training program a year before being moved to a permanent assignment.
3. The present solutions that has been suggested are not adequate.
4. At times while typing and editing, the text on your screen may not look correct.
5. All employees are asked to cut back on energy waste by the manager.
6. The benefits of an on-line catalog are
    1. We will be able to keep records up-to-date;
    2. Broad access to the catalog system from any networked terminal on campus;
    3. The consolidation of the main catalog and the catalogs in the departmental and branch libraries;
    4. Cost savings.
7. You can take advantage of several banking services. Such as automatic withdrawal of a house or car payment and direct deposit of your pay check.
8. As a freshman, business administration was intriguing to me.
9. Thank you for the help you gave Joanne Jackson and myself.
10. I know from my business experience that good communication among people and departments are essential in running a successful corporation.

B.10   Writing Numbers

Revise the following sentences to correct errors in writing numbers.

1. 60% percent of the respondents hope to hold internships before they graduate.
2. 1992 marked the formal beginning of the European Economic Community.
3. In the year two thousand, twenty percent of the H-1B visas for immigrants with high-tech skills went to Indians.
4. More than 70,000,000 working Americans lack an employer-sponsored retirement plan.
5. The company's sales have risen to $16 million but it lost five million dollars.

B.11   Using Plurals and Possessives

Choose the right word for each sentence.

1. Many Canadian (companies, company's) are competing effectively in the global market.
2. We can move your (families, family's) furniture safely and efficiently.
3. The (managers, manager's) ability to listen is just as important as his or her technical knowledge.
4. A (memos, memo's) style can build goodwill.
5. (Social workers, social worker's) should tell clients about services available in the community.
6. The (companies, company's) benefits plan should be checked periodically to make sure it continues to serve the needs of employees.
7. Information about the new community makes the (families, family's) move easier.
8. The (managers, manager's) all have open-door policies.
9. (Memos, memo's) are sent to other workers in the same organization.
10. Burnout affects a (social workers, social worker's) productivity as well as his or her morale.

B.12   Choosing the Right Word

Choose the right word for each sentence.

1. Exercise is (good, well) for patients who have had open-heart surgery.
2. This response is atypical, but it is not (unique, unusual).
3. The personnel department continues its (roll, role) of compiling reports for the federal government.
4. The Accounting Club expects (its, it's) members to come to meetings and participate in activities.
5. Part of the fun of any vacation is (cite, sight, site)-seeing.
6. The (lectern, podium) was too high for the short speaker.

7. The (residence, residents) of the complex have asked for more parking spaces.
8. Please order more letterhead (stationary, stationery).
9. The closing of the plant will (affect, effect) house prices in the area.
10. Better communication (among, between) design and production could enable us to produce products more efficiently.

B.13 Choosing the Right Word

Choose the right word for each sentence.
1. The audit revealed a small (amount, number) of errors.
2. Diet beverages have (fewer, less) calories than regular drinks.
3. In her speech, she (implied, inferred) that the vote would be close.
4. We need to redesign the stand so that the catalog is eye-level instead of (laying, lying) on the desk.
5. (Their, There, They're) is some evidence that (their, there, they're) thinking of changing (their, there, they're) policy.
6. The settlement isn't yet in writing; if one side wanted to back out of the (oral, verbal) agreement, it could.
7. In (affect, effect), we're creating a new department.
8. The firm will be hiring new (personal, personnel) in three departments this year.
9. Several customers have asked that we carry more campus merchandise, (i.e., e.g.,) pillows and mugs with the college seal.
10. We have investigated all of the possible solutions (accept, except) adding a turning lane.

B.14 Choosing the Right Word

Choose the right word for each sentence.
1. The author (cites, sights, sites) four reasons for computer phobia.
2. The error was (do, due) to inexperience.
3. (Your, you're) doing a good job motivating (your, you're) subordinates.
4. One of the basic (principals, principles) of business communication is "Consider the reader."
5. I (implied, inferred) from the article that interest rates would go up.
6. Working papers generally are (composed, comprised) of working trial balance, assembly sheets, adjusting entries, audit schedules, and audit memos.
7. Eliminating time clocks will improve employee (moral, morale).
8. The (principal, principle) variable is the trigger price mechanism.
9. (Its, It's) (to, too, two) soon (to, too, two) tell whether the conversion (to, too, two) computerized billing will save as much time as we hope.
10. Formal training programs (complement, compliment) on-the-job opportunities for professional growth.

B.15 Tracking Your Own Mechanical Errors

Analyze the mechanical errors (grammar, punctuation, word use, and typos) in each of your papers.
- How many different errors are marked on each paper?
- Which three errors do you make most often?
- Is the number of errors constant in each paper, or does the number increase or decrease during the term?

As Your Instructor Directs,
a. Correct each of the mechanical errors in one or more papers.
b. Deliberately write two new sentences in which you make each of your three most common errors. Then write the correct version of each sentence.
c. Write a memo to your instructor discussing your increasing mastery of mechanical correctness during the semester or quarter.
d. Briefly explain to the class how to avoid one kind of error in grammar, punctuation, or word use.

C

Making and Communicating Meaning

Communication Channels in Organizations

A Model of the Communication Process

Principles of Semantics

- Perception Involves the Perceiver as Well as What Is Perceived.
- Observations, Inferences, and Judgments Are Not the Same Thing.
- No Two Things Are Ever Exactly Alike.
- Things Change Significantly with Time.

- Most *Either–Or* Classifications Are Not Legitimate.
- A Statement Is Never the Whole Story.
- Words Are Not Identical to the Objects They Represent.
- The Symbols Used in Communication Must Stand for Essentially the Same Thing in the Minds of the Sender and the Receiver.

Summary of Key Points

Many miscommunications arise not because people genuinely disagree but because they use symbols to mean different things and make different assumptions. **Communication theory** attempts to explain what happens when we communicate. **Semantics** is the study of the way our behavior is influenced by the words and other symbols we use to communicate. (Sometimes it is called **general semantics** to distinguish it from more narrow meanings of *semantics*.) Because semantics deals with the way we perceive and process information, conflicts that "are just a matter of semantics" may be serious. Depending on the situation, it may or may not be possible to find words that everyone can endorse.

Communication theory and semantics both show why and where communication can break down. They are most useful for persuasion in difficult situations, working and writing in groups, and writing reports. This appendix suggests what we can do—as writers and speakers—to get more of our meaning across to other people and—as readers and listeners—to more accurately understand the messages that we receive.

Communication Channels in Organizations

Channels vary in speed, accuracy of transmission, cost, number of messages carried, number of people reached, efficiency, and ability to promote goodwill. Depending on the audience, your purposes, and the situation, one channel may be better than another.

Oral channels are better for group decision making, allow misunderstandings to be cleared up more quickly, and seem more personal. Shorter communication channels are more accurate than longer chains. And all-channel patterns, where everyone can communicate with everyone else, produce better group decisions and more satisfaction. Figure C.1 illustrates some of the communication channels that exist in organizations.

Managers choose channels based on their familiarity with the channel and on the situation. Lamar Reinsch and Raymond Beswick found that voice mail was the preferred channel when employees on one shift needed to communicate with those on another. Administrative, professional, and technical workers were less likely to use voice mail for complex or negative messages or for messages that needed to be documented in writing. In fact, for important messages when the cost of miscommunication was high, managers usually used two different channels, for example, talking to someone about a written memo.[1]

FIGURE C.1 Examples of Communication Patterns in Organizations

Direct channel from A to B

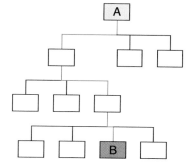

A must go through other people to get to B.

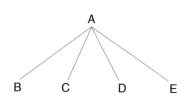

A can send messages to four people simultaneously. They must go through A to send messages to each other.

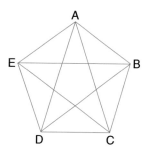

A can send messages to four people simultaneously. They can send messages directly to each other.

FIGURE C.2   A Model of Two-Person Communication with Feedback

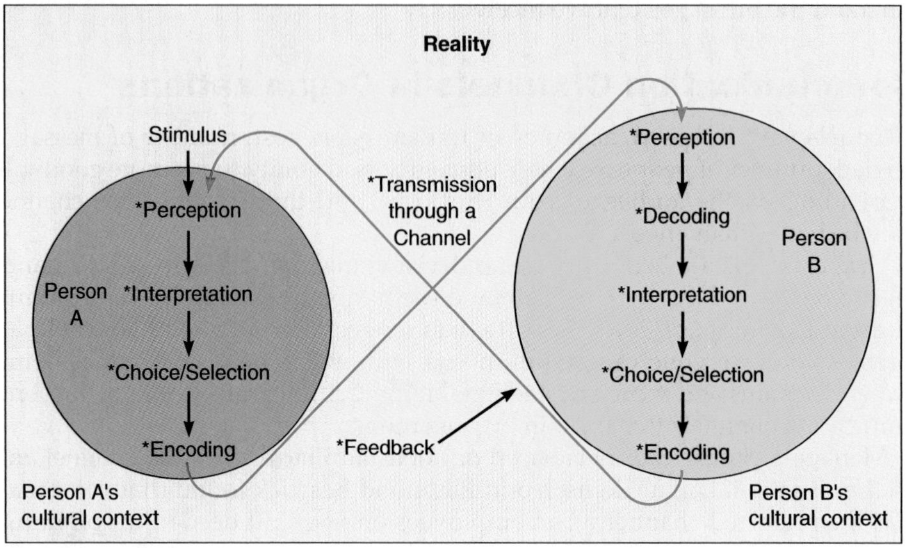

*Noise (and miscommunication) can occur here.

Channel choice may also be influenced by organizational culture. At Microsoft, e-mail is the preferred channel, and new employees have to learn to use it effectively.

A Model of the Communication Process

The following model of the communication process drastically simplifies what is perhaps the most complex human activity. However, even a simplified model can give us a sense of the complexity of the communication process. And the model is useful in helping us see where and why miscommunication occurs. Figure C.2 shows the basic process that occurs when one person tries to communicate ideas to someone else.

The process begins when Person A (let's call him Alex) perceives some stimulus. Here we are talking about literal **perception:** the ability to see, to hear, to taste, to smell, to touch. Next, Alex **interprets** what he has perceived. Is it important? Unusual? The next step is **choice** or **selection:** Alex decides what information he wishes to send to Person B (whom we'll call Barbara). Now Alex is ready to put his ideas into words. (Some people argue that we can think only in words and would put this stage before interpretation and choice.) Words are not the only way to convey ideas; gestures, clothing, and pictures can carry meaning nonverbally. The stage of putting ideas into any of these symbols is called **encoding.** Then Alex must **transmit** the message to Barbara using some **channel.** Channels include memos, phone calls, meetings, billboards, TV ads, and e-mail, to name just a few.

To receive the message, Barbara must first perceive it. Then she must **decode** it, that is, extract meaning from the symbols. Barbara then repeats the steps Alex has gone through: interpreting the information, choosing a response, and encoding it. The response Barbara sends to Alex is called **feedback.** Feedback may be direct and immediate or indirect and delayed; it may be verbal or nonverbal.

Noise can interfere with every aspect of the communication process. Noise may be physical or psychological. Physical noise could be a phone line with static, a lawn mower roaring outside a classroom, or handwriting that is hard to read. Psychological noise could include not liking a speaker, being concerned about something other than the message, or already having one's mind made up on an issue.

Channel overload occurs when the channel cannot handle all the messages that are being sent. A small business may have only two phone lines; no one else can get through if both lines are in use. **Information overload** occurs when more messages are transmitted than the human receiver can handle. Some receivers process information "first come, first served." Some may try to select the most important messages and ignore others. A third way is to depend on abstracts or summaries prepared by other people. None of these ways is completely satisfactory.

Here's how the process might work in an organizational situation:

Perception and Speed*

Seattle wanted people to drive more slowly over the bridge on the West Seattle Freeway. A sign posting a 40-mph speed limit didn't work. So the authorities changed the name of the road—to the West Seattle Bridge. It worked: people slowed down. The change in perception caused by the name change called for different behavior.

*Based on Gloria Pfeif to Kitty Locker, September 6, 1997.

Alex is an inspector for a state Department of Public Health. He inspects nursing homes to be sure that they meet state standards. Answering some of the questions on the form calls only for **perception** (Does each resident have a separate bed?). Others depend on **interpretation** as well as perception (Do residents receive appropriate care?). Today Alex is appalled at the condition of the Olde Folks Inne. He must **choose** details to put in his report to document his judgment that Olde Folks violates state standards.

Alex **encodes** his information in words only; he didn't think to bring a camera along, and he doesn't think a drawing or a table is necessary. The **channel** he chooses is the standard format for inspection reports in his office. He **transmits** his report to his boss, who may forward it to the attorney general's office if the violations are sufficiently severe.

Barbara is a lawyer in the attorney general's office. She gets Alex's report about three weeks after he wrote it (the **channel** isn't very fast) but doesn't read the report for another two weeks because she's so busy. Barbara is experiencing **information overload:** she cannot deal with messages as fast as they arrive.

When Barbara finally reads Alex's report, she **perceives** the typed document and **decodes** it. There are some technical terms in the report (Alex has talked about § 302.1.a of the State Code for Nursing Homes), which she understands since she's an expert in this area. She must **interpret** Alex's information. Are the violations severe enough to warrant filing a case against Olde Folks? She thinks they are. Furthermore, the governor made a speech three months ago promising to curb abuses in nursing homes, so clearing up this case will make her and her office look good.

Barbara **chooses** points that she wants to check on; she **encodes** her questions in simple, direct language and **transmits** her message to Alex by a phone call. Her questions serve as **feedback.** Alex learns that his report is on target but that at several points Barbara needs more information. (It isn't enough to say that residents are *neglected*; Barbara needs measurable, objective data to prove her case.)

The initial communication circuit expands. Barbara makes an appointment to visit the nursing home with Alex to collect the evidence she needs and interview some of the residents. She adds these **perceptions** to the information Alex has already given her. In her office after the visit, Barbara will **interpret** the evidence, **choose** the strongest arguments, and **encode** and **transmit** messages designed to make the nursing home make the necessary improvements voluntarily. She'll try persuasion and negotiation first; if they fail, she'll **encode** and **transmit** the documents necessary to file a suit against the nursing home.

The example above represents successful communication. But things don't always work so well. At every stage, both Alex and Barbara could misperceive, misinterpret, choose badly, encode poorly, and choose inappropriate channels.

Freshness Is in the Eye of the Beholder*

Stew Leonard's food store in Norwalk, Connecticut, is one of the most successful supermarkets in the United States. Part of the success comes from listening to customers—and giving them what they ask for.

At a focus group meeting, a woman complained that the store didn't sell fresh fish. The fish sales rep, who was also at the meeting, protested: the fish came fresh every morning, some from the Fulton Fish Market, some from the Boston Piers. But the customer held her ground. To her, fish on a Styrofoam plate in plastic wrap didn't look fresh.

What did the Leonards do? "We set up a fish bar with ice in it . . . it's the same price as over in the package. Our packaged fish didn't decrease at all, but we doubled our fish sales. We were doing about 15,000 pounds a week; now we're doing 30,000 pounds a week."

*Based on "In Search of Excellence: The Film," transcript by John Nathan (Waltham, MA: Nathan-Tyler Productions, 1985), 6–8; and Joanne Kaufman, "In the Moo: Shopping at Stew Leonard's," *The Wall Street Journal*, September 17, 1987, 28.

Miscommunication can also occur because different people have different frames of reference. We always interpret messages in light of our personal experiences, our cultures (◀ p. 293) and subcultures, and even the point in history at which we live.

Principles of Semantics

Semantic principles offer guidelines for improving communication. The basic principles of semantics may be expressed in eight statements. In the list below, the principles are linked to the parts of the communication model they explain.

Perception

1.   Perception involves the perceiver as well as what is perceived.

Interpretation

2.   Observations, inferences, and judgments are not the same thing.
3.   No two things are ever exactly alike.
4.   Things change significantly with time.
5.   Most *either–or* classifications are not legitimate.

Choice

6.   A statement is never the whole story.

Encoding and decoding

7.   Words are not identical to the objects they represent.
8.   The symbols used in communication must stand for essentially the same thing in the minds of the sender and the receiver.

Let's look at each of these principles.

1. Perception Involves the Perceiver as Well as What Is Perceived.

What we see is conditioned by what we are able to see, what we have seen in the past, what we are prepared to see, and what we want to see.

Our ability to perceive is limited first of all by our senses. Some people cannot distinguish between red and green; some people need glasses to see or hearing aids to hear. Perception is also affected by context. A line may appear longer or shorter depending on arrows at its ends (Figure C.3a). A circle may appear bigger or smaller depending on the circle around it (Figure C.3b). Parallel lines may appear slanted when other lines cross them (Figure C.3c). A symbol may appear to be the letter *S* or the number *5* depending on whether it's part of a word or a number (Figure C.3d).

Perceptions can even shape reality. In one school, a group of researchers gave teachers their students' aptitude scores, telling the teachers that they wanted to see whether high-scoring children really learned more quickly. At the end of the term, the high-aptitude children indeed scored higher on achievement tests than their classmates did. At this point, the researchers revealed the truth: the aptitude scores they had given the teachers had no relation to the students' real scores. The children who learned the most were not the smartest ones, but rather those the teachers *perceived* to be the smartest—those they expected to learn most easily. Evidently, by nonverbal feedback, extra attention, or some other means, the teachers enabled these children to learn more, whether or not they really were "smart."[2]

This experiment has implications for supervisors as well as teachers, for it suggests that our own expectations may shape the performances we get from those we evaluate.

FIGURE C.3   How Context Affects Perception

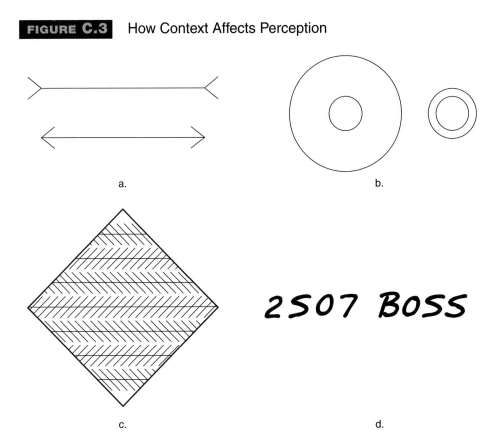

a.

b.

c.

d.

General Inference*

Our battalion reported to the recreation-theater for a briefing by the new general. Among the topics he spoke about was safety. "How many of you wore your seat belts on the way over here?" he asked us. Of the 400 soldiers present, only a few raised their hands.

The general, obviously annoyed, began to berate us for not following regulations. Then his aide leaned over to him. "Excuse me, sir," he whispered. "Their battalion area is across the street, so most of them walked."

*Quoted from "Humor in Uniform," *Reader's Digest,* July 1993, 111.

Perception is also affected by what we want to see. Most people have a tendency to attribute their own feelings to other people as well; we tend to repress ideas that are unpleasant or threatening. We may tune out messages we think will challenge our own positions; we seek messages that support the positions we have taken. The most avid readers of car ads are people who have just bought that make of car and who want to be reassured that they made the right choice.[3]

Use these correctives to check the accuracy of your perceptions:

1. Recognize that everyone's perception will be in some measure biased; the person who sees only reality does not exist.

2. Recognize that different positions cause us to view reality differently and to make different inferences from what we observe. When you disagree with someone, try to go back to the original observation to see if a difference in perception is at the root of the conflict.

3. If a new idea comes along that does not fit neatly into your worldview, recognize that your worldview, not the challenging idea, may need rethinking.

2. Observations, Inferences, and Judgments Are Not the Same Thing.

Ten minutes before lunchtime, Jan is talking on the phone. Her manager thinks, "I don't believe it! She's talking again. Doesn't she ever work?" Jan is talking to a potential customer; she sees the call as part of her job, since it may eventually lead to a sale. She can't understand why her manager doesn't think she's serious about her career.

The Camera Lies*

The truthfulness of photographic images has been vastly overrated. . . . [Cameras] can distort the viewer's interpretation of reality in at least six ways:

- The angle of view is critical, as football fans know well from instant replays. From one angle of view, the receiver is in bounds; from another, it's no catch.

- The framing of an image extracts only a portion of a scene. . . . What lies beyond the edge of the frame could lead to a completely different reading of the situation.

- Timing also removes context, by isolating a fraction of a second in time . . . Was the Congressman truly asleep or just blinking?

- Under- or overexposure can . . . wash out detail in parts of an image, deleting essential information.

- The lens itself modifies perspective. A telephoto lens makes foreground and background objects appear much closer to each other than they really are.

- Reproduction size significantly alters perception of content. . . . [Details can be emphasized by blowing up the photo; patterns can be hidden when the photo doesn't show] "the whole picture."

*Quoted from A. G., "Photographic Truth: Fact or Fiction," *NADTP Journal*, September 1993, 16–18.

Jan's manager sees a woman talking on the phone; he assumes that she's wasting time. He has jumped to the wrong conclusion about the meaning of her behavior. But, as Tim R. V. Davis points out, we are usually less interested in an action than in what we think that action means.[4] And interpretation invariably creates the possibility of error.

Semanticists would say that Jan's boss is confusing observations and inferences. To a semanticist, an **observation** is a statement that you yourself have verified. An **inference** is a statement that you have not personally verified, but whose truth or falsity could be established, either now or in the future. A **judgment** or an **opinion** is a statement that can never be verified, since it includes terms that cannot be measured objectively. Let's look at some examples.

1. The book you are reading is titled *Business and Administrative Communication.*
2. The author teaches at The Ohio State University.
3. The book is the best college text in business communication.

Statement 1 is an observation: you can verify it by checking the cover and title page. Statement 2 is an inference. It seems reasonable, based on what the title page says, but you don't know that of your own knowledge. (Even if the statement was true when the book went to press, is it still true?) However, you could check the truth of the statement if you wanted to take the time and trouble to do so. Statement 3 is a judgment. There is no way to prove that it is true, because people will have different notions of what makes a textbook the "best."

Semanticists claim that only observations are facts. Consider this statement:

Scientists first cloned mammals in 1997.

Is that a fact? Very few people reading this book observed the birth of the cloned sheep in Scotland in person. Most of us saw pictures of the sheep on TV or read about it in newspapers and newsmagazines. We accept statements about the cloning as fact because we trust the TV announcers who reported it then and the books that record it now. But all of us have seen images on TV that were fiction, not fact. Digital imaging allows editors to alter pictures. Indeed, photo studios routinely use digital imaging technology to "restore" the hair a high school senior had shaved off or to remove pimples or prom dates.[5] Nor is printed information necessarily true.

Usually, we call statements *facts* if nearly everyone in our culture accepts them as true. But something is not necessarily true just because large numbers of people believe it. Before Columbus's discovery of America, nearly everyone believed that the world was flat. If one defines *facts* not as widely shared beliefs but as observations, there are almost no facts. Almost everything we know we take on someone else's authority rather than on our own. Even much of what we know by observation may be inference rather than direct observation. Furthermore, observations vary from person to person, since different people will have verified different things.

In everyday life and in business, you have to make decisions based on inferences ("That driver whose right turn signal is blinking intends to turn right." "I will live long enough to need a retirement fund." "The sales figures I've been given are accurate.") and even on judgments ("We have too much money tied up in long-term investments."). What should you as a reader or writer do?

As both a reader and writer,

1. Check to see whether a statement is an observation, an inference, or a judgment.

As a reader or listener making decisions based on information you get from other people,

2. Estimate the accuracy of the inference by comparing it to your experiences with the source and with this kind of situation. If the cost of making a mistake is high, try to get more information.

As a writer or speaker trying to persuade people,

3. Use measurable statements, not just statements that contain value terms that will mean different things to different people.

> Not: Buying a slag grinder would be a good investment.
>
> But: Buying a slag grinder will enable us to save $25,000 on the Moreland order alone.

4. Label your inferences so that your audience can distinguish between what you know to be the case and what you think, assume, believe, or judge to be true. In the following examples, the italicized words remind readers that the statements are inferences.

> *He predicts* that the stock market *could* move up an additional 10% to 20% during the next 12 to 18 months.
>
> *The results of our survey suggest* that employees will accept the proposed limits on health care benefits only if benefits for top management are also frozen or cut.

3. No Two Things Are Ever Exactly Alike.

We make sense of the world by grouping things into categories. Once we have categories, we do not have to evaluate each new experience independently; instead, we simply assign it to a category and then make the response we find appropriate to that category.

Unfortunately, this convenient lumping can lead to **stereotyping:** putting similar people or events into a single category, even though significant differences exist. A list of the customers whose accounts are overdue, for example, may include several different kinds of people:

- A good customer who is behind on bills because of a temporary setback.
- A marginal risk who won't pay the bill until forced to do so.
- Someone whose record-keeping is poor and who has honestly forgotten to pay.
- Someone who claims that he or she never received the merchandise or that the amount of the bill is in error and who is delaying payment until the dispute is settled.

The approach that would be needed to get a customer in the second category to pay would be unnecessary and even offensive if used with customers in other groups. Different "delinquent" customers need to be treated differently.

Generalizing—faultily—on the basis of experience is a particular problem when our experience is limited to one or two cases. Suppose, for example, that someone has an Asian supervisor who isn't a good boss. If the supervisor is the only Asian boss the employee has ever known, the employee may conclude that Asians don't make good supervisors. If the same employee has an Anglo supervisor who isn't a good boss, he or she is less likely to assume that Anglos can't be good supervisors. Because we see many Anglo supervisors, some of whom are better than others, it is easy to recognize that the weakness of an individual doesn't condemn the whole group.

To guard against stereotyping, you should

1. Recognize significant differences as well as similarities. The members of any one group are not identical.

2. Be sure that any analogy you use to make your point clear is accurate at the point of comparison.

But Things Are Different Now*

Conventional wisdom is that US companies can't sell unaltered appliances in Japan: Japanese houses are just too small for them. Conventional wisdom is no longer true.

The Japanese discount chain Kojima sells GE appliances. Between June 1995 and June 1996, GE's share of the Japanese refrigerator market went from 1% to 3%.

Why the change? Two factors seem responsible: more Japanese women continue to work after marriage and can't shop daily for food. And Japan's weak economy has made consumers interested in saving money. A GE refrigerator costs about half as much as a smaller Japanese model.

True, the larger model won't fit in small kitchenettes. Buyers solve that problem by putting the US refrigerators in their living rooms.

*Based on Morihiko Shirouzu, "Flouting 'Rules' Sells GE Fridges in Japan," *The Wall Street Journal*, October 31, 1995, B1.

The Word Is Not Connected to the Object

- Octoberfest is held in September.
- The Big 10 has 11 teams.
- The principal ingredient in sweetbread is neither sugar nor bread but the cooked pancreas or thymus of a young animal, usually a calf.
- Wild rice isn't necessarily wild. Nearly all the wild rice on grocery-store shelves is commercially cultivated in rice paddies and turned and watered by machines. The Ojibway in Minnesota harvest true wild rice by hand.

4. Things Change Significantly with Time.

If you keep up with the stock market, with commodity prices, or with interest rates, you know that things (especially prices) change significantly with time.

People change too. The sales representative who was once judged too abrasive to make a good supervisor may have mellowed by now; employees who accepted management dictates without question 20 years ago may be more critical; the student who almost flunked out freshman year may have settled down, solved his or her problems, and become an excellent prospect for employment or graduate school.

Someone who does not recognize that prices, situations, and people change is guilty of making a **frozen evaluation.** The following corrections help us remember not to freeze evaluations:

1. Date statements. The price of IBM stock on October 20, 1993, is not the price of IBM stock on January 3, 2003.
2. Provide a frame of reference so that your reader has some basis for comparing grades, profits, injuries, percentages, or whatever the relevant criterion may be.
3. Periodically retest your assumptions about people, businesses, products, and services to make sure that your evaluations apply to the present situation.

5. Most *Either–Or* Classifications Are Not Legitimate.

A common logical fallacy is **polarization:** trying to force the reader into a position by arguing that there are only two possible positions, one of which is clearly unacceptable:

> Either the supervisor runs this department with a firm hand, or anarchy will take over and the work will never get done.

Very few areas of life allow only two options. Running a department "with a firm hand" is only one of several possible leadership styles; sharing authority with or even transferring it entirely to subordinates need not result in anarchy.

Even people who admit that there are more than two possible positions may still limit the options unnecessarily. Imposing limits that do not exist in reality is called **blindering,** after the blinders that horses wear. Blindering can lead to polarization.

Sometimes blindering is responsible for bad questions in surveys:

> Do you own _____ , rent _____ , or live with your parents _____ ?

At first glance, that may seem to cover the options. But what about someone who lives with a friend or with relatives other than parents? What about a minister who lives in a parsonage or manse furnished by the church as part of the minister's compensation? The minister does not own the house, but neither does he or she rent it. Depending on what the makers of the questionnaire really want to know, better questions would be:

How much is your housing worth a month?

How much do you pay a month for your housing?

Polarization sharpens divisions between people and obscures the common ground on which they could forge a decision that everyone could live with. Blindering prevents our seeing creative solutions to the problems we face. Here are some correctives:

1. Recognize the complexities of a situation. Resist the temptation to over-simplify.
2. Whenever you see only two alternatives, consciously search for a third, and maybe even a fourth or fifth, before you make your decision.
3. Redefine the question or problem to get at the real issue.

Don't ask: How can I as a manager show that I'm in control?

Ask: How can we improve productivity in this unit?

6. A Statement Is Never the Whole Story.

It is impossible to know everything; it is impossible to tell someone everything. Thinking that we know everything about a subject or can communicate everything about it that is important is the fallacy semanticists call **allness.** When we assume that a statement contains all the important information, or when the context is omitted (deliberately or inadvertently), meanings are inevitably twisted.

For example, you've probably read that US investments suffer because US families save far less than do Japanese families. But, according to several economists, this statement overlooks differences in what counts as savings and as investments. Many US families own their own homes, yet their equity isn't considered "savings." Few Japanese own homes; their "savings" are more likely to be in stocks and bonds. Economist Fumio Hayashi points out that Japanese accounting values depreciation at historical cost figures, thus understating the value of assets and making investments look higher. Furthermore, the United States counts government spending—even on schools, roads, and warships—as consumption. The Japanese system considers such expenditures to be investments.[7] When these differences are considered, the alleged gap between the two countries' savings and investment rates disappears.

Since, even with the best intentions, we cannot include everything, what can we do to avoid misstatements by implication?

1. Recognize that the reports you get are filtered; you are not getting all the facts, and you are almost certainly getting inferences as well as observations.
2. Check the correspondence you send out to make sure you have provided the background information the reader needs to interpret your message accurately.

7. Words Are Not Identical to the Objects They Represent.

People perceive objects and think of ideas; they attach labels to those objects and ideas. Other labels could be substituted without changing reality. Indeed, the ability to attach a new label to an object—to attach a different meaning to it—is a key element of creative intelligence. In the **semantic triangle** in Figure C.4, there is no base, no connection between the thing and the word that symbolizes it. People, who name things and use words, provide the only connection.

We often respond to the label rather than to reality. Our degree of distress during a bleak economic period is likely to be as much a product of the label given the period as it is of the rate of unemployment: a *slowdown* doesn't sound as bad as a *recession,* and even that is better than a *depression.* Labeling a book a *best-seller* is sure to increase sales. Billy Joel put the song "You're Only Human" on his "Greatest Hits" album before he had even released it as a single.

Because people respond to symbols, organizations choose names carefully. Corporate name changes raise stock prices 2.4% "solely because of name changes."[8] In World War II, a Navy ship changed its call signal from SAP-WORTH to HELLCAT—with a marked improvement in morale.[9]

The Map Is Not the Territory*

Traveling over the United States in a balloon, Huck Finn expects the world to look just like the maps he has seen:

". . . [If] we was going so fast we ought to be past Illinois, oughtn't we?"

"Certainly."

"Well, we ain't."

"What's the reason we ain't?"

"I know by the color. We're right over Illinois yet. And you can see for yourself that Indiana ain't in sight."

"I wonder what's the matter with you, Huck. You know by the *color?*"

"Yes, of course I do."

"What's the color got to do with it?"

"It's got everything to do with it. Illinois is green, Indiana is pink. You show me any pink down here, if you can. No, sir; it's green."

"Indiana *pink?* Why, what a lie!"

"It ain't no lie; I've seen it on the map, and it's pink."

*Quoted from Mark Twain, *Tom Sawyer Abroad,* Chap. 3, *The Family Mark Twain* (New York: Harper, 1935), 1101–02.

What's in a Name? I*

FIGURE C.4   Semantic Triangle

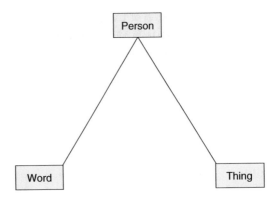

Responding to the symbol rather than to reality, "confusing the map with the territory," is called **intensionalism.** Advertising works in part because we respond intensionally to symbols. A man working at a flea market noticed that garden supplies went quickly, but no one was buying broom handles. He bought the entire supply of broom handles for a dime each, put up a sign in his own booth advertising "Tomato stakes—25¢ each," and sold all 300 in two hours.[10] The characteristics of the wooden poles hadn't changed, but the symbol had, and people responded differently to the new symbol.

Since we must use symbols to communicate, it's hard to avoid treating symbols as if they were reality. Semanticists suggest these correctives:

1. Support general statements and evaluations with specific evidence or examples.
2. Check your own responses to make sure that your decisions are based not on labels but on valid, logical arguments.

8. The Symbols Used in Communication Must Stand for Essentially the Same Thing in the Minds of the Sender and the Receiver.

Communication depends on symbols; if those symbols mean different things to the people who use them, communication will fail. **Bypassing** occurs when two people use the same symbol to mean different things.

"Virtual signs" exist in computer feeds to TV screens but not in reality. Fans watching the Philadelphia Phillies on TV see large ads for Coca-Cola or for the team's Web site on the wall behind the batter. But the ads aren't really there. They're generated by computer for the TV audience. Fans at the ball park just see a blank wall.

Bypassing creates misunderstandings. A factory employee who had been absent frequently notified his supervisor that he would not be at work the next day. The supervisor said "OK," meaning only that he had heard what the worker had said and was acknowledging having heard it. The worker thought the *OK* signified approval, that is, that his absence was acceptable. When he received a written warning notice for poor attendance, he felt he was being treated unfairly and filed a grievance against management.

Until we learn to look into each other's minds, we can't be certain that symbols mean exactly the same things to us as they do to the people with whom we communicate. But there are some measures that will help us avoid bypassing:

1. Be sensitive to contexts.
2. Consider the other person. Given his or her background and situation, what is he or she likely to mean?
3. Mirror what the other person has said by putting it into your own words, and let him or her check it for accuracy. (Note: use different words for the key ideas. If you use exactly the same word, you still won't be able to tell if you and the other person mean the same thing by it.)
4. Ask questions.

Timothy Hanz, 10, decorates a hamburger with squirts of Heinz's new "E-Z Squirt" bottled green ketchup at a commercial photo shoot in Pittsburgh, Friday, July 7, 2000. "A lot of kids are going to love it," Hanz said. "I told one guy about it, and he's like 'No way!' I'll draw stuff with it and eat a lot more ketchup." (AP Photo/Keith Srakocic)

What's in a Name? II*

Twenty years ago, no one could sell portabella mushrooms. But they weren't called portabellas.

In the 1970s, when exotic cultivated mushrooms became a market segment, growers began to remarket the mature, brown mushrooms that were out of favor. In the 1980s, the name *portabella* emerged.

Now, at the turn of the century, portabellas are featured in chefs' signature dishes. In grocery stores, portabellas cost as much as steak. And growers can't keep up with demand.

It helps to have a beautiful name.

*Based on Kim Pierce, "Meaty Portabella Mushrooms Are Springing Up All Over: Change of Name Promotes Interest in Giant, Unglamorous Fungi," *The Columbus Dispatch*, May 31, 1995, 6H.

Summary of Key Points

- **Communication theory** attempts to explain what happens when we communicate. **Semantics** is the study of the way our behavior is influenced by the words and other symbols we use to communicate. Communication theory and semantics both show why and where communication can break down and what we can do to communicate more effectively.

- Because semantics deals with the way we perceive and process information, conflicts that are "just a matter of semantics" may be serious. Depending on the situation, it may or may not be possible to find words that everyone in the group can endorse.

- The best channel for a message will depend on the audience, the sender's purposes, and the situation. Channel choice may be shaped by the organizational culture.

- **Channel overload** occurs when a channel cannot handle all the messages being sent. **Information overload** occurs when the receiver cannot process all the messages that arrive. Both kinds of overload require some sort of selection to determine which messages will be sent and which ones will be attended to.

- A sender goes through the following steps: **perception, interpretation, choice** or **selection, encoding,** transmitting the message through a **channel.** The receiver perceives the message, **decodes** it, interprets it, chooses a response, encodes the response, and transmits it. The message transmitted to the original sender is called **feedback. Noise** is anything that interferes with communication; it can be both physical and psychological. Miscommunication can occur at every point in the communication process.

- Eight principles of semantics will help us avoid errors in perception, interpretation, choice, and encoding and decoding.

Perception

1. Perception involves the perceiver as well as what is perceived.

Interpretation

2. **Observations** are statements you yourself have verified. **Inferences** are statements that have not yet been verified but that could be. **Judgments** can never be proven, since they depend not on measurable quantities but on values.

3. No two things are ever exactly alike.

4. Things change significantly with time. Violating this principle produces **frozen evaluations.**

5. Most *either–or* classifications are not legitimate. Seeing only two alternatives is called **polarization.** Assuming limits that do not exist is called **blindering.**

Choice

6. A statement is never the whole story. Thinking that one can know or tell everything is called **allness.**

Encoding and Decoding

7. Words are not identical to the objects they represent. The **semantic triangle** shows that the only link between word and object is the person who uses the word.

8. The symbols used in communication must stand for essentially the same thing in the minds of the sender and the receiver. When the sender and the receiver use the same symbol to mean different things, **bypassing** occurs.

APPENDIX C   Exercises

C.1   Choosing a Channel to Reach a Specific Audience

Suppose that your business, government agency, or non-profit group had a product, service, or program targeted for each of the following audiences. What would be the best channel(s) to reach people in that group in your city? Would that channel reach all group members?

a.   Macintosh users.

b.   People who own mutual funds.

c.   Teenagers who do the family grocery shopping.

d.   People who bowl.

e.   Muslims.

f.   Parents whose children play team sports.

g.   Native Americans/Native Canadians.

h.   Lawyers.

i.   People who have Web sites.

j.   People who use wheelchairs.

C.2   Choosing a Channel to Convey a Specific Message

Assume that you're the campaign manager for a campus, local, or state race. (Pick a real candidate and a real race.) What would be the advantages and disadvantages of each of the following channels as media to carry ads for your side?

a.   Ad in the campus newspaper.

b.   Posters around campus.

c.   Ad in the local newspaper.

d.   Ad on a local radio station after midnight.

e.   Ad on the local TV station during the local news show.

f.   Ads on billboards.

g.   Ads on yard signs.

h.   Flyers distributed door-to-door.

i.   Ad on cable TV.

C.3   Dealing with Channel and Information Overload

In each of the following situations, identify ways that people could deal with the overloads described. What are the consequences of the methods that might be used?

a.   When a radio station announces a prize for the ninth caller, dozens of people try to phone in.

b.   After Bill Gates's e-mail address is printed in a magazine, he gets 5,000 messages in three days.

c.   A car buyer in the United States can choose from 572 makes and models.

d.   At State University, every accounting senior with a GPA of "B" or better wants to interview for jobs with

the Big Five accounting firms, but each firm will interview only 34 seniors at the school.

e.   A major freeway is closed for repairs.

f.   System capacity allows only two of every five calls on cellular phones to get through.

g.   A student wants to attend a lecture by a prominent speaker the night before a paper is due.

h.   A sales representative's job requires him to be on the road four nights a week, but he wants to spend more time with his family.

C.4   Separating Observations, Inferences, and Judgments

Indicate whether each of the following statements is an observation, an inference, or a judgment.

a.   This statement is printed in black ink on a page edged in orange.

b.   All the exercises and problems in this book are printed on pages edged in orange.

c.   Printing the problems on pages with colored edges makes them easier to find.

d.   Five years from now, 90% of the college texts designed for business courses will use at least two colors of ink.

e.   Color printing makes textbooks more interesting.

C.5   Separating Observations, Inferences, and Judgments

Indicate whether each of the following statements is an observation, an inference, or a judgment.

a.   There is a chair in this room.

b.   The Dow Jones Industrial Average closed above 7000 for the first time in February 1997.

c.   High stock prices are a sign that the economy is healthy.

d.   Accounting majors get good jobs.

e.   All the people in this room will be employed three years from today.

f.   It's better to be 75% right and 100% on time than 100% right and a week late.

g.   This statement is a complete sentence.

C.6   Separating Observations, Inferences, and Judgments

Pick a topic and write a statement of observation, a statement of inference, and a statement of judgment about it.

C.7   Explaining Bypassing

1. Show how the following statements could produce bypassing.
   a. The house needs painting badly.
   b. I made reservations for seven.
   c. If you think our servers are rude, you should see the manager.

2. Bypassing is the basis of many jokes. Find a joke that depends on bypassing and share it with the class.

C.8   Identifying Semantic Errors

Match each of the following statements with the semantic error it represents.

1. Allness
2. Frozen evaluation
3. Intensionalism
4. Polarization
5. Stereotyping
   a. All Australians are cricket maniacs.
   b. We tried that two years ago and it didn't work. There's no point in trying it again.
   c. My subordinate isn't looking at me while I talk to him. He must be rebelling against my authority.
   d. *The New York Times* prints all the news that's fit to print.
   e. Junk mail wastes paper and money.
   f. He applied for a job last year, and we hired someone else. There's no reason to consider him for our jobs this year.
   g. If we grant pay increases, we will have to raise our cost to customers.
   h. I swear to tell the truth, the whole truth, and nothing but the truth.
   i. Women are more nurturing than men are.
   j. Any man who wears a Brooks Brothers suit will be politically and fiscally conservative.

C.9   Verbal Map-Reality Test

Directions: If a statement is *true under all circumstances,* check the line in the "True" column. If the statement is *ever false* or if its truth *cannot be determined,* put a check in the "False" column.

True	False	
____	____	1. A statement is either true or false.
____	____	2. 1 + 1 = 2
____	____	3. A college education is a good thing to have.
____	____	4. A person is dead when he or she has no heartbeat.
____	____	5. No one wants to die.
____	____	6. Roses are red.
____	____	7. The sum of the angles of a triangle is 180 degrees.
____	____	8. All people are born equal.
____	____	9. Freedom of speech is good.
____	____	10. Do unto others as you would have them do unto you.

Source: Adapted from "Advertising as Communication: How To Test Your Semantic I.Q.," Harry E. Maynard, Printer's Ink, December 11, 1964, 52.

C.10   Inference-Observation Tests

Directions: You will read a brief story. Assume that all the information in the story is *accurate* and *true.* You will then read statements about the story. Answer them in order. You may reread the story as you answer the questions, but DO NOT go back to fill in answers or change answers once you have marked them.

As you read each statement, determine whether the statement is

"T"—on the basis of the information presented in the story, the statement is definitely true.

"F"—on the basis of the information presented in the story, the statement is definitely false.

"?"—the statement may be true (or false) but on the basis of the information presented in the story one cannot be sure. (Mark "?" if any part of the statement is doubtful.)

Sample Story

The only vehicle parked in front of 619 Oak Street is a blue van. The words "Valley Cable TV Plumber" are spelled in large black letters across the side of the van.

Statements about the Sample Story

1. The color of the van in front of 619 Oak Street is blue. T F ?
2. There is no lettering on the side of the van parked in front of 619 Oak Street. T F ?
3. The people at 619 Oak Street have cable TV. T F ?
4. The blue van parked in front of 619 Oak Street belongs to Valley Cable TV. T F ?

Test Story

Babe Smith has been killed. Police have rounded up six suspects, all of whom are gangsters. All of them are known to have been near the scene of the killing at the approximate time that it occurred. All had substantial motives for wanting Smith killed. However, one of the suspected gangsters, Slinky Sam, has positively been cleared of guilt.

Statements about the Story

1. Slinky Sam is known to have been near the scene of the killing of Babe Smith. T F ?
2. All six of the rounded-up gangsters were known to have been near the scene of the murder. T F ?
3. Only Slinky Sam has been cleared of guilt. T F ?
4. All six of the rounded-up suspects were near the scene of Smith's killing at the approximate time that it took place. T F ?
5. The police do not know who killed Smith. T F ?
6. All six suspects are known to have been near the scene of the foul deed. T F ?
7. Smith's murderer did not confess of his or her own free will. T F ?
8. Slinky Sam was not cleared of guilt. T F ?
9. It is known that the six suspects were in the vicinity of the cold-blooded assassination. T F ?

Source: Test by William Haney, in Harry E. Maynard, "Advertising as Communication: How to Test Your Semantic I.Q.," *Printer's Ink,* December 11, 1964, 53.

C.11   Removing Blinders

To solve the following problems, you may need to remove some "blinders."

1. How can the following be true:

   A = 3

   B = 4

   But A + B = 5

2. How can you drop an egg six feet through the air over a hard surface without breaking the egg?

3. How can you, with one line, turn VII into the number 8?

   How can you, with one line, turn IX into the number 6?

4. Finish the alphabet, putting each letter above or below the line according to the pattern below:

A		EF	HI
	BCD	G	J

5. When men and women are on an elevator and all of them are getting off on the seventh floor, who should get off first?

6. Why are 2000 US dollars worth more than 1999 US dollars?

7. Their is four errors in this sentence. Can you find them?

8. How can you rearrange the letters in the words *new door* to make one word?

9. Six glasses are in a row. The first three are full of juice; the second three are empty. How can you move just one glass to arrange them so that full and empty glasses alternate?

10. Separate all nine dots into their own individual spaces by drawing two squares.

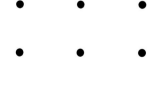

C.12   Identifying Logos

Find four corporate logos. Do all your classmates recognize all the logos? Which logos seem to be especially effective symbols for their organizations? What makes them so effective?

Crafting Logical Arguments

The Toulmin Model

How Much of the Full Toulmin Model to Use

Using Toulmin Logic to Craft Arguments

Summary of Key Points

Any argument has a better chance if it is logically sound and well presented. Tight logic is crucial when you face a hostile audience hoping to defeat you by picking holes in your argument. To make your logic convincing,

- Give evidence and specific supporting details.
- Connect the parts of your argument.
- Respond to possible objections
- Limit your claim to make it more persuasive.

While any system of logic will help you craft solid arguments, **Toulmin logic,** developed by Stephen Toulmin,[1] is particularly useful for business communication since it can help you both to see whether an argument is valid and to decide how much—or what kind of—evidence you need to provide.

The Toulmin Model

In everyday life, the first part of the argument to emerge is frequently the **claim** we wish to make. When the reader is already on our side, all we have to do is state the claim. But when the reader resists the claim, we must support it with **data** or **evidence.**

Just providing evidence may not be enough in difficult situations. The reader has to see the relationship between the evidence and the claim. If the reader doesn't see the relationship (doesn't know it, agree with it, or happen to think of it at the moment), he or she won't be convinced. Adding more evidence won't help. Instead, we need to spell out the assumption or **bridge** that links the evidence to the claim. (In the old movie *If It's Tuesday, This Must Be Belgium,* the bridge is that we're on a whirlwind package trip through Europe that sticks to the itinerary. Without that assumption, there would be no bridge between the evidence that today is Tuesday and a claim about where we are.)

If the audience may disagree with the bridge, we need to prove it. When the proof is made explicit, the statement supporting the bridge is called the **foundation.** Sometimes the reader may accept the bridge but think of a **counterclaim** that negates the claim. If a counterargument exists, we must provide a **rebuttal** to it to be convincing.

Here's an example, labeling the parts of an argument that a college sports team needs to communicate more often with high school athletes it wants to recruit.

Claim:	Better communication will improve our recruiting record.
Evidence:	We are losing recruits to other schools.
Bridge:	Recruits don't necessarily go to the most prestigious school they can. Instead, recruits are more likely to choose schools that communicate with them often during the recruiting process.
Foundation:	Research shows that frequency and quality of communication were key factors in influencing recruits to attend a specific school. Communication strengthened recruits' initial interest and helped overcome objections. Our informal surveys of recruits show that they receive more mail and phone calls from other schools than from us.
Counterclaim:	Our communication might be poor. Frequent communication might hurt rather than help.
Rebuttal:	We will hire a consultant to help our coaches write effective letters.

Many claims cannot be made with 100% certainty. If the claim is only *probably* and not *necessarily* true, we need to **limit** it. You can limit a claim with the words *probably, help,* and *may be* and with explicit disclaimers: "These results are accurate within ±5.6%." "This projection is based on surveys taken October 28th." Qualifying your claims will build your credibility as a person who promises only what you can deliver.

In a paragraph, the parts of the Toulmin model can come in almost any order; choose the one that makes ideas flow most smoothly. In a longer document—a letter, memo, or report—claims, once you prove them, become data or evidence (now that the reader accepts them) that can be used to support bigger claims. Thus logic becomes a pyramid: small claims support medium-sized claims, which, when proven, in turn support major claims.

How Much of the Full Toulmin Model to Use

It is possible to outline the full Toulmin model for any claim, even simple ones such as "Your order will arrive Thursday." However, it is not always necessary to do so. Decide how much of the model to use by analyzing the reader and the situation.

The following guidelines can help.

1. **Make both the claim and the evidence explicit** unless you are *sure* the reader will accept what you say totally without questions. Present obvious evidence in a subordinate clause beginning with "since" or "because" to avoid giving the impression that this information is new and surprising.

> Since employers prefer job candidates with work experience, we should set up an internship program for our students.

Here the claim "we need an internship program" is supported by evidence in the introductory subordinate clause: "employers prefer candidates with experience."

Limiting Statements in Accounting Reports*

Accountants carefully limit the claims they make in their reports. The following paragraph from a review contains four limiting phrases:

> Based on our review we are not aware of any material modifications that should be made to the accompanying financial statements in order for them to be in conformity with generally accepted accounting principles.

"Based on our review" and "we are not aware" acknowledge that evidence may exist which the auditors have not seen. To say that "material modifications" are not needed leaves the door open for possible minor improvements. Finally, "generally accepted accounting principles" is itself limited. CPAs are not claiming that these principles are unchanging or that everyone in the world accepts them.

*Based on Aletha S. Hendrickson, "How to Appear Reliable without Being Liable: C.P.A. Writing in Its Rhetorical Context," *Worlds of Writing: Teaching and Learning in Different Discourse Communities,* ed. Carolyn Matalene (New York: Random House, 1989), 308–13.

Using Logic in an Environmental Restoration Report*

Battelle's Environmental Restoration department produces final reports that deliver the results of lengthy research to a wide variety of readers.

In our discourse community, the most common kinds of evidence are measurements and calculations. For example, if writers want to recommend one particular strategy for cleaning up a contaminated site, they can support this claim logically with evidence ranging from tables of raw analytic data and graphics that illustrate geological contours at the site to specific terms for the level of technology development (emerging, conventional, innovative) and estimates of the cost of cleanup.

Limiting claims appropriately is important. For example, one recent exchange between writers centered on whether data tended to "support" or to "strongly support" the final recommendations. At that point, I was able to point out that language in preceding analytic sections more often expressed ambiguity rather than certainty, so the word "strongly" was dropped. The difference between "support" and "strongly support" can determine whether a client spends more than $500,000 to take remedial action at a particular site.

*Quoted from Tom Wilk to Kitty Locker, April 10, 1999.

2. **Include the bridge**
   a. **If it is new information to the reader.**
   b. **If the reader may have heard the bridge but forgotten it.**
   c. **If the reader may disagree with the bridge.**
   d. **If invalid as well as valid bridges exist.**

> All of the money saved in the cost-reduction program will go into salaries and benefits, not into research and development, executive bonuses, or stockholder dividends. Therefore, employees will benefit if the company saves money.

The first sentence is a bridge connecting saving money to the claim, "employees will benefit." The bridge is necessary because invalid bridges exist: any money saved might be spent on several things other than salaries and benefits.

3. **Make the foundation explicit**
   a. **If it is new information to the reader.**
   b. **If the reader will disagree with the bridge.**
   c. **If invalid as well as valid foundations exist.**
   d. **If there are arbitrary demands for documentation (e.g., in a term paper or a paper you are submitting for publication, where you must indicate your sources for each fact).**

> XYZ university will have trouble developing a top-20 football team because its academic standards are high. After practicing four hours a day, football players don't have the time or energy to complete complex, lengthy assignments. Long practices are necessary both to reduce the risk of injury and to make the moves automatic.

The implicit bridge here is "good football players can't meet high academic standards." Readers who think of the possible but invalid foundation "Good football players are dumb" will reject the argument. Giving the valid foundation (the last two sentences) makes the argument more persuasive.

4. **Always offer rebuttals to counterclaims.** Failure to dispose of loopholes is, after failure to provide a valid bridge, probably the most common cause of unconvincing—and unaccepted—recommendations.

> Three of our best customers got busy signals for two straight hours Monday. Business was slow Monday: quotes were down 11%, and the logs compiled by the inside sales reps don't show many outgoing business calls. But the phones were busy, and it seems likely that they were tied up with personal calls.

A reader who accepts the evidence "our phones were tied up" may offer the counterclaim "all the calls were to business customers." If that claim were true, customers would get busy signals even though no one was making personal calls. The middle sentence rebuts that counterclaim by showing that business activity was down. That rebuttal is crucial to making convincing the claim in the last clause: the phones were tied up with personal calls.

5. **Limit any claim whose truth is uncertain or relative.**

> This procedure should produce more accurate results.

The word *should* limits the claim. Without it, we would be promising that the procedure would definitely bring an improvement. But many things could go wrong. Limiting the claim makes it more persuasive because it is now more realistic.

Using Toulmin Logic to Craft Arguments

Each of the following arguments is unconvincing, but the solutions differ.

Argument 1	By using XTROCUT tubing, you can cut production time and reduce scrap loss.
Problem with argument	This argument needs evidence to support each of its claims.
Revised argument	Because XTROCUT comes in the lengths and shapes you use most often, you spend less time cutting down longer tubes. Since you can order just the length you want, you don't waste 2 feet every time you need a 10-foot tube.
Argument 2	The workers I talked to were split 50/50. The workers at our plant don't agree whether the benefits package is adequate.
Problem with argument	No bridge shows that the "workers I talked to" were a representative or sufficiently large sample. The audience may also wonder whether things have changed since the date of the poll.
Revised argument	I talked to a random sample of 60 workers. They were split 50/50. Last week, the workers didn't agree whether the benefits package is adequate.
Argument 3	Our national advertising campaign will run during the most popular TV shows this month. This ad campaign will increase our sales dramatically.
Problem with argument	Such a claim cannot be made with certainty: too many variables affect sales.
Revised argument	Our national advertising campaign will run during the most popular TV shows this month. This ad campaign will support our sales reps' efforts to increase sales 5% over last month's.

Specific supporting details show that you've thought through your argument. For example, Kris McKnight handed her boss 16 pages of supporting documentation to argue that she could be more effective working out of her home and on the road rather than in the organization's regional office. Part of her reason for wanting to telecommute was personal. But her proposal emphasized the benefits to the organization.[2] Anne Fisher advises including specific details about how you'll spend your time ("8 AM to 9 AM: Read and answer e-mail. Reply to voice mail. Check in with secretary.").[3] A small request—to telecommute one day a week for two months—gives you a chance to prove your claims with the strongest proof of all: personal experience.

In a job application letter, the major claim is "I can do the job." That major claim rests on several smaller claims: "I have the necessary technical skills," "I work well with people," and "I have relevant experience." But each of these smaller claims needs support before it is convincing in supporting the major claim. For example, to prove that she had relevant experience, a student might describe the cost accounting system she developed for a small business, enabling it to save money. She could support that claim by giving details (evidence) about her contribution (to rebut the counterargument that she only used an already-written software package) and by being specific about how

FIGURE D.1   A Problem-Solving Memo

Inter-office Memorandum

Date: February 19, 2004

To: All Sales Representatives

From: James Christopher Smith   *JCS*   *Common ground as subject line*

Subject: Improving Service of Customers' Phone Orders

Writer as problem solver

Common ground

All of you have told me that your customers are experiencing difficulties in placing orders because all the phone lines are tied up, and that some customers are ordering from other wholesalers as a result. This is causing you a loss in sales commissions.

Evidence

The recent opening of the Johnson Wholesale House in Decatur has made competition in our field of wholesale drugs even keener. With the addition of this new warehouse, Johnson can service customers in all our sales areas almost as quickly as we can, and for approximately the same price. This new availability makes it even easier for our customers to call Johnson's instead of us. In fact, Glenn and Jack report that Walgreen's has increased its business with Johnson's from a sixth to a third of its total drug business. Sue and Jerry also say that several of the small independent drug stores in central Illinois, such as the ones in Effingham and Tuscola, have switched to Johnson's from us. With competition as fierce as this, we must make ordering from us a quick and easy operation.

Rebuttal of counter-claim

Most orders are phoned in between 9:30 and 11:30 in the morning and 1:00 and 2:00 in the afternoon, according to the times indicated on the order forms from last month. Computer records of our phone use, however, show that the lines are tied up throughout the day, usually by calls from the sales department. In order to relieve congestion, then, it is necessary to reduce phone activity in the sales department.

Solution presented impersonally

This reduction can be made by using the pay phones for personal calls during the peak ordering hours. Calls on company business should be made during non-peak hours too, if possible. This will enable us to keep more lines open during the peak ordering hours without spending money on costly new lines.

Additional reader benefits

With the lines open to incoming calls, customers will find that they can place their orders quickly and easily. This will encourage them to keep calling us instead of our competitors, which can mean greater sales for you. In addition, good service helps build goodwill which may enable you to get a bigger share of your customers' business. The easy phone ordering service will also serve you as an additional selling point for new customers.

Links action to solution of problem

In order to improve customer relations and realize greater sales, then, use the pay phones for personal calls between the peak hours of 9:30-11:30 and 1:00-2:00, and make outgoing business calls during non-peak hours.

Asks for action; tells readers exactly what to do

the system saved money and how much money it saved. The amount of money limits the claim and makes it more convincing. How specific the applicant needs to be—whether a statement can stand on its own as evidence or whether it first needs to be treated as a claim and proved—depends on how critically the reader will scrutinize the logic. If people who can do cost accounting are in short supply, the simple claim "I can do it" may net an interview. But if the job market is tight, proof will be necessary.

Figure D.1 is a problem-solving persuasive message written to persuade employees not to make personal calls on office phones. The comments in the margins identify the words, phrases, sentences, or paragraphs that

1. Build a common ground.
2. Offer evidence of the problem.
3. Prove that the problem hurts the organization.
4. Rebut the counterclaim that phones are tied up on business, not personal, calls.
5. Present the solution to the problem in general terms.
6. Present the complete solution in specific terms.
7. Picture the problem being solved.
8. Limit the claims about additional reader benefits that may arise from the solution but are not certain to occur.
9. Ask for action.
10. Create a win–win solution and build an image of the writer as someone who's on the same side as readers, helping them to solve their problems and achieve their goals.

Summary of Key Points

- To make your logic convincing,
  - Give evidence and specific supporting details.
  - Connect the parts of your argument.
  - Respond to possible objections.
  - Limit your claim to make it more persuasive.
- In Toulmin logic, the **claim** is the point we want the audience to accept. **Evidence** is material the audience already accepts. The **bridge** is the assumption that allows us to infer the claim from the evidence. The **foundation** supports (proves) the bridge. **Counterclaims** are statements that invalidate the claim even when the evidence and bridge are sound. The **rebuttal** answers the counterclaim. The **limiter** shows under what circumstances, or with what limitations, the claim is true.
- Use these guidelines to determine how much of the full Toulmin model to use:
  1. Make both the claim and the evidence explicit.
  2. Include the bridge
     a. If it is new information to the reader.
     b. If the reader may have heard the bridge but forgotten it.
     c. If the reader may disagree with the bridge.
     d. If invalid as well as valid bridges exist.
  3. Make the foundation explicit
     a. If the reader will disagree with the bridge.
     b. If invalid as well as valid foundations exist.
     c. If there are arbitrary demands for documentation.

4. Always offer rebuttals to loopholes the reader may find in the main claim.

5. Limit any claim whose truth is uncertain or relative.

APPENDIX D   Exercises

Getting Started

D.1   Using Toulmin Logic

In each of the following arguments, identify the claim and the evidence (if any). What bridge could link the evidence to the claim? Is it valid? Why or why not?

1. When you work harder, our customers are more satisfied. And that in turn raises the price of the company's stock.

2. Tom majored in accounting and he got five job offers. I should major in accounting, too.

3. I've worked for two large companies and hated both of them. I'd be happier starting my own business.

4. Of all the applicants, Bob got the highest score on the test. He's the person who should get the job.

5. Last month we spent 34% more on paper than we did six months ago. People are either wasting it or stealing it.

6. The vote on whether to move to a four-day workweek was 50/50. Our employees can never agree on whether or not a shorter workweek would be beneficial.

7. The vote on whether to move to a four-day workweek was split 50/50. Our employees don't care whether or not we change the workweek.

8. Since profits are falling, we need to downsize.

9. Customers already believe that our microwave meals taste better than other brands. So we should use our new advertising campaign to stress other advantages, such as their convenience or nutrition.

10. This company is a team. And just as every player does what the coach says, so each of you needs to run the game plan that your manager creates.

D.2   Brainstorming Evidence

Brainstorm ways to support each of the following claims. What kinds of evidence could you use? What bridges would be necessary? What counterclaims would you need to refute?

1. Many students are interested in serving as Big Brothers and Big Sisters.

2. I have a solid understanding of accounting principles.

3. Stocks should be part of every retirement plan.

4. Today's cellular phones are too dangerous to use while driving.

5. Our city should provide more support to help people start small businesses.

D.3   Rebutting Counterclaims

The Southwest School System has several computer classrooms for students to use, but teachers do not have individual desktop computers. The school board is considering a proposal to buy computers and to replace the courier system of hand delivery of documents with e-mail.

Brainstorm ways to answer each of the following counterclaims:

1. "People won't use computers if they have them."

2. "Learning to use the computers will take time. People will spend more time getting mail than they do now."

3. "By the time you buy computers and pay for the energy and maintenance they need and for printer supplies, it won't be any cheaper to use e-mail than to pay people to drive from building to building to deliver intersystem mail."

4. "People will just print out copies of documents, so the cost of paper won't go down. And if we're going to print hundreds of copies of a document, it's more efficient to print copies centrally."

D.4   Analyzing Arguments

Analyze the arguments in one or more of the following kinds of documents. For each, identify the claim and (if present) the evidence, the bridge, the foundation, rebuttals to counterclaims, and limiters. What additional parts (if any) are needed to make the argument convincing?

1. An article in a business periodical or Web site recommending that it is or is not a good idea to buy a particular company's stock.

2. A recruiting brochure or Web page explaining why a company is a good place to work.

3. The CEO's letter in an annual report arguing that the company is well positioned for the coming year.

4. A fund-raising letter arguing that the organization is doing good work and is a deserving candidate for financial gifts.

5. A letter of recommendation recommending a candidate for a job or for a promotion.

6. Material from your city's chamber of commerce presenting your city as a good place to live and work.

7. An editorial in *The Wall Street Journal* or *Business Week* recommending economic policy.

A

abstract   A summary of a report, specifying the recommendations and the reasons for them. Also called an executive summary.

acknowledgment responses   Nods, smiles, frowns, and words that let a speaker know you are listening.

active listening   Feeding back the literal meaning or the emotional content or both so that the speaker knows that the listener has heard and understood.

active verb   A verb that describes the action of the grammatical subject of the sentence.

adjustment   The response to a claim letter. If the company agrees to grant a refund, the amount due will be adjusted.

alliteration   A sound pattern occurring when several words begin with the same sound.

allness   The semantic error of assuming it is possible to know or communicate everything that is important about a topic.

alternating pattern   Discussing the alternatives first as they relate to the first criterion, then as they relate to the second criterion, and so on: ABC, ABC, ABC.

AMS Simplified format   A letter format that omits the salutation and complimentary close and lines everything up at the left margin.

analytical report   A report that interprets information.

argument   The reasons or logic offered to persuade the audience.

assumptions   Statements that are not proven in a report, but on which the recommendations are based.

average   See *mean.*

B

bar chart   A visual consisting of parallel bars or rectangles that represent specific sets of data.

behavioral interviews   Job interviews that ask candidates to describe actual behaviors they have used in the past in specific situations.

bias-free language   Language that does not discriminate against people on the basis of sex, physical condition, race, age, or any other category.

blind ads   Job listings that do not list the company's name.

blind copies   Copies sent to other recipients that are not listed on the original letter or memo.

blindering   Imposing limits that do not exist in reality.

block format   In letters, a format in which inside address, date, and signature block are lined up at the left margin. In résumés, a format in which dates are listed in one column and job titles and descriptions in another. This format emphasizes work history.

blocking   Disagreeing with every idea that is proposed in a meeting.

blueprint   An overview or forecast that tells the reader what you will discuss in a section or an entire report.

body language   Nonverbal communication conveyed by posture and movement, eye contact, facial expressions, and gestures.

boilerplate   Language from a previous document that a writer includes in a new document. Writers use boilerplate both to save time and energy and to use language that has already been approved by the organization's legal staff.

boxhead   Used in tables, the boxhead is the variable whose label is at the top.

brainstorming   A method of generating ideas by recording everything people in a group think of, without judging or evaluating the ideas.

branching question   Question that sends respondents who answer differently to different parts of the questionnaire. Allows respondents to answer only those questions that are relevant to their experience.

bridge (in prospecting job letters)   A sentence that connects the attention-getter to the body of a letter.

bridge (in *Toulmin logic***)**   The general principle that authorizes making the step between the claim and the evidence in an argument.

brochure   Booklet (often part of a direct mailing) that gives more information about a product or organization.

buffer   A neutral or positive statement designed to allow the writer to bury, or buffer, the negative message.

build goodwill   To create a good image of yourself and of your organization—the kind of image that makes people want to do business with you.

bullets   Large round dots or squares that set off items in a list. When you are giving examples, but the number is not exact and the order does not matter, use bullets to set off items.

businessese   A kind of jargon including unnecessary words. Some words were common 200–300 years ago but are no longer part of spoken English. Some have never been used outside of business writing. All of these terms should be omitted.

business plan   A document written to raise capital for a new business venture.

buying time with limited agreement   Agreeing with the small part of a criticism that one does accept as true.

bypassing   Miscommunication that occurs when two people use the same symbol to mean different things.

C

case   The grammatical role a noun or pronoun plays in a sentence. The nominative case is used for the subject of a clause, the possessive to show who or what something belongs to, the objective case for the object of a verb or a preposition.

central selling point   A super reader benefit, big enough to motivate readers by itself, but also serving as an umbrella to cover other benefits and to unify the message.

chain   The body of a direct mail letter, providing the logical and emotional links that move readers from interest to the action the writer wants.

channel   The physical means by which a message is sent. Written channels include memos, letters, and billboards. Oral channels include phone calls, speeches, and face-to-face conversations.

channel overload   The inability of a channel to carry all the messages that are being sent.

chartjunk   Decoration that is irrelevant to a visual and that may be misleading.

checking for feelings   Identifying the emotions that the previous speaker seemed to be expressing verbally or nonverbally.

checking for inferences   Trying to identify the unspoken content or feelings implied by what the previous speaker has actually said.

choice or selection   The decision to include or omit information in a message.

chronological résumé   A résumé that lists what you did in a time line, starting with the most recent events and going backward in reverse chronology.

citation   Attributing a quotation or other idea to a source in the body of the report.

claim   The part of an argument that the speaker or writer wants the audience to agree with.

claim letter   A letter seeking a replacement or refund.

clip art   Predrawn images that you can import into your newsletter, sign, or graph.

close   The ending of a document.

closed body position   Includes keeping the arms and legs crossed and close to the body. Suggests physical and psychological discomfort, defending oneself, and shutting the other person out. Also called a defensive body position.

closed question   Question with a limited number of possible responses.

closure report   A report summarizing completed research that does not result in action or recommendation.

clowning   Making unproductive jokes and diverting the group from its task.

clustering   A method of thinking up ideas by writing the central topic in the middle of the page, circling it, writing down the ideas that topic suggests, and circling them.

cognitive dissonance   A theory which posits that it is psychologically uncomfortable to hold two ideas that are dissonant or conflicting. The theory of cognitive dissonance explains that people will resolve dissonance by deciding that one of the ideas is less important, by rejecting one of the ideas, or by constructing a third idea that has room for both of the conflicting ideas.

cold list   A list used in marketing of people with no prior connection to your group.

collaborative writing   Working with other writers to produce a single document.

collection letter   A letter asking a customer to pay for goods and services received.

collection series   A series of letters asking customers to pay for goods and services they have already received. Early letters in the series assume that the reader intends to pay but final letters threaten legal action if the bill is not paid.

comma splice or comma fault   Using a comma to join two independent clauses. To correct, use a semicolon, subordi-

nate one of the clauses, or use a period and start a new sentence.

common ground   Values and goals that the writer and reader share.

communication theory   A theory explaining what happens when we communicate and where miscommunication can occur.

complaint letter   A letter that challenges a policy or tries to get a decision changed.

complex sentence   Sentence with one main clause and one subordinate clause.

complimentary close   The words after the body of the letter and before the signature. *Sincerely* and *Cordially* are the most commonly used complimentary closes in business letters.

compound sentence   Sentence with two main clauses joined by a conjunction.

conclusions   Section of a report that restates the main points.

conflict resolution   Strategies for getting at the real issue, keeping discussion open, and minimizing hurt feelings so that people can find a solution that feels good to everyone involved.

connotations   The emotional colorings or associations that accompany a word.

contact letter   Letter written to keep in touch with customer or donor.

convenience sample   A group of subjects to whom the researcher has easy access.

conversational style   Conversational patterns such as speed and volume of speaking, pauses between speakers, whether questions are direct or indirect. When different speakers assign different meanings to a specific pattern, miscommunication results.

coordinating   Planning work, giving directions, fitting together contributions of group members.

coordination   The third stage in the life of a task group, when the group finds, organizes, and interprets information and examines alternatives and assumptions. This is the longest of the four stages.

counterclaim   In Toulmin logic, a statement whose truth would negate the truth of the main claim.

credibility   The audience's response to the source of the message as a believable one.

criteria   The standards used to evaluate or weigh the factors in a decision.

critical activities   Activities that must be done on time if a project is to be completed by its due date.

critical incident   An important event that illustrates a subordinate's behavior.

crop   To trim a photograph to fit a specific space. Also, photographs are cropped to delete visual information that is unnecessary or unwanted.

culture   The unconscious patterns of behavior and beliefs that are common to a people, nation, or organization.

cutaway drawings or schematic diagrams　Line drawings that depict the hidden or interior portions of an object.

cycling　The process of sending a document from writer to superior to writer to yet another superior for several rounds of revisions before the document is approved.

D

dangling modifier　A phrase that modifies a word that is not actually in a sentence. To correct a dangling modifier, recast the modifier as a subordinate clause or revise the sentence so its subject or object can be modified by the now-dangling phrase.

data　Facts or figures from which conclusions can be drawn.

decode　To extract meaning from symbols.

decorative visual　A visual that makes the speaker's points more memorable but that does not convey numerical data.

defensive body position　See *closed body position.*

demographic characteristics　Measurable features of an audience that can be counted objectively: age, sex, race, education level, income, etc.

denotation　A word's literal or "dictionary" meaning. Most common words in English have more than one denotation. Context usually makes it clear which of several meanings is appropriate.

dependent clause　See *subordinate clause.*

descriptive abstract　A listing of the topics an article or report covers that tells how thoroughly each topic is treated but does not summarize what is said about each topic.

deviation bar charts　Bar charts that identify positive and negative values, or winners and losers.

dingbats　Small symbols such as arrows, pointing fingers, and so forth that are part of a typeface.

direct mail　A form of direct marketing that asks for an order, inquiry, or contribution directly from the reader.

direct mail package　The outer envelope of a direct mail letter and everything that goes in it: the letter, brochures, samples, secondary letters, reply card, and reply envelope.

direct marketing　All advertisements that ask for an order, inquiry, or contribution directly from the reader. Includes direct mail, catalogs, telemarketing (telephone sales), and newspaper and TV ads with 800 numbers to place an order.

direct request pattern　A pattern of organization that makes the request directly in the first and last paragraphs.

directed subject line　A subject line that makes clear the writer's stance on the issue.

discourse community　A group of people who share assumptions about what channels, formats, and styles to use for communication, what topics to discuss and how to discuss them, and what constitutes evidence.

divided pattern　Discussing each alternative completely before going on to the next alternative: AAA, BBB, CCC.

document design　The process of writing, organizing, and laying out a document so that it can be easily used by the intended audience.

documentation　Providing full bibliographic information so that interested readers can go to the original source of material used in a report.

dominating　Trying to run a group by ordering, shutting out others, and insisting on one's own way.

dot chart　A chart that shows correlations or other large data sets. Dot charts have labeled horizontal and vertical axes.

dot planning　A way for large groups to set priorities; involves assigning colored dots to ideas.

E

early letter　A collection letter that is gentle. An early letter assumes that the reader intends to pay but has forgotten or has met with temporary reverses.

editing　Checking the draft to see that it satisfies the requirements of good English and the principles of business writing. Unlike revision, which can produce major changes in meaning, editing focuses on the surface of writing.

ego-involvement　The emotional commitment the audience has to its position.

elimination of alternatives　A pattern of organization for reports that discusses the problem and its causes, the impractical solutions and their weaknesses, and finally the solution the writer favors.

ellipses　Spaced dots used in reports to indicate that words have been omitted from quoted material and in direct mail to give the effect of pauses in speech.

emotional appeal　Making the audience want to do what the writer or speaker asks.

empathy　The ability to put oneself in someone else's shoes, to *feel with* that person.

enclosure　A document that accompanies a letter.

encoding　Putting ideas into symbols.

enunciate　To voice all the sounds of each word while speaking.

evaluating　Measuring the draft against your goals and the requirements of the situation and audience. Anything produced during each stage of the writing process can be evaluated, not just the final draft.

evidence　Facts or data the audience already accepts.

exaggeration　Making something sound bigger or more important than it really is.

executive summary　See *abstract.*

expectancy theory　A theory that argues that motivation is based on the expectation of being rewarded for performance and the importance of the reward.

extensionalism　Inspecting and responding to reality itself.

external audiences　Audiences who are not part of the writer's organization.

external documents　Documents that go to people in another organization.

external report　Report written by a consultant for an organization of which he or she is not a permanent employee.

extranets　Web pages for customers and suppliers.

extrinsic benefits　Benefits that are "added on"; they are not a necessary part of the product or action.

eye contact　Looking another person directly in the eye.

F

feasibility report A report that evaluates two or more possible alternatives and recommends one of them. Doing nothing is always one alternative.

feedback The receiver's response to a message.

figure Any visual that is not a table.

five Ws and H Questions that must be answered early in a press release: who, what, when, where, why, and how.

fixed typeface A typeface in which each letter has the same width on the page. Sometimes called *typewriter typeface.*

flaming Sending out an angry e-mail message before thinking about the implications of venting one's anger.

focus groups Small groups who come in to talk with a skilled leader about a potential product.

forced choice A choice in which each item is ranked against every other item. Used to discover which of a large number of criteria are crucial.

form letter A prewritten, fill-in-the-blank letter designed to fit standard situations.

formal meetings Meetings run under strict rules, like the rules of parliamentary procedure summarized in *Robert's Rules of Order.*

formal report A report containing formal elements such as a title page, a transmittal, a table of contents, and an abstract.

formalization The fourth and last stage in the life of a task group, when the group makes and formalizes its decision.

format The parts of a document and the way they are arranged on a page.

formation The second stage in the life of a task group, when members choose a leader and define the problem they must solve.

foundation In Toulmin logic, a statement proving the truth of a bridge.

freewriting A kind of writing uninhibited by any constraints. Freewriting may be useful in overcoming writer's block, among other things.

frozen evaluation An assessment that does not take into account the possibility of change.

fused sentence The result when two or more sentences are joined with neither punctuation nor conjunctions.

G

Gantt charts Bar charts used to show schedules. Gantt charts are most commonly used in proposals.

gatekeeper The audience with the power to decide whether your message is sent on to other audiences. Some gatekeepers are also initial audiences.

gathering Physically getting the background data you need. It can include informal and formal research or simply getting the letter to which you're responding.

general semantics The study of the ways behavior is influenced by the words and other symbols used to communicate.

gerund The *-ing* form of a verb; grammatically, it is a verb used as a noun.

getting feedback Asking someone else to evaluate your work. Feedback is useful at every stage of the writing process, not just during composition of the final draft.

glossary A list of terms used in a report with their definitions.

good appeal An appeal in direct marketing that offers believable descriptions of benefits, links the benefits of the product or service to a need or desire that motivates the reader, makes the reader want to read the letter, and motivates the reader to act.

good mailing list A mailing list used in direct marketing that has accurate addresses and is a good match to the product.

good product A product that appeals to a specific segment of people, is not readily available in stores, is mailable, and provides an adequate profit margin.

good service or cause A service or cause that fills an identifiable need.

goodwill The value of a business beyond its tangible assets, including its reputation and patronage. Also, a favorable condition and overall atmosphere of trust that can be fostered between parties conducting business.

goodwill ending Shift of emphasis away from the message to the reader. A goodwill ending is positive, personal, and forward-looking and suggests that serving the reader is the real concern.

goodwill presentation A presentation that entertains and validates the audience.

grammar checker Software program that flags errors or doubtful usage.

grapevine An organization's informal informational network that carries gossip and rumors as well as accurate information.

grid system A means of designing layout by imposing columns on a page and lining up graphic elements within the columns.

ground rules Procedural rules adopted by groups to make meetings run smoothly.

grouped bar chart A bar chart that allows the viewer to compare several aspects of each item or several items over time.

groupthink The tendency for a group to reward agreement and directly or indirectly punish dissent.

guided discussion A presentation in which the speaker presents the questions or issues that both speaker and audience have agreed on in advance. Instead of functioning as an expert with all the answers, the speaker serves as a facilitator to help the audience tap its own knowledge.

H

headings Words or short phrases that group points and divide your letter, memo, or report into sections.

hearing Perceiving sounds. (Not the same thing as listening.)

hidden job market Jobs that are never advertised but that may be available or may be created for the right candidate.

hidden negatives Words that are not negative in themselves, but become negative in context.

high-context culture A culture in which most information is inferred from the context, rather than being spelled out explicitly in words.

histogram A bar chart using pictures, asterisks, or points to represent a unit of the data.

I

impersonal expression A sentence that attributes actions to inanimate objects, designed to avoid placing blame on a reader.

indented format A format for résumés in which items that are logically equivalent begin at the same horizontal space, with carryover lines indented three spaces. Indented format emphasizes job titles.

independent clause See *main clause.*

inference A statement that has not yet been verified but whose truth or falsity could be established, either now or in the future.

infinitive The form of the verb that is preceded by *to.*

inform To explain something or tell the audience something.

informal meetings Loosely run meetings in which votes are not taken on every point.

informal report A report using letter or memo format.

information interview An interview in which you talk to someone who works in the area you hope to enter to find out what the day-to-day work involves and how you can best prepare to enter that field.

information overload A condition in which a human receiver cannot process all the messages he or she receives.

information report A report that collects data for the reader but does not recommend action.

informational messages In a group, messages focusing on the problem, data, and possible solutions.

informative message Message to which the reader's basic reaction will be neutral.

informative presentation A presentation that informs or teaches the audience.

informative report A report that provides information.

inside address The reader's name and address; put below the date and above the salutation in most letter formats.

initial audience The audience that assigns the message and routes it to other audiences.

intensionalism An unconscious response to a symbol rather than reality.

interactive presentation A conversation in which the seller uses questions to determine the buyer's needs, probe objections, and gain provisional and then final commitment to the purchase.

intercultural competence The ability to communicate sensitively with people from other cultures and countries, based on an understanding of cultural differences.

internal audiences Audiences in the writer's organization.

internal document Document written for other employees in the same organization.

internal documentation Providing information about a source in the text itself rather than in footnotes or endnotes.

internal report Reports written by employees for use only in their organization.

interpersonal communication Communication between people.

interpersonal messages In a group, messages promoting friendliness, cooperation, and group loyalty.

interpret To determine the significance or importance of a message.

interview Structured conversation with someone who is able to give you useful information.

intranet A Web page just for employees.

intrapreneurs Innovators who work within organizations.

intrinsic motivators Benefits that come automatically from using a product or doing something.

introduction The part of a report that states the purpose and scope of the report. The introduction may also include limitations, assumptions, methods, criteria, and definitions.

J

jargon There are two kinds of jargon. The first kind is the specialized terminology of a technical field. The second is businessese, outdated words that do not have technical meanings and are not used in other forms of English.

judgment See *opinion.*

judgment sample A group of subjects whose views seem useful.

justification report Report that justifies the need for a purchase, an investment, a new personnel line, or a change in procedure.

justified margins Margins that end evenly on the right side of the page.

K

keywords Words used in a résumé to summarize areas of expertise, qualifications.

keywords Words describing the content of an article used to permit computer searches for information on a topic.

knot The action close of a direct mail letter, which harnesses the motivation you have created and turns it into action.

L

landscape graphs Line graphs with the area below the line filled in are sometimes called landscape graphs.

late letter A collection letter that threatens legal action if the bill is not paid.

letter Short document using block, modified, or AMS simplified letter format that goes to readers outside your organization.

letterhead Stationery with the organization's name, logo, address, and telephone number printed on the page.

limit In Toulmin logic, a boundary placed on a claim that cannot be made with 100% certainty.

limitations Problems or factors that limit the validity of the recommendations of a report.

line graph A visual consisting of lines that show trends or allow the viewer to interpolate values between the observed values.

listening Decoding and interpreting sounds correctly.

low-context culture A culture in which most information is conveyed explicitly in words rather than being inferred from context.

M

mailing list The list of names and addresses to which a direct mail letter is sent.

main clause A group of words that can stand by itself as a complete sentence. Also called an independent clause.

Maslow's hierarchy of needs Five levels of human need posited by Abraham H. Maslow. They include physical needs, the need for safety and security, for love and belonging, for esteem and recognition, and for self-actualization.

mean The average. Found by adding up all the numbers and dividing by the number of numbers.

median The middle number.

memo Document using memo format sent to readers in your organization.

methods section The section of a report or survey describing how the data were gathered.

middle letter A collection letter that is more assertive than an early letter. Middle letters may offer to negotiate a schedule for repayment if the reader is not able to pay the whole bill immediately, remind the reader of the importance of good credit, educate the reader about credit, or explain why the creditor must have prompt payment.

minutes Records of a meeting, listing the items discussed, the results of votes, and the persons responsible for carrying out follow-up steps.

mirror question Question that paraphrases the content of the answer an interviewee gave to the last question.

misplaced modifier A word or phrase that appears to modify another element of the sentence than the writer intended.

mixed abstract An abstract that has characteristics of both summary and descriptive abstracts: it contains the thesis or recommendation and proof, but also contains statements about the article or report.

mixed punctuation Using a colon after the salutation and a comma after the complimentary close in a letter.

mode The most frequent number.

modified block format A letter format in which the inside address, date, and signature block are lined up with each other one-half or one-third of the way over on the page.

modifier A word or phrase giving more information about another word in a sentence.

monochronic culture Culture in which people do only one important activity at a time.

monologue presentation A presentation in which the speaker speaks without interruption. The presentation is planned and is delivered without deviation.

multiple graphs Three or more simple stories juxtaposed to create a more powerful story.

Myers-Briggs Type Indicator A scale that categorizes people on four dimensions: introvert-extravert; sensing-intuitive; thinking-feeling; and perceiving-judging.

N

negative message A message in which basic information conveyed is negative; the reader is expected to be disappointed or angry.

noise Any physical or psychological interference in a message.

nominative case The grammatical form used for the subject of a clause. *I, we, he, she,* and *they* are nominative pronouns.

nonagist Refers to words, images, or behaviors that do not discriminate against people on the basis of age.

nonracist Refers to words, images, or behaviors that do not discriminate against people on the basis of race.

nonrestrictive clause A clause giving extra but unessential information about a noun or pronoun. Because the information is extra, commas separate the clause from the word it modifies.

nonsexist language Language that treats both sexes neutrally, that does not make assumptions about the proper gender for a job, and that does not imply that men are superior to or take precedence over women.

nonverbal communication Communication that does not use words.

normal interview A job interview with some questions that the interviewer expects to be easy, some questions that present an opportunity to showcase strong points, and some questions that probe any weaknesses evident from the résumé.

noun–pronoun agreement Having a pronoun be the same number (singular or plural) and the same person (first, second, or third) as the noun it refers to.

O

objective case The grammatical form used for the object of a verb or preposition. *Me, us, him, her,* and *them* are objective pronouns.

observation In semantics, a statement that you yourself have verified.

omnibus motion A motion that allows a group to vote on several related items in a single vote. Saves time in formal meetings with long agendas.

open body position Includes keeping the arms and legs uncrossed and away from the body. Suggests physical and psychological comfort and openness.

open punctuation Using no punctuation after the salutation and the complimentary close.

open question Question with an unlimited number of possible responses.

opinion A statement that can never be verified, since it includes terms that cannot be measured objectively. Also called a judgment.

organization   The order in which ideas are arranged in a message.

organizational culture   The values, attitudes, and philosophies shared by people in an organization that shape its messages and its reward structure.

orientation   The first stage in the life of a task group, when members meet and begin to define their task.

outpull   To bring in a bigger response than another version of the same direct mailing.

outsourcing   Going outside the company for products and services that once were made by the company's employees.

P

package   The outer envelope and everything that goes in it in a direct mailing.

paired bar chart   A bar chart that shows the correlation between two items.

paired graphs   Two or more simple stories juxtaposed to create a more powerful story.

parallel structure   Putting words or ideas that share the same role in the sentence's logic in the same grammatical form.

paraphrase   To repeat in your own words the verbal content of what the previous speaker said.

passive verb   A verb that describes action done to the grammatical subject of the sentence.

people-first language   Language that names the person first, then the condition: "people with mental retardation." Used to avoid implying that the condition defines the person's potential.

perception   The ability to see, to hear, to taste, to smell, to touch.

performance appraisals   Supervisors' written evaluations of their subordinates.

persona   The "author" or character who allegedly writes a letter; the voice that a writer assumes in creating a document.

personal space   The distance someone wants between him- or herself and other people in ordinary, nonintimate interchanges.

personalized   A form letter that is adapted to the individual reader by including the reader's name and address and perhaps other information.

persuade   To motivate and convince the audience to act.

persuasive presentation   A presentation that motivates the audience to act or to believe.

pie chart   A circular chart whose sections represent percentages of a given quantity.

pitch   The highness or lowness of a sound. Low-pitched sounds are closer to the bass notes on a piano; high-pitched sounds are closer to the high notes.

planning   All the thinking done about a subject and the means of achieving your purposes. Planning takes place not only when devising strategies for the document as a whole, but also when generating "miniplans" that govern sentences or paragraphs.

polarization   A logical fallacy that argues there are only two possible positions, one of which is clearly unacceptable.

polychronic culture   Culture in which people do several things at once.

population   The group a researcher wants to make statements about.

positive emphasis   Focusing on the positive rather than the negative aspects of a situation.

positive or good news message   Message to which the reader's reaction will be positive.

possessive case   The grammatical form used to indicate possession or ownership. *My, our, his, hers, its,* and *their* are possessive pronouns.

post office abbreviations   Two-letter abbreviations for states and provinces.

prepositions   Words that indicate relationships, for example, *with, in, under, at.*

presenting problem   The problem that surfaces as the subject of disagreement. The presenting problem is often not the real problem.

primary audience   The audience who will make a decision or act on the basis of a message.

primary research   Research that gathers new information.

pro-and-con pattern   A pattern of organization for reports that presents all the arguments for an alternative and then all the arguments against it.

probe question   A follow-up question designed to get more information about an answer or to get at specific aspects of a topic.

problem-solving pattern   A pattern of organization that describes a problem that affects the reader before offering a solution to the problem.

procedural messages   Messages focusing on a group's methods: how it makes decisions, who does what, when assignments are due.

process of writing   What people actually do when they write. Most researchers would agree that the writing process can include eight parts: planning, gathering, writing, evaluating, getting feedback, revising, editing, and proofreading.

product of writing   The final written document.

progress report   A statement of the work done during a period of time and the work proposed for the next period.

proofreading   Checking the final copy to see that it's free from typographical errors.

proportional typeface   A typeface in which some letters are wider than other letters (for example, *w* is wider than *i*).

proposal   Document that suggests a method for finding information or solving a problem.

prospecting letter   A job application letter written to companies that have not announced openings but where you'd like to work.

psychographic characteristics   Human characteristics that are qualitative rather than quantitative: values, beliefs, goals, and lifestyles.

psychological description   Description of a product or service in terms of reader benefits.

psychological reactance   Phenomenon occurring when a reader reacts to a negative message by asserting freedom in some other arena.

purpose statement The statement in a proposal or a report specifying the organizational problem, the technical questions that must be answered to solve the problem, and the rhetorical purpose of the report (to explain, to recommend, to request, to propose).

Q

quadrant analysis A way of analyzing numerical data that sets up two factors of interest and two criteria (forming four sections, or quadrants).

questionnaire List of questions for people to answer in a survey.

R

ragged right margins Margins that do not end evenly on the right side of the page.

random cluster sample A random sample of subjects at each of a random sample of locations. This method is faster and cheaper when face-to-face interviews are required.

random sample A sample for which each person of the population theoretically has an equal chance of being chosen.

reader benefits Benefits or advantages that the reader gets by using the writer's services, buying the writer's products, following the writer's policies, or adopting the writer's ideas. Reader benefits can exist for policies and ideas as well as for goods and services.

rebuttal In Toulmin logic, the refutation of a counterclaim.

recommendation report A report that recommends action.

recommendations Section of a report that specifies items for action.

reference line A *subject line* that refers the reader to another document (usually a numbered one, such as an invoice).

referral interview Interviews you schedule to learn about current job opportunities in your field and to get referrals to other people who may have the power to create a job for you. Useful for tapping into unadvertised jobs and the hidden job market.

release date Date a report will be made available to the public.

request To ask the audience to take an easy or routine action.

request for proposal (RFP) A statement of the service or product that an agency wants; a bid for proposals to provide that service or product.

reply card A card or form designed to make it easy for the reader to respond to a direct mail letter. A good reply card not only leaves space for the reader to fill in mailing and ordering information but also repeats the central selling point, basic product information, and price.

respondents The people who fill out a questionnaire; also called subjects.

response rate The percentage of subjects receiving a questionnaire who agree to answer the questions.

restrictive clause A clause limiting or restricting the meaning of a noun or pronoun. Because its information is essential, no commas separate the clause from the word it restricts.

résumé A persuasive summary of your qualifications for employment.

reverse chronology Starting with the most recent job or degree and going backward. Pattern of organization used for chronological résumés.

revising Making changes in the draft: adding, deleting, substituting, or rearranging. Revision can be changes in single words, but more often it means major additions, deletions, or substitutions, as the writer measures the draft against purpose and audience and reshapes the document to make it more effective.

RFP See *request for proposal.*

rhetorical purpose The effect the writer or speaker hopes to have on the audience (to inform, to persuade, to build goodwill).

rhyme Repetition of the final vowel sounds, and if the words end with consonants, the final consonant sounds.

rhythm The repetition of a pattern of accented and unaccented syllables.

rival hypotheses Alternate factors that might explain observed results.

roll out To send to the whole list of recipients the version of a direct mail letter that performed better in a test of part of the list.

rule of three The rule explaining that when a series of three items are logically parallel, the last will receive the most emphasis.

run-on sentence A sentence containing several main clauses strung together with *and, but, or, so,* or *for.*

S

salutation The greeting in a letter: "Dear Ms. Smith."

sample (*in a direct mail package*) A product included to give the reader something to touch.

sample (*in research*) The portion of the population a researcher actually studies.

sans serif Literally, *without serifs.* Typeface whose letters lack bases or flicks. Helvetica and Geneva are examples of sans serif typefaces.

saves the reader's time The result of a message whose style, organization, and visual impact help the reader to read, understand, and act on the information as quickly as possible.

scope statement A statement in a proposal or report specifying the subjects the report covers and how broadly or deeply it covers them.

secondary audience The audience affected by the decision or action. These people may be asked by the primary audience to comment on a message or to implement ideas after they've been approved.

secondary letters Additional letters in a direct mail package. Often on smaller paper, these letters may be to readers who have decided not to accept the offer, from people who have benefited from the charity in the past, and from recognized people corroborating the claims made in the main letter.

secondary research Research retrieving data someone else gathered.

segmented, subdivided, or stacked bars Bars in a bar chart that sum components of an item.

semantic triangle A triangle without a base, a graphic portrayal of the idea that people provide the only connection between words and things.

semantics or general semantics The study of the ways behavior is influenced by the words and other symbols used to communicate.

sentence fragment A group of words that are not a complete sentence but that are punctuated as if they were a complete sentence.

sentence outline An outline using complete sentences that lists the sentences proving the thesis and the points proving each of those sentences. A sentence outline is the basis for a summary abstract.

serif The little extensions from the main strokes on the *r* and *g* and other letters. Times Roman and Courier are examples of serif typefaces.

sexist interview A stress interview in which questions are biased against one sex. Many sexist questions mask a legitimate concern. The best strategy is to respond as you would to a stress question: rephrase it and treat it as a legitimate request for information.

signpost An explicit statement of the place that a speaker or writer has reached: "Now we come to the third point."

simple random sample A random sample generated by using a list of all members of a population and a random digit table.

simple sentence Sentence with one main clause.

situational interviews Job interviews in which candidates are asked to describe what they would do in specific hypothetical situations.

skills résumé A résumé organized around the skills you've used, rather than the date or the job in which you used them.

solicited letter A job letter written when you know that the company is hiring.

spot visuals Informal visuals that are inserted directly into text. Spot visuals do not have numbers or titles.

standard agenda A seven-step process for solving problems.

star The attention-getting opener of a direct mail letter.

star-chain-knot pattern A pattern of persuasion that consists of an attention-getting opener (star), a body with logical and emotional links (chain), an an action close (knot).

stereotyping Putting similar people or events into a single category, even though significant differences exist.

storyboard A visual representation of the structure of a document, with a rectangle representing each page or unit. An alternative to outlining as a method of organizing material.

strategy A plan for reaching your specific goals with a specific audience.

stratified random sample A sample generated by first dividing the sample into the same proportion of subgroups as exists in the population and then taking a random sam-ple for each subgroup. This method enables a researcher to be sure that all important subgroups are included in the sample.

stress Emphasis given to one or more words in a sentence.

stress interview A job interview that deliberately puts the applicant under stress, physical or psychological. Here it's important to change the conditions that create physical stress and to meet psychological stress by rephrasing questions in less inflammatory terms and treating them as requests for information.

structured interview An interview that follows a detailed list of questions prepared in advance.

stub The variable listed on the side in a table.

subject line The title of the document, used to file and retrieve the document. A subject line tells readers why they need to read the document and provides a framework in which to set what you're about to say.

subjects The people studied in an experiment, focus group, or survey.

subordinate A group of words containing a subject and a verb but that cannot stand by itself as a complete sentence. Also called a dependent clause.

summarizing Restating and relating major points, pulling ideas together.

summary abstract The logical skeleton of an article or report, containing the thesis or recommendation and its proof.

summary sentence or paragraph A sentence or paragraph listing in order the topics that following sentences or paragraphs will discuss.

survey A method of getting information from a large group of people.

systematic random sample A random sample generated by setting up a template for a random entry on a page, choosing a random interval, and then taking the name at that entry on every page at the interval. A systematic random sample is often used when the researcher has a phone book.

T

table Numbers or words arrayed in rows and columns.

talking heads Headings that are detailed enough to provide an overview of the material in the sections they introduce.

target audience The audience one tries to reach with a mailing: people who are likely to be interested in buying the product, using the service, or contributing to the cause.

teaser copy Words written on the envelope to get the reader's attention and persuade him or her to open the envelope.

10-K report A report filed with the Securities and Exchange Commission summarizing the firm's financial performance; an informative document.

thank-you note A note thanking someone for helping you.

threat A statement, explicit or implied, that someone will be punished if he or she does or doesn't do something.

tone The implied attitude of the author toward the reader and the subject.

tone of voice The rising or falling inflection that indicates whether a group of words is a question or a statement, whether the speaker is uncertain or confident, whether a statement is sincere or sarcastic.

topic heading   A heading that focuses on the structure of a report. Topic headings give little information.

topic outline   An outline listing the main points and the subpoints under each main point. A topic outline is the basis for the table of contents of a report.

topic sentence   A sentence that introduces or summarizes the main idea in a paragraph. A topic sentence may be either stated or implied, and it may come anywhere in the paragraph.

Toulmin logic   A model, developed by Stephen Toulmin, useful in planning and in presenting arguments.

transmit   To send a message.

transitions   Words, phrases, or sentences that show the connections between ideas.

transmittal   A memo or letter explaining why something is being sent.

truncated code   Symbols such as asterisks that turn up other forms of a keyword in a computer search.

truncated graphs   Graphs with part of the scale missing.

two-margin or **block format**   A format for résumés in which dates are listed in one column and job titles and descriptions in another. This format emphasizes work history.

U

umbrella sentence or paragraph   A sentence or paragraph listing in order the topics that following sentences or paragraphs will discuss.

understatement   Downplaying or minimizing the size or features of something.

unity   Using only one idea or topic in a paragraph or other piece of writing.

unjustified margins   Margins that do not end evenly on the right side of the page.

unstructured interview   An interview based on three or four main questions prepared in advance and other questions that build on what the interviewee says.

V

venting   Expressing pent-up anger and frustration.

verbal communication   Communication that uses words; may be either oral or written.

vested interest   The emotional stake readers have in something if they benefit from keeping things just as they are.

vicarious participation   An emotional strategy in fund-raising letters based on the idea that by donating money, readers participate vicariously in work they are not able to do personally.

visual impact   The visual "first impression" you get when you look at a page.

volume   The loudness or softness of a voice or other sound.

W

watchdog audience   An audience that has political, social, or economic power and that may base future actions on its evaluation of your message.

white space   The empty space on the page. White space emphasizes material that it separates from the rest of the text.

wild card   Symbols such as asterisks that turn up other forms of a keyword in a computer search. See also *truncated code.*

withdrawing   Being silent in meetings, not contributing, not helping with the work, not attending meetings.

wordiness   Taking more words than necessary to express an idea.

works cited   The sources specifically referred to in a report.

works consulted   Sources read during the research for a report but not mentioned specifically in the report.

writing   The act of putting words on paper or on a screen, or of dictating words to a machine or a secretary.

Y

you-attitude   A style of writing that looks at things from the reader's point of view, emphasizes what the reader wants to know, respects the reader's intelligence, and protects the reader's ego. Using *you* probably increases you-attitude in positive situations. In negative situations or conflict, avoid *you* since that word will attack the reader.

Chapter 1

1. Albert R. Karr, "Work Week," *The Wall Street Journal,* December 29, 1998, A1.

2. Anne Fisher, "Ask Annie," *Fortune,* March 1, 1999, 242.

3. Hal Lancaster, "Making the Break from Middle Manager to a Seat at the Top," *The Wall Street Journal,* July 7, 1998, B1.

4. Robyn D. Clarke, "A New Labor Day," *Black Enterprise,* February 2001, 98.

5. Anne Fisher, "The High Cost of Living and Not Writing Well," *Fortune,* December 7, 1998, 244.

6. Elaine Viets, "Voice Mail Converts Boss into a Secretary," *The Columbus Dispatch,* August 10, 1995, 3E; Rochelle Sharpe, "Work Week," *The Wall Street Journal,* September 26, 1995, A1.

7. Henry Mintzberg, *The Nature of Managerial Work* (New York: Harper & Row, 1973), 32, 65.

8. Frederick K. Moss, "Perceptions of Communication in the Corporate Community," *Journal of Business and Technical Communication* 9.1 (January 1995): 67.

9. John Kotter, *The General Managers* (1982), summarized in Alan Deutschman, "The CEO's Secret of Managing Time," *Fortune,* June 1, 1992, 140.

10. "1996 Cost of a Business Letter" (Chicago: Dartnell/From 9 to 5, September 30, 1996), 1.

11. Dianna Booher, *Cutting Paperwork in the Corporate Culture* (New York: Facts on File, 1986), 24.

12. Claudia MonPere McIsaac and Mary Ann Aschauer, "Proposal Writing at Atherton Jordan, Inc.: An Ethnographic Study," *Management Communication Quarterly* 3 (1990): 535.

13. Elizabeth Allen, "Excellence in Public Relations & Communication Management," IABC/Dayton Awards Banquet, Dayton, OH, July 12, 1990.

14. Murray Raphel, "Comes the Revolution," *Direct Marketing,* May 2001, 61.

15. James R. Rosenfield, "Tackling the Tough Topics," *Direct Marketing,* June 2001, 4.

16. Nicholas G. Carr, "The Economics of Customer Satisfaction," *Harvard Business Review,* March–April 1999, 17–18; Emily Barker, "High-Test Education," *Inc.,* July 2001, 81–82; and "The Store That Stark Built," *Inc.,* August 2001, 46.

17. "June 2000 Star of the Month," www.southwest.com/careers/stars/star_June00.html, visited site July 12, 2001; Jill Rosenfeld, "No Room for Mediocrity," *Fast Company,* September 2001, 160; and Susan Greco, "Fanatics," *Inc.,* April 2001, 47.

18. "Small Business 2001," *Inc., State of Small Business 2001,* 18; Nina Munk, "The Price of Freedom," *New York Times Magazine,* March 5, 2000, 52; and Small Business Administration, "Small Business Frequently Asked Questions," www.sba.gov/advo/stats/sbfaq.html, July 16, 2001, visited site August 26, 2001.

19. L. D. DeSimone, George N. Hatsopoulous, Charles P. Holt, et al., "How Can Big Companies Keep the Entrepreneurial Spirit Alive?" *Harvard Business Review,* November–December 1995, 183–92.

20. Doug Garr, "Inside Out-Sourcing," *Fortune,* Summer 2001, 85–92; and Greco, "Fanatics," 47.

21. John Hilikirk, "Listening to Workers Pays Off," *USA Today,* April 2, 1993, 1B–2B.

22. "Teams: A Formula for Success," *Inc.,* May 1996, 111.

23. Pet Engardio, "Smart Globalization," *BusinessWeek,* August 27, 2001, 132–36; Mickael Arndt and Pete Engardio, "Diebold," *BusinessWeek,* August 27, 2001, 138.

24. Dawn Blalock, "Study Shows Many Execs Are Quick to Write Off Ethics," *The Wall Street Journal,* March 26, 1996, C1.

25. Thomas Petzinger, Jr., "The Front Lines: This Auditing Team Wants You to Create a Moral Organization," *The Wall Street Journal,* January 19, 1996, B1.

26. Clarke, "A New Labor Day," 96; Tony Schwartz, "While the Balance of Power Has Already Begun to Shift, Most Male CEOs Still Don't Get It," *Fast Company,* December 1999, 366; and Pamela Kruger, "Jobs for Life," *Fast Company,* May, 2000, 236–52.

27. Keith H. Hammonds, "Balancing Work and Family," *BusinessWeek,* September 16, 1996, 74.

28. Sue Shellenbarger, "New Training Methods Allow Jobs to Intrude Further Into Off Hours," *The Wall Street Journal,* July 11, 2001, B1; and Lori Lewis, "Critical Issues in Communications: Applications to Business," Panel, Association for Business Communication Western Regional Conference, Boise, ID, April 12, 1996.

29. Alessandra Bianchi, "Mission Improbable," *Inc.,* September 1996, 75.

30. Jörgen Sandberg, "Understanding Competence at Work," *Harvard Business Review,* March 2001, 24–28.

31. Rahul Jacob, "Why Some Customers Are More Equal Than Others," *Fortune,* September 19, 1994, 222, 224.

32. "A Master Class in Radical Change," *Fortune,* December 13, 1993, 82–83.

33. Eric Abrahamson, "Change Without Pain," *Harvard Business Review,* July–August 2000, 75–79; and "Change Is Changing," *Harvard Business Review,* April 2001, 125.

34. "The List: Hit the Net, Then the Met," *BusinessWeek,* January 29, 2001, 8; Paul C. Judge, "How I Saved $100 Million on the Web," *Fast Company,* February 2001, 174–81.

35. Brian Caulfield, "Talk Is Cheap. And Good for Sales, Too," *Business 2.0,* April 2001, 114.

36. Jennifer Reingold and Marcia Stepanek, "The Boom," *BusinessWeek,* February 14, 2000, 116.

37. This process was inspired by a process developed by Francis W. Weeks, *Principles of Business Communication* (Champaign, IL: Stipes, 1973), 45.

Chapter 2

1. Sue Shellenbarger, "Companies Are Finding It Really Pays to Be Nice to Employees," *The Wall Street Journal,* July 22, 1998, B1.

2. Jim Collins, "Level 5 Leadership: The Triumph of Humility and Fierce Resolve," *Harvard Business Review,* January 2001, 66–76; Alan M. Webber, "Danger: Toxic Company," *Fast Company,* November 1998, 152–59.

3. Charles Burck, "Learning from a Master," *Fortune,* December 27, 1993, 144; Kathy Casto, "Assumptions about Audience in Negative Messages," Association for Business Communication Midwest Conference, Kansas City, MO, April 30–May 2, 1987; and John P. Wanous and A. Colella, "Future Directions in Organizational Entry Research," *Research in Personnel/Human Resource Management,* ed. Kenneth Rowland and G. Ferris (Greenwich, CT: JAI Press, 1990).

4. Annette N. Shelby and N. Lamar Reinsch, Jr., "Positive Emphasis and You-Attitude: An Empirical Study," *Journal of Business Communication* 32, no. 4 (October 1995): 303–27.

5. Alan Farnham, "Are You Smart Enough to Keep Your Job?" *Fortune,* January 15, 1996, 42.

6. Mark A. Sherman, "Adjectival Negation and the Comprehension of Multiply Negated Sentences," *Journal of Verbal Learning and Verbal Behavior* 15 (1976): 143–57.

7. Margaret Baker Graham and Carol David, "Power and Politeness: Administrative Writing in an 'Organized Anarchy,'" *Journal of Business and Technical Communication* 10, no. 1 (January 1996): 5–27.

8. John Hagge and Charles Kostelnick, "Linguistic Politeness in Professional Prose: A Discourse Analysis of Auditors' Suggestion Letters, with Implications for Business Communication Pedagogy," *Written Communication* 6, no. 3 (July 1989): 312–39.

9. Brad Edmondson, "What Do You Call a Dark-Skinned Person?" *American Demographics,* October 1993, 9.

10. "The Internet's Next Niche," *American Demographics,* September 2000, 18.

11. Marilyn A. Dyrud, "An Exploration of Gender Bias in Computer Clip Art," *Business Communication Quarterly* 60, no. 4 (December 1997): 30–51.

Chapter 3

1. Audiences 1, 3, and 4 are based on J. C. Mathes and Dwight Stevenson, *Designing Technical Reports: Writing for Audiences in Organizations,* 2nd ed. (New York: Macmillan, 1991), 40. The fifth audience is suggested by Vincent J. Brown, "Facing Multiple Audiences in Engineering and R&D Writing: The Social Context of a Technical Report," *Journal of Technical Writing and Communication* 24, no. 1 (1994): 67–75.

2. Isabel Briggs Myers, *Introduction to Type* (Palo Alto, CA: Consulting Psychologists Press, 1980). The material in this section follows Myers's paper.

3. Isabel Briggs Myers and Mary H. McCaulley, *Manual: A Guide to the Development and Use of the Myers-Briggs Type Indicator* (Palo Alto, CA: Consulting Psychologists Press, 1985), 251, 248, respectively.

4. Matt Siegel, "The Perils of Culture Conflict," *Fortune,* November 9, 1998, 258.

5. Kitty O. Locker, "What Makes a Collaborative Writing Team Successful? A Case Study of Lawyers and Social Service Workers in a State Agency," *New Visions of Collaborative Writing,* ed. Janis Forman (Portsmouth, NH: Boynton/Cook, 1991), 52–54.

6. Daniel Pearl, "UPS Takes On Air-Express Competition," *The Wall Street Journal,* December 20, 1990, A4.

7. Keith Naughton, "How Ford's F-150 Lapped the Competition," *BusinessWeek,* July 29, 1996, 74–76.

8. Gabrielle Sándor, "Attitude (Not Age) Defines the Mature Market," *American Demographics,* January 1994, 18–21.

9. Eric N. Berkowitz, Roger A. Kerin, Steven W. Hartley, and William Rudelius, *Marketing,* 3rd ed. (Homewood, IL: Irwin, 1992), 126; and Carla Marinucci, "Marketers Have Word for You," *San Francisco Examiner,* in *The Columbus Dispatch,* December 23, 1987, B1–B2.

10. Alan W. H. Grant and Leonard A. Schlesinger, "Realize Your Customers' Full Profit Potential," *Harvard Business Review,* September–October 1995, 65–66.

11. Linda Driskill, "Negotiating Differences among Readers and Writers" (Paper presented at the Conference on College Composition and Communication, San Diego, CA, March 31–April 3, 1993).

12. Frederick Herzberg, "One More Time: How Do You Motivate Employees," *Harvard Business Review* September–October 1987, 109–20.

13. Glenn Burkins, "Work Week," *The Wall Street Journal,* February 13, 1996, B1.

14. Robyn D. Clarke, "More Than Money," *Black Enterprise,* June 2000, 89; and Charles Fishman, "Sanity Inc.," *Fast Company,* January 1999, 85–99.

15. Kevin Leo, "Effective Copy and Graphics," DADM/DMEF Direct Marketing Institute for Professors, Northbrook, IL, May 31–June 3, 1983.

16. Abraham H. Maslow, *Motivation and Personality* (New York: Harper & Row, 1954).

17. Cf. Tove Helland Hammer and H. Peter Dachler, "A Test of Some Assumptions Underlying the Path-Goal Model of Supervision: Some Suggested Conceptual Modifications," *Organizational Behavior and Human Performance* 14 (1975): 73.

18. Edward E. Lawler, III, *Motivation in Work Organizations* (Monterey, CA: Brooks/Cole, 1973), 59. Lawler also notes a third obstacle: people may settle for performance and rewards that are just OK. Offering reader benefits, however, does nothing to affect this obstacle.

19. Rachel Spilka, "Orality and Literacy in the Workplace: Process- and Text-Based Strategies for Multiple Audience Adaptation," *Journal of Business and Technical Communication* 4, no. 1 (January 1990): 44–67.

Chapter 4

1. Robert L. Brown, Jr., and Carl G. Herndl, "An Ethnographic Study of Corporate Writing: Job Status as Reflected in Written Text," *Functional Approaches to Writing: A Research Perspective,* ed. Barbara Couture (Norwood, NJ: Ablex, 1986), 16–19, 22–23.

2. Linda Flower, *Problem-Solving Strategies for Writing,* 3rd ed., (New York: Harcourt Brace Jovanovich, 1989), 38.

3. James Suchan and Robert Colucci, "An Analysis of Communication Efficiency between High-Impact and Bureaucratic Written Communication," *Management Communication Quarterly* 2, no. 4 (May 1989): 464–73.

4. Hilvard G. Rogers and F. William Brown, "The Impact of Writing Style on Compliance with Instructions." *Journal of Technical Writing and Communication* 23, no. 1 (1993): 53–71.

5. Gretchen Glasscock, "My Favorite Bookmarks," *Fast Company,* October 1999, 62.

6. Mary Ellen Podmolik, "New Rule Raises Stakes for Minority Shop Owners," *Advertising Age,* February 28, 2000, 34; and Hersch Doby, "Changing the Rules," *Black Enterprise,* April 2000, 23.

7. Caleb Solomon, "Clearing the Air: EPA–Amoco Study of Refinery Finds Pollution Rules Focusing on Wrong Part of It," *The Wall Street Journal,* March 29, 1993, A6.

8. Interoffice memo in a steel company.

9. Quoted by Emery Hutchison, "Things My Mother Never Taught Me about Writing," *Journal of Organizational Communications,* Winter 1972, 20.

10. Sign in front of a Kentucky Fried Chicken franchise in Bloomington, IN, July 13, 1984.

11. Philip B. Crosby, *Quality Is Free: The Art of Making Quality Certain* (New York: New American Library, 1979), 79–84.

12. Jaguar ad, *The Wall Street Journal,* September 29, 2000, A20.

13. *News-Gazette,* Champaign-Urbana, IL, January 16, 1979, C-8.

14. Richard C. Anderson, "Concretization and Sentence Learning," *Journal of Educational Psychology* 66, no. 2 (1974): 179–83.

15. Harris B. Savin and Ellen Perchonock, "Grammatical Structure and the Immediate Recall of English Sentences," *Journal of Verbal Learning and Verbal Behavior* 4 (1965): 348–53; and Pamela Layton and Adrian J. Simpson, "Deep Structure in Sentence Comprehension," *Journal of Verbal Learning and Verbal Behavior* 14 (1975): 658–64.

16. E. B. Coleman, "The Comprehensibility of Several Grammatical Transformations," *Journal of Applied Psychology* 48, no. 3 (1964): 186–90; Keith Rayner, "Visual Attention in Reading: Eye Movements Reflect Cognitive Processes,"

Memory and Cognition 5 (1977): 443–48; and Lloyd Bostian and Ann C. Thering, "Scientists: Can They Read What They Write?" *Journal of Technical Writing and Communication* 17 (1987): 417–27.

17. Arn Tibbetts, "Ten Rules for Writing Readably," *Journal of Business Communication* 18, no. 4 (Fall 1981): 55–59.

18. Thomas N. Huckin, "A Cognitive Approach to Readability," *New Essays in Technical and Scientific Communication: Research, Theory, Practice*, ed. Paul V. Anderson, R. John Brockmann, and Carolyn R. Miller (Farmingdale, NY: Baywood, 1983), 93–98.

19. Janice C. Redish and Jack Selzer, "The Place of Readability Formulas in Technical Communication," *Technical Communication* 32, no. 4 (1985): 46–52.

20. James Suchan and Ronald Dulek, "A Reassessment of Clarity in Written Managerial Communications," *Management Communication Quarterly* 4, no. 1 (August 1990): 93–97.

Chapter 5

1. See especially Linda Flower and John R. Hayes, "The Cognition of Discovery: Defining a Rhetorical Problem," *College Composition and Communication* 31 (February 1980): 21–32; Rose, *Writer's Block*; and the essays in two collections: Charles R. Cooper and Lee Odell, *Research on Composing: Points of Departure* (Urbana, IL: National Council of Teachers of English, 1978), and Mike Rose, ed., *When a Writer Can't Write: Studies in Writer's Block and Other Composing-Process Problems* (New York: Guilford Press, 1985).

2. Rebecca E. Burnett, "Content and Commas: How Attitudes Shape a Communication-Across-the-Curriculum Program," Association for Business Communication Convention, Orlando, FL, November 1–4, 1995.

3. W. Ross Winterowd and John Nixon, *The Contemporary Writer: A Practical Rhetoric*, 3rd ed. (San Diego: Harcourt Brace Jovanovich, 1989), 37.

4. George H. Jensen and John K. DiTiberio, *Personality and the Teaching of Composition* (Norwood, NJ: Ablex, 1989), 42.

5. Mike Rose, *Writer's Block: The Cognitive Dimension*, published for Conference on College Composition and Communication (Carbondale, IL: Southern Illinois University Press, 1984), 36.

6. Peter Elbow, *Writing with Power: Techniques for Mastering the Writing Process* (New York: Oxford University Press, 1981), 15–20.

7. See Gabriela Lusser Rico, *Writing the Natural Way* (Los Angeles: J. P. Tarcher, 1983), 10.

8. Rachel Spilka, "Orality and Literacy in the Workplace: Process- and Text-Based Strategies for Multiple Audience Adaptation," *Journal of Business and Technical Communication* 4, no. 1 (January 1990): 44–67.

9. Fred Reynolds, "What Adult Work-World Writers Have Taught Me About Adult Work-World Writing," *Professional Writing in Context: Lessons from Teaching and Consulting in Worlds of Work* (Hillsdale, NJ: Lawrence Erlbaum Associates, 1995), 18–21.

10. Raymond W. Beswick, "Communicating in the Automated Office," American Business Communication Association International Convention, New Orleans, LA, October 20, 1982.

11. Dianna Booher, *Cutting Paperwork in the Corporate Culture* (New York: Facts on File Publications, 1986), 23.

12. Susan D. Kleimann, "The Complexity of Workplace Review," *Technical Communication* 38, no. 4 (1991): 520–26.

13. This three-step process is modeled on the one suggested by Barbara L. Shwom and Penny L. Hirsch, "Managing the Drafting Process: Creating a New Model for the Workplace," *Bulletin of the Association for Business Communication* 57, no. 2 (June 1994): 1–10.

14. Glenn J Broadhead and Richard C. Freed, *The Variables of Composition: Process and Product in a Business Setting*, Conference on College Composition and Communication Studies in Writing and Rhetoric (Carbondale, IL: Southern Illinois University Press, 1986), 57.

15. This list of five actions is adapted from Robert Boice, "Writing Blocks and Tacit Knowledge," *Journal of Higher Education* 64, no. 1 (January/February 1993), 41–43.

16. Christina Haas, "How the Writing Medium Shapes the Writing Process: Effects of Word Processing on Planning," *Research in the Teaching of English* 23, no. 2 (May 1989): 181; and Christina Haas, "'Seeing It on the Screen Isn't Really Seeing It': Computer Writers' Reading Problems," *Critical Perspectives on Computers and Composition Instruction*, ed. Gail Hawisher and Cynthia Selfe (New York: Teachers College Press, 1989), 18–23.

Chapter 6

1. Linda Reynolds, "The Legibility of Printed Scientific and Technical Information," *Information Design*, ed. Ronald Easterby and Harm Zwaga (New York: John Wiley & Sons, 1984), 187–208.

2. For a review of the events and an analysis of the management problems, see J. C. Mathes, "Three Mile Island: The Management Communication Role," *Engineering Management International* 3 (1986): 261–68.

3. Bruch Tognazzini, "The Butterfly Ballot: Anatomy of a Disaster," *Ask Tog*, January 2001, www.asktog.com/columns/042ButterflyBallot.html, visited site September 4, 2001.

4. George A. Miller, "The Magical Number Seven, Plus or Minus Two: Some Limits on Our Capacity for Processing Information," *Psychological Review* 63, no. 2 (March 1956): 81–97.

5. Once we know how to read English, the brain first looks to see whether an array of letters follows the rules of spelling. If it does, the brain then treats the array as a word (even if it isn't one, such as *tweal*). The shape is processed in individual letters only when the shape is not enough to suggest meaning. Jerry E. Bishop, "Word Processing: Research on Stroke Victims Yields Clues to the Brain's Capacity to Create Language," *The Wall Street Journal*, October 12, 1993, A6.

6. David Matis, "The Graphic Design of Text," *Intercom*, February 1996, 23.

7. M. Gregory and E. C. Poulton, "Even versus Uneven Right-Hand Margins and the Rate of Comprehension of Reading," *Ergonomics* 13 (1970): 427–34.

8. Russell N. Baird, Arthur T. Turnbull, and Duncan McDonald, *The Graphics of Communication: Typography, Layout, Design, Production*, 5th ed. (New York: Holt, Rinehart & Winston, 1987), 37.

9. Philip M. Rubens, "A Reader's View of Text and Graphics: Implications for Transactional Text," *Journal of Technical Writing and Communication* 16, nos. 1–2 (1986): 78.

10. M. E. Wrolstad, "Adult Preferences in Typography: Exploring the Function of Design," *Journalism Quarterly* 37 (Winter 1960): 211–23; summarized in Rolf F. Rehe, "Typography: How to Make It Most Legible," Design Research International, Carmel, IN, 57.

11. Elizabeth Keyes, "Typography, Color, and Information Structure," *Technical Communication*, 40, no. 4 (November 1993): 652; and Joseph Koncelik, "Design, Aging,

Ethics, and the Law" (Paper presented in Columbus, OH, May 6, 1993).

12. Marilyn A. Dyrud, "An Exploration of Gender Bias in Computer Clip Art," *Business Communication Quarterly* 60, no. 4 (December 1997): 30–51.

13. Jakob Nielsen, "Top Ten Mistakes in Web Design," May 1996, www.useit.com/alertbox/9605.html.

14. Jakob Nielsen, "Why You Only Need to Test With 5 Users," *Jakob Neilsen's Alertbox*, March 19, 2000, www.useit.com/alertbox/20000319.html, visited site September 4, 2001.

Chapter 7

1. Thomas L. Fernandez and Roger N. Conaway, "Writing Business Letters II: Essential Elements Revisited," *1996 Refereed Proceedings*, Association for Business Communication Southwest Region, ed. Marsha L. Bayless, 65–68.

2. In a study of 483 subject lines written by managers and MBA students, Priscilla S. Rogers found that the average subject line was 5 words; only 10% of the subject lines used 10 or more words ("A Taxonomy for Memorandum Subject Lines," *Journal of Business and Technical Communication* 4, no. 2 [September 1990]: 28–29).

3. Deborah Tannen, *That's Not What I Meant: How Conversational Style Makes or Breaks Your Relationships with Others* (New York: Morrow, 1986), 108.

4. Richard C. Whitely, *The Customer-Driven Company* (Reading, MA: Addison-Wesley, 1991), 39–40.

5. An earlier version of this problem, the sample solutions, and the discussion appeared in Francis W. Weeks and Kitty O. Locker, *Business Writing Cases and Problems* (Champaign, IL: Stipes, 1980), 40–44.

Chapter 8

1. Deborah Tannen, *Talking from 9 to 5: Women and Men in the Workplace: Language, Sex, and Power* (New York: Avon, 1994), 43–52.

2. Ilan Mochari, "The Talking Cure," *Inc.,* November 2001, 123.

3. Ibid.; and Joann S. Lublin, "More Companies Cut Little Perks," *The Wall Street Journal*, January 4, 2001, B4.

4. Kitty O. Locker, "Factors in Reader Responses to Negative Letters: Experimental Evidence for Changing What We Teach," *Journal of Business and Technical Communication*, 13, no. 1 (January 1999): 21.

5. Ibid., 25–26.

6. Sharon S. Brehm and Jack W. Brehm, *Psychological Reactance: A Theory of Freedom and Control* (New York: Academic Press, 1981), 3.

7. Carol David, "Rereading Bad News: Policy and Procedural Memos and Bad News Lore," Association for Business Communication Annual Convention, Montreal, Canada, October 27–30, 1993.

8. Leslie N. Vreeland, "SEC 'Cop' Has Eye on Mutual Funds," *Columbus Dispatch*, July 21, 1987, 3F.

9. Frederick M. Jablin and Kathleen Krone, "Characteristics of Rejection Letters and Their Effects on Job Applicants," *Written Communication* 1, no. 4 (October 1984): 387–406; and Carlos Tejada, "Work Week," *The Wall Street Journal*, October 23, 2001, A1.

10. John D. Pettit, "An Analysis of the Effects of Various Message Presentations on Communicatee Responses," Ph.D. diss. Louisiana State University, 1969; and Jack D. Eure, "Applicability of American Written Business Communication Principles across Cultural Boundaries in Mexico," *Journal of Business Communication* 14 (1976): 51–63.

11. Elizabeth A. McCord, "The Business Writer, the Law, and Routine Business Communication: A Legal and Rhetorical Analysis," *Journal of Business and Technical Communication* 5, no. 2 (1991): 183.

12. Gabriella Stern, "Companies Discover That Some Firings Backfire into Costly Defamation Suits," *The Wall Street Journal*, May 5, 1993, B1.

Chapter 9

1. Art Kleiner, "Flexing Their Mussels," *Garbage*, July/August 1992, 50.

2. Alan Farnham, "You're So Vain," *Fortune*, September 9, 1996, 78–80.

3. The first and the last two are identified by Jay A. Conger, "The Necessary Art of Persuasion," *Harvard Business Review*, May–June 1998, 88.

4. J. C. Mathes and Dwight W. Stevenson, *Designing Technical Reports: Writing for Audiences in Organizations* (Indianapolis: Bobbs-Merrill, 1979), 18–19.

5. James Suchan and Ron Dulek, "Toward a Better Understanding of Reader Analysis," *Journal of Business Communication* 25, no. 2 (Spring 1988): 40.

6. Frances Harrington, "Formulaic Patterns versus Pressures of Circumstances: A Rhetoric of Business Situations," Conference on College Composition and Communication, New Orleans, LA, March 17–19, 1986.

7. Min-Sun Kim and Steven R. Wilson, "A Cross-Cultural Comparison of Implicit Theories of Requesting," *Communication Monographs* 61, no. 3 (September 1994): 210–35.

8. Kathleen J. Krone and John T. Ludlum, "An Organizational Perspective on Interpersonal Influence," in *Seeking Compliance: The Production of Personal Influence Messages*, ed. James Price Dillard (Scottsdale, AZ: Gorsuch Scarisbrick, 1990), 123–42.

9. "Sell Prospects by Using Their Motivational Triggers," *Personal Selling Power*, October 1993, 48.

10. Walter R. Nord, "Beyond the Teaching Machine: The Neglected Area of Operant Conditioning in the Theory and Practice of Management," *Organizational Behavior and Human Performance* 4 (1969): 375–401.

11. Priscilla S. Rogers, "A Taxonomy for the Composition of Memorandum Subject Lines: Facilitating Writer Choice in Managerial Contexts," *Journal of Business and Technical Communication* 4, no. 2 (September 1990): 21–43.

12. See John Nathan, "In Search of Excellence: The Film" (Waltham, MA: Nathan/Tyler Productions, 1985), 9–14.

13. Karen Lowry Miller and David Woodruff, "The Man Who's Selling Japan on Jeeps," *Business Week*, July 19, 1993, 56–57.

14. Daniel J. O'Keefe, *Persuasion* (Newbury Park, CA: Sage, 1990), 168; Joanne Martin and Melanie E. Powers, "Truth or Corporate Propaganda," *Organizational Symbolism*, ed. Louis R. Pondy, Thomas C. Dandridge, Gareth Morgan, and Peter J. Frost (Greenwich, CT: JAI Press, 1983), 97–107; and Dean C. Kazoleas, "A Comparison of the Persuasive Effectiveness of Qualitative versus Quantitative Evidence: A Test of Explanatory Hypotheses," *Communication Quarterly*, 41, no. 1 (Winter 1993): 40–50.

15. Thomas Petzinger, Jr., "A Banc One Executive Credits His Success to Mastering Dyslexia," *The Wall Street Journal*, April 24, 1998, B1.

16. Daniel Dieterich to Kitty Locker, March 24, 1993.

17. "Phoning Slow Payers Pays Off," *Inc.*, July 1996, 95.

18. An earlier draft of this problem and analysis appeared in Francis W. Weeks and Kitty O. Locker, *Business Writing Problems and Cases* (Champaign, IL: Stipes, 1980), 78–81.

Chapter 10

1. "Direct Marketing . . . An Aspect of Total Marketing," *Direct Marketing*, April 2001, 2.
2. Ernan Roman, "More for Your Money," *Inc.*, September 1992, 113; and Con Squires, "Using Personalization to Increase Response," *Fund Raising Management*, August 1993, 51.
3. James R. Rosenfield, "Junk Mail, 2001: Physical and Virtual," *Direct Marketing*, March 2001, 28.
4. Sandra Yin, "Mail Openers," *American Demographics*, October 2001, 20–21.
5. This pattern is an adaptation of the Star-Chain-Hook pattern developed by Cy Frailey in the 1930s.
6. John D. Beard, David L. Williams, and J. Patrick Kelly, "The Long versus the Short Letter: A Large Sample Study of a Direct-Mail Campaign," *Journal of Direct Marketing* 4, no. 12 (Winter 1990): 13–20.
7. Ray Jutkins, "All about Post and Post Post Scripts—A Key Element in Direct Mail," *Direct Marketing*, January 1997, 44.
8. Eileen Daspin, "How to Give More," *The Wall Street Journal*, October 2, 1998, W1, W4.
9. Jane Maas, *Better Brochures, Catalogs and Mailing Pieces* (New York: St. Martin's Press, 1981), 98–99.
10. Maxwell Sackheim, *My First Sixty-Five Years in Advertising* (Blue Ridge Summit, PA: Tab Books, 1975), 97–100.

Chapter 11

1. Brenda Arbeláez, statement to Kitty Locker, December 12, 1996.
2. Yadong Luo, *Partnering with Chinese Firms: Lessons for International Managers* (Burlington, VT: Ashgate, 2000), 217.
3. Gail Edmondson. "See the World, Erase Its Borders," *BusinessWeek*, August 28, 2000, 113.
4. Mark Clifford and Manjeet Kripalani, "Different Countries, Adjoining Cubicles," *BusinessWeek*, August 28, 2000, 182–84.
5. Joann S. Lublin, "An Overseas Stint Can Be a Ticket to the Top," *The Wall Street Journal*, January 29, 1996, B1.
6. Rob Norton, "Exploding the Myths about Growth," *Fortune*, November 25, 1996, 84.
7. See, for example, W. B. Johnson and A. E. Packer, *Workforce 2000* (Indianapolis: Hudson Institute, 1987). The population estimates are unchanged; see Robyn D. Clarke, "The Future Is Now," *Black Enterprise*, February 2000, 99.
8. Bureau of the Census, *Statistical Abstract of the United States 1997*, Table 22, pp. 22–23.
9. Cited in Farai Chideya, *The Color of Our Future* (New York: Morrow, 1999), 17.
10. "Amazing Numbers," *Selling Power*, September 1996, 28.
11. Charles W. Holmes, "U.S. More Diverse by the Decade," *The Columbus Dispatch*, March 13, 2001, A1; and Nicholas Kulish, "Census Survey Uncovers More About U.S.," *The Wall Street Journal*, August 6, 2001, B4.
12. Timothy Aeppel, "A 3Com Factory Hires a Lot of Immigrants, Gets Mix of Languages," *The Wall Street Journal*, March 30, 1998, A1, A12.
13. Albert R. Karr, "Work Week," *The Wall Street Journal*, April 18, 2000, A1.
14. David A. Victor, *International Business Communication* (New York: HarperCollins, 1992), 148–60.
15. John Webb and Michael Keene, "The Impact of Discourse Communities on International Professional Communication," in *Exploring the Rhetoric of International Professional Communication: An Agenda for Teachers and Researchers*, ed. Carl R. Lovitt with Dixie Goswami (Amityville, NY: Baywood, 1999), 81–109.
16. Christina Haas and Jeffrey L. Funk, "'Shared Information': Some Observations of Communication in Japanese Technical Settings," *Technical Communication* 36, no. 4 (November 1989): 365.
17. William Ruch, *Corporate Communication: A Comparison of Japanese and American Practices* (Westport, CT: Quorum Books, 1984), 5–6.
18. Paula J. Pomerenke, "Cultural Influences on Formulating Arguments in Marketing Reports," Modern Language Association Convention, Toronto, Canada, December 27–30, 1993.
19. Laray M. Barna, "Stumbling Blocks in Intercultural Communication," in *Intercultural Communication*, ed. Larry A. Samovar and Richard E. Porter (Belmont, CA: Wadsworth, 1985), 331.
20. Carmen Judith Nine-Curt, "Hispanic-Anglo Conflicts in Nonverbal Communication," in *Perspectivas Pedagogicas*, ed. I. Abino et al. (Universidad de Puerto Rico, 1983), 235.
21. Laurence Wylie, *Beaux Gestes: A Guide to French Body Talk* (Cambridge, MA: Undergraduate Press, 1977), xi.
22. Marjorie Fink Vargas, *Louder than Words* (Ames: Iowa State University Press, 1986), 47.
23. Michael Argyle, *Bodily Communication* (New York: International University Press, 1975), 89.
24. Jerrold J. Merchant, "Korean Interpersonal Patterns: Implications for Korean/American Intercultural Communication," *Communication* 9 (October 1980): 65.
25. Argyle, *Bodily Communication*, 92.
26. Ray L. Birdwhistell, *Kinesics and Context: Essays on Body Motion Communication* (Philadelphia: University of Philadelphia Press, 1970), 30–31.
27. Edward T. Hall and Mildred Reed Hall, *Hidden Differences* (Hamburg, West Germany: Stern Magazine, 1983), 47.
28. Jack Seward, *The Japanese* (New York: Morrow, 1972), 37.
29. Birdwhistell, *Kinesics and Context*, 81.
30. Glenna Dod and Gergana Kuneva, "*Yes* or *No*: Communication Barriers Between Bulgaria and the United States," ABC Canadian, Eastern US, Southeastern US Joint Regional Conference, Nashville, TN, March 30–April 1, 2000.
31. Paul Ekman, Wallace V. Friesen, and John Bear, "The International Language of Gestures," *Psychology Today* 18, no. 5 (May 1984): 64.
32. Nine-Curt, "Hispanic-Anglo Conflicts," 234.
33. Baxter, 1970, reported in Marianne LaFrance, "Gender Gestures: Sex, Sex-Role, and Nonverbal Communication," in *Gender and Nonverbal Behavior*, ed. Clara Mayo and Nancy M. Henley (New York: Springer-Verlag, 1981), 130.
34. Nine-Curt, "Hispanic-Anglo Conflicts," 238.
35. Khamdi Amnatvong, interview with the author, Columbus, OH, August 1987.
36. Brenda Major, "Gender Patterns in Touching Behavior," in *Gender and Nonverbal Behavior*, ed. Clara Mayo and Nancy M. Henley (New York: Springer-Verlag, 1981), 26, 28.
37. Mike McKeever to Kitty Locker, June 25, 2001.
38. Natalie Porter and Florence Gies, "Women and Nonverbal Leadership Cues: When Seeing Is Not Believing," in *Gender and Nonverbal Behavior*, ed. Clara Mayo and Nancy M. Henley (New York: Springer-Verlag, 1981), 48–49.
39. Robert C. Christopher, *Second to None: American Companies in Japan* (New York: Crown, 1986), 102–3.
40. Edward Twitchell Hall, *Hidden Differences: Doing Business with the Japanese* (Garden City, NY: Anchor-Doubleday, 1987), 25.
41. Lawrence B. Nadler, Marjorie Keeshan Nadler, and Benjamin J. Broome, "Culture and the Management of Conflict Situations," in *Communication, Culture, and Organizational*

Processes, ed. William B. Gudykunst, Lea P. Stewart, and Stella Ting-Toomey (Beverly Hills, CA: Sage, 1985), 103.

42. Argyle, *Bodily Communication,* 90.

43. Carl Quintanilla, "Work Week," *The Wall Street Journal,* August 13, 1996, A1; Mary Ritchie Key, *Paralanguage and Kinesics* (Metuchen, NJ: Scarecrow, 1975), 23; Fred Hitzhusen, conversation with Kitty Locker, January 31, 1988; and William Horton, "The Almost Universal Language: Graphics for International Documents," *Technical Communication* 40, no. 4(1993): 687.

44. David Stipp, "Mirror, Mirror on the Wall, Who's the Fairest of Them All?" *Fortune,* September 9, 1996, 87.

45. Vincent O'Neill, "Training the Multi-Cultural Manager," Sixth Annual EMU Conference on Languages and Communication for World Business and the Professions, Ann Arbor, MI, May 7–9, 1987.

46. Akihisa Kumayama, comment during discussion, Sixth Annual EMU Conference on Languages and Communication for World Business and the Professions, Ann Arbor, MI, May 7–9, 1987.

47. Muriel Saville-Troike, "An Integrated Theory of Communication," in *Perspectives on Silence,* ed. Deborah Tannen and Muriel Saville-Troike (Norwood, NJ: Ablex, 1985), 10–11.

48. A. Jann Davis, *Listening and Responding* (St. Louis: Mosby, 1984), 43.

49. Marcia Sweezey to BizCom, September 14, 1992.

Chapter 12

1. For a full account of the accident, see Andrew D. Wolvin and Caroline Gwynn Coakely, *Listening,* 3rd ed. (Dubuque, IA: William C. Brown, 1988), 10–11.

2. Molefi Asante and Alice Davis, "Black and White Communication: Analyzing Work Place Encounters," *Journal of Black Studies* 16, no. 1 (September 1985): 87–90.

3. Thomas Gordon with Judith Gordon Sands, *P.E.T. in Action* (New York: Wyden, 1976), 83.

4. Thomas J. Knutson, "Communication in Small Decision-Making Groups: In Search of Excellence," *Journal for Specialists in Group Work* 10, no. 1 (March 1985): 28–37. The next four paragraphs summarize Knutson's analysis.

5. For a fuller listing of roles in groups, see David W. Johnson and Frank P. Johnson, *Joining Together: Group Theory and Group Skills,* 6th ed. (Englewood Cliffs, NJ: Prentice Hall, 1997), 20–21.

6. Beatrice Schultz, "Argumentativeness: Its Effect in Group Decision-Making and Its Role in Leadership Perception," *Communication Quarterly* 30, no. 4 (Fall 1982): 374–75; Dennis S. Gouran and B. Aubrey Fisher, "The Functions of Human Communication in the Formation, Maintenance, and Performance of Small Groups," in *Handbook of Rhetorical and Communication Theory,* ed. Carroll C. Arnold and John Waite Bowers (Boston: Allyn and Bacon, 1984), 640; Curt Bechler and Scott D. Johnson, "Leadership and Listening: A Study of Member Perceptions," *Small Group Research* 26, no. 1 (February 1995): 77–85; and Scott D. Johnson and Curt Bechler, "Examining the Relationship between Listening Effectiveness and Leadership Emergence: Perceptions, Behaviors, and Recall," *Small Group Research* 29, no. 3 (August 1998): 452–71.

7. H. Lloyd Goodall, Jr., *Small Group Communications in Organizations,* 2nd ed. (Dubuque, IA: William C. Brown, 1990), 39–40.

8. Nance L. Harper and Lawrence R. Askling, "Group Communication and Quality of Task Solution in a Media Production Organization," *Communication Monographs* 47, no. 2 (June 1980): 77–100.

9. Rebecca E. Burnett, "Conflict in Collaborative Decision-Making," in *Professional Communication: The Social Perspective,* ed. Nancy Roundy Blyler and Charlotte Thralls (Newbury Park, CA: Sage, 1993), 144–62.

10. Kimberly A. Freeman, "Attitudes Toward Work in Project Groups as Predictors of Academic Performance," *Small Group Research* 27, no. 2 (May 1996): 265–82.

11. Solomon F. Asch, "Opinions and Social Pressure," *Scientific American* 193, no. 5 (November 1955): 31–35. For a review of recent literature on groupthink, see Marc D. Street, "Groupthink: An Examination of Theoretical Issues, Implications, and Future Research Suggestions," *Small Group Research* 28, no. 1 (February 1997): 72–93.

12. Poppy Lauretta McLeod, Sharon Alisa Lobel; Taylor H. Cox, Jr., "Ethnic Diversity and Creativity in Small Groups," *Small Group Research* 27, no. 2 (May 1996): 248–64; and Leisa D. Sargent and Christina Sue-Chan, "Does Diversity Affect Efficacy? The Intervening Role of Cohesion and Task Interdependence," *Small Group Research* 32 (2001): 426–50.

13. Deborah Tannen, *That's Not What I Meant!* (New York: William Morrow, 1986).

14. Karen Ritchie, "Marketing to Generation X," *American Demographics,* April 1995, 34–36.

15. Thomas Kochman, *Black and White Styles in Conflict* (Chicago: University of Chicago Press, 1981), 103.

16. Daniel N. Maltz and Ruth A. Borker, "A Cultural Approach to Male-Female Miscommunication," in *Language and Social Identity,* ed. John J. Gumperz (Cambridge: Cambridge University Press, 1982), 202.

17. Thomas Kochman, *Black and White Styles in Conflict* (Chicago: University of Chicago Press, 1981), 44–45.

18. David S. Jalajas and Robert I. Sutton, "Feuds in Student Groups: Coping with Whiners, Martyrs, Saboteurs, Bullies, and Deadbeats," *Mastering Management Education: Innovations in Teaching Effectiveness,* ed. Charles M. Vance (Newbury Park, CA: Sage, 1993), 217–27.

19. Nancy Schullery and Beth Hoger, "Business Advocacy for Students in Small Groups," Association for Business Communication Annual Convention, San Antonio, TX, November 9–11, 1998.

20. Jeffrey A. Fadiman, "Intercultural Invisibility: Deciphering the 'Subliminal' Marketing Message in Afro-Asian Commerce," Sixth Annual Conference on Languages and Communication for World Business and the Professions, Ann Arbor, MI, May 8–9, 1987.

21. Raymond L. Gordon, *Living in Latin America* (Skokie, IL: National Textbook, 1974), 41.

22. M. B., "The New Girls' Club," *Inc.,* March 1999, 88.

23. Eric Matson, "The Seven Deadly Sins of Meetings," *Fast Company Handbook of the Business Revolution,* 1997, 30.

24. Lisa Ede and Andrea Lunsford, *Singular Texts/Plural Authors: Perspectives on Collaborative Writing* (Carbondale, IL: Southern Illinois Press, 1990), 60.

25. Rebecca Burnett, "Characterizing Conflict in Collaborative Relationships: The Nature of Decision-Making During Coauthoring." PhD dissertation, Carnegie-Mellon University, Pittsburgh, PA, 1991.

26. Kitty O. Locker, "What Makes a Collaborative Writing Team Successful? A Case Study of Lawyers and Social Service Workers in a State Agency," in *New Visions in Collaborative Writing,* ed. Janis Forman (Portsmouth, NJ: Boynton, 1991), 37–52.

27. Ede and Lunsford, *Singular Texts/Plural Authors,* 66.

28. Meg Morgan, Nancy Allen, Teresa Moore, Dianne Atkinson, and Craig Snow, "Collaborative Writing in the Classroom," *The Bulletin of the Association for Business Communication* 50, no. 3 (September 1987): 22.

Chapter 13

1. For a useful taxonomy of proposals, see Richard C. Freed and David D. Roberts, "The Nature, Classification, and Generic Structure of Proposals," *Journal of Technical Writing and Communication* 19, no. 4 (1989): 317–51.
2. Donna Kienzler, e-mail to Kitty Locker, November 5, 1998.
3. Dana Milbank, "Scientists Have to Beat the Bushes for Money to Stay in Business," *The Wall Street Journal,* November 7, 1990, A1.
4. Anne Fisher, "Six Ways to Supercharge Your Career," *Fortune,* January 13, 1997, 48; and Patti Douglas to Kitty Locker, January 26, 1994.
5. Patti Douglas to Kitty Locker, January 26, 1994.
6. Christine Peterson Barabas, *Technical Writing in a Corporate Culture: A Study of the Nature of Information* (Norwood, NJ: Ablex Publishing, 1990), 327.
7. Pamela Paul, "School Vouchers," *American Demographics,* September 2001, 26.
8. David B. Wolfe, "Targeting the Mature Mind," *American Demographics,* March 1994, 34.
9. Janice M. Lauer and J. William Asher, *Composition Research: Empirical Designs* (New York: Oxford University Press, 1986), 66.
10. Irving Crespi, quoted in W. Joseph Campbell, "Phone Surveys Becoming Unreliable, Pollsters Say," *Columbus Dispatch,* February 21, 1988, 8F.
11. Alison Stein Wellner, "The National Headcount," *American Demographics,* March 2001, s12.
12. Earl E. McDowell, Bridget Mrolza, and Emmy Reppe, "An Investigation of the Interviewing Practices of Technical Writers in Their World of Work," in *Interviewing Practices for Technical Writers,* ed. Earl E. McDowell (Amityville, NY: Baywood Publishing, 1991), 207.
13. Thomas Hunter, "Pulitzer Winner Discusses Interviewing," *IABC Communication World,* April 1985, 13–14.
14. Joshua Macht, "The New Market Research," *Inc.,* July 1998, 90–92.
15. Macht, 92–93.
16. Phaedra Hise, "The Camera Doesn't Lie," *Inc.,* October 1993, 35.

Chapter 14

1. Michael Schrage, "Take the Lazy Way Out? That's Far Too Much Work," *Fortune,* February 5, 2001, 212.
2. Cynthia Crossen, "Diaper Debate: A Case Study of Tactical Research," *The Wall Street Journal,* May 17 1994, B8.
3. "The Incredible Shrinking Failure Rate," *Inc.,* October 1993, 58.
4. Cynthia Crossen, "Margin of Error: Studies Galore Support Products and Positions, but Are They Reliable?" *The Wall Street Journal,* November 14, 1991, A1, A7.
5. "Whirlpool: How to Listen to Consumers," *Fortune,* January 11, 1993, 77.
6. Peter Lynch with John Rothchild, *One Up on Wall Street: How to Use What You Already Know to Make Money in the Market* (New York: Fireside-Simon & Schuster, 2000), 189.
7. Patricia Sullivan, "Reporting Negative Research Results," and Kitty O. Locker to Pat Sullivan, June 8, 1990.
8. Michael L. Keene, conversation with Kitty Locker, May 17, 1988.

9. Jeanne H. Halpern, phone interview with Kitty Locker, January 21, 1994.
10. James Paradis, David Dobrin, and Richard Miller, "Writing at Exxon ITD: Notes on the Writing Environment of an R&D Organization," in *Writing in Nonacademic Settings* (New York: Guilford, 1985), 300–2.
11. George A. Miller, "The Magical Number Seven, Plus or Minus Two: Some Limits on Our Capacity for Processing Information," *Psychological Review* 63, no. 2 (March 1956): 81–97.
12. Dwight W. Stevenson, Business and Technical Writing Teachers' Roundtable, Purdue, West Lafayette, IN, October 19–20, 1986.
13. Frederick Rose, "In Wake of Cost Cuts, Many Firms Sweep Their History Out the Door," *The Wall Street Journal,* December 21, 1987, 21.
14. Thomas E. Pinelli, Virginia M. Cordle, and Raymond F. Vondran, "The Function of Report Components in the Screening and Reading of Technical Reports," *Journal of Technical Writing and Communication* 14, no. 2 (1984): 92.

Chapter 15

1. Barbara Rosewicz, "Consumer Lobbies Gain Ground on Capitol Hill by Parlaying Tactics, Timing on Banking Bills," *The Wall Street Journal,* October 5, 1987, 46.
2. "GM's $2 Billion Quarterly Loss Biggest Ever," AP, *The Columbus Dispatch,* November 1, 1990, 1B; and Joseph B. White and Paul Ingrassia, "Huge GM Write-Off Positions Automaker To Show New Growth," *The Wall Street Journal,* November 1, 1990, A1.
3. Karen Springer, "Finally, the Free Lunch?" *Newsweek,* February 1, 1999, 57.
4. Gene Zelazny, *Say It with Charts: The Executive's Guide to Successful Presentations,* 4th ed. (New York: McGraw-Hill, 2001), 52.
5. Most of these guidelines are given by Zelazny, *Say It With Charts.*
6. W. S. Cleveland and R. McGill, "Graphical Perception: Theory, Experiments, and Application to the Development of Graphic Methods," *Journal of the American Statistical Association* 79, nos. 3 & 7 (1984): 531–53; cited in Jeffry K. Cochran, Sheri A. Albrecht, and Yvonne A. Greene, "Guidelines for Evaluating Graphical Designs: A Framework Based on Human Perception Skills," *Technical Communication* 36, no. 1 (February 1989): 27.
7. L. G. Thorell and W. J. Smith, *Using Computer Color Effectively: An Illustrated Reference* (Englewood Cliffs, NJ: Prentice Hall, 1990), 12–13; William Horton, "The Almost Universal Language: Graphics for International Documents," *Technical Communication* 40, no. 4 (1993): 687; and Thyra Rauch, "IBM Visual Interface Design," *The STC Usability PIC Newsletter,* January 1996, 3.
8. Thorell and Smith, *Using Computer Color Effectively,* 13.
9. Ibid., 49–51, 214–15.
10. Edward R. Tufte, *The Visual Display of Quantitative Information* (Cheshire, CT: Graphics Press, 1983), 113.
11. Thophilus Addo, "The Effects of Dimensionality in Computer Graphics," *Journal of Business Communication* 31, no. 4 (October 1994): 253–65.
12. Kathleen Deveny, "What's Wrong with This Picture? Utility's Glasses Are Never Empty," *The Wall Street Journal,* May 25, 1995, B1.
13. Day Mines *1974 Annual Report,* 1; reproduced in Tufte, *The Visual Display of Quantitative Information,* 54.

Chapter 16

1. Dan Gilmore, "Putting on a Powerful Presentation," *Hemispheres*, March 1996, 31–32.

2. Linda Driskill, "How the Language of Presentations Can Encourage or Discourage Audience Participation," paper presented at the Conference on College Composition and Communication, Cincinnati, OH, March 18–21, 1992.

3. Anne Fisher, "Willy Loman Couldn't Cut It," *Fortune*, November 11, 1996, 210.

4. Roy Alexander, *Power Speech: Why It's Vital to You* (New York: AMACOM, 1986), 156.

5. Robert S. Mills, conversation with Kitty Locker, March 10, 1988.

6. Phil Theibert, "Speechwriters of the World, Get Lost!" *The Wall Street Journal*, August 2, 1993, A10.

7. "A Study of the Effects of the Use of Overhead Transparencies on Business Meetings," Wharton Applied Research Center, reported in Martha Jewett and Rita Margolies, eds., *How to Run Better Business Meetings: A Reference Guide for Managers* (New York: McGraw-Hill, 1987), 109–10; and Tad Simmons, "Multimedia or Bust," *Presentations*, February 2000, 44, 48–50.

8. University of Minnesota/3M Study, reported in Martha Jewett and Rita Margolies, eds., *How to Run Better Business Meetings: A Reference Guide for Managers* (New York: McGraw-Hill, 1987), 115.

9. Stephen E. Lucas, *The Art of Public Speaking*, 2nd ed. (New York: Random House, 1986), 248.

10. John Case, "A Company of Businesspeople," *Inc.*, April 1993, 90.

11. Edward J. Hegarty, *Humor and Eloquence in Public Speaking* (West Nyack, NY: Parker, 1976), 204.

12. Based on Jewett and Margolies, *How to Run Better Business Meetings: A Reference Guide for Managers*, 183–85.

13. The comparison is taken from Jim Martin, "National Debt: Pennies to Heaven," *The Wall Street Journal*, February 22, 1988, 18.

14. Andy Rooney, "World Has Lost Mental Magician," Tribune Media Syndicate, *The Columbus Dispatch*, February 22, 1988, 7A.

15. Some studies have shown that previews and reviews increase comprehension; other studies have found no effect. For a summary of the research see Kenneth D. Frandsen and Donald R. Clement, "The Functions of Human Communication in Informing: Communicating and Processing Information," *Handbook of Rhetorical and Communication Theory*, ed. Carroll C. Arnold and John Waite Bowers (Boston: Allyn and Bacon, 1984), 340–41.

16. S. A. Beebe, "Eye Contact: A Nonverbal Determinant of Speaker Credibility," *Speech Teacher* 23 (1974): 21–25; cited in Marjorie Fink Vargas, *Louder than Words* (Ames: Iowa State University Press, 1986), 61–62.

17. J. Wills, "An Empirical Study of the Behavioral Characteristics of Sincere and Insincere Speakers," Ph.D. diss., University of Southern California, 1961; cited in Vargas, *Louder than Words*, 62.

18. George W. Fluharty and Harold R. Ross, *Public Speaking* (New York: Barnes & Noble, 1981), 162–63.

19. Ralph Proodian, "Mind the Tip of Your Tongue," *The Wall Street Journal*, May 4, 1992, A20.

20. Stephen E. Lucas, *The Art of Public Speaking*, 2nd ed. (New York: Random House, 1986), 243.

21. Ralph Proodian, "Raspy Throat? Read This, Mr. President," *The Wall Street Journal*, January 25, 1993, A14.

22. Michael Waldholz, "Lab Notes," *The Wall Street Journal*, March 19, 1991, B1.

23. George B. Ray, "Vocally Cued Personality Prototypes: An Implicit Personality Theory Approach," *Communication Monographs* 53, no. 3 (1986): 266–76.

Chapter 17

1. Elizabeth Blackburn-Brockman and Kelly Belanger, "One Page or Two? A National Study of CPA Recruiters' Preferences for Résumé Length, *The Journal of Business Communication* 38 (2001): 29–45.

2. Davida H. Charney, Jack Rayman, and Linda Ferreira-Buckley, "How Writing Quality Influences Readers' Judgments of Résumés in Business and Engineering," *Journal of Business and Technical Communication* 6, no. 1 (January 1992): 38–74.

3. Vincent S. Di Salvo and Janet K. Larsen, "A Contingency Approach to Communication Skill Importance: The Impact of Occupation, Direction, and Position," *The Journal of Business Communication* 24, no. 3 (Summer 1987): 13.

4. Carl Quintanilla, "Coming Back," *The Wall Street Journal*, February 22, 1996, R10.

5. LeAne Rutherford, "Five Fatal Résumé Mistakes," *Business Week's Guide to Careers* 4, no. 3 (Spring/Summer 1986): 60–62.

6. Phil Elder, "The Trade Secrets of Employment Interviews," Association for Business Communication Midwest Convention, Kansas City, MO, May 2, 1987.

7. Kitty O. Locker, Gianna M. Marsella, Alisha C. Rohde, and Paula C. Weston, "Electronic Résumés: Lessons from *Fortune* 500, *Inc.* 500, and Big Six CPA Firms," Association for Business Communication Annual Convention, Chicago, IL, November 6–9, 1996.

8. This section is based on Kirsten Dixon, "Crafting an E-Mail Résumé," *BusinessWeek*, November 13, 2001.

9. Locker, Marsella, and Rohde, "Electronic Résumés."

10. T. T. Sekine, "Employment Portfolios in the Nineties," Association for Business Communication Midwest Convention, Indianapolis, IN, April 20–22, 1995.

11. Beverly H. Nelson, William P. Gallé, and Donna W. Luse, "Electronic Job Search and Placement," Association for Business Communication Convention, Orlando, FL, November 1–4, 1995.

12. Resumix, "Preparing the Ideal Scannable Resume," [www.resumix.com] October 16, 1996.

13. Taunee Besson, *The Wall Street Journal National Employment Business Weekly: Résumés*, 3rd ed. (New York: J Wiley S, 1999), 263.

14. Besson, *Résumés*, 263.

Chapter 18

1. Pierre Mornell, *Games Companies Play: The Job Hunter's Guide to Playing Smart & Winning Big in the High-Stakes Hiring Game* (Berkeley, CA: Ten Speed Press, 2000), 25.

Chapter 19

1. Thomas Petzinger, Jr., "Lewis Roland's Knack for Finding Truckers Keeps Firm Rolling," *The Wall Street Journal*, December 1, 1995, B1.

2. Bill Breen and Anna Muoio, "PeoplePalooza," *Fast Company*, November 2000, 88.

3. Rachel Emma Silverman, "Why Are You So Dressed Up? Do You Have a Job Interview?" *The Wall Street Journal*, April 17, 2001, B1.

4. The Catalyst Staff, *Marketing Yourself* (New York: G. P. Putnam's Sons, 1980), 179.

5. Lopez, "Firms Force Job Seekers to Jump through Hoops," *The Wall Street Journal*, October 6, 1993, B1.

6. Donna Stine Kienzler, letter to Ann Granacki, April 6, 1988.

7. Joel Bowman, "Using NLP to Improve Classroom Communication," Association for Business Communication Regional Conference, Lexington, KY, April 9–11, 1992.

8. Christopher Conte, "Labor Letter," *The Wall Street Journal*, October 19, 1993, A1.

9. *Marketing Yourself*, 101.

10. Claud Dotson, comment at the Association for Business Communication Western Regional Conference, Boise, ID, April 13, 1996.

11. Kate Wendleton, *Through the Brick Wall: How to Job-Hunt in a Tight Market* (New York: Villard Books, 1992), 244.

12. Ray Robinson, quoted by Dick Friedman, "The Interview as Mating Ritual," *Working Woman*, April 1987, 107.

13. Rachel Emma Silverman, "Great Expectations," *The Wall Street Journal*, July 25, 2000, B10.

14. Wendleton, *Through the Brick Wall*, 278.

Appendix C

1. N. L. Reinsch, Jr., and Raymond W. Beswick, "Voice Mail versus Conventional Channels: A Cost Minimization Analysis of Individuals' Preferences," *Academy of Management Journal* 11, no. 4 (1990): 801–16.

2. Robert Rosenthal, *Pygmalion in the Classroom* (New York: Holt, Rinehart, and Winston, 1968).

3. Danuta Ehrlich, Isaiah Guttman, Peter Schonbach, and Judson Mills, "Postdecision Exposure to Relevant Information," *Journal of Abnormal and Social Psychology* 54 (1957): 98–102; summarized in Elliot Aronson, *The Social Animal* (San Francisco: W. H. Freeman, 1972), 101.

4. Tim R. V. Davis, "Managing Culture at the Bottom," in *Gaining Control of the Corporate Culture*, ed. Ralph H. Kilman, Mary J. Saxton, Roy Serpa, and Associates (San Francisco: Jossey-Bass Publishers, 1985), 175.

5. "Photo Touch-Up Can Add a Tux, Lose a Girl Friend," *The Columbus Dispatch*, July 13, 1999, 1B.

6. Paulette Thomas, "Work Week," *The Wall Street Journal*, October 29, 1996, B1.

7. Paul Craig Roberts, "America's 'Savings Crisis' Is a Chimera," *BusinessWeek*, February 12, 1990, 20.

8. William M. Bulkeley, "A Firm by Any Other Name Means Likely Rise in Stock, Research Finds," *The Wall Street Journal*, July 10, 1987, 22.

9. Elmo R. Zumwalt, Jr., *On Watch: A Memoir* (New York: Times Books, 1976), 189; cited in Thomas J. Peters and Robert H. Waterman, Jr., *In Search of Excellence: Lessons from America's Best-Run Companies* (New York: Warner, 1992, 263–64.

10. Roger Trench, "All in a Day's Work," *Readers' Digest*, September 1989, 138.

Appendix D

1. See Stephen Toulmin, *The Uses of Argument* (Cambridge, UK: Cambridge University Press, 1958).

2. Diana Kunde, "Many Workers Afraid to Ask Boss for Flextime," *The Columbus Dispatch*, February 15, 1998, 27J.

3. Anne Fisher, "How Do I Persuade My Boss to Let Me Work at Home?" *Fortune*, November 9, 1998, 264.

Chapter 1

Page 3: Courtesy of Dave Siefert; p. 12: © Rich Frishman; p. 13: Courtesy of Haystack Toys; p. 15: Michael Greenlar/The Image Works; p. 16: Copyright © 1999 The Condé Nast Publications Inc. All rights reserved. Reprinted by permission. Photograph by Aaron Caplan; p. 19: © 2000 Rocky Kneten.

Chapter 2

Page 33: Courtesy of Stephen Hlibok; p. 41: Kitty O. Locker, by permission of Joseph-Beth Booksellers; p. 49: Bill Sikes/AP/ Wide World Photos.

Chapter 3

Page 57: Courtesy of Catarino Lopez; p. 61, above: © Ken Burris; below: © Barbel Schmidt; p. 64: Courtesy of Claritas, Inc., © 2001; p. 65: Courtesy Cisco Systems, Inc.; p. 72: Whirlpool Corporation.

Chapter 4

Page 85: Courtesy of Wei Shen; p. 89: Courtesy Iomega; p. 94: Courtesy of California Dried Plum Board.

Chapter 5

Page 111: Courtesy of Daniel R. Zevchik.

Chapter 6

Page 125: Courtesy of Susan Kleimann.

Chapter 7

Page 147: Courtesy of Diana Sun; p. 160: © 2001 Tim Pott Photography; p. 161: Courtesy of Siemens AG/ShareNet.

Chapter 8

Page 181: Courtesy of Rajani J. Kamath; p. 193: Courtesy Schwinn Bicycle.

Chapter 9

Page 211: © Dewey Chapman; p. 214: Courtesy of Target Corporation; p. 221: © Gregg Goldman; p. 234: David Umberger/ AP/Wide World Photos.

Chapter 10

Page 253: Courtesy of Linda Westphal; p. 254: John Thoeming; p. 259: Courtesy of Ducati.

Chapter 11

Page 289: Courtesy of Stefania Pinton; p. 295: AP/Wide World Photos; p. 297: © Jessica Wecker 1999.

Chapter 12

Page 315: Courtesy of Valeria Maltoni; p. 317: Marnie Crawford Samuelson; p. 333: © Deborah Mesa-Pelly.

Chapter 13

Page 347: Courtesy of James B. Lane; p. 350: © Karen Moskowitz; p. 373: Rim Light/ PhotoLink/PhotoDisc, Volume 21 Retail, Shopping and Small Business; p. 375: Courtesy of Frito-Lay Corporation.

Chapter 14

Page 389: Courtesy of Diane Kokal; p. 397: Courtesy of UPS Creative Media; p. 404: Photo by Mike Watiker, Courtesy of Medflight of Ohio.

Chapter 15

Page 441: Courtesy of Cindy Huffman.

Chapter 16

Page 465: Courtesy of Guy Kawasaki, Garage Technology Ventures (www.garage.com); p. 470: © Junebug Clark/Photo Researchers.

Chapter 17

Page 485: Courtesy of Kevin Slakey.

Chapter 18

Page 519: Courtesy of Teresa Moburg; p. 529: Courtesy of Bruce Mau Design, Toronto; p. 531: © Christopher Hartlove.

Chapter 19

Page 545: Courtesy of Tim R. Moore; p. 547: © Rick Rickman/Matrix; p. 553: Copyright © Danny Turner. All rights reserved.

Appendix C

Page 622: Courtesy Princeton Video Image (www.pvimage.com); p. 623: Keith Srakocic/AP/ Wide World Photos.

SERIOUS FUN

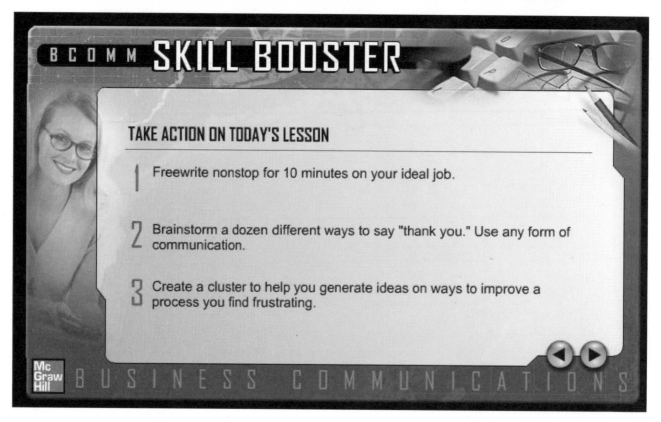

BCOMM SKILL BOOSTER

TAKE ACTION ON TODAY'S LESSON

1 Freewrite nonstop for 10 minutes on your ideal job.

2 Brainstorm a dozen different ways to say "thank you." Use any form of communication.

3 Create a cluster to help you generate ideas on ways to improve a process you find frustrating.

BUSINESS COMMUNICATIONS

The *BComm Skill Booster* is an Internet-based reinforcement system that delivers fun, interactive lessons directly to your computer, whether in a lab or in the privacy of your own room.

To use the *BComm Skill Booster*, you simply download a thin browser client called The Motivator, through which you set usage preferences and activate lessons. While lessons are dispersed according to a schedule determined by your professor, you may choose to receive them at a time most convenient to you.

When you register for the Skill Booster you receive a series of 15-minute lessons at regular intervals. Each lesson is built on the four-step system:

1 **Core Principle.** Each lesson focuses on one topic.

2 **Lesson Overview.** Read a brief, motivational review of the topic.

3 **Action Steps.** Three practical actions for each lesson help you learn by exercising your knowledge and skills in your daily life.

4 **Reinforcements.** Interact and learn through various fun tools: Quotations, Reality Checks, Quick Quizzes, FixIt! Exercises, and Dig Deeper Web links.

Each new textbook comes with a **FREE** password card. Access the text Web site (www.mhhe.com/locker6e) and follow the links to register for the Skill Booster.

Learning with the *BComm Skill Booster* is more than just a way to prep for a test or a term paper: It provides you with the rare satisfaction of using what you learn and seeing that it works.